MITCHELL WAITE
Signature Series

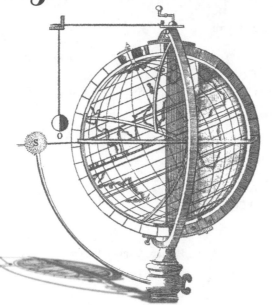

OBJECT-ORIENTED DESIGN IN JAVA™

STEPHEN GILBERT AND BILL McCARTY

Waite Group Press™
A Division of Macmillan Computer Publishing
Corte Madera, CA

PUBLISHER: Mitchell Waite

ASSOCIATE PUBLISHER: Charles Drucker

EXECUTIVE EDITOR: Susan Walton

ACQUISITIONS EDITOR: Susan Walton

PROJECT DEVELOPMENT EDITOR: Laura Brown

CONTENT EDITOR: Scott Rhoades

TECHNICAL EDITOR: Keith Ermel

PROJECT EDITOR: Maureen A. McDaniel

COPY EDITORS: Susan Shaw Dunn, Kate Givens, Tonya R. Simpson, Kate Talbot, Dana Rhodes Lesh

MANAGING EDITOR: Jodi Jensen

INDEXER: Erika Millen

INDEXING MANAGER: Johnna L. VanHoose

EDITORIAL ASSISTANT: Carmela Carvajal

SOFTWARE SPECIALIST Dan Scherf

PRODUCTION MANAGER: Cecile Kaufman

PRODUCTION TEAM SUPERVISOR: Brad Chinn

COVER DESIGNER: Sandra Schroeder

INTERIOR DESIGNER: Diana Jean Parks

PRODUCTION: Marcia Deboy, Michael Dietsch, Jennifer Earhart, Cynthia Fields, Maureen West

© 1998 by The Waite Group, Inc.®

Published by Waite Group Press ™

200 Tamal Plaza, Corte Madera, CA 94925

Waite Group Press™ is a division of Macmillan Computer Publishing.

Printed in the United States of America

00   10 9 8 7 6 5 4

Library of Congress Cataloging-in-Publication Data: 97-46425

International Standard Book Number: 1-57169-134-0

About the Authors

Bill McCarty teaches Management Information Systems and Computer Science at Azusa Pacific University. He holds a B.S. in Computer Science, and a Ph.D. in the Management of Information Systems from The Claremont Graduate School. He learned to write computer programs using the IBM 1130 while still a high school student back in the days of the IBM model 026 keypunch. Although on cold days he misses the warmth provided by the 026's vacuum tubes, he finds Southern California winters, for the most part, bearable. He passes them by reading and by writing software in the cheery solitude of his condo, which he shares with his wife, two children, three cats, and an unknown number of software bugs.

Stephen Gilbert teaches computer science at Orange Coast College in Costa Mesa, California. Steve saw his first computer play tic-tac-toe in the summer of 1960 and wanted one of his own ever since. When he purchased his first machine, a Vic-20 (which he subsequently trained to play an unbeatable game), his life took a sudden turn after years spent as a carpenter, chicken picker, and offset press operator. Since then, he has been a programmer and systems designer for DRI Management Systems of Newport Beach, as well as for other clients in California, Oregon, and Washington. Steve holds a B.S. degree in Business Computer Methods from California State University at Long Beach, and an M.S. degree in Applied Computer Science and Technology from Azusa Pacific University. Having long ago given up his ambition of becoming a professional surfer, he can still be found sitting on the Newport Beach pier with his wife Kathleen, or his children, Judah and Hosanna, whenever the surf's up.

Steve and Bill are the co-authors of *Mitchell Waite Signature Series: Object-Oriented Programming in Java*.

Contents

Table of Contents

Acknowledgments

Stephen Gilbert: This has been a year of change. In the midst of starting a new job and preparing an entirely new set of courses, I received an email from Bill McCarty, suggesting that we work together on a book about object-oriented design, using Java. Bill, as is his usual habit, was abuzz with a half-dozen wild and crazy ideas, and his enthusiasm was infectious. Nevertheless, it was with no little trepidation that I approached my wife, expecting to hear the words that would come most naturally to my tongue, were our situations reversed: "Not again!!!?" (or words to that effect). Instead of discouraging me, however, my wife Kathleen and my children, Hosanna and Judah, picked up the slack and gave me the time I needed to finish the project. My gratitude to them knows no bounds.

Finally, in a year of change, I'd be remiss if I failed to acknowledge the one constant in my life—the care and guidance of my Lord, Jesus Christ. In the words of the old hymn, "I don't know who holds tomorrow, but I know who holds my hand."

Bill McCarty: Jennifer, my wife, and Patrick and Sara, my children, who patiently answered the phone or made lunch while Dad wrote "another book," deserve most of the credit for this work. After all, they did most of the real work. As they've finally figured out, I'd much rather write than answer the phone or make lunch.

The remainder of the real work was done by my co-author, Stephen Gilbert, who regularly turned my terse and stultifying prose into something delightful. Thanks, Steve, let's do it again some time!

I also thank the "author and finisher of [my] faith" (Heb. 12:2, KJV), of whom it is written, "Not by works of righteousness which we have done, but according to His mercy He saved us, by the washing of regeneration and the renewing of the Holy Ghost" (Titus 3:5, KJV).

Stephen Gilbert and Bill McCarty: We want to thank the wonderful folks at the Waite Group, whose expertise is matched only by their kindness. Mitch, Charlie, Robert, Susan, Laura, Andrea, Dan, and "honorary Waite Groupers" Scott and Keith: you guys are the greatest! Thanks so much for all your help and encouragement, without which this book would be a mere dream.

We also want to thank the many professors who reviewed chapter manuscripts, patiently bearing with our inchoate expressions and all-too-frequent errors, and graciously offering numerous improvements. Prof. Leon Tabak of Cornell College was a particularly abundant source of suggestions that substantially improved the quality of the book. Errors, omissions, bad style, and corny humor should not be laid at their doorstep, but at ours.

Introduction

What Is This Book About, and How Is it Different?

Why does the world need another book on design? More to the point, why should *you* read *this* book on object-oriented design in Java? A trip to `amazon.com`, the Internet bookstore where you can find almost any book ever written, reveals over 200 titles that contain the word *design* or *designing* applied to computers or programming. If you decided to read one of these books each week, it would take you more than four years to finish the current crop. Even narrowing the field to books whose titles contain the words *design* and *object-oriented*, still yields a hefty 75 possibilities. Contemplating that task, you may find yourself agreeing with King Solomon, who wrote several thousand years ago: "Of making many books there is no end; and in much study there is a weariness of the flesh."

Why are there so many books on software design? A cynic would suggest that books on design flourish for the same reason that books on dieting fill the bookstores: because their readers have a boundless hope that *this* regime will work! While there might be some justification for this viewpoint—you don't have to travel far to find a program that is hard to use or that breaks down regularly—a more fundamental reason is that different software developers mean different things by the word *design*.

You've probably heard the ancient Indian legend (or read John Godfrey Saxe's version) of the six blind men examining an elephant. Each of them feels only a portion of the elephant—the side, a tusk, the trunk, or a leg—and each concludes that the elephant is like a wall, a spear, a snake, or a tree.

Books on software design exhibit similar tendencies. Authors coming from a software-engineering background see design in terms of specifications and blueprints; those from the information systems world think of an activity of the software development life cycle, along with their favorite diagrams; the database analysts think of normalization and entity-relationships; those immersed in computer-human interaction naturally see design as the specification of dialogs between people and machines; those responsible for interface design view design from a perspective that emphasizes visual integrity and communication. Like the blind men in the story, each of these constituencies has its own view on design, and each view is correct and valuable. But none of them is the whole story.

Our Viewpoint

In writing *Object-Oriented Design in Java*, we have tried to keep in mind two objectives. Our first objective was to avoid too narrow and specific a focus. We believe that design is important in every aspect of software development, and that every developer should have a toolkit of different design techniques and methods to call on. While your "real job" may require an in-depth knowledge of database design, GUI craftsmanship, or object and class design, such specialized knowledge is no substitute for a broad understanding of the design issues and techniques that are used throughout the software development process. You will find this book especially valuable if you are

- A student who has learned to program in Java, and you now find yourself asking "How does this all fit together?" Learning a programming language is a little like learning the syntax and semantics of English: you may have learned how to write and speak grammatically, but such knowledge doesn't prepare you to write a poem or a detective novel or a business letter. It is a necessary condition, but it is not sufficient. *Object-Oriented Design in Java* will help you to put the pieces of fundamental programming knowledge together, helping you to build software products that perform their intended function efficiently and effectively, and are a pleasure to use.

- A small software developer who, literally, "has to do it all." The introduction of Java and the use of the Internet for software distribution and marketing have revived the fortunes of the independent developer, who only a few years ago was considered an endangered species. *Object-Oriented Design in Java* will help you make sure that you've "touched all the bases" in developing your product.

- A technical manager or developer involved in corporate software development or Information Technology. *Object-Oriented Design in Java* will not only teach you the basics of each design perspective, but will also let you see where each of the parts of design "fit together." Thus, even if you are already an expert in interface design, you can use this text to learn about database design. And, should the occasion arise, the "To Learn More" sections at the end of each chapter will give you a set of references that you can use for further, in-depth study.

Because software design draws from such a wide range of related disciplines, it's impossible for a single book to cover every aspect of design comprehensively. Yet, we believe it's useful and important for designers to know something about each of the disciplines that bears on the practice of design. Of course, not everyone will agree with our choice of that "something." A reader with a strong background in, say, software engineering might bemoan our failure to cover one or more topics the reader thinks important. Like the blind man who believes an elephant is like a tree, such a reader might wish this book had a bigger trunk or more branches. But, just as an elephant is not a tree, design is not software engineering. Neither is it information systems, database analysis and design, computer-human interaction, nor interface design.

In designing the book, we worked hard to include all the fundamentals, the things a practicing designer needs to know and is called on to apply on a daily basis. Because in each chapter we wanted to write more than we could, each chapter includes a section titled "To Learn More," which lists books and articles that can help you further explore topics of personal interest and relevance. We expect you'll find *Object-Oriented Design in Java* a useful book for both study and reference.

Our Method

Besides adopting a "breadth-first" viewpoint, our objective was to adopt a specific method of presentation. *Object-Oriented Design in Java* is a book that was written to teach a wide variety of object-oriented design techniques to Java programmers. Design books with an Information-Systems or Software-Engineering bent usually begin by teaching analysis, followed by design and implementation. This book is different because the basic elements of object-oriented design are presented *beginning with the implementation*, and the design notations and methods are then built upon this concrete example.

Albert Schweitzer (the philosopher, physician, musician, clergyman, missionary, and writer on theology who won the 1952 Nobel Peace Prize) once remarked that there are three ways to learn—by example, by example, and by example. We find it easier to learn by going from the concrete to the abstract than from the abstract to the concrete, and we think you will too. For example, in Chapter 4, following a brief problem statement, we show you how to model a solution using the Java language. This chapter provides specific instruction on writing classes and presents several rules of thumb (heuristics) you can use to build more reliable and reusable classes. This chapter, which uses an informal, intuitive approach to class and object design, is followed (rather than preceded) by a chapter on systematic analysis (use case and CRC cards) and class/object notations. Following what we call the "round-trip" methodology, the next chapter then introduces you to a case study that is worked out "from scratch."

This same pattern is followed through the rest of the book:

- Present a concept by creating an implementation example.

- Discuss and present informal design measures and heuristics.

- Show how to represent that implementation using a design notation (we use the Unified Modeling Language, which we believe is already assuming the status of a de facto standard for object modeling) or by following a software process.

- Come full circle, answering the question: "What do you do with a blank sheet of paper?"

A Preliminary Briefing

Though browsing through the table of contents will give you some idea whether you'll actually find this book helpful, reading the next few pages might be more useful; a table of contents shows you only titles and subtitles, it doesn't tell you how the various chapters are related to each other.

Though the focus of *Object-Oriented Design in Java* is concrete and practical, the first two chapters start out in a very different vein by presenting the concepts and vocabulary of design and object-oriented development. Why start with two conceptual chapters rather than just "jumping right in?" If you've ever taken a journalism course in school, one of the first things you learned was to ask "who, what, why, where, and how." Most of this book is devoted to how, but without some understanding of who, what, where, and (especially) why, the how just doesn't make much sense. What's the purpose of learning, for example, how to encapsulate information if you don't know why it is important to do so?

The following sections provide an overview of what you'll find in each chapter.

CHAPTER 1: WHAT IS DESIGN AND WHY IS IT NEEDED?

How are building design (architecture), graphic design, industrial design, and software design similar? What *kind* of activity is design? In the software arena, there are different viewpoints; some believe software design is a science, others an engineering field, still others feel it is like art or drama. Despite these different perspectives, all designers deal with the common concepts of modeling, abstraction, and structuring. The second half of the chapter turns from general design issues to those specific to *software design*—software abstraction mechanisms and software design methodologies.

CHAPTER 2: OBJECT-ORIENTED SOFTWARE DEVELOPMENT

Moving on from design in general, this chapter covers two specific concepts that underlay object-oriented design. Just as structured design was built on the technology of structured programming, so object-oriented design is built on the concepts embodied in object-oriented programming: objects, classes, encapsulation, inheritance and polymorphism. The second half of the chapter is devoted to the idea that software has a life-cycle—that it is conceived, created, used, repaired and retired—and that design is involved in each of the phases of a software product.

CHAPTER 3: TEACH YOURSELF JAVA IN 21 MINUTES

This chapter won't make you an instant Java guru, but it will equip you with enough understanding of the Java language to allow you to follow the rest of the text. Starting with the mechanics of writing Java programs, this chapter discusses the syntax of creating classes (including attributes and methods), shows how flow of control works in Java, and provides a brief overview of Java's facilities for input and output.

CHAPTER 4: ENCAPSULATION: CLASSES AND METHODS

There may be "no bad boys," but there are bad classes galore. This chapter is intended to help you avoid some of the mistakes those who went before you have made. The chapter helps you get a quick start by dissecting a summary paragraph and then helping you decide on the first "big-picture" decision in class design: what is visible, and to whom. Detailed instructions for implementing methods and state are followed by guidelines for creating robust classes.

CHAPTER 5: DESIGNING CLASSES AND OBJECTS

Whereas Chapter 4 showed you how to design a class using Java code, this chapter shows you how that code can be represented using graphical software models. You are introduced to different class and object notations, using the Java code as a model. Most of the mistakes in software design are not coding errors, but communication errors between you, the designer, and your clients. This chapter concludes by introducing two powerful (and fun!) techniques for heading off those kinds of errors: use-case diagrams and Class-Responsibility-Collaboration (CRC) Cards.

CHAPTER 6: ROUND-TRIP DESIGN: A CASE STUDY

This chapter takes the tools you acquired in Chapters 4 and 5 and shows you how they can be applied in a "round-trip" manner, taking you through the entire design lifecycle. You first identify the problem and use a context diagram to represent the bounds of the system. Using CRC cards and use-case scenarios, you incrementally discover the classes and objects needed to create your design. Class diagrams help you to model the attributes and interfaces of each of the classes you design. The chapter finishes up by providing some guidance on drawing the user interface, implementing your design in Java, and testing the resulting design.

CHAPTER 7: OBJECT RELATIONSHIPS: IMPLEMENTING ASSOCIATIONS

Though designing individual classes and objects is important, most object-oriented programs involve collaboration by multiple objects. This chapter focuses on implementing relationships in which one object uses the services of another object: an association. You will learn how to write code for one-way and bi-directional associations. The chapter finishes by giving you a set of rules that will help you keep your objects from "bad company."

CHAPTER 8: OBJECT RELATIONSHIPS: COMPOSITIONS AND COLLECTIONS

This chapter focuses on a special kind of object relationship: composition, building objects from multiple parts. Composition is perhaps the most important tool for simplifying object-oriented software designs. The chapter shows you how and when to use composition and how to model composition relationships using Unified Modeling Language.

CHAPTER 9: IMPLEMENTING CLASS RELATIONSHIPS: INHERITANCE AND INTERFACES

While Chapters 7 and 8 look at associations between objects, this chapter begins a look at how classes can be related to each other. In Java, these different relationships are implemented using inheritance, abstract classes, and interfaces. The chapter walks you through the semantics of each of these relationships (what, for example, does it mean to say that a class implements an interface?) and then turns to the actual techniques used to create class hierarchies, interfaces, and abstract classes. The rules of thumb presented at the end of the chapter will help you to design usable inheritance and interface relationships.

CHAPTER 10: DESIGNING WITH INHERITANCE AND INTERFACES: A CASE STUDY

This chapter introduces you to notations that allow you to capture inheritance relationships between classes. The second half of this chapter features a case study using inheritance.

CHAPTER 11: PATTERNS: PROVEN DESIGNS

While the analysis and design methods presented in the first 10 chapters will help you when you have an entirely new problem, this chapter will help you to learn from the past. Based on ideas from the field of architecture, the proponents of the "patterns movement" insist that there are recurring design problems in software, each of which has one or more good solutions. By capturing the essence of the solution in a pattern, the programmer is free from the necessity to "reinvent the wheel." This chapter introduces you to the basic pattern form, shows you how to read and find new patterns, and then walks you through the implementation of many of the basic patterns you will use again and again.

CHAPTER 12: DESIGNING CONCURRENT OBJECTS

Java is a multi-threaded language. That means it is possible to write programs where several things are happening at once. The related design issues—and problems—are new to many programmers. The central problem in concurrent programs is dealing with contention for resources, which can manifest itself in race conditions or in deadlock. You'll learn how to avoid these problems, as well as explore some of the additional design issues inherent in developing distributed applications.

CHAPTER 13: DESIGNING REMOTE OBJECTS

Not only can Java programs do several things "at once," but the individual parts of an application—the classes and objects—no longer have to execute on a single computer. This chapter shows you how to design distributed applications using RMI and CORBA—the most widely used technologies for distributed computing in Java. You'll also learn a notation for representing the interactions of remote objects, and a set of rules for designing distributed systems.

CHAPTER 14: DESIGNING PERSISTENT OBJECTS: DATABASE DESIGN AND IMPLEMENTATION

One oft-forgotten part of designing an application is designing the persistent data that is a major part of many applications. Java comes with a facility (JDBC) that allows you to store your data in a wide variety of popular relational databases. Of course, you can't just throw your data into such a database; it must be carefully designed to avoid corrupting your data. This chapter will give you the information you need to do that. Starting with relational database concepts such as creating and manipulating tables, you'll walk through the logical design of a database, learning the widely used ERD notation. Finally, you'll learn how the technique called *normalization* can help you avoid missing or redundant data.

CHAPTER 15: USER INTERFACE DESIGN AND IMPLEMENTATION

One of the chief attractions of Java is the Abstract Window Toolkit (AWT) that provides a cross-platform graphical-user interface. Chapter 15 provides you with the concrete help you'll need to make your applications and applets both more usable and better looking. The chapter concludes with a wide range of design guidelines you can use to improve your Java programs.

CHAPTER 16: DESIGNING WITH COMPONENTS

Microsoft's Visual Basic popularized the idea of drag-and-drop component programming. Now Java has its own component model—Java Beans—that works wherever Java does; that is, everywhere. A Java Bean is a small Java program that can be visually manipulated in a design tool like Symantec's Visual Café for Java or Borland's JBuilder. In fact, Java Beans are what make such Java development tools possible. In this chapter, you learn how to use the Java Beans facilities to design, make, and package your own reusable components.

CHAPTER 17: DESIGNING WITH CLASS LIBRARIES

Just as the availability of patterns and components has freed the software designer from much of the drudgery required in the past, so class libraries enable you to build your programs on proven code that is pre-tested and in wide use. One example of such a class library is the AWT for constructing graphical interfaces. Another is the Java Generic Library (JGL, pronounced "jiggle"), which is provided by ObjectSpace. The library includes a rich set of containers and algorithms which this chapter walks you through.

CHAPTER 18: ARCHITECTURES: DESIGN-IN-THE-HUGE

As a programmer, you make design decisions every day. Some decisions are small ("what should I name this variable?") while others are large ("what classes should I use, and how should they be related to each other?"). The largest design decisions are architectural decisions—decisions about how applications should be packaged and deployed, and how applications should communicate with each other. This chapter walks you through the fundamental program architectures including LAN-based, client-server, and distributed architectures, and provides guidance you'll find helpful when it comes time for you to ask, "How should this application be deployed?"

What You Need: System and Software Requirements

Because Java runs on many platforms, you can use this book as a guide to developing Java programs for almost any operating system or computer. Java does require a fast processor, ample memory, and 256-color (or better) video support. Check the configuration requirements of the Java development tool you plan to use against the capabilities of your system.

The sample programs were developed and tested using the Java Developer's Kit, version 1.1.5, under Microsoft Windows 95 and Windows NT 4.0. Applets were tested using Microsoft Internet Explorer, version 4.0, and Netscape Navigator 4.04, with the Netscape-provided patch supporting Java 1.1.

The CD-ROM

The companion CD-ROM includes all the listings in the book and a few that couldn't be included in the book, due to size. The CD-ROM also includes the Java Developer's Kit (JDK) 1.1.5 for Microsoft Windows 95 and Microsoft Windows NT 4.0, and several useful design tools and utilities.

To install the JDK or other software on the CD-ROM, simply follow the instructions on the CD-ROM. Be sure to check the read-me file for special instructions.

1

What Is Design and Why Is it Needed?

"Reality: what a concept!" - Robin Williams

It's later than normal, almost an hour later. On Fridays you always try to leave by 3:30 so you'll have time to stop for takeout and still get home by 5:30. Now, as you approach the door of the small shop where you've picked up your dinner a hundred times before, your steps slow. Unconsciously you tell yourself, "This time it will be different." The front door is closed, but the smells from inside seem—if it were possible—to come right through the glass. You grab the big, brass, door handle, look straight at the large prominent sign that says PUSH, and give the handle a pull—exactly like you have done every other time in the years you've been coming here. "D'oh!" you exclaim, sounding very much like Homer Simpson, but already thinking about what you'll order.

Have you ever had an experience like this? Why is it that you, an intelligent, educated person can't read a large, prominently displayed sign, and follow a one-word instruction? Why does everyone pull instead of push when presented with a door like the one shown in Figure 1.1?

The answer is really very simple: because the door handle itself is a sign, a sign that says more fundamentally and forcefully than the written sign above it, "PULL!!!" The problem is not with your ability to read, but with the "designers" of the building who

FIGURE 1.1
What does this door say to you?

combined an inward-opening front door with a door-pull instead of a push-plate. Someone made a fundamental design error, and all the user-friendly instructions in the world won't fix it.

What is design? What are the design fields, and how are building design (architecture), graphic design, industrial design, and software design similar? As you ask these questions, you'll discover many different viewpoints: those who see design as science, those who claim design for engineering, those who feel design is an art, and those who insist that design is (or should be) a profession like law or medicine. This chapter explores those ideas as well as the common concepts of modeling, abstraction, and structuring, and how all of these ideas relate to developing software; after all, what you really want to do is to turn out a great program, right?

In this chapter, you will learn

- How to distinguish between different design philosophies and viewpoints.

- Why design is needed.

- How to describe the basic goals of design: "firmness, commodity, and delight."

- How to recognize the basic problems of design: essential and accidental complexity.

- How the fundamental tools of design—models, abstraction, and decomposition—can be used to attack the basic problems of design.

- How software abstraction mechanisms can be used to simplify the building of software, enabling you to build better programs.

- How software design methodologies help the software designer approach different parts of the design problem.

- How object-oriented design and structured design are related, and the basic terms common to each.

What Is Design?

"One of the main reasons most computer software is so abysmal is that it's not designed at all, but merely engineered."

You might be surprised to find out that these are not the words of some disgruntled Luddite or some ivory-tower academician. The speaker was Mitch Kapor, the designer of one of the most popular software packages of all time (Lotus 1-2-3) and also the author of "A Software Design Manifesto." Originally given as the keynote address at Esther Dyson's PC forum in 1990, Kapor's manifesto has been widely reprinted in the ensuing years. In it, he argues for the creation of a new type of software professional: the software designer, who fulfills the role that an architect does in building construction, making sure that a building meets the needs of its inhabitants.

Most everyone would agree with Kapor, (although, after your latest software crash, you might think that software is neither designed nor engineered). How to actually design good software is the real question.

The ancient Roman architect Vitruvius considered a similar question: what makes a good building? In his treatise *De Architectura Libri Dece* (*Ten Books on Architecture*), written in 29 B.C., he proposed three principles that many think provide a good starting point for evaluating software designs. A well-designed building, said Vitruvius, should have the qualities of commodity, firmness, and delight. Notice, as shown in Figure 1.2, that a product that balances commodity, firmness, and delight does not necessarily possess an equal amount of each. Most people think a good cup of coffee should contain more coffee than cream or sugar.

When you buy a software package, you want it to do exactly what the box says it will do. This is the characteristic of commodity—the program is effective in the sense of being well fit for its purpose. You also want the program to be well built: you want it be as fast and small as possible, and to continue working in a wide range of situations. This is the characteristic of firmness. Finally, you want your software to be attractive and pleasant to use. In a sense, you "live inside" your software, and it's important that the interface be both functional and aesthetic. This is the quality of delight.

Each of these qualities is important. Good-looking software that doesn't run well or is hard to use is no better than software that is fast and efficient (that is, software that uses as few resources as possible) but doesn't do what you want or does it in an ugly or unappealing way. Software designers, like all of us, tend to see the design process through their own particular lenses and to concentrate on one specific aspect or method of designing programs. Some see software development as a scientific endeavor. Others see it as an engineering exercise. Still others think of designing computer programs as artistic expression, like painting or music (see Figure 1.3).

" Software designers tend to see the design process through their own particular lenses. "

FIGURE 1.2

A good design balances the qualities of commodity, delight, and firmness

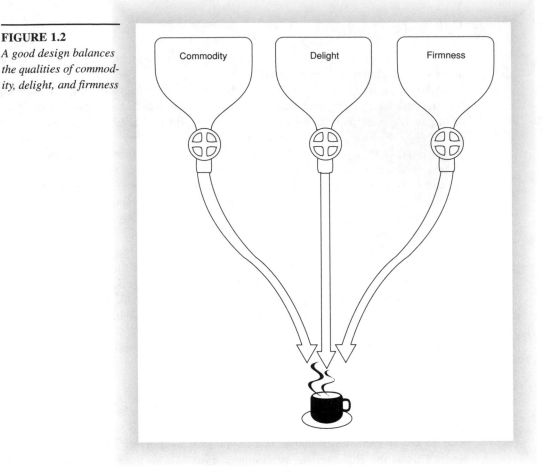

DESIGN AS SCIENCE

How do you become a lawyer or doctor? You go to law school or medical school. But, what do you study if you want to design computer software? If you're just embarking on your academic career and you ask this question, almost certainly you'll be encouraged to major in Computer Science. Are software designers scientists, and, if so, what does such a science entail?

You might have heard the old joke, "You can tell if something's a science—it doesn't have the word science in its name." And there's some truth to this observation. All of us agree that physics and astronomy and chemistry—the so-called hard sciences—are really sciences. But how about political science or military science or social science? How are the so-called "soft" sciences diffcrent from physics and geology?

FIGURE 1.3

The designer: scientist, engineer, or artist?

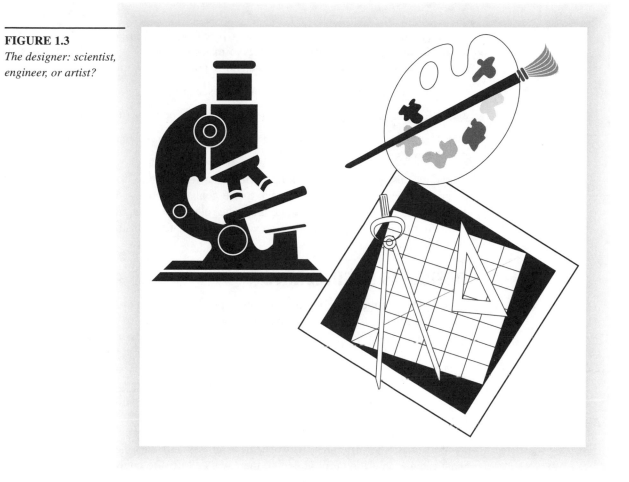

FIGURE 1.3

The designer: scientist, engineer, or artist?

Nobel prize winner Herbert Simon, one of the founders of the Computer Science department at MIT, attempted to answer this question in his 1969 book, *The Sciences of the Artificial*. According to Simon, there really are two sorts of sciences:

- The natural sciences—physics, chemistry, biology, and geology—which are concerned with the discovery of the natural world—finding out "how" things work, and building workable theories of explanation.

- The artificial sciences—political science, the social sciences, engineering, and computer science—which study things that have been built by humans, rather than naturally existing phenomena. Unlike the natural sciences, the artificial sciences are concerned with how things should work, not merely how things do work. An engineer wants to find the best way to build a bridge and a doctor wants to find the most effective method of treatment. All of these are issues of design.

Science, then, is about the study and discovery of general principles (theories), and the artificial sciences apply those theories to man-made artifacts, including the design of software. Software design, from the scientific point of view, includes

- Theories that deal with structure and representation.
- Rigorous and formal techniques for evaluating properties of designs.
- Formal methods for choosing the optimal (or at least a satisfactory) design from a set of possible designs.

Reading this, you may be thinking, "what does that have to do with writing a word processor or spreadsheet?" Think back to the goals of design—to create artifacts that exhibit firmness, commodity, and delight. The role of the computer scientist is to provide an objective, rigorous, theoretical foundation for constructing software that exhibits firmness.

DESIGN AS ENGINEERING

"The scientist builds in order to study; the engineer studies in order to build."

These are the words of the universally acknowledged father of software engineering, Fred Brooks, who was also the founder of the Computer Science Department at the University of North Carolina at Chapel Hill. His book, *The Mythical Man Month* (recently re-released in a 20th anniversary edition), was written after the completion of one of the largest software development projects ever attempted: the design and construction of the operating system for the IBM System/360. For those designing or managing the construction of a software product, it remains a unique and indispensable information resource, as the 250,000 purchasers of the first edition will attest.

For Brooks, the difference between the engineer and the scientist is not so much what they do, but the purpose behind their work. Software engineers design software in much the same way that mechanical engineers design bridges, industrial engineers design cars, and construction engineers design houses and auditoriums. What does the software engineer design? Tools: tools for writing, tools for computing, tools for communicating. The software engineer succeeds only to the extent that he builds a useful tool. To quote Brooks, "That swordsmith is successful whose clients die of old age."

"This is more like it," you might be thinking. "I understand that engineering is about building things, and it seems obvious that the software that I use could benefit from some engineering techniques." You're right. Like the computer scientist, those who see software design as engineering are concerned with the quality of "firmness." Building on the foundation of computer science—the fundamental data structures and algorithms discovered and constructed there—the software engineer builds "things that work."

Many of the techniques discussed in this book, such as the various diagramming techniques and the rules of thumb about class design, have their origin in the software engineering community. Software engineering is essential for well-designed software, but, as Kapor pointed out, it is not enough.

DESIGN AS ART

Figure 1.4 asks whether software development is an art. If so, are software developers artists? How far can the notion of "art" be stretched? "Look," said the hopeful student to his long-suffering advisor, "everyone who watches Michael Jordan play says he's a real artist. So why can't I get art units for playing basketball?" The reason, of course, is similar to the reason that computer science students don't receive foreign language credit for learning C, Pascal, or Java: because the word "language" means something different in each context. The same can be said for the word "art." In one sense, a good basketball player is an artist, but in another, very real sense, basketball players are not artists at all.

What, exactly, do we mean when we talk about design as art? The fine arts—painting, drawing, sculpture—exist to provide an aesthetic experience. Though it's conceivable that you could write a program whose primary purpose was aesthetic, in the

FIGURE 1.4

Is software development an art?

ordinary course of things you'll probably never do that. But, if we consider the applied arts—the construction of artifacts that are both useful and aesthetic—then software design certainly is one of the arts, in much the same way that graphic design or industrial design is.

The purpose of graphic design is to create documents such as books and magazines in which the aesthetic structure, the use of type and color and layout, serves the message that the piece conveys in a way that the reader can readily appreciate. In industrial design, the designer tries to create appliances or automobiles that are both attractive and functional. Of course, balancing functionality and aesthetics is not always easy. Think of the tail-fins on the 1958 Cadillac! Though at the time many people thought them attractive, most people today see the non-functional tail-fins as a case of wretched excess (see Figure 1.5).

"Well, I don't know," you might be saying to yourself. "I'm not really artistic, and it seems like all this stuff is just a little superfluous." You have a point. Adding an "artistic" gloss to an aging and infirm superstructure is seldom successful—just as gold plating does nothing to improve the beauty of the lily. You might even find yourself writing software that has no visible interface—embedded or systems software, for example. In such cases, arguing for "good-looking" programs is a misplaced concern.

Most of you, though, will write software for other people to use, and when you do, you take on the role of the artist-designer, striving to inspire delight, as well as commodity and firmness. This is a difficult role. Software (at least good software) doesn't just lie there and look pretty. Instead, it involves its user in an interactive experience. Not only do you want your program to look cool, you want it to act cool as well.

The demands of your role resemble those under which a playwright works. You must strive to get all the actors to line up and say their lines in a way that leaves the audience begging for more. However, your job is tougher still. The piece you've been commissioned to write is a more like a "murder-mystery dinner" where the actors and

FIGURE 1.5

Design requires balancing functionality and aesthetics

the audience intermingle. Your job is made doubly difficult because you have to antici-pate the unscripted actions of your diners, and provide contingent lines for your play-ers to use when things go off on a tangent.

If all this seems a little vague and abstract to you, you'll be happy to know that designing software that is attractive and a pleasure to use does not require an "artistic temperament," or the talent of pop artist David Hockney or playwright Neil Simon. Chapter 15, "User Interface Design and Implementation," will lead you through the processes, tools, and techniques that will make your software more than just another pretty face.

DESIGN AS ARCHITECTURE

" In the end, the architect designs neither for beauty nor for durabil-ity, but for the client. "

If "firmness" is the special purview of the engineer-designer, then "delight" has a sim-ilar place in the world of the artist-designer. Yet, concentrating on firmness and delight is not enough; the designer must also be concerned with commodity, balancing form and function. In this regard, many software designers see a close parallel between their role and that of the architect. This analogy was the central theme of Mitch Kapor's "A Software Design Manifesto," and the similarities between software design and architecture have greatly influenced the "patterns" movement, which you'll read about in Chapter 11, "Patterns: Proven Designs."

Like the artist, the architect wants to build structures that are visually pleasing; visual design is central to every architect's training. But, like the engineer, the architect wants to build structures that stand the test of time. The science of materials and construction techniques is an important part of an architect's training. In the end, the architect designs neither for beauty nor for durability, but for the client. The architect's goal is to build a structure that meets the client's needs.

The Process of Design

"So," you say, "you've talked about science and engineering and art and architecture. Let's not beat around the bush! Just what is design? How do you go about it?" Those are two very good questions, and they deserve a direct, if not exhaustive, answer:

- Design is preliminary; it's done before construction. Designing and building a house are two different activities.

- Design uses models. One dictionary definition of design is "to plan by making preliminary sketches or outlines." A design may use several different models, but the models are all distinct from the creation.

- Design has a goal: to create artifacts for human use. The designer acts as an agent for the client, and needs to ask "does it work?" not only in the mechanical sense of running without error, but "does it work?" in the larger sense of meeting the needs of the client.

🔹 Design is a process, yet the same process may not be applicable to every artifact. A process appropriate for designing a computer game might place a high emphasis on spontaneity and creative intuition, while a process used to develop a heart monitor or a missile-defense system might, appropriately, be much more formal and rigorous.

WHY DESIGN IS NEEDED

If you are a student who has written a few programs, or if you write software for your own use, you might be asking, "Why bother? Why not just start coding?" Or, in the immortal words of the Bard, "Just do it!" (Well, maybe Shakespeare didn't write exactly that.) Though some software projects may not need a long or formal design process, nobody with substantial experience sits down at the keyboard and just bangs away with no thought or reason. And, though an informal design process might be appropriate for most of the work you do, learning about more formal processes can help you to consider aspects of software design you have previously ignored.

Design is the planning process you go through before you build something. But again, why bother to plan at all? The major reason is that it's cheaper to change your mind while you're planning something than after it's half built. This is true for buildings, of course; erasing a line on a blueprint is much less expensive than ripping out a wall. For software, the same thing is true. A change that may cost $100 to make while you are designing your program can cost $1,000 to make after parts of the program are already built, simply because so many other parts have to be adjusted. And, if you find you have to make the change after the program is finished and in operation, the same change can cost $10,000 or more. "Look before you leap," is more than just a hoary old cliché.

More broadly, design involves an attitude that seeks to identify alternatives and intelligently choose an appropriate course of action. Good design involves analysis, reflection, and the development of insight. The way in which design is done has changed over time, as such insights have accumulated.

In the 16th century, if you wanted to build a house, you wouldn't work from a set of blueprints created by an architect and given to a contractor. Instead, you would hire a master-builder who would build your house based on his own experience and the experience of the master-builder who had trained him. Today, the development of a common language—the blueprint—and a common process (supported by such things as the Uniform Building Code and the licensing of building contractors) enables you to build a house by any number of firms, with little variation in the output of the finished product. This "separation of concerns" is one of the factors that leads to a more efficient process (see Figure 1.6).

Today, if you decide to build a house, your architect acts as your agent, making sure that the house meets your needs. To do this, the architect uses many different types of models—not only blueprints, but sketches, mock-ups, and even style books of common house types and floor plans, as you can see in Figure 1.6. Normally, as a client

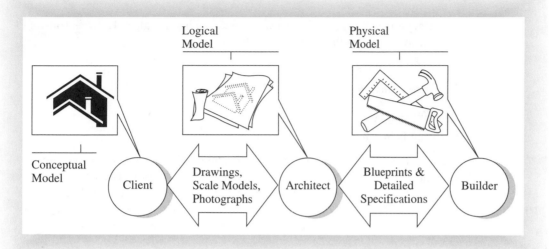

FIGURE 1.6

Client, architect, and builder: The architect constructs a logical model from the client's conceptual model and communicates that model to the builder

you review the sketches and mock-ups, whereas the building contractor relies on the blueprints. These models help the parties communicate and record the respective decisions they make. Your builder does not decide, halfway through construction, to add a stairway to the west wing—at least not without consulting the architect. This whole system works because of the availability of different models—at several levels of detail and abstraction—and a common agreement among all the parties about how those models correspond to reality.

THE PROBLEMS OF DESIGN: WHY IS SOFTWARE HARD?

If design—the use of planning and models—has been so successful in architecture and engineering, why can't we just apply to software the same principles used to make buildings, bridges, and cars? Is designing a piece of software the same as designing a bridge—or a computer? There is a lot of evidence to suggest it is not; that software design is fundamentally more difficult than engineering skyscrapers. Professor Brooks, in his famous article, "No Silver Bullet," tells us why.

Perhaps you've had a dream like this. You are sitting at the dinner table talking to your family, or perhaps you are taking a walk with your sweetheart. You turn to look into each other's eyes, and, as you watch, your loved ones turn into something different—something horrible. You wake in a sweat, with your heart pounding. This primordial fear—the familiar changing into the unknowable and fearful—is at the heart of the medieval legend of the werewolf. In the modern retelling of the legend, the only hope for deliverance is the "magical" effect of a silver bullet. And, if you've ever worked on a piece of software that seems to have grown ravenous and rapacious, the metaphor seems especially apt.

Why is designing software more difficult than designing a bridge? Because software has four essential qualities that resist easy solutions:

- Software is complex.
- Software is unprincipled.
- Software changes.
- Software is invisible.

Software is complex because it contains so many "moving parts." A modern jet fighter plane may contain a few thousand moving parts. A software system of even moderate size may contain tens of thousands of lines of code, each of which must correctly "mesh" with the rest of the system. Every additional line of code, every new condition or event, leads to the possibility of new conditions, previously unconsidered, or overlooked.

Software is "unprincipled" because there are no known fundamental and unifying laws that can cause software programs to "make sense." Software programs are written not to conform to a regular universe, but to the arbitrary, capricious, and illogical mind of man.

Software changes because it is so malleable. Although the London Bridge was moved to Lake Havasu, Arizona, that was an event both expensive and uncommon in bridge-building lore. (Plus, the bridge remained essentially unchanged.) By contrast, software is moved, twisted, and distorted with such regularity, and with such little foresight, that it's a wonder that any of it works at all.

Finally, software is invisible. Any design problem involves two translation steps. The first step is the translation of a mental or conceptual model to an abstract model. Suppose you decide to splurge on a new, custom designed hot-rod. Your conceptual model is the picture in your mind. The designer's first task is to translate your mental model into a specification. This specification may include textual parts—the type of engine, and the brand of tires—but most of the specification will be visual: sketches, scale models, and photographs of similar cars. When designing software, this translation is much more difficult, as Figure 1.7 shows. Prototypes and interface builders have done much to make the "external face" of a program visible, and software engineering diagramming techniques are of considerable value; but, in the final analysis, the "mapping" between an abstract model and a finished software product is much more tenuous than that for buildings, cars, or dresses.

> *"Software is complex because it contains so many 'moving parts.'"*

The Designer's Toolbox

Software, then, because of its very nature, is hard to design. But hard is not impossible, and, while the problems presented by complexity, change, and invisibility don't have magical solutions, they do have solutions.

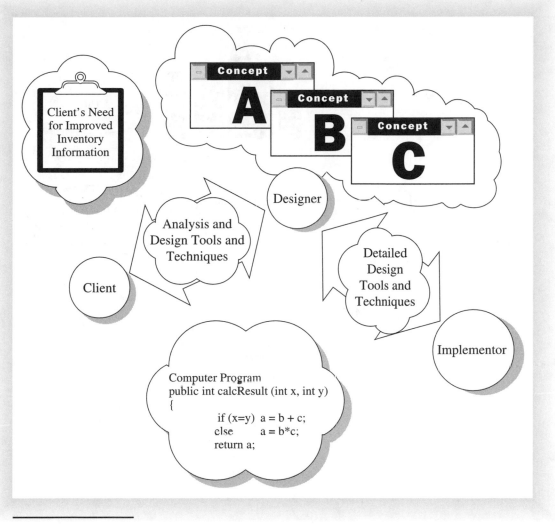

FIGURE 1.7

User, software designer, and programmer: a lack of visibility

MODELING AND MODELS

You've seen the word *model* bandied about, but what, exactly, is a model? A model is a representation of something else: something real or imaginary. A model can be textual, mathematical, graphical, or can use some other form of symbolic representation (see Figure 1.8). The supply-demand curve in economics is a model of a social interaction. J.R.R. Tolkien's *The Lord of the Rings* is a literary model of an imaginary world. A map is a model of our physical world.

FIGURE 1.8

What is a model?

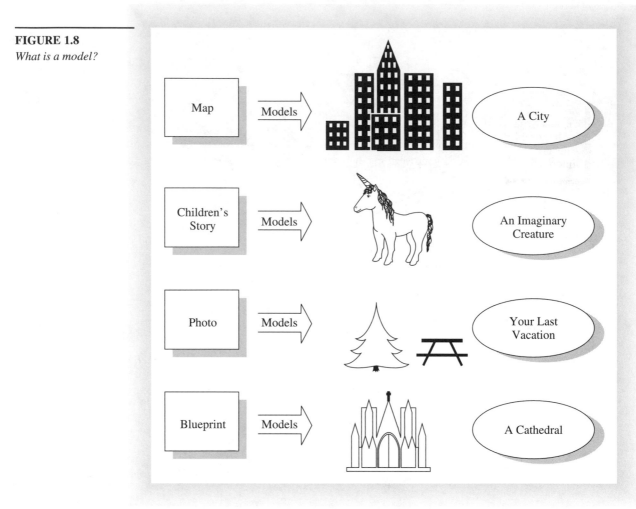

How is a model different from what it represents? A model is an abstraction. The globe on your desk is not the real earth; your Thomas' Guide is not really your town; Tolkien's novel is not Middle Earth; supply and demand is not the buying and selling of hot dogs and off-road vehicles. Instead, abstraction lets us model the thing we're studying by ignoring the irrelevant elements and concentrating on the essential.

ABSTRACTION, COMPLEXITY, HIERARCHY, AND DECOMPOSITION

"Why on earth," you say, "would I want to ignore details? What do I gain from that?" A good way to illustrate the importance of ignoring details is to compare a street map with a photograph of the same area taken by a LandSat satellite (see Figure 1.9).

Taken from space by high-resolution cameras, the satellite photo will let you count the blades of grass on your lawn. Yet, with all this incredible detail, it's almost entirely useless for finding your way across town. It doesn't have too little detail for this purpose; it has too much.

As you've already seen, one of the essential elements that makes software hard is its complexity. Human limitations—our memories and our senses of perception—prevent us from comprehending and dealing with very complex situations without the help of a simplifying model. For instance, social systems simplify our relationships with each other by proscribing behavior (through laws) and describing roles (through government).

You can use such models both to understand the world, and as a tool to create artifacts. Faced with the multitude of different animals in the world, you group similar animals together into classes based on their similarities to each other. You can arrange those classes into a "pyramid" (or hierarchy) based on the similarities of each class to other classes (see Figure 1.10). When you encounter a creature that is 1/4 inch high and has six legs, you put it in the insect category. Creating such categories gives you a mental tool you can use to deal with individual animals. Can you imagine what your life would be like if you didn't do this? If you were bitten by a snake, you'd have no reason to avoid others.

A special form of classification, decomposition, is useful as a tool for creating solutions, not merely for understanding. Decomposition is not merely recognizing similar "things," but recognizing that most big things can be broken into simpler things, and

> *" Abstraction lets us ignore the irrelevant elements and concentrate on the essential. "*

FIGURE 1.9

Which is clearer, a street map or a satellite map?

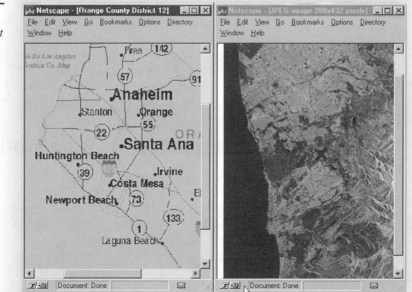

FIGURE 1.10

Abstraction and hierarchies in the animal world

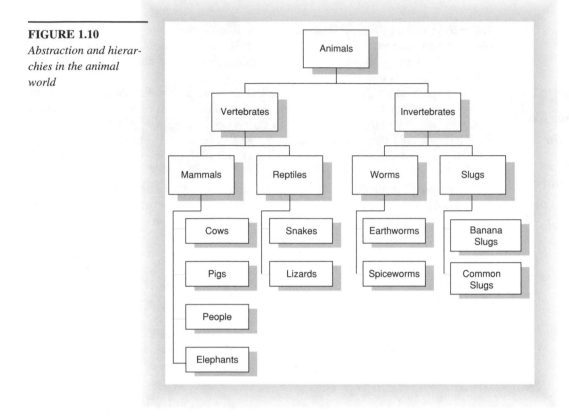

those simpler things into still simpler things. Trees have branches, leaves (or needles), roots, bark, and trunk, and the countless types of trees have innumerable variations. But, when you decompose a tree you find it is composed of simpler structures known as cells, and that the cells themselves are composed of simpler pieces yet—molecules and atoms. Most human artifacts exhibit similar structure, and such structure can usually be described in the form of a hierarchy or decomposition.

Design Solutions in the Software World

Architects have been designing buildings for thousands of years, and thinking about design nearly as long. Vitruvius wrote his books laying down the principles of firmness, commodity, and delight over two thousand years ago. In comparison, the computer was invented yesterday, and we may someday regard today's latest software creation the same way we regard Stonehenge in comparison to the Acropolis. Perhaps the golden age of software development is just ahead.

SOFTWARE ABSTRACTION MECHANISMS

Short though the history of software design has been, the ideas of abstraction, decomposition, and hierarchy have played an important part. Originally, computers were somewhat simple, and programmers could keep all the relevant details straight in their minds. As programs got larger and (subsequently) more complex, these principles were used to create various software abstraction mechanisms that were brought to bear in an attempt to master complexity.

The first programmers worked almost directly with the "naked" machine. A very thin abstraction, numbering memory locations to give some order to their seemingly unlimited (perhaps 12K) reserve of memory, was the only concession. Unfortunately, even 12K of memory, which seems laughably small today, is too much complexity for our brains to handle. Named variables (the ability to refer to GROSS_PAY instead of location AF3CH) enabled programmers to handle more complex problems by hiding an unnecessary detail—the actual physical location where GROSS_PAY was stored (see Figure 1.11).

FIGURE 1.11

Machine language versus assembly language

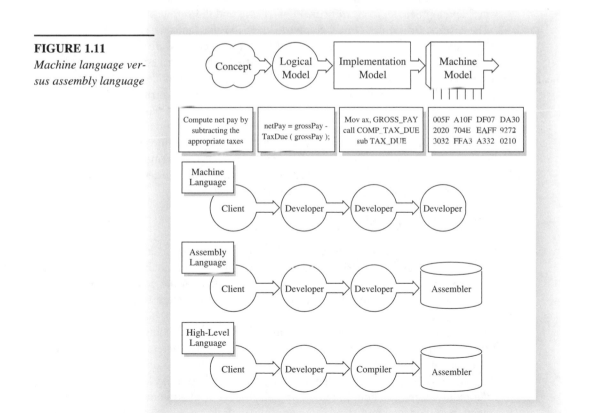

Just as the ability to name variables enabled programmers to hold bigger "chunks" of a program in their minds at a time, the ability to name sections of code (called *named subroutines*) enabled them to think of their programs in still larger pieces. These two advances, both of which involved ignoring irrelevant details, increased the productivity of programmers more than ten-fold. So, what do you suppose they did? That's right, they wrote programs that were ten times larger, and then some. And, just as you might expect, the additional complexity rendered those programs unmaintainable and unreliable.

THE SOFTWARE CRISIS AND STRUCTURED PROGRAMMING

In the late 1960s, the Department of Defense (DOD) was one of the largest purchasers of custom-made software. No doubt you've heard the stories of the $900 ash-trays. But even for folks accustomed to those sorts of apparent extravagances, the problems with software had gotten out of hand. In a pair of conferences sponsored by the North Atlantic Treaty Organization (NATO), two memorable terms were added to the software development lexicon: *software engineering* and the *software crisis*.

The term *software crisis* was coined to describe the fact that software was consistently late, over budget, and buggy. "Why can't we get software on time, at the price agreed upon, and why doesn't it work as specified?" NATO asked. The prescription of the experts at the conference was to endorse an engineering model. Once software was engineered—like bridges or weapons systems—bugs, cost overruns, and late delivery would be a thing of the past. With 25 years hindsight, it's easy to see that things weren't so simple; nevertheless, the techniques promoted and developed as a result of the proclamation of the software crisis, did, in fact raise the level of abstraction, increase the robustness (firmness) of the software that was written, and open the way for much larger programs to be written. Of course, this started the same cycle of improvement followed by rising expectations all over again.

SPECIFIC DESIGN TECHNIQUES

Structured programming, one set of techniques popularized as a means of combating the software crisis, was designed to make software more readable and maintainable. Because, as the DOD researchers discovered, over 75% of the cost of a software system occurs during maintenance, it made sense to concentrate efforts on techniques to reduce that effort.

The first of these techniques was to simplify the "flow of control" inside programs. *Flow of control* is simply the sequence in which program statements are executed. In early computer programs, all or most program execution was controlled by the unconditional branch—the infamous goto. Although, at the machine level, gotos were still required, by using the goto to build more abstract control structures—the loop and the selection statement—and then programming entirely in terms of those higher-level constructs, programmers were able to eliminate a whole class of common errors and thus, increased their ability to write and understand more complex programs.

If hiding the "actual" flow of control inside the computer was a success, the technique of hiding or limiting the access to data was an even greater success. Researchers discovered that many common software errors of the time were caused by two subroutines inadvertently modifying a piece of data that both used. The invention of local variables—and David Parnas' ideas on data hiding, modularization, and abstract data types—were responsible for the next advance in the creation of "firm" software. Each of these was an attempt to hide more of the details of the problem and only show the relevant information.

Software Design Methodologies

In applying the abstraction mechanisms that were developed during the "years of crisis" to help in mastering software complexity, programmers began to follow, and encourage others to follow, software development methodologies. A methodology is simply a prescribed way of using abstraction mechanisms.

Methodologies consist of three things:

- A process—the step-by-step activities and related deliverables that are used to model and construct software.

- A notation—a representation, often graphical, of the subsystems that make up a system and the way they interact.

- A set of heuristics—rules of thumb or figures of merit that give the designer guidance about how the artifact being built should work.

STRUCTURED DESIGN AND OBJECT-ORIENTED DESIGN

Software design methodologies were developed to exploit the abstraction mechanisms that were introduced with better programming techniques. Developed in the 1970s, structured design takes the best practices of structured programming and adds a graphical notation and a development process.

The primary abstraction mechanism in procedural languages is the subroutine, sometimes called a function, which operates on a piece of data. The primary design decision in a procedural program is apportioning the work of the program among specialized subroutines. Because of this, the shape or morphology of a system developed using structured design almost always takes the form of a tree, with centralized control invested in the top or main module (see Figure 1.12).

Object-oriented design (OOD), in a similar manner, arose from the ideas introduced in object-oriented programming with SmallTalk and Simula. In an OOD system, the primary abstraction mechanism is the class, which you'll meet in greater depth in the next chapter, and will be using throughout the book. A *class* is a combination of both data and the legal operations that can be performed on that data. The data in an OOD

FIGURE 1.12
A structure chart

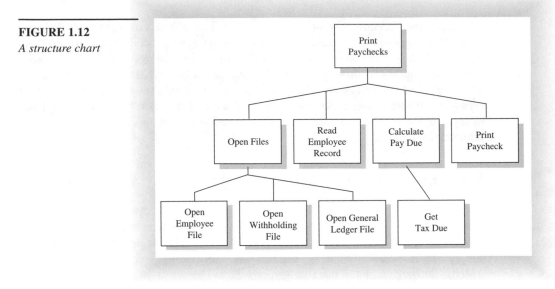

system, rather than being passed between operations (subprograms), is hidden and protected from access by other parts of the program, by means of a principle called encapsulation. This is simply a refinement of the ideas of data hiding that began with local variables and abstract data types.

The flow of control in an object-oriented program is also different from that within a structured program. Instead of superior and subordinate subroutines, the action in the program occurs as objects (instances of a class) interact with each other by sending messages (see Figure 1.13).

FIGURE 1.13
Object interactions

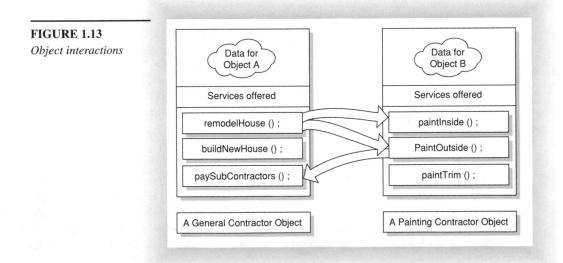

" In an OOD system, the primary abstraction mechanism is the class. "

One way to think about the difference between structured designs and OO designs is to think about the difference between a centralized (planned) economy and a free-market economy. In a planned economy, decisions about who should produce what, and about what will be sold in the marketplace, are made at the top. In a free-market economy, the economy runs itself by the interaction of millions of autonomous, independent decisions. You could say that the major difference between structured and OO systems is the degree to which intelligence (and thus flow-of-control) is vertical or horizontal.

Summary

Design is the process of creating artifacts for human use. While you can look at design from a scientific, an engineering, or an artistic point of view, the successful designer needs to draw from each of these traditions to produce artifacts that exhibit firmness, commodity, and delight. As a software designer, you want your creations to work correctly and efficiently (firmness), to meet the actual needs of your users (commodity), and to do so with style and aesthetic pleasure (delight).

Design has several characteristics. First, design is preliminary—you design before you construct. Second, design involves constructing abstract models that will help in construction. Third, design has a goal: to create artifacts that meet the needs of their users. Finally, design is a process, with different degrees of formality, each appropriate to the product.

Design is needed for two reasons. First, changes done during the planning stage are less expensive than changes initiated during or after construction. Second, by consciously separating the concerns of the client from the concerns of the builder, you can build software that is both more efficient and more effective.

Although no one would build a house without a set of plans, introducing design into the software process has not yet been as successful. Why is software so hard to design? Because software is very complex, because software is very easy to change (though not easy to change correctly), and because software is essentially invisible. The correspondence between an architect's sketch—or even a blueprint—and the finished building is a visual one, which makes it easier for the architect to communicate with clients.

Despite the difficulties present in designing software, the would-be designer is not left without tools. Abstraction is the mental tool that lets you ignore irrelevant details, and concentrate on the important parts of the problem. In software development, the two most important abstraction mechanisms are decomposition and classification. As a designer, you can use these techniques to construct models that enable you to graphically or textually represent a particular abstraction so you can communicate with others about your design.

Software development methodologies are collections of such models (represented using established notations), along with a prescribed process for applying them. The structured design methodologies were based on breaking a problem down into "units of work" called procedures. The object-oriented design methods break a problem down into semi-autonomous agents, which cooperate to make the artifact work. In this sense, object-oriented design is much more like industrial design or electrical engineering, where elemental components are arranged in sub-assemblies, which are then combined to make the whole.

Questions

1. A designer approaching a software product from the engineering perspective would most likely be concerned with the quality of _____.

2. When you ignore irrelevant or extraneous details, you are using the process of _____.

3. A map, a novel, and a blueprint are all examples of a _____ of something real or imaginary.

4. An effective way to understand a complex process is to break it into smaller pieces, using the process called _____.

5. A software designer who was primarily concerned with creating attractive buttons and screen layouts would be focusing on the design quality of _____.

6. Software is hard to construct because it is
   a. Expensive, complex, and buggy.
   b. Complex, easily changed, and invisible.
   c. Hard to change, hard to fix, and hard to understand.
   d. Invisible, prone to errors, obscure.

7. A software development methodology uses a _____ to represent a set of models, and prescribes a _____ for using those models.

8. A designer acts as an agent for the client, designing artifacts that meet the client's needs. Her designs will exhibit the quality of _____ if she is successful.

9. The abstraction process of _____ allows us to tell the difference between a garden hose and a rattlesnake.

10. A primary reason for designing a program before writing it is because it is _____ to make a change to a design than to a shipping program.

Exercises

1. Design a process for baking a cake, building a dog house, driving a car, or producing a newsletter, by breaking down the individual steps necessary to accomplish the task. You may create any number of subtasks.

2. Design a plan for accomplishing the task you designed in Exercise 1, assuming that you will use a team of three or four people. Assign each person a particular responsibility, list the resources each person will need, and make sure you account for the necessary communication between team members.

3. Change the design in Exercise 2, so that your hypothetical team members can work simultaneously. Does this make your design simpler or more complex?

4. Change the design in Exercise 2 so that you don't have to know what resources each person needs. Does this make the task simpler or more complex?

5. Suppose you were asked by the Federal Aviation Administration to design a software system to control the nation's air traffic. Which of the design characteristics—firmness, commodity, delight—would be most important, and why?

6. For each of the design qualities, discuss what kind of software products are most affected by that quality and what kind are least affected by it.

7. Spend 10 minutes making a list of all of the audio CDs you can think of. Now use the abstraction mechanism of classification to put each CD in a category. Do some CDs fit in more than one category? Are some categories subcategories of others? Could you combine some categories into larger categories?

To Learn More

The classic book treating design as a scientific subject was written by the cofounder of the Computer Science program at MIT, Herbert Simon. *The Sciences of the Artificial* is a set of essays that make thought-provoking, if difficult, reading. Would-be designers should give Chapter 5, "The Science of Design," and Chapter 7, "The Architecture of Complexity," a special look.

Looking at software design from the engineering and management perspective is Frederick Brooks Jr.'s *The Mythical Man Month*. The best known and most widely read book on software development, MMM was recently re-released in a 20th anniversary edition. If you think that a 20-year-old book on software design and development couldn't have anything to say to you, pick up a copy and you'll find yourself very pleasantly surprised. This is one book everyone in software design should own.

When Terry Winograd, Stanford University Professor of Computer Science, set out to hold a conference on software design, the unexpected result was the many different perspectives of those represented. Another unexpected result was the publication of *Bringing Design to Software*, which gives each of those different hearings a platform. This book, which leads off with Mitch Kapor's "A Software Design Manifesto," provides the broadest view on software design as a user-centered activity. Each essay is interesting in its own right, and is supplemented by case studies of actual software products and the design issues that they illustrate.

Finally, a book that attempts to reconcile the engineering and user-centered design camps in software development is Nathaniel Borenstein's *Programming As If People Mattered: Friendly Programs, Software Engineering, and Other Noble Delusions*. Written as a series of anecdotes, this book will be especially helpful to the programmer or software engineer who wants to learn about adding "commodity" to her programs. If you still can't decide whether computer science is really a science, you'll want to read Chapter 20, "The Ivory Tower."

2

Object-Oriented Software Development

Have you ever wondered why some organizations refer to the group responsible for computers and information systems as "data processing"? Structured programming and structured design (which grew out of structured programming) understand the mission of software as that of processing data. Structured programming and structured design are focused on the changes programs make in transforming input data to output data, seeing computer programs as action-oriented. The early name of the computer programming profession—data processing—reflects this procedural perspective.

Object-oriented programming and design emphasize the view that software systems model the real world. Objects within an object-oriented system may still transform input data to output data, but this is not the only possible way to organize an object-oriented program.

From an object-oriented perspective, the group responsible for computers and information systems might aptly be named the Business Object Portfolio (BOP) group. Their function, as you'll see, is to assemble and maintain a portfolio of objects that model their organization's processes.

If your age is over twenty and you're therefore less than enthusiastic about the prospect of being called a BOPper, never fear. You can choose to work in the health care industry, in which case you may come to be known HOPper (for "Health care Object Portfolio") or MOPper (for "Medical Object Portfolio"). That's decidedly better than working in law enforcement, where you might come to be known as a COPper (for "Crime Object Portfolio"), or working in agriculture, where you might come to be known as a CROPper (for "Crop Rotation Object Portfolio").

In this chapter you will learn:

◆ How structured design exploits the organization inherent in routine business procedures.

◆ How the principles of structured design tend to break down when systems become large and complex.

◆ How the object-oriented paradigm differs from the structured paradigm.

◆ How the concepts of class and object and the principles of encapsulation, inheritance, and polymorphism define the object-oriented paradigm.

◆ How various processes are used to design and develop software and how each has strengths and weaknesses.

Procedural Programs

Computer programs, whether designed based on structured design or object-oriented design, usually model some process that exists in the real world. A payroll program, for example, models the manual process that a real business goes through when it pays its employees. In a small business, the process might work something like this:

1. Get the list of employees from the file over by the coffee machine.
2. Get the federal and state withholding schedules out of the bottom right drawer of the desk.
3. Get the general ledger from the supervisor's office.
4. For each employee on the list, do the following:
   A. Get the amount of pay from the employee record.
   B. Calculate the amount of taxes due, based on the withholding schedules.
   C. Calculate the net pay by subtracting the deductions and withholding from the gross pay.
   D. Prepare the check.
   E. Record the check in the general ledger.
5. Take the stack of checks to the boss to be signed.
6. Mail the checks at the post office.
7. Return the general ledger, withholding schedules, and list of employees to their regular places.

Most of these operations could be performed by a computer, though the computer wouldn't do them exactly the same way the payroll clerk would. When written as part of a computer program, the steps necessary to carry out a task are called a *process*. Each step within a process is known as a *procedure*. When a procedure is long or complex, it may consist of several steps, called subprocedures or simply procedures.

Procedures are the blocks used to build structured programs. A typical payroll program, for example, would contain procedures to open and read the files, perform the payroll calculations, and print the checks. By using direct deposit, the program might even "sign" and "mail" the checks. Figure 2.1 shows how such a program might be structured.

Figure 2.1 represents a computerized payroll process. Each of the boxes in Figure 2.1 represents a procedure that carries out a series of steps. Each procedure receives input data, processes the data, and transmits the results of its processing, either to a subsequent procedure or to a human. Data is fed to the procedures in much the same way that raw materials are fed to an assembly line—except the procedures produce information rather than cars or toasters.

A useful property of structured programs is that the "shape" of the solution (that is, the program) closely models the shape of the problem. Each of the procedures of the structured program in Figure 2.1 relates to one or more of the steps in the process for manually preparing payroll checks. Structured programs are designed by means of *procedural decomposition*. Using procedural decomposition, a designer studies the problem and attempts to break it apart by identifying a series of actions that solve it. When a designer is asked to automate an existing business process, the design process is often simple because procedural decomposition is easy to perform. The designer merely uses the steps of the manual process to identify the actions that the program must perform. Because these steps have successfully kept the business from devolving into chaos, using them as the basis for a computer program may be less risky that trying an entirely new series of steps.

Think again, though, about what would happen to the manual payroll process in your imaginary business if it grew to 20,000 employees instead of 20. The employee file could no longer be kept in the filing cabinet over by the coffee machine. Fred, the part-time bookkeeper, could no longer finish his work each Tuesday afternoon. And,

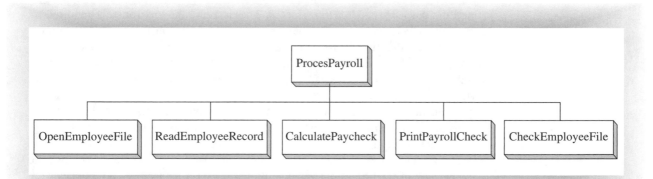

FIGURE 2.1
A procedural payroll program

most importantly, the boss, who previously signed every check and would likely notice if Ms. Smallie's check had $1,000 written on it, instead of $100, could no longer sign each check personally—there simply wouldn't be enough remaining time to properly watch over the business.

When businesses grow, they change their structure to handle the added complexity caused by their growth. Finance departments, vice-presidents, controllers, and auditors are added because the simple structure that worked fine for a 20-person company is no longer adequate.

Computer programs can suffer from a similar malady. The procedural paradigm (*paradigm* is just a fancy word for pattern) works fine for automating routine office processes, like preparing payroll checks. But it fails to offer sufficient structure when applied to many other kinds of problems, such as simulations and interactive environments. If you've been around a while, you might remember when the main job of computer programmers and designers was writing programs that solved "assembly-line" problems like payroll, batch accounting, and monthly invoicing. Things are different today. Instead of being assigned to write a data-processing program to tally the month-end statements, a bank programmer is more likely to be responsible for writing code to control the ATM or the bank's new World Wide Web site. A programmer for a stock broker might design automatic trading programs instead of a simple client billing application.

Such interactive or "reactive" programs are much more complex than traditional data-processing applications, because the flow of control is no longer linear. Data doesn't come in at the start of the program, flow through a number of predefined procedures, and exit at the end, relaxed and refreshed. In a reactive program, the procedure `DoThingC()` might be called first, second, last, or not at all—unlike the procedural program where `DoThingC()` always follows `DoThingA()` and `DoThingB()`.

Look back at Figure 2.1. What does it look like? A pyramid, right? The pyramid structure occurs because of the hierarchical nature of control in the program. `ReadEmployeeRecord()` relies on the fact that `ProcessPayroll()` has already performed the `OpenEmployeeFile()` process. The data and the environment required by `ReadEmployeeRecord()` are available only because the `OpenEmployeeFile()` procedure has been called first. If you attempt to write an interactive program that uses procedures as its basic building block, however, the program structure no longer resembles a neat pyramid. Instead, it begins to look like a dense web of interconnections.

If you remember your first programming class, this might set off a light bulb. Before the advent of structured programming, back in the days of "iron men," when "big-iron" was not merely metaphorical, computer programs were largely monolithic—they had no procedures at all. Thus, when a programmer needed to execute a piece of code in another part of the program, an unconditional branch was used; such branches were called `gotos`. As programs got larger, the typical path of program execution began to resemble a large web. Such code became known as *spaghetti code*, code that was difficult or impossible to understand and thus difficult or impossible to maintain, fix, or change.

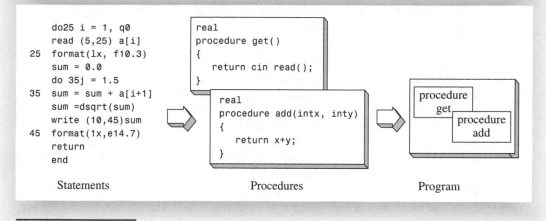

```
      do25 i = 1, q0
      read (5,25) a[i]
 25   format(1x, f10.3)
      sum = 0.0
      do 35j = 1.5
 35   sum = sum + a[i+1]
      sum =dsqrt(sum)
      write (10,45)sum
 45   format(1x,e14.7)
      return
      end
```

Statements

```
real
procedure get()
{
    return cin read();
}
```

```
real
procedure add(intx, inty)
{
    return x+y;
}
```

Procedures

```
procedure
get
    procedure
    add
```

Program

FIGURE 2.2

Procedures as an organizing unit

The underlying problem was that programs were organized as a collection of source statements. Too many "blocks" (that is, source statements) were required to build large programs. To solve this problem, structured programming introduced the procedure as a second, larger organizing unit, as shown in Figure 2.2. Source statements were used to build procedures, but procedures (not source statements) were used to build programs. Thus, the number of blocks required to build a program decreased, reducing the complexity of the program.

Object-Oriented Programs

Object-oriented programming attacks the complexity of today's programs in a similar fashion. By grouping procedures into still larger organizing units called *objects*, programs require fewer blocks and are, therefore, simpler.

O O P : I S N O T H I N G N E W ?

Studying object-oriented programming, it's hard not to notice the fact that different folks have very different views when it comes to OOP. Reading various OOP books and papers, it almost seems that people are talking about entirely different things. When you finally cut through all the rhetoric, though, there are two points of view: the revolutionary and the evolutionary. The advocate of the revolutionary view loudly proclaims that OOP is so different from traditional programming that you have to learn programming over again from scratch. The evolutionists, in contrast, say that OOP is really just new packaging of old concepts. Perhaps there's some truth, as well as some error, in each of these views.

Continued...

OOP: IS NOTHING NEW? Continued...

The evolutionists are correct when they assert that it is possible to write clear, well-commented, understandable code in a procedural language, and that it is possible to write incomprehensible, unmaintainable code in an object-oriented language. The evolutionist generally fails to recognize, however, that an OOP program is organized in a fundamentally different manner than a procedural program.

The revolutionist is right in pointing out that the OOP design process uses different tools and different types of abstraction, and that no amount of functional decomposition will ever yield an object-oriented program. The revolutionist overestimates, perhaps, the value of such an object-oriented design when weighed against factors of clarity and understandability. A well-designed and implemented procedural program is definitely to be preferred over a poorly conceived and written OOP program. OOP and object-oriented languages provide tools to express ideas clearly, but are not instant, automatic panaceas.

" An object-oriented program is a collection of objects that are organized for, and cooperate toward, the accomplishment of some goal. "

Five fundamental concepts govern object-oriented programs:

- Objects
- Classes
- Encapsulation
- Inheritance
- Polymorphism

What Are Objects?

Just as procedures are used to build structured programs, objects are used to build object-oriented programs. An object-oriented program is a collection of objects that are organized for, and cooperate toward, the accomplishment of some goal. Every object:

- **Contains data.** The data stores information that describes the state of the object.

- **Has a set of defined behaviors.** These behaviors are the things that the object "knows" how to do and are triggered by sending the object a message.

- **Has an individual identity.** This makes it possible to distinguish one object from another, just as it's possible to distinguish one program variable from another.

Like the records or structures used in procedural programs, objects contain data. In this sense, an object looks very much like one of the employee records that would be used in the payroll program you saw in the last section. An object's data is used to represent the object's state. For example, data within an employee object might indicate whether an employee is full-time or part-time, hourly or salaried.

Unlike the employee record within a procedural program, however, an employee object can also contain operations. These operations may be used to read or change the object's data. In this sense, an object acts like a small "mini-program" that carries its own data around on its back, as shown in Figure 2.3.

If you want to do something to an object, or want to know something about it, you "ask it" to perform one of its operations. In object-oriented parlance, you *send it a message*. In response, it performs some behavior. The second characteristic of an object, then, is that it has some built-in behavior: An employee object may know how to tell you its salary, or how to print itself out to a mailing-address label.

The third characteristic of an object is that every object has a unique identity. This doesn't mean that every object necessarily has an ID number, or a "primary key" like you find in relational databases. Objects are very much like program variables in a procedural language. The integer variables i and j may have exactly the same value—say 3—and yet they are distinct variables, stored at different locations within the computer's memory. Changing the value of i to 4, for example, does not change the value of j. Similarly, two employee objects that represent the identical twins who work in shipping, Fred and Ned, may have similar data contents, yet still be distinct objects.

FIGURE 2.3

Objects have data, operations, and identity

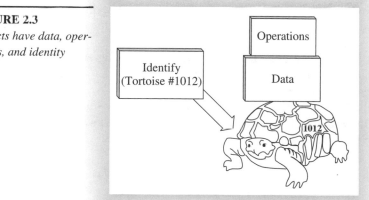

O O P   T E R M I N O L O G Y

Much, but not all, of the terminology used in object-oriented programming is the same from programming language to programming language. However, knowing about the differences in terminology might help you avoid some confusion when you find yourself "talking objects" to a Smalltalk or Object Pascal or C++ programmer. In Java, the operations of an object or class are called *methods*, just as in Smalltalk. C++ programmers call methods *member functions*. While Smalltalk programmers always speak of *sending a message*, C++ programmers tend to refer to *calling a member function*. Java programmers tend to split the difference, and speak either of sending a message to an object, or calling an object's method, depending on whether it is the sender or the recipient of the message that is the focus of discussion.

An Object Example

When a book on object-oriented programming attempts to introduce you to objects, it usually begins by discussing objects in the "real world"—things like animals, or plants, or vehicles. It does this for a very good reason. One of the advantages of object-oriented programming is that program objects have a much closer correspondence to objects in the real world than do the procedures of structured programs, which have operations but lack data. Still, unless you're writing an application for a zoo or a botanist's convention, you may have a hard time trying to apply what you learn from your textbook—how to model a marmoset—to the actual programs you find yourself writing.

In an effort to avoid that difficulty, let's start out by looking at some of the objects you'll really use in your Java programs. Figure 2.4 shows the `LabelsGalore` applet, which features an ensemble of talented objects.

If you want to run the applet for yourself, the HTML file you'll need is shown in Listing 2.1. The applet features some animation that isn't obvious in Figure 2.4, so by all means run the applet if you can.

Listing 2.1 LabelsGalore.html

```
<HTML>
<HEAD>
<TITLE> The LabelsGalore Applet </TITLE>
</HEAD>
<BODY>
<H1> The LabelsGalore </H1>
<HR>
<H2> A family of Label objects </H2>
<BR>
<APPLET CODE=LabelsGalore HEIGHT=300 WIDTH=500>
</APPLET>
</BODY>
</HTML>
```

FIGURE 2.4

*Running the
LabelsGalore applet*

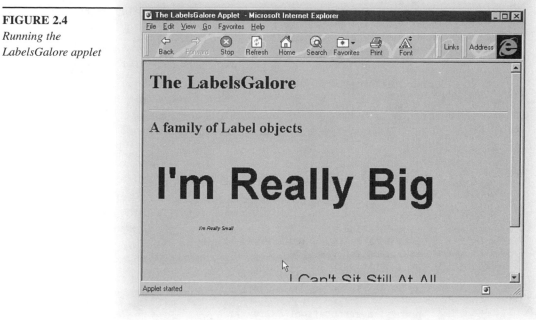

The Java source code for the applet is shown in Listing 2.2. Chapter 3, "Teach Yourself Java in 21 Minutes," introduces you to the Java language, but, even if you can't yet understand much of what you read, see if you can pick out the objects. If you can't spot them, don't despair. The next section will walk you through the highlights of the code.

Listing 2.2 LabelsGalore.java

```java
//  LabelsGalore.java
//  Creating and sending messages to Label objects

import java.awt.*;
import java.applet.*;
import java.util.Random;

public class LabelsGalore extends Applet
                          implements Runnable
{
  Label gigantica = new Label( "I'm Really Big" );
  Label miniscula = new Label( "I'm Really Small" );
  Label nervosica = new Label( "I Can't Sit Still At All" );

  Thread runner;
  int vx = 1, vy = 1;

  public void init( )
  {
    gigantica.setFont( new Font("Serif",     Font.BOLD,   72));
    miniscula.setFont( new Font("SanSerif",  Font.ITALIC,  8));
```

```
        nervosica.setFont( new Font("Monospaced", Font.PLAIN,  28));
        add( gigantica );
        add( miniscula );
        add( nervosica );
    }

    public void run()
    {
        Random randomizer = new Random( );
        int dx, dy;

        while ( true )
        {
            dx = (int) (randomizer.nextFloat() * 50);
            dy = (int) (randomizer.nextFloat() * 50);

            Point location = nervosica.getLocation( );

            if ( location.x < -100 ) vx =  1;
            if ( location.x >  300 ) vx = -1;
            if ( location.y <  100 ) vy =  1;
            if ( location.y >  300 ) vy = -1;
            dx = location.x + ( dx * vx );
            dy = location.y + ( dy * vy );

            nervosica.setLocation( dx, dy );

            try { runner.sleep( 500 ); }
            catch ( InterruptedException e ) { }
        }
    }

    public void start( )
    {
        if ( runner == null )
        {
            runner = new Thread( this );
            runner.start();
        }
    }

    public void stop( )
    {
        if ( runner != null )
        {
            runner.stop();
            runner = null;
        }
    }
}
```

Objects, State, and Identity

The LabelsGalore applet creates and uses eight objects. Working together, these objects comprise the program:

- The three `Label` objects, `gigantica`, `miniscula`, and `nervosica`. These names represent the identity of each of the three objects.

- Each `Label` object also uses a `Font` object to change the way that it displays characters.

- A `Random` object named `randomizer`. `Random` objects act as "factories" for producing pseudo-random numbers. The object `randomizer` is used to generate the pixel coordinates sent to the `Label` `nervosica`.

- A `Thread` object named `runner`. Java is a multithreaded language (able to execute different methods simultaneously). The `Thread` object is responsible for executing the code that keeps `nervosica` moving around the screen.

- A `Point` object named `location`, which is used to hold `nervosica`'s current location.

Actually, there is one other object involved in this program, which you may not have noticed. The program itself becomes an `Applet` object when your browser loads the Web page it resides on. You'll learn more about this in the next chapter.

Rather than trying to dissect each of these objects, let's just take a closer look at the three `Label` objects, `gigantica`, `miniscula`, and `nervosica`—named, of course, after the legendary ancient circus performers. As you've learned, every object has three characteristics—identity, state, and behavior. You've already seen that the name of each `Label` represents its identity. What could a `Label` store as its state? Because the purpose of a `Label` is to display textual information on the screen, what type of data does a `Label` object need to perform this task? You can likely identify these three:

- The text that `Label` displays.

- The position where the text is displayed on the screen.

- The font or typeface used to display the text.

`Label` objects, as implemented in Java's AWT, actually have a few more attributes such as alignment, but these three are the essential ones. When each `Label` object is created in `LabelsGalore.java`, the text that each `Label` displays is provided as an argument, and each `Label` stores this bit of data away "inside" itself:

```
Label gigantica = new Label( "I'm Really Big" );
Label miniscula = new Label( "I'm Really Small" );
Label nervosica = new Label( "I Can't Sit Still At All" );
```

Again, it's not important that you understand the specific Java syntax that is used to create these `Label`s—help with that is coming soon enough. It is important that you understand that each of these `Label`s—`gigantica`, `miniscula`, and `nervosica`—has some data that it is individually responsible for managing.

What Do Labels Do?

One mark of an enjoyable movie is that you're not really aware, when you're watching it, that it's a movie at all. A poor film announces its presence, but a good one allows you to suspend your disbelief and savor the experience. Working with objects and thinking in an object-oriented manner benefit from a similar attitude. A well-designed program object lets you forget that it's a program object, directing your attention instead to the real-world object it represents.

> *A well-designed program object lets you forget that it's a program object, directing your attention instead to the real-world object it represents.*

This is particularly helpful in considering the third characteristic of objects, behavior. Those programmers who have spent many years working with a procedural language sometimes experience a sticking point here. All this talk of sending messages and objects that "know" how to do something, or "behave" in a certain way, strikes them as unnecessarily anthropomorphic. If you find yourself in this situation—struggling to understand how an object "really" works—please just step back and consider Arthur C. Clarke's famous maxim: "Any sufficiently advanced technology is indistinguishable from magic." A well-designed object, like a well-cast magical spell, works even if you don't fully understand why.

> *A well-designed object, like a well-cast magical spell, works even if you don't fully understand why.*

A `Label` is a fairly simple object, as objects go, and can't do all that much. What kind of things can you tell a `Label` to do? Another way of asking the same thing is, "What messages does a `Label` object respond to?" Most objects, and `Labels` are no exception, respond to messages that

- Allow you to change their internal state. One attribute of a `Label` is the `Font` it uses to display its data. By sending the `setFont()` message to a `Label`, you can have it display itself using a different `Font` than the one it originally assumes:

```
gigantica.setFont( new Font("Serif",     Font.BOLD,   72));
miniscula.setFont( new Font("SanSerif",  Font.ITALIC,  8));
nervosica.setFont( new Font("Monospaced", Font.PLAIN,  28));
```

- Ask the object to tell you something about itself. If you ask it, a `Label` object will tell you its coordinates on the screen. You can do this by sending it the `getLocation()` message, just as in the `LabelsGalore` applet:

```
Point location = nervosica.getLocation();
```

- Ask the object to do something. The `Label` object `nervosica` will move itself to a new position on the screen when you send it the `setLocation()` message, like this:

```
nervosica.setLocation( dx, dy );
```

What Are Classes?

If Java programs are built from collections of objects, then what are classes? Are they collections of "student" objects? No, classes are the blueprints that are used to create

> **" You will never actually write the code for an object: what you write is the pattern that is used to make objects. "**

> **" A class defines the attributes and behaviors that each object created from the class will possess. "**

objects. You will never actually write the code for an object: what you write is the pattern that is used to make objects. The distinction between classes and objects is sometimes subtle, but it is basic to a good understanding of object-oriented design.

One helpful way to think about the relationship between classes and objects is to think about the similar relationship between types and variables in a procedural programming language. When you talk about the type of a variable—integer, floating-point, or string—you are using shorthand to describe the range of data that the variable can store, as well as the operations that can be performed on that variable. For instance, integer variables cannot hold fractional numbers. Similarly, you can multiply integers and floating-point numbers, but you can do spell-checking only on strings.

Notice that variables hold values; types do not. A type is merely an abstraction. To actually hold an integer value, you have to create an integer variable. A variable is an integer if it follows the "blueprint" for creating integers, specified as the integer type. Rules within the integer type determine what data integers store, and how integers act. Individual integers, i, j, and k, are called *instances* of the integer type.

Objects and classes have a similar relationship. A class defines the attributes and behaviors that each object created from the class will possess. The class is the blueprint that is used to create objects. In writing Java programs, you use classes created by others, and you define new classes that are used to create new sorts of objects of your own device. Creating new classes involves a two-part process:

- Define the attributes that objects created from your class will use to store their state.

- Define the messages you want your objects to understand and the steps involved in responding to these messages. For each message, create a procedure, called a *method*, that implements these steps.

Chapter 3, "Teach Yourself Java in 21 Minutes," guides you through the syntax necessary to define classes in Java, while Chapter 5, "Designing Classes and Objects," shows you how to design classes that are both robust and maintainable.

What Is Encapsulation?

Unlike objects and classes, encapsulation is not a Java language element. Instead, encapsulation is a technique you'll use to create well-designed classes. Just as writing a successful action novel involves application of techniques intended to create a suspenseful mood, writing well-designed object-oriented classes demands that you apply the technique of encapsulation.

"Fine," you say. "I'd be happy to pay attention to encapsulation, if only I knew what it is. It sounds like something astronauts have to go through. Just what is it?" No sooner asked than answered: Encapsulation is the process of packaging your program, dividing each of its classes into two distinct parts: the *interface* and the *implementation*.

" Writing well-designed object-oriented classes demands that you apply the technique of encapsulation. "

"Wait a second," you respond. "You've already said that classes have two parts: attributes and methods. Are the interface and implementation two new parts, or are these just new terms for attributes and methods?" Neither one.

Your objects are made of attributes and methods. Some of these attributes and methods are publicly available, visible from outside the object: These are the interface. Other attributes and methods are reserved for the private use of the object itself: These are the implementation. Separating the interface from the implementation is the most fundamental design decision you make when you design an object-oriented program.

To see the value of dividing interface from implementation, look at an example you're already familiar with: the automobile. The interface of an automobile is relatively simple and uniform: the steering wheel, the gas pedal, and the brake. You only have to learn to drive once. You don't have to take new lessons whenever the fall line of cars appears. In contrast, the internal workings of the car—the ignition, number of cylinders, fuel-injection, and so on—can change dramatically from year to year. If you had to directly interact with the ignition system for each different type of automobile, you'd find yourself having great difficulty even getting your new car started. As it stands, even if you're flying to a faraway place, you can make a car reservation without fear that you'll be unable to drive the car you're assigned.

A well-designed class has these same characteristics. The interface completely describes how the users (sometimes called *clients*) of your class interact with it. In almost every case this means that the attributes of your class will be hidden, and that users will use the class's methods to modify its data.

You can see this at work in the `Label` objects you met in the `LabelsGalore` applet. When you send the `Label nervosica` the `getLocation()` message, it gives you back the `Label`'s location as a `Point` object. But, that's not necessarily the way that `Label`s store this piece of information. If the `Label` class exposed this attribute and users interacted with it directly, a change to the class might cause programs that use `Label`s to quit working. For example, changing the data type of the location coordinates from integer to float-point might cause client programs that expect integer coordinates to choke. Separating the actual data storage (implementation) from the method used to obtain the information (interface) means that you can change the insides of a class without affecting those who use the class. You'll see how this can be done in Chapter 4, "Encapsulation: Classes and Methods."

What Is Inheritance?

The second design decision made while designing a class is the structure of its inheritance hierarchy. Encapsulation is necessary for creating robust classes that can be easily changed. Inheritance is concerned with "families" of classes and their relationships.

If you were to take a look at the source code for the `Label` class provided with the Java Development Kit, you might be surprised to find that the `Label` class does not define a method called `setLocation()`. "How can that be?" you ask. "I just saw you send the `setLocation()` message to the `Label nervosica`. Where's the corresponding `setLocation()` method?" The answer to your question is simple. A `Label` knows how

" The true value of inheritance is as a powerful organizing abstraction. "

to respond to the `setLocation()` message because every `Label` receives a `setLocation()` method through inheritance.

Figure 2.5 shows the inheritance hierarchy for part of the Java Abstract Windowing Toolkit. Notice that the `Label` class appears below the `Component` class. All the classes appearing below `Component`—`Button`, `TextField`, and `Panel`, in addition to `Label`—are *subclasses* of the `Component` class. The `Component` class, which is called a *superclass*, defines the attributes and behaviors that are common to all its subclasses. A subclass, like `Label`, needs to define only those ways in which it is a specialization of its superclass. It automatically inherits all the attributes and methods of its superclass.

There are two chief advantages in defining such inheritance relationships between classes. The first is purely Pragmatic: if you write a `setLocation()` method within the `Component` class, you don't have to include a `setLocation()` method in any of the classes descended from `Component`. Each subclass of `Component` inherits the `setLocation()` method included in the superclass. Thus, when writing a subclass that describes a new kind of `Component`, you have all sorts of functionality already built in.

This is the advantage most commonly cited for using inheritance. However, it is not the whole story. When procedures were first used in programming languages, they were promoted primarily as a way of reducing redundant code. Their greatest strength, however, proved to be their facility as a tool to organize and conquer complexity in the computer. The true value of inheritance is as a powerful organizing abstraction. Whereas using procedures allows you to divide complex problems into simpler parts, using inheritance allows you to see commonalties and to factor them out, placing them in a more general superclass.

Structured programming was based on abstraction by decomposition. Object-oriented programming includes decomposition as an abstraction mechanism, but supplements it with inheritance, which is based on abstraction by classification. The power of hierarchical classification can be seen in Figure 2.6, which depicts its use in the natural sciences. There it has been a powerful tool for organizing information about the millions of types of animal and plant life on our planet.

FIGURE 2.5

A portion of the Java Abstract Windowing Toolkit hierarchy

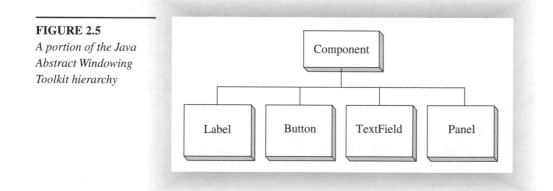

FIGURE 2.6
Abstraction by hierar-
chical classification

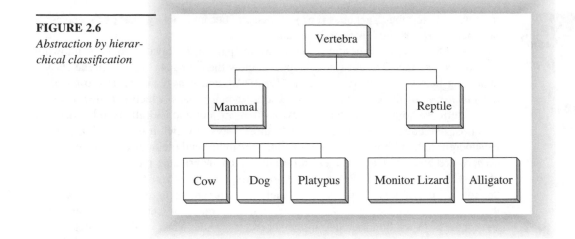

What Is Polymorphism?

> *Polymorphism works together with encapsulation and inheritance to simplify the flow of control in an object-oriented program.*

The final, fundamental principle used in object-oriented programming is *polymorphism*. From the Greek word meaning "many shapes," polymorphism works together with encapsulation and inheritance to simplify the flow of control in an object-oriented program.

Flow of control, knowing what happens next, is the Achilles heel of computer programs: It is the chief cause of complexity, because, without tracing through an unlimited number of pathways, you cannot examine all the possible states of your objects. Thus you can't exhaustively test your programs. Early attempts at structured programming were attempts to simplify program flow of control: Unconditional branches gave way to the canonical constructs of sequence, selection, and iteration. In a similar way, the use of polymorphism simplifies the sending of messages to objects that are related to one another through inheritance.

When a message is sent to an object, that object must have a method defined to respond to that message. When classes are connected in an inheritance hierarchy, all the subclasses of a parent class automatically inherit their parent's interface. Anything that a superclass object can do, a subclass object can also do. For example, if class *A* is a subclass of class *B*, then an *A* object can do anything a *B* object can do. In this practical sense, an *A* object *is* a *B* object. Because of this, the inheritance relationship is sometimes called an *ISA relationship*.

Although a subclass object responds to the same messages that a superclass object does, the message need not trigger the same behavior. It simply needs to be understood. Each subclass can rely on the superclass to define the appropriate response or define a new, specialized response. Therefore, each of the subclasses is able to respond differently—polymorphically or according to its nature, so to speak—to the same message. This is what is meant by "many shapes."

A simple example should make this clear. Suppose you are writing a Java program that is going to mimic the well-known desktop metaphor. You want your users to be able to drop a wide variety of things on the desktop, which they can then move or manipulate in a standard way. For instance, you'd like to be able to double-click the mouse on an item to activate it. Of course, different items should respond differently when activated. When you double-click on the little notebook icon, you want a notepad program to launch, and when you double-click on the modem icon, you want to connect to the Internet.

Without polymorphism, you would have to send a distinct message to each type of icon. You'd have to send a "launch" message to the notebook icon and a "connect" message to the modem icon. Polymorphism allows you to send the same "double-click" message to either type of icon. The icon knows whether it's a notebook icon or a modem icon, and responds appropriately.

To use polymorphism in this example, you might first create a class, `DesktopObject`, having a method `doubleClick()`. You could then extend the `DesktopObject` class by defining two subclasses, `NotepadObject` and `ModemObject`. Next, you could define a customized `doubleClick()` method in the `NotepadObject`, causing it to open a notepad. Finally, you could define another customized `doubleClick()` method in the `ModemObject`, causing it to make a phone call. This way, an object of either type would act properly when it received a `doubleClick()` message.

The beauty of polymorphism is that your program can now work with `NotepadObjects` and `ModemObjects` as though they were the more generic `DesktopObjects`. You don't need to be at all concerned about whether a given `DesktopObject` is a `NotepadObject` or a `ModemObject`. Any `DesktopObject` knows how to respond to a `doubleClick()` message. Moreover, each will respond in its own appropriate way, as shown in Figure 2.7.

FIGURE 2.7
Polymorphism simplifies programs

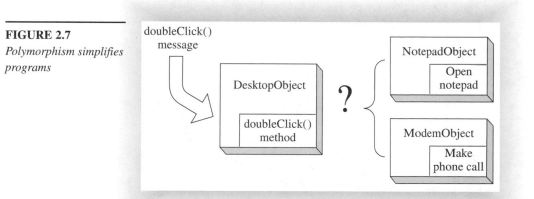

Software Development

Now that you've learned something about the structure of modern software systems, it's appropriate to learn more about how such systems are built. Most modern software systems are too large to be built by an individual in a timely manner. As Figure 2.8 shows, a well-organized team will consistently outrace an individual. In principle, a large system could be built by a solo programmer, but while a system is being built, the world does not stand still. If a system requires a long time to build, the users' needs will likely change. When the solo programmer finally presents the users with the finished system, it may not meet their changed needs. Worse still, it may be less expensive to start over than to struggle to modify the outdated system to meet the users' current needs.

To avoid this problem, software development is usually a team activity. By developing software as a team, programmers hope to deliver the system more rapidly. Of course, performing an activity as a team does not guarantee that the activity will be completed more rapidly.

For teamwork to succeed, it must be possible to separate the activity into discrete units. This is not always possible; some activities are nonseparable. Fred Brooks cites child bearing as an example of a nonseparable task. The nine-month schedule cannot be accelerated to a single month by assembling a team of nine women, each of whom performs 1/9 the total work in a single month.

Another example is the ubiquitous high school algebra problem that goes something like this: "If Fred can mow the lawn in 1/2 hour and Bob can mow the lawn in 1/3 hour, how long will it take the two of them to mow the lawn together?"

Your high school algebra teacher insisted that the answer was something less than 1/3 hour, but if you know much about teamwork, you know that your teacher's answer is wrong. First of all, it's not possible to beat Bob's time unless the boys have two lawn mowers. Most families have only a single lawn mower, so this would be a doubtful assumption. Of course, if Bob and Fred live near one another, Bob can bring his lawn mower to Fred's house. But, some time will be required to transport the lawn mower. Unless the houses are quite nearby, this may offset the advantage of having two mowers.

FIGURE 2.8

Large systems take a single programmer too long to build

And, there are further problems. If Fred mows the front lawn while Bob mows the back lawn, all may go well. But if both try to mow the front lawn at the same time, there may be an accident. Or, they may spend time dodging one another and the debris ejected by the mowers, reducing their mutual efficiency. As Figure 2.9 shows, there's an even greater risk that they may stop to play one-on-one until it's too dark to mow either lawn.

Most likely, as the parent of any teenager will attest, it will take Fred and Bob longer to mow the lawn together than it would take Fred alone. The boys will spend most of the afternoon listening to music, snacking, or watching MTV. Only as darkness approaches, and only after repeated, stern admonishments by a determined parent, will the lawn be mowed at all. As it turns out, the basic principles of lawn mowing don't seem as mathematical as your algebra teacher insisted.

What Is the SDLC?

> *" Conway's law states that the structure of a software system resembles the structure of the team that built it. "*

Software design, as you've seen, has as much to do with the human process of software development as it does with technical issues such as performance or aesthetic issues such as elegance. Conway's law, a well-known maxim of software development, states that the structure of a software system resembles the structure of the team that built it. For example, if a team of five programmers builds a system, there's a good chance that the system will consist of five modules.

After several decades of collective software development experience, the software development community has learned a bit about how to "mow" software, taking account of factors like Conway's law. One important product of community insight is the *structured development life cycle* or SDLC.

As shown in Figure 2.10, the SDLC breaks the process of developing software into several activities. These activities are performed more or less sequentially, one following another. You'll learn about the activities of the SDLC in detail in a moment. But, the big picture of the SDLC is simply this: Some software development tasks must be

FIGURE 2.9

A team may take longer to complete an activity

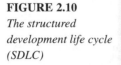

FIGURE 2.10
The structured development life cycle (SDLC)

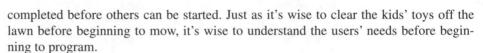

completed before others can be started. Just as it's wise to clear the kids' toys off the lawn before beginning to mow, it's wise to understand the users' needs before beginning to program.

The SDLC is based on the manufacturing product development cycle, shown in Figure 2.11. The manufacturing product development cycle helps focus attention on the importance of assessing the existence of a market before committing funds to product design, the importance of product design to manufacturing efficiency, and so on.

A helpful way of better understanding the SDLC is by means of an analogy. Building a software system is much like building a house. Great care must be taken in laying the foundation of a house, because the entire structure rests on the foundation. A weak or malformed foundation is no basis for a high-quality home.

After the foundation has been poured, the frame is erected on it. The frame, in turn, is important because it must support the walls, which are only as sturdy and durable as the frame and the foundation. The entire house is built, layer by layer, each new component depending on the integrity of the previous components.

The software community came to realize that the same is true of a software system. Software development activities are not completed in isolation. Each part of the process is used as the basis for performing subsequent parts. And, each is only as strong as the parts that support it. The parts of a software system, of course, are not as tangible as those of a house. Nevertheless, they are real.

Look back to Figure 2.10, which shows the SDLC, and identify the components of the SDLC: Requirements Analysis, Design, Programming, Testing, and Operation. The following subsections describe each of these components in detail.

FIGURE 2.11
The manufacturing product development cycle

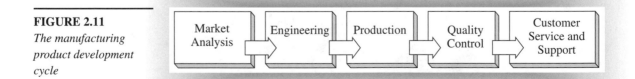

REQUIREMENTS ANALYSIS

The Requirements Analysis activity forms the foundation of the SDLC. Requirements Analysis identifies the goals that the system must achieve. Sometimes a system is intended to solve a problem; other times a system is intended to capitalize on an opportunity. Either way, the Requirements Analysis activity spells out the problem or opportunity. It then identifies the set of discrete requirements that a system must satisfy in order to achieve its goal.

The Requirements Analysis activity aims at building a bridge between two groups. The managers and users who want the system form one group. The programmers who will build the system form the other. In most organizations, these groups are very different. The managers and users talk about costs, customers, and sports, while the programmers talk about CPUs, co-routines, and caches. The managers and users are concerned about what the system will do; the programmers are concerned about how the software will be structured, what new technologies can be used, and what they will learn while writing it. Often, you can recognize members of each group by their distinctive dress. Managers and users wear business attire; programmers wear whatever was on top of the clothing pile.

"The Requirements Analysis activity aims at building a bridge between two groups."

It is crucial that the two groups transcend their cultural differences and arrive at a common understanding of what the proposed system will do. Otherwise, enormous sums of money may be expended in building the "wrong" system. Software development history is replete with such examples. In one of the most notable examples, a major U.S. bank spent over $100 million in building a system that it was never able to use.

Often, communication among the managers, users, and programmers is imperfect. As shown in Figure 2.12, small misunderstandings about what the system should do are often amplified during system development, to the point that the users sometimes cannot see the similarity between what they wanted and what the programmers delivered.

Software developers have learned that producing a document that summarizes the findings of the Requirements Analysis activity helps avoid misunderstanding. A well-written document provides objectivity often lacking in the collective memories of the Requirements Analysis team, which tend to be incomplete and are sometimes inaccurate. Such a document is referred to as a Requirements Specification, because it specifies and describes the requirements that the system must satisfy.

Of course, if a system is simple and its requirements are few, it may not be necessary to produce a Requirements Specification. However, even when it's not strictly necessary, a Requirements Specification can be a useful document. When system development is done by outside consultants, the Requirements Specification is usually considered part of the contract between the consultants and their client. If a dispute arises, a court of law will likely focus on the Requirements Specification in determining whether the consultants did, or did not, fulfill their obligations. Even when system development is done internally, the Requirements Specification can help system developers avoid being unfairly blamed when users are unhappy with a delivered system.

FIGURE 2.12

Small misunderstandings are often amplified

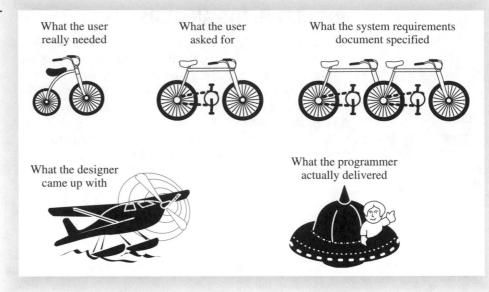

Whether the Requirements Specification takes the form of a multivolume catalog of requirements or a simple one-page memorandum, it's an important tool for the software developer.

Because it focuses on understanding the users' wants and needs, the Requirements Analysis activity involves a great deal of interaction between the users and the programmers. Usually the Requirements Analysis team includes both users and programmers. Often, managers are included as well. Requirements Analysis teams go about their work in a variety of ways. Almost always, however, the team will meet and discuss the problem, interview workers who understand the problem, and collect important documents related to the current system. When they have reached an agreement on what the system must do, the team will draft a Requirements Specification that records their findings.

In drafting the Software Requirements Specification, the team will try to produce a document that has these qualities:

- **Correctness.** The specification should correctly identify and describe each of the requirements the system must satisfy. The specification should be without error.

- **Completeness.** The specification should include every relevant requirement.

- **Consistency.** The specification should not contain conflicting requirements. For example, it should not state in one section that the system must run on an IBM-compatible PC and state in another section that the system must run on a Macintosh.

🔹 *Clarity*. The specification should be written in language understandable by both users and programmers.

Often, the Requirements Specification will include a numbered list of requirements. Numbering the requirements makes it easy to refer to a particular requirement, which is very helpful later in the software development process when it's necessary to show which parts of the system implement each requirement.

Table 2.1 summarizes the Requirements Analysis activity of the SDLC.

TABLE 2.1
SUMMARY OF THE REQUIREMENTS ANALYSIS ACTIVITY OF THE SDLC

Goal	Determine and document the requirements that the system must satisfy.
Participants	Team consisting of users, managers, and programmers.
Means	Meet and discuss the problem or opportunity the system addresses, interview knowledgeable workers, collect relevant documents.
Product	Software Requirements Specification that documents findings of the team.

DESIGN

The Design activity of the SDLC builds on the work of the Requirements Analysis activity. Like the other parts of the SDLC, it's better termed an activity than a phase, because design may begin a bit before the Requirement Analysis activity is finished. During the Design activity, a team consisting mainly of programmers decides how the software system should satisfy the requirements identified during Requirements Analysis.

Because design is the subject of this book, you might correctly guess that it's a big subject—too big to be adequately explained in the next several paragraphs. As a starting point for understanding design within the context of the Design activity of the SDLC, think of design as involving decisions about the structure of the software system. During the Design activity, system developers decide what the major parts of the software system should be, which requirements each will implement, and how the parts of the software system should work together.

The remainder of this book will teach you a variety of ways to approach these tasks. You'll learn about the following:

🔹 **Design processes**, which describe steps you should follow in designing software.

🔹 **Design notations**, which describe models or pictures you can use to document and communicate your designs.

🔹 **Design heuristics**, which help you decide among design alternatives.

Design heuristics are particularly important. There's usually no one "right" way to structure the system—each alternative has its own strengths and weaknesses. Finding a structure that has many of the most important strengths and few of the most serious weaknesses is what design is about. Heuristics help you in this search.

Table 2.2 summarizes the Design activity of the SDLC.

TABLE 2.2
SUMMARY OF THE DESIGN ACTIVITY OF THE SDLC

Goal	Determine the structure of the software system.
Participants	Mainly system developers, with some user assistance.
Means	Study of the Requirements Specification and analysis of alternative designs that might satisfy the requirements.
Product	System design.

PROGRAMMING

After the system has been designed, it can be programmed. Little must be said about programming, because you are presumed to know something about programming already. A few words about programming in relation to design are in order, however.

Ideally, individual programmers or teams of programmers can work separately on the various parts of the system identified in the design. This is how good design accelerates software development. From this perspective, design seems more important managerially than technically.

As you know from experience, however, good designs make the work of the programmer much easier, and bad designs make it much more difficult. Design has both managerial and technical dimensions.

Table 2.3 summarizes the Programming activity of the SDLC.

TABLE 2.3
SUMMARY OF THE PROGRAMMING ACTIVITY OF THE SDLC

Goal	Implement the software units specified by the design.
Participants	Programmers or teams of programmers.
Means	Programming languages and tools.
Product	Source code.

TESTING

After the software units specified by the design have been implemented, they can be combined and tested. Most organizations encourage, or even require, programmers to test their work as part of the programming activity. This practice is called *unit testing*, because it is the individual programmer's unit of work that is the subject of the testing.

Novice programmers are sometimes surprised to learn that testing cannot end with unit testing. If all the units have passed their tests, they reason, then the entire system must be OK.

This thinking is based on a simple but prevalent mathematical fallacy. Your high school algebra teacher taught you that a + b = (a + b). However, in the world of software, a + b < (a + b). In fact, structured design gurus Stevens and Constantine refer to this inequality as perhaps the most fundamental principle of software engineering. A more familiar way of expressing this idea is the saying, "The whole is greater than the sum of the parts."

Some years ago, scientists studying the chemistry of the human body determined that humans are composed mainly of water, along with some carbon, and a few handfuls of other assorted substances. They calculated that the value of these components was only a few dollars. None of us, however, would likely sell our body for such a small sum. The value of a whole, live human is far more than the value of the chemicals that constitute the human body.

Applied to software testing, this lesson means that we must test not only the individual software units, but the system as a whole. Just because units A and B seem to work individually does not mean that they will work together as intended—they may well prove to be "incompatible."

Although the focus of this book is on design, a few further words about testing are in order, owing to widespread misunderstanding of the aims and limits of testing. As computer scientist Edsger Dijkstra put it, "Testing can show only the presence of bugs, never their absence." It is not possible to prove that a system is free of errors by testing it, because the number of possible system inputs is almost always practically infinite. Though every test case may work perfectly, there always remain some inputs that have not been tested. Any one or more of these could expose a serious software bug.

HOW MANY TEST CASES DOES IT TAKE?

How many test cases would it take to completely test a program whose only input is a single 10-character field? Because each character can assume any one of 256 possible values, there are 256^{10} possible test cases. If your computer could run ten million test cases per second, it would require 3.8 billion years to run all the test cases— roughly the age of planet Earth.

As if that weren't enough, consider how long it would take you to go through the results, determining whether each of the program's answers was right or wrong. Then, consider also that most real computer programs have much more than a mere 10 characters of input.

Conclusion: It's a practical impossibility to completely test most computer programs.

Moreover, the sad experience of software developers is that our ability to improve the quality of bug-ridden software is more limited than we realize. A significant umber of attempts to repair known bugs fail. Worse, these attempts themselves regularly introduce new bugs.

The best approach would seem to be to avoid software bugs in the first place. Certainly there are promising techniques for reducing the number of bugs introduced during software development; however, no one has been bold enough to suggest that any technique can entirely eliminate bugs. "Just do it right the first time" seems a laudable but unattainable goal for software developers.

Why then do we test software? One reason is that we do find and fix more bugs than we introduce. On the balance, software quality improves because of testing. Another, more subtle reason is that software testing allows us to assess the quality of software. When software is found to have low quality, we may not know exactly what to do about it. But, knowing before we deliver the software that we have a quality problem seems better than learning of the problem after we've delivered the software. Timely information gives us a greater range of options.

Table 2.4 summarizes the Testing activity of the SDLC.

> " *'Just do it right the first time' seems a laudable but unattainable goal for software developers.* "

TABLE 2.4
SUMMARY OF THE TESTING ACTIVITY OF THE SDLC

Goal	Assess and improve the quality of the software.
Participants	Programmers and testers. Limited user participation.
Means	Execution of test cases.
Product	Logs of tests performed and report summarizing conclusions about software quality.

OPERATION

The ultimate goal of Requirements Analysis, Design, Programming, and Testing is to deliver a system that is satisfactory for operation. Hopefully, the system will remain in operation for an extended period, during which it may be adapted to meet new requirements or run on new platforms, or fixed when troublesome bugs are discovered.

Though software is intangible, it suffers from the phenomenon of aging no less than do mechanical systems. As the world changes, users' needs and expectations change. As a software system is repeatedly modified, its original clarity and elegance progressively diminish. Over time, it becomes both less useful and more difficult to change. At some point, the high costs of operating the system will compel its abandonment or replacement.

Table 2.5 summarizes the Operation activity of the SDLC.

TABLE 2.5
SUMMARY OF THE OPERATION ACTIVITY OF THE SDLC

Goal	Solve a problem or realize an opportunity, using a software system.
Participants	Users and managers. Limited participation of programmers who maintain and adapt software.
Means	Execution of delivered software system.
Product	Improved organizational efficiency and effectiveness.

Alternative Models: Variations on the Theme

" When software development activities can be constrained to downstream movement, the software development process can be controlled. "

The SDLC is not the only way to develop software. Most organizations, however, do use something more or less like the SDLC. Given the popularity of the SDLC, why would an organization choose some other way of developing software?

A popular variation on the SDLC is the *waterfall model*, which emphasizes several features implicit in the SDLC. First, as shown in Figure 2.13, the waterfall model is a one-way model. Water flows downward, from an upstream phase to a downstream phase; but it does not flow in reverse, from a downstream phase to an upstream phase. Organizations that use the waterfall model strive to cause their software development activities to move like water, only downstream. After Requirements Analysis has been completed, requirements issues are not revisited. Instead, development activity focuses on Design, then on Programming, and then on Testing. The activities of the SDLC become the time-sequenced phases of the waterfall model.

When software development activities can be constrained to downstream movement, the software development process can be controlled. If analysis is estimated to require 10% of total software development resources, after analysis is complete the project can be said to be 10% complete. No such statement can be made if, for example, it is possible to move from Design back to Requirements Analysis.

An organization using the waterfall model marks the progress of its software development process by the products or documents produced by each phase. These documents are usually carefully prepared and formally reviewed in the hope that the risk of needing to return to a previous phase can be eliminated. This approach is often referred to as *document-driven* software development.

If software development were a sport, all would be well. A football game never moves from the second quarter back to the first quarter and a baseball game never moves from the fourth inning back to the second inning. Things are not so simple, however, in the world of software.

What if, for example, a design flaw is discovered during programming? Should the flaw be ignored in the interest of following the waterfall model? No. Even the developers of the waterfall model recognized the need for limited backtracking to handle

FIGURE 2.13

*The waterfall model of
software development*

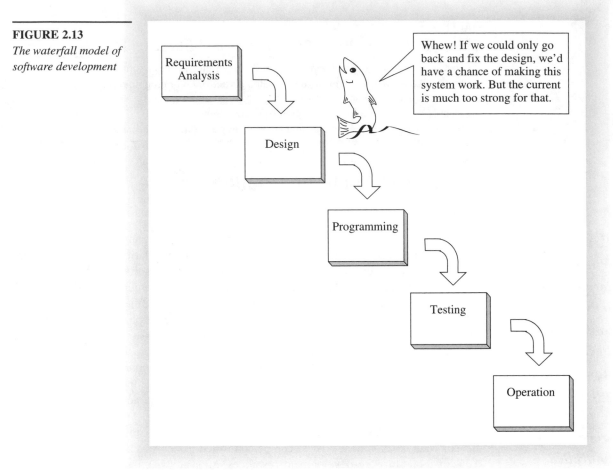

exceptions. Their hope was that it would seldom be necessary to move back beyond the previous phase, and that the amount of backtracking would be small in relation to total project effort. It seems that a software waterfall must occasionally flow upstream after all.

Still, the waterfall model tends to inhibit the amount of backtracking that actually occurs. Software developers are sometimes understandably reluctant to undergo the scrutiny that attends an admission that a mistake has been made and that a previous phase must be revisited. Often a conspiracy of silence results, in which software developers know that a previous phase should be revisited but refuse to acknowledge this openly. In the best of circumstances, they somehow manage to deliver a working system. In the worst of circumstances, they eventually deliver a system that is fatally flawed.

TOP-DOWN AND BOTTOM-UP

The SDLC and waterfall models are within a class of models called *top-down* models. Software development under a top-down model moves from the general and abstract to the specific and concrete. For example, requirements that specify what must be done, but not how it must be done, lead eventually to source code that solves a particular problem.

Top-down models are characterized by plans and other documents that are used to represent the system before it's complete. These plans and documents are used in much the same way that the equations of aeronautical engineering are used to test an aircraft design. The equations cannot tell a design team everything about aircraft performance. Eventually, a test pilot must take a prototype out for a spin. However, it's a foolhardy test pilot who would step into a prototype that has not had its equations checked and cross-checked.

Just as it takes time and money to test an aircraft design using aeronautical theory, it takes time and money to build the Requirements Specification and other documents of the SDLC and waterfall models. In some cases, more time and money may be expended to develop the documents than is expended to develop the source code. Because the goal of a software development project is source code, not documents, it's reasonable to ask, "How much documentation is enough?" Recall that the conviction of those using the SDLC or waterfall models is that planning and documentation done early will help avoid misdirected efforts later in the project. The right amount of planning and documentation depends on the nature of the project, among other factors. But, clearly, more is not inevitably better. As soon as reasonable, we need to complete the analysis of the documents that represent the software system and get on with the business of building the real system.

This realization has led some to adopt a *bottom-up* approach to software development. Bottom-up development resembles the wind tunnel testing of an experimental aircraft, which uses a physical model of the aircraft rather than a system of equations. More can be learned about the performance of the aircraft from wind tunnel testing than from analysis of design equations, but building the model for the wind tunnel is more expensive and time consuming than analyzing the design equations.

Two main forms of bottom-up software development are popular: the *prototyping model* and the *incremental development model*.

THE PROTOTYPING MODEL

Software developers using the prototyping model do not prepare an elaborate Requirements Specification, because they have learned that users often don't read, or don't understand, the Requirements Specification. They know that many users relate better to a concrete, tangible representation of the system than to words, so they provide users with a prototype. The prototype itself may take any of a number of forms, from drawings of input and request screens to a runnable, but stripped down, version of the system.

The most common approach to prototyping provides the user with a runnable mockup of the system that lets the user see how the system will be used. The mockup resembles a Hollywood residential street, where you can see the front of every building, but if you step up and open the door, you see grass and trees where you expected to find the living room.

In the prototype, all the various buttons and text fields can be seen on the screen. The user can click the buttons and type text into the text fields. But, when a user clicks OK, little or nothing happens. The system includes only a user interface—the processing logic and database logic are omitted. This works because, to the users, the user interface *is* the system. The processing logic and database logic are invisible to users, who see only the user interface.

Given the prototype, the users can experiment with the user interface and confirm, or deny, that the developer has understood the users' needs. The developer can modify the prototype to conform to the users' clarified needs, or the developer can throw the prototype away and start fresh. Eventually, the developer adds the processing logic and database logic and delivers a working system.

The prototyping model works best on small- or medium-sized systems. Some developers, however, use a variation of the prototyping model when building large systems. They use prototypes to help them understand the users' needs. Once they believe they thoroughly understand what's required, they draft a traditional Requirements Specification. This way all the requirements are explicit, rather than merely implicit within the final prototype. This facilitates checking of the results of all the downstream phases.

Why doesn't every developer choose to prototype? The prototyping model has its weaknesses, just like every other approach:

- **Inadequate system design**—The prototype is often modified many times before the users pronounce it satisfactory. By the time it's run the gauntlet, it may be held together by little more than "chewing gum and baling wire." This may lead to performance or maintenance problems during operation. A possible countermeasure is to throw away the prototype, rather than using it as the basis of the delivered system. This interesting approach combines the bottom-up prototyping process with a traditional top-down development process, potentially securing the advantages of each.

- **Runaway user expectations**—Often users see the prototype as so much like the system they want that they can't understand why the fully capable system is anything other than right around the corner. They may pressure developers to deliver the final system so rapidly that inadequate attention is paid to quality, resulting in performance or maintenance problems during operation. A possible countermeasure is user education that helps users understand early in the project how the prototype differs from a real system.

INCREMENTAL DEVELOPMENT

The incremental model stands midway between prototyping and top-down development. A significant problem with top-down development is that nothing is complete until everything is complete. The user does not see any part of the system for weeks, months, or sometimes years, after the Requirements Specification is done. A significant problem with prototyping is the absence of an overall plan. The developers don't really know what the user wants until they submit a satisfactory prototype.

To avoid these problems, developers using the incremental model strive to break the system up into small pieces and deliver the first of these as quickly as possible. This way, the developers receive important feedback on whether they've correctly understood the users' needs and the users get a working part of the system very quickly. Subsequent pieces of the system can incorporate lessons learned in delivering early pieces.

Of course, it's not always easy to divide a system into a series of useful chunks. Moreover, some effort goes into delivering and installing each system chunk. In total, this effort is usually more than would be required if the system were delivered as a unit.

> *" A significant problem with prototyping is the absence of an overall plan. "*

A CONTINUUM OF DEVELOPMENT MODELS

Rather than thinking of the waterfall model, prototyping, and incremental development as fixed opposites, it seems more useful to think of them as points within a continuum. By thinking of the various models as lying on a continuum, you're encouraged to ask questions about your projects rather than reflexively choosing a familiar development model that may not be well suited to the project. Figure 2.14 shows the continuum of development models.

Granularity refers to the relative size of each delivery made during the project. Prototyping is based on small granularity, whereas the waterfall model, with its single delivery, is based on high granularity. Formality refers to the amount of documentation generated during system development. As Figure 2.14 shows, prototyping tends to have low formality, whereas the waterfall model has high formality.

Summary

Structured design leads to procedural programs that transform input data to output data. This paradigm tends to break down when systems become large and complex. Object-oriented design can address a wider range of problems, and larger and more complex systems, than structured design.

Objects have three basic properties: identity, state, and behavior. Classes are used as patterns that describe the possible states and behavior of objects.

Encapsulation divides an object into an externally visible portion called an interface, and a private portion called an implementation. Inheritance allows similar objects to share common properties. Polymorphism allows objects to respond to identical messages in individual ways.

FIGURE 2.14

The continuum of development models

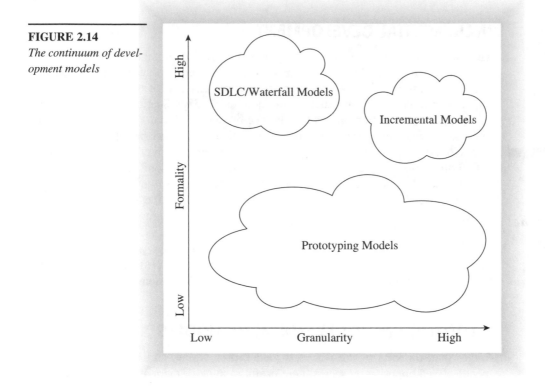

The SDLC is a popular process for developing software that identifies five main activities: Requirements Analysis, Design, Programming, Testing, and Operation. Top-down processes, like the SDLC, stress planning and control; bottom-up processes stress experimentation and adaptation. Prototyping, a bottom-up process, lets the user see a model of the system early in the development process. Incremental development, which has elements of both top-down and bottom-up processes, delivers a system in a series of versions, each providing new or enhanced capability.

Questions

1. The principle of combining, in an object, the data that describes its state and the operations that can be performed on the data is called _____.

2. The data and operations of an object that are visible externally comprise its _____.

3. The data and operations of an object that are *not* visible externally comprise its _____.

4. The principle of _____ allows object-oriented designers to classify objects based on similarity of properties.

5. The principle of _____ allows objects that belong to different classes to respond distinctively to identical messages.

6. The _____ activity of the SDLC involves understanding and documenting user requirement.

7. The _____ activity of the SDLC involves choosing a system structure capable of satisfying the Requirements Specification.

8. During the _____ activity of the SDLC, the software is actually written.

9. The _____ activity of the SDLC aims at ensuring the software is of suitable quality.

10. A _____ is a pattern, or blueprint, used to construct actual _____.

11. A development process that uses experimental software to better understand user requirements is _____.

Exercises

1. How is a customer service system designed using structured design likely to differ from one designed using object-oriented design?

2. If you and a team of five programmers were responsible for developing an order-entry system to be delivered in four months, what sort of development process would you use? Discuss the alternatives and defend your choice.

3. Show how the SDLC, prototyping, and incremental development can be used together to develop different parts of a system or during different phases of system development.

To Learn More

The following books will help you learn more about structured design:

📚 Yourdon, E. and Constantine, L. *Structured Design, 2nd. ed.* Englewood Cliffs, New Jersey: Prentice-Hall, 1979.

📚 Page-Jones, M. *The Practical Guide to Structured Systems Design, 2nd ed.* Englewood Cliffs, New Jersey: Prentice-Hall, 1988.

The following books will help you learn more about software processes:

📚 Degrace, P. and Stahl, L. *Wicked Problems, Righteous Solutions: A Catalog of Modern Software Engineering Paradigms.* Englewood Cliffs, New Jersey: Yourdon Press, 1990.

📚 Pressman, R. *Software Engineering: A Practitioner's Approach.* New York: McGraw Hill, 1996.

3

Teach Yourself Java in 21 Minutes

Have you ever read a magazine article about some inventor who got rich by inventing something simple—say the cardboard box—and said to yourself, "I could do that?" Or, perhaps you've seen the latest musical group on MTV, or read a new detective novel, and thought the same thing. What do all these accomplishments have in common? They all seem to have a low barrier to entry. Most of us can afford a word processor, an electric guitar, or a legal pad and a number two pencil on which to sketch our latest brilliant invention. But, once you break down and buy that new Stratocaster or Gibson, things start to look a little different; you actually have to learn how to play! And, if you persist, your dreams of MTV fame will only be realized once you master the fundamentals.

Writing software is a little like that. Everyone, novice and expert alike, has access to the same tools. To become an expert, however, you have to master the fundamentals. Just as a novelist spends time learning syntax, sentence structure, and paragraph development before embarking on her magnum opus, you need to learn about the software mechanics that can form the building-blocks for your next killer app. This chapter provides a quick and condensed overview of Java. If you are new to programming, you'll want to pick up an introductory text on the subject. (Of course, we recommend *Object-Oriented Programming in Java* by Gilbert and McCarty, available from the Waite Group Press.) If you already know how to program in a high-level language such as Pascal, C, C++, or a modern dialect of BASIC, you'll find this chapter adequate, if not exhaustive, as an introduction to Java.

In Chapter 2, "Object-Oriented Software Development," you were introduced to the fundamental concepts of object-oriented programming: objects, classes, encapsulation, inheritance, and polymorphism. In addition, you learned a little about different strategies or development models that software writers use to move their creations from a spark of intuition to a shrink-wrapped package you can purchase at your local SoftwareWorld. While most of the rest of this book is devoted to exploring those strategies, tactics, processes and methodologies, this chapter is a little different. In this chapter you will learn:

- How to create and run Java applications and applets

- The syntax (or language rules) for creating new classes

- How to define object attributes using both primitive types and object types

- How to specify the behavior of your classes by writing methods

- How to use sequence, selection, and iteration to control the way your methods work

- How to respond to events from the user or the system

- How to use the Abstract Window Toolkit (AWT) to build graphical user interface (GUI) style applications

The Mechanics of Writing Java Programs

" One of the coolest features of Java is its cross-platform binary portability."

One of the coolest features of Java is its cross-platform binary portability. This means that the very same program you run on your Macintosh or your Sun SPARC machine will also run under Windows or OS/2. Not only will the same program run unchanged on all these machines, but you can also develop your programs on whichever type of machine you prefer. How do you do that, and what resources do you need?

To write, test, and run Java programs, you will need three pieces of software. Fortunately, each of these items is both widely available and (generally) free: an ideal combination! You will need the following:

- **A text editor**—You will use a text editor to write your actual Java programs. A text editor is like a word processor, except that the files it creates do not contain any formatting codes. If you are using Windows 95 or NT, you can use the Notepad program or MS-DOS Edit. In the Macintosh world, you will want to use a program like SimpleText. For all you UNIX aficionados, vi or emacs will be your tool of choice. You can, if you like, use a word-processing program like Microsoft Word, Lotus WordPro, or WordPerfect, but you will have to remember to save your files without any extra formatting—as plain text or ASCII.

- **Development tools**—These are the programs you will use to turn your Java programs into executable code, and to test and debug your applets and applications. Usually these tools will be packaged as either a kit of individual tools, or as an application program that combines the various tools into one integrated program (called an IDE, short for "integrated development environment"). The Java Development Kit (JDK) from JavaSoft is included on the CD-ROM that comes with this book, or you can download the latest version from `http://www.javasoft.com`. The JDK contains separate versions of the development kit for Windows 95/NT, Sun Solaris, and Macintosh. Microsoft has created its own software development kit that you can use if you are developing your programs on Windows 95/NT. Called the Java Software Development Kit (SDK), it features very fast compilation and can be downloaded free of charge from `http://www.microsoft.com`.

There is also a wide variety of commercial software packages you can purchase for developing Java programs. Some of the better known products are Microsoft's Visual J++, Symantec's Visual Café for Java, Metrowerk's Code Warrior (for the Macintosh and Windows), and Sun's Java Workshop. Each of these IDEs has some features not available in the JDK, such as a visual source code debugger or visual layout of graphical interfaces. Any program you can write with an IDE, though, you can also write with one of the free software development kits.

- **A Java-enabled web browser**—You will use this to run and test your applets in their native environment. Netscape's Navigator and Microsoft's Internet Explorer have captured most of the market, but there are other browsers you might want to try, such as Sun's HotJava, which is written entirely in Java itself. Strictly speaking, a Web browser is not absolutely necessary for you to develop Java programs, because the JDK includes appletviewer, a program for viewing applets; neither is an Internet connection mandatory. A text editor and the JDK are the bare minimum you need to get started, but a Web browser and an Internet account will make your work a lot more fun!

EDIT, COMPILE, DEBUG, RUN

After you have set up your programming environment and installed the JDK, SDK, or the IDE you will be using, you're ready to start writing Java programs. Before you get started though, you'll find it handy to get a bird's-eye view of the process you will go through in developing your applications.

The first step in creating a Java application or applet is to use your editor to create a text file. Java programs use two types of files, one called source code and the other called object code or machine code. The first type of file contains the Java language programs you write with your text editor. The filenames must end with the file extension `.java`. (A file extension is added as a suffix to the end of a filename, separated from the rest of the file by a period or dot). Every source code file contains the definition for a single class that is publicly visible, and, unlike many programming languages you might be familiar with, the name of the file and the name of the class must be identical. Each source file may also contain other "helper" classes, but each file can contain only one public class, which is visible to the rest of your program.

Once you have finished writing your source code, the second step is to translate your source code into the object code instructions that can be read by the Java runtime environment (called the Java Virtual Machine or VM). In Java, this object code is called *byte code*. The process of translating your source code into machine code is called *compiling*, and is the job of a tool called a *compiler*. In the JDK, the compiler is a program called javac, which is shorthand for *java compiler*. If you have used your text editor to create a class definition for a class called Robotz, (saved in a text file named Robotz.java), you can compile your source code by typing

```
javac Robotz.java
```

and the javac compiler will turn your source code definition into object code, storing it in a file named Robotz.class. Be sure to use uppercase and lowercase letters exactly as shown in the line above. Even if you're using a Windows 95 or Windows NT command window, neither of which is case sensitive, the Java compiler and other programs *are* case sensitive. They will not properly process your command if you use the wrong case.

Remember

Use your text editor to create Java source code files that have the extension .java. Use your compiler to translate your source code file into machine code. The compiler will give your machine code file a .class extension, as you can see in Figure 3.1.

The third step in developing a Java program is called debugging. *Debugging* is a euphemism for finding and fixing the mistakes that you made when writing your program. There are three basic types of mistakes: syntax errors, semantic errors, and runtime errors.

Syntax errors simply mean that you have broken the grammatical rules of the Java language. You may have misspelled a word, or punctuated a line of code incorrectly. When you have a syntax error in your program, the Java compiler refuses to create the machine code from your source code, and prints out a message telling you what the compiler thinks the problem is. When you get such an error you must examine it carefully, correct the offending code using your text editor, and then try recompiling your application. You continue this cycle until the compiler stops giving you error messages.

Semantic errors are more difficult to detect than syntax errors, which the Java compiler flags for you. A semantic error is an error in the meaning of a computer statement: if you subtracted the sales tax in your program when you should have added it, for example, you've created a semantic error. The usual way to find semantic errors is by testing your program with predefined inputs and outputs. This is, as you might expect, an extremely arduous process, but it can mean the difference between a successful product and a real disaster.

A *runtime error* is an error that occurs because of some unexpected environmental condition. Trying to open a file that doesn't exist or to read from a closed socket are

FIGURE 3.1

Editing and compiling a Java program

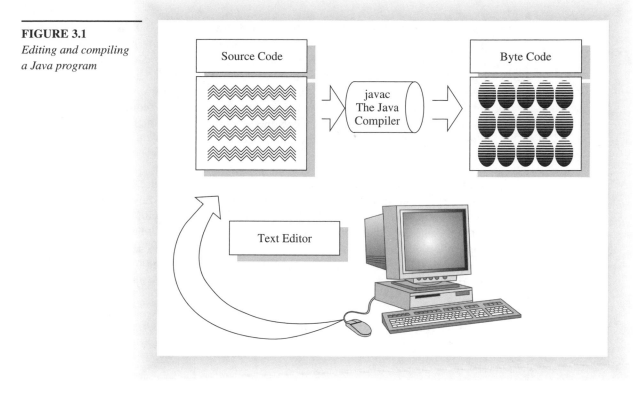

examples of runtime errors. Runtime errors have some characteristics of both syntax errors and semantic errors. Like a syntax error, Java tells you when one occurs. With syntax errors, the Java compiler announces your mistake; with runtime errors, the Java VM does the honors. Like semantic errors, however, runtime errors are discovered when you run your program, not when you compile it. Because a program may run correctly one time (when the server was working correctly for example) and create a runtime error the next, runtime errors are fixed not by correcting the source code, but by writing code to deal with the exceptional environmental conditions that cause them. Such conditions are called *exceptions*, and the code you write is called an exception handler.

After your program is completed and (reasonably) bug free, it's time for you to deploy your application. Java provides two different ways to deliver and run your programs: as an application or as an applet.

APPLICATIONS, APPLETS, AND BROWSERS

A Java application is, in many ways, similar to many of the programs you currently run on your computer. Once you have successfully written and compiled your Java application, you deliver the resulting .class files to your users on a disk or over the

Internet using FTP. The user then installs and executes the program on his own computer...more or less. The machine code stored in a .class file is not *really* machine code for your Macintosh or Pentium; instead it is machine code for the Java VM. To execute a Java application, you thus have to "start" the VM before you can load the Java application. In Windows 95/NT and UNIX, this is done from a command window by using the program named *java* and passing the name of the compiled application as an argument. Figure 3.2 illustrates how this works. To run the Robotz.class you compiled in the previous section, you would type

```
java Robotz
```

Notice that you don't add the extension .class when running a Java application. If you forget and tack it on, the java program lets you know that it can't find Robotz.class.class. This behavior is a little inconsistent with that of the compiler. Simply remember that you *do* include the .java extension when you compile your application's source file(s), and that you *do not* include the .class extension when you run the application. Again, be careful to use uppercase and lowercase letters in all the right places. Your operating system may not be case sensitive, but the java program is.

The second way you can deliver a Java program to your users is to embed the program in an HTML Web page. A program embedded in a Web page is called an *applet*, and will be automatically downloaded and executed whenever someone uses a Web

FIGURE 3.2

Running a Java application using the java interpreter

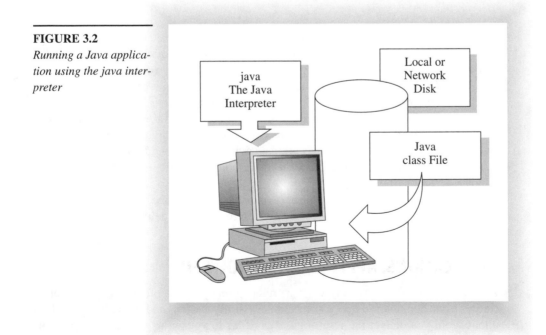

browser to access that Web page. Applets still require a Java Virtual Machine to execute, but the VM is invisibly loaded (and provided) by your Web browser.

Adding an applet to a Web page is done the same way as adding any other element to a Web page: through the use of an HTML tag. The tag to add an applet is called, not surprisingly, <APPLET>. When you add an <APPLET> tag to a Web page, you have to provide three additional pieces of information:

- The name of the object code file. Use the CODE= attribute to specify this.

- The width of the applet in pixels. Use the WIDTH= attribute to specify this.

- The height of the applet in pixels. Use the HEIGHT= attribute to specify this.

If the Robotz.java program were written as an applet, you could display it in a Web page by adding the following lines to the body of your .HTML file:

```
<APPLET CODE=Robotz.class HEIGHT=300 WIDTH=500>
</APPLET>
```

In the CODE= attribute, the .class extension is optional. As when you're using javac and java, the case of the class name is significant. This means CODE=Robotz is fine, but CODE=ROBOTZ or CODE=Robotz.CLASS is not. Figure 3.3 shows how applets are loaded into your computer over the Web.

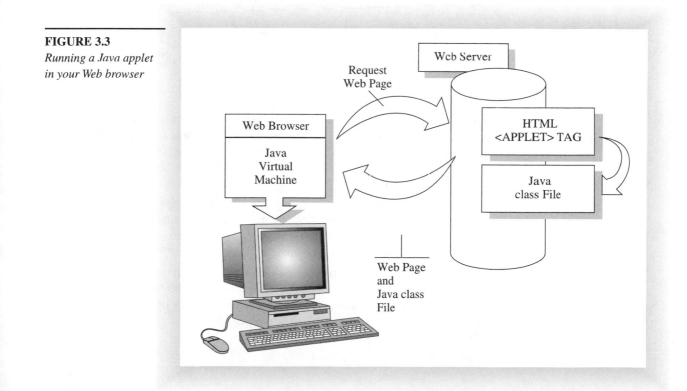

FIGURE 3.3

Running a Java applet in your Web browser

If you've worked on the Internet for any length of time, you're probably aware of some of the dangers that lurk there. One of those dangers is the possibility of getting a computer virus from running a program downloaded over the Net. Because Java applets are downloaded automatically when a viewer accesses the Web page in which the applet is embedded, there could be risk of inadvertently downloading a *hostile applet*, a program that could format your hard disk, steal private information, or worse. To forestall this possibility, the designers of Java imposed several security restrictions on Java applets. Java applets cannot read or write files on your local file system, cannot run any programs on your local machine, and cannot connect you to a machine other than the one the applet originates from. If your Java program needs to do any of these things, you will have to deliver it as an application rather than an applet.

Your First Java Program

"Context is everything," a wise man once said, and the quickest way to see how the Java development process works in context is to put your own hands on the keyboard and try it yourself. Listing 3.1 contains the source code for the `Robotz` Java applet that simulates a group of timid robots, deathly afraid of being poked by a mouse pointer. Although the listing may initially seem rather long and forbidding, you'll find it a good learning tool as you study the basics of the Java language. After you have the applet running, you'll take it apart, line by line, until you've seen what makes the robots tick. To start:

1. Use your text editor to create the program `Robotz.java`, copying Listing 3.1.

2. Create the Java machine code by compiling your source code using the Java compiler, javac:

```
javac Robotz.java
```

   If you have typed everything accurately, javac will silently create the file `Robotz.class`. If not, it will tell you what you did wrong. Correct your error and recompile. (Of course, if typing is not really your cup of tea, you can just copy the source code from the CD-ROM included in this book, but that's not really as much fun!)

3. Use your text editor to create an `.HTML` file to hold your applet, by copying Listing 3.2, `TimidRobotz.html`. Notice that, unlike the name of the Java file, the name of the `.HTML` file is not significant—that is, it does not have to be named the same as the applet it contains.

4. Finally, you can run your applet in either of two ways: through your Web browser or by using the appletviewer utility provided with the JDK. After your Web browser is running, you can run your applet by opening the `.HTML` file using your browser's local file opening capabilities. To run your applet under appletviewer, simply type

```
appletviewer TimidRobotz.html
```

from the console window. Notice that when the application is run from appletviewer rather than the browser, none of the additional HTML tags is displayed. Nevertheless, when developing applets, you'll often find using appletviewer a simpler and better alternative than firing up your Web browser.

After you have the Robotz applet up and running, move your mouse pointer around the screen and try to catch one of the little guys. As you can see from Figure 3.4, catching one is not the easiest of tasks. When you're finished, come on back here to dissect the Robotz.java program and see how it works.

Listing 3.1 Robotz.java

```java
// Robotz.java
// A first java program

import java.applet.*;
import java.awt.*;
import java.awt.event.*;

public class Robotz extends Applet
{
    public void init()
    {
        add( new Robot( Color.blue ) );
        add( new Robot( Color.red   ) );
        add( new Robot( Color.green) );
    }
}

class Robot extends    Canvas
            implements MouseMotionListener
{
    private Color myColor;
    private Point myLocation;

    public Robot( Color theColor )
    {
        myColor = theColor;
        setSize( 50, 50 );
        setBackground( theColor );
        addMouseMotionListener( this );
    }

    public void mouseMoved( MouseEvent evt )
    {
        myLocation = getLocation( );
        int dx = evt.getX( ), dy = evt.getY( );
        if ( dx > 25 )
            dx = dx - 50;
        if ( dy > 25 )
            dy = dy - 50;

        setLocation( myLocation.x + dx,
                     myLocation.y + dy );
    }
```

```
    public void mouseDragged( MouseEvent evt )
    {
        myLocation = getLocation();
        setLocation( myLocation.x + (evt.getX( ) - 25),
                     myLocation.y + (evt.getY( ) - 25));
    }

    public void paint( Graphics g )
    {
        g.drawLine( 10, 40, 40, 40 );
        g.drawRect( 15,  5,  5, 15 );
        g.drawRect( 30,  5,  5, 15 );
    }
}
```

Listing 3.2 TimidRobotz.html

```
<HTML>
<TITLE> TimidRobotz.html: The Robotz applet in action </TITLE>
<BODY>
<H1> Everyone's a Little Shy </H1>
<HR>
This is the Robotz applet. <BR>
Move your mouse over the Robot
objects and they'll run away. <BR>
(Hint: Trying to catch them is a real drag!!!)
<HR>
<APPLET CODE=Robotz.class HEIGHT=200 WIDTH = 300 >
</APPLET>
</BODY>
</HTML>
```

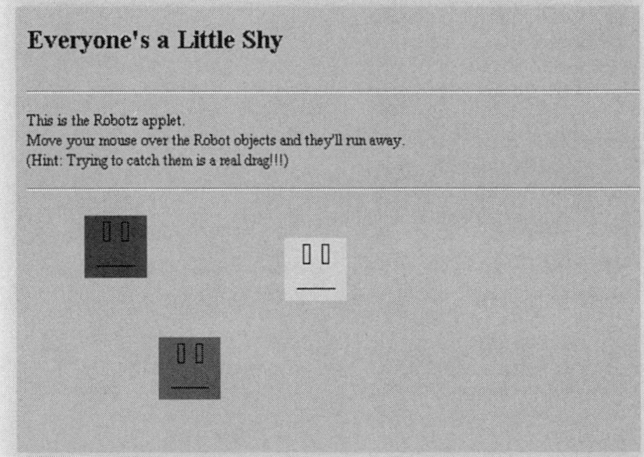

FIGURE 3.4

Running the Robotz applet

CREATING A NEW CLASS

When you first look at `Robotz.java`, it may seem intimidating and complex. One of the tools that you can use to conquer that complexity is structure. Once you step back and look at the "big picture," the important points stand out and the details recede into the background. `Robotz.java`, like all Java programs, is organized as a set of class definitions. Take a brief scan through the code; how many class definitions can you find?

If you answered two, you're correct. `Robotz.java` contains the definition for the `Robotz` class that uses three objects of the `Robot` class. The definition of the `Robot` class is also contained inside the `Robotz.java` source file, as you can see in Figure 3.5. The definition of a class consists of two parts: the class header (think of it as a brief title), followed by the class body. The body of the class is where the attributes (called *fields* in Java) and operations or behavior (called *methods* in Java) are defined. The class definitions for the `Robotz` class and the `Robot` class are structured like this:

```
public class Robotz extends Applet
{
    // Attribute and method definitions go here
}

class Robot extends    Canvas
            implements MouseMotionListener
{
    // Attribute and method definitions go here
}
```

The body of a class definition is enclosed in curly braces ({}), which, in Java as in C and C++, roughly mean "begin a section" and "end a section." (The technical term for such a section is a "block.") The line of code before the class body is the class header. Let's start by deciphering that first, and then you'll be better prepared to continue dissecting one of these virtual creatures.

Keywords and Identifiers

The header for the Robotz class consists of five words:

```
public class Robotz extends Applet
```

Some of these words are part of the Java language, and some of them are names that you can change. The words that are part of the Java language are called *keywords*. Keywords cannot be changed, and when you use them you must spell them correctly, including the case. If you've come from another programming language, such as BASIC, FORTRAN, or Pascal, where case is not significant, remembering that `public` and `Public` are not the same thing can be difficult. The keywords in this header are `public`, `class`, and `extends`. What do these mean?

Remember that a class definition acts like a blueprint or pattern that can be used to create objects. The first two of these keywords, `public class`, instruct Java to create a definition for a class that is publicly available, one that can be used by any other class. Each Java source code file can have only one `public class` definition. As you

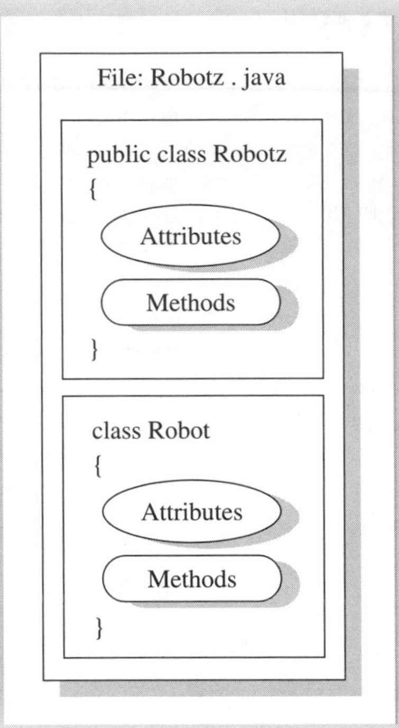

FIGURE 3.5

A Java source code file can contain many class definitions, each consisting of attribute and method definitions

noticed, `Robotz.java` contains two class definitions, but the definition for the `Robot` class does not start with the keyword `public`.

The second type of word that can appear in a Java program is called an *identifier*. An identifier is simply a name that you supply for the objects, classes, attributes, and methods that you create. While the spelling and usage of Java keywords is fixed and proscribed by the Java language, identifiers are at the mercy of your imagination, subject to a few simple rules:

- Identifiers must start with an alphabetic character, the special underline symbol (_), or the dollar sign ($).

- In addition to these characters, identifiers can contain the digits 0 through 9.

- Upper- and lowercase are significant in identifiers. Thus, you can have two different classes, one named `Cat`, and the other named `cat` (although this is seldom a good idea!).

The identifiers in the `Robotz` class header include the word `Robotz`, which you defined when writing the class, and the word `Applet`, which another programmer defined and which you'll meet when you look at the `extends` keyword shortly.

Extending and Importing

As you saw, the word Robotz is an identifier that you created. You could have, just as easily, named the class GangOfThree (remembering to rename the file that contains it to GangOfThree.java, of course), or anything else you liked. But what about the other name you looked at, the word Applet? That is not a name that you, the programmer, chose. You have to use that word, and it must be spelled exactly as you see (including capitalization). However, unlike the word extends (which precedes it), Applet is not a keyword. Applet is the name of a class that is supplied with the Java Development Kit (JDK). Java comes with a wide variety of pre-built classes, but such classes are not a part of the Java language itself.

The keyword extends, written right in front of the word Applet, is how you tell the Java compiler that this new class, Robotz, is based on (or is a kind of) the class Applet. If you recall the last chapter and think that this sounds a lot like inheritance, you're right on target. The keyword extends is used in Java to specify the superclass (or parent class) when you are writing a new class. If you leave out the extends clause of a class definition, Java assumes you want to extend the most basic Java class, Object.

Java is a relatively sparse and simple language. When the designers of Java wanted to add a new feature, they didn't usually add it to the language, but instead, they created libraries of classes (called *packages*) that you can include inside your program. Thus, if you have no need for any of the features of the Applet class, your program does not have to carry them around, as it would if Applet were part of the Java language.

To use one of these packages of classes, you have to let your program know that you intend to use it by employing the import statement. You use the import statement to tell Java the full name of the package that contains the class you want to use. In the Robotz applet, we are using (or *importing*) classes from three different packages: the java.applet package, the java.awt package, and the java.awt.event package. We let the compiler know we are going to do this by adding these three lines at the top of our program:

```
import java.applet.*;
import java.awt.*;
import java.awt.event.*;
```

The asterisk (*) after the name of the java.applet package tells the compiler to make all the classes in the package available to your program. Because the program only uses the Applet class from that package, you could have just as easily have written:

```
import java.applet.Applet;
```

In fact, because you are only using one class from the package, and that class is only referenced one time, you could just as easily use the fully qualified class name when declaring the Robotz class, like this:

```
public class Robotz extends java.applet.Applet
{
    // Attribute and method definitions go here
}
```

> *The attributes of a class (called fields in Java) determine what kind of values (or state) each object that is created from the class will contain.*

and not include the import statement at all. Adding the import statements to your program does not actually add the classes to your code, however, so most programmers find it easiest to use imports liberally. (If you are coming from a C or C++ background, you might be tempted to think of import as the equivalent of the #include pre-processor directive found in those languages. This can be a little misleading, because the import statement does not cause a header file to be processed, as #include does. Neither does it cause code to be inserted into your program; it merely qualifies the names of classes referenced by your program.)

THE CLASS BODY

The body of your class definition is where you define the attributes and methods of your class. The attributes of the class (called *fields* in Java) determine what kind of values (or *state*) each object that is created from the class will contain. The methods of the class determine what messages the object responds to, as well as define the specific behavior that is performed when each message is received.

Braces, Whitespace, and Convention

> *The methods of a class determine what messages the object responds to, as well as define the specific behavior that is performed when each message is received.*

In Java, braces ({}) are used as begin and end markers sometimes called delimiters. Every class starts with an opening brace ({) (after the header declaration) and ends with a closing brace (}). Braces are also used to delimit the bodies of methods, blocks of code that are used in loops and selection statements, and in initializer expressions for arrays.

Java programs give you almost unlimited freedom in the way you arrange the elements on the page. Unlike COBOL or FORTRAN, Java is a free-form language. This simply means that where you put spaces and line breaks is (usually) a matter of taste. However, spacing, indentation, and layout are very important in making your code readable and understandable to other programmers—even though the Java compiler couldn't care less. Program layout helps you, and others who read your code, to make sense out of complex class definitions by providing structure—just like sentences, paragraphs, and chapters provide structure for a text book or novel.

How can you lay out your code so it's easily understood and read? The easiest way is to use a set of common programming conventions. A convention is just the common way a community has decided to do something. Such conventions can be formalized (as in a programming style guide for a particular company), or they can be informal agreements that are simply widely accepted. In the Java community, there are three widely accepted programming conventions that will make your programs easier to read and understand:

- Put each statement on a single line.

- Indent lines of code inside control flow statements.

- Use standard naming and capitalization conventions for the identifiers you create. The most basic of these are:

Mixed case, capitalized names for classes and packages. Individual words in a name are also capitalized like this: `MyFirstClass`, `AnotherClassExample`.

Mixed case names are also used for regular fields and methods, but the name does not start with a capital letter. Some examples: `customerName`, `totalSales`, `calculatePayroll()`.

Constant identifiers commonly use all uppercase identifiers, with the individual words separated by underscores like: `A_CONSTANT_FIELD`.

Finally, some Java programmers like to make the difference between local variables and fields explicit by using all lowercase letters for local variables, splitting the individual words with an underscore like this: `some_local_variable`. One limitation of this convention is that you cannot tell by looking whether a variable is a field or a local variable, unless the identifier has multiple words.

State and Behavior

You've already seen that every class definition you write has two parts:

- The definitions of the attributes that are particular to your class. You will define these using declaration statements, as you'll see in the next section.

- The definitions of the methods that provide the behavior for your class and its objects. Each of these definitions looks a little like a class definition; it is composed of a header section, and a body section. However, the body of a method contains very different stuff than the body of a class, because the method body contains the actual instructions that implement the method's behavior.

DEFINING ATTRIBUTES

The attributes of a class store the state of an object (or class). A class can have many attributes, or it may have none (as the `Robotz` class illustrates). To define an attribute you use a definition statement that follows this pattern:

```
[ MODIFIERS]    TYPE    attributeName    [ = <initial value>    ];
```

How can you interpret this pattern? The two sections enclosed in brackets (`[]`) are optional—you don't have to include them, but you may. The required sections include:

- The type of the attribute, which determines what kind and range of values it can hold.

- The name you want the attribute to have. You have to follow the naming rules for Java identifiers; in addition, you'll want to follow the common naming conventions given previously.

🌑 The semicolon that ends the definition statement (all statements in Java end with a semicolon).

Look at these examples from the `Robot` class (the second class defined in `Robotz.java`):

```
private Color myColor;
private Point myLocation;
```

The `Robot` class has two fields that each `Robot` object uses to store its color and its location on the screen. The name of the attribute that stores the color is `myColor`, whereas the attribute that stores the location is named `myLocation`.

The type of the field `myColor` is `Color`, a class defined in the `java.awt` package. The type of the field `myLocation` is `Point`, which is also defined inside `java.awt`. (AWT stands for Abstract Window Toolkit. These are the classes that give you the ability to create graphical user interface (GUI) programs in Java.)

Both `myColor` and `myLocation` also use the optional modifier `private`. When a field within a class is declared `private`, only the methods in that class have access to it. As you'll discover in Chapter 4, "Encapsulation: Classes and Methods," this type of "data hiding" is one of the fundamental principles for building robust and maintainable classes.

Neither `myLocation` nor `myColor` uses an optional initializer section that specifies an initial value. Of course, every attribute should always have a value. In the case of the `Robot` class, the field `myColor` is initialized when each `Robot` object is created, and `myLocation` is updated automatically whenever the mouse is moved or dragged over a `Robot` object. If you wanted to provide an initial value for these two attributes (although it doesn't make much sense in this context), you could do it like this:

```
private Color myColor      = Color.red;
private Point myLocation    = new Point( 50, 50 );
```

> *" There are two basic kinds of attributes: those that are specific to each object that is created from the class, and those that are shared among all class objects. "*

There are two basic kinds of attributes: those that are specific to each object that is created from the class, and those that are shared among all class objects. Object-specific attributes—like `myLocation` and `myColor`—are called *fields* or *instance variables*, while those that are class-wide are called *class variables*. If you had some information that you wanted all `Robot`s to share—say the current `Robot` population for example—you could create a class variable by prefixing the field definition with the keyword `static`. Here is how you could add such a field to the `Robot` class:

```
static private int robotPopulation = 0;
```

To use this field whenever you create a new `Robot`, you would add one to the `robotPopulation` field, and then all of the `Robot`s currently in existence would be able to access it. Note, though, that this example makes `robotPopulation` a private field; the `Robot`s all know how many of them there are, but none of the other classes or objects in your programs can get that information. Figure 3.6 shows all the pieces you'll need to define class and object attributes.

The discussion about attributes has been, so far, a little cavalier. Attributes have appeared rather magically when you needed them. What exactly is an attribute? An

FIGURE 3.6

Specifying class and object attributes

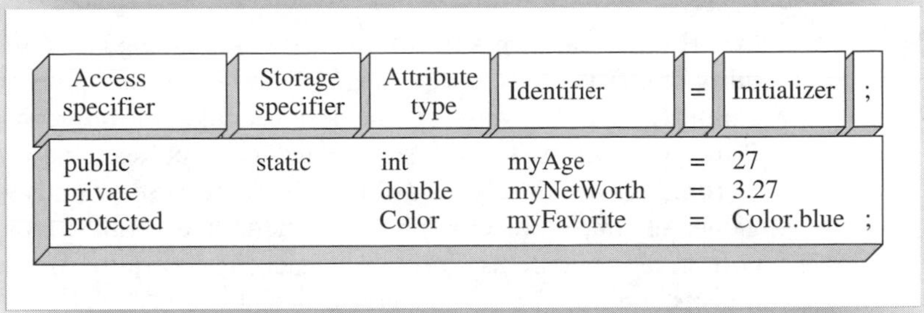

Access specifier	Storage specifier	Attribute type	Identifier	=	Initializer	;
public	static	int	myAge	=	27	
private		double	myNetWorth	=	3.27	
protected		Color	myFavorite	=	Color.blue	;

attribute is simply a place or storage location where you are going to store a specific kind of information. Java has very specific kinds of information or data that it can handle, and the Java language requires that you specify exactly what kind of information will be stored in a field when you name it. Because of this, Java is said to be a strongly typed language. The advantage of strong typing is that it helps you find certain errors in your program while you are writing it, instead of after it has been released.

There are two general kinds of data objects that Java can use for attributes: primitive types and objects. Normally, your programs will be designed around collections of objects, but, as you implement your designs, you will frequently be called upon to use primitive types for a variety of purposes.

Primitive Types

Recall from Chapter 2 that objects contain both state and behavior. Unlike objects, primitive types are data objects that:

- Consist of a single value.

- Are manipulated by using operators, rather than by sending messages.

- Cannot be extended by creating new types or operations.

- Store values, whereas object types store references. This is a fundamental difference and the source of much confusion for programmers coming from different language backgrounds.

> *" The advantage of strong typing is that it helps you find certain errors in your program while you are writing it, instead of after it has been released."*

WHY PRIMITIVES?

If Java provides object types that, in some sense, mirror the capabilities of the primitive types, then what is the purpose of providing primitive types at all? Some object-oriented languages have no primitive types; in these pure OO languages, the only entities are objects. Other "hybrid" languages like Java and C++ have retained

Continued...

Why Primitives? Continued...

the primitive data types from earlier, structured languages, for purposes of compatibility or efficiency. As a new language, Java was not burdened with backwards compatibility (like C++ was), but the designers of Java *were* concerned with efficiency. Primitive types require less storage and less processing power than object types.

Primitives are closely related to objects, because primitives can be used to store the values of simple object attributes. A thermometer object, for example, might store the current temperature as a primitive value. The purpose of primitives is not to supplant objects, but to make objects more efficient.

The primitive types supplied with Java fall into four different families: the integers, the floating-points, the characters, and the booleans. Each of these primitive types also has a doppelganger or proxy that lives in the object world and provides the services of that realm to its less advanced brethren.

The Integer Family

The integer family is used to represent signed whole (counting) numbers. This family has four different members, byte, short, int, and long. Each of these uses a different amount of storage in memory, and thus each can represent a successively larger range of values. Table 3.1 shows the range of values that each integer type can represent.

TABLE 3.1
THE INTEGER DATA TYPES

Type	Storage Required	Smallest Value	Largest Value
byte	1 byte	−128	127
short	2 bytes	−32,768	32,767
int	4 bytes	−2,147,483,648	2,147,483,647
long	8 bytes	−9,223,372,036, 854,775,808	9,223,372,036, 854,775,807

To create an integer field in your class definition, you follow the pattern presented earlier. Listing 3.3 shows a class with four field definitions, each of which is given an initial value.

Listing 3.3 IntegerStore.java

```
public class IntegerStore
{
    private byte    aBigByte   =   127;
    private short   aBigShort  =   32767;
    private int     aBigInt    =   214783647;
    private long    aBigLong   =   9223372036854775807L;

    // Methods to manipulate or use these fields would go here
}
```

Just as you saw in the Robot class, each field begins with the private declaration, followed by the type of the field and an initializing expression. Here, integer literals are used to specify a starting value (in this case, the largest value that can be stored in each type) that will be used when any IntegerStore objects are created.

Integer literals are written as numerals, with no decimal points or commas. If you attempt to store a literal value in a field that is too small to hold that value—trying to put 128 into a byte field for example—the compiler will give you an error message and refuse to compile your code. If you look closely at the last line in IntegerStore, you'll note an L appended to the literal value assigned to aBigLong. Internally, all integer literals are stored as ints by default. The L at the end of aBigLong simply tells the compiler to store this literal value as a long instead of an int. If you fail to do this, the Java compiler will, again, issue an error message and your program will remain uncompiled.

Because each integer type occupies a finite amount of memory, what happens when you add one to an integer that is already full? If you've ever seen the odometer on an automobile roll over, you might have some idea, but you would not be entirely correct. Because integers in Java are processed as two's-complement signed numbers, when you add one to a field holding the largest value for that integer type, rather than rolling over to zero like that old Ford you owned in college, it instead rolls over to the smallest negative number that the integer type can represent. Though Java will warn you if you attempt to store a value that is too large when you are creating an integer field, it will not tell you when your integer accidentally "overflows."

The Floating-Point Family

In Java, the floating-point family consists of two members: the float and the double. Floating-point values, unlike integer values, can have a fractional part. Just as longs use more memory than ints, and thus can represent a wider range of values, so doubles use twice the storage as floats and can also represent a larger range of values. However, because floating-point numbers represent approximate values (unlike integers), the extra storage used to store a double also means that doubles can represent those values to a greater precision than can floats. Table 3.2 shows the storage and precision requirements for the floating-point family.

TABLE 3.2
floats AND doubles

Type	Size	Approx. Precision	Approx. Min Value	Approx. Max Value (Decimal digits)
float	4 bytes	7 digits	±1.40E–45	±3.40E+38
double	8 bytes	15 digits	±4.94E–324	±1.79E+308

Floating-point fields are created in your class definition using almost the same pattern you followed for the integers. Similar to the previous example, Listing 3.4 shows a class with four field definitions, each of which is given an initial value.

Listing 3.4 FloatingStore.java

```java
//  Defining each of the floating point types

public class FloatingStore
{
    private float   aSmallFloat =    .0032128F;
    private float   aLargeFloat =    2.345E7F;
    private double  aBigDouble  =    9223372036854775808.0;
    private double  aTinyDouble =    0.214783647e-89;

    // Methods to manipulate these fields would go here
}
```

Each of these four fields is initialized by using the assignment operator (=) to store a floating-point literal in the field. As you can see, there is a wider variety of ways to write floating-point literals than you saw with integer literals. In the simplest form, a floating-point literal is written as a decimal number. If the literal is to be stored into a float field, you must append the suffix 'F' or 'f' to the value. Literal floating point values written without the suffix are created as doubles and Java will refuse to store a double value inside a float—even if the current value of the double would fit.

In addition to using decimal notation to specify floating-point literals, you can also use scientific or exponential notation. These are both methods of writing very large numbers more easily, especially given Java's refusal to accept commas in numeric literals. If you wanted to write the number six billion, two-hundred and thirty-three million, five-hundred and twenty-two thousand, one hundred and ninety-three dollars and fifty-two cents, you could do it in any of these three ways:

```java
6233522193.52;          // Decimal notation
6.23352219352E9         // Scientific notation
0.623352219352E10       // Exponential notation
```

The advantage of scientific and exponential notation is, of course, that you are less likely to be off by a billion or so dollars than when you have to count decimal places with your fingers! When using this method of writing literals, the actual number is written with the first non-zero digit to the left (scientific) or right (exponential) of the decimal point. The number is followed by 'E' or 'e' and then the number of places that you want to move the decimal point when the number is "decoded." If the exponent is a negative number (as in aTinyDouble above), the decimal point is shifted to the left, filling with zeros. Otherwise, the decimal point is shifted to the right.

The Characters

The first computers were seen as large calculators: number-crunchers extraordinaire! Little could their designers have realized that by the end of the decade the most common use of computers would be to manipulate text, not numbers. Because of the importance of text, Java has a primitive type devoted entirely to characters: the char type.

In Java a char is a 16-bit unsigned integer value that stands for a Unicode character. Unicode is an international encoding standard that enables Java programs to represent most of the characters used in most of the world's alphabets. Earlier programming languages used the ASCII encoding standard and thus could only represent the 128 characters common in English and a few other Western European languages.

Like the floating-point family of primitives, there are several ways you can specify a char literal:

- The easiest way is to type the literal character using your keyboard. Put the value inside single quotes. This works fine if the character you want to use is represented on your keyboard. To define a field that initially stores the value A, you would write:

```
private char    theCharacterA    = 'A';
```

- You can also simply use the integral Unicode encoding value in your initialization (not using any quotes) like this:

```
private char    theCharacterA    = 65;
```

- Alternatively, you can use an *escape sequence* to specify a particular character. Escape sequences consist of two parts: the escape character and the escape value. In Java, as in the C language, the escape character is the backslash character (\). When Java encounters the escape character in a character declaration, it treats the next value as a special character and applies a set of translation rules. Table 3.3 lists the common escape codes and the Unicode characters that they stand for. Unicode escape sequences can be used anywhere you use characters in Java; not only as literal values for char fields, but in Strings as well.

TABLE 3.3
ESCAPE SEQUENCES FOR char LITERALS

Sequence	Meaning
\b	Backspace (\u0008)
\t	Tab (\u0009)
\n	Newline (\u000A)
\f	Form feed (\u000C)
\r	Return (\u000D)
\"	Double quote (\u0022)
\'	Single quote (\u0027)
\\	Backslash (\u005C)
\ddd	Any character, specified by octal digits *ddd*

The Booleans

The last, and simplest, of the primitive data types is the `booleans`. A `boolean` can hold only one of two possible values: `true` or `false`. In your classes, you'll use `boolean` fields wherever such a binary state is appropriate: a switch that can be on or off, or a widget that is either finished or not.

Although `boolean` fields are useful for modeling such binary information in your classes, the most common use of `boolean` values is in making decisions for loops and selections. Such `boolean` values are normally the results of expressions rather than being stored in fields and variables.

Object, String, and Array Types

Although primitive types are common in procedural programs, you will find object types much more common in Java programs. The two attributes in the `Robot` class, `myColor` and `myLocation`, are both object types. How are object types different from primitive types? There are two primary differences:

- Objects consist of both attributes and methods, whereas primitives consist of exactly one single value and are manipulated by means of operators.

- Object types are stored (and manipulated) as references instead of as values. We say that objects have reference semantics whereas primitives have value semantics. Object variables do not store their actual attribute values. Instead, Java controls the storage of the actual values and gives you, the programmer, a reference or handle that allows you to use those values. The major consequence of this is that two different object variables may, in fact, refer to the same object.

> *" Object types are stored (and manipulated) as references instead of as values. "*

Java has two other data types that are similar to object types: the `String` and the array. Most of us are familiar with `Strings`, which are lines of text composed of characters. In Java, `Strings` act a little differently than strings in C or Pascal or BASIC, each of which treats strings in its own idiosyncratic way. The major difference between Java `Strings` and strings in these other languages is that Java `Strings` are immutable: once you create a `String`, you can't change it. However, because `Strings` are reference types (like objects), you can easily cause a `String` variable to refer to another `String`. This all sounds more confusing than it is, so perhaps an example will set things straight:

```
String firstName    = "Barney";
String lastName     = "Google";

lastName  = firstName;   // both variables refer to the same string
firstName = "Carney";    // both variables again have distinct values
```

This example creates two `String` variables, `firstName` and `lastName`, each of which is initialized to refer to an actual value: the `String` literals `Barney` and `Google` respectively. Notice that `String` literals are surrounded by double quotes (`"`), unlike characters, which use the single quote character (`'`).

In the third line, the assignment of firstName to lastName has the effect of causing both String variables to refer to exactly the same String literal: the word Barney. If Strings were allowed to change, any changes made to lastName would also change firstName, because both String variables refer to the same actual String. Finally, in the last line, firstName is again changed to refer to a new String literal, the word Carney.

If you're a C programmer, you may be wondering what happened to the string literal Google when firstName was assigned to lastName. Java's automatic garbage collection makes sure that objects without references are reclaimed by the system.

Memory Management and new

When you created the String variable lastName you gave it a value by assigning a String literal, just as you did for the primitive types like ints and floats. Other object types, however, lack literals. To assign a value to an object variable, you'll normally go through two steps: first, tell Java to create a new object, and then use assignment to store the reference to the new object in your field.

To create a new object, Java uses the operator called new. The new operator is used in conjunction with a special factory method that is defined (implicitly or explicitly) in every class. This special factory method is responsible for taking the class definition (recall that a class definition is a blueprint for creating an object), creating a new object, and returning a reference to that new object to the caller.

This special factory method (called a *constructor*) is always named exactly the same as the name of the type of object you are trying to create. If you are trying to create a ToyFrog object, name the constructor method ToyFrog(); when you are trying to create a ToyRobot object, name the constructor (surprise!) ToyRobot(). If you were creating a Playroom class that required one of each, your class definition might look like Listing 3.5.

```
Listing 3.5 Playroom.java
//  Defining some object variables

public class PlayRoom
{
    private ToyFrog    myFrog    =    new ToyFrog( );
    private ToyRobot   myRobot   =    new ToyRobot( );

    // Methods to manipulate these fields would go here
}

//  Definitions for the Robot and Frog classes could
//  appear here or in another file accessible to the
//  PlayRoom class
class ToyFrog
{
}
class ToyRobot
{
}
```

Sometimes, constructors require additional information in order to construct a suitable object for you. A class can actually have several constructors, each using a different set of information to construct customized objects upon demand. Moreover, the new operator, and the related object constructors, can be used anywhere you need to create an object, not just when assigning values to class fields.

Now that you've looked at the way attributes are defined in Java, it's time to turn your attention to the second task you'll face when writing classes: defining methods. And, what better introduction than to look at a method that uses both the new operator and the Robot class constructor to create the three Robots that appear in the Robotz applet?

```
public void init()
{
    add( new Robot( Color.blue ) );
    add( new Robot( Color.red  ) );
    add( new Robot( Color.green) );
}
```

DEFINING METHODS

" A method definition describes the steps that your class will perform to accomplish a particular operation."

A method definition describes the steps that your class will perform to accomplish a particular operation. If you'll take a look at the init() method that ended the previous section, you'll see the two parts of a method definition: the header and the body. The body of a method definition, like the body of a class, is enclosed within curly braces ({}). Each method definition, however, is placed inside the body of its class definition.

The header for a method body consists of five parts, which you can see in Figure 3.7:

- **An access specifier that defines who is able to use this method**—If the access specifier is public (as in this example), anyone can call this method; if the method is declared private, only methods in the same class are permitted to use this method; if the protected specifier is used, methods in this class and methods in any subclasses may also use this method; finally, if no specifier is present (called package access), methods in any classes in this particular package or directory may access this method.

- **The type of value that will be returned when the method is invoked or called**—Methods that only perform an action and don't return any information should use the special type void. Methods may return a single primitive type, an object (possibly a String), or an array. When you invoke a method, you may choose to use the returned value, but you don't have to. (However, if a method returns a value, and is well designed, there is seldom a reason to ignore the return value).

- **The name of the method**—This name must follow the rules for creating Java identifiers, should observe the common Java naming conventions, and should give the caller some idea of what the method is going to do. By looking at the name of the init() method, you probably have some idea of what it is going to do; if the method were named xyz(), you would have no such confidence.

- **A pair of parentheses that are used to hold the information that is passed to the method**—Even if a method requires no additional information, you must include the parentheses.

- **An optional list of parameters, which provides information that customizes the behavior of the method**—For example, a method that computes a square root would require its user to provide a number to use for the calculation; a method that connects to a URL might need the user to pass a String representing the URL. To specify a parameter, you write the type of the parameter and then provide a name that can be used inside the method to refer to the parameter. A method can have more than one parameter; simply separate each parameter definition with a comma.

FIGURE 3.7

The parts of a method

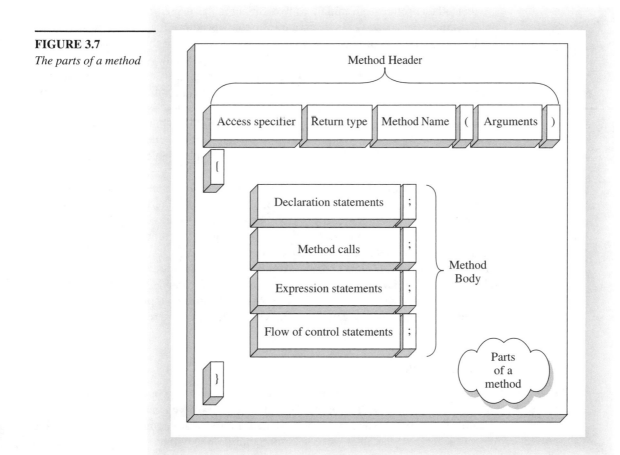

The Method Body: Statements, Expressions, and Operations

The bodies of a class's methods are where the real work of an object-oriented program takes place. The body of a method consists of statements. You might think of statements as the sentences of the Java language. Each statement, ended by a semicolon, usually performs a single operation or calculation. You will use several kinds of statements to write your Java methods.

Declaration Statements

Declaration statements enable you to create local variables using either primitives or objects. You've already seen one type of declaration statement when you saw how to create an object's attributes. Creating local variables is very similar. Look at line three of the method named `mouseMoved( )` in the `Robot` class:

```
int dx = evt.getX( ), dy = evt.getY( );
```

This method declares and initializes two `int` variables named `dx` and `dy`. Local variables, unlike fields, serve as temporary storage locations for values needed by a method for a calculation. Here the values `dx` and `dy` represent the amount each `Robot` object will have to move when it receives the `mouseMoved( )` message.

The major difference between defining fields and defining local variables is that you cannot use any of the optional access specifiers or storage modifiers (like `static`) on local variables. When you create a field, you have the option of keeping that field `private` (recommended), or of sharing it with some larger community. Local variables, by contrast, can only be seen inside the methods where they are created. In Java you can create a variable anywhere inside the method, but it is only usable after it has been created.

Besides this restricted visibility, local variables also have an abbreviated lifetime compared to fields. A field exists as long as the object that contains it exists. A local variable exists only as long as the method that created it is executing. If a method is invoked several times, a new local variable is created each time; thus the value of a local variable is not retained between method calls.

Finally, local variables must be initialized before they are used; they do not receive a default value like fields do. If you attempt to use a local variable without initializing it, the Java compiler will not compile your program. In this example, `dx` and `dy` are initialized by sending a message to a `MouseEvent` object called `evt` that has been passed as a parameter to the `mouseMoved( )` method.

Method Calls

The second major type of statement that you can use inside your methods is one that invokes another method. Indeed, looking at `Robotz.java` you can see that most of the statements are of this variety. Object-oriented programs are composed of cooperating objects, so one of your chief ways of getting things done will be to ask other objects to give you a hand.

The general form of making a method call is:

```
Receiver.Message( [argument [, argument ...]] );
```

The receiver is the object you want to send the message to. (An alternative way to think of this is that the receiver is the object you want to perform the work.) The message is the name of the method you want performed. If a method requires you to pass some information, put the necessary information in the parentheses after the method name. Again, an example from `Robotz.java` should prove helpful. The body of the `paint()` method, which each `Robot` object uses to draw its face, looks like this:

```
public void paint( Graphics g )
{
    g.drawLine( 10, 40, 40, 40 );
    g.drawRect( 15,  5,  5, 15 );
    g.drawRect( 30,  5,  5, 15 );
}
```

Notice that the `paint()` method takes a single argument, a `Graphics` object, which has been named g here. You don't have to know what a `Graphics` object is to see that it responds to both the `drawLine()` and `drawRect()` messages. In each of the three method invocations that make up the body of `paint()`, the `Graphics` object g is the receiver of the message. The message is either `drawLine` or `drawRect`, and each time the method is called a different set of arguments is passed, resulting in a line drawn for the mouth and a set of rectangles drawn for each eye. Notice how the same method call (`drawRect()`) can be customized to draw either a right or left eye, by simply varying the value of the arguments that are passed to the method.

If you look closely at `Robotz.java`, however, you'll find a number of method calls that don't seem to have any receiver. For example, the body of the `init()` method in the `Robotz` class looks like this:

```
public void init()
{
    add( new Robot( Color.blue ) );
    add( new Robot( Color.red  ) );
    add( new Robot( Color.green) );
}
```

The `init()` method makes three calls to the `add()` method, each time passing a different `Robot` object. Who is the receiver of the `add` message? It might not be immediately obvious, but when you call a method, that method can exist in two different places: in the current class you're working on, or in another class. When you call a method that exists in another class, you need to have an object to send that method to. However, when you call a method that exists in the class you are currently working on, you don't need another object; when you leave out the receiver in a method call you are, in effect, saying "send this message to me!" This is such a common situation that "me" has even been given a name: in Java, the current object is specified by use of the keyword `this`. If you like, you can explicitly use `this` whenever you make a method call where the current object is the receiver:

```
this.add( new Robot( Color.red  ) );
```

Expression Statements

The third major type of statement that you can use inside the body of your methods is the expression statement. An expression statement is, formally, "a combination of operands and operators, that, when evaluated, produces a value." In real life, that simply means you can write statements that perform some calculation. Here is an example of an expression statement from the mouseMoved() method in the Robot class:

```
dx = dx - 50;
```

The operands in this expression statement are the local variable dx and the constant integer 50. The operators used are the subtraction operator (–) and the assignment operator (=). Expressions and expression statements are not exactly the same thing. An expression statement is a full expression that ends with a semicolon; it may include any number of intermediate, or sub-expressions.

This example includes two sub-expressions. The first, dx – 50, uses the operands (just another word for a data value) dx and 50 to produce another value, the result of the expression. The second expression is the assignment expression, dx = <result-from-the-first-expression>. If you come from a Pascal or BASIC background, you might object at this point and say, "No, dx – 50 is an expression, but the rest is simply an assignment statement, saving the value of that expression." In Java however, as in C and C++, the assignment operator produces a value, just like any other operator, and it can be used inside expressions. If you have two integer variables, dx and dy, and you want to set them both equal to 0, the following expression statement will do so:

```
dx = dy = 0;
```

This statement first evaluates the expression, dy = 0. Part of the process of evaluating the expression is performing the operation of assignment. Once this operation is completed, the value of the expression is calculated. With the assignment operator, the value of the assignment expression is the value of the variable after assignment. It is this temporary value (the result of the expression) that is assigned to dx.

Java has a very rich set of operators that can be used to create expressions. Table 3.4 lists the operators that you can use. Expressions using the operators at the top of the list will be performed before operators at the bottom of the list. This sort of hierarchy is termed operator precedence. If you look at the list, you'll see that multiplication is higher on the list than addition, so when Java evaluates the expression

```
a = 3 + 5 * 0;
```

it produces the value 3 (adding 3 to 5 * 0), rather than the value 0 (first adding 3 and 5 to produce 8, and then multiplying by 0).

When operators are at the same level of precedence, a second rule kicks in, called the rule of associativity. This one is simple to remember; for every operator except assignment, simply evaluate the expressions left to right. Thus the expression

```
a = 3 * 3 / 7;
```

yields the value 1 (dividing the integer 9 by the integer 7, with the remainder discarded), rather than the value 0 (multiplying 3 times the result of dividing 3 by 7).

TABLE 3.4
JAVA'S OPERATORS AND PRECEDENCE (ABRIDGED)

Operator	Type	Meaning
++, --	Numeric	Pre/post increment, decrement
+, -	Numeric	Unary plus and unary minus
!	Boolean	Logical negation
*, /, %	Numeric	Multiply, divide, modulus
+, -	Numeric	Add, subtract
+	String	Concatenate
<, <=, >, >=	Numeric	Inequality
==, !=	Primitive	Equality, not equal
==, !=	Object	Identity, not identical
&&	Boolean	Logical AND
||	Boolean	Logical OR
?:	Boolean, any	Conditional operator
=	Variable, any	Assignment

" Flow-of-control statements give your programs the ability to make decisions, and to keep working on a problem until it's done. "

Before you leave expression statements, there is one last thing you should think about: what kind of things can be used as operands? So far, the examples you've seen have all used variables and literals. In addition to these, you can also use method calls, provided a method returns a value of the correct type. Take a brief look at the method, mouseDragged(), from the Robot class:

```java
public void mouseDragged( MouseEvent evt )
{
    myLocation = getLocation();
    setLocation( myLocation.x + (evt.getX( ) - 25),
                 myLocation.y + (evt.getY( ) - 25));
}
```

The statement myLocation = getLocation() is an expression statement that uses a method call to provide a value for the assignment. The second line is a method call statement that uses two expressions to calculate the arguments passed to the method. Notice how an expression can include a variable (myLocation.x), an integer literal (25), and a method call (evt.getX()).

Flow of Control

The fourth and last kind of statement that can appear in a method body is called a flow-of-control statement. These give your programs the ability to make decisions and to keep working on a problem until it's done.

Creating variables, assigning values, and performing calculations are all important parts of any computer program, but restricting your software to these features would mean that every program would do exactly the same thing exactly the same way every time it was run. To provide any sort of "intelligence," computer programs need two additional abilities.

Most computer programs have to operate on different types of data. A payroll program cannot just make simple calculations—multiplying your salary by 20% to determine the amount of taxes to withhold, for example. The actual situation is much more complex. The program has to take into account, as a minimum, the amount of your salary (withholding rates are progressive) and the number of deductions you'll claim. To perform this type of operation, the computer needs a selection or branching capability; it needs to be able to execute a particular series of statements based on a condition.

In addition, programs need to be somewhat general, handling entire categories of problems rather than specific problems. The author of the payroll program could, in fact, write a separate program for every employee in the company; when a new employee was hired, a new program could be written. A better solution however, is the ability to perform repetitive processing, applying the single payroll program to each employee, until all the employees have been processed. This capability is called iteration or looping.

Finally, for modern programs, this model is not entirely sufficient. Much of today's software does not simply process some finite stream of inputs (employee payroll records) and produce some predetermined output (weekly paychecks). Instead, today's systems have become highly interactive. The popularity of systems like the Macintosh and Microsoft Windows has led to the need to work with *reactive* systems—programs whose flow-of-control is not neatly linear, but instead is described as a set of stimulus-response behaviors. Such systems are called *event-driven* programs.

Java provides methods for working with each of these control structures and program architectures.

SELECTION: MAKING CHOICES

Java has two basic language facilities for making choices: the `if-else` construct and the `switch`. The `if` statement makes its decision by evaluating a `boolean` value or condition, whereas the `switch` statement branches based on an integer-valued expression.

The `if-else` Statements

The general form of the `if-else` statement in Java looks like this:

```
if ( boolean expression )
    statement;
else
    statement
```

An `if` statement consists of two parts: a test condition and a results section (see Figure 3.8). When the compiler executes the `if` statement it first evaluates the `boolean` condition inside the parentheses. If the result is `true`, the statement on the line below the `if` will be executed; if the condition is `false`, the statement on the line below the `else` is executed.

FIGURE 3.8

The parts of an `if-else`
selection statement

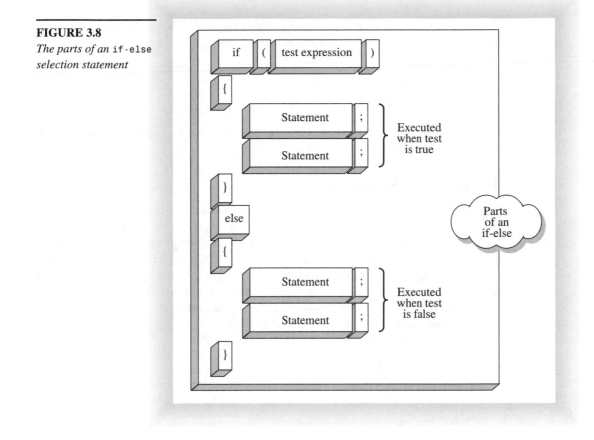

You don't need to include the `else` portion; it's optional. The parentheses surrounding the `boolean` condition are part of the syntax and are required. Although you can use a `boolean` variable for this test condition, you will normally use one of the relational operators (`>`, `<`, `>=`, `<=`, `==`) to form a `boolean` expression. These `boolean` expressions can be combined with the logical operators AND (`&&`), OR (`¦¦`), and NOT (`!`), to form complex expressions.

In the `mouseMoved()` method in the `Robot` class, the `if` statement is used to restrict the values of `dx` and `dy` to values between 25 and `-25`, causing the `Robot` to move to the left when the mouse is moved over its right half, and move to the right when the robot is moved over its left half:

```
if ( dx > 25 )
    dx = dx - 50;
if ( dy > 25 )
    dy = dy - 50;
```

If you want to execute more than one statement in a branch, you have to enclose the statements in braces; then Java will treat them as a single statement, like this:

```
if ( dx > 25 )
{
    dx = dx - 50;
....// other statements
}
```

If you forget the braces, Java executes the lines after the first statement unconditionally, despite your attractive indentation.

The `switch` Statement

The second form of selection statement in Java is the `switch` statement, which allows you to decide between multiple branches based on a numeric calculation. This is similar to the `case` statement found in other programming languages (with a few unexpected behaviors). If you're wondering why the designers of Java used the word `switch` instead of the more common `case`, remember that Java is syntactically descended from the C and C++ languages, developed at AT&T's Bell Laboratories where thinking in terms of telephone switches is the most natural thing in the world. Figure 3.9 shows the parts of the `switch` statement.

The general form of the `switch` statement looks like this:

```
switch ( integer expression )
{
    case 1:
        // Statement
        break;
    case 2:
        // Statement
        break;
    default:
        // Statement
        break;
}
```

When Java encounters a `switch` statement, it first evaluates the integer expression in the parentheses after the keyword `switch`. It then scans each of the `case` sections looking for a match. Each of the `case` expressions must evaluate to an integer constant (not variable) value. If such a match is found, an unconditional jump is executed to that location, where the rest of the code inside the braces of the `switch` body is executed. If no such match is found, a jump is made to the (optional) `default` case if one is provided.

Normally, a `break` statement is used as the last statement inside each of the `case` conditions, but this is not required by the syntax of the `switch` statement. As a result, it is very easy to forget to include a `break`, and have the code in the remaining `cases` execute. This is the most common error made in writing the `switch` statement.

FIGURE 3.9

The parts of a switch
selection statement

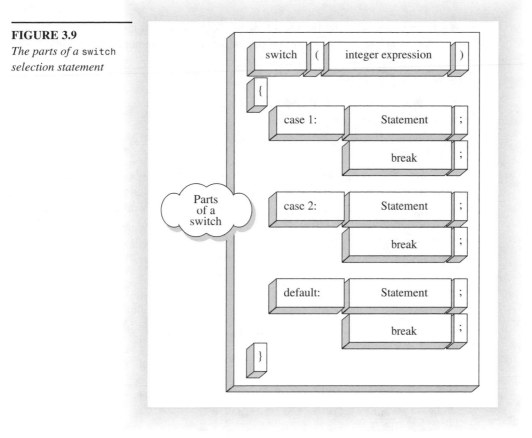

ITERATION: LOOPING

Like selection, iteration is one of the fundamental control structures upon which all modern software is built. Java, like the C/C++ programming languages, has three different iteration or looping structures: while, an entry-condition loop; do-while, an exit-condition loop; and for, an all-purpose loop especially well suited for building counted loops.

All loops consist of two major parts: the loop condition, which determines how long the loop will continue to execute, and the loop body, which contains the statements that are executed repetitively while the loop executes. In operation, the loop condition is tested and if it is found true, all of the statements inside the loop body are executed, after which the loop condition is tested again. If the loop condition is placed before the body of the loop, it is possible (if the condition is false) for the statements inside the body to never be executed. This is an entry-condition loop.

By contrast, the loop condition can be placed after the body of the loop. The do-while loop works this way. It always executes the statements inside its body at least once, because the loop condition is not tested until after the do-while executes the statements within its loop body. One final consideration deserves comment: In every loop it is imperative that the loop body include statements that move the loop closer to completion. An endless or dead loop is one of the most common programming errors.

The `while` Loop

The simplest loop in Java is the `while` loop, which you can see in Figure 3.10. This loop has the basic form:

```
while ( boolean condition )
    Statement;
```

Like the `if` statement, the `boolean` condition in a `while` loop must be enclosed in parentheses. The loop body is assumed to be one statement long. If you want to execute multiple statements in your loop body (as you almost always will), you can include braces around the loop body. Finally, you'll need to "set things up" so you know what's going to happen when the loop starts. A more typical `while` loop that includes multiple statements and initialization has this basic form:

FIGURE 3.10

The parts of a `while` *loop*

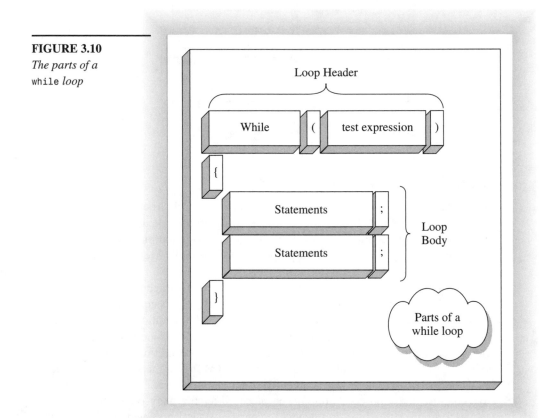

```
// Initialize loop condition
while ( boolean condition )
{
    // Statements
    // Update loop condition
}
```

A short example with a code fragment that executes 10 times should prove the value of this "template":

```
int loopCounter = 0;       //  Set up the loop variable
while ( loopCounter < 10 )  //  Test the loop condition
{
    // Statements
    loopCounter++;          //  Update the loop expression
}
```

If you forget to set up the loop variable, you can't be sure that the loop won't execute more or fewer times than you want. If you forget to update the loop expression at the bottom, the loop will execute forever. If you leave off the braces in this example, the statements in the first line of code after the test condition will execute, again, forever.

The for Loop

Because this is such a common pattern—initialize, test, update—Java gives you a loop that puts all of these features in one place for easy access. The for loop is probably the most used loop in Java. You can see the for loop illustrated in Figure 3.11. The basic form of the for loop is:

```
for ( initializer; test condition; update expression )
    // Statement;
```

Instead of just putting a single boolean condition inside the parentheses, like the while loop does, the for loop puts three expressions, separated by semicolons. The first expression, usually called the *initializer*, is where you set up the loop, giving values to any variables that are tested. The initializer expression in a for loop is only executed once, and it is always executed, regardless of whether the test condition is true or false.

The test condition is a boolean expression that works just like the test condition in a while loop. The expression is evaluated and, if found true, the statements in the body of the loop are executed sequentially. But, there is an important difference between the while loop and the for loop. When a while loop has finished executing its loop body, it evaluates its test condition. However, before a for loop evaluates its test condition, it first evaluates its *update expression*.

Like the while loop, you'll almost always want to enclose the body of the for loop in braces to avoid unexpected and unpleasant results. Like the more generalized form of the while loop, the normal for loop can be based on a pattern like this:

```
for ( int loopCounter = 0; loopCounter < 10; i++ )
{
    // Statements
}
```

FIGURE 3.11

The parts of a for *loop*

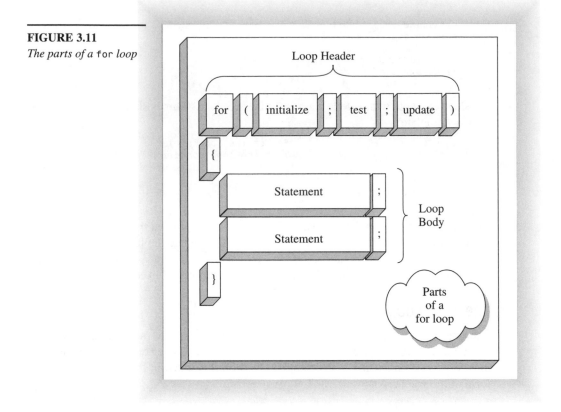

The local variable loopCounter is local to the statements inside the body of the for loop, unlike its use in the while loop example.

The do-while Loop

Java has one last form of loop, used less frequently than the other two, called the do-while loop. The do-while loop is an exit-condition loop, so it will always execute its statements at least once. The basic form of the do-while loop looks like this:

```
do
    // Statement
while ( boolean condition );
```

Note that, unlike the while loop, the do-while loop has a semicolon after the boolean condition. (Putting a semicolon after the condition in a while loop is almost always an error.) Like the other loops, you use braces to have your loop perform multiple statements. The generalized form of the loop you saw previously would look like this rewritten as a do-while loop:

```
int loopCounter = 0;
do
{
```

```
    // Statements
    loopCounter++;
while ( loopCounter < 10 );
```

You can see the do-while loop illustrated in Figure 3.12.

EVENTS: STIMULUS AND RESPONSE

Sequence, selection, and iteration are the basic building blocks of structured programming. However, if you take a look at Robotz.java, you'll immediately notice that there are no loops. Does this mean that the Robotz applet simply executes all of the statements in the code and then stops? No, not at all. Robotz is an example of a reactive or event-driven system.

Most computer systems involve some sort of interaction with the user of the program. In bygone years, if you wanted to write an interactive program, you were responsible for reading the keyboard and the mouse yourself. Normally the code that did this would be placed in a large, endless loop that continuously monitored or polled

FIGURE 3.12

The parts of a do-while *loop*

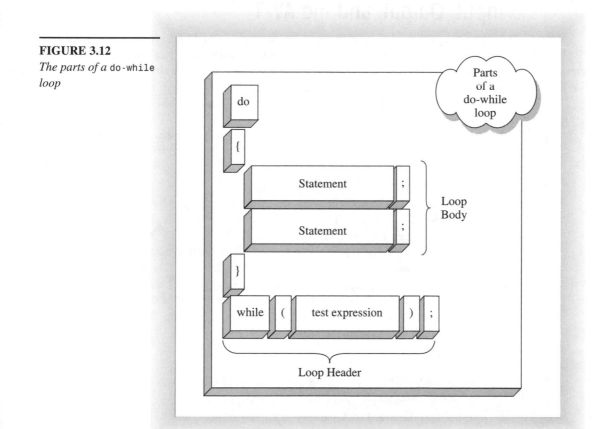

those devices. The problem with this scheme is that each program took exclusive control of the mouse and keyboard so that other programs couldn't use them.

When computers first started to use hard disks, a similar problem arose. If my program took control of the hardware and wrote data to track 50, sector 27, how was your program supposed to know that, and avoid overwriting my files? In response to this, software developers invented disk operating systems that allow us all to work with a virtual file system, rather than working with the actual disk-drive and controller hardware.

Event-driven, graphical operating systems like the Macintosh OS and Windows 95/NT perform a similar function for the mouse and keyboard that earlier systems did for the file system. In an event-driven system, the mouse, keyboard, and display all belong to the operating system, rather than to your program. If the user moves the mouse over one of the windows you've created, or if the user clicks a button on your form, or types a character into a text field, the operating system sends your program a message telling you that such an event has occurred.

Input, Output, and the AWT

Java programs should run, unchanged, on the Mac and on your Windows 95/NT machine, yet each of those operating systems has a different event notification system, incompatible with the others. This created a little bit of a problem. The solution the designers of Java arrived at was to create their own event handling system that sits on top of the native system provided by your operating system. This Java event system is part of the Abstract Window Toolkit or AWT.

The AWT actually has two different schemes for handling events: the current version (the 1.1 event model), and an earlier version (the 1.0 event model). As explained in the introduction, this book uses the 1.1 event model. Responding to events in your programs is a three-step process:

1. First, you have to notify the AWT that you are willing to handle certain types of events. If you don't tell Java that you're able to receive messages for a particular type of event, it won't send them to you. To tell the AWT that your class is able to listen for an event, you add a line that says your class implements one of the AWT "listener" interfaces. The class `Robotz` doesn't listen for any events; thus, Java doesn't send any to it. The class `Robot`, however, wants to know whenever the mouse is moved or dragged over one of its objects, and so it advertises its ability to handle those messages, by having the line

```
implements MouseMotionListener
```

in its header. This is your class's declaration of eligibility.

You'll learn more about the `implements` keyword, and the corresponding `interface` keyword, in Chapter 9, "Implementing Class Relationships: Inheritance and Interfaces," and Chapter 10, "Designing with Inheritance and Interfaces: A Case Study."

2. Now that you've asserted your ability to handle events, the next step is to register a listener. Essentially, you have to tell the AWT where to send the event messages. The line

```
addMouseMotionListener( this );
```

is the last line of the constructor method `Robot()`. The `Robot()` method will be called whenever anyone (in this example the `Robotz` class) creates a `Robot` object. The effect of this line is to make sure that every `Robot` object receives the messages in the `MouseMotionListener` interface whenever the mouse moves over the surface of that `Robot`.

3. The final step in handling events is to write methods to handle the messages that will be sent to you. Every set of events you "subscribe" to requires you to write a different set of methods. Because you subscribed to the `MouseMotionListener` interface, Java sends you two messages: `mouseMoved` when the mouse moves across the surface of your `Robot`, and `mouseDragged`, when the mouse is moved and the dragging button is depressed. If you only want to do something when one of these events occurs, you still have to write the method for the event you're not interested in, but you can leave the method body empty.

Applets and Applet Methods

By this time, you should have a pretty good feel for how the `Robotz` applet works. You saw that the `Robotz` class has a single method, `init()`, that creates three `Robot` objects using the `new` operator and calling the `add()` method to place them on its surface. At that point, the work of the `Robotz` applet is done; the rest of the work will be done by the `Robots` themselves.

You've seen how the `Robot` class calls a constructor whenever a `Robot` object is created. The constructor is responsible for initializing each of the attributes of a `Robot` object as it is created. This constructor is also responsible for registering each `Robot` so that it receives event messages from the operating system. Finally you saw how the `Robot` class writes the `mouseMoved()` and `mouseDragged()` methods to respond to those event messages.

You might still be wondering about two things, however. Who called the `init()` method and who called the `paint()` method? Are these part of the event system? Well, yes and no.

The `init()` method is invoked by either your Web browser or the appletviewer application whenever either loads a program that is derived from the `Applet` class. This is only one of several messages that can be sent to your applet by your Web browser. You can write methods to respond to each of these messages (called the applet life-cycle methods). The `paint()` method, by contrast, is called by the operating system whenever the surface of your applet needs to be redrawn. Remember that in an event-driven operating system, the display is the property of the operating system (OS). The OS doesn't know what you want the faces of your `Robots` to look like, but it tells you when it thinks that they need to be repainted. You can see how this works by starting the `Robotz` applet and then dragging another window so that your applet is partially obscured. When you remove the window, Java calls the `paint()` method in your applet to touch up the marred visages.

That Thing Called `main()` Is Just a Bit Arcane

Unlike applets, which have a family of life-cycle methods, Java applications have only one special method: `main()`. C and C++ programmers recognize `main()`, because C and C++ programs have a special function by that name. But, just what does the `main()` method do? If you pose this question to 10 C or C++ programmers, you're likely to get ten answers that, if not identical, will recognizably mean the same thing. "The `main()` method," they'll say, "is where every C program starts executing." In C and C++, each program can have only a single `main()` function, and programmers are no more confused about the meaning of `main()` than they are about the meaning of life in general; perhaps even less so. All that changes in Java.

In Java, asking "what does `main()` mean" can lead your brain into an existential paradox that has a myriad of equally correct, or equally incorrect, answers. Is `main()` the entry point to your application, as it is in C++? Well…, yes, no, sometimes, and perhaps; all these are valid answers. This confusion arises because there is no division between Java programs and Java objects like there is in languages like C++ or Object Pascal. In Java

- Each class in a program can have its own `main()` method.

- The user may decide to start the program using the `main()` method of any class in the application.

To understand what's going on, let's take a look at an example.

A `main()` EXAMPLE

Suppose you have two versatile and talented classes, the `Dancers` and the `Singers`. Because you realize that a Java program is, at its heart, a collection of cooperating agents, you give each class a `main()` method, which enables it to cooperate with the other class for the purpose of putting on a performance. The `Dancer` class might look like this:

```
//  A class that dances around

public class Dancer
{
  public void dance(String step)
  {
    /* Do dancing stuff here */
```

```
      System.out.println("Do a little "+ step +" right here");
    }

    public static void main(String[] args)
    {
      Dancer fred   = new Dancer();
      Dancer ginger = new Dancer();
      Singer frank  = new Singer();
      fred.dance("waltz");
      ginger.dance("fandango");
      fred.dance("macarena");
      frank.sing("Rainy-day Women");
      ginger.dance("tango");
    }
  }
```

Like the Dancer class, the Singer class has also been designed to be cooperative. Its main() method creates the Dancer fred, and puts him to work, along with a few Singers as well. The Singer class looks like this:

```
//  A musical class

public class Singer
{
  public void sing(String tune)
  {
    /* do singing stuff */
    System.out.println("Croon the tune, " + tune +", right here.");
  }

  public static void main(String[] args)
  {
    Singer frank = new Singer();
    Singer sammy = new Singer();
    Singer tony  = new Singer();
    Dancer dean  = new Dancer();

    frank.sing("Born on the Bayou");
    sammy.sing("The Gates of Eden");
    frank.sing("All Along the Watchtower");
    tony.sing("Maggie's Farm");
    dean.dance("twist");
    frank.sing("My Way");
  }
}
```

You can run this program by using the Java interpreter (java), which starts executing the main() method in the class you specify at runtime. If you invoke the main() method in the Singer class, you'll see a performance that looks like this:

```
C:> java Singer
Croon the tune, Born on the Bayou, right here.
Croon the tune, The Gates of Eden, right here.
Croon the tune, All Along the Watchtower, right here.
Croon the tune, Maggie's Farm, right here.
Do a little twist right here
Croon the tune, My Way, right here.
```

On the other hand, if you put the `Dancer` class in charge, the performance that ensues goes like this:

```
C:> java Dancer
Do a little waltz right here
Do a little fandango right here
Do a little macarena right here
Croon the tune, Rainy-day Women, right here.
Do a little tango right here
```

When you try and analyze what is going on here, it's important to keep a few facts at the forefront of your mind:

- Unlike C programs, Java programs can have several `main()` methods.

- Even if your class has a `main()` method, it will never be executed unless that class is invoked by the Java interpreter. It is easy to confuse the class constructor, which is called every time an object is created, and the `main()` method, which is only called when the class is used to "start-up" a Java program.

- Like C programs, only one `main()` method will act as the "entry point" or starting position each time your program runs. Unlike C programs, however, the `main()` method that performs this service is determined at runtime, not when you compile your program.

GUIDELINES FOR USING `main()`

By now, you may be more confused than when you started. So, what *does* `main()` mean, and how *should* you use the `main()` method in your programs? Here are two guidelines for using `main()` that will help clear the confusion, and keep your Java classes from becoming hopelessly intertwined:

1. Make a clear distinction between *application* classes and the working classes in your design. An application class is designed to act as an entry-point and overall manager for your application. Because the Java language does not enforce this distinction, you will have to do so by convention. One such useful convention is to add an "App" suffix to all such classes like this: `EmailApp, WriterApp`.

2. For every other class, resist the urge to use the `main()` method as a "test bed" to exercise each of the methods and features of the class. Instead, you should forego writing `main()` at all. Although using each class's `main()` method as a place for test-code has some appeal, in the final analysis, the drawbacks outweigh the advantages. Test code placed in a `main()` method is compiled into byte-codes and is delivered along with your finished application, making it larger and subsequently more sluggish. Furthermore, if you put a test-bed `main()` method in every class, you cannot prevent users from running your test code, without actually *commenting out* the main method when testing is complete. (Commenting out refers to the practice of placing comment

markers around some part of your program that you wish to remain in the source code, but you don't want to appear in the byte code.) You *should* write a test-bed program for every class you develop, but keeping the test code outside of your working classes is probably a better strategy.

Summary

This chapter has introduced you to the mechanics of writing Java programs and the basics of the Java language. To write and test Java programs, you use a text editor to write source code files, the javac compiler to turn those source files into executable code, and a Web browser, the java interpreter, or the appletviewer application to run your finished programs.

Java source code files are composed of class definitions. Every source file must contain exactly one publicly accessible class, but it can contain other, non-public classes. The source file must be named exactly the same as the public class it contains, except that the file has a .java extension. A class definition has two parts, a header, which acts a little like a title, and a body, which contains the definitions of the classes attributes and methods.

When you define attributes, you can use both primitive types—integers, floating-point numbers, characters, and logical values—and object types. Attributes that hold primitive types can each hold a single value and are manipulated by operators inside the methods of your class; attributes are built from object types and hold references to objects, rather than the objects themselves. When defining attributes, you have several choices to make. The most important of these is whether the attributes should be visible outside the class or whether their visibility should be restricted to the classes methods by using the access specifier private. To support encapsulation, you will usually make all of your attributes private. In addition, you can choose to provide separate copies of each attribute for each object, or you can create attributes that are shared among all instances of a class by using the keyword static.

In addition to defining attributes, you also define the methods for your class. Unlike attributes, the methods of a class are usually public. Like class definitions, a method definition has two parts: a header and a body. The header of a method declares the type of value that method produces (if any) as well as the kind of arguments the method requires to perform its work. The body of a method consists of the steps necessary to carry out the operations the method performs.

The body of a method is composed of statements, which fall into four general categories:

- Declaration statements enable you to create local variables, used to hold temporary values.

- Method call statements enable you to ask other objects to perform an operation; these are perhaps the most common statements in an object-oriented program.

● Expression statements enable you to assign a value to a variable or perform some other calculation.

● Flow of control statements enable you to make your methods act "intelligently" by giving them the ability to make decisions or repetitively perform some operation.

Many of the methods you will write will be written in response to events from the operating system or from your Web browser. The `init()` message is sent to an applet when it first loads, the `mouseMoved()` and `mouseDragged()` messages are sent to those objects that register to listen for them, and the `paint()` message is sent by the operating system to all objects that need to redraw themselves.

Java applications begin by executing the `main()` method of the class specified as the argument of the `java` command. Any Java class can include a `main()` method, but it's good to distinguish application classes from working classes and provide a `main()` method only for application classes.

Questions

1. The _____ code for a Java program is created by using a text editor, and the _____ code is created by compiling the source code with the Java compiler, _____.

2. A Java program that runs in the context of a web browser is called an _____, whereas a program that runs by using the java interpreter is called an _____.

3. Java source code files are composed of _____ definitions.

   a. byte code

   b. class

   c. data

   d. method

4. Every Java source file can contain only one _____ class, but may include other helper classes, provided they are not created with _____ access.

5. The public class `JaguarButton` must be contained in the file named _____.

6. In a class definition, the _____ describe the attributes of the object, whereas the _____ define its behavior.

7. Methods and fields can have access specifiers that determine their visibility. If you want to create a field that is only accessible by the methods of the same class, you would use the access specifier _____.

    a. package

    b. private

    c. protected

    d. public

8. True or false. Every object created from a class will contain individual fields for every defined attribute except those declared final, which will be shared among all members of the class.

9. Two differences between primitive types and objects are: An object can store _____, whereas a primitive stores a _____. Objects are manipulated by using _____, whereas primitives use _____ for the same purpose.

10. True or false. To support the principle of encapsulation, you will usually make the fields in your class public, while making your methods private.

Exercises

1. Type in and compile `IntegerStore.java`. When it compiles without errors, make the following changes, recompiling after each change, and record the error messages that appear. What rules can you discover? (Remember to restore the changes after each test.)

    Initialize the field `aBigByte` with `128`.

    Remove the `L` from the field `aBigLong`.

    Add an `L` to the end of the value stored in `aBigShort`.

2. Type in and compile `FloatingStore.java`. When it compiles without errors, make the following changes, recompiling after each change. Record the error messages that appear. What rules can you discover? (Remember to restore the changes after each test.)

    Remove the `F` from the end of `aSmallFloat`.

    Change the type of `aTinyDouble` to `int`.

    Create a new `int` variable called `aTinyInt`. Initialize it by storing the value `1.0`. Then try `1.0E1`. Can you store any numbers with a decimal point into `aTinyInt`?

    Store the value `1.75F` in the field `aBigDouble`. Does that work? If so, why?

3. Compile and run the `PlayRoom.java` program using the javac compiler and the java interpreter. What error message do you get? Now add the following method inside the body of the `PlayRoom` class. Compile and run the program, recording your results. How many objects can you find in this method?

```
public static void main(String[] args)
{
  PlayRoom myApp = new PlayRoom();

  System.out.println( myApp.myFrog );
  System.out.println( myApp.myRobot );
}
```

4. Still using `PlayRoom.java`, create a constructor for both the `ToyFrog` and `ToyRobot` classes. Add a line of text inside each constructor that uses `System.out.println()` to print a message to the console announcing that the specific constructor has been called. (The line `System.out.println("Hi Mom");` prints the `String` "Hi Mom" to the console.)

5. Modify `Robotz.java` to add two more `Robots` to the applet. Use your web browser to look up the color constants in the `Color` class (which is in the `java.awt` package) in the documentation that came with the JDK, and give your two new `Robots` some different colors.

6. Modify the logic in either the `mouseMoved()` method or the `mouseDragged()` method of the `Robot` class to change the behavior of the `Robots`. Compile and test your changes in appletviewer.

To Learn More

There is no lack of books for those who want to learn Java. Wading through them all is a little more difficult. As a general introduction, Laura Lemay's *Teach Yourself Java in 21 Days* is probably the most popular. The Waite Group's *Java 1.1 Interactive Course*, also by Laura Lemay, features an effective interactive format that includes questions and exercises. For those who want to learn programming and Java at the same time, bear with us one more time as we recommend Gilbert and McCarty's *Object-Oriented Programming in Java* by the Waite Group Press. Experienced programmers may prefer *The Java Programming Language*, by Ken Arnold and James Gosling—the creator of Java. Intermediate programmers should look at Cornell and Horstman's *Core Java*.

The Web has a wide variety of resources for learning Java. At the official JavaSoft site, you can download the Java Developer's Kit and review online documentation and API specifications. There's even an online tutorial. The URL is `http://www.javasoft.com`.

Seeing is sometimes believing. Sometimes it's learning too. If you're one of those who find it easier to learn through hearing and seeing something explained and illustrated, rather than through reading and doing, you might appreciate some of the new multimedia applications that help you learn Java. The Waite Group Press has published *Talk Java To Me*, while MindQ Publishing has a series of interactive CD-ROMs that cover all aspects of Java software development. See them on the Web at `http://www.waite.mcp.com` and `http://www.mindq.com`, respectively.

4

Encapsulation: Classes and Methods

"This is not a pipe." Painstakingly, word-by-word, you thumb through your worn English–French dictionary. You pause for a second and think. "I must be missing something," you say to yourself and start again from the beginning. "Ceci n'est pas une pipe." The translation comes out the same the second time around: "This is not a pipe." "But," you protest as you stand staring at Rene Magritte's famous 1926 painting, "it *is* a pipe. A big brown pipe. Why does it have 'This is not a pipe' written across the bottom?" Frustrated, you pick up your backpack and head for the exit, muttering to yourself, "Artists!"

Of course, Magritte was right. The painting hanging there on the museum wall is *not* a pipe. It is a *painting* of a pipe—a model, if you will. Even the word—pipe—is, itself, a model of the real thing. In this chapter, you will meet two software models that represent a real piece of software: the summary paragraph and the class definition (implemented as Java source code). In this chapter, you will step into the role of designer, working for a client who wants a filing program or a notepad program. You will be responsible for translating the client's ideas into a logical model that can be understood by the computer (as you can see in Figure 4.1).

"Wait just a minute," you say. "I understand that a summary paragraph is a model, but Java source code is what we're trying to build. Source code is not a model, it's the artifact!"

FIGURE 4.1

*The software designer
translates the client's
ideas into a model the
computer can under-
stand*

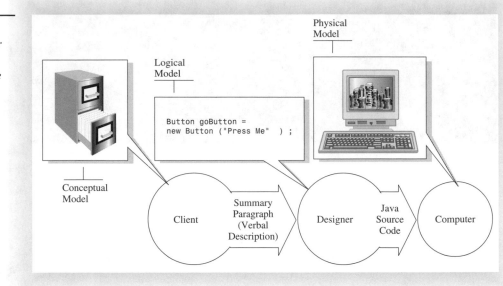

Well, just reflect on that for a minute. Is the Java source code really the artifact you're trying to create? If you gave the finished source code to your users, would they be satisfied? Could your accountant keep the source code for your spreadsheet program in his desk and pull it out to perform a calculation? No. Source code is a model; a very concrete and specific kind of model: one that can be understood by people (you hope) and, with the help of a translator, understood by the computer. As a software designer, it's easy to think of your source code as your goal when you write programs. Perhaps, following Magritte, you'd do better to add this line to the top of every file: "This is not a program."

Much of the complexity surrounding software design exists because software requires a two-step translation: First you must translate the user's concept into a logical solution, and then you must translate the logical solution into a physical design. Chapter 5, "Designing Classes and Objects," focuses on logical modeling—how you can be sure your design captures the client's concept. This chapter concentrates on techniques for designing simple, reliable, physical (implementation) models: the creation of a model that is understood and correct in both the human and the machine sphere. You will learn:

- More about how to differentiate between interface and implementation

- How to use a summary paragraph to discover the *environment* your objects will live in, the client objects that will use them, and the *functionality* they must implement

🍃 How to use the Java documentation tool, *javadoc*, to provide essential documentation for your users

🍃 How to recognize common object-design pitfalls: the Data Warehouse Trap, the Spectral Object Trap, and the Multiple-Personality Trap

🍃 How to evaluate strategies for handling errors and exceptions

Designing a Robot

Suppose you were given the job of designing a household robot. How would you go about it? Where would you start?

Some would begin by describing what the robot looked like. You might draw a sketch or describe its appearance in words or by example, comparing it to R2D2, C3PO, or Pathfinder's Sojourner Truth. Others might describe the construction of the robot. "I'd use an array of off-the-shelf microprocessors for the central controller, and a set of gallium-arsenide biochemical batteries mounted over traction-driven treads," you might say.

One way of describing any kind of object is in terms of its appearance and the physical (or logical) components that make it up. But another, equally valid, way to describe (or design) an object is to state what it does. As Figure 4.2 illustrates, this is often the client's main concern.

WHAT IT IS OR WHAT IT DOES?

Take a few minutes and think about the functionality you'd want in a household robot. What kinds of things should it do? Suppose you had to write the software that would control such a robot in Java. If you took a piece of paper and wrote a list of methods, you might come up with something like this:

🍃 `start()`

🍃 `stop()` (This is the method you always want to implement first!)

🍃 `faster()`, `slower()`

🍃 `forward()`, `backward()`

🍃 `left()`, `right()`

🍃 `extendArm()`, `contractArm()`

🍃 `openHand()`, `closeHand()`

FIGURE 4.2

*From the client's point
of view, what an object
does is often more
important than its com-
position*

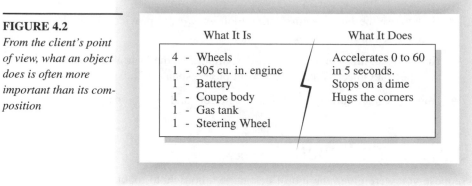

With a little thought you'd probably be able to come up with an even larger set of methods that a general-purpose household robot should be able to perform. Using just this set of methods, however, you could create a remote control that wouldn't look much different than a video-game controller, and that wouldn't be much bigger than the remote control for your TV. You could use a joystick for the left-right/forward-backward movement as well as for the speed settings. A single button could handle the on/off functions. A second joystick control could manipulate the robot's arm.

The question is, how would you know if you have the right set of methods? Is this minimal set adequate, or do you need more methods or perhaps different methods? How can you tell if your robot does the right things?

TRYING IT OUT

Imagine that you went ahead and built your robot, using this specification. Six months later, your robot has been successfully tested and manufactured. Heedless to the possible consequences, you head on down to Sears to purchase one for your spouse's birthday. (It might be wise to have a backup gift, just in case!) Proudly you unpack the pieces in the living room. After a quick trip down to the nearby 7-Eleven convenience store for a set of batteries to power the remote control, you hand it over.

Truthfully, you've done an amazing job. The remote control is so well designed that even a novice can drive the robot around the house. The robot's arm is a pleasure to use. It can pick up an egg without breaking it, turn a faucet, or pound a nail, all with equal skill. Perhaps a little giddy, you suggest a practical demonstration of your robot's usefulness: vacuuming the living room.

Retrieving the remote, you navigate your creation over to the broom closet, which it easily opens. Out comes your ever-faithful Hoover, which "Robo" deftly plugs into the power outlet. You use the robot's arm to start up the vacuum, and use the joystick to start it running around the room. Bzzzzzzzzzzzzt. It makes a pass along the far wall of the living room. You have a little difficulty turning it around, but figure you'll get the hang of it soon. Anyway, Aunt Matilda was never your favorite aunt, and she'll probably never notice that the lamp she gave you for Christmas is missing.

Bzzzzzzzzzzzzzzt. You make another pass. You're relieved to find that turning around is much easier the second time. Fifteen minutes later, you've vacuumed the entire room and the Hoover is again safely stowed in the closet.

THE FIRST RULE OF DESIGN

How many times will you (or your significant other) use your robot to vacuum the living room? The answer is almost certain: exactly one. Why is that? What was wrong with your design? Why didn't your robot turn out to be more useful? The problem is that you've failed to differentiate between the *interface* and *implementation*:

- The interface of a well-designed object (whether that object is a robot or a software object) describes the services that the client wants accomplished.

- The implementation of an object is the manner in which it performs its job. The user of a household robot doesn't want to move it forward or backward or make it go fast or slow. All those methods are implementation details; they are the things that the robot has to be able to do to carry out its work. The robot's owner doesn't care about them, and would rather not have to know about them.

> *" Encapsulation hides the nonessential. "*

Encapsulation hides the nonessential, as you can see in Figure 4.3. Rather than forward() and backward() methods, a truly useful robot would have methods with names like vacuumHouse(), doLaundry(), cookDinner(). A *really* useful robot would let you tell it what you wanted done and then have only a single method, run()!

Abstraction and Encapsulation: The First Iteration

You aren't going to be building any robots in this chapter, but the process you'll use in designing objects and classes is similar to what you did with your robot. Where do you start when designing your objects and classes? Do you start from a high-level view and work down, or start at the bottom and work up? Do you think about the data first and then think about the methods, or vice-versa?

The purpose of a well-designed class is to model an abstraction from the client's point of view. This means you should *always* start by designing a minimal public interface, because the public interface is the *only* thing that the client will see. Just as an architect tries to put herself in the place of her clients—"Would I want to use this kitchen? How would I feel with the bedroom so close to the living-room?"—the good class designer begins by thinking about a class from the point of view of the client.

There are some complicating subtleties here. For example, consider the case of an architect designing an apartment building for a client. The client will probably not actually live in one of the apartments. But, the client will pay the architect's fee and

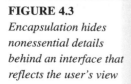

FIGURE 4.3

Encapsulation hides nonessential details behind an interface that reflects the user's view

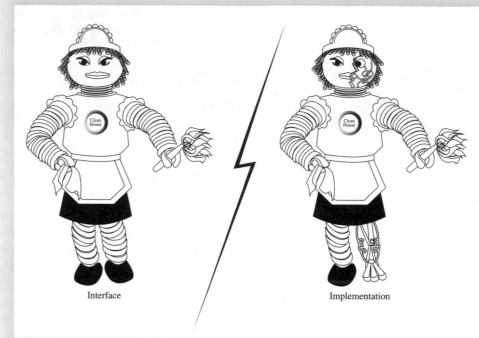

thus has the right to decide how big the closets should be and how much water the hot water tank will hold. Of course, an apartment resident might have very different ideas about closet size and hot water capacity.

In the software world, you would refer to the apartment resident as the *user*. Users actually run the software you design and implement. Clients, on the other hand, pay the bills and make the decisions. Sometimes the client and the user are the same person, but more often they are not.

When the client and user are separate individuals, your task as a designer is made more complex. It's your job to please the client, who pays your fee and therefore gets to make the decisions. But, it's also your job to help the client understand the user's perspective. A successful system must meet the needs of *both* the client and the user. The architect who accedes without comment to the client's hasty decision to limit each apartment to 3 gallons of hot water per day will not ultimately have a happy client, however much lower the utility bills may be.

WHO, WHERE, AND WHAT

Separating the public interface from the details of the private implementation is the first, and most basic, task in designing classes and objects. Designing such a public interface involves identifying:

- **The client objects (who):** What objects are going to use the services of your class? The human users of your system will be represented within it by objects, called client objects or actors, which send messages to your objects and receive information in return.

- **The environment (where):** What is the environment in which your design will be implemented? The environment includes things like the computer hardware and software that will run your program, and the software tools available to help you build it. The environment imposes limits on how your interface is actually designed. An ideal interface for a robot may be doWhatImThinking(), but limitations in the real world do not currently render that feasible.

- **The required functionality (what):** What should the object do? This functionality is described from the user's point of view. Many—sometimes most—of the methods you define will be necessary, yet will not appear in the public interface.

WRITING IT DOWN

When you design the public interface of your class, you are involved in a process of abstraction—trying to find the essential elements that your users need. You really don't need a computer for this. You can start with a pencil and a blank piece of paper. (Of course, if you want to use your computer, there's nothing wrong with that; you just won't start by writing code.) You're ready to start finding out "who," "where," and "what," as Figure 4.4 illustrates.

If you were designing a Clock object, for instance, you'd ask, "Who will want to use my Clock, where will they use it, and what will those users want it to do?" Unless you're building an application for a clock-repair shop, you'll find only two essential services: getTime() and setTime().

As you write down your ideas, you'll undoubtedly come up with a good many things that you just know your object must do—your robot, for example, had to move forward and backward. Don't throw those ideas away; keep a separate sheet of paper for those kind of details, because you'll need them later. You might also come up with physical (data) details. File them away also. For now, try and put yourself in the place of the user, and blithely ignore any details that are not essential.

FIGURE 4.4

Designing a new class begins by asking who will use your objects, under what circumstances, and what your objects will be required to do

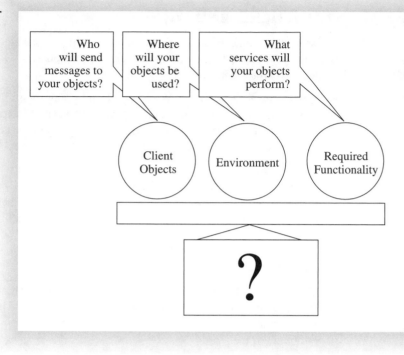

 Remember

Abstraction is concentration on the essential. A well-designed class begins with a public interface that operates at the user's level of abstraction.

Of course that's easy to say when talking about robots and clocks. But, just how does that work when applied to a real Java program? Let's take a look.

Client Objects, Environment, and Functionality

Every class design starts with a set of requirements. In fact, for the majority of programs that are written, discovering the right requirements is often more difficult than writing the code, and is more error-prone. You'll return to this subject in the next few chapters when you learn about the very powerful CRC technique. Right now, though, you'll start with just a summary paragraph describing the class you'll build in the rest of the chapter.

Most non-trivial design projects require you to consider the relationships and interactions between different classes. Description and explanation of such relationships take up a large portion of this book. Finding a project where the class design problem can stand alone is difficult. Fortunately, there is one convenient area where you can design meaningful standalone classes: by designing a component for Java's Abstract Windowing Toolkit (AWT).

With JDK 1.1, Java has added the ability to create lightweight components; that is, GUI components that are not derived from the AWT's `Canvas` or `Panel` classes, and that do not require the cooperation of native peer components. These lightweight components can thus be written in pure Java, which allows you to easily add new components beyond the basic ones already contained in the AWT. One easy-to-design, yet really cool, component is a progress bar like the one that appears in Microsoft Word when reading a file, or in Netscape Navigator when performing a long download. The Java 1.1 AWT does not include such a component, so this is your opportunity to build something really useful.

EXAMINING THE SPECIFICATION

As a specification, this description of a progress bar leaves a little to be desired. A good first step in class design is to describe, in a single paragraph, exactly what the class you are building should do. A summary paragraph for the `ProgressBar` class could look something like this:

A progress bar is a rectangular area of the screen that looks like a small window. It's used when a long operation is taking place, to graphically display how much of the operation has been completed, usually by using means of a filled region consisting of two different colors.

A summary paragraph describes the problem and requirements in an informal way. Even a somewhat vague and imprecise document such as this can be used as a starting point. From this description (and maybe a sketch like that shown in Figure 4.5), can you identify the users, environment, and functionality required for your new `ProgressBar` component?

> *"[F]or the majority of programs that are written, discovering the right requirements is often more difficult than writing the code, and is more error-prone."*

> *"A summary paragraph describes the problem and requirements in an informal way."*

FIGURE 4.5
The pieces of a `ProgressBar`

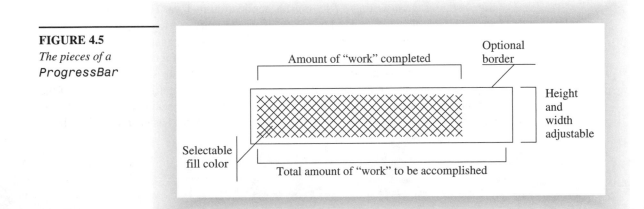

The environmental limitations are probably the easiest to discern. The specification says that the ProgressBar class should be a lightweight component—that is, a component derived directly from the AWT's Component class or Container class. Thus, with these environmental restrictions, you'll be able to use your objects in an applet or in a GUI-based application, but they won't work in a text-mode application.

FINDING THE CLIENT OBJECTS

Discovering the client objects (the objects that will send messages to, and receive information from, the progress bar) in the summary paragraph is a little more difficult.

The first client object will be any object that needs to keep the user informed about the processing of a lengthy operation. The second client object is the container that holds your component, which will tell it to repaint itself or ask it for information, such as its preferred or minimum size, when it comes time to lay it out. This second client object is the AWT framework itself.

Remember

Client objects include anyone or anything that sends messages to your object.

For both of these client objects, your task will be to create an interface that conforms to their needs. The major difference between these two client objects is that the AWT client object's requirements are already precisely specified, whereas the user-level interface will be designed by you.

PUBLIC OPERATIONS

Now that you've identified the environment and clients for your class, all that's left is to determine what public operations are required. In other words, what public methods will your client objects need to call? What do the client objects who use your ProgressBar class want your objects to do?

To answer this question, you start by asking another question, "What do I need to do to use a progress bar?" And, you answer *that* question by putting yourself in your client objects' shoes and asking "How would I use a progress bar?" Think about the different situations when you might need one. Here's one to consider.

Suppose you were writing a file transfer application in Java. How would you use a ProgressBar object? What kind of messages would you have to send to get it to work right? To put the question another way, "What should a ProgressBar object do?"

First, notice that a progress bar shows the *relative* amount of a task that is completed; the size of a progress bar doesn't tell you anything about the size of the task to be completed. You can use the same size ProgressBar object, regardless of the size of the file you are transferring. When the bar is half filled, it just means that the transfer is half done; it doesn't mean that any particular number of bytes has been transferred.

To work like this, every `ProgressBar` object has to store the total amount of work to be done—the extent of the job, so to speak. The first essential requirement of the public interface, then, is the ability to construct a `ProgressBar` object by providing it with the size of the job to be completed. A client object should be able to construct a `ProgressBar` to process `1000` bytes like this:

```
ProgressBar pBar = new ProgressBar( 1000 );
```

Besides constructing a progress bar, the objects that use the `ProgressBar` class will need to keep the object informed about the progress of the task. In this sense, it is the responsibility of the client object to tell the `ProgressBar` object to update itself. It can do this by telling the object *how much* of the job is completed. Think of this as the current value of the job. To tell the `ProgressBar` object, `theBar`, that the transfer is half done, you should be able to write:

```
theBar.setValue( 500 );
```

In actual practice, you'd normally use a `ProgressBar` object in a loop, something like this:

```
//    Set up file transfer, open socket, etc.
//    Find out total size of transfer and store in variable nSize
ProgressBar theBar = new ProgressBar( nSize );
//    Add theBar to a container where it can be displayed
int bytesRead = 0;
while ( bytesRead < nSize )
{
    // Read some bytes, store number read in nRead
    bytesRead += nRead;
    theBar.setValue( bytesRead );
}
```

Remember

The best way to discover the necessary public operations of a class is to put yourself in your client objects' shoes. Think about how your objects are used before considering how they will be built.

THE AWT CLIENT OBJECT

The constructor and `setValue()` method may meet the minimal needs of objects that use your class, but remember that the `ProgressBar` class actually has two client objects. The second client object—the container that holds your component—has a clearly defined set of methods that must be serviced. These methods are imposed by the environment (that is, the AWT framework). They include `getPreferredSize()`, `getMinimumSize()`, and `paint()`, which work together to allow your component to size and display itself correctly. To work within their environment, these methods must be `public`; nevertheless, they are not part of the public interface in the same sense that the other methods are. They are necessary for your progress bar to carry out its work, but like forward and backward movement of the household robot, they are only implementation details from the logical point of view.

At this point, your design (which is illustrated in Figure 4.6) consists of

- **An environment:** A lightweight component working in the context of the AWT.

- **Two client objects:** The objects that use your progress bar and the framework those objects are placed in.

- **Four requirements or behaviors that will comprise the minimal public interface:**

  The ability to construct a `ProgressBar` by providing it with the total amount of work to be done.

  The ability to update a `ProgressBar` you've constructed by telling it how much work has currently been accomplished.

  The ability to display your `ProgressBar` by overriding the AWT's `paint()` method.

  The ability to size your object in response to `getMinimumSize()` and `getPreferredSize()` messages.

Implementing the Interface

You're just about ready to lay down your pencil and create the first implementation of your design. In the next few sections, you'll write all of the methods necessary for a robust and full-featured progress bar. For right now, you're only interested in seeing if you have correctly defined a minimal public interface. Then you'll cycle back and iteratively refine your design until you're satisfied.

To create your implementation, you'll use three common techniques. The first technique is to use a *template* that acts as a checklist to make sure you don't forget anything. The second technique is to implement a `main()` method that really acts more like a `test()` method; you'll use the `main()` method to exercise each method in your class. The third technique is to use the console window to view debugging output during development, by writing *stubs*—methods that simply announce themselves when called.

FIGURE 4.6

The environment, client objects, and services required for the `ProgressBar` *class*

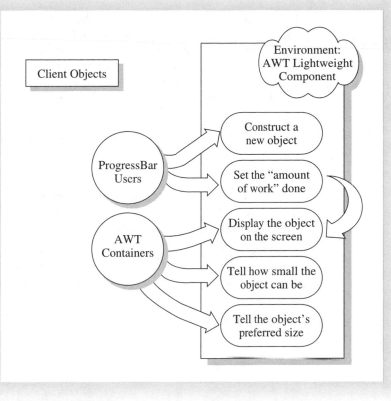

USING A TEMPLATE

No matter how photographic your memory, using it to remember trivial details is a waste of brain power. A programming template is simply a "skeleton" program that you use to create a new class. You stick inside the template all the little niggly details that you otherwise seem always to get wrong, so you don't have to remember them.

But, handy as that is, that's not the most important advantage of using a template. Using a template allows you to arrange your programs in a consistent way that facilitates good design and helps you to avoid making silly mistakes. Listing 4.1, `ClassTemplate.txt`, is an example of such a template that you can use in your programs. Notice that it is divided into four major sections:

💠 **Constructors:** These are where you'll put the operations that construct your objects.

🔹 **Public Interface:** This is the section where you'll put all the methods that are called from outside your program. If you have multiple client objects (as the ProgressBar class does), you'll want to duplicate the Public Interface section for each client object. This section is, itself, subdivided into four different sections: constants, mutators, accessors, and the common object interface. You'll learn more about each of these later in this chapter.

🔹 **Class and Object Attributes:** This is the section in your program where the data is stored. The users of your class will not directly interact with this section, and so it is placed after the public sections that they will normally deal with.

🔹 **Testing Methods:** For all classes except an application class, the main() method is used as a test-bed to try out the various methods and to compare them against the design requirements.

You may want to have a whole directory of such templates, one for each of the common programming situations you encounter—applet with threads, applet without threads, applet with image, application with a closeable frame, and so on.

Remember

A good implementation begins with a template. A template remembers necessary but logically non-essential details so you can concentrate on the essential. A template helps you to logically organize your class so the important parts stand out.

```
Listing 4.1 ClassTemplate.txt
//   OOD in Java
//   Class design template file
//

package <package name> ;
import  <packages>     ;

public class <ClassName>  extends      <Superclass>
                          implements   <Interface>,
                                       <Interface>
{
  //   ==========================================
  //          CONSTRUCTORS
  //   ==========================================

  //   ==========================================
  //          PUBLIC INTERFACE
  //   ==========================================

  /*   --Class Constants--------------- */

  /*   --Mutators--------------------- */
```

```
/*  --Accessors-------------------- */

/*  --Common Interface------------- */

//  Want String conversion for output?
//  public String toString();

//  Logical equality necessary?
//  public boolean equals( Object obj );

//  Need to copy objects?
//  protected Object clone()
//            throws CloneNotSupportedException;

//  Need to release resources at cleanup?
//  protected void finalize()
//            throws Throwable;

//  ========================================
//     PRIVATE METHODS
//  ========================================

//  ========================================
//     CLASS AND OBJECT ATTRIBUTES
//  ========================================

//  ========================================
//     TEST METHODS
//  ========================================
//  For individual classes use main() as test
//  public static void main( String[] args );

}
```

USING A STUB

To test out your design, you'll use a tried-and-true old programmer's trick, called a *stub*. When you write a stub, all you do is create an empty method. You must declare the correct number of arguments and give each method the correct name. In addition, if a method returns a value—an int, say—you have to make sure that your stub method returns a value of the correct type.

The body of a stub method, however, contains only two things. First, it contains a line that "announces" that the method has been entered, along with the values of the arguments passed in. In Java this is done by using System.out.println() to print out the name of the method along with the arguments. A related trick is to define a private method called dbg() and use it, rather than using System.out.println(). If you use System.out.println(), when it comes time to deploy your code, you'll have to systematically comment out each of these output statements. If you use a dbg() method, you only have to comment out the single line that its body contains.

Remember

Write stubs before you write method bodies. Stubs allow you to test your interface.

The second thing that a stub method may contain is an outline of the steps necessary to perform that particular operation. There are two big advantages to doing this. The first one is that it helps you make sure you know how to write the code; if you can't write out the steps in simple English, it's not going to get any easier when you have to write them in Java. The second advantage is that the comments in the code will help you understand the program after it's been written. This will make it easier to repair or modify the program.

You've undoubtedly been lectured about commenting your code since your very first programming class, and perhaps you've found it a burden. Commenting before you write code—instead of trying to remember what you did last week—creates better comments and helps you create better designs. Here, for instance, is the `paint()` method from `ProgressBar.java`, written as a stub with comments:

```java
public void paint( Graphics g )
{
  dbg( "paint( " + g +" )");

  // 1. Calculate border and "inside" rectangles
  // 2. Calculate size of the "fill" area
  // 3. Paint entire background with background color
  // 4. Draw appropriate border
  // 5. Draw filled area
}
```

Remember

Write it in English before you write it in Java. If you can't explain in English what your objects should do, you aren't ready to begin writing code.

JAVA MECHANICS

To begin implementing your design, first create an empty directory and copy `ClassTemplate.txt` into it. Rename `ClassTemplate.txt` to `ProgressBar.java` (if you're using Windows 95, you can ignore its warning about changing the file's extension name). If you've had some Java programming experience, you might like to strike out on your own. Otherwise, you can look at Listing 4.2. You should:

1. Change the comment at the top of the file to reflect the name of the file. Remove the line containing the keyword `package`, and import the `java.awt.*` package.

2. Name the class `ProgressBar` and `extend` the `Component` class. This will be a lightweight component. You can remove both of the `implements` clauses from the template.

3. Add a constructor to the Constructors section, one that accepts a single argument representing the size of the job to be done. You don't have to worry about storing the value just yet—that will come soon enough. Just have the constructor announce itself by using a stub as previously described. (If constructors don't make a lot of sense to you right now, you'll find them discussed under the heading "Constructing Objects," later in the chapter.)

4. Create a method called `setValue()` that takes a single parameter value representing the amount of the job that has been completed. As with the constructor, don't worry about storing the data. Simply have the method announce itself, using a stub as you did with the constructor.

5. Write stubs for each of the three AWT `public` methods, `paint()`, `getMinimumSize()`, and `getPreferredSize()`. You can look up the documentation by using the help facility provided by your development environment, or simply look at Listing 4.2 to find the signatures for each method. You'll actually have to return a value for each of the sizing methods, but for right now, that value just acts like a placeholder.

6. Write a `public static void main(String [] args)` method that first creates a `Frame` object and then creates three `ProgressBar` objects, adding each one to the `Frame`. Finally, send the `setValue()` message to each of the `ProgressBar` objects.

Compile and run your application, using the `javac` compiler and the `java` interpreter, like this:

```
javac ProgressBar.java
java ProgressBar
```

When you run your application, you should see each stub being called in the console window, as shown in Figure 4.7. Your `ProgressBar` objects don't show up on the `Frame` window you created, of course, because you haven't written any code in the `paint()` method. You may notice that the `Labels` that display the value of each `ProgressBar` object aren't very helpful. Don't be concerned; things will get better. For right now, congratulations: you've designed your first class! (To close the `Frame`, select the console window and press [Ctrl]-[C]. The `Frame` cannot be closed by using the mouse, unless you program it to implement the `WindowListener` interface, which really isn't necessary for a test method.)

```
Listing 4.2 ProgressBar.java (Initial Version)
//  ProgressBar.java
//     A class for OOD in Java, Chapter 4

//
import java.awt.*;

public class ProgressBar extends Component
{
  //  ============================================
```

```java
//          CONSTRUCTORS
//   =========================================
public ProgressBar( int extent )
{
  dbg( "ProgressBar( " + extent + " )" );
}


//   =========================================
//        PUBLIC INTERFACE: User Client
//   =========================================

/*   --Mutators--------------------- */
//
public void setValue( int value )
{
  dbg( "setValue( " + value +" )");
}


//   ===================================================
//        PUBLIC INTERFACE: AWT Client
//   ===================================================
public void paint( Graphics g )
{
  dbg( "paint( " + g +" )");

  // 1. Calculate border and "inside" rectangles
  // 2. Calculate size of the "fill" area
  // 3. Paint entire background with background color
  // 4. Draw appropriate border
  // 5. Draw filled area
}

public Dimension getPreferredSize(  )
{
  dbg( "getPreferredSize() called" );
  return getMinimumSize();
}

public Dimension getMinimumSize(  )
{
  dbg( "getMinimumSize() called" );
  return new Dimension( 100, 20 );
}

//   =========================================
//        TESTING METHODS
//   =========================================
public static void main( String[] args )
{
```

```
      Frame f = new Frame();
      f.setLayout( new FlowLayout() );

      ProgressBar pb1 = new ProgressBar( 1000 );
      pb1.setValue( 50 );
      f.add( pb1 );
      f.add( new Label("pb1 = " + pb1));

      ProgressBar pb2 = new ProgressBar( 2000 );
      pb2.setSize( 200, 20 );
      pb2.setValue( 500 );
      f.add( pb2 );
      f.add( new Label("pb2 = " + pb2));

      ProgressBar pb3 = new ProgressBar( 700 );
      pb3.setValue( 650 );
      f.add( pb3 );
      f.add( new Label("pb3 = " + pb3));

      f.setBackground( Color.lightGray );
      f.setSize( 400, 500 );
      f.setVisible( true );
   }

   private static void dbg( String msg )
   {
      System.out.println( msg );
   }
}
```

As a finished component, of course, your `ProgressBar` still leaves a little to be desired. Surely your boss is not going to be real happy with a progress bar that just prints a few messages out to the console. Nevertheless, you can be fairly certain that this minimal design does, in fact, work. If you're anxious to begin writing code in earnest—making the `ProgressBar` paint on the screen, for instance—try to hang on a little longer. After you've refined the design specification just a bit, you'll be ready to take on the rest of the class.

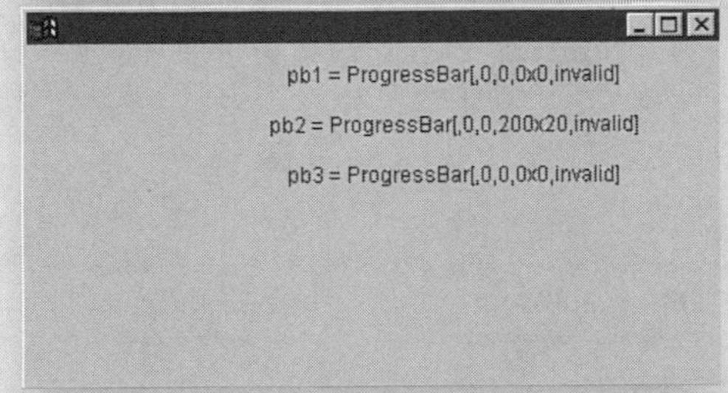

FIGURE 4.7

Running Version 1 of the `ProgressBar` *component*

```
pb1 = ProgressBar[,0,0,0x0,invalid]

pb2 = ProgressBar[,0,0,200x20,invalid]

pb3 = ProgressBar[,0,0,0x0,invalid]
```

ROUND TRIP: REFINING THE INTERFACE

" Designing a class is really an iterative process: you design a little, code a little, test a little, and then go back and design a little more."

Designing a class is really an iterative process: you design a little, code a little, test a little, and then go back and design a little more. One very useful technique—once you have the minimal interface written—is to pretend that you are one of your object's client objects. How do you do that? Simple: begin writing programs that use your object, and see if it really does everything you want. The Zenos applet, shown here in Listing 4.3 (Zenos.java) and Listing 4.4 (ZenoApplet.html), uses the progress bar you've designed.

Listing 4.3 Zenos.java

```java
//  Zenos.java
//  An applet to test the ProgressBar class
//
//  SDG - 7/21/97

import  java.awt.*;
import  java.applet.*;
import  java.awt.event.*;

public class Zenos  extends      Applet


implements  Runnable,

 ActionListener
{
  //  ==========================================
  //       APPLET METHODS
  //  ==========================================
  /*  --Initialization---------------- */
  public void init()
  {
    theBar.setForeground( Color.red );
    theBar.setSize( 250, 20 );
    add( theBar );
    add( startButton );
    add( stopButton  );
    add( resetButton );
    add( valLabel );

    stopButton.setEnabled( false );
    startButton.addActionListener( this );
    stopButton.addActionListener( this );
    resetButton.addActionListener( this );
  }

  //  ==========================================
  //       IMPLEMENT RUNNABLE
  //  ==========================================
  public void run()
  {
    int amtRemains = TOTAL_SIZE - curValue;

    while ( true )
    {
```

```
      curValue += (int) ((double) amtRemains / 2.0);
      amtRemains = TOTAL_SIZE - curValue;

      theBar.setValue( curValue );
      double pValue = theBar.getPercent() * 100.0;
      double decimals = pValue - (int) pValue;
      decimals *= 1.0E38;
      String out = "" + ((int) pValue) + "." + ((long) decimals);
      valLabel.setText( "" + out + " %");
      System.out.println( out );
      repaint();

      if ( theBar.isFull() )
      {
        theThread.stop();
        theThread = null;
        return;
      }

      try { Thread.sleep( 1000 ); }
      catch (InterruptedException e ) { }
    }
  }

  // ==========================================
  //      IMPLEMENT ACTIONLISTENER
  // ==========================================
  public void actionPerformed( ActionEvent ae )
  {
    if ( ae.getSource() == startButton )
    {
      if ( theBar.isFull() )
        return;

      if ( theThread == null )
      {
        startButton.setEnabled( false );
        stopButton.setEnabled( true);

        theThread = new Thread( this );
        theThread.start();
      }
    }
    else  //  both stop and reset
    {
      if ( theThread != null )
      {
        theThread.stop();
        theThread = null;
        startButton.setEnabled( true );
        stopButton.setEnabled( false );
      }
      if ( ae.getSource() == resetButton )
      {
        curValue = 0;
        theBar.setValue( 0 );
      }
```

```
    }
  }

  // ==========================================
  //     CLASS ATTRIBUTES
  // ==========================================
  private Button   startButton = new Button( "Start" );
  private Button   stopButton  = new Button( "Stop"  );
  private Button   resetButton = new Button( "Reset" );
  private Label    instruction = new Label( "Press Start" );
  private Label    valLabel    = new Label( "0 %            " );
  private int      curValue    = 0;

  static  final int TOTAL_SIZE = 1000;

  private ProgressBar theBar   = new ProgressBar( TOTAL_SIZE );

  private Thread  theThread    = null;

}
```

Listing 4.4 ZenoApplet.html

```
<HTML>
<HEAD>
<TITLE>Solving Zeno's Paradox</TITLE>
</HEAD>
<BODY>
<H1>Another look at Zeno's Paradox</H1>
<HR>
<APPLET CODE=Zenos HEIGHT=50 WIDTH=500> </APPLET>
<HR>
<H2>Zeno of Elea (495 - 435 B.C.)</H2>
How long does it take an arrow to go from one
point to another. Zeno, the ancient Greek philosopher,
argued, "forever!" Since before an arrow can travel
half-way to it's target, it must travel a quarter of
the distance, and before that, 1/8th. Since you can
continue this on into infinity, Zeno argued that motion
was impossible.<BR>
This applet examines a similar problem. It creates a
ProgressBar object, 1000 units long. It then fills
1/2 the distance. On each succeeding pass, it
fills 1/2 the remaining distance. How long will it
take to fill the whole ProgressBar?

</BODY>
</HTML>
```

The Zenos applet contains three Buttons (startButton, stopButton, and resetButton), a ProgressBar object (theBar), and a Label (valLabel). Zenos.java implements the Runnable interface, which means it includes a method called run() that is activated by starting and stopping a Thread object. The applet also implements the ActionListener interface, which it uses to respond to presses of any of the three Buttons. The applet works like this:

1. The init() method, which is called when the applet is loaded by appletviewer or your Web browser, begins by setting the foreground color of the ProgressBar (theBar) to red, and setting its size to 250 pixels wide and 20 pixels high. The ProgressBar, the Buttons, and the Label are then added to the surface of the applet. Finally, the stopButton is disabled (because the program is not yet running), and the applet registers to receive actionPerformed() messages from each of the three Buttons (by sending the addActionListener() message to each in turn).

2. When any Button is pressed, the actionPerformed() method is invoked, and the getSource() method of the ActionEvent class is used to tell which Button sent the message. If the startButton was pressed, the applet's Thread is started up (indirectly calling the run() method), the stopButton is enabled, and the startButton is disabled. If the stopButton is pressed, the Thread object is stopped (thereby terminating the run() method), and the startButton is re-enabled. Finally, if the resetButton is pressed, it stops the Thread from running, and, in addition, resets the values of the ProgressBar back to start.

3. The run() method of the applet—called whenever the Thread object, theThread, is started—performs the work of updating the ProgressBar. Using the field variables curValue and TOTALSIZE, it continually calculates one-half of the unfinished portion of the ProgressBar, and then updates theBar. You've already seen the setValue() method, from your previous design, but the run() method uses a few others that may be useful. The isFull() method tells you when the value of the ProgressBar equals its extent. The getPercent() method asks the ProgressBar object how much of its work is done.

Paradoxically, the real advantage of writing code that uses your class is that it gets you out of the "implementation" mind-set. Because your client objects represent your program's human user, thinking in terms of the client objects puts you in the user's shoes. You're led to consider afresh the user's needs.

You have to think of this as a fact-finding exercise, however. The danger is that you'll fall victim to "featuritis." If you find yourself adding lots of methods because you, or your human clients and users, think they would be neat or handy, you should stop and think twice. Your design goal for the public interface is that it should be minimal and complete.

> *" Paradoxically, the real advantage of writing code that uses your class is that it gets you out of the "implementation" mind-set. "*

Remember

To paraphrase Einstein, "Make your interface as simple as possible, but no simpler."

DESIGNING THE IMPLEMENTATION

Obviously, one of the problems with this technique is that you can't run your applet until you actually implement the code for your `ProgressBar`. But that's just a detail!

By using your initial template as a checklist, you can go through each of its sections, asking yourself, "What will this section contribute to a complete and minimal interface?" Before you know it, you'll have your `ProgressBar` up and running. Let's take a look at the two major design tasks you have to consider: implementing state and implementing methods.

Implementing State

The attributes of your objects store its state, or characteristics. You define those attributes when you write your class. You can define three types of attributes:

- Object attributes or fields, which will store the individual state for every object.

- Class attributes, which store a single value or object that is shared among all objects of a class.

- Class constants, which store a single attribute or value that is shared among all the objects of a class and that are usable by objects outside of the class as well.

THE PRIME DIRECTIVE: HIDE YOUR DATA

> *"If there is one thing you can take away from this book that will improve your designs, it is this: all data should be private."*

There are several things you should consider when designing the fields that will hold the data for your class, but one rule stands out above all the others: all object and class attributes should be declared as `private`, without exception. This rule should be embossed on your mind (and perhaps hung on your wall, as Figure 4.8 illustrates) the same way that an earlier generation learned that `goto`s were synonymous with evil incarnate. If there is one thing you can take away from this book that will improve your designs, it is this: all data should be `private`.

FIGURE 4.8

The Prime Directive of encapsulation—make the details `private`

There is one major advantage in making the data in your program `private`: it "uncouples" your interface from your implementation. Suppose you've written a program that has a `public` data field called, for the sake of originality, x. Now, suppose that you have thousands of lines of code that refer directly to this variable x, reading and setting its value. Now suppose, for whatever reason, you're required to make a change to the variable; you have to change its name or its data type or even what it represents—perhaps you were storing Cartesian coordinates and now you have to use polar coordinates. Every line of code that previously used x directly is now going to have to be located and changed. If, on the other hand, the representation of x was hidden and the value was changed or read only through a method, only that method has to change.

Remember

All state variables, without exception, should be declared as `private` fields. The choice is really yours: hide your data and make one change when the time comes, or use `public` data and spend the rest of your life doing mindless maintenance on your own programs.

"OK," you say, "if all of the data in my programs is `private`, then how am I supposed to use it? I suppose that, rather than just making a single `public` field named x, you now want me to make the field `private`, and write getX() and setX() methods. That's a whole lot more work, and my program will run slower as a result. I just don't think it's worth it!"

You're partially right. You should make the field x `private`. (You should also use a more descriptive name than x, but that's another topic!) But you don't necessarily—and you shouldn't generally—write getX() and setX() methods. This is a common tendency that programmers coming from a procedural background fall into. Why do you want to getX() and setX()? What do you want with the information? Why isn't the object doing that work for you? When designing classes, there are three different design errors you can fall into:

- **The Data Warehouse Trap**—An object is *not* a repository for data that the rest of your program will use. Your objects should contain both data and the methods that work on that data. If you find yourself with classes that have lots of data elements and almost every element has a get() or set() method, you may be falling into this trap. Objects should *do* something, not just sit there!

- **The Spectral Object Trap**—An object is *not* just a collection of methods that you pass data to. If a class has no data elements, and if most of the methods in the class are `static` methods, then what you have is a procedural *module*. A module is not an object. If you find a class like that, ask yourself, "Why is the data I'm working on stored in a different place than the operations that work on the data?" Remember, an object contains both data and the operations that are performed on the data. Objects with no data are ghosts (specters)!

⬤ **The Multiple Personality Trap**—An object should model *one* abstraction. It should be one kind of thing. Structured designers called this principle *cohesion*. Every class should be highly cohesive, meaning that every data element and every method should contribute to that one abstraction. Usually, a multiple personality error is obvious from the name of the class: the SpreadSheetAndWordProcessor class is an example. Even if you have an integrated class such as this, both the SpreadSheet class and the WordProcessor class should be separate classes in your design. Even if the name doesn't tip you off, looking at the data fields may. If you have separate fields for SpreadSheet documents and WordProcessor documents, and one group of methods works with one document and another group works with the other, then your object has a multiple-personality disorder. Fortunately the remedy—splitting the class in two—is less expensive (and perhaps more effective) than therapy.

Let's take a look at your class, ProgressBar.java, and see what kinds of attributes you'll need.

OBJECT AND CLASS ATTRIBUTES

If you look back at your initial design, you can probably easily identify two of the attributes you'll need: extent and value. The extent field stores the amount of work that each ProgressBar object will do: 1,000 bytes of data to be transferred, or 32 characters to be input. Your ProgressBar objects will initialize the extent and value fields when each object is constructed (see the constructor section later in this chapter) and will update the value field as often as the client sees fit, through the setValue() method, also discussed later in this chapter.

Can you think of any other data fields you'll need? Well, how about data that represents the physical appearance of the ProgressBar when it's displayed? You'll need to store the height of the bar, its width, its color, and where it's located on the screen. Each of those things is important and each ProgressBar object has to store that information, but you don't need to define new data fields to hold them because each ProgressBar object already has such fields!

As you might recall, the ProgressBar class extends the Component class, so ProgressBars already contain all of the fields that define their "Componentness." Now, it's true that you don't know the names or storage details of those fields. You don't know if the background color is stored as a Color object or as part of an array, or in some entirely different way. You do know—from reading the JDK documentation for the Component class—that you can change the background color simply by sending a Component the setBackground() message. Users of your ProgressBar objects can send them any of the messages that they can send to Components, and you don't have to write any code to support those messages.

Are there any special facilities you'd like your `ProgressBar` to have, facilities that don't come free as a consequence of also being a `Component` object? One thing that might come in handy is the ability to put a border around your `ProgressBar`. Sometimes, a programmer might have already set up his display, and want only the "interior" part of the bar to be painted. Other times, a simple plain line around the bar might be more appropriate. You might think that most folks, though, will want to use the cool, sunken 3D look you've come up with. When it comes time to render the actual `ProgressBar`, you'll have to know which style the programmer prefers. That requires you to store that value in a field called `borderStyle`.

All three fields (object attributes) you want to use can be stored as integers and they should all use `private` access. Go ahead and modify the "Class and Object Attributes" section of `ProgressBar.java`, adding the following lines:

```
//    ==========================================
//        CLASS AND OBJECT ATTRIBUTES
//    ==========================================
private int extent;
private int value;
private int borderStyle;
```

CONSTANT ATTRIBUTES

Because you've decided to offer three different border styles with your `ProgressBar`, how do you expect programmers to tell which one they want? Your first inclination might be to add `setSunkenBorder()`, `setPlainBorder()`, or `setNoBorder()` methods, but that means programmers must first construct a `ProgressBar` and then set the border style. You'd like to avoid that if possible by having your programmers supply a border style when they create their `ProgressBar` objects. Thus, you'll want to pass the border style as an argument to the constructor.

That doesn't quite answer the first question though; how should programmers tell you which style they want? One solution is to have them use a `String` representing the name, like `SunkenBorder`, `PlainBorder`, or `NoBorder`. This is a common way to tell a `BorderLayout` which quadrant to place your component in. A second method is to simply assign numbers to each style; thus, no border would be `0`, a plain border would be `1`, a sunken border would be `2`, and so on.

The problem with this scheme is that it relies on our weakest facility as humans—that of recall. People are much better with association than just remembering that `2` stands for `SunkenBorder`. To make the most of this fact, Java allows you to associate constants with specific identifiers. You do this by declaring a field, just as you did for the object attributes, and then prefixing the field type with the keywords `static final`. By convention, constant identifiers appear in all capital letters, with underscores used to separate words, like this: `CONSTANT_IDENTIFIER`.

All the constant numbers you use in your code should be `static final` constants. A good rule of thumb is to question any numbers that appear in source code other than `0`, `1`, or `-1`. However, there are two types of constants. The first type of constant can be a value that is used only in an internal calculation. These constants should be declared as `private static final` and should be placed just ahead of the object attributes.

The other sort of constant you'll use is an identifier that you want programmers who use your class to use instead of remembering numbers like `0`, `1`, and `2`. These constants should be declared as `public static final`, and should be placed as the first entry in the "Public Interface" section of your class where they can be easily seen. For the `ProgressBar` class, you'll want three identifiers—`NONE`, `PLAIN`, and `SUNKEN`. Programmers will refer to `ProgressBar.NONE`, but inside your class, you can just use `NONE`. Drawing a border requires that the actual bars be drawn in different sizes (the borders each take up some room), so you can use the size difference between the inner and outer rectangles as the constant values. (Be warned, though, that if you decide to add more border styles that also consume eight pixels, you won't be able to differentiate between them.) To add these three identifiers, put the following lines in the section marked Constants:

```
/*  --Constants----------------------- */
public static final int NONE    = 0;
public static final int PLAIN   = 4;
public static final int SUNKEN  = 8;
```

Remember

Use `static final` constants instead of literals. As a human, your weakest facility is recall and your strongest is recognition. Named constants play to your strengths.

Writing Methods

Writing code that is bug-free, efficient, and elegant is a skill that comes only with much practice. But, even if you have that skill, designing a set of methods for a class is a little different. You are no longer writing methods in isolation; you now have to ask yourself, "What methods do I write, and how do those methods work together?"

In deciding which methods go into an interface, you have two sorts of yardsticks against which to measure your efforts. The first yardstick is the general, object-oriented design goals that an interface should achieve. The second yardstick is a checklist to make sure you've considered all the types of methods your class should have.

In evaluating the public interface of your class, ask yourself the following questions:

- Does the interface represent, or model, a single abstraction? You've already seen cohesion discussed in the context of multiple-personality classes. Cohesion is also important when evaluating methods. You may be tempted to put a `static MessageBox()` method in your `GeneralLedger` class, just for convenience sake. Resist the temptation. If you give in, it is only a matter of time before you find the `GeneralLedger` class used in all sorts of situations that have nothing to do with accounting, simply to use the `MessageBox()` method. Classes are not collections of autonomous methods. Make sure each method contributes to the intended behavior of your object.

- Does each method represent, or model, a single operation? That is, are the methods themselves internally cohesive? If you are building a `Report` class for an accounting module, don't use a method like `doMonthEnd()`, which, in turn, creates a financial statement, a trial balance, and a payroll report. If you do, you can be certain that next month the `doMonthEnd()` method will have to be modified when your boss decides she doesn't need the trial balance. Instead, the code that creates each of these reports should be contained in its own method.

- Does the class do everything it needs to do, and no more? If programs that use your objects rely primarily on `get()` and `set()` methods, this may be a sign that your interface is not complete, that client objects are having to process your object's data. On the other hand, if there are methods that are not used, don't clutter up your interface with them. While it's nice if a class solves a very general problem, excessive generality creates very congested, and thus hard-to-use, interfaces. If programmers can't find operations provided by your class, they won't use them.

- Is your interface easy to use? Your interface should be designed around the problem your class solves, not the details of your implementation. Methods that require long argument lists or complex calculations clamor for simplification. A method in an accounting package that requires its input as a hexadecimal number would be one example, but a programmer's productivity class that requires addresses in decimal might be another. The important thing to remember is that ease of use must be evaluated from the user's perspective.

- Use a checklist of common operations that all classes should understand. Use your checklist to make sure that you have considered how objects are constructed, copied (or assigned), and destroyed. Make sure you've dealt with the difference between identity and equality if ordering or sorting of objects is important. Finally, when you design your class, consider including methods to test, debug, and print the state of your objects; don't leave these methods for later.

Remember

Evaluate your methods by asking whether each method contributes to a single abstraction, whether each method is internally cohesive, and whether each method is necessary, useful, and easy to use.

DOCUMENTING METHODS

" If programmers can't find operations provided by your class, they won't use them. "

Writing the documentation for your users is a thankless task that less responsible programmers strive to avoid. Java, however, comes with a tool, called javadoc, that creates HTML documentation for your classes, making the job less of a chore. You're probably already familiar with the style of documentation produced by javadoc, because it was used to produce the online documentation that comes with the JDK. The real significance of javadoc for the designer, however, is its advantage as an abstraction tool. By running javadoc on your classes as you develop them, you can strip away all but the essentials, and see the underlying structure of your class.

Using javadoc is a two-step process. The first step is to use a special comment symbol to mark the beginning of each method and class. A javadoc comment begins with the symbol /** and ends, like a regular multiline comment, with */. Then, in between these two symbols, you put the lines of text that you want to appear in your documentation. In addition, there are several special tags that can be used inside a javadoc comment, tags that have meaning to the javadoc compiler. Some of these tags can be used only in front of a method, and some of them are valid only when used in front of a class. As you continue to examine the methods in ProgressBar.java, you'll notice javadoc comments before each one. Here, for example, is the javadoc comment that precedes the class declaration:

```
/**
 * ProgressBar - a class for OOD in Java, Chapter 4.<BR>
 *
 * A lightweight component based on the Component
 * class. A lightweight component doesn't use a window
 * handle, has no peers, and can contain transparent
 * areas. <BR><BR>
 *
 * The progress bar is a component that can be used to
 * keep your user informed about the progress of some
 * lengthy operation. Ideal candidates are file transfers,
 * printing operations, loading resources, and so on. <BR><BR>
 *
 * To use a progress bar you have to first know the size
 * of the job that will be processed. This can be the number
 * of bytes in a file, and so on. As each portion of the job is
 * processed, you notify the progress bar with the new
 * value, which then updates the display. <BR><BR>
 *
 * @version Version 1.0 - the finished first-cut
 * @author Stephen Gilbert, Bill McCarty
 *
 */
```

Continued...

DOCUMENTING METHODS Continued...

Because the output produced by `javadoc` is HTML text, you can insert HTML tags as you see fit (although you should avoid including structural tags like `<H1>`, and so on). After you have created a source file using `javadoc` comments, the next step is to use the file to create the actual documentation. To create the documentation file `ProgressBar.html` from the source code file `Progress.java` you use the following command:

```
javadoc -notree -noindex ProgressBar.java
```

This produces documentation that you can view in your Web browser, as shown in Figure 4.9. If you provide a package name instead of the name of a single class, `javadoc` produces documentation for the entire package. The documentation normally includes an extensive index and inheritance tree file; these were excluded from this example. The generated HTML uses several graphical images that are stored in an `images` directory underneath the directory where the documentation resides. By copying an `images` directory from the Java JDK documentation, your own documentation can have the same cool buttons and titles as the standard JDK documentation.

CONSTRUCTING OBJECTS

Object constructors (sometimes called constructor methods) have only a single purpose in life: to correctly initialize each and every data field when a new object is created. Constructors, however, don't operate in a vacuum; you can't simply write a constructor and think that's all there is to object initialization. You have to be aware of how your constructors interact with superclass constructors and with Java's built-in object-initialization facilities.

FIGURE 4.9
Progressbar.java documentation produced by `javadoc`

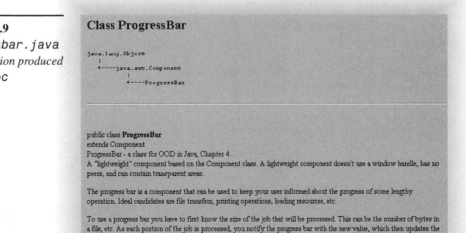

When Java creates an object, it first creates the "superclass part" of the object, as Figure 4.10 illustrates. It does this by calling your class's superclass constructor as the first statement in every constructor. In the case of the `ProgressBar` class, that means the constructor for the `Component` class is called first, because `ProgressBar` is a subclass of the `Component` class. (Of course, the `Component` constructor first calls the constructor of *its* superclass, and so on, until the constructor for the `Object`—or root—class is reached.)

Because a superclass may have several (overloaded) constructors, you are given the opportunity to specify which superclass constructor you wish to call by invoking the `super()` method. If you don't add a `super()` method as the first statement of your constructor, Java implicitly calls your superclass's no-argument—or default—constructor. When the superclass constructor returns (whether invoked explicitly or implicitly), each attribute of your object is then initialized in order, using any initialization values or expressions that were provided when the fields were defined. After that, the rest of the constructor executes.

The Working Constructor

How do you design a constructor? The first question you should ask is "What does it take to make a valid object?" A valid object is one that has every field initialized and all of the class invariants satisfied. A class invariant is simply a logical condition that applies to the data or state of your object. A `Fraction` class, for instance, that contains the fields `numerator` and `denominator` represented by integers should make sure that the `denominator` field is never zero. This is a class invariant.

FIGURE 4.10

Object construction

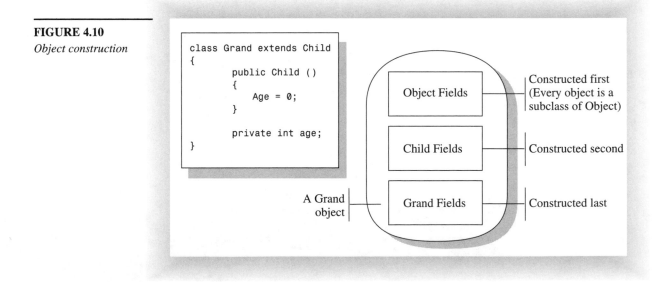

" You should always construct your objects in a valid state."

You should always construct your objects in a valid state. Avoid writing constructors that first create invalid objects, and then require another method call (create() or open(), for instance) before the objects can be used.

However, this can be more difficult than you might imagine. It's sometimes hard to think of meaningful values for all data fields. If you create a MyDate class, for instance, what should you use for the default value? January 1, 1980, or what? In such cases, you may want to prohibit default construction by not providing a default constructor. If you don't provide any constructor at all, Java will "write" one for you, but once you provide a constructor, Java no longer provides the invisible default constructor.

If the values passed to a constructor don't permit the construction of a valid object, the constructor should throw an exception rather than construct an invalid object. That way, the method that invoked the new operator can catch the exception and deal appropriately with the problem.

Remember

> Design your constructors so that all fields are initialized and all class invariants satisfied. Construct only legitimate objects.

What does the working constructor for your ProgressBar class have to do? Well, first, it doesn't make much sense to write a no-argument (default) constructor, simply because the client must know how "big" the job is before creating a ProgressBar. If the client doesn't know how big the job is, then there's no way a ProgressBar object can be expected to take any intelligent action. So, to construct a ProgressBar object, your users *must* provide a value for the extent. In addition, since you added (or are going to add!) the ability to use different borders, the user will have to supply that information as well. With these requirements, the working constructor for the ProgressBar class should look something like this:

```
//   ==========================================
//        CONSTRUCTORS
//   ==========================================
/**
 * Working constructor
 * @param extent the "size" of the job to be processed
 * @param borderStyle NONE, PLAIN, or SUNKEN
 */
public ProgressBar( int extent, int borderStyle )
{
  dbg( "ProgressBar( " + extent +", " + borderStyle +" )" );
if ( extent < 0 )
{
  dbg(" ERROR: ProgressBar.extent cannot be negative");
  extent = 0;
}
  this.extent = extent;
  this.borderStyle = borderStyle;
  this.value  = 0;
}
```

Place this code in the Constructors section of your program. Notice the @param javadoc tag in the javadoc comment preceding the method body. When processed, this produces the documentation that you see in Figure 4.11.

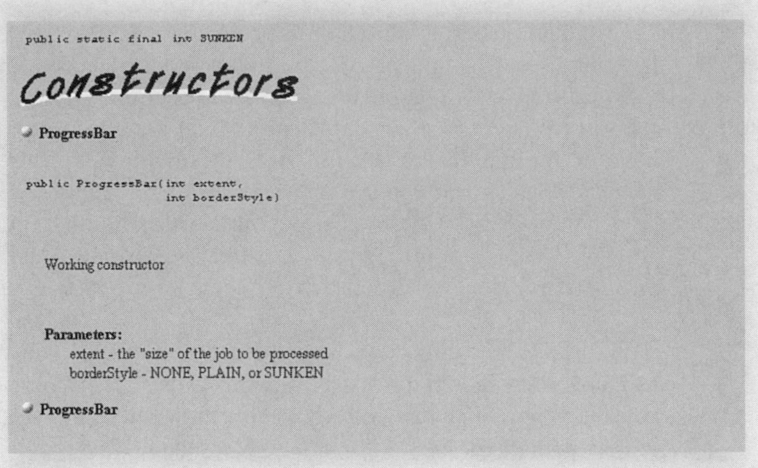

FIGURE 4.11
*The ProgressBar
constructor in*
`javadoc`

```
public static final int SUNKEN
```

Constructors

* ProgressBar

```
public ProgressBar(int extent,
                   int borderStyle)
```

Working constructor

Parameters:
    extent - the "size" of the job to be processed
    borderStyle - NONE, PLAIN, or SUNKEN

* ProgressBar

The actual body of the constructor uses the `dbg()` stub method to print to the console the parameter values received, and then initializes the `extent` and `borderStyle` fields. When the constructor arguments and the field names are the same, you can refer to the field values as `this.extent`, and so on. This is a common Java idiom much used in constructors; in other programming languages it is often considered bad form to name a parameter the same as a data field. Note that the `extent` argument used to construct the `ProgressBar` object is assumed to be greater than `0` and is set to `0` if it is not. See the sidebar, "Exceptions, Assertions, and Defense" to take a look at this issue.

EXCEPTIONS, ASSERTIONS, AND DEFENSE

The most problematic part of designing software is dealing with possible errors. As a designer, you have to consider two things:

    What can go wrong?

    What should I do about it?

Think about the `ProgressBar` class for a moment. What can go wrong when your client tries to create a `ProgressBar` object? The system could run out of resources; the programmer could specify a border style that doesn't exist (by using a literal integer instead of the constants you provided); or the programmer could supply a negative extent. Think for an instant about the last case. Your `ProgressBar` class assumes the

Continued...

EXCEPTIONS, ASSERTIONS, AND DEFENSE Continued...

invariant condition (`extent >= 0`). To preserve this condition in your constructor, you have four choices (a fifth choice, returning an error code, is available to regular methods, but not to constructors). You may:

- **Simply ignore the problem.** This is the most popular strategy (based on the amount of code that uses it). You just assume that everyone who uses your class will never make a mistake, and that, if they do, they deserve whatever happens. A more charitable explanation for the widespread use of this technique is the mistaken belief that the cost of checking and handling possible errors is greater than the cost incurred should the error occur. This may be true for one-time, throw-away routines, but it's seldom true for production code. And, unfortunately, that one-time, throw-away routine has a tendency to stick around for longer than you expect. Even for one-time code you have to consider possible error conditions, so it's not much more work to think about how to handle them while you're at it.

- **Test the value and stop the program.** This is a favorite technique of former C programmers who write an `assert()` method like the following:

```
public void assert( boolean theCondition, String theMessage)
{
  if ( ! theCondition )
  {
    System.out.println( theMessage );
    System.exit(0);
  }
}
```

  `Assert()` methods (and classes) can vary in their complexity and sophistication. By redefining the `assert()` method to have a null body or test a class constant, the result of failing an assertion can be switched on for testing and switched off for production code. The important thing to understand about assertions, however, is that the class that uses the `assert()` method is deciding what to do about errors. This responsibility is usually better left to its client objects.

- **Fix the mistake.** This third way to handle errors is usually called "defensive" programming. In defensive programming, you assume that errors may occur, and therefore check for them. You also assume that the users will want to continue the program—exactly the opposite assumption the `assert()` method makes. To allow this to occur, you set invalid values to a known state. The problem with defensive programming is that it fails to alert the caller when something goes amiss. If you do use defensive techniques—as the constructor for the `ProgressBar` class does for the `extent` argument—be sure you also notify the programmer if possible.

Continued...

EXCEPTIONS, ASSERTIONS, AND DEFENSE Continued...

    ❧ **Throw an exception**. In Java, this is the preferred way to deal with errors of this sort. When your class throws an exception, you allow the user of your class to decide what to do about the error that occurred. However, mimicking the behavior of a program that uses defensive techniques is not always possible when using exceptions. In most designs, exceptions can take the place of assertions, but they cannot easily replace defensive programming.

A good rule of thumb for deciding between these options is the rule of "least astonishment." You want to follow the strategy that is least surprising to your users. For some errors, this will be assertions or exceptions; for others it will be defensive programming. In `ProgressBar.java`, a defensive strategy was chosen because it seems most in keeping with how the rest of the AWT acts—it seemed the least surprising option.

Remember

Consider the possibility of failure and handle failure in the least astonishing way.

Overloaded Constructors

Only after you've decided on what your constructor should do, should you consider whether you need more than one constructor. You should generally write the working constructor—that is, the constructor that requires you to specify all the user-selectable inputs—as the first constructor.

There are two reasons for this. First, writing the working constructor requires you to decide what data items users can initialize and what data items your class is responsible for. Second, you'll want to write the working constructor first because all the other constructors can be (and should be) written in terms of the working constructor.

Because the end result of every constructor should be a valid object, overloaded constructors simply provide multiple views on the "one true way" to construct your object. If you write completely separate constructors, you run the risk that, due to a programming error, an object constructed via constructor A will exhibit subtly different behavior from one constructed by constructor B. That's a situation you should avoid.

What kind of overloaded constructors make sense for the `ProgressBar` class? You may, for instance, decide that most users of your `ProgressBar` class will want to use the SUNKEN style borders, and would prefer that they not have to supply that information when they do. Because Java does not have default arguments (though C++ does), you can accomplish your goal by using an overloaded constructor.

You can have as many constructors as you want, but each must have a unique combination of argument count, order, and type. This unique combination, along with the name of the class, forms the argument's *signature*. Thus, if you implement a constructor that takes only a single integer argument—unlike the working constructor above, which takes two—Java looks at the signature and sees a different method. This second constructor is called an overloaded constructor.

When it comes time for you to actually implement this second constructor, you should not attempt to duplicate all the code you wrote for the first constructor (as was previously mentioned). Really, what you'd like is to simply call the first constructor, but just pass SUNKEN as the second argument. Constructors, however, are not methods. You cannot call them directly, except as an argument to the new operator. Instead, Java gives you the ability to call another constructor (only from within a constructor) by using the this() method. The arguments you pass to this() are evaluated to determine which constructor to invoke. To provide such a capability to ProgressBar.java, add the following code just under the constructor you previously wrote:

```
/**
 * Constructs a ProgressBar using default size
 * @param extent the "size" of the job to be processed
 */
public ProgressBar( int extent)
{
   this( extent, SUNKEN );
}
```

Remember

Define overloaded constructors in terms of a working constructor. If you find yourself duplicating construction code in multiple constructors, you've created a potential point of failure.

MODIFYING STATE (MUTATORS)

In third-generation programming languages like Pascal, a distinction is generally made between subprograms that return information (functions) and subprograms that perform an action (procedures). As in C and C++, all the methods in Java are written using a functional format, as if they returned a value. Those methods that only perform an action are marked by the keyword void, which appears in the method header in the place where the type of the return value is normally specified.

In object-oriented designs, rather than categorizing methods as procedures or functions, a much more useful dichotomy is to divide them into those methods whose operations change the state of the object and those methods which only provide information. Methods that change the fields of an object are called *mutator* methods and are usually placed right after the "Constants" subheading in the "Public Interface" section of your program. Most of the interesting behavior of an object causes it to change state, so mutators are placed where they can easily be found.

As with constructors, you must be certain that mutator methods preserve the invariants of your class. To return to the `Fraction` class, every method that changes the field `denominator`—and that would include many, if not most, of the methods you'd want in a `Fraction` class—should check before returning to make sure the invariant condition still holds, and act accordingly. In addition to the options you had when writing constructors, mutator methods can also return a value that can, in some instances, be used as an error code.

For the `ProgressBar` class, you've already identified the main mutator method, `setValue()`. At first glance, `setValue()` seems straightforward; all it has to do is to update the value field in the `ProgressBar` object. One danger, however, of mutator methods is that they can quickly degenerate into an end-run around encapsulation. The user of the `ProgressBar` class shouldn't (and probably doesn't) care that the `ProgressBar` class has a field called `value`, because that's an implementation detail. Looking from the client's point of view, you just want to tell the `ProgressBar` object that you have some more work done, and therefore it should update itself. Methods should tell an object to perform some meaningful behavior, not act as a way to read and write `private` data.

Remember

Mutator methods should perform a meaningful operation and should leave your object in a valid state. Don't use mutators to break encapsulation by exposing a private field.

Given those constraints, your `setValue()` method should cause your object to:

1. Update its internal state to reflect the fact that you've accomplished another chunk of work. Client objects shouldn't care how this is accomplished or how the results of the work are stored.

2. Reflect the fact that more of the job has been accomplished. Because the `ProgressBar` object talks to the outside world through its display, this can be accomplished by calling the `repaint()` method, asking the AWT to schedule a `paint()`.

3. Ensure that the internal state of the `ProgressBar` object remains consistent—that none of the invariant conditions have been abrogated. From a logical point of view, it doesn't make any sense for the amount-of-work-completed variable (`value`) to be larger than the total-size-of-the-job variable (`extent`). You'll have to check and act on that condition.

The following code addresses each of these requirements, and can be added to your program under the Mutators subheading, in the Public Interface section:

```
/*  --Mutators--------------------- */
/**
 * Tells the ProgressBar "how much" is done <BR>
 * Causes the bar to repaint itself <BR>
 * <BR>
 * Invariant: value <= extent
 *
```

```
    * @param value the new value that is "done"
    *
    */
  public void setValue( int value )
  {
    dbg( "setValue( " + value +" )");
    if ( value > extent )
      this.value = extent;
    else
      this.value = value;
    repaint();
  }
```

PROVIDING INFORMATION (ACCESSORS)

The second major type of service that a class offers its client objects is access to information. Unlike mutator methods, accessor methods should not put your object into an invalid state; therefore, there is no need to consider class invariants or error-handling strategies. Carefully note, however, the difference between *should not* and *cannot*. The C++ programming language allows you to declare a method as const; when you do so, the compiler warns you if statements in that method change the object's state (although the mechanism is by no means foolproof). Java has no such facility, and so it's up to you to be doubly vigilant in making sure that accessor methods don't change the state of their objects.

Unfortunately, in Java it is surprisingly easy for this to occur. In Java, an object variable does not contain an object value; it merely *refers* to an object value. Because of this, when your accessor method returns a reference to an object, the caller may be able to modify your object. Most likely that's *not* what you want. Just to make the point perfectly clear, consider the code in Listing 4.5, GoodKid.java.

> " *In Java, an object variable does not contain an object value; it merely refers to an object value.* "

Listing 4.5 GoodKid.java

```
//  GoodKid.Java
//
//  Every GoodKid is constructed so that it stays at
//  a certain position. This position is relative to
//  the static final field HOME. The GoodKid class
//  has NO mutators or accessors, so only their
//  creators know where they are.
//
import java.awt.*;

public class GoodKid extends Component
{
  public static final Point HOME = new Point( 100, 100 );
  public static final Point SIZE = new Point( 25, 25 );

  private Point myLocation;

  public GoodKid( int hPos, int vPos )
  {
```

```
    setSize( SIZE.x, SIZE.y );
    myLocation = new Point( hPos, vPos );
  }

  public void paint( Graphics g )
  {
    setLocation( HOME.x + myLocation.x,
                 HOME.y + myLocation.y );
    g.fillOval( 0, 0, SIZE.x - 1, SIZE.y - 1 );
  }
}
```

The GoodKid class looks like the epitome of well-behaved encapsulation. The field myLocation is private, and is set only in the constructor. In the paint() method, each GoodKid object is returned to its proper place, just in case anything was moved. If there was ever a class that a programmer should have confidence in, GoodKid seems to be the one.

The PiedPiper class, which you can see in Listing 4.6, Listing 4.7, and Figure 4.12, shows that things are not as simple as they seem. Even though the PiedPiper has no access to the private data encapsulated inside each GoodKid object, it does have access to the public static field HOME. By using the setLocation() mutator on GoodKid.HOME, the Piper is able to lead the children astray.

Listing 4.6 PiedPiper.java

```
//  PiedPiper.java
//
//  Makes the GoodKids follow the mouse
//  By REDEFINING the static final "constant" GoodKid.HOME
//
import java.awt.*;

import java.applet.*;
import java.awt.event.*;

public class PiedPiper  extends    Applet
                        implements MouseMotionListener
{
  public void init()
  {
    setLayout( null );
    add( new GoodKid( -20, -20 ) );
    add( new GoodKid( -20,  20 ) );
    add( new GoodKid(  20, -20 ) );
    add( new GoodKid(  20,  20 ) );

    addMouseMotionListener( this );
  }

  public void mouseDragged( MouseEvent evt ) {}
  public void mouseMoved( MouseEvent evt )
  {
    Point bad = GoodKid.HOME;
    bad.setLocation( evt.getX(), evt.getY() );
    repaint();
  }
}
```

Listing 4.7 PiedPiper.html

```
<HTML>
<HEAD>
<TITLE>Using the GoodKid Class</TITLE>
</HEAD>
<BODY>
<H1>The Pied Piper of Hamelin</H1>
<HR>
In medieval legend, the town of Hamelin was plagued with rats.
(Today, of course, we call them mice.) <BR>
To rid the town, the merchants and elders of Hamelin
hired a piper, who lead the rats away with his music. <BR>
When not rewarded, the piper returned and lead the town's
children away likewise. <P>
The cyberian descendents of the elders of Hamelin, never
let this lesson stray far from their minds. They always
make their data private or static final. But is it enough?
<HR>
<APPLET CODE=PiedPiper WIDTH=500 HEIGHT=200>
</APPLET>
</BODY>
</HTML>
```

The HOME field is specified as final, therefore its value cannot be changed. However, HOME does not contain a Point, it merely refers to a Point. As long as HOME always refers to the same Point, its value has not changed.

Unfortunately, this doesn't rule out the possibility that some of the attributes of the Point might be changed. The PiedPiper exploits this loophole, changing the X and Y values associated with the Point. The value of HOME does not change, it always refers to the same Point. But, the Point unexpectedly comes to have a new location.

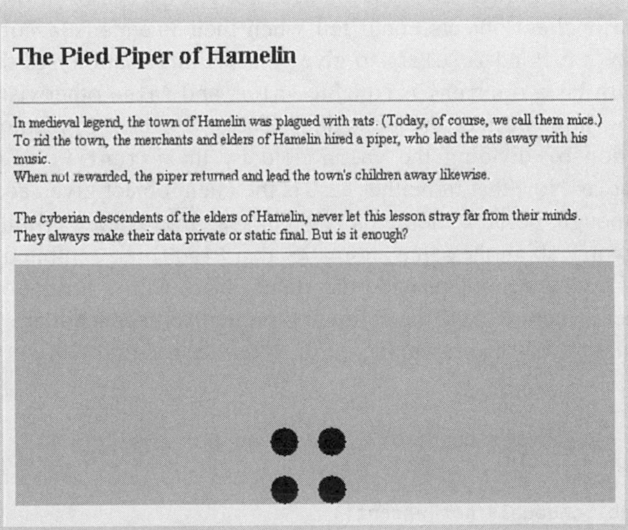

FIGURE 4.12
Running the PiedPiper applet

The Pied Piper of Hamelin

In medieval legend, the town of Hamelin was plagued with rats. (Today, of course, we call them mice.)
To rid the town, the merchants and elders of Hamelin hired a piper, who lead the rats away with his music.
When not rewarded, the piper returned and lead the town's children away likewise.

The cyberian descendents of the elders of Hamelin, never let this lesson stray far from their minds.
They always make their data private or static final. But is it enough?

You might feel that you could avoid this problem by making HOME a private field and using an accessor to return its value. However, if this is done naively, like this:

```
private static final Point HOME = new Point( 100, 100);
public static Point getHOME() { return HOME; }
```

the problem is not alleviated at all. The PiedPiper can change the field just as easily as before. To avoid this potential time-bomb, you *must* make sure that accessor methods return only values, *never* references.

How, you wonder, do you do that when objects are always represented by references? Do you use only primitive types (which are returned by value) as data members? No, that's not the answer. Instead, when working with object types and accessors, make sure that all accesses receive a *copy* of the object or, better yet, don't return access to individual fields at all. If the outside world just *has* to know the location of HOME, you can safely publish it like this:

```
private static final Point HOME = getHOME();
public static Point getHOME( return new Point( 100, 100 ));
```

Now, inside the class you can refer to the static field HOME (which should be more efficient than constructing a new Point object each time). Outsiders, however, will only get a *copy* of HOME, and they won't be able to lead the GoodKids off the screen.

Remember

In a well-designed class, objects provide services for clients; they don't just store data to be used elsewhere in the program. If you find yourself with many getThisField() accessor methods, you may have fallen into the Data Warehouse Trap. Data and the operations on that data belong together.

Although your original design contained no accessor methods, writing ZenoApplet.java revealed the need for two pieces of information. First, it would be nice if client objects could tell when their ProgressBar objects were full. You can write a method isFull() to give you this information. All that isFull() has to do is return true if extent is equal to value, and false otherwise. You might also want to know how much of the job is done. The getPercent() method can give you this information by dividing the value field by the extent field, returning the result as a double. Note that in neither case is the client object given access to the private fields (although, because the fields in ProgressBar.java are primitives, you would not have to worry about the same anomalies that PiedPiper exhibited). Instead, both isFull() and getPercent() provide the client object with information without revealing their inner structure. Add the following section to ProgressBar.java, just underneath the Mutators subheading, in the Public Interface section.:

```
/*   --Accessors--------------------- */
/**
  * Returns percent of job done as a double
  *
  */
public double getPercent()
{
```

```
    return (double) value / extent;
}

/**
  * Returns true if extent and value are same
  *
  */
public boolean isFull()
{
  dbg( "isFull = " + ( extent == value ) );
  return ( extent == value );
}
```

THE COMMON-OBJECT INTERFACE

When designing a class, most of your focus will, rightly, be on accessors and mutators. To make your objects fit for public habitation, however, you should also implement a minimal interface that all objects understand. In Java, this is the interface described by the root class, `Object`.

Because every object in Java is an `Object`, your objects should know how to do the things that `Object`s do! You should ask yourself whether objects of your new class need:

> *Because every object in Java is an `Object`, your objects should know how to do the things that `Object`s do!*

- To perform `String` conversion for output. If so, you'll want to override the `toString()` method.

- To compare themselves to other objects. If you have to sequentially order or otherwise distinguish one object of your class from another, you should override the `equals()` method. Make sure you understand the difference between identity (two object variables that refer to the same object in memory) and equality (two objects that have the same logical contents). The == operator compares identity in Java, and is seldom useful when used on objects. The `equals()` method compares logical equivalence, and you must override it in your class if this concept is important.

- To copy themselves. If you need to make copies of objects you should consider writing a method that does so. If your class has fields that are themselves objects, you will need to override the `clone()` method to provide a deep copy instead of simply a replication of references. Chapter 17, "Designing With Class Libraries," will show you how to do this.

- To clean up or release resources. If so, you may need to override the `finalize()` method, which is called before an object is garbage collected. In reality, however, you'll seldom need to do this if you explicitly release the resources you acquire once you're done with them.

For the `ProgressBar` class, you won't need to write most of these methods. You won't, generally, want to copy, compare, or clean up `ProgressBar` objects. However, the ability to inspect a `ProgressBar` object by simply printing it out to the console does have some value, so you'll probably want to override the `toString()` method. When writing the `toString()` method, you can format the output in any way that makes sense to you.

If you recall that `ProgressBar` extends `Component`, you may realize that the `toString()` method for `ProgressBar` would be considerably easier to write if it could invoke the `toString()` method of `Component`. The descriptive information supplied by `Component.toString()` could then be supplemented with the distinctive information specific to a `ProgressBar`. The good news is that this is easy to accomplish: sending `toString()` to a special receiver called `super` will forward the `toString()` message up the inheritance hierarchy to `Component`. Add the following lines to `ProgressBar.java`, just below the Accessor subheading, still in the Public Interface section:

```
/*  --Common Interface-------------- */

/**
  * Returns extent, value, and borderStyle
  *
  */
public String toString()
{
  String retStr = super.toString();
  retStr += "[ value=" + value;
  retStr += ", extent=" + extent;
  retStr += ", borderStyle=" + borderStyle + "]";
  dbg( "toString() = " + retStr );

  return retStr;
}
```

SERVICING THE AWT

When you first started the design for your `ProgressBar`, you identified two different client objects. One, of course, was created by the programmer who wanted to use your `ProgressBar`; the other client object was Java's Abstract Window Toolkit, which provides you with the framework to actually display your `ProgressBar` objects. The AWT's `Component` superclass provides several methods that you can override, methods which are called by the AWT as necessary.

Listing 4.8 shows the Public Interface section, which is dedicated to the AWT client object. Whereas you could have interspersed these methods with the other `public` methods, organizing the interface by client object allows you to concentrate on one problem at a time. This section includes the following methods:

- `getMinimumSize()`, which tells the AWT's layout manager not to resize a `ProgressBar` object to less than 20 pixels high and 100 pixels wide.

- `getPreferredSize()`, which tells the layout manager to use the actual size if one has been explicitly set (using the `setSize()` method that `ProgressBar` inherits from `Component`), or to use the value returned from `getMinimumSize()` otherwise.

🔹 paint(), the most important of these methods, which gives the AWT precise, step-by-step instructions for rendering your ProgressBar. Unless you override the paint() method, nothing will be displayed and your ProgressBar class ends up being, well, a little pointless!

Both getMinimumSize() and getPreferredSize() are relatively self-explanatory, but the paint() method deserves a few words of explanation. To paint() a ProgressBar object, you want to complete the five steps you had earlier added to the first draft of ProgressBar.java:

1. Allow enough space to draw your border. Because each possible border means that the interior bar will have to be a different height and width, the first order of business is to calculate and create this inner rectangle.

2. Transform the logical size of the ProgressBar, stored in the field extent, to the actual physical rectangle available for drawing the bar.

3. Fill the interior of the bar with the background color, because lightweight components do not automatically do this. (That's how they provide the useful ability to have transparent backgrounds.)

4. Draw the appropriate border.

5. Draw the interior bar itself.

The actual code for each of these operations is an implementation detail, and is thus contained in methods located in the next section.

Listing 4.8 The AWT Public Interface section for ProgressBar.java

```
// ========================================================
//      PUBLIC INTERFACE: AWT Client
// ========================================================
/**
 * Called by AWT when component must repaint itself
 *
 */
public void paint( Graphics g )
{
  dbg( "paint( " + g +" )");

  // 1. Calculate border and "inside" rectangles

    Rectangle rect   = getBounds();
    rect.x = rect.y = 0;

    Rectangle inside = new Rectangle( rect );
    inside.grow( -(borderStyle/2), -(borderStyle/2) );

  // 2. Calculate size of the "fill" area

    float pixPerUnit = (((float) inside.width) / extent);
    inside.width     = (int) (pixPerUnit * value);
```

```
        // 3. Paint entire background with background color

          g.setColor( getBackground() );
          g.fillRect( rect.x, rect.y, rect.width, rect.height );

        // 4. Draw appropriate border

          if      ( borderStyle == SUNKEN ) drawSunkenBorder( g, rect );
          else if ( borderStyle == PLAIN ) drawPlainBorder( g, rect );

        // 5. Draw filled area

          drawInterior( g, inside );

    }

    /**
      * Tells the AWT the preferred size of a ProgressBar
      *
      */
    public Dimension getPreferredSize(  )
    {
      dbg( "getPreferredSize() called" );
      Rectangle r = getBounds();
      if ( r.width == 0 ¦¦ r.height == 0 )
        return getMinimumSize();
      else
        return new Dimension( r.width, r.height );
    }

    /**
      * Tells the AWT how "small" the bar is willing to go
      *
      */
    public Dimension getMinimumSize(  )
    {
      dbg( "getMinimumSize() called" );
      return new Dimension( 100, 20 );
    }
```

THE PRIVATE AND PROTECTED SECTION

There are still two steps necessary before you can loose your ProgressBar class on the waiting world. You have to actually draw the bar on the screen, and you must test it.

The Private and Protected section of the classes you design should contain implementation details that the rest of the class—and certainly other classes—should not rely on. Just as you put the constructors and public methods first when implementing the other sections, here you should put the protected methods—those that can be overridden in a subclass, before the private methods.

ProgressBar.java has one protected method, drawInterior(), which you can see in Listing 4.9. This method simply fills the interior rectangle calculated earlier with the value contained in the component's foreground color. The reason the method is protected, rather than private, is to allow you to create derived classes that display the bar in a different manner—like Microsoft-style progress bars, for instance—or to use a different color.

Listing 4.9 The protected and private methods of ProgressBar.java

```
//  =========================================
//      PROTECTED AND PRIVATE METHODS
//  =========================================
/**
  * Draws the actual "bar" itself. Override to draw differently
  * @param g Graphics context object
  * @param inside Rectangle for drawing inside
  *
  */
protected void drawInterior( Graphics g, Rectangle inside )
{
  g.setColor( getForeground() );
  g.fillRect( inside.x, inside.y, inside.width, inside.height );
}

/**
  * Draws a single line border in foreground color
  * @param g Graphics context object
  * @param rect Rectangle representing size of ProgressBar
  *
  */
private void drawPlainBorder( Graphics g, Rectangle rect )
{
  g.setColor( getForeground() );
  g.drawRect( rect.x, rect.y, rect.width-1, rect.height-1 );
}

/**
  * Draws a 3D "sunken" border 2 pixels deep
  * @param g Graphics context object
  * @param rect Rectangle representing size of ProgressBar
  *
  */
private void drawSunkenBorder( Graphics g, Rectangle rect )
{
  g.setColor( getBackground().darker().darker() );
  g.drawLine( 0, 0, rect.width-1, 0 );
  g.drawLine( 0, 1, rect.width-2, 1 );
  g.drawLine( 0, 0, 0, rect.height-1);
  g.drawLine( 1, 0, 1, rect.height-2);

  g.setColor( getBackground().brighter().brighter() );
  g.drawLine( 0, rect.height-1, rect.width, rect.height-1 );
  g.drawLine( 1, rect.height-2, rect.width, rect.height-2 );
  g.drawLine( rect.width-1, 1, rect.width-1, rect.height-1 );
  g.drawLine( rect.width-2, 2, rect.width-2, rect.height-2 );
}
```

The other two methods, drawPlainBorder() and drawSunkenBorder(), are private methods that were moved out of the paint() method simply to unclutter the code and make it easier to understand. You may feel that drawSunkenBorder() is such a handy routine that it should be made public so you can use it anywhere you need to draw a sunken style border. As soon as you use it that way, however, you will find yourself creating invisible ProgressBar objects, simply to be able to use the drawSunkenBorder() method.

Remember

Classes are not function libraries. If you find yourself creating unneeded objects just to use their methods, you've fallen into the "spectral object trap" and you need to make those methods private.

Testing Your Work

After you've added these methods to ProgressBar.java, you're ready to test it out. Modify your main() method so it looks like the one shown in Listing 4.10. This uses some of the new accessors and the ProgressBar's new toString() method to print out a little more information than before. Now compile the program like you did before, using

```
javac ProgressBar.java
```

and run the resulting .class file by typing the following:

```
java ProgressBar
```

You should see a Frame window that now contains three ProgressBar objects, like that shown in Figure 4.13, along with some information about each object. If you have some difficulty getting the program to compile, you can copy a completed version from the CD-ROM.

Listing 4.10 The main() method of ProgressBar.java

```
//    =========================================
//        TESTING METHODS
//    =========================================
/**
 * Tests the class by creating three ProgressBar objects
 * The PBApplet programs tests the actual operation
 *
 */
public static void main( String[] args )
{
  Frame f = new Frame();
  f.setLayout( new FlowLayout() );
  ProgressBar pb1 = new ProgressBar( 1000, ProgressBar.NONE );
  f.add( pb1 );
  pb1.setValue( 50 );
  f.add( new Label(" % = " + (int)(pb1.getPercent() * 100)));
  f.add( new Label("pb1 = " + pb1));

  ProgressBar pb2 = new ProgressBar( 1000, ProgressBar.SUNKEN );
  pb2.setSize( 200, 20 );
```

```
        pb2.setBackground( Color.lightGray );
        pb2.setForeground( Color.blue );
        f.add( pb2 );
        pb2.setValue( 500 );
        f.add( new Label(" % = " + (int)(pb2.getPercent() * 100)));
        f.add( new Label("pb2 = " + pb2));

        ProgressBar pb3 = new ProgressBar( 1000, ProgressBar.PLAIN );
        f.add( pb3 );
        pb3.setValue( 999 );
        f.add( new Label(" % = " + (int)(pb3.getPercent() * 100)));
        f.add( new Label("pb3 = " + pb3));

        f.setBackground( Color.lightGray );
        f.setSize( 300, 300 );
        f.setVisible( true );
    }

    // -------------------------------------------
    // dbg() method
    //    Used to print a debug string to the console
    // -------------------------------------------
    /**
     * Prints a debug string to the console
     *
     */
    private static void dbg( String msg )
    {
      System.out.println( msg );
    }
```

After you've got the test method running, use appletviewer or a Web browser that supports JDK 1.1 and try out ZenoApplet.html (which you can see in Figure 4.14) to see if the philosopher Zeno was right when he proposed that motion was intrinsically impossible!

FIGURE 4.13
Running
ProgressBar.java

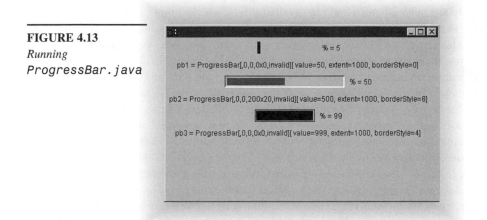

FIGURE 4.14

Running the Zeno applet

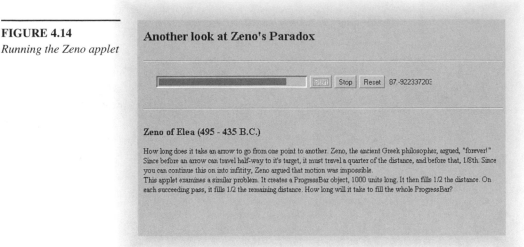

Summary

Design is the process of turning your client's ideas into something useful. The first step in designing a software program is translating your client's conceptual model (what's wanted) into a logical—and then a physical—model, which can finally be translated into executable form and run on a computer. In this chapter, you learned how to translate a client's description (in the form of a summary paragraph) into a source code model that can be compiled by the Java compiler.

A well-designed class is divided into a public section, called the interface, and a private section, called the implementation. Applying the principles of abstraction and encapsulation involves first deciding which parts of your class are essential for its use (abstraction), and then wrapping everything else up in an opaque package where the details are hidden from view (encapsulation). When deciding on which parts of your class should be public, put yourself in your client objects' position; the public interface of your class should be as small and easy to use as possible, yet complete enough to perform its intended purpose.

The data in your program should be private, and the data and methods should work together to present client objects with a single abstraction. Classes that contain multiple abstractions should be broken into cohesive classes. You should not create classes that contain only methods, because a class is not a subroutine library. Neither should you create classes that contain mostly data (with methods to get and set that data), because an object is not a data warehouse. Your methods should all use the attributes of your class. Also, each attribute should be used by some method, and not simply stored for processing by some imaginary external routine.

The methods in your class should be internally cohesive; each method should do only one thing. You should use a template to structure your class, and a checklist to make sure you have considered all the necessary details in your design. You should make sure that your constructors initialize each field in your class and that they create all objects in a valid state. Make sure you know what the invariant conditions are for your class, and be certain your constructors maintain those conditions. Write your working constructor first, and then write overloaded constructors in terms of the working constructor.

Check mutator methods to see that each maintains the invariants of your class. When errors occur, consider different error-handling strategies and adopt the strategy that does the least harm and that provokes the least surprise. When you use accessor methods, be careful not to return a reference to private data. If you have accessor methods that should return a private data field that refers to an object, you should return a copy of the field or create an immutable interface.

Questions

1. For any kind of object, one way of looking at it is to describe its _____, whereas an equally valid way is to describe its

    _____.

2. The _____ of a well-designed object describes the services that the client of the object wants performed.

3. The _____ of an object is the manner or techniques it uses to carry out its functions.

4. When designing classes, abstraction is the process of discovering the _____ behavior of an object. These behaviors are used to construct the object's _____.

5. The purpose of a well-designed class is to model an _____ from the user's point of view.

6. The first step in designing a class begins by identifying the class's _____, _____, and _____.

7. A _____ describes the client's conceptual model in an informal way.

8. Your object's client is anyone or anything that sends your object

    _____.

9. Three common techniques that will help you implement your designs are to begin with a _____, write a _____ method that exercises your class, and use _____ methods to refine your interface before looking at the details.

10. Your class will define three types of attributes: _____, which store the state of each individual object; _____ attributes, which share state among all members of the class; and _____ class attributes, which store unchanging state.

11. The "Prime Directive" for object attributes is that all state variables should be declared _____.

12. An object contains both _____ and _____ that operate on that data. Objects with no _____ are ghosts!

13. The principle of _____ says that every class should model a single abstraction.

14. Using static final constants allows you to use your facility for _____, rather than rely on _____.

15. When constructing an object, Java gives you the opportunity to decide which superclass constructor should by called first, by using the _____ method.

16. To write all of your constructors in terms of the working constructor, you can use the special _____ method.

17. The most important consideration when writing constructors is to make sure that all fields are _____ and that all _____ are satisfied.

18. When dealing with errors that occur in your methods, you have the options of doing nothing, stopping the program after testing (by writing an _____ method), fixing the mistake (which is called _____ programming), or _____, which is the preferred way of dealing with errors in Java.

19. Methods that change the state of an object (called _____) must be very careful to preserve the invariants of the class.

20. Methods that return information to the client without changing the state of the object are called _____.

Exercises

1. On a sheet of paper, list the method names that would represent the public interface for a car, a refrigerator, a pencil, a trumpet, and a calculator.

2. Why do you think that the interface for an airliner (represented by its cockpit control panel) is more complex than that of your automobile? Is it simply that an airliner is a more complex machine? What would be some of the ramifications of simplifying the interface? What does your answer tell you about the limitations of abstraction?

3. Using the public interface you developed for the car in Exercise 1, list the private operations and attributes for your automobile. Take your list, and write a class definition for an automobile. Write stubs for each of the public methods. Write a main method that tests each of the methods in your class.

4. If you're part of a class or study group, divide your classmates into equal groups A and B. Divide each group into teams of two or three. Have each team in group A write a summary paragraph that describes a software component (taking 15 or 20 minutes). Shuffle the examples and have each team in group B take one component. While Group B creates a Java class definition, Group A should write a Java program that uses the software component they described. Group B should write the public interface and a list of data members—you don't have to list private methods. This should take about one-half hour. At the end of that time, have both groups get together and compare their work.

5. If you are in a class or study group, choose a large software product like Microsoft Word or Netscape Navigator and list the classes that you think would be necessary to build that application. Take two of the classes that most of you agreed upon, and describe their public interfaces.

To Learn More

Specific advice for designing good classes and objects in Java is still rare; however, there are several books that focus on general object-oriented principles, or that are geared toward another language yet contain useful advice.

Steve McConnell's *Code Complete* falls into neither of these categories, yet is immensely useful for practical, real-world knowledge that will stand you in good stead in any language.

Scott Meyers' *Effective C++* and Alan Holub's *Enough Rope to Shoot Yourself in the Foot* are both geared toward C and C++ programmers. The specific C++ implementation issues that comprise the majority of both these books will not necessarily be helpful, but the sections on class and object design both provide useful information for the Java programmer.

Arthur J. Riel's *Object-Oriented Design Heuristics* addresses general rules for partitioning methods and data between classes and is clear and easy to read.

Some of the most interesting advice is found on the Web, and some of the most helpful (especially if you come from a C++ background) is the "Java Cookbook," a guide to porting C++ programs to Java written by Dr. Mark Davis at Taligent. Despite the title, even non C++ programmers will find something they can use. The address is `http://www.taligent.com/Technology/WhitePapers/PortingPaper/index.html`.

Also helpful are the numerous Java coding standards. Although they frequently deal with purely implementation details, they also have some good advice for doing detailed, physical design. Two of the best are Doug Lea's "Draft Java Coding Standard," and Scott Ambler's "Java Coding Standards." You can find these at `http://g.oswego.edu/dl/html/javaCodingStd.html` and `http://www.AmbySoft.com/javaCodingStandards.pdf`.

Designing Classes and Objects

"So," Jason began, leaning forward in his chair with what he hoped was a disarming smile. "You've certainly been busy. Why don't you tell me what you've done." Because Jason was one of the company's most skilled programmers, he'd been assigned by the boss, Mr. Markey, to mentor Barney, a new intern on loan from marketing.

Across the conference room table, Barney sat up straight in his chair and rested his elbows on the table, returning Jason's smile. With no hint of self-consciousness, and with an admirable enthusiasm, he started right in.

"Busy? I'll say!" Barney exclaimed, pointing to the foot-high pile of listing paper sitting between them. "I was up half the night working on this job. Mr. Markey told me it was really important to make sure that everyone in the company got entered into the new scheduling system, so Sam and I were here until 11:30 writing the new classes. There are almost 1,200 of them."

"Mr. Markey had you write 1,200 classes to be added to the new system?" Jason was careful to keep his tone neutral, and to keep an encouraging smile on his face, but he couldn't quite keep the shock out of his voice. "Can I take a look?" he asked, reaching for the sheet on the top of the pile. The listings were neatly printed in very small type, sideways and two to a page. Jason silently calculated the lines of code as he started to read:

```java
public class AndersonJane
{
  private String lastName  = "Anderson";
  private String firstName = "Jane";
```

```
private int    ID_No    = 107325;
  . . .
public AndersonJane(String name)
{
  . . .
```

Keeping the smile on his face, he reached for a handful of sheets this time. He quickly flipped through them. Every class followed the same pattern: each was named after a different employee, had the fields initialized to proper values, and had a different constructor name. Jason struggled lamely to find something encouraging to say. "Very nice formatting. Alphabetizing the names was a nice touch as well," was the best he could come up with. Barney's grin let him know he had succeeded. Now for the hard part.

"Tell me," Jason asked, in what he hoped was a non-threatening manner, "where's the code that adds all the employees to the scheduling system?" Jason was surprised to find that Barney brightened even further.

"Oh," he began, "that's why I'm here. Mr. Markey told me that you're the Java expert. He said that once I got finished, I should bring the code down here, and we could hook it up together."

Just because someone can define the word *class* and write a Java class header and class body, they're not automatically able to recognize what should, and should not, be represented as a class. In the previous chapters, you've learned the fundamentals of object-oriented programming. Many software developers stop learning at that point. Rather than pressing on to study design, they approach every programming problem afresh, as though each new program had no relationship to programs previously written. Rather than working out a suitable design in advance, they solve each design problem as it comes up.

Their approach is somewhat similar to that of chimpanzee art: give a chimp a brush, a canvas, and some oil paints, stand back, and watch the fun. The chimp may have a fine understanding of how to apply the paint to the brush and the brush to the canvas, but the chimp does not give great significance to concepts like shape, texture, and color. Though some people may like the resulting "art," it falls short of the work of a talented human artist who understands the elements of artistic design.

Similarly, the results of programming without design are often less than satisfactory. If the resulting program works at all, it's likely to be difficult to understand and maintain.

This effect is magnified when programmers work as a team. Without an agreed design, members of the team discover design issues one by one, as they program. Often, they resolve these issues in ways that are inconsistent with the assumptions and decisions of other team members. When it comes time to bolt together the software components built by team members, the team often discovers that the parts don't fit. Design is essential to effective teamwork.

Building on the knowledge of object-oriented programming you gained in previous chapters, this chapter begins your study of object-oriented design. In this chapter you will learn:

- How to analyze a problem and write a summary paragraph

- How to identify the classes and objects of your system

- How to identify the attributes and methods of the classes of your system

- How to sketch a user interface for your system

- How to draw object interaction diagrams that show how messages are passed from object to object within your system

- Some handy rules of thumb for designing classes and objects

The Renter Applet

Figure 5.1 shows the Renter applet, which models the interaction between a renter and a lender. The model is not perfect. For example, the renter can return items that haven't even been rented. But, by omitting some of the finer points of renting, the program is made simpler. And, a simple program better serves the immediate purpose of illustrating important design principles. Later, you'll have an opportunity to extend the program so that it more realistically models the real world.

The user interface of the Renter applet includes two buttons: Rent and Return. By clicking the Rent button, the user (who plays the role of the renter) can rent a software bug. Notice that the program doesn't give the user a selection of bugs from which to choose—all bugs are considered to be the same. The number of remaining bugs that

FIGURE 5.1

The Renter applet

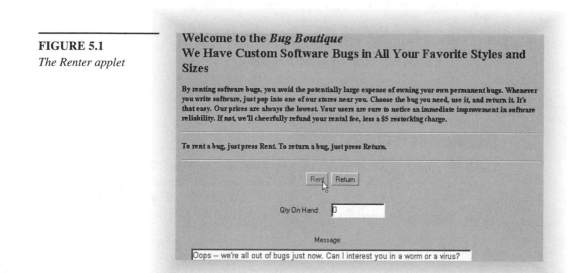

the lender has on hand is displayed in a text box. Below that text box is another text box, which is used to display messages from the lender.

When the renter rents a bug, the number of remaining bugs is decremented and a message from the lender is displayed. If the renter attempts to rent a bug when none remain, the lender responds with an error message, which is displayed in the Message text box.

The renter can return a bug simply by clicking the Return button. The applet updates the number of remaining bugs and displays a message from the lender. As mentioned, the renter can return a bug even before one has been rented. This simplification does-n't bother the cheerful but unsophisticated lender, who appreciates the increase in the inventory of bugs, even if it's a phantom increase.

The HTML file used to execute the applet is shown in Listing 5.1.

Listing 5.1 Renter.html

```
<HTML>
<HEAD>
<TITLE>The Software Renter: Custom Bugs in All Sizes </TITLE>
</HEAD>
<BODY>
<H1>Welcome to the <I>Bug Boutique</I>
<BR>
We Have Custom Software Bugs in All Your Favorite Styles and Sizes
</H1>
<H4>By renting software bugs, you avoid the potentially large
expense of owning your own permanent bugs. Whenever you write
software, just pop into one of our stores near you. Choose the
bug you need, use it, and return it. It's that easy. Our prices
are always the lowest. Your users are sure to notice an immediate
improvement in software reliability. If not, we'll cheerfully
refund your rental fee, less a $5 restocking charge.
<HR>
To rent a bug, just press Rent.
To return a bug, just press Return.
<HR></H4>
<APPLET CODE=Renter WIDTH=500 HEIGHT=150>
</APPLET>
</BODY>
</HTML>
```

THE Renter CLASS

The Renter applet consists of two classes, Renter and Lender. The source file for the Renter class is shown as Listing 5.2. See what you can learn by dissecting the Renter class: take a look at the class and identify its methods and attributes. Then, determine which are part of the interface of the class, and which are part of the implementation.

Listing 5.2 Renter.java

```
//  Renter.java

import   java.applet.*;
import   java.awt.*;
import   java.awt.event.*;
```

```
public class Renter
        extends     Applet
        implements ActionListener

{
  //   =========================================
  //           APPLET METHODS
  //   =========================================
  /*  —Initialization— — — — — — —- */
  public void init()
  {
    setLayout( new GridLayout(3, 1));
    Panel north = new Panel( );
    north.setLayout(new FlowLayout( ));
    north.add(theRentButton);
    north.add(theReturnButton);
    add(north);

    Panel center = new Panel( );
    center.setLayout(new FlowLayout( ));
    center.add(new Label("Qty On Hand: "));
    center.add(theQtyOnHand);
    add(center);

    Panel south = new Panel( );
    south.setLayout(new FlowLayout( ));
    south.add(new Label("Message: "));
    south.add(theMessage);
    add(south);

    theRentButton.addActionListener(this);
    theReturnButton.addActionListener(this);

    displayQtyOnHand( );
  }

  //   =========================================
  //         IMPLEMENT ACTIONLISTENER
  //   =========================================
  public void actionPerformed( ActionEvent ae )
  {
    System.out.println("Event: " + ae);
    Object source = ae.getSource( );

    if (source == theRentButton)
      theLender.rentItem(this);
    else if (source == theReturnButton)
      theLender.returnItem(this);
    displayQtyOnHand();
  }

  //   =========================================
  //           PUBLIC INTERFACE
  //   =========================================

  /*  —Mutators— — — — — — — — — — —- */
  public void tellResult(String msg)
  {
    theMessage.setText(msg);
  }
```

```
//  =========================================
//      PRIVATE METHODS
//  =========================================
private void displayQtyOnHand()
{
  int onhand = theLender.getQtyOnHand( );
  theQtyOnHand.setText("" + onhand);
}

//  =========================================
//      CLASS ATTRIBUTES
//  =========================================
private final static int INITIAL_QTY = 5;
private Lender     theLender = new Lender( INITIAL_QTY );

private Button     theRentButton   = new Button( "Rent" );
private Button     theReturnButton = new Button( "Return" );
private TextField theQtyOnHand     = new TextField( 10 );
private TextField theMessage       = new TextField( 64 );
}
```

Your findings should be similar to those in Table 5.1, which shows the methods and attributes of the Renter class. Remember that methods are shown with parentheses following the name of the method. Remember also that public methods and attributes are part of the interface of a class, but private methods and attributes are part of the implementation of a class.

TABLE 5.1
METHODS AND ATTRIBUTES OF THE Renter CLASS

Method/Attribute	Type
init()	Interface
actionPerformed()	Interface
tellResult()	Interface
displayQtyOnHand()	Implementation
INITIAL_QTY	Implementation
theLender	Implementation
theRentButton	Implementation
theReturnButton	Implementation
theQtyOnHand	Implementation
theMessage	Implementation

When studying a class, you may find that constructing a table like Table 5.1 helps you to understand the class. Notice that most of the methods and attributes of the Renter class are part of its implementation, not its interface. The interface, which is the part of the class that is visible to other classes, is smaller and simpler than the implementation. This is typical of classes generally, and is one mark of a good design.

Remember

A good design hides much of the complexity of a class in the implementation of the class. Ideally, the interface of a class should be small and simple.

THE Lender CLASS

Listing 5.3 shows the source file for the Lender class. Take a look at it, identify the methods and attributes, and allocate them to the class interface or implementation, just as you did for the Renter class.

" The interface... is smaller and simpler than the implementation. This is typical of classes generally, and is one mark of a good design. "

Listing 5.3 Lender.java

```java
//  Lender.java

public class Lender
{
  //  ============================================
  //        CONSTRUCTORS
  //  ============================================

  public Lender(int qty)
  {
    theQtyOnHand = qty;
  }

  //  ============================================
  //        PUBLIC INTERFACE
  //  ============================================

  /*  —Mutators— — — — — — — — — —· */
  public boolean rentItem(Renter renter)
  {
    if (theQtyOnHand > 0)
    {
      theQtyOnHand -= 1;
      renter.tellResult("Thanks for your business — " +
                        "come back soon.");
      return true;
    }
    renter.tellResult("Oops — we're all out of bugs just now."+
                      " Can I interest you in a worm or a virus?");
    return false;
  }

  public void returnItem(Renter renter)
  {
    theQtyOnHand += 1;
    renter.tellResult("Thanks for returning the bug promptly.");
  }

  /*  —Accessors— — — — — — — — — — */
  public int getQtyOnHand()
  {
    return theQtyOnHand;
  }
```

```
//   ==========================================
//       CLASS AND OBJECT ATTRIBUTES
//   ==========================================
private int theQtyOnHand;

}
```

Table 5.2 shows what you should have found. Notice that the table identifies the constructor, Lender(), as a method. This is not strictly correct, but it's more convenient than treating constructors separately.

TABLE 5.2
METHODS AND ATTRIBUTES OF THE Lender CLASS

Method/Attribute	Type
Lender()	Interface
rentItem()	Interface
returnItem()	Interface
getQtyOnHand()	Interface
theQtyOnHand	Implementation

As you can see, the interface of the Lender class is larger than the implementation. Is this a symptom of poor design? Though such is often the case, it is not the case here. The Lender class is so simple that there just isn't much implementation needed.

Remember

A class with more interface than implementation is not always a badly designed class. Often, a very simple class will have more interface than implementation.

A Design Process

Now that you've studied the structure of the Renter class and the Lender class, you may be wondering how that structure came about: What process did the designer follow? Recall from Chapter 2, "Object-Oriented Software Development," that design is an activity within a larger process, the software development process. As you learned, there are many possible ways of performing the software development process. Consequently, you should not be surprised to learn that there are many possible ways to perform the design activity.

This chapter introduces you to one approach that can be effectively applied to a variety of problems. The references at the end of the chapter will help you discover other ways of performing the design activity that may be more suitable for problems of the sort you regularly deal with.

The design process consists of these four steps:

1. Determine the requirements.
2. Identify the classes and objects.
3. Describe the object collaborations and the classes.
4. Sketch the user interface.

Figure 5.2 illustrates this design process. Although the figure does not indicate it (for the sake of simplicity), the design process is exploratory and iterative. Each step may take the designer forward to the following step or back to a preceding step. If it seems to the designer as though a tentative design is going nowhere, the designer may abandon it and restart the entire process.

Because a design can always be improved, design is a process without a "stopping rule." The decision to cease looking for a better design has less to do with the design itself than with circumstances such as the time remaining on the schedule or the amount of energy the designer has left.

The same is true of the individual steps of the design process. The decision to move from one step to the other is made rather subjectively. The good news is that this poses no serious risk, because it's always possible to revisit the decision.

FIGURE 5.2
The object-oriented design process

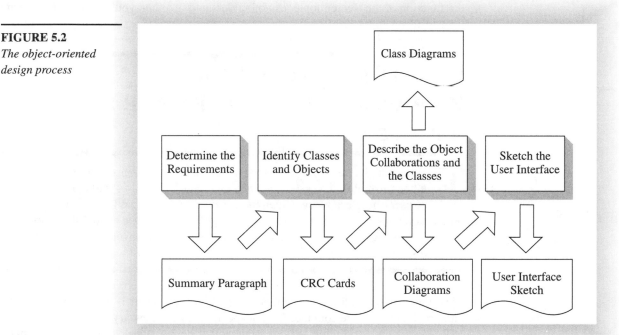

Determining the Requirements

The first step of object-oriented design is to determine the general requirements the program must satisfy. Of course, you're unlikely to completely and accurately specify the requirements right away. As you proceed, you'll undoubtedly uncover new requirements and you'll better understand previously identified requirements. But, one must start somewhere. Remember that design is iterative. The trick is to get something down on paper and *then* study it and improve it. Don't try to perfectly form the idea in your head before writing it down. The simple act of writing will often help you form your ideas.

A good way to begin to determine the program requirements is to write a summary paragraph. The summary paragraph should view the system from a functional perspective, focusing on the inputs and outputs of the system and on its external behavior. In effect, it should describe the interface of the program rather than the implementation of the program. Often, the paragraph is called a problem summary paragraph. You may wonder why it's not called a solution summary paragraph. The answer is simple. Because the paragraph doesn't spell out a specific solution, but merely identifies elements that must characterize *any* acceptable solution, it is more focused on the problem than on the solution.

Don't read ahead. Instead, stop now and write a summary paragraph that describes the function of the Renter applet as you understand it. When you're finished, compare your results with what follows.

PROBLEM SUMMARY PARAGRAPH FOR THE RENTER APPLET

The Renter applet tracks the inventory (that is, a count) of bugs. Initially, there are five bugs available. The user can rent a bug, which decreases the remaining inventory. The user can return a bug, which increases the inventory. Whenever a bug is rented or returned, the applet displays a message confirming the action. If the user tries to rent a bug when none are available (that is, when the inventory is zero), the applet displays an error message.

Did you identify all the actions that the applet must perform? If not, study the sample paragraph until you are convinced that it specifies no unnecessary action.

Did you identify additional actions, actions that do not appear in the summary paragraph? Remember that the summary paragraph given above describes the applet as written. Perhaps, for example, you believe that allowing the user to return a bug that was never actually rented is an oversimplification. If so, it was appropriate for you to include actions that prevent this from happening. Check any actions you added and convince yourself that they're really necessary, or cross them out of your summary paragraph.

Identifying Classes and Objects

The next step in the object-oriented design process is to identify the classes and objects that will comprise the program. Your summary paragraph will help you do this.

An effective way to identify classes and objects is by preparing what are known as *CRC cards*. The name *CRC card* stands for *class-responsibility-collaboration card*. To create CRC cards, find some 3×5 index cards. If you don't have any 3×5 index cards, you can use a larger size or even 8-1/2×11 paper. The handy thing about 3×5 cards is their small size, which prevents you from putting too much detail on a single card, and their weight, which keeps them in place. Sheets of paper tend to be randomly redistributed every time a high-volume air conditioning system kicks in, which can get annoying.

Each CRC card describes a single class in terms of the data attributes, responsibilities, and collaborations of the class. The responsibilities of a class are simply the messages it responds to (that is, the public methods it contains). The collaborations (or, collaborators, if you prefer) of a class are simply other classes that interact with the class by sending it messages or receiving messages from it.

More precisely, it is the objects of a class—not the class itself—that send or receive messages. However, it's convenient to speak in terms of messages sent by or received by a class, because any object of the class can send or receive such messages. Though this practice can sometimes be confusing, particularly for beginners, it is common; you should strive to grow accustomed to it, without forgetting that the usage is not really quite right.

> *" The name CRC card stands for class-responsibility-collaboration card. "*

PREPARING CRC CARDS FROM A COMPLETED DESIGN

To learn how to prepare CRC cards, you'll first study CRC cards that describe the Renter and Lender classes presented earlier. By comparing the CRC cards with an actual design, you'll better understand the relationship between the CRC cards and the design. In the next subsection, you'll learn how to prepare CRC cards from a problem summary paragraph.

Figure 5.3 shows a CRC card prepared for the Renter class. Notice how the front of the card identifies the class by name. Responsibilities are listed in the left-hand column, and corresponding collaborations are listed in the right-hand column. The back of the card gives a short description of the class and lists the attributes of the class. This is a subset of the information presented earlier in Table 5.1. Look back to that table and try to determine whether you can identify the information that appears there, but does not appear on the CRC card.

Class: Renter		Attributes:
		Lender object
Responsibilities:	**Collaborations:**	initial inventory quantity
		(for constructing Lender object)
rent item	Lender	
return item	Lender	The renter class provides a user interface that
display message from lender	N/A	allows the user to rent and return software bugs.
		It acts as a client object, making requests
		of the Lender object.
(Front of card)		(Back of card)

FIGURE 5.3

A CRC card for the
Renter class

You should have found that Table 5.1 includes implementation information that is not included in the CRC card for the Renter class. In other words, the CRC card represents the Renter class at a higher level of abstraction. Moreover, the attributes and responsibilities listed on the CRC card are listed using very general names rather than the names used in the Java program. Remember that CRC cards are prepared very early in the system design activity, long before code is actually written. It would be premature to attempt to identify fields and methods with Java-style names at the time CRC cards are written.

Another significant difference between Table 5.1 and the CRC card is that the CRC card lists two responsibilities, "rent item" and "return item," that do not appear in Table 5.1. Certainly, these are operations that a Renter object must be able to perform. Why, then, don't they appear in Table 5.1? The operations are embedded within the actionPerformed() method of the Renter class. Because Table 5.1 lists the methods of the Renter class, it does not include these operations implemented within the actionPerformed method. They're *logically* present within the actionPerformed() method, but they do not have distinct identities as the methods within the Renter class do.

It would certainly be possible to rewrite the Renter class to include two new methods, rentItem() and returnItem(). This would make it easier to spot the operations performed by Renter objects. But, it would also make the class somewhat longer.

Design involves a myriad of such decisions, wherein each alternative gains you something, but only at a price. Knowing which to choose is no simple matter. That's why good designs are usually the result of an iterative process. You make a decision that you later see was more costly than you'd originally thought. A conscientious designer will go back and try the other alternative. A lazy designer continues on course, sailing as blithely as the Titanic through a forest of icebergs. Because you're planning on being a conscientious designer, let's rewrite Renter.java to make the hidden operations more explicit. Listing 5.4 shows the relevant fragment of code.

Listing 5.4 The revised Renter class (partial listing)

```
//    =========================================
//       IMPLEMENT ACTIONLISTENER
//    =========================================
public void actionPerformed( ActionEvent ae )
{
  System.out.println("Event: " + ae);
  Object source = ae.getSource( );

  if (source == theRentButton)
    rentItem();
  else if (source == theReturnButton)
    returnItem();
}

public void rentItem()
{
  theLender.rentItem(this);
  displayQtyOnHand();
}

public void returnItem()
{
  theLender.returnItem(this);
  displayQtyOnHand();
}
```

This change has the added virtue of separating the operations performed by the class from the user interface (that is, the `actionPerformed()` method). This will make it easier to change the user interface, should that become necessary, because the `rentItem()` and `returnItem()` methods can be conveniently invoked by the revised user interface code.

Remember

Separating operations from the user interface that invokes them often yields a more maintainable program.

Okay, now it's your turn. Grab a 3×5 card and write a CRC card for the Lender class. Refer to Table 5.2 or Listing 5.3 for help. When you're done, compare your results with the CRC card shown in Figure 5.4.

How did you do? Did you find all the relevant attributes, responsibilities, and collaborations? If not, consider why the missing items are needed by the class. Did you find any additional attributes, responsibilities, or collaborations? If so, ask yourself whether they *must* be included in the class, or whether they merely represent one way of implementing an important interface.

PREPARING CRC CARDS FROM A PROBLEM SUMMARY STATEMENT

In the real world, CRC cards are prepared from a problem summary statement rather than from a completed design. The good news is that preparing them from a problem

Class: Lender	Attributes:
Responsibilities: Collaborations:	current inventory quality
rent item Renter return item Renter Supply current inventory Renter quantity	The Lender object tracks the inventory of bugs. It services requests sent by the Renter object.
(Front of card)	(Back of card)

FIGURE 5.4
A CRC card for the
Lender class

summary statement is only a little more difficult than preparing them from a completed design. Remember that as long as you keep iterating, design mistakes don't count. Thomas Edison, the famous inventor, offered the following maxim, which is a good design motto: "I failed my way to success."

Remember

Every design alternative examined and rejected leaves you with fewer alternatives to choose from. As long as you've picked a design problem that has a solution, every failure brings you one step closer to success. Of course, analyzing your failures and learning from them, rather than trying random alternatives, makes the process more efficient.

" Remember that as long as you keep iterating, design mistakes don't count. "

Chapter 6, "Round-Trip Design: A Case Study," presents a case study that will lead you through the entire design process, including the preparation of CRC cards, using an example problem. For now, here are some suggested ways of finding classes, responsibilities, and collaborations lurking in your problem statement:

- **Classes**—Read through the problem summary statement and identify nouns and noun phrases, placing them on a list. When the list is complete, review it for possible classes, which may be (for example) physical objects, concepts, categories of objects, or attributes of other objects.

- **Responsibilities**—Responsibilities relate to actions. A good starting place for finding responsibilities is in the verbs of the problem summary statement. List the verbs, decide which of them represent responsibilities that must be discharged by some class, and allocate each such responsibility to a class.

- **Collaborations**—After you've identified the classes and their responsibilities, finding the collaborations is easy. Simply scan the list of responsibilities of each class and identify any other classes it needs in order to fulfill its responsibilities. List these as its collaborations.

Finding the Classes

Look back to the problem summary statement and identify the noun and verb phrases it contains. Do this now, before reading further, so you can compare your results with those in Table 5.3.

TABLE 5.3
NOUNS AND VERBS OF THE PROBLEM SUMMARY STATEMENT

Nouns	Verbs
Renter applet	track inventory
bugs	rent bug
inventory	decrease inventory
user	return bug
message	increase inventory
	display message

Does your list resemble the one in Table 5.3? If you're missing one or more items, add them to your list. If you have extra items, stay tuned: you may have correctly identified some important items that are implicit in the problem summary statement.

Notice that the list of nouns and verbs is only vaguely similar to the CRC cards shown earlier. Remember that the list is a starting point. Moving from the list to the actual CRC cards is not automatic, and not always easy. Again, that's why design is iterative—don't be concerned.

Consider the list of nouns, which is intended to help you identify classes. The list has five nouns, but only two classes are described by CRC cards. How did this come about? The Renter class, you may recall, is an applet that represents the user (that is, the renter). The Renter class accounts for two of the four candidate classes appearing in the noun list: *Renter applet* and *user*.

What about the Lender class? Where did it come from? Often it's necessary that the design include classes that are merely implicit in the problem summary statement. The Lender class is such a class. Although it does not appear explicitly in the problem summary statement, you know that if there is a renter, there must be a lender.

What if you failed to make this important deduction? A subsequent step of the design process would help you realize your omission. At that point you'd create a CRC card for the class.

What about other classes implicit in the problem summary statement? For example, Thomas Aquinas concluded that there must be a "first cause" standing behind every action—does Aquinas's first cause need to be included on a CRC card? No, it doesn't. You want your design to be as sleek and elegant as possible. Cluttering it with classes whose responsibilities you only dimly realize runs counter to this goal.

Remember that the problem statement is intended to establish a fence around the system. The fence is not a perfect one, so you shouldn't worry too much when you discover a necessary class not mentioned in the problem statement or find that a class mentioned in the problem statement is not really necessary. However, when you find one of these imperfections, take that as a clue to revisit the problem statement, revising it when appropriate. Don't mindlessly add classes not found in the problem summary statement or mindlessly refuse to remove classes that do appear in the problem summary statement, if you find they contribute little to the design.

What about the remaining nouns, *bugs* and *inventory*? These really point to a single thing, an inventory of bugs. Why doesn't this class appear as a CRC card? Recall that in the Lender class the inventory was represented as an int, a primitive type. Conceptually, the inventory *does* represent an object. If you created a CRC card for the inventory, you did a good thing. But, later in the design you'll see that the demands the problem summary statement places on the inventory are quite simple. So simple, in fact, that the inventory can be represented using a Java primitive type, rather than an object.

Of course, you could insist on having it your way and represent the inventory as a third class. This, too, would be okay. In fact, you might find it easier to extend the capabilities of the program if the inventory were represented as an object rather than a primitive. Design decisions, like this one, often have no obvious right and wrong answers. A lot depends on what happens tomorrow (like a request to extend the inventory-related information tracked by the program), which is often anybody's guess. Certainly, when you *can* anticipate the future, you should attempt to accommodate it in your design. It's just that you won't often be wise and fortunate enough to be able to do this. If your forecasts are highly accurate, you can earn a great deal more money on Wall Street or in Las Vegas than by working as a software designer.

The final noun, *message*, is likewise not found on the CRC cards. It's implicit, however, in the responsibility of the Renter, which must be able to display a message sent by the Lender. Recall that the Renter provides the user interface, so the Lender cannot display the message. There's even an associated object in the source code—the TextField named theMessage. Why then is there no CRC card for the noun *message*? Well, it would not be wrong to have included one. But, the message doesn't seem to be a very important part of the program. The fact that it can be implemented using a standard component is a hint that this is the case. If you chose to include it, give yourself a pat on the back for having been very thorough and don't be further concerned.

> *" Design decisions…often have no obvious right and wrong answers. A lot depends on what happens tomorrow… "*

Discovering Responsibilities

The relationship between the verbs and the responsibilities is a little simpler, at least in this case. You won't always be so blessed. The *track inventory* verb is really a general term that refers to *decrease inventory* and *increase inventory*. These two actions are closely related to the operations of renting an item and returning an item, respectively. By combining the related responsibilities inherent in these five verbs, you're left with just two: renting an item and returning an item. Both the Renter and the Lender share these responsibilities, because each must act in concert to discharge them. Therefore, each CRC card includes both responsibilities.

This leaves you the *display message* verb to consider. This is a responsibility of the `Renter` class, and is shown on its CRC card.

If you review the CRC cards, you'll notice that the `Lender` class includes a responsibility that did not arise from the list of verbs. However, a careful reading of the problem summary statement shows that it includes the phrase *when the inventory is zero*. Yes, the verb phrase *is zero* was missed when the list was made. Usually some important verb phrases are missed. You'll discover these in a subsequent design step, at which point you can add the related responsibility to the appropriate CRC card.

Here, the verb phrase *is zero* implies that there is some way of determining the current inventory level. Thus, the `Lender` is responsible for reporting the current inventory quantity, as shown on the CRC card for the `Lender` class.

Describing the Object Collaborations and the Classes

After you've prepared the CRC cards, it's time to focus on the collaborations. By examining the collaborations, you may identify an important class you missed when preparing the CRC cards. You simply add a CRC card for any such class. You may also discover that a class for which you prepared a CRC card is not as important as it initially seemed. For any such class, you allocate its responsibilities and attributes to other classes and discard its CRC card. Finally, to document the collaborations you discover, you prepare a series of collaboration diagrams. This section shows you how.

PREPARING COLLABORATION DIAGRAMS

Just as CRC cards helped you discover classes, *use-case scenarios* help you discover and describe collaborations. A use-case is simply a transaction or a sequence of related operations that the system performs in response to a user request or event. In the Renter applet, two transactions are obvious: the user can rent a bug or the user can return a bug.

To apply the use-case scenario technique, you spread your CRC cards across a flat surface and walk through each use-case (transaction). During the walk-through, you try to identify the objects involved in the use-case and the messages they exchange. It's helpful to move the CRC cards around, grouping them so that classes that often collaborate are located near one another. If you have a magnetic white board, you can fasten the CRC cards to it and draw lines between the classes, showing the messages involved in a use-case.

To document the use-cases, you should prepare a series of *collaboration diagrams*. Several styles of collaboration diagrams are commonly used. Figure 5.5 shows a collaboration diagram for the use-case of renting a bug.

FIGURE 5.5

*A collaboration diagram
for the Rent use-case*

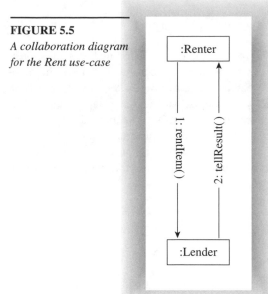

The diagram shows two objects, one `Renter` object and one `Lender` object, that exchange two messages. The first message, `rentItem()`, is sent by the `Renter` object to the `Lender` object. The second message, `tellResult()`, is a response sent by the `Lender` to the `Renter`. Notice that each message is numbered so that its sequence of execution is explicit.

In the diagram, the two objects are named using their class names. More generally, objects are named using the form *objectName : className*. This technique can handle the possibility that multiple objects of a single class interact in a use-case. Where specific object names are not needed, as in Figure 5.5, the form *: className* is used. Including the colon makes it clear that a class name, not an object name, is meant.

Now, it's your turn once again. Before reading on, draw your own collaboration diagram for the Return use-case. You can look back at the CRC cards and the problem summary statement for help. When you're done, compare your results with Figure 5.6.

Hopefully, your diagram closely resembles that shown in Figure 5.6. If not, study the differences between your diagram and Figure 5.6, and look back at Figure 5.5 to determine where you went wrong.

The goal of walking through the use-cases is not simply to produce the collaboration diagrams. Helpful though the diagrams are, they're not the most important part of this step of the design process. Often, as you walk through a transaction, you'll discover the need for additional attributes, the need to collaborate with additional classes beyond those identified on the CRC cards, or even the need to define additional classes. Whenever you find such a discrepancy, you should iterate: Go back and correct the CRC cards, re-check your bearings, and resume forward movement.

FIGURE 5.6

*A collaboration diagram
for the Return use-case*

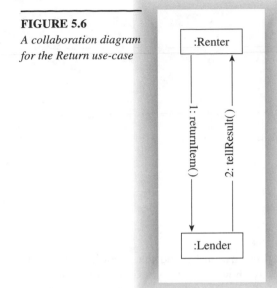

How do you prepare use-case diagrams without being able to cheat by looking at source code or lists of methods? The techniques taught in Chapter 7 will provide considerable help. It turns out that there are several common ways in which objects interact. By knowing these ways, you can quickly focus your attention on the most salient possibilities. Constructing an interaction diagram is then pretty much a piece of cake.

For now, strive to use the principle of decomposition to simplify the problem. Begin a fresh collaboration diagram for each use-case by drawing rectangles for each collaborating object, as shown on the CRC cards. Then, break the action involved in the use-case into a series of steps, identifying a message that triggers each step. Simply label the collaboration diagram with these messages and you're done.

Don't fret too much about getting things right the first time. Remember that, because design is iterative, you'll get (at least) a second chance.

PREPARING CLASS DIAGRAMS

Though CRC cards are helpful during design, they're not very convenient for later reference. After you've completed the collaboration diagrams, you transfer information from each CRC card onto a class diagram. Figure 5.7 shows a class diagram of the Renter class. As you can see, like the CRC cards, a class diagram describes the attributes and methods of a class.

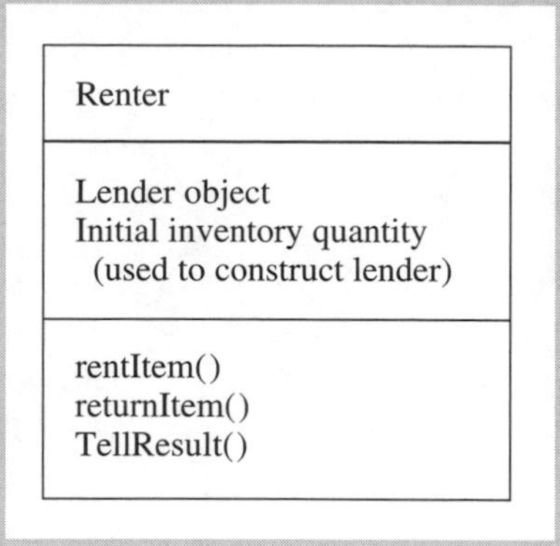

FIGURE 5.7
A class diagram of the
Renter class

Renter
Lender object Initial inventory quantity (used to construct lender)
rentItem( ) returnItem( ) TellResult( )

Class diagrams, however, can include information beyond that recorded on a CRC card. For attributes, the class diagram may show the data type and initial value. For methods, the class diagram may show the arguments, their data types, and the return data type. Figure 5.8 shows an example of a more detailed class diagram.

The syntax used to describe attributes in the detailed class diagram is

```
attribute : type = initialValue
```

where *attribute* is the name of the attribute, *type* is its data type, and *initialValue* is its initial value. Either the type and its associated colon (:) or the initial value and its associated equal sign (=) may be omitted. The syntax used to describe methods is

```
returnType method (argumentList)
```

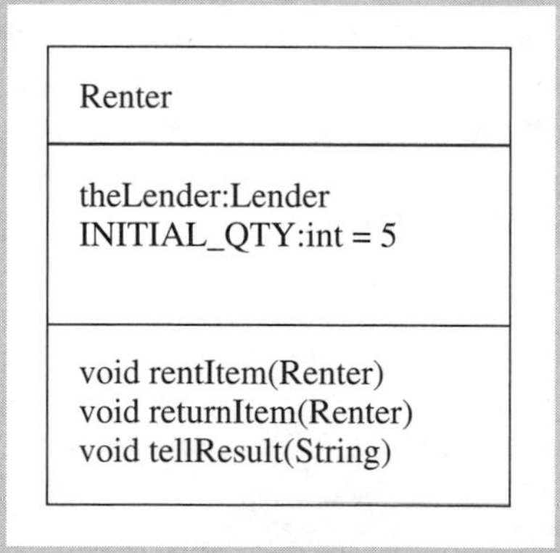

FIGURE 5.8
A more detailed class
diagram of the
Renter class

Renter
theLender:Lender INITIAL_QTY:int = 5
void rentItem(Renter) void returnItem(Renter) void tellResult(String)

where *method* is the name of the method, `argumentList` is an optional list of arguments, and `returnType` is the data type returned by the method. Entries within the argument list are separated by commas, each entry taking the same form as that given previously to describe attributes. The return data type and its associated colon can be omitted.

You can use the detailed form of the class diagram to document the implementation, as well as the interface, of a class. This is done by prefixing the keyword `public` or `private`, as appropriate, to the line describing each attribute or method. This is not shown in the figure, but you'll use this technique in later chapters.

How do you decide between the style of class diagram shown in Figure 5.7 and that shown in Figure 5.8? Simple. Your class diagram should include all the information you know. If you've decided what data type or initial value an attribute should have, then you should note it on the class diagram. Don't compel yourself to include information of which you're not yet certain. Before implementation begins, you must decide all the data types and so forth. But, many trips through the design activity may occur before you arrive at that point.

Now it's your turn. Before reading on, review the CRC card for the `Lender` class and draw a class diagram for the class. If you want, you can look back to the source code for the class and draw a detailed class diagram. When you're done, compare your results with the diagram shown as Figure 5.9.

The figure shows a detailed class diagram. If you drew a conceptual diagram rather than a detailed diagram, your version will lack some of the features shown.

Sketching the User Interface

The final step in designing an object-oriented program is designing its user interface. Chapter 15 addresses user interface design in detail. For now, a few words of explanation and advice will suffice.

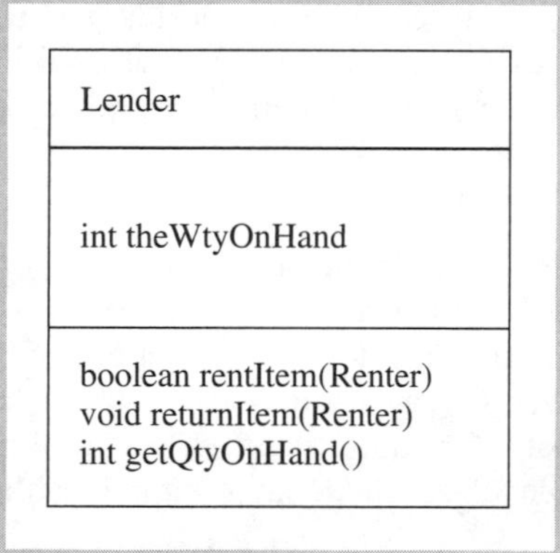

FIGURE 5.9

A detailed class diagram of the Lender class

Lender
int theWtyOnHand
boolean rentItem(Renter) void returnItem(Renter) int getQtyOnHand()

The user interface is important to the user, because it's the part of the system that's visible. It's important to show the user, as soon and as accurately as possible, what the user interface will look like.

To a system user, the user interface *is* the system.

You can sketch a user interface using pencil and paper, or you can use a drawing program. But, the best way to sketch a user interface is using your Java interactive development environment (IDE). Many IDEs provide facilities that help you lay out a user interface, letting you (for example) place buttons and text boxes on the screen and arrange them appropriately.

If your IDE provides such a facility, then by all means use it. Lay out a sample user interface and print it, if your IDE provides a way to do so. Otherwise, capture the screen and use a paint program or word processor to print the user interface.

Better still, if time is available, create a prototype of the user interface. A *prototype* is simply a working model of your finished program. Give a copy of the prototype to the user so the user can try it out. Often, you'll receive valuable feedback. Translation: often the user will tell you in clear terms that you've completely misunderstood what's required. As uncomfortable as this may be, it's better to learn this now than after you've spent weeks or months implementing an unsatisfactory system.

Remember

" [T]he best way to sketch a user interface is using your Java interactive development environment (IDE). "

Rules of Thumb for Designing Classes and Objects

Here are some useful rules of thumb for designing classes and objects. Not all of them will apply in every case and there's at least one case where any given one will lead you astray. But, every one of them is useful often enough to be worth knowing and considering as you design:

- **Minimize collaborations between classes.** It's stressful meeting the expectations of one's many fans: a class that collaborates too widely is likely to die of an early heart attack. Consider splitting such a case into two or more classes or reallocating its responsibilities among several other classes. Otherwise, changes to the highly collaborative class will compel changes to its collaborating classes. Each such change will spread across your system like a tidal wave across a flat beach.

- **Beware the hermit.** In a simple design like that of the Renter applet, it's common to have "hermit" classes that are used to instantiate only a single object or messages that handle only a count of one. This is a possible sign of trouble, however, in real-world systems, which generally handle greater volumes of information and therefore need more sociable objects. Often, for example, users who today want to be able to rent a single item in a transaction turn out tomorrow to want to be able to rent multiple items: be prepared.

⚫ **Allocate responsibility equitably.** You can eliminate classes that don't collaborate at all, but you should also question classes that have limited collaboration. Perhaps another class has too much responsibility, some of which should be transferred to its thinner partners.

⚫ **Prune unproductive responsibilities.** You can eliminate any responsibilities that are not called on by any collaborators. They contribute nothing and are, therefore, not deserving of the effort involved in implementing them.

Summary

The steps of the object-oriented design process presented in this chapter are

1. Determine the requirements.
2. Identify the classes and objects.
3. Describe the object collaborations and the classes.
4. Sketch the user interface.

To determine the requirements, it's helpful to write a problem summary paragraph. Focusing on the nouns and verbs of the problem summary paragraph will help you to identify the classes, responsibilities, and collaborations the program must provide. These are recorded using CRC cards, which also list the data attributes of each class. Object collaborations are studied by walking through the use-cases for the system and preparing collaboration diagrams that describe the use-cases. Data is transferred from CRC cards to class diagrams, which are more convenient to reference during subsequent software development activities.

The final step of object-oriented design is designing the user interface. The user interface is important because it is visible to the user. Prototyping is a useful tool for modeling the user interface.

The object-oriented design process is iterative. Steps are performed multiple times and earlier steps are revisited as necessary in order to satisfactorily resolve design issues.

Questions

1. Analysis of a system begins by writing a _____ paragraph.
   a. Problem summary
   b. Solution summary
   c. Transaction summary
   d. Use-case

2. CRC cards are used to identify _____, responsibilities, and _____.

3. When an object sends a message to another object, the two objects are said to _____.

    a. collaborate

    b. communicate

    c. server

    d. transact

4. An object that receives a message has the _____ for handling it.

5. A collaboration diagram depicts the sequence in which objects exchange messages in a single _____ scenario.

6. A class diagram specifies the _____ and _____ of a class.

7. To a system user, the user interface is the _____.

8. The design process is _____, meaning that the process and its steps may be performed multiple times.

    a. inaccurate

    b. iterative

    c. open

    d. tentative

9. A good tool for helping the user visualize the user interface is _____.

10. A detailed class diagram may show the implementation of a class as well as the interface of the class (true/false).

Exercises

1. Write a problem summary statement that describes a system that could be used by a library to administer its circulation system. The system should include provisions for fines due for late return and for handling lost items.

2. Write a problem summary statement that describes a system that could be used by a bank to control its ATM machines. The system should allow customers to make both deposits and withdrawals.

3. Write a problem summary statement that describes a customer support system that could operate on the Web. The system should allow customers to post questions and requests, and to view questions and answers posted by others. The system should track open questions so that customer support representatives can address the oldest pending questions before moving on to newer ones.

4. For any of your problem summary statements prepared for exercises 1–3, prepare a set of CRC cards that further describes the system.

5. For any of your problem summary statements prepared for exercises 1–3, prepare collaboration diagrams that further describe the system.

6. For any of your problem summary statements prepared for exercises 1–3 , prepare class diagrams that further describe the system.

7. For any of your problem summary statements prepared for exercises 1–3 , prepare a user interface sketch that further describes the system.

8. For any of your problem summary statements prepared for exercises 1–3 , prepare a Java user interface prototype that further describes the system.

To Learn More

The following books will help you learn more about designing objects and classes.

The first book of a series that will present Unified Modeling Language (UML), an important *de facto* standardization of notations for modeling object-oriented software, is:

Fowler, Martin, with Kendall Scott. *UML Distilled: Applying the Standard Object Modeling Language.* Reading, Massachusetts: Addison-Wesley, 1997.

These books present the approach to object-oriented analysis and design developed by Grady Booch:

Booch, Grady. *Object-Oriented Analysis and Design with Applications, 2nd ed.* Redwood City, California: Benjamin/Cummings, 1994.

White, Iseult. *Using the Booch Method: A Rational Approach.* Redwood City, California: Benjamin/Cummings, 1994.

Useful books describing other approaches to object-oriented design include the following:

Rumbaugh, James, et al. *Object-Oriented Modeling and Design.* Englewood Cliffs, New Jersey: Prentice Hall, 1991.

Wirfs-Brock, Rebecca, Brian Wilkerson, and Lauren Wiener. *Designing Object-Oriented Software.* Englewood Cliffs, New Jersey: Prentice Hall, 1990.

Wilkinson, Nancy. *Using CRC Cards: An Informal Approach to Object-Oriented Development.* New York: SIGS, 1995.

The following book is focused on C++. Nevertheless, many of its clearly stated principles apply equally well to the design and implementation of Java programs:

Horstmann, Cay. *Mastering Object-Oriented Design in C++.* New York: John Wiley & Sons, 1995.

6

Round-Trip Design: A Case Study

In the previous chapters, you learned techniques for implementing and designing robust classes and objects. But as you saw in Chapter 2, object-oriented design involves more than technology and notation; it also involves a process and the people who implement that process. In this chapter, you'll follow the design of a larger program, from the problem summary statement through the sketch of the user interface. Subsequent chapters will expand on what you've learned, looking closely at specific techniques and issues.

The centerpiece case study of this chapter completes the round-trip journey you began in Chapter 4, "Encapsulation: Classes and Methods." There, you first learned how to take a concept and create a working model by using the Java programming language. Then, in Chapter 5, "Designing Classes and Objects," you took some code and used it as a point of reference for learning how to prepare various object-oriented design artifacts: a problem summary statement, CRC cards, class diagrams, collaboration diagrams, and a user-interface sketch.

Normally, however, you won't write the software first and then prepare the design; usually things work the other way around. This chapter simulates a real-world situation much more faithfully. You won't begin with code. Instead, you will begin with a mere idea inside a user's head. From this idea—given sweat, tenacity, and the principles of object-oriented design—a program eventually emerges. You won't study the program itself in this chapter, although you'll take the design far enough that only your Java programming skills will stand between you and a working program. Later chapters will present principles of database design and network design necessary to

> *" From a mere idea—given sweat, tenacity, and the principles of object-oriented design—a program eventually emerges. "*

scale up the program into an industrial-strength application, ready for full-scale deployment and use.

This chapter introduces no new design techniques or notations, but does show how design is actually done—including the good, the bad, and the ugly. You'll view the members of a design team through the eyes of one Jason D'Naught, lead designer and doughnut aficionado. Pay careful attention to Jason's observations; he is an experienced (but not infallible) designer, who *usually* knows how things should be done. He doesn't always succeed in moving events down an ideal path, however. Jason's observations will help you distinguish what happens from what should happen.

In this chapter you will learn:

- How to apply object-oriented techniques to a medium-sized program

- How the object-oriented design process can be performed by a team

- How the object-oriented design process involves iteration—moving between different activities, which might themselves involve cycles of repetition

- How doughnuts and related foodstuffs act to facilitate the design process

Day 1: The System Concept

"I've sure enjoyed these last few weeks," you think to yourself, as you prepare for the morning's meeting. "It's been great being able to catch up on the backlog of technical journals and being able to attend that conference on using genetic algorithms to test object-oriented software."

"Still," you reflect, returning to the reality of the moment, "it'll be good to be back in the design saddle again. And this new system that Dawn mentioned sounds like a real time-saver for everyone. That expense report accounting system I did last year just about ruined my reputation; I guess not everyone is a fan of efficiency."

Glancing at your watch, which blinks 9:27 a.m., you start to head out for the meeting when you realize that you don't recall where it's being held. "Hey, this new scheduling system would be real handy right now," you think to yourself as you dig through the stack of memos piled on the corner of your desk.

"Aha, there it is. Archaeological order is once again shown to be the most efficient ordering! Let's see, conference room #2 at 9:30 a.m. Hmm, conference room #2—oh yeah, that's the one over in building #4." At a brisk trot you begin the 10-minute walk, knowing it's unlikely that you'll be the last to arrive, despite your late start.

AT THE MEETING

Arriving at conference room #2 you see that, just as you'd hoped, several others haven't yet arrived. You greet those present in abbreviated fashion, having spotted an open box of doughnuts at the opposite end of the long conference table. "First things first," you murmur under your breath, making a beeline for the refreshments.

Long accustomed to the beauty of the New England autumn, you scarcely notice the landscape framed by the long window of the conference room. Swooping toward the box, you hope that there's a chocolate eclair waiting there for you, but your hopes are dashed. Settling for a chocolate doughnut with chocolate sprinkles, you turn your attention to the steam rising from a coffee urn atop the credenza that runs along the far wall. Selecting a generous mug, you pour yourself an equally generous portion of the hot coffee. Inhaling the aroma before you taste, you note a disagreeable hint of hazelnut. Your taste confirms the accusation. "Trick coffee," you think. "Still, better than no coffee at all."

Snagging a second consolation doughnut on the way, you navigate around the cape formed by the end of the table and return to your seat. Soon, you perceive the combined effect of the coffee's caffeine and the doughnut's sugar as it kicks in. "Ahh," you sigh, entering that strange combination of hyperalertness and relaxation produced by your morning feast.

THE TEAM ARRIVES

Just then, two more participants arrive and Dawn Davis urges everyone to take their seats. Aware that the meeting will soon begin, you focus your temporarily enhanced mental powers on the task of reviewing what you know about the other members of the project team:

- **Dawn Davis, manager of Human Resources**. Dawn is the originator of the system concept you're here to discuss and is also responsible for convening the current meeting. After reviewing her proposal for a meeting scheduling system, the Information Systems Steering Committee gave her the responsibility for directing the system implementation project. On other projects, that role has often fallen to you. However, you don't relish the social and political tasks that the role requires, and so you're grateful they'll be on someone else's plate this time around.

- **Fred Farnsworth**. Fred is a new guy in your department. As your boss, the director of Information Systems, explained it to you, Fred is here to "learn the ropes" from you, so that subsequently he can take responsibility for designing and programming systems. Observing that Fred is a decade or more years your senior, you wonder how it is that he finds himself in such a junior role at this point in his career.

- **Barney Rupert**. The new intern, lately departed from the Marketing department, now seems more or less on permanent assignment to the Information Systems area. He is in his late 20s—bright, ever enthusiastic, and talkative. Apparently, he's here to represent the interests and concerns of office staff who'll use the proposed system.

- **Barbara Baskin**. Barbara ("call me Barb") represents the Engineering department. You and Barb have worked together on earlier projects. You know her to be sober-minded and direct, qualities you value and admire in a project team member. You know you won't get any fluff or waffle from Barb, that she'll get right down to business, tell you what she knows and what she wants, and then stand back and let you work. As you see it, her presence is a favorable sign.

Your thoughts are interrupted by Dawn's take-charge voice, as she calls the meeting to order and distributes the meeting agenda. After making the preliminary introductions, Dawn explains that several others will soon be added to the project team, and that this initial project team meeting will wrap up before lunch. Subsequent meetings, she tells the team, will be held daily at the same time and place, until the system is ready to hand over to the programmers.

INTRODUCING THE PLAN

"I'm going to start by giving you an overview of the proposed system," begins Dawn, simultaneously switching on the overhead projector at the end of the conference table and passing out a thick packet to each team member. Dimming the lights, Dawn begins to recite the proposal she recently presented to the Information Systems Steering Committee, and your interest flags a little.

"All these proposals look the same," you observe to yourself, "Costs, benefits, justification, risks—when does it end?" Always one to prefer actually developing a system to arguing about whether a system should—or should not—be developed, you're relieved when the talk turns to specifics.

"The program we're going to build," Dawn continues, "is a scheduling system that will allow our workers to quickly and easily schedule meetings with other individuals and groups. It will be deployed over our organizational intranet and, if some security issues can be worked out, will be available on the Internet as well. Then you'll be able to schedule meetings or check and update your schedule from anywhere in the world. Even in its first incarnation, we expect that the program can do a lot to make it easier for our workers to communicate.

"Since this is a general-purpose program," Dawn went on, "we first considered buying a package, instead of building it. Many on the IS Steering Committee still favor such an approach. The majority agree, however, that building our own system will allow us to better integrate the scheduling system with our other information systems. And by designing this system to be implemented as a Java applet, we hope to easily deploy it throughout the company. Anyone with a Web browser and a password can access the system—there will be no additional software to install. In the future, perhaps all of our software will be built like this. Of course, that depends on how well things go with this project."

"Boy, nothing like starting with a bit of pressure," you think, as the room lights are returned to their pre-presentation intensity. To your surprise, Dawn announces a 10-minute break. "Wow," you note, after examining your watch, "it's 10:30 already."

As the others leave the room to check for phone messages or email, you casually wander over to the doughnut box, where you discover a single remaining donut, one decorated with rainbow sprinkles. Feeling you've earned it by your patient attention during Dawn's presentation, you snag it and commence munching, savoring contentedly the gooey, sweet icing you know to be high in saturated fats.

JASON HAS A PROBLEM

Promptly at 10:40, as several of the others are just entering the room to resume their places around the table, Dawn reconvenes the meeting. "Jason," you hear her say, as mention of your name snaps your mind from doughnut-land back to the here and now, "will facilitate the second half of today's session, during which we'll jointly develop a problem summary statement."

Instantly forcing down the last bite of doughnut and biting back the urge to protest, you rise to your feet and to the occasion. Grabbing a bright blue dry erase marker left randomly on the table by participants of a previous meeting, you stride toward the whiteboard, greeting the project team as you go, in your best take-charge voice, "Okay, folks, let's get started.

"This morning we're going to try and nail down exactly what features and functions our new meeting scheduling system should have. It's important that we have as much input as possible, and I want all of you to feel free to offer any suggestions at all. There's no such thing as a stupid suggestion," you continue in your most reassuring tone, "so please just jump right in. What do you think that the scheduling system should do in order to achieve these benefits Dawn has identified?"

"It should let us describe our own daily schedules and let us schedule meetings with others, based on mutual availability," suggests Barb.

"Great," you offer as encouragement to Barb and the others. You know your job will be made easier if suggestions flow freely. Using the blue marker, you write the functions identified by Barb as separate, numbered items:

1. Let workers describe their schedules.

2. Let workers schedule meetings with others, based on mutual availability.

"What else?" you ask.

"Well, wouldn't it be great if the system kept track of everybody's birthday?" suggests Barney. "Then, we could use it to plan parties. We'd never miss anybody's birthday again. And holidays. The system should keep track of holidays. Then, if a group of us want to go skiing or something, we could put that into the system and everybody would know all the details and more people would be able to come with us. This'll be *sooo* cool."

Knowing from experience that too much critical analysis can stifle creative problem solving, you add Barney's suggestions to the list, even though you're convinced they're irrelevant or worse:

3. Keep track of workers' birthdays.

4. Keep track of holidays.

5. Help plan holiday outings.

Dawn, you notice, is holding back, allowing you to take control of the meeting. As a system development veteran, you surmise that she's confident the group will converge on a proper problem summary statement without much direct input from her. Preferring to reserve her leadership prerogatives for the inevitable squabbles yet to come, she's apparently holding her fire.

" Too much critical analysis can stifle creative problem solving. "

Your technical cohort, Fred, pipes up with a suggestion. "We really need to make sure that everyone has the latest TCP/IP drivers," he states with great conviction, "and we should consider adding LZH compression to the message store; otherwise, it'll be too slow over dial-up." You know that this is neither the time nor place for considering such technical details, but you also want to keep ideas flowing. Mechanically, you add Fred's misplaced concerns to the growing list:

6. Use the latest TCP/IP drivers.

7. Use LZH compression techniques.

"What else?" you ask. When, after some seconds, no additional ideas have surfaced, you suggest that the group review and discuss the functions identified so far. This, you explain, may lead the group to discover additional functions or help them understand why one or more of the functions already on the list should be removed.

Barney asks warily, "What's a TCP/IP driver anyway?" In response, Fred begins a technical lecture on the relative merits of different TCP/IP stacks, protocols, and implementations. You note that his grasp of the technical principles is impressive, but that his lack of audience awareness is even more impressive. Barney obviously has no idea what Fred means.

Breaking in on Fred, you muster your most authoritative tones, "Really, these are implementation issues that are better addressed later by the programmers than now by us. Fred, you've got some great ideas here. Why don't you draft a short memo that will help the programmers better understand the issues involved in choosing a TCP/IP stack? We can leave that decision to them and move on." As you pronounce a judgment of doom on Fred's contribution, you simultaneously line through items 6 and 7 on the whiteboard, in an attempt to demonstrate finally your control of the situation. Looking at Fred, you notice he doesn't seem all that unhappy. Apparently, your suggestion that he help educate the programmers sufficiently softened the blow of rejecting his contributions.

"What about the remaining functions?" you ask. A lively discussion ensues, at the end of which you're instructed to line out items 3 and 5. According to the consensus view, the system should keep track of holidays, but not birthdays or worker outings. Barney seems disappointed, but the disappointment is only sufficient to reduce his enthusiasm to about 125 percent that of the typical person. He's still as enthusiastic and talkative as ever, you note.

Discovering that it's almost time for lunch, Dawn brings the meeting to a close, directing you to draft a problem summary statement for review at tomorrow's meeting. As you and the others file out of the conference room, you're pleased to have made it through the session in one piece. Although you weren't initially happy to discover so late your role in the meeting, you now realize that you've been spared the several hours of preparation you'd have spent if Dawn had notified you earlier to be prepared to lead the session. "Looking at it that way, it almost sounds good," you conclude.

AFTER THE MEETING: THE PROBLEM SUMMARY STATEMENT

Back at your office after lunch, you begin drafting the problem summary statement. You've hardly begun when Dawn drops by. "So, how'd you think it went?" she asks.

"I'd say things are off to a good start," you offer, deciding not to raise the issue of being put on the spot. Anxious, however, to avoid a repeat, you ask, "What's on tap for tomorrow?"

"I thought we'd do that thing with the index cards," she responds, obviously referring to CRC cards. "Can you handle the session?" she asks.

"No problem," you reply casually, thinking yourself lucky to have advance notice.

"Great! I'll see you there," you hear, as Dawn vanishes down the hallway before you can ask any questions.

Settling down to work on the problem summary statement again, you come up with the following:

Meeting Scheduling System: Problem Summary Statement

The meeting scheduling system lets workers specify their schedules and lets them organize meetings with others, based on mutual availability. The system also tracks company holidays, preventing workers from attempting to schedule a meeting when no one is likely to be available.

Thinking how awkward it can be to have a computer prevent you from doing something you want to do, you revise the statement slightly, changing the part about *preventing* to *informing*. Then, thinking about work schedules, you realize that many people have the same, or nearly the same, work schedule from week to week. It would be helpful if the system allowed users to enter a standard schedule. Then they could make adjustments for just those days that fail to fit the standard schedule. This would simplify considerably the task of entering the schedule. You decide to add this function to the problem summary statement. If the others object, you can simply remove it.

Noticing that it's time to pick up the kids for soccer, you quickly key the changes and click the Print button. Checking the output for accuracy, you place it on top of your desk, where it will be easy to find tomorrow morning. Having done your duty for the day, you race to the parking lot and head off to chauffeur the kids.

LESSONS LEARNED: DAY 1

The first step in any software-development process is assembling a team and defining your product. A joint session spent drafting a problem statement is a good way to develop both. At this stage, you can't have too much input. As a facilitator, you can use the simple brainstorming technique Jason employed—listing features on a white-board—to get the other team members involved and to get them to feel that they have a part in the project.

As a leader, it's important that you don't dictate the system features but allow them to emerge from the process. On the other hand, you need to keep the discussion on track. Jason illustrated skill in both areas by accepting Barney's birthday suggestions without comment, allowing the group consensus to eliminate them, and by deflecting Fred's attempts to introduce technical details into the discussion.

> *"When drafting a problem statement, you can never have too much input."*

> *"As a leader, it's important that you don't dictate the system features but allow them to emerge from the process."*

Day 2: Preparing CRC Cards

The next morning you arrive as usual around 9 a.m. You're relieved to discover that you've received no hot emails overnight. All you need to do is make copies of the problem summary statement and get over to conference room #2 by 9:30. Knowing that the office copier is probably still stiff from a night of rest, you print several additional copies of the problem summary statement with your office printer. As you dash out the door, you remember that today you'll be doing CRC cards. You grab a pack of 3×5 index cards out of your top-right desk drawer and get on your way again.

Arriving a few minutes early, you find that Barney is the only team member already on station. He greets you and immediately begins to share his disappointment over yesterday's outcome, attempting to cajole you into breaking ranks with the team consensus. "If only the new scheduling system could track birthdays, I just know everyone would love it." Fortunately, Dawn arrives before you can respond, and you're spared the need to reply, as Dawn and Barney take up another subject of conversation. Grabbing a doughnut and some coffee, you count your blessings.

Soon the others arrive and Dawn calls the meeting to order. "You made copies of the problem summary statement for everyone, didn't you, Jason? Why don't you hand them out and we'll take a look?" she asks, more by way of command than question. You move around the room, passing out your revised problem summary statement, which looks like this:

Meeting Scheduling System: Problem Summary Statement

The meeting scheduling system lets workers specify their schedules and lets them organize meetings with others, based on mutual availability. The system also tracks company holidays, informing workers who attempt to schedule a meeting when no one is likely to be available.

The system allows a user to enter a standard work schedule. The schedule for a given week is based on this standard schedule, but the user can modify it as needed to handle schedule differences that arise from week to week.

You point out the function you added and explain how it will make it easier for workers to enter their schedule in the system. There's some discussion, a good part of which is off-track. But when you call for the question, even if some fail to understand your change, all agree to it—at least no disagreement is voiced. You're relieved you don't have to explain the change a second time.

Dawn then remembers to explain that no final decision has yet been made on additional members of the project team. For the time being, the present group will be the entire team. Although some team members seem concerned that this means fewer shoulders to carry the load, you're privately relieved. You know that things will proceed much more quickly with a smaller group. And you're confident that this group has all the knowledge of the organization required to make good decisions relating to this project. "When it comes to project teams, small really is beautiful," you remind yourself. "It's sort of like what Einstein said about models. You could say that a team should 'be as small as possible, but no smaller.'"

CRAZY RANDOM CHOICES?

Preliminary business out of the way, Dawn motions for you to come back to the head of the table. "Jason is going to lead the rest of our meeting this morning," she says, heading for her seat at the back of the room. "I understand we're going to create CRC cards today."

To your surprise, Barb, never known for her spontaneous humor, speaks up. "What's the CRC stand for Jason? Crazy random choices?" Still looking at Dawn, you notice she's suppressing a grin. The rest of the team is smiling.

"Don't you watch *E.R.*?" chimes in Barney. "It's how they resuscitate people when their heart stops." The team is quietly chuckling now, as Dawn speaks up. "That's CPR, Barney, not CRC. Why don't you give us a little introduction to CRC cards, Jason?"

Barney, with his irrepressible enthusiasm, seems none the worse for the correction, and you're thankful for the opportunity to get things back on track.

"Yesterday," you start in, "we talked about what we wanted the new scheduling system to do—its functionality. But software is made up of pieces or parts. In the programming language we use, Java, those parts are called *classes*. Now I know that many of you have no programming background," you hastily interject, noticing that Barney's smile is fading a bit. "We aren't here to ask you to learn about programming. Instead, we're going to define the classes inside our system from the inside out, by defining what each part is supposed to do."

"We're going to start by looking at a single function that you might want the new system to accomplish—schedule a meeting, for instance—and then we'll look at the steps and the parts necessary to accomplish that. We call each of these functions a 'use case,' and we call the steps that each part (class) needs to accomplish the 'class responsibilities.' That's where the *CR* in CRC comes from—it stands for Class Responsibility. The final *C* stands for Collaboration. As we look at the system, we'll all discover that some classes will have to work together—that is, collaborate—with other classes."

By now, you have the entire team's attention, although you notice that Barney still looks a little dubious. Putting on your most confident and reassuring smile, you look right at him and say, "Ready? Let's get started. Take the problem statement in front of you and underline the nouns and verbs."

Moving to the front of the room, you divide the whiteboard into two halves, using a vertical line. On the left section of the board, you write the heading *Noun Phrases*. On the right, you add *Verb Phrases*. To get things moving, you go around the room, asking each member to read one noun phrase and one verb phrase from the problem summary statement in front of them. As each phrase is called out, you record it on the board. When you're done, the board looks like this:

Noun Phrases	Verb Phrases
Worker	Specify schedule
Schedule	Organize meeting
Meeting	Enter standard schedule
Holiday	Enter schedule modifications
Standard schedule	
Schedule modification	

"Not bad!" you say, hoping to keep things going. "We've already defined our set of tentative classes." By using the index cards, you create CRC cards for each of the following:

- Worker
- Schedule
- Standard schedule
- Meeting
- Holiday

You get no further than this when Dawn announces a break. As everyone scurries off, you stay behind and ponder the evolving design, fortified with a fresh mug of joe and an opulent eclair inexplicably overlooked by the others. By the time the rest of the team returns, after you lick the last smudge of custard off your thumb and refill your mug, you are ready to pick up right where you left off, almost as though there'd been no hiatus.

REFINING THE CLASSES

"Generally," you explain, "some of the tentative classes aren't classes at all, but merely attributes of classes. Does anyone see any examples of this in our list of tentative classes?"

"Well," Barb removes her pen from her mouth, but not quite before she begins to speak, "I see Schedule and Standard Schedule as attributes of Worker, and I'd prefer that we renamed the Worker class to Participant to emphasize the Worker's role that's relevant here."

Hearing no objection, you set aside the cards for Schedule and Standard Schedule. You cross out *Worker* and replace it with *Participant* on the CRC card that will represent the Participant class. Finally, you add the attributes Schedule and Standard Schedule to the back of the card.

"Okay, now let's add a brief description to the back of each CRC card," you direct the group. Within a short period, the group has settled on the following descriptions:

- Participant—A worker who is scheduled to attend a meeting

- Meeting—A group of workers who come together at a set time and place and work together for a set interval

- Holiday—An interval during which, by company policy, no one is available for meetings

"Just a second," interrupts Dawn, "I think we need another class. Every meeting occurs someplace—an office or a conference room, for example. Currently, we keep a schedule for the conference rooms, to avoid workers scheduling simultaneous meetings. I think the system should handle that function."

Everyone readily agrees, so you create a CRC card for the new class, describing it as

Location—A place where a meeting is to be held.

"I have some other classes, too," offers Fred. "We need a class to represent the user interface and another to represent the database back end."

"You're right, Fred," you begin, hoping not to step too heavily on Fred's technical toes, "these objects will have to be persistent and so we'll need a database of some sort. And the interface to that database should be represented as a class. But I'd like to put that issue off for a bit. I do agree with your suggestion to add a class that stands in for the user. Let's call it User."

The others pay little heed to your discussion with Fred, seeing it as shop talk of little relevance to them. You know that making this call yourself was a little beyond your role as facilitator. But much time could have been wasted on issues not yet ripe for decision. You create the CRC card for the User class, describing it as follows:

User: the worker interacting with the system.

ENUMERABLE ATTRIBUTES

Now, starting with the Participant class, you take the classes one by one, inviting team members to identify the data attributes of each class. You encourage the team to call out attributes without arguing about whether a given attribute is needed. As you explain, "There'll be plenty of time for discussion in a moment. The goal now is to come up with as complete a list as possible within a short time."

When a minute or so has passed without anyone proposing a new attribute, you find the team has arrived at the following list of candidate attributes for `Participant`:

- Name
- Employee number
- Office location
- Telephone number
- Email address
- Birth date
- Schedule

You now ask the team to consider which, if any, of the attributes aren't really needed. Fred, having had obvious difficulty suppressing his urge to speak, suggests deletion of the `Birth date` attribute. The others, except Barney, quickly agree and Barney himself finally accedes, chagrined that he has again failed to establish a mandate for birthday tracking.

Barb initiates a discussion of the need to include office location. Some argue that workers with offices in building #3 may need extra time to travel to a meeting location in some other building, so it's important to know who these workers are. Others point out that the worker should be responsible for arriving on time. In the end, all agree to delete the attribute.

Dawn asks whether the system needs to include the worker's name, because the employee number can be used to access that information in the human resources database. Knowing the poor reputation for reliability of the human resources system, you suggest that it would be best not to integrate the two systems. Dawn agrees and the others follow her lead.

You continue in similar fashion until each candidate class has been discussed. As lunch draws near, the back sides of the CRC cards identify the following attributes:

Class	Attributes
Participant	Employee number Name Telephone number Email address Schedule
Meeting	Meeting name Schedule Location Participants
User	Employee number

Class	Attributes
Location	Room number
	Capacity
	Schedule
Holiday	Holiday name
	Schedule

You realize that you haven't had time to discuss responsibilities, let alone collaborations between classes, but today they're serving meatloaf (your favorite) in the company cafeteria. Because you're eager to beat the lunch-time rush, you don't want to hold the meeting over. When Dawn asks whether you're done for the day, you answer in the affirmative, figuring you can work out some of the remaining details on your own. Racing past the others, you head for the cafeteria, hoping to get a place near the head of the line.

THE WRAP UP: DAY 2

After a hearty lunch including two portions of meatloaf and a piece of chocolate cream pie (washed down with some Jolt cola), you head back to your office to finish up today's work and prepare for tomorrow morning's meeting. The main tasks remaining from today's session are identifying the responsibilities and the collaborations. To prepare for tomorrow's session, you decide to identify several use-case scenarios the group can walk through.

Before you know it, it's nearly quitting time, and you decide to wing it during tomorrow's meeting rather than stay overtime to complete your preparation. You shut down the computer and head for the door. Just before you're out of earshot, you hear your phone ringing. Worried that something serious has gone wrong with the shipping system that just went live, you reverse course to answer the call. You're relieved to find that it's your wife, calling to ask you to pick up some canned green beans on the way home. "No problem," you promise.

"They'll go great with dinner—your favorite," she offers, proud of her solicitude. "Meatloaf."

"Some days," you reflect happily during the drive home, "you just can't get enough of a good thing."

LESSONS LEARNED: DAY 2

An object-oriented design is composed of cooperating objects. One useful technique for deciding which objects belong in your system is the CRC or Class-Responsibility-Collaboration card technique. Requiring no sophisticated software, the CRC card technique is ideally suited for group design activities.

" When working with CRC cards, don't be too quick to eliminate classes and attributes, because removing them later is simple. "

Begin your CRC session by working with the problem statement that outlines the functions your software system is supposed to perform. Then, have the session participants underline the noun phrases in the problem statement. For each noun phrase, prepare a CRC card. These cards represent potential classes. The list of potential classes is then either expanded or contracted through group discussion. After a set of classes is agreed on, use the back of each card to record the attributes of each class. Don't be too quick to eliminate classes and attributes, because removing them later is simple; after all, they're not cast in code yet. Nevertheless, you want to avoid adding classes that are tied to the implementation or technical issues.

Day 3: Called on Account of Dawn

When you arrive the next morning at conference room #2, you're surprised to find that neither doughnuts nor coffee await you. Puzzled, you check your watch. "It's 9:25—not that early," you mumble. As you start to take a seat near the place usually occupied by the donuts, John, Dawn's secretary, strolls in. "Hi, Jason," he greets you cheerfully, "Dawn can't make it today, so she asked me to come by and tell you. I tried to reach you by phone, but I guess you'd already left for the meeting. Anyhow, she'll be available tomorrow, so you can all meet here at the usual time."

"Thanks," you murmur, now twice disappointed. Heading back to your office, you stop long enough at the office vending machines to purchase their insipid coffee and a three-day-old Danish.

Knowing that you should take advantage of the delay to better prepare for tomorrow's meeting, you instead spend the remainder of the day surfing the Web and catching up on technical journals. "Boy, wouldn't it be great to have a 100Mbps data link at home," you sigh as the graphics on a Web page load apparently instantaneously.

LESSONS LEARNED: DAY 3

In the immortal words of Forrest Gump, "You never know what you're gonna get." When running a software project, it's easy to make plans and schedules without taking unanticipated events into account. A wise project leader allows enough slack to make up for a day spent surfing the Web.

Day 4: Drawing Collaboration Diagrams

Mindful of your mistake in arriving early the previous day, you precisely time the departure from your office so that today you'll arrive right on time, which you do. The others are already assembled. They greet you and point you to the coffee and doughnuts. You're pleased to discover that it's real coffee this morning—French extra roast—rather than that Hazelnut Delight or whatever it is they've been serving.

Equipped with a chocolate eclair and a capacious mug of hot coffee, you take your seat just as Dawn calls the meeting to order. She turns the meeting over to you.

"What we'd like to do today," you begin, while distributing the CRC cards around the table, "is work on responsibilities and collaborations. To do that, we're going to do a little play acting. Each of you take a single card, which represents one of the classes we already defined. If you think you don't know anything about how that class should work, feel free to exchange it with someone else."

Barney is happy to receive the card for the Holiday class, but Fred exchanges his Meeting card for Dawn's User card, feeling he knows more about user interfaces than meetings. Beyond the one exchange, no one has any questions or objections. "Probably because they don't yet understand what collaborations are about," you muse to yourself. To the group you offer, "Okay, let's move on to collaboration diagrams. I think what we've been doing will make more sense to you once we begin work on them."

EXPLORING USE CASES

"When we first wrote up the system definition, you described what you thought the system should do. Now, I'd like you to expand on that idea. We want to divide the system functions into specific operations and then elaborate on each of them. We don't care about the internal operation of the system just now. What we're interested in is how a user would make use of the system. We call these situations use cases, or scenarios. You might like to think of them as little dramas.

"Let me give you an example," you continue. "One function you've defined for the system is to schedule a meeting between participants. So, let's start by exploring that scenario. What happens when…," you ask, reaching for a name out of the air, "Tarzan uses the system to schedule a meeting with Cheetah, both of whom have wide-open schedules?" Barb seems somewhat annoyed by your choice of scenario but says nothing.

"Well," says Fred, "I hold the User card, so I'm the one who gets the ball rolling."

"Great," you respond, "hold up that card so the others can see it. Now what is it, exactly, that you do?"

"Hmm, let's see. I'm Tarzan and I tell the system that I want a meeting with Cheetah. But I'm not sure who gets that message. I guess I could send a message to Barb, since she holds the Participant card. Cheetah would be a Participant, I assume."

"Barb, how would you handle that request?" you ask.

"I'm not sure," says Barb. "I'd have to check my schedule and see when I'm free. But how would I know when Tarzan is available?"

"I can help you there," responds Fred. "I really need to be talking to two Participant objects, one representing Tarzan and one representing Cheetah. I'll ask each to tell me their schedule and then I'll see where they match up."

"Wait a minute, wait a minute!" Barney interjects, waiving his hand in the air for attention. "I thought you were Tarzan, and I thought Tarzan was the user. How can Tarzan be both the user and a participant? I'm confused."

"Good, that's a very good point, Barney," you applaud verbally, glad that he's getting involved and wondering how Fred will handle the question.

"Yes, I see the problem," Fred responds. "I was really speaking inaccurately when I said that I was Tarzan. Really, anybody who's authorized could set up a meeting. Perhaps Tarzan's secretary. The user doesn't need to be any particular person."

"Good point," you reply. "Does that make sense to you Barney?" Barney replies in the affirmative, and you turn your attention back to Fred. "Now you've determined when the meeting can take place. What happens next?"

"Well, I need to actually book the meeting," answers Fred. "Oops—I can't do that unless a room is free at selected time. I need to ask Barb—she's got the Location class, right—if there's a room free. If there is, then I need to book the room and block out the time on the meeting participants' schedules."

"Great, now we're really getting somewhere," you observe. "Let's see if I can sketch this scenario as a collaboration diagram. Using the whiteboard, you make a sketch similar to Figure 6.1.

ASSIGNING RESPONSIBILITIES

"Now, we need to transfer the responsibilities we've just identified to the CRC cards," you say. "Each of you that's holding a card from this scenario, put each of your class's responsibilities in the left column and the related collaborator opposite it, in the right column. Everybody done? Okay, Barb, let's see what you've got."

Barb shows you the CRC card for Participant, which looks like Figure 6.2.

"And what about Location?" you ask. Barb's second card looks like Figure 6.3.

"Fred, what have you got for User?" you query. Fred shows you and the others his card, which looks like Figure 6.4.

FIGURE 6.1

The Tarzan-meets-Cheetah use case

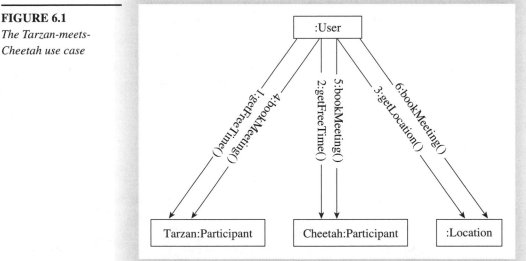

```
Class: Participant                      Participant: a worker who is scheduled to
                                        attend a meeting
Responsibilities:
                                        Attributes:
getFreeTime()
bookMeeting()                           Employee number
                                        Name
                                        Telephone number
                                        Email address
                                        Schedule


        (Front of card)                         (Back of card)
```

FIGURE 6.2
The CRC card for the
Participant class

```
Class: Location                         Location: a place where a meeting is to be held

Responsibilities:                       Attributes:

getLocation()                           Room number
bookMeeting()                           Capacity
                                        Schedule


        (Front of card)                         (Back of card)
```

FIGURE 6.3
The CRC card for the
Location class

"Good. You show a responsibility called setMeeting(), which requires collaboration from Participant and Location."

"Thanks," says Fred, "but why doesn't Barb show these collaborations on her Participant and Location cards?"

"Remember," you explain, "that a collaboration is when a class needs help from another class to perform its responsibility. The class is the client in a client/server relationship with its collaborator. Barb was correct in not showing the collaborations, since she's seeing the message from the server side."

```
Class: User                          User: the worker interacting with the system

Responsibilities:                    Attributes:

setMeeting()         Participant, Location   Employee number



                (Front of card)                              (Back of card)
```

FIGURE 6.4
The CRC card for the
User class

ALTERNATIVE SCENARIOS

"That was super," you announce, changing the subject. "Let's try another. What if Batman, Robin, and Catwoman want to get together, but Catwoman's completely booked?" Again, you employ fictional details intended to elicit creative behavior.

"In that case," answers Dawn, "we'd have three participants rather than two. And no meeting would get booked. It wouldn't require any new responsibilities or anything."

"Okay, then, we don't need to walk through that one," you concede. "What happens when Santa attempts to book a meeting with Mrs. Claus on December 25?"

"Oh, I don't allow that," insists Barney, who holds the `Holiday` card.

"But *how* do you get the opportunity to prevent it?" asks Dawn. "The `Holiday` class doesn't appear on the collaboration diagram."

"Then we need to fix it," demands Barney.

"Right you are," you respond cheerfully. You're pleased that the team has gotten into the process and is contributing freely. Adding a few lines to the collaboration drawing, you come up with something like Figure 6.5.

"Okay, Barney, do you know how to add the responsibility to your card?" you ask.

"I think so. Is this right?" he asks, showing you his card for `Holiday` (see Figure 6.6).

Happy that he's got it right (because you secretly dreaded the thought of again dampening his enthusiasm), you almost shout, "Yes! That's great—you've got it!

"Can anyone think of any scenarios dealing with setting a meeting that might need additional responsibilities?" you ask. "If so, we need to study them."

Barb offers a possibility, and then rejects it herself: "Well, you might have a situation where there's no available room large enough to handle the meeting, but that's just a truncation of the first scenario we looked at. Nothing new as far as I can tell."

FIGURE 6.5

The Santa-meets-Mrs.
Claus use case

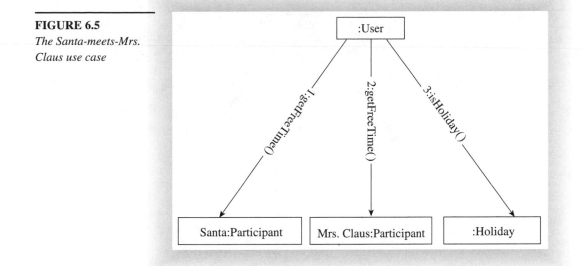

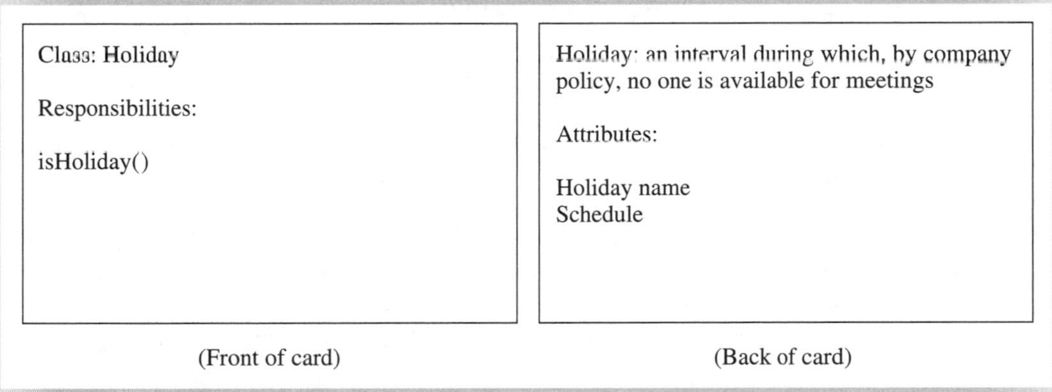

FIGURE 6.6

The CRC card for the
Holiday class

Because the others have no further ideas, you decide to move on. "What happens when a user wants to cancel a meeting—say, Tarzan's meeting with Cheetah?" you ask.

"Well, I'm the user interface, so I'm the first to know about it," says Fred. "I suppose I simply inform Cheetah and cancel the reservation of the Location. Let me see if I can draw it."

You stand aside to make room. After a few moments, he steps away from the board and you see something along the lines of Figure 6.7.

FIGURE 6.7

Tarzan cancels his meeting with Cheetah

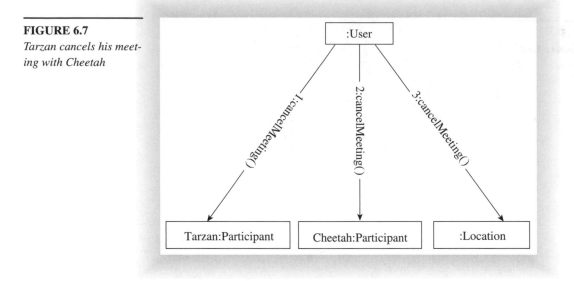

FINDING WHO'S WHO

"Wait a minute," enjoins Barb. "How do you know who the participants in the meeting are? Who is it that you send the `cancelMeeting()` message to?"

"Hmm, you've got a point," agrees Fred. "Still, if I know the time and location of the meeting, I could ask `Participant` to tell me who's booked for it."

"I could help out here," Dawn speaks up. "I have the `Meeting` class, which could hold a list of meeting participants. Then you wouldn't have to ask `Participant` at all."

A general discussion ensues, without a clear consensus. Hanging back initially, you now step in. "Often we run into a situation such as this," you explain, "where neither of two choices is clearly the best. What's usually best is simply to pick one or the other. Later, if it becomes clear that we've made the wrong choice, we can change our minds. That's the beauty of working with CRC cards and diagrams, rather than program source code."

"But which way should we do it?" asks Barney.

"I like to keep things as simple as possible," you explain. "I recommend we handle it Fred's way. Unless the `Meeting` class offers us some important benefit we can't see right now, Fred's way is better. Besides, the `Meeting` class has no responsibilities so far. Unless we uncover some as we go along, we may not need the `Meeting` class at all. Eliminating a class could make the design simpler and reduce the time it takes to implement the system," you point out, hoping to appeal to the team's desire to get the system up as soon as possible.

"So, what does the cancellation scenario look like? It seems we need to add a responsibility to `Participant` in order to make everything work right." Adjusting the diagram, you end up with a drawing like Figure 6.8.

FIGURE 6.8

Revised drawing: Tarzan cancels his meeting with Cheetah

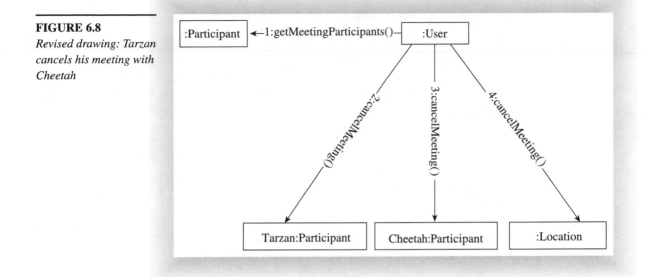

"And what about the CRC card for `Participant`? Barb, did you catch the change it needs?"

"You bet," answers Barb, who shows the team her revised CRC card, which now includes the `getMeetingParticipants()` responsibility.

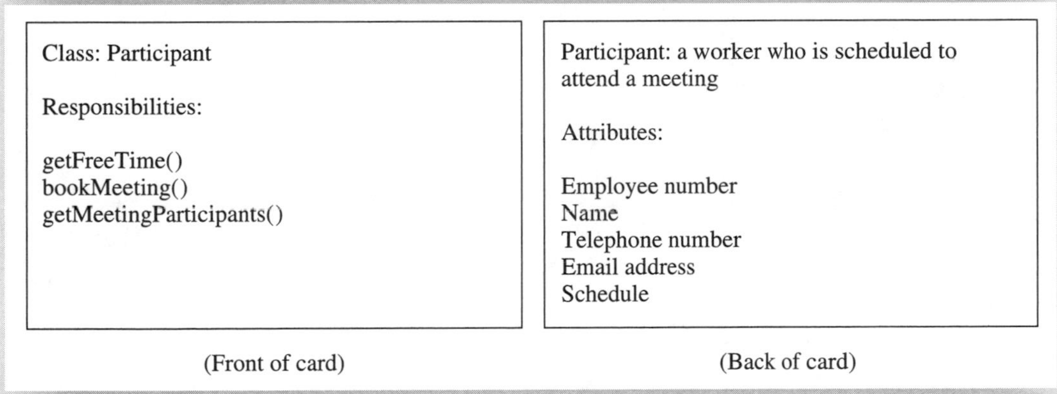

Class: Participant Responsibilities: getFreeTime() bookMeeting() getMeetingParticipants()	Participant: a worker who is scheduled to attend a meeting Attributes: Employee number Name Telephone number Email address Schedule
(Front of card)	(Back of card)

FIGURE 6.9

Revised CRC card for the Participant class

SCHEDULE MATTERS

Pleased by their accurate work, you move on. "Let's look now at the way a user establishes his or her schedule within the system. Fred, how do you deal with that?"

Fred thinks aloud, "Well, there are two aspects to this. One involves initially establishing a schedule. The other involves tweaking the schedule as, from time to time, you find out you're going to be away from the office or whatever."

"Sounds good. Let's start with the first case because that seems simpler," you suggest. "What happens when I want to enter my schedule for next week?"

Fred pipes up, "Well, as usual, I get things started. I guess my move is to talk to your `Participant` object and tell it to extend its schedule."

"Like this?" you ask, quickly sketching on the whiteboard a collaboration diagram similar to Figure 6.10.

"That looks good to me," responds Barb. "I just need to add the `addFreeTime()` method to the `Participant` class. I don't need a collaborator, so it's straightforward to do."

"Okay, what about blocking out time that won't be available?" you ask.

"That's equally easy," says Barb. "I simply need another responsibility, call it `subtractFreeTime()`, that blocks out the specified time block. Here, I'll show you the card." Her card looks like Figure 6.11.

"Are you tracking this, Fred?" asks Barb.

"No problem," answers Fred. "Here's what I've got so far." His card resembles Figure 6.12.

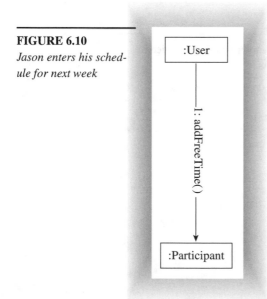

FIGURE 6.10

Jason enters his schedule for next week

Class: Participant	Participant: a worker who is scheduled to attend a meeting
Responsibilities:	Attributes:
getFreeTime() bookMeeting() getMeetingParticipants() addFreeTime() subtractFreeTime()	Employee number Name Telephone number Email address Schedule
(Front of card)	(Back of card)

FIGURE 6.11
Revised CRC card for the Participant *class*

Class: User	User: the worker interacting with the system
Responsibilities:	Attributes:
getMeeting() Participant, Location cancelMeeting() Participant, Location addFreeTime() Participant subtractFreeTime() Participant	Employee number
(Front of card)	(Back of card)

FIGURE 6.12
Revised CRC card for the User *class*

"Looks good to me," observes Barb. You and the others express agreement.

Fred raises a new issue. "One thing I've been missing," he says, "is how the schedules are stored. I mean, the Participant class and the Location class each have a schedule attribute. Shouldn't it be an object of some sort?"

"Good idea," you agree. "Let's create a CRC card for a Schedule class. How about we represent the time-related part of the schedule as a set of ordered pairs: a begin time and an end time. Each member of the set can also specify a location or a code that means 'free' to handle the meeting-related part." You quickly prepare a CRC card like the one in Figure 6.13.

```
┌─────────────────────────────────┐  ┌─────────────────────────────────┐
│ Class: Schedule                 │  │ Schedule: a set of time intervals, each marked │
│                                 │  │ as "free" or booked to a specified location │
│ Responsibilities:               │  │                                 │
│                                 │  │ Attributes:                     │
│ isFree()                        │  │                                 │
│ locationAtTime()                │  │ BeginTime                       │
│                                 │  │ EndTime                         │
│                                 │  │ Location                        │
│                                 │  │                                 │
└─────────────────────────────────┘  └─────────────────────────────────┘
        (Front of card)                      (Back of card)
```

FIGURE 6.13

CRC card for the
Schedule class

An inexplicable gnawing sensation in your stomach prompts you to glance at your watch. You're amazed to see that the team has worked almost completely through the lunch hour. Apparently everyone has been too engrossed in the task to notice. "Can anyone think of any other scenarios we need to consider?" you ask, but no one responds.

After an interval, Dawn revisits an earlier question. "What about my Meeting class? Is it not needed after all?"

"It appears not," you answer, hedging your bet. "But someone may come up with something new. Why don't you hang on to the card until tomorrow? Otherwise, it appears we're done for the day."

You notice looks of surprise as the team members discover how time has flown by. "See you all tomorrow, same time, same place," chimes Dawn, as the team members scatter to grab a quick bite before attending to afternoon duties.

THE WRAP UP: DAY 4

Hoping to get a leg up on tomorrow's meeting, you spend some time preparing class diagrams from the CRC cards. The process is mostly mechanical, so you don't really need user input to do it. The risk is that someone has come up with an additional scenario that will require modification of the identified classes. Although that would cost you some work, you'd be pleased to learn about the need for change now, rather than after the programs are written. Looking at it that way, you don't feel you're risking much in venturing ahead.

Rather than create detailed class diagrams, you decide to prepare conceptual class diagrams that everyone on the team can review. Then, you and Fred can add the more technical details that the others won't care about anyway. Soon, your completed suite of diagrams numbers five, and you decide to call it a day.

LESSONS LEARNED: DAY 4

Before you can determine the responsibilities of a class, you need to know what users expect the system to do. The easiest way to do that is by working through use-case scenarios. A scenario is developed by asking, "What happens when the user does this?" Remember, you're not interested in determining what actually happens at the technical level—that is, which records are deleted or which database tables affected. Instead, you're interested in describing system interactions from the user's point of view: "If I withdraw money from my bank account, the ATM machine gives me some money and a receipt, and my bank balance is reduced."

Unlike other group activities, working through scenarios requires participants to take on the roles of the classes they represent. When the participants get past their initial reluctance and can "suspend their disbelief," it can be quite an effective technique. Dangers, however, lie in straying into technical details or failing to separate the conceptual responsibilities of each class from the implementation details that may arise later. If you find the conversation shifting to primary keys or other computer lingo, you need to move away from the "real" world and back into the world where objects and classes are really alive.

> *" When developing use-case scenarios, you're interested in describing system interactions from the user's point of view. "*

Day 5: The End in Sight

Next morning, you're a little late to arrive, due to a freight train that blocked a street during the morning rush. The others are all seated, reviewing yesterday's work as you enter. Apologizing to all, you take your seat so quickly that you forget to grab a doughnut. Fortunately, the coffee is within grabbing distance, so you pour yourself a cup.

Dawn, knowing little about class diagrams, has obviously been stalling and is eager to turn the meeting over to you. "Jason," she directs, "why don't you get us started doing the class diagrams?"

"Okay," you respond, "but first let me ask if anyone has thought of any additional scenarios we need to consider. What about it, folks?"

Receiving a unanimous "no," you proceed with your agenda. Passing around copies of the class diagrams you prepared yesterday afternoon, you start off with a general description of what each diagram is intended to show.

REVIEWING CLASS DIAGRAMS

"Yesterday, we all designed a set of CRC cards. These were for our benefit as we worked through the design. When we turn our work over to the programmers, however, they'll work from something called class diagrams. Let's take a look at the diagram for the User class, which you'll find on top of your handouts." Your diagram resembles Figure 6.14.

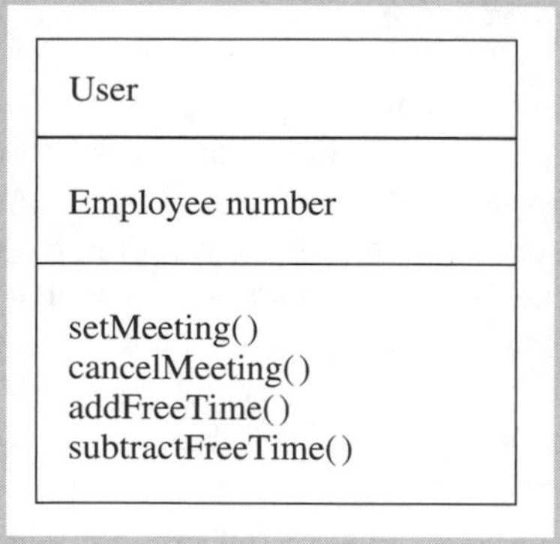

FIGURE 6.14

Class diagram of the **User** *class*

User
Employee number
setMeeting( ) cancelMeeting( ) addFreeTime( ) subtractFreeTime( )

"Notice how closely this follows the CRC card you developed yesterday," you start in. By using the overhead projector and your new laser pointer, you highlight the overhead projected at the front of the room. "At the top is the name that was on the CRC card," you continue. "This is the class diagram for the user class. The remainder of the card is divided into attributes and methods. The only attribute of the employee class is the Employee Number. The methods should also look familiar. They are just the responsibilities you defined yesterday.

"Let's take a look at another class. Here's the participant class, which is obviously the most complex," you say as you switch to the transparency shown in Figure 6.15.

The room is silent for a second as all the members study the diagrams on the table in front of them, looking up at the overhead as if they were different. Tentatively, Barney raises his hand. Hopefully, you ask, "Go ahead, Barney."

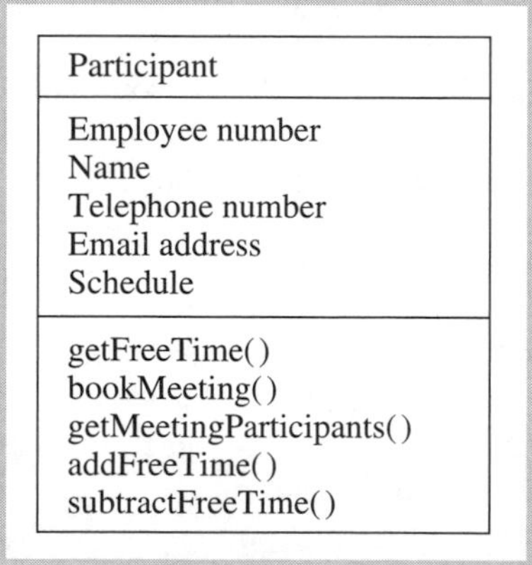

FIGURE 6.15

Class diagram of the **Participant** *class*

Participant
Employee number Name Telephone number Email address Schedule
getFreeTime( ) bookMeeting( ) getMeetingParticipants( ) addFreeTime( ) subtractFreeTime( )

"I've got a couple questions," starts Barney slowly, picking up speed as he continues. "I notice that we've included the `Employee Name` with the `Participant` class because, if I remember right, we didn't want to integrate this system with the HR system at this time. Why do we only include the `Employee Number` with the `User` class, then?"

Before you can answer, Barney continues. "My second question is why the `Participant` class has `Schedule` as one of its attributes. I thought that `Schedule` was a separate class."

Surprised at the astuteness of Barney's questions, you take a moment to compose just the right answer. "Very good questions," you begin. "First, it's not only the `Participant` class that has a `Schedule` as an attribute. Other classes do as well. For instance, here's the `Location` class. Notice that one of its attributes is a `Schedule`." You point to a diagram resembling Figure 6.16.

"Remember the third *C* in CRC cards?" you go on. "It stands for *Collaboration*. Every time one class collaborates with another class, it requires an instance of that class (called an object) to perform the required services. Thus, for every collaboration, you're likely to find that the collaborating class is listed as an attribute. Notice here, the `Holiday` class uses the `Schedule` class as well," you say as you point to a diagram resembling Figure 6.17.

"I understood about the collaborations," interjected Barney. "For some reason, however, I sort of thought that attributes were, like, parts of other objects. I guess I thought that the collaborations would be shown in some other way." When Barney falls silent for a moment, you use the respite to put the final class diagram, the `Location` class, on the overhead (see Figure 6.18).

Barney isn't quite finished, however. "What about the `Employee Name` and `Employee Number` thing?" You think for a second, trying to determine how much information you need to impart, and opt for the most straightforward explanation.

"Even though we won't be hooking up to the HR system at this time, we still don't want to store more information than we must. By defining the `Employee Name` attribute

FIGURE 6.16

Class diagram of the `Location` class

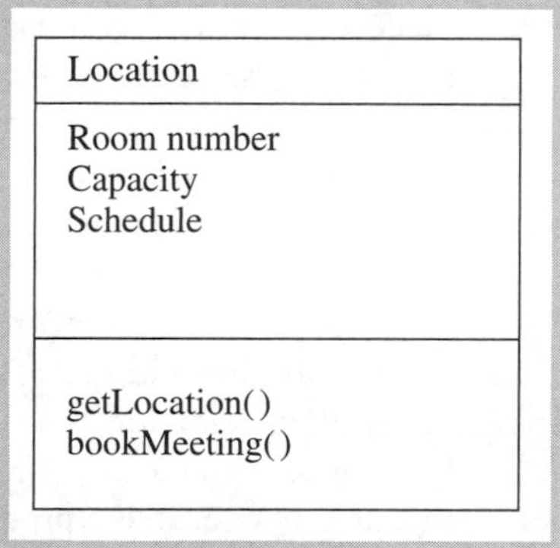

Location
Room number Capacity Schedule
getLocation() bookMeeting()

```
┌─────────────────────────┐
│ Holiday                 │
├─────────────────────────┤
│ Holiday name            │
│ Schedule                │
│                         │
├─────────────────────────┤
│                         │
│ isHoliday()             │
│                         │
└─────────────────────────┘
```

```
┌─────────────────────────┐
│ Schedule                │
├─────────────────────────┤
│ BeginTime               │
│ EndTime                 │
│ Location                │
├─────────────────────────┤
│ isFree()                │
│ locationAtTime()        │
│                         │
└─────────────────────────┘
```

only in the Participant class, we make it available to every other class in the system, yet store it only once. That way, when we finally do hook up with the HR system, we'll only have one extra copy of the Employee Name instead of the two we'd have if we stored it in both Participant and User."

You're pleased to see that Barney not only accepts your reasoning but also seems to be shaking his head in agreement. Briefly you ask for more questions and are pleased to find that there are none.

"Well, then, it looks as though this will be a short meeting," you promise. "Here's what remains. Fred and I will work this morning and this afternoon to refine the class diagrams to include additional technical information. We'll then cobble together a user-interface prototype that we'll demonstrate tomorrow morning. Given your acceptance of the prototype, we'll turn this project over to the programmers, stand back, and await Christmas morning."

INTERFACE AND PROTOTYPE

Dawn thanks everyone for coming, nods appreciatively in your direction, and joins the others as they return to their offices. Fred stays behind to work with you on the detailed class diagrams and the prototype.

Deciding to pre-empt what you believe is a likely question from Fred, you explain, "This design is going to need some tweaking here and there because these objects have to have persistence. It won't work for all the data to be lost every time someone cuts power to the server. We'll have to design an interface to a relational database. But that can wait. For now, let's focus on specifying the details of the interfaces and getting a user-interface prototype up and running.

"Okay by me," Fred declines to argue. "Let's get to it." An hour or so of work is sufficient to produce detailed class diagrams that include data types for attributes, method parameters, and method return values.

You then leave Fred the task of quickly hacking the prototype. You know that, by using a visually oriented Java IDE, this task can be done in an hour or so. You return to your respective offices, you to check your email and Fred to write code.

Later that afternoon you check with Fred to find out how he's progressing. The user interface he's built looks simple enough to use and seems to support the necessary functions (see Figure 6.19).

You're pleased and you tell him so. "Thanks," he mumbles, unsure how to respond.

FIGURE 6.19

The ScheduleMatic user interface

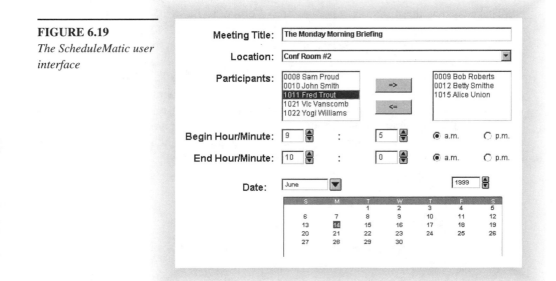

LESSONS LEARNED: DAY 5

Hide the details! Some things work well in a group setting, and others just don't. Many a project manager has attempted to make drawing class diagrams a loose group project and has become bogged down in a quagmire of endless discussions on arrowheads, lines, and figures. You can avoid this pitfall by assigning responsibility for this task to a single person or, if the project is larger and can be divided into modules, a subgroup. If you're a technically inclined person, you might be surprised to find out that not every one of your colleagues finds creating detailed diagrams to be an exciting or rewarding experience!

Although creating class diagrams should be a solo activity, reviewing them should not. You may feel that you've carefully captured the essence of your CRC card sessions, but when the CRC cards are put away and the class diagrams are put up on the wall, you might be surprised to find that you've completely misunderstood what was required. The extra effort necessary to educate your team to understand the meaning of your finished diagrams will be well worth the effort.

Finally, when creating a set of class diagrams, make sure you create them at a conceptual level that's appropriate for the group you're presenting them to. Diagrams meant for the implementers should include more detailed information than those meant for designing and approving the product's functionality.

" Hide the details! Many a project manager...has become bogged down in a quagmire of endless discussions on arrowheads, lines, and figures. "

Day 6: Demonstrating the Prototype

The next day, the team assembles in Fred's office, to be nearer the computer. Fred demonstrates the prototype, and team members spend some time trying it out. You and Fred are equally pleased to see how much everyone likes the system.

You promise to turn the design over to programming that very afternoon and to keep the team members posted on the progress of implementation. To celebrate completion of the design, Dawn treats the team to lunch at a local restaurant, one you've never visited. Already unsure what she may have in mind, your fears are confirmed when you see the large and gaudy sign that adorns the face of the building, Lo Fat's Faux Food Buffet, and the smaller sign proclaiming the day's special dish, Sweet and Sour Tofu Bits. "I wonder if they have tofu meatloaf," you're startled to find yourself asking no one in particular—but happily, no one has heard you.

Summary

Designing software combines technical issues and a process for harnessing the expertise of different people in support of a common goal. Most of this book is about the technical issues surrounding software development; this chapter is a peek into the process involved. The process discussed in this chapter isn't meant to be definitive but includes steps and techniques that will usually be found in any process you adopt.

The software development process begins by assembling a team and defining your product. A joint session spent developing a problem statement is a good way to develop both. The facilitator can use a simple brainstorming technique—listing features on a whiteboard—to get the other team members involved. The facilitator must not dictate the system features but allow them to emerge from the process while keeping the discussion on track. It's important to achieve consensus at this stage.

After deciding what your product will do, the next step is to "discover the objects" in your system. One useful technique for doing this is the CRC, or Class-Responsibility-Collaboration, card technique. Using CRC cards requires no sophisticated software and is well suited for group-design activities. CRC sessions begin by having participants underline the noun phrases in the problem statement. A CRC card is prepared for each noun phrase, representing a potential class. Through group discussion, the set of classes is either expanded or contracted. When a set of classes is agreed on, the back of each card is used to record the attributes of each class.

The third step in the software design process is to assign responsibilities to each of your classes by "play acting" with the proposed system. These play-acting scripts are called *use-case scenarios*. A scenario is developed by asking, "What happens when the user does this?" You're not interested in determining what actually happens at the technical level; instead, you're interested in describing system interactions from the user's point of view.

Technical details, such as class diagrams, are difficult to do in a group setting, so preparing them should be delegated to skilled individuals. The resulting product, however, should be reviewed by the entire team. Finally, when running a software project, make allowances for the unexpected by allowing slack time.

Questions

1. The first step in the software development process is to prepare a

   a. Summary paragraph

   b. List of features

   c. Plate of doughnuts

   d. All of the above

2. The summary paragraph concisely lists

   a. The hardware that the system will run on

   b. The programming language to be used in implementation

   c. What the software should do, from the user's perspective

   d. Which database manager should be used for storing the data

3. Working together in a group is most effective for
   a. Ironing out technical details that might arise as the design is finalized
   b. Finalizing the inheritance hierarchy to be used in your design
   c. Defining requirements and brainstorming general classes and their responsibilities
   d. Nothing. Everything that can be done in a group can be done better by individuals.

4. The CRC card technique uses index cards, each of which represents
   a. Crazy Random Choices
   b. Class Responsibility Collaborations
   c. Civilian Regular Communications
   d. Class Requirements and Connections

5. When using CRC cards as an analysis technique, you
   a. Underline nouns in the problem statement, trying to discover candidate classes
   b. Start with the responsibilities and wait until later to work out who does what
   c. Discover the attributes necessary and later group them into classes.
   d. Create a module structure chart, starting with the main method

6. Class diagrams prepared for team approval should generally
   a. Be conceptual rather than technically complete
   b. Be omitted, because team members don't want to be bothered with details
   c. Make no use of inheritance because that just confuses people
   d. Use colorful icons and many lines so that team members can remain interested

7. Role playing, play acting, use cases, and scenarios are all useful techniques for discovering
   a. Class attributes
   b. Candidate classes
   c. Class responsibilities
   d. Future box-office stars

8. Because things can go wrong, a wise manager will always
   a. Prepare for every contingency
   b. Hire extra people to make up for those who don't perform adequately
   c. Lock the office doors before the employees can get out
   d. Build "slack time" into the schedule to provide a buffer against unforeseen circumstances

To Learn More

Most of the time, the success of your process project will depend less on what you're building than on who's on your team. Even if you're not a manager, you'll benefit from the insights in these books that focus on the "human side" of software development:

- Constantine, Larry L. *Constantine on Peopleware*. New Jersey: Hall Computer Books, 1995.

- DeMarco, Tom and Timothy Lister. *Peopleware: Productive Projects and Teams*. New York: Dorset House Publishing Co., 1987.

- DeMarco, Tom and Timothy Lister. *Software State-of-the-Art: Selected Papers*. New York: Dorset House Publishing Co., 1990. In this resource, DeMarco and Lister collected a group of papers dedicated to current practice in software development. One particular article makes purchasing this hefty volume worthwhile and may change your mind—David Parnas's article, "A Rational Design Process: How and Why to Fake It," which was originally published in the *IEEE Transactions on Software Engineering*, Vol. SE-12, No. 2.

- McConnell, Steve. *Rapid Development: Taming Wild Software Schedules*. Redmond, Washington: Microsoft Press, 1996. This volume by McConnell, who penned one of the definitive collections of software construction lore, is devoted not only to peopleware but also to managing the software development process in general.

7

Object Relationships: Implementing Associations

Frantically you punch at the unfamiliar buttons on the radio of the shiny new rental car, wishing you'd had the sense to adjust it before you pulled onto the freeway. The static only gets louder and more irritating as you try each obscurely labeled knob and slider in turn. Finally, just before you pull over and get out your emergency tool kit, you find the tuning button—inexplicably marked with a plus sign—and are rewarded by the refreshing sound of human speech.

"…and then, like, he said, I'm just not ready for that kind of commitment, you know? What is it with men, Jerry? Like last week…"

You jab the tuning button.

"…at 5, Arnoldo's got the scoop. Don't miss Alien Invaders, and the Women Who Lo…"

Jab.

"…violence erupted for the second time today in the capital city of…"

"…the President said he was willing to compromise if only…"

"…secret to raising happy children is setting…"

Jab. Jab. Jab.

"…and Mama's in the Statehouse, and Daddy's in the pen."

Jab.

Finally! Music. Sitting back in your seat, you let the vibration of the steel guitar wash over you, at peace with the world.

Relationships. We spend much of our lives coping with the problems they involve. Every relationship involves responsibility: because you're a parent, you must do this-and-that, and because you're a citizen you must do thus-and-so. Pile on enough relationships and life gets overwhelming. Unfortunately, you can't escape relationships by immigrating to the world of objects. Although objects participate in different kinds of relationships than you do and have different sorts of responsibilities, relationships play a central role in software design. Describing, defining, and working on the relationships between classes and objects is one of the chief occupations of the object-oriented designer.

The next four chapters concentrate on teaching your objects and classes to form healthy relationships. In this chapter and the next, you'll study *association relationships*—relationships between objects in which the objects exchange messages. In later chapters, you'll study *inheritance relationships*—relationships between classes in which objects of one class inherit data and behavior from another class. In this chapter you will learn:

- How to differentiate between *association*, *composition*, and *simple association* relationships

- How to implement associations by using *referential attributes* and *temporary objects*

- How to evaluate association relationships based on the criterion of *coupling*

- How to choose between different strategies for implementing a *uses* relationship

- How to implement *cardinality* constraints on an association

The Basics of Relationships

In real life, relationships are an important building block used to organize society. When you were born, you formed a parent-child relationship with your parents. As you grew up, you formed relationships with different people, groups, and things. You might have joined the scouts, owned a car, gotten married, or eaten a chili dog. Each of these relationships implies certain rights and responsibilities between yourself and the other partners in the relationship.

If you own your car, for example, you have the right to drive it and sell it; this is inherent in the *owns-a* relationship. If you try to perform the sell() operation on an automobile with which you don't have an *owns-a* relationship, you're likely to form a new relationship with the rest of society—the *inmate* relationship.

When designing object-oriented software, discovering the classes and objects you'll need is a first step, closely tied up with the task of discovering the responsibilities that each object assumes. Until now, however, one messy little detail has been swept under the rug: how are classes and objects related to each other?

Think about the `ProgressBar` class presented in Chapter 4. `ProgressBar` is a simple, standalone class. But, in fact, `ProgressBar` couldn't do its work—or even exist—without the cooperation and collaboration of several other classes and objects. You couldn't create a `ProgressBar` unless the `Component` class already existed. You couldn't `paint()` without the collaboration of a `Graphics` object. A `ProgressBar` would have no place to live without the cooperation of a friendly `Container` object. While it's important that all your objects be well behaved, it's equally important that they participate in stable relationships. As in real life, failure to do so can lead to disaster.

"No man is an island," wrote 16th-Century poet John Donne. Today he might well have added, "No object is an island either." Java programs are communities of objects that collaborate to accomplish a goal. For that collaboration to be effective, Java communities—like human communities—must be organized. Like human communities as well, not just any organization will do; the form must follow the function. The chain-of-command organization that works so well in the military isn't going to be as successful when you want to take your date to dinner and a movie; you're liable to end up eating alone.

One way to decide whether a particular organizational strategy is likely to be successful is to rely on simple rules, usually formed from past experience. Such rules are called *heuristics*.

" Java communities— like human communities— must be organized."

RELATIONSHIP HEURISTICS

"Don't put all your eggs in one basket."

This well-known cliché is an example of a relationship heuristic or rule of thumb. If all your eggs are in one basket and something happens to the basket, you've lost all your eggs. If you've put a portion of your eggs in several different baskets, a disaster befalling one basket won't have as great an impact on your ability to serve your customers a tasty omelet.

Such heuristics are not always reliable, but they work often enough to prove their worth. You could, for example, scatter your eggs so widely you forget where you put them. In that case, you would have been better off if you had left them in one basket. Fortunately, such results are rare.

When you design objects and classes, you rely on a similar set of rules, each designed to reduce the risk of some "bad thing" happening to your program. For instance:

- Make all your data private to reduce the effects of changing your implementation.

- Create a simple public interface that hides the internal working of your class.

- Create highly cohesive classes. Each class should model a single abstraction.

These, and a host of other similar rules, help you design classes and objects that are robust, easy to use, and resistant to the unintended side effects of inevitable change.

Are there also rules for designing the relationships between objects? Yes. In fact, there are really two kinds of rules:

- Rules that help you decide which kind of relationship will be most effective

- Rules that help you implement a particular relationship most effectively

First things first, however. Before you can decide which relationship to use and how best to implement it, you need to know what's available. To resurrect another hoary cliché, "To the man with only a hammer, everything is a nail." The first step toward expanding your relationship repertoire is to differentiate between object relationships and class relationships.

OBJECT AND CLASS REVIEW

" The Constitution is not the government; it merely provides the blueprint for implementing an actual government. "

The differences between objects and classes can sometimes be confusing. Frequently, the terms are used interchangeably, but, in fact, they are quite different things. Remember from Chapter 2 that objects are instances of a particular class. An object is not a class. A class acts like a blueprint that defines the attributes and behavior of each object. You can—usually—create numerous objects from a single class.

If you have difficulty keeping these two concepts straight, just think of the difference between writing a program and running a program. When you write a Java program, you define a set of classes by specifying attributes and methods. This is the *static structure* of your program. But when you run your application or applet, that static structure comes alive and your class definitions are used to create objects. It is the objects in your program that interact and send messages to each other and store different values.

This relationship is much like the one between the U.S. Constitution and the government. The Constitution describes the different branches of the government as well as the relationships between them. But the Constitution is not the government; it merely provides the blueprint for implementing an actual government. When you want to write a letter complaining about how things are going, you don't send it to the Constitution—you send it to your member of Congress. In a sense, your individual member of Congress is an object made possible by the Constitution class.

Remember

An object is not a class: it's a member, or instance, of a class. A class acts like a blueprint that defines the attributes and methods common to its (potentially many) instances.

INTRODUCING OBJECT AND CLASS RELATIONSHIPS

When you use Java, you write class definitions. When you run your program, it becomes a community of interacting objects. Just as objects and classes are different, a Java program really has two basic types of relationships: *class relationships* and *object relationships*.

As a simple analogy, you might think of class relationships as similar to genetic relationships in the real world. No matter how you get along with your parents, children, or aunts and uncles, your actual relationship to such "blood relatives" is fixed and unchanging. Barring time travel (as in *Back to the Future*), your parents will always be your parents.

As with genetic relationships, class relationships always involve inheritance. This fixed or mandatory relationship is sometimes called the *is-a* relationship. You can say that the Button class *is-a* Component because it is derived from the Component class. Each individual Button object always has this fixed relationship to the Component class. It has no "choice" in the matter. Class relationships are the subject of Chapter 9, "Implementing Class Relationships: Inheritance and Interfaces," and Chapter 10, "Designing with Inheritance and Interfaces: A Case Study."

Object relationships—called *associations*—are the relationships objects use to work together. If you think about the people you interact with outside your family, you'll see that you also have a wide variety of relationships. You purchase food from a grocery store, you may attend class at a local college, you might belong to a professional organization like the Association for Computing Machinery (ACM). All these relationships are different from the fixed relationships you have with your parents and children. These are all forms of association.

Kinds of Associations

Object relationships or associations are more flexible than class relationships and come in a wider variety. Because object relationships don't involve inheritance, you might say that object relationships are made, not born. Objects can work together in three different ways:

- An object can use another object to do some work. This is called an *association*, *acquaintance*, or *uses* relationship.

- A complex object may be composed of several simpler parts. This is called a *composition* relationship, although sometimes it's also called *aggregation* or *containment* relationship. Composition will be covered in Chapter 8, "Object Relationships: Compositions and Collections."

- When two objects depend on each other but don't directly interact, a *simple* or *weak association* is formed.

In reality, there aren't just three forms of association. These somewhat simplistic categories make it easier for you to analyze the collaborations between objects, but don't be surprised if you have difficulty "fitting" a particular collaboration into one of these pigeonholes. As with all simplifications, the truth is frequently more complex.

The underlying principle behind these categories is found in the idea of *coupling*, which measures the mutual dependence of two objects on each other. If each of two objects participating in a relationship cannot exist without the other, the objects are very highly coupled. If each object can exist independently but cannot perform some operation without the other, the objects are less highly coupled. If the relationship between two objects is "purely formal"—that is, the objects don't interact or share data at all—the coupling between them is nonexistent. Figure 7.1 shows this entire range of coupling and places the weak association, association, and composition relationships on that continuum.

In general, you want to create classes that are as loosely coupled as possible while still being able to efficiently carry out their responsibilities. This goal is laudable; however, most of the time the nature of the problem itself will dictate the type of association you must use.

Before you look at each of these forms of association, let's first examine a preliminary concept that affects all three forms: *cardinality*.

> *" In general, you want to create classes that are as loosely coupled as possible while still being able to efficiently carry out their responsibilities. "*

How Many? A Cardinal Question

Suppose that you were given the task of teaching an alien species how to shop for, say, a new computer. What would you do? (Of course, if you have children, you've already found yourself in a similar position.) You'd certainly teach the aliens to ask about features: Does it have enough memory? Is it fast enough? How about disk storage? You'd also teach them to compare prices and features between competing brands: the Andromeda V may be state-of-the-art, but the HedKrache 7—which has 90 percent of the Andromeda's capabilities—is only half the price. Finally, you'd teach them to read consumer reviews and tap into the Internet to learn about reliability.

FIGURE 7.1
Coupling between objects

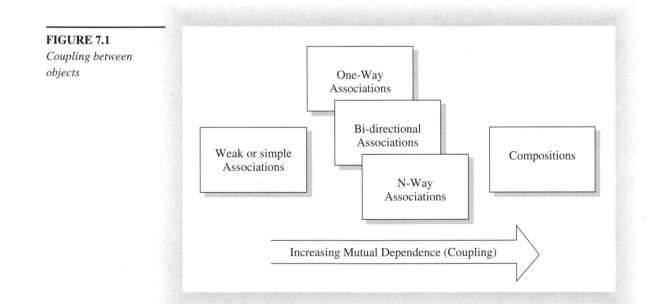

When you buy a new computer or car, or when you decide on a career or a school or a mate, it's important to ask questions, but they have to be the right questions! When you design associations between objects, regardless of the type of association, you should ask yourself these questions:

- How many objects will participate in the association?

- Is the association *mandatory* or *optional*?

Let's take a look at an example. Rather than work with aliens or robots, you'll look at a Java application you might expect to find in a typical business: a `SalesInvoice` object. This same example will be continued and further elaborated in the next chapter.

Figure 7.2 shows an invoice of the kind you might find in almost any organization. Get yourself a pencil and paper and take a minute to write down a list of collaborating objects you find explicit or implicit there. When you're finished, compare your list to Table 7.1, remembering that discovering objects is not an exact science. Your list may include more objects or fewer. The important thing is that you consider all the requirements. You might find that simply circling the relevant parts on the invoice, as Figure 7.3 illustrates, is a helpful exercise.

TABLE 7.1
COLLABORATING OBJECTS IN THE `SalesInvoice` OBJECT

Object	Description
Customer	Purchased the product
Recipient	Ship the product here
SalesPerson	Who took the order
LineItems	The things purchased

ANALYZING THE SALES INVOICE

The `Customer` is the person you send the bill to. You might ship your product to the same person. A `Customer` object should have name and address information, so your invoice gets sent to the right address. You'll also want some credit-worthiness information and maybe some links to the `Customer`'s buying history.

The `Recipient` is the person you send your product to. Because the `Recipient` isn't necessarily paying the bill, you don't need the same kind of credit information you would for a `Customer`. If your business is the sort where the `Customers` and the `Recipients` are normally different—a florist, for instance—you may want to maintain the distinction between a `Customer` and a `Recipient`. In many retail or mail-order (Web-order?) applications, however, the `Customer` and `Recipient` are almost always the same. In this kind of situation, it makes sense to use a single class for both `Customer` and `Recipient`. That's what we'll do here.

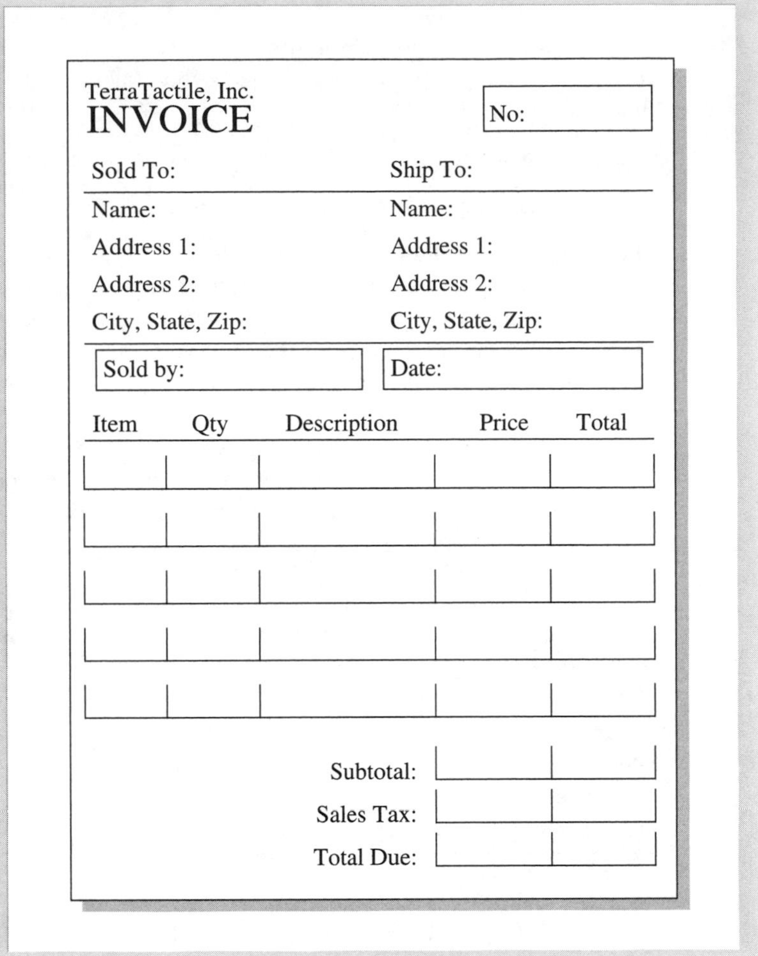

FIGURE 7.2

A sales invoice

> TerraTactile, Inc.
> # INVOICE   No:
>
> Sold To: Ship To:
>
> Name: Name:
> Address 1:   Address 1:
> Address 2:   Address 2:
> City, State, Zip: City, State, Zip:
>
> Sold by: Date:
>
> Item   Qty   Description   Price   Total
>
>
>
>
>
>   Subtotal:
>   Sales Tax:
>   Total Due:

The SalesPerson is the person who took the order. You need to know who that is because you need to pay sales commissions based on the number of units they sold.

Finally, the LineItem objects store the actual items sold, with the quantities of each item. The LineItem class is perhaps the most important part of the application—the key abstraction, if you will. If you get the LineItem class wrong, you're liable to lose track of how much you sold and how much each item cost.

FIGURE 7.3

Circling the collaborating objects

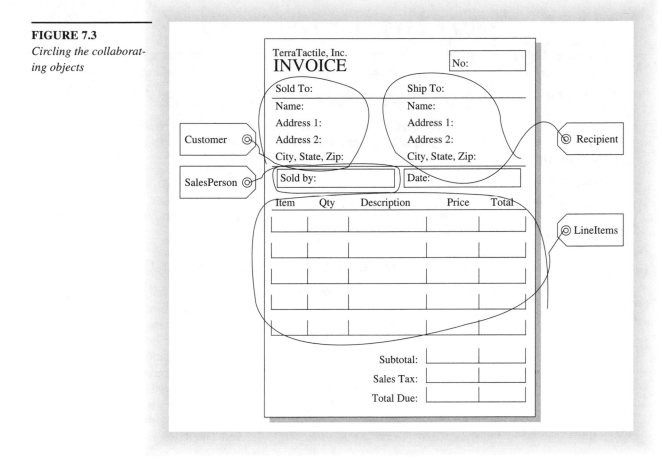

But truthfully, each object in your SalesInvoice is equally important; you want to make sure that you sell to credit-worthy customers, ship your products to the right address, charge the correct amount, ship the correct number, and pay your sales force what they've earned. Your SalesInvoice program really is a community of objects, and it's important that you get them working together as a team. First, you need to set some ground rules to specifically define the cardinality constraints your objects will observe.

WHAT IS CARDINALITY?

Cardinality refers to the number of objects that participate in an association and whether their participation is optional or mandatory. Look at the five objects you've defined: the `Customer`, the `Recipient`, the `SalesPerson`, the `LineItem`, and the `SalesInvoice` object itself, and ask yourself the following questions:

- Which objects collaborate with which other objects? You may want to draw some simple collaboration diagrams like those shown in Chapters 5 and 6.

- How many objects participate in each collaboration?

- Is the collaboration mandatory or optional?

Take a second and write out your list. When you're finished, come back to the discussion below and see how you did.

ANALYZING `SalesInvoice` COLLABORATIONS

Every `SalesInvoice` object collaborates with only one `Customer` object. You may wish you could bill the same invoice to more than one `Customer`, but that would be illegal as well as unethical. Also, every `SalesInvoice` object *must* have a `Customer`—you can't send out a bill without one. Thus, from the `SalesInvoice` point of view, the cardinality of the association is 1, and it is a *mandatory* association.

Every relationship has two sides, however, and from the `Customer`'s point of view, things look a little different. First, a `Customer` may have ordered products from you on many different occasions—in fact, you desperately hope that is the case. You may also have `Customers` who haven't ordered anything from you—perhaps they just moved into town and opened an account, or maybe you purchased a large mailing list of potential `Customers`. From the `Customer`'s point of view, then, the cardinality of the association is 0..n (meaning a single `Customer` can be associated with zero or more invoices). Because the lower bound is 0, the association is optional. Figure 7.4 shows the `SalesInvoice`-`Customer` association.

What about the `Recipient`? As with the `Customer`, you can ship the product to only one address, so it would seem as though the cardinality of the `Recipient` association should be the same as that of the `Customer`. But is that true? For most businesses, as

FIGURE 7.4
The `SalesInvoice`-`Customer` association

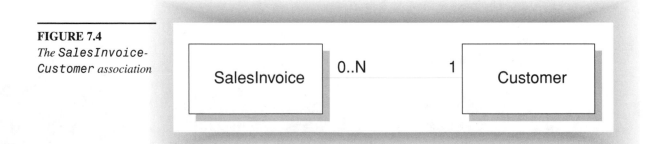

previously mentioned, products are shipped to the Customers who purchase them. Thus, it is not necessary for every SalesInvoice object to have a Recipient. If there is no Recipient, the product is simply shipped to the Customer. Thus, the cardinality of the SalesInvoice-Recipient association is 0..1, and it is optional.

From the Recipient's side of the fence, the relationship looks superficially like the Customer-SalesInvoice association, but here, too, a closer look reveals a difference. Although you may have Customers who have never ordered a product (for the reasons mentioned previously), you'll never have Recipients who haven't received a product; they become Recipients because some Customer decides to ship them something! Thus, a Recipient must be the target of at least one SalesInvoice, but may actually be associated with many. The cardinality of the Recipient-SalesInvoice association is thus 1..n, and it is mandatory. Figure 7.5 shows the SalesInvoice-Recipient association.

The cardinality of the SalesInvoice-SalesPerson association is identical to that of the SalesInvoice-Customer association. Every SalesInvoice must be written by only one SalesPerson, and the relationship is mandatory. Just as you can have Customers who have not yet ordered a product, however, you can also have SalesPersons who have not yet written a SalesInvoice; perhaps they are new hires or just not very good at their job. Because you pay them only on commission, you're not really concerned. From the SalesPerson's perspective, the cardinality is 0..n, and it is optional. Figure 7.6 illustrates the SalesInvoice-SalesPerson association.

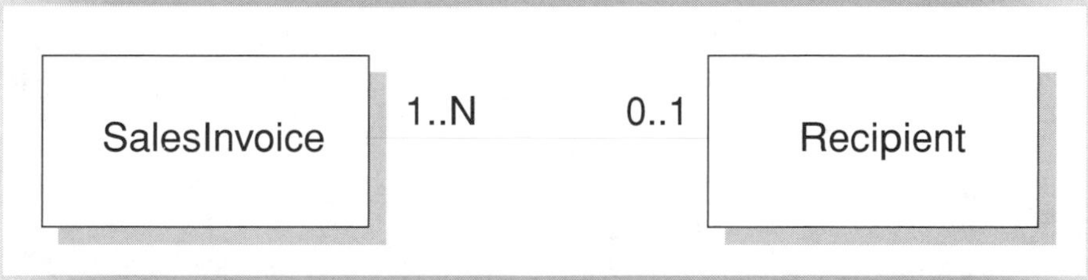

FIGURE 7.5
The SalesInvoice-Recipient association

FIGURE 7.6
The SalesInvoice-SalesPerson association

The last association to define is that of the `SalesInvoice` and the `LineItems` appearing on the invoice. Each `LineItem` object encapsulates information about the quantity of products, which products, and the price. The `LineItem` objects also offer input and output services to the `SalesInvoice`. Because you're only interested in the cardinality of the association at this point, you can put off thinking about the type of collaboration until later. Looking at Figure 7.3, you can see that every `SalesInvoice` has 5 `LineItem` objects. Or does it? Really, what you mean is that every invoice can have at most five `LineItem` objects. If you assume you'll never create a `SalesInvoice` for 0 items (why keep that around?), you can see that the cardinality of the `SalesInvoice`-`LineItem` association is `1..5`, and that it is a mandatory association.

By this point, you're becoming an old hand at this, and you realize that you also have to look at the association from the side of the `LineItem`. Can you have a `LineItem` object that isn't associated with a `SalesInvoice`? No. Can a `LineItem` be associated with more than one `SalesInvoice`? Again, no. You cannot bill two different `Customers` for the same item. Because every `LineItem` must appear on exactly one `SalesInvoice`, the cardinality of this association is 1, and it is a mandatory association. Figure 7.7 shows the `SalesInvoice`-`LineItem` association.

> *" Every relationship needs some rules, even if they're informal and unspoken. "*

SUMMARY OF `SalesInvoice` CARDINALITY

Every relationship needs some rules, even if they're informal and unspoken. The first rule in an association relationship is the membership criteria—who gets to join? The cardinality constraints lay out the answers to this fundamental question. Table 7.2 reiterates the objects you've investigated so far, and the cardinality of their associations.

TABLE 7.2
THE CARDINALITY OF THE `SalesInvoice` ASSOCIATIONS

Association	Cardinality	Optional/ Mandatory
SalesInvoice-Customer	1	Mandatory
Customer-SalesInvoice	0..n	Optional
SalesInvoice-Recipient	0..1	Optional
Recipient-SalesInvoice	1..n	Mandatory
SalesInvoice-SalesPerson	1	Mandatory
SalesPerson-SalesInvoice	0..n	Optional
SalesInvoice-LineItem	1..5	Mandatory
LineItem-SalesInvoice	1	Mandatory

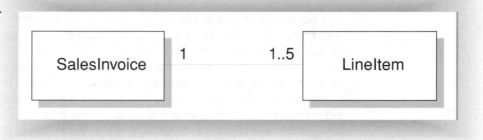

FIGURE 7.7
The SalesInvoice-LineItem association

ASSOCIATIONS AND MESSAGES

To implement an association, you not only have to know about the cardinality of the association, you also have to know how messages will be passed. Will `SalesInvoice` objects send messages to `LineItems`? How about `LineItems` sending messages to `SalesInvoice` objects? To find out this type of information, you'll have to do some additional design work, classifying each relationship by using the categories given previously:

- *Uses relationship*, in which objects communicate via messages

- *Composition relationship*, in which an object is composed of other objects

- *Simple association*, in which objects depend on one another but do not directly interact

By using the `SalesInvoice` class, let's start by looking at the most common type of association between objects—the *uses* relationship.

> *" Whenever one object sends a message to another object, a uses relationship is established... "*

Objects That Use Objects

Whenever one object sends a message to another object, a *uses* relationship is established between the object that sends the message and the object that receives it. In real life you use a similar terminology. When you call PizzaLand for a double pepperoni, you establish a *uses* relationship. You probably use a certain grocer or dry cleaner; you may use your local library. All of these are instances of *uses* relationships from the real world.

One defining characteristic of the *uses* relationship is that it doesn't require the same level of commitment as other relationships. If you decide you'd rather have Szechwan take-out next time you're hungry, you have no binding ties to PizzaLand. Similarly, with objects, the *uses* relationship generally implies a lower level of coupling between objects than inheritance or containment relationships do.

    Uses relationships among objects all boil down to message passing. Does an object send messages to or receive messages from another object? If so, a *uses* relationship exists between those two objects. What *uses* relationships can you find in the SalesInvoice class? To answer that question, you'll have to revisit the collaborations between the objects you've identified. A simple collaboration diagram, like that shown in Figure 7.8, can help you as you work.

SalesInvoiceS AND CustomerS: WHO USES WHOM?

The first class you identified was the Customer class. Does a SalesInvoice object send messages to a Customer object (or to the Customer class)? Yes, certainly. A SalesInvoice object will have to ask its Customer object for the Customer's credit balance, and will have to ask the Customer object where to send the bill. The SalesInvoice object thus sends several messages to the Customer object. You can say that a SalesInvoice uses a Customer object.

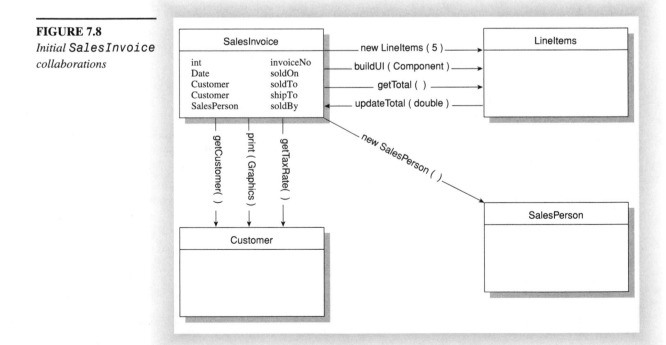

FIGURE 7.8
Initial SalesInvoice collaborations

Let's turn that around. Does a `Customer` object send messages to the `SalesInvoice` object? No, it really doesn't need to. A `Customer` object can exist and has meaning independently from a `SalesInvoice` object. A `Customer` object really doesn't even know that it's associated with a `SalesInvoice` object. It might just as easily be part of a `MailingList` collection or simply stand on its own. The designer Grady Booch calls objects like `Customer` *server objects*, because they provide services to the association but don't send messages. (Of course, `Customer` objects aren't pure server objects, because they do send messages to, and use, other objects. In the Java world, it's rare to find a class that uses no other objects and sends no messages.)

This means that the `SalesInvoice`-`Customer` association is a single-direction, mandatory association that implements a *uses* relationship. It's a *uses* relationship because the `SalesInvoice` sends messages to the `Customer` object. It's single direction because the messages flow in only one direction. It's mandatory because every `SalesInvoice` must have a `Customer`.

> **Remember**
>
> **If an object sends messages to another object, even if that object doesn't send messages back, a *uses* relationship exists between the objects. The *uses* relationship will normally be the dominant relationship in object-oriented programs.**

IMPLEMENTATION: WHERE DOES THE CUSTOMER COME FROM?

If you sit back and think for a second, you'll realize that the first task you face in implementing a *uses* relationship between your `SalesInvoice` object and a `Customer` object is answering the question, "Where do you get a `Customer`?" After thinking about it for a few minutes, you might come up with a solution. Rather than fix on the first solution that comes along, though, you should realize that your `SalesInvoice` object can get hold of a `Customer` in several different ways, and each method has its own advantages and disadvantages. In fact, Arthur Riel, in his book *Object-Oriented Design Heuristics*, describes six different techniques for implementing a *uses* relationship. Let's analyze some of the different possibilities.

Customers as Arguments

Because the `SalesInvoice` association is a mandatory association (that is, you can't have a `SalesInvoice` without a `Customer`), and because as a conscientious designer you always try to make sure your constructors create only valid objects, your first attempt might look something like Listing 7.1.

Listing 7.1. A First Attempt at Implementing the
SalesInvoice-Customer Association

```
public class SalesInvoice
{
  //  --Constructors-----------------------------------------
  public SalesInvoice( Customer soldTo )
  {
    this.soldTo = soldTo;
    //  Other initializations
  }
  //  Details omitted
  //  --Class and Object Attributes-----------------------
  private Customer     soldTo;
}
```

The `SalesInvoice` class shown in Listing 7.1 has a constructor that takes a `Customer` object as an argument. The `Customer` object passed to the constructor is stored in the referential attribute `soldTo`. A *referential attribute* is an object field that refers to another object, even though that object isn't logically contained in the class that holds the field.

Although this solution solves both the mandatory and validity constraints, it lacks a little something in practicality. Users of the class have to get hold of a fully constructed `Customer` before they can start. Moving the analogy back to the paper forms you started with, it would be like a salesperson filling out a credit application before starting to fill in the `SalesOrder`.

Creating Your Own Customers

For some business transactions (buying a house or car, for instance), it might be entirely appropriate to fill out a credit application before the sale. For others, it's overkill. Listing 7.2 shows a second possible solution.

Listing 7.2. A Second Attempt at Implementing the
SalesInvoice-Customer Association

```
public class SalesInvoice
{
  //  --Constructors-----------------------------------------
  public SalesInvoice( ... )
  {
    this.soldTo = new Customer();
    //  Other initializations
  }
  //  Details omitted
  //  --Class and Object Attributes-----------------------
  private Customer     soldTo;
}
```

This version of the `SalesInvoice` class constructs its own `Customer` object, rather than require the user of the class to supply a fully constructed one. Like your first attempt, this `Customer` object is likewise stored in the referential attribute, `soldTo`. This solution may seem attractive if you're in a business where you never get any repeat `Customers` but, if that is the case, why hold on to the `Customer` abstraction at all? You'd be better off simply selling everything to "Cash Customer." The advantage of having `Customer` objects is that they can exist on their own.

Third-Party Customers

A third solution, shown in Listing 7.3, satisfies the need for `Customers` that can exist independently.

```
Listing 7.3. A Third Attempt at Implementing the
SalesInvoice-Customer Association
public class SalesInvoice
{
  //  --Constructors-----------------------------------------
  public SalesInvoice( int custNo, ... )
  {
    this.soldTo = CustomerDB.getCustomer(custNo);
    //  Other initializations
  }
  //  Details omitted
  //  --Class and Object Attributes----------------------
  private Customer    soldTo;
}
```

Listing 7.3 assumes that a repository of `Customers` (here contained in the `CustomerDB` class) keeps track of all `Customer` objects. In Listing 7.3, that's done through a simple, static, non-persistent array. In a real application, the static method `CustomerDB.getCustomer()` would look up a `Customer` in your database and return a copy of the `Customer` for you to use.

This has the advantage of working very much like the problem you're modeling. Have you ever bought anything at a store where you had an account—perhaps a video store? What happens when you go to the checkout counter? The first thing the clerk will do is ask you for your "customer number." The sales clerk then sends the information you supply to an "oracle" somewhere who knows all about your purchasing habits and buying history. If you haven't returned that rented copy of *My Dinner with Andre*, the oracle will know.

Furthermore, this solution has the advantage of "spinning-off" parts of the `Customer` abstraction that are necessary for the `Customer` class to work, but aren't purely part of the `Customer` abstraction itself. In most applications, you will divide your implementation into different layers. One of the most common methods of layering your class is to split off the user-interface code and the data-storage code into separate, tightly coupled classes that work together. Figure 7.9 shows such a partitioning scheme used for the `Customer` class.

FIGURE 7.9

*Partitioning the
Customer class*

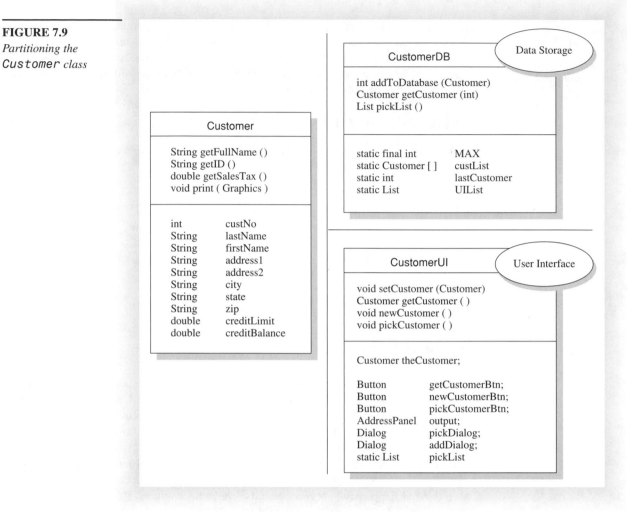

Combining Constructors and Mutators

Unfortunately, this solution suffers from the same failing as your very first; it requires you to supply a valid customer number (instead of a valid Customer object) to fill out a SalesInvoice. You're back to filling out a credit application before you can sell a CD to a new Customer.

The solution to this dilemma is the same solution used at your local video store. If you want to purchase a video, all you need is cash. If you want to rent a video, however, the store needs to get more information from you. You can make your

SalesInvoice class act like this by giving it two constructors: use the no-argument constructor when you want to create a new SalesInvoice object. It gets its Customer object by calling CustomerDB.getCustomer(), which returns the generic "Cash Customer." Inside your SalesInvoice class you can use another method—attached to a "Change Customer" Button, for instance—to allow the SalesInvoice object to change the Customer object that it's associated with. Listing 7.4 shows the constructors for a SalesInvoice class that implements this design. (You can find the entire class on the CD-ROM.)

```
Listing 7.4. Implementing the SalesInvoice-Customer
Association with Two Constructors
public class SalesInvoice
{
  // ==========================================
  //          CONSTRUCTORS
  // ==========================================
  public SalesInvoice( Customer    soldTo,
                       Customer    shipTo,
                       SalesPerson soldBy,
                       LineItems   items )
  {
    this.soldTo = soldTo;
    this.shipTo = shipTo;
    this.soldBy = soldBy;
    this.items  = items;
  }

  public SalesInvoice( )
  {
    this( Customer.getCustomer(0),
          null,
          new SalesPerson(),
          null
        );
    this.items = new LineItems(5, this );
  }
  // Details omitted
  // ==========================================
  //        CLASS AND OBJECT ATTRIBUTES
  // ==========================================
  private Customer    soldTo;
  private Customer    shipTo;
  private SalesPerson soldBy;
  private LineItems   items;
}
```

Other Ways to Use an Object

Each method you've looked at so far relies on the SalesInvoice class to store a referential attribute, soldTo, in its private interface. Can you create a *uses* relationship without storing such attributes? Yes, and in many cases you should. Let's look at the two most popular methods you can use.

PASSING AN ARGUMENT

If you find yourself driving through a strange town and you stop at a convenience store for a cup of coffee, you don't want the clerk to ask you to fill out a credit application. As far as you're concerned, you don't want that kind of relationship.

Sometimes, an object may similarly have a very short and transitory relationship with another object. You may need to use an object only during the execution of a single method. In that case, you might choose to have the method take as an argument an instance of the object it uses, much like the paint(Graphics g) method does with its Graphics object. This is appropriate when:

"Sometimes, an object may similarly have a very short and transitory relationship with another object."

- The object you're going to use will be used only in a single method, and the state of that object doesn't need to be (or positively *shouldn't* be) retained between calls.

- The object you have to use carries with it some immediate state information that must be renewed each time the method is called. For instance, a paint() method should get a new copy of its Graphics context on each call, because the state of the Graphics context may change.

- The object you're using is easily constructed outside your class environment. If, however, it's easier for you (in the using class) to construct the object you want to use from scratch (because of some special knowledge), use the next technique (creating objects on-the-fly).

- If an identical object is constructed over and over, or if it's very time-consuming to construct an object and you need to use it more than once, you should use a referential attribute to hold a reference to the object you'll use, rather than pass it as an argument or create it on-the-fly.

CREATING OBJECTS ON-THE-FLY

A second way to get an object that will be used in only a single method is to create it inside the method itself. If you need to modify the Graphics context of an applet inside a method, you would use some code like this:

```
public void doSomeGraphicsThing()
{
  Graphics g = getGraphics();
  g.setFont(...);
  g.dispose();
}
```

This has several advantages over passing a Graphics object to doSomeGraphicsThing(). First, it makes calling the method easier. Rather than have to create an object first and then pass it to your object to use, another class can simply call doSomeGraphicsThing() like this:

```
SomeObject obj = new SomeObject();
obj.doSomeGraphicsThing();
```

rather than have to do this:

```
SomeObject obj = new SomeObject();
Graphics g = obj.getGraphics();
obj.doSomeGraphicsThing( g );
```

Second, the code where the `Graphics` object is created inside the method is inherently more maintainable. If, for instance, you change how a `Graphics` object is obtained—perhaps you need to switch from `getGraphics()` to `getExtendedGraphics()`—you'll need to change the method name only once if you've created it inside the method where it's used. Otherwise, you'll find yourself hunting through reams of source code, looking for `getGraphics()` method invocations.

Creating an object inside a method is called for when the using object has special knowledge that is required to create the object that it will use. For a very simple example, consider a class—here named `Used`—that has some `private` text that it wishes to display, as shown in Listing 7.5. Obviously, the `TestMethods` class has to do less work to use `methodOne()`, where the `Label` is created as a local variable, than it does to use `methodTwo()`, where the text for the `Label` is passed in as an argument. In fact, if the `Used` class didn't provide the accessor method, `getPrivateText()`, the `TestMethods` class could not even use `methodTwo()` at all.

Listing 7.5. Passing an Object Versus Creating It On-the-Fly

```
//  TestMethods.java
import java.awt.*;
import java.applet.*;

public class TestMethods extends Applet
{
  public void init()
  {
    Used usedObject = new Used();
    add( usedObject.methodOne() );
    add( usedObject.methodTwo(
        usedObject.getPrivateText() ));
  }
}

class Used
{
  public Label methodOne()
  {
    return new Label( privateText );
  }

  public Label methodTwo(String text)
  {
    return new Label( text );
  }

  public String getPrivateText()
  {
```

```
    return privateText;
  }

  private String privateText = "This is some private text";
}
```

Rules for Using Objects

In Java, you can implement the *uses* relationship in several different ways: by use of a referential attribute, by way of a supplied argument to a method, or by creating an instance inside a method. Each technique has advantages and drawbacks.

You should use a referential attribute when

- The object needs to be directed from several different methods, or the object stores persistent state information between method calls.

- The object you are going to use is used repeatedly.

- The object you are going to use is very expensive or time consuming to construct, and you will use the object more than once.

You should pass the object you'll use as an argument when

- The object you want to use will be used only in a single method.

- It's easier to construct the object you want to use outside your class. This is the case when the object you're going to use brings in some information supplied by the caller.

You should construct the object you want to use on-the-fly—that is, inside the method where it's used—when

- The object will be used in only that method.

- The invoking object has information needed to construct the object that will be used, information that would be more difficult or impossible for an outside caller to supply.

Optional Associations: `SalesInvoice` and `Recipient`

If you look back at Table 7.1, notice that the major difference between the `SalesInvoice-Customer` association and the `SalesInvoice-Recipient` association is that the `SalesInvoice-Recipient` association is optional rather than mandatory. You could, if you wanted, make this relationship mandatory, but making it optional allows you to look at how you can implement such optional associations in Java.

An optional `Recipient` association means that the `shipTo` field contained in the `SalesInvoice` class can refer to either a valid `Customer` object (because in this example you have made the decision to represent `Customers` and `Recipients` by using a single class) or a `null` value. What does this mean for the way you implement your class? First, it means that the constructors for the `SalesInvoice` class don't need to pass in a valid value for `shipTo`. If you look at the constructors shown in Listing 7.4, you'll see that `shipTo` is passed the `null` value. Second, it means that any code that could possibly manipulate the `shipTo` value must first check to see whether it's `null`. This is the major difficulty you'll encounter when you want to implement optional relationships: they make the code more complex.

> **" This is the major difficulty you'll encounter when you want to implement optional relationships: they make the code more complex. "**

One problem you'll encounter, for example, is simply the need to display the information about the `soldTo` and `shipTo` objects in your `SalesInvoice`. If the `shipTo` field is `null`, you'll have to use the information from the `soldTo` field. That leads you to write code like this:

```
Button     soldToBtn = new Button(" Sold To ");
Button     shipToBtn = new Button(" Ship To ");
TextField soldIDTxt = new TextField( soldTo.getID(), 5 );
TextField shipIDTxt = new TextField( 5 );
if ( shipTo == null )
{
   shipIDTxt.setText( "" + soldTo.getID() );
}
else
{
   shipIDTxt.setText( "" + shipTo.getID() );
}
```

Notice how much more work the initialization of the `TextField` `shipIDTxt` requires than its compatriot `soldIDTxt`. Anywhere you have an optional association such as this, you'll find similar code designed to handle both the case where the association exists and the case where the association is `null`.

By now, you're probably thinking that, if possible, you should make all associations mandatory. Although it's true that mandatory associations result in simpler code, if the problem you are trying to solve demands an optional association, it's usually not a good idea to create a "fake" association just for simplicity's sake. For example, adding phantom dependents—where the `Employee-Dependent` relationship is optional—may create more problems than it solves.

In the `SalesInvoice` case, however, there *is* a simpler solution. You decided to make the `Recipient` association optional because your company didn't want to store separate files for people who purchased items and the people they were shipped to. The simpler solution is to initialize the `shipTo` field to the same `Customer` object as the `soldTo` field when creating a new object. This is perhaps a clearer understanding of the actual problem, in any case. It's not that the `SalesInvoice-Recipient` relationship is really optional; instead, you can say that both the `Customer` (`soldTo`) and the `Recipient` (`shipTo`) may refer to the same object.

Examining the `Customer` Associations

As you saw in Figure 7.9, the `Customer` class has been divided into three pieces—`Customer`, `CustomerDB`, and `CustomerUI`—each with its own responsibilities and methods. Although the code for these three classes is too large to be reprinted in its entirety here, looking at the associations between these parts can help you understand different methods of association and the tradeoffs required.

`Customer` AND `CustomerDB`

The simplest of the three classes is the `CustomerDB` class—simplest mainly because it's just a proxy for an actual database class that would be used in a production application. Actually storing and retrieving the data from a real database would be somewhat more involved than shown here. Instead, however, the `CustomerDB` class contains a simple `static` array, with a reference to each and every `Customer` in existence.

Let's look first at the interactions between the `SalesInvoice` class and the `CustomerDB` class. The `Customer` class sends a single message to the `CustomerDB` class. Every time a new `Customer` object is constructed, the last line in the `Customer` constructor (shown as Listing 7.6) makes a call to the `static` method `CustomerDB.addToDatabase()`, passing the newly constructed `Customer` as the argument. The method then proceeds to save the `Customer` in the database.

Listing 7.6. The Constructor of the Customer Class

```
public class Customer
{
  protected Customer( String lastName, String firstName,
                      String address1, String address2,
                      String city, String state, String zip,
                      double creditLimit, double creditBalance
                    )
  {
    this.lastName    = lastName;
    this.firstName   = firstName;
    this.address1    = address1;
    this.address2    = address2;
    this.city        = city;
    this.state       = state;
    this.zip         = zip;
    this.creditLimit    = creditLimit;
    this.creditBalance  = creditBalance;

    this.custNo = CustomerDB.addToDatabase(this);
  }
  //  Details omitted
}
```

The `CustomerDB` class, shown in Listing 7.7, likewise sends messages to `Customer` objects. The `CustomerDB` class not only keeps track of all `Customers` created, but also keeps a `List` of their names in the field named `uiList`. This `List` is retrieved by the

CustomerUI class when it needs to display a "picklist" for selecting customers. By making the uiList static, the List needs to be created only one time, and changes to it are immediately available to all clients of CustomerDB.

Listing 7.7. CustomerDB.java

```
// CustomerDB.java
// Simple version
//
import java.awt.*;

public class CustomerDB
{
  //  --Add a Customer to the "database"------------------
  public static int addToDatabase(Customer newCustomer )
  {
    int custNo = lastCustomer++;

    custList[custNo] = newCustomer;
    uiList.add( custList[custNo].getFullName() );
    return custNo;
  }

  public static List pickList()  { return uiList; }

  public static Customer getCustomer( int custNo )
  {
    // This application simplisticly looks up the
    // index value in the custList array
    if (custNo >= lastCustomer)
      custNo = 0;
    return custList[custNo];
  }

  //  =========================================
  //        STATIC FIELDS (In lieu of persistence)
  //  =========================================
  private static final int  MAX          = 100;
  private static Customer[] custList      = new Customer[MAX];
  private static int        lastCustomer  = 0;
  private static List       uiList        = new List();

  // Make sure the Customer List always contains the
  // "default" customer, "Cash"
  static
  {
    new Customer( "Customer", "Cash", "", "", "", "WA", "",
                  0.0, 0.0 );
  }
}
```

Because Customer objects and the CustomerDB class send messages to each other, the relationship is a *bidirectional* association. If you think about it for a moment, you'll realize that a bidirectional association has intrinsically tighter coupling than a one-way association like the `SalesInvoice-Customer` association. That's because a one-way association allows one of the partners—`Customer` in this case—to exist independently. In a bidirectional association, neither class can exist without the other.

Because of this tighter coupling, any time you need a `Customer` object, you must bring along the `CustomerDB` class as well. For this reason, you should avoid bidirectional associations except for classes that can be treated as a unit. Figure 7.10 shows the associations between the `Customer` and `CustomerDB` class.

> *A bidirectional association has intrinsically tighter coupling than a one-way association like the `SalesInvoice-Customer` association.*

CustomerUI ASSOCIATIONS

The `CustomerUI` class provides the "visible" input and output facilities for the `Customer` class. As usual, the user interface accounts for a very large percentage of the total lines of code devoted to the `Customer` abstraction. The `CustomerUI` class provides these services:

- The ability to add a `Customer` to the database interactively using a form. This is done through the `addNewCustomer()` method, which is triggered by an `ActionListener` object attached to the `newCustomerBtn` `Button`.

- The ability to select a customer from the `CustomerDB` database by choosing the name from a picklist. This functionality is embodied inside an `ActionListener` object attached to a `Button` named, appropriately, `pickCustomerBtn`.

- A user interface object—created by constructing an instance of `CustomerUI`—which can be added to an application or applet to provide access to the other services. A `CustomerUI` object contains a reference to a `Customer` object. This object is originally attached when the `CustomerUI` object is created, but may be set or retrieved by using the accessors `getCustomer()` and `setCustomer()`. Also, each `CustomerUI` object contains two `Buttons`, triggering (respectively) the `addNewCustomer` and the `pickCustomer` actions, and a special type of `Panel` used to display a formatted representation of the `Customer` referenced.

FIGURE 7.10
The `Customer-CustomerDB` association

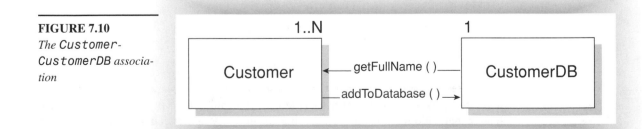

If this seems a little too complex, stepping through a simple scenario should make the relationship clear. The steps needed to use a `CustomerUI` object are as follows:

1. Create an instance of the `CustomerUI` object. To construct a `CustomerUI` object, you must pass in a `Customer`. If you want to use something other than the default `Button` text, Pick Customer and New Customer, you should pass in your preferred descriptions as well. The `SalesInvoice` class creates two `CustomerUI` objects in the attribute section—one attached to the `soldTo` field and the other attached to the `shipTo` field:

```
//  --UI Fields---------------------------------------
private CustomerUI soldToUI = new CustomerUI(SoldTo, " Sold To ");
private CustomerUI shipToUI = new CustomerUI(ShipTo, " Ship To ");
```

2. Add the `CustomerUI` object to your interface, just like you would any other `Panel`. The `SalesInvoice` class does this in its `buildUI()` method, using the following lines:

```
// 2. Add the soldTo and shipTo UI elements
    Panel top = new Panel();
    top.setLayout( new GridLayout(1, 2) );
    f.add( top, "North" );
    top.add( soldToUI );
    top.add( shipToUI );
```

3. After the `CustomerUI` objects are added to your application or applet, they will manage and display the `Customer` information for you. To retrieve the `Customer` reference contained in the `CustomerUI` object, you can use its `getCustomer()` method. You don't have to do anything at all to activate the `pickCustomer()` or `addNewCustomer()` behavior.

Figure 7.11 shows you how the `SalesInvoice` user interface looks after adding the `CustomerUI` objects. Notice that the default, Cash Customer, is selected for both the `SoldTo` and `ShipTo` fields. You don't have to do anything to display the Customer information.

Figure 7.12 shows what happens when you select the Add New `Button` by using the `shipToUI` `CustomerUI` object.

You may fill in the form and then use either the Save or Cancel `Buttons`. If you choose Cancel, the `SalesInvoice` remains the same. If you choose Add, the `CustomerUI` object constructs a new `Customer` (which it adds to the database), and then assigns it to its own internal `Customer` reference. Notice that the `CustomerUI` object doesn't update the `soldTo` or `shipTo` fields inside the `SalesInvoice` object. The `CustomerUI` object does not "know" it's inside a `SalesInvoice` object. By not tying the `CustomerUI` class to the `SalesInvoice` class, you're free to drop a `CustomerUI` object into a `MailingList` form and have it work without change.

Most of the time, rather than add new `Customers`, the `CustomerUI` object will help you select existing `Customers`. It does this through its `pickCustomer()` method, which queries the `List` object maintained by the `CustomerDB` class to find the names of all the existing `Customer` objects. Figure 7.13 shows how this looks.

Figure 7.14 shows each `CustomerUI` association.

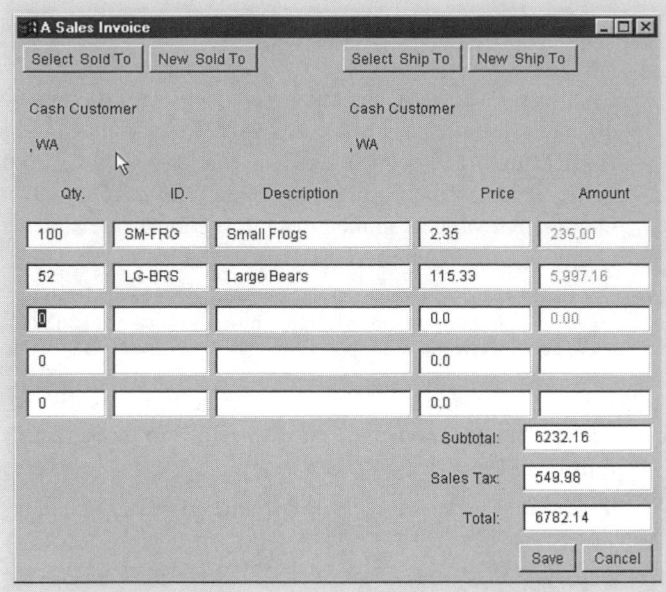

FIGURE 7.11
Adding a CustomerUI
object to a
SalesInvoice *form*

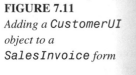

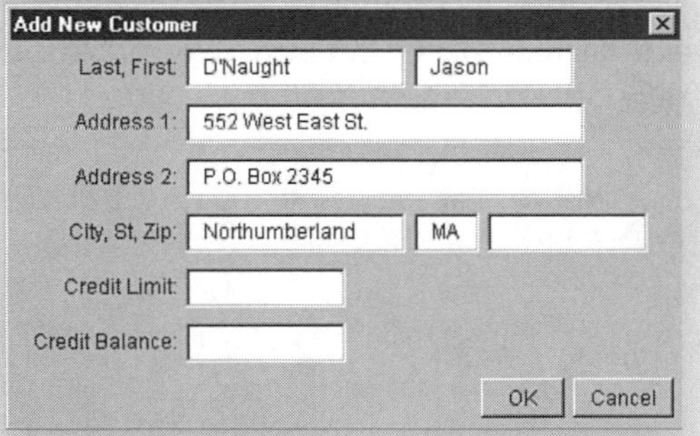

FIGURE 7.12
Adding a new
Customer *by using a*
CustomerUI *object*

FIGURE 7.13
Selecting an existing
Customer *by using a*
CustomerUI *object*

FIGURE 7.14
The CustomerUI associations

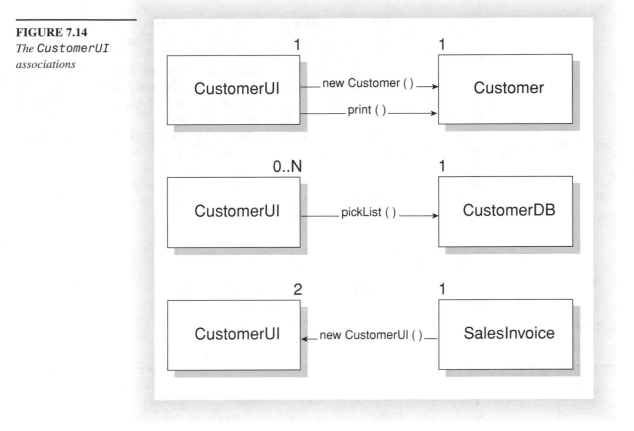

Weak Associations: SalesInvoice and SalesPerson

Most of the "work" done inside the SalesInvoice class is done by the LineItem objects that hold information about the number of items you've sold, how much each item costs, and, subsequently, how much money you've made. The relationship between these LineItems and the SalesInvoice class is a much closer relationship than you've seen so far: the relationship of containment. In the first half of the next chapter, you'll take a look at that relationship.

This chapter still has one loose end to tie up, however. What do you make of the relationship between SalesPerson and SalesInvoice? If you'll look back, you'll see that no messages seem to be flowing between the SalesPerson and the SalesInvoice object. Can you then just eliminate the SalesPerson attribute from the SalesInvoice class altogether? No, not really. At the end of each month or week, you'll have to add up all the SalesInvoices and pay each SalesPerson the appropriate commission. Should you then attempt to send some messages between the SalesPerson and

`SalesInvoice` object, so you don't end up with a "Data Warehouse" class? Again, the answer has to be negative. It makes no sense to initiate meaningless messages just to satisfy some rule of thumb.

In fact, the relationship between `SalesInvoice` and `SalesPerson` is not uncommon—it's known as a *weak association*. A weak association exists whenever you have an association where no messages are exchanged, but the association is necessary to the success of the overall abstraction you're trying to model.

The real danger you face when confronted with a potential weak association is determining whether it's really necessary for the abstraction you are working with. Clearly, `SalesPerson` is necessary for an invoicing application if you hope to continue selling products past the first payday. On the other hand, `InvoiceSupplier` probably won't be a necessary field. When you run out of invoices, simply check your Rolodex for the name of the person from whom you bought them.

> *" A weak association exists whenever you have an association where no messages are exchanged, but the association is necessary to the success of the overall abstraction... "*

Summary

Describing and defining the relationships between objects and classes is one of the biggest jobs you'll undertake as an object-oriented designer. By breaking up the types of relationships into different categories, and then applying experience-based rules of thumb (heuristics), you can save yourself from creating dysfunctional object communities.

The first relationship distinction is between inheritance-based relationships—that is, relationships between classes, and object-based relationships or associations. An inheritance-based relationship is a mandatory relationship, much like your relationship with your parents. Every subclass object must contain all the fields and methods of its superclass, although it may modify them. By contrast, object relationships are more flexible.

The cardinality of a relationship is the lower bound and the upper bound on the number of objects that participate in it. The lower bound may be zero or one, and the upper bound may be one or many, represented by n.

There are three basic types of object relationships. When one class sends messages to an instance of another class, that's called an association or a *uses relationship*. This is the most common type of relationship in an object-oriented program. When an object logically contains another object, that's called a *composition* or *aggregation relationship*; composition is the subject of Chapter 8. Finally, when an object has an association with an object of another class, yet they don't exchange messages, it is called a *weak* or *simple association*.

There are several different ways to implement a *uses* relationship. The most common method is to include an object attribute that's used to refer to the other object. The object may be obtained as an argument to a method, from a global "supplier" class, or may be constructed inside the method on-the-fly. Each method has different advantages and disadvantages.

Questions

1. Experience-based rules that help you decide which relationships to implement and the best way to implement them are called _____.

2. A relationship where no messages are passed between two objects, yet the relationship cannot be eliminated, is called a _____ or _____ association.

3. A _____ relationship exists between two objects when one object sends messages to another object.

4. The relationship between a car and its engine is what kind of association?

   a. Weak association

   b. *Uses* relationship

   c. Inheritance

   d. Composition relationship

5. In the following code fragment, what is the relationship between the `BigApp` object and the `CustomDialog` object?

```
public class BigApp extends Applet
{
  public void getInput()
  {
    CustomDialog d = new CustomDialog();
    d.show();
    d.dispose();
  }
}
```

   a. Weak association

   b. *Uses* relationship

   c. Inheritance

   d. Composition relationship

6. True or false. You should always implement a *uses* relationship by means of a referential attribute.

7. True or false. Using a referential attribute means that the class holding the attribute has a containing or composition relationship with the attribute.

8. True or false. Weak associations can always be eliminated.

9. Complete the following code segment, showing two ways you could supply a `Graphics` object for the `paintMe()` method to complete its work:

```
public class PaintThis extends Applet
{
    public void init()
    {

    }
    public void paintMe(                )
    {
```

```
        g.setBackground( Color.red );
        repaint();
    }
}
```

10. The term used to describe the mutual dependence of two objects on each other is _____. All things being equal, _____ is better than _____.

Exercises

1. Print out the source listing for `CustomerUI.java`. This chapter has described the associations between `CustomerUI` and the other classes in the `SalesInvoice` application. What other object relationships exist inside the `CustomerUI` class? (Hint: `CustomerUI` uses several of the `AWT` classes to do things it's too busy to do.)

2. Take the case study from Chapter 6 and update the collaboration diagrams to add cardinality information.

3. Design Challenge: While the `Customer` abstraction was broken up into the `CustomerUI`, `CustomerDB`, and `Customer` classes, the `SalesInvoice` class was not similarly divided. Design the classes necessary to divide `SalesInvoice` into `SalesInvoiceUI`, `SalesInvoiceDB`, and `SalesInvoice`.

4. Coding Challenge I: Look up the documentation for the `java.util.Vector` class and modify the `CustomerDB` class to use a `Vector` rather than an array.

5. Coding Challenge II: Implement the `SalesPerson` class. You can use the `Customer` abstraction as a model.

6. Create a set of class diagrams and interaction diagrams that show how you would design a simple piggy-bank system. Feel free to invent classes, like "Coin Sensor," that you might not feel comfortable building in real life.

To Learn More

Associations are one of the fundamental parts of object-oriented design. Unfortunately, each author and each methodology has a different take on what an association is and how to define and refine it. Furthermore, each different methodology uses a slightly different meaning when they talk about associations. To get a different take on each issue, you can read the following publications:

- Booch, Grady. *Object-Oriented Analysis and Design with Applications,* 2nd ed. Redwood City, California: Benjamin/Cummings, 1994.

- Rumbaugh, James, et al. *Object-Oriented Modeling and Design.* Englewood Cliffs, New Jersey: Prentice Hall, 1991.

8

Object Relationships: Compositions and Collections

"Beep," pause, "beep," pause, "beep."

Your head snaps up from the manual you were browsing while waiting for your computer to boot. There on-screen, instead of the colorful logo you expected and a triumphant "Ta-da!" sits a solitary line of silent gray text on a plain black background:

```
02-Keyboard Failure
```

What do you do? If your VCR, microwave oven, or popcorn popper stopped working, you'd probably immediately pull out the yellow pages and begin searching for an appliance repair shop. It's unlikely, however, that the dire-sounding message appearing on your monitor will trigger same sort of behavior. Instead, you'll first follow the keyboard cord to the back of the computer, make sure that it's plugged in, and then restart your computer. If the same thing happens again, you'll unplug the keyboard, trot on down to your local Computer Warehouse store and pick up a new keyboard—maybe one of those nice new ergonomic models! Only then, if that fails, will you think about looking for a repair shop.

Why do you react differently to your computer failing than you would to your VCR breaking down? Is it because you're some sort of computer guru? Not really. Even very ordinary, everyday computer users think nothing of replacing a keyboard or monitor. Many who would never dream of unscrewing the top on their VCR routinely open up their computer case and install a new sound board or hard drive. Modern PC systems are different from VCRs; PC systems are modular, rather than integrated like the VCR. Your PC is composed of self-contained parts that interact by using well-defined interfaces; these parts are easily tested and replaced without affecting the rest of your system.

Like hardware, software too can be composed of parts that are tightly "wired" together (like your VCR), or it can be built in layers (*subsystems*), with each subsystem acting independently from the others, and with more complex systems made from differing arrangements of less complex and more fundamental parts.

This chapter will teach you how to combine objects to build more complex, composite objects, while hiding unnecessary complexity from the user. You will learn:

> *" Like hardware, software too can be composed of parts that are tightly 'wired' together, or it can be built in layers..."*

- How hierarchy and decomposition can aid you in creating and understanding complex systems
- How to implement composite objects by combining simpler objects
- How to simplify the use of complex objects by providing a simpler interface that delegates its responsibilities to its subsystems
- How Java's inner classes allow you to simplify the communication between composite objects and their parts
- How to use the Unified Modeling Language (UML) notation to represent composite objects and their dynamic interactions
- How to use arrays in Java to create multivalued objects and implement 1..n associations

Associates and Aggregates

In Chapter 7, "Object Relationships: Implementing Associations," you looked at two of the three different types of association relationships: *weak associations*, where related objects don't send messages to each other, and *uses* relationships, where objects do send messages to each other. Although it's possible to create object-oriented programs by using only these relationships, you'll quickly find yourself overwhelmed by complexity if you do so. The third type of association, *composition*, provides a way to bring structure to your programs that the other mechanisms don't provide.

COMPOSITION: THE *PART-OF* RELATIONSHIP

Sometimes, the best way to describe the relationship between two objects is to say that one object contains another object. It seems intuitive and natural to say that a car contains an engine, a university contains colleges, or a house contains a kitchen. Whenever a particular object is composed of other objects, and those objects are included as object fields, the new object is known as a *compound*, *aggregate*, or *composite* object. (Although some designers make a distinction between the words *aggregation* and *composition*—defining *composition* as a strong form of aggregation—in this chapter we'll use the two words interchangeably.)

Figure 8.1 shows the relationship between a car and its parts using the Unified Modeling Language (UML) notation. You can read more about UML later in this chapter, but for now, you can see that a car consists of four wheels, an engine, a body, from two to four seats, and a "user interface." The interface itself includes a steering wheel, a gas pedal, and a brake.

Several other terms are commonly used to label this relationship. You might hear it referred to as a *hasA* relationship because, in ordinary English, you can say a car *hasA* engine, and a house *hasA* kitchen. It is also called the *whole-part* or *part-of* relationship. No matter what it's called, though, the idea remains the same: individual objects can be combined to create a more complex and useful object. And just as a *uses* association implies greater coupling between its members than a weak association, so too the *part-of* relationship implies greater mutual dependence than the simple *uses* association.

Using composition is one of the key techniques you can use in your battle against complexity. Let's see how.

> *" Composition provides a way to bring structure to your programs that other mechanisms don't provide. "*

FIGURE 8.1

A car is composed of parts

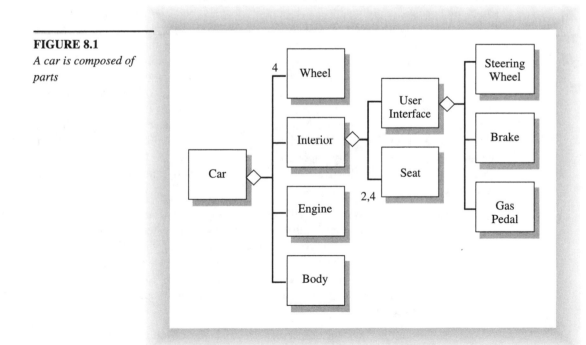

No matter what it's called, the idea remains the same: individual objects can be combined to create a more complex and useful object.

Complexity and order: look around and you'll see these two opposing forces on every hand...

COMPOSITION AND COMPLEXITY

"[A]fter all, complicated tasks usually do inherently require complex algorithms, and this implies a myriad of details. And the details are the jungle in which the devil hides. The only salvation lies in structure."

As this quote from Niklaus Wirth, the creator of Pascal, reminds us, building software is hard, even when using object-oriented techniques, because things are always threatening to get out of hand. Your clients might want to add a new feature, or you may find yourself having to accommodate new hardware or a new operating system. Unfortunately, if you're not careful, adding support for that new piece of hardware or adding that new feature can introduce instabilities and problems that can bring your whole system falling down, like the proverbial house of cards. In an instant, it seems, your working program can become too complex to understand or fix.

The bane of software construction is complexity. Even when you start with a simple, well understood problem, before you know it, you can end up with a contraption that would do Rube Goldberg (the cartoonist famous for his drawings of excessively complicated, zany machines) proud. Does it have to be like this? Maybe not.

Complexity and order: look around and you'll see these two opposing forces on every hand, not just in software development. Think of the wide varieties of plant and animal life in the world, and then realize that everything you see is composed of the same fundamental building blocks: atoms, molecules, and elements. How can such simple pieces produce such extensive diversity, without disintegrating into a chaotic mess? The answer lies in *structure*, a very specific kind of structure.

In an article titled "The Architecture of Complexity," first published in 1962, Nobel Prize winner Herbert Simon outlined some basic organizational principles that govern stable complex systems. When you write programs, instead of simply connecting objects together in random ways, you can use these principles to create systems that continue to work when your environment changes. Because Java programs are designed to work unchanged on a variety of platforms, the ability to remain stable in the face of change is especially important.

What are the principles that Dr. Simon discovered? Briefly, they include these four observations:

- Stable complex systems usually take the form of a *hierarchy*, where each system is built of simpler subsystems, and each subsystem is built from simpler subsystems still. You may already be familiar with this principle because it forms the basis for *functional decomposition*, the method behind procedural software development. In object-oriented design, you apply the same principle to composition—building complex objects from simpler pieces.

- Stable complex systems are *nearly decomposable*. That means you can identify the parts that make up the system and can tell the difference between interactions *between* the parts and interactions *inside* the parts. Stable systems have fewer links between their parts than they do inside the parts. Thus, a modular stereo system, with simple links between the speakers, turntable, and amplifier, is inherently more stable than an integrated system, which isn't easily decomposable.

- Stable complex systems are almost always composed of only a few different kinds of subsystems, arranged in different combinations. Those subsystems, in turn, are generally composed of only a few different kinds of parts.

- Stable complex systems that work have almost always evolved from simple systems that worked. Rather than build a new system from scratch—reinventing the wheel—the new system builds on the proven designs that went before it.

Composition—building relatively independent subsystems using simple parts—is the technique you'll most often use to apply Dr. Simon's insights to your own software designs. Although these observations don't provide a cookbook for constructing your Java programs, they do give you a yardstick for measuring the quality of your designs. Let's look at the details you'll need to master to implement composite relationships in Java.

COMPOSITION RELATIONSHIPS IN JAVA

As a Java programmer, you're already familiar with the composition relationship in practice because it's used extensively to create user interface code with Java's Abstract Window Toolkit (AWT). By adding `Buttons`, `TextFields`, and `LayoutManagers` to a `Panel` object, you easily create new compound objects, which you then add to the surface of your applications or applets. With composition, however, rather than simply add the components to a `Panel`, you create a new class with your `Buttons` and `TextFields` as fields or parts inside your new object.

If you've been paying close attention, you may wonder at this point what's the difference between this new *part-of* relationship and a simple *uses* relationship. After all, as you saw in Chapter 7, the main way in which both weak associations and *uses* relationships are implemented is by embedding a reference to the associate as a field inside the class definition. Does this mean that those relationships are also composition relationships? Not at all.

The distinction between the three forms of association is a *semantic* distinction, not an *implementation* distinction. In Java, it's likely that all three forms—weak association, *uses* relationship, and *part-of* relationship—will be represented in exactly the same way when the code is written. That's one reason it's so hard for CASE (Computer-Aided Software Engineering) tool vendors to create a program that draws object-model diagrams from source code. Because the implementation of each relationship is likely to be identical, there's no way for the program to tell which kind of relationship is intended.

How, then, does the meaning of a composition relationship differ from that of an association relationship? Let's take a look.

COMPOSITION VERSUS ASSOCIATION

Despite what the heading of this section might seem to imply, composition relationships are also a form of association. Specifically, composition is a strong form of the *uses* relationship. For composition to exist, either the parts or the whole must send messages to each other. If an object contains other objects and doesn't send messages to those objects, such a relationship is a weak association, not a containment relationship. Thus, it's something of a misnomer to speak of composition as entirely distinct from association.

Unlike a regular *uses* relationship, however, a composition relationship implies that one class (the whole) is made up of other objects (the parts). Composition is thus a whole-part relationship, where:

- One object is physically built from other objects—for example, a custom user-interface component built from more basic components.

- An object represents a logical whole, composed of smaller parts. A company may be composed of finance, production, and marketing departments, for instance.

- Each part belongs to only a single whole. This is a useful test you can use to differentiate between composition and *uses* relationships. For instance, in the `SalesInvoice` application, a single `Customer` may have placed several orders, and thus be referenced on several `SalesInvoices`. Therefore, the `SalesInvoice` doesn't *contain* a `Customer` object.

- Each part lives and dies with the whole. In the `SalesInvoice` application, you certainly wouldn't want your `Customers` disappearing every time you deleted a `SalesInvoice` object. Therefore, this relationship is a *uses* relationship, not a composition relationship. You would, however, want the `LineItems` to disappear with the rest of the `SalesInvoice` when you deleted it. This second relationship is a composition relationship.

As you can see, a meaningful distinction really exists between the composition relationship and the *uses* relationship. And, as you'll see later, the composition relationship provides several advantages over a simple *uses* relationships, chief among them the ability to hide unnecessary details from the users of your objects.

CREATING A COMPOSITE OBJECT: THE LABELED `TextField`

Let's begin looking at composition by building a simple class that solves a recurring problem. You're already familiar with this problem if you've spent any time creating applications with Java's AWT—the problem of adding a `Label` to a `TextField`.

For many business applications, an input form is the heart of the program. Users first enter some information into fields on the form, the data is validated, and finally it's sent off to the rest of the application for processing. To make sure that the user knows

" Composition provides several advantages over a simple uses relationship, chief among them the ability to hide unnecessary details from the users of your objects."

what to enter, you usually attach a `Label` to each field. If you're a developer making the transition to Java from some other development environment, you'll quickly discover that although Java has `TextFields` you can use for input and `Label` objects you can use to display text, it doesn't have a built-in class that combines both. If you try sending the `setText()` message to a `TextField` object, you'll quickly find that your command doesn't label the `TextField`, but instead fills it with text. And, look as you may, you'll find no `setLabel()` method to help. Fortunately, by using composition, it's easy to build an aggregate object that meets your needs.

Listing 8.1, `LTextField.java` (the L stands for *Labeled*), shows the implementation of a very simple class that allows you to label a `TextField` object.

Listing 8.1 LTextField.java

```java
//  A Labeled TextField class
import java.awt.*;

public class LTextField extends Panel
{
  // --Constructors-----------------------------------
  public LTextField(String name, int size, int lWidth)
  {
    theLabel = new FixedWidthLabel(name, Label.RIGHT, lWidth);
    theText  = new TextField(size);
    add(theLabel);
    add(theText);
  }

  // --Accessors--------------------------------------
  public String getText() { return theText.getText(); }

  // --Mutators---------------------------------------
  public void setLabel(String newLabel)
  {
    theLabel.setText(newLabel);
  }

  // --Object Attributes------------------------------
  private FixedWidthLabel theLabel;
  private TextField       theText;

  // --Private inner class----------------------------
  private class FixedWidthLabel extends Label
  {
    public FixedWidthLabel(String s, int align, int columns)
    {
      super(s, align);
      this.columns = columns;
    }

    public Dimension getPreferredSize()
    {
      Dimension d = super.getPreferredSize();
      FontMetrics fm = getFontMetrics(getFont());
      int pixPerCol = fm.charWidth('o');
      return new Dimension(pixPerCol * columns, d.height);
```

```
    }
    private int columns;
  }
}
```

The `LTextField` class, which extends the `Panel` class, contains as `private` fields two other objects: a `TextField` object named `theText`, and a `FixedWidthLabel` object named `theLabel`. Every time you create an `LTextField` object, it will consist of these two parts: its `TextField` and its `FixedWidthLabel`. The definition for the `FixedWidthLabel` class is implemented as a `private`, named, inner class inside the body of the `LTextField` class itself. (See the following sidebar for more information on this Java 1.1 feature.) The `FixedWidthLabel` class is the key to neatly lining up your input areas and their associated text. A regular AWT `Label` is dynamically sized according to the text it contains. The `FixedWidthLabel` class, by contrast, accepts an additional argument in its constructor, just as the `TextField` class does. Regardless of the size of the text it contains, the `FixedWidthLabel` uses the integer value you specify to set its width.

COMPOSITE CLASSES WITH INNER CLASSES

Inner classes, new to Java 1.1, are an ideal way to implement a whole-part relationship in cases where the parts are unique to the subsystem you're building. This occurs most often when you're writing classes to handle various user-interface generated events. To create an inner class, you simply define the body of one class inside the body of another class like this:

```
public class LTextField extends Panel
{
  private class FixedWidthLabel extends Label
  {
    // attributes and methods from the FixedWidthLabel class
  }
}
```

The enclosing class (`LTextField`) can then create as many copies of the inner class (`FixedWidthLabel`) as it needs. Because `FixedWidthLabel` was declared as a private class, only the `LTextField` class can use it.

As shown, the `FixedWidthLabel` class really derives no advantage from being an inner class except that its name is hidden inside the `LTextField` class. If the name `FixedWidthLabel` could possibly clash with another class of the same name used in the same system, this would be helpful. By making `FixedWidthLabel` an inner class, you can avoid "polluting" the global namespace, much the same way that local variables restrict their scope to the method they're declared in.

Continued

COMPOSITE CLASSES WITH INNER CLASSES Continued...

A more interesting use of inner classes, however, is to *increase* the coupling between a contained part and the object that contains it. One characteristic of stable complex systems is that the parts *inside* the subsystem are more tightly coupled to each other than the different subsystems are to each other. Thus, you want to increase intra-system (internal) coupling and decrease inter-system (external) coupling.

Inner classes support this by allowing the inner class access to the data environment of the object that contains it. Thus, inside the FixedWidthLabel class you could use the fields theLabel and theText, which are declared inside LTextField, but LTextField wouldn't have access to the column field declared inside the FixedWidthLabel class. (Currently, certain environments—notably, Microsoft's version of Java—don't allow you to access the private fields of an enclosing class from an inner class. If you want to make sure that your code will interoperate in these conditions, you'll want to specify protected access for those fields that must be visible in the inner class.)

In the LTextField class, notice that the FixedWidthLabel object, theLabel, is initialized inside the LTextField constructor just like any other field:

```
theLabel = new FixedWidthLabel(name, Label.RIGHT, lWidth);
```

The new inner class syntax also allows you to create new classes by supplying a class definition as part of the constructor call:

```
MouseAdapter ma = new MouseAdaptor() { ... class methods go here };
```

You can even create *anonymous* inner classes by passing a class constructor to any method that expects to receive a particular object:

```
myButton.addActionListener(new ActionListener()
{
    public void actionPerformed(ActionEvent ae)
    {
        // Code for anonymous ActionListener object here
    }
});
```

Anonymous inner classes might be better called "objects of an anonymous inner class." The preceding code creates an inner class that extends ActionListener but overrides ActionListener.actionPerformed(). It goes on to actually instantiate an object, which is used as the parameter to the addActionListener method. The anonymous inner class feature is used mostly for creating event handlers, which tend to be highly specific for each individual class.

The most important characteristic of the LTextField class is that its parts—the FixedWidthLabel and TextField—are encapsulated as part of its state. Users of the LTextField class have no more access to these internal parts of the LTextField than the average driver has to the fuel-injection system inside an automobile. Instead, users are presented with a simplified interface consisting of the following:

🔹 A single constructor that requires a `String` for the field description, the number of columns to use for the `TextField`, and the number of columns to use for the `FixedWidthLabel`. Users who don't need descriptive text in front of their fields can pass in the empty `String` (`""`), along with the appropriate number of columns for the `TextField` and the label.

🔹 An accessor method, `getText()`, that asks its `TextField` part for the text it contains, and then passes it back to the caller.

🔹 A mutator method, `setLabel()`, that allows you to change the descriptive text associated with an input field.

Composite objects serve a purpose very similar to functional decomposition in procedural programs. By hiding non-essential details inside a class, and then replacing those details with a simpler interface, composition allows you to concentrate on the task at hand without getting bogged down in minutia, much the way procedures allowed an earlier generation to see their programs at a higher level of abstraction. As an example of this effect, look at the `LTextFieldUser` applet in Listing 8.2, which creates a simple name and address form, very similar to the one you created for the `Customer` class.

Listing 8.2 LTextFieldUser.java

```java
//  Using the Labeled TextField class
import java.awt.*;
import java.awt.event.*;
import java.applet.*;

public class LTextFieldUser extends Applet
{
  public void init()
  {
    setLayout(new FlowLayout(FlowLayout.LEFT));
    add(new LTextField("Name : ",            40, 15));
    add(new LTextField("Address : ",         40, 15));
    add(new LTextField("City, State, Zip : ", 15, 15));
    add(new LTextField("",                     2,  0));
    add(new LTextField("",                    10,  0));
  }
}
```

As you can see, creating an `LTextField` object is as easy as creating a regular `TextField`, and certainly simpler than creating both a `TextField` and `Label` together and then trying to line them up. By specifying the same number of columns for the `Name`, `Address`, and `City-State-Zip` labels (using the last argument to the `LTextField()` constructor), you ensure that all the `TextFields` will nicely line up when placed on your applet. Use the sample HTML file in Listing 8.3, `LTextFieldUser`, and see for yourself.

Listing 8.3 LTextFieldUser.html

```
<HTML>
<HEAD>
<TITLE>Using the LTextField Class</TITLE>
</HEAD>
<BODY>
<H1>Name and Address</H1>
<HR>
<APPLET CODE=LTextFieldUser HEIGHT=300 WIDTH=400>
</APPLET>
</BODY>
</HTML>
```

As you can see from Figure 8.2, each field is lined up neatly, all with a minimum of work.

Rules of Thumb for Composition

Iteration—trying out a design, noting its deficiencies, and then building a better model—is an essential component of object-oriented modeling. However, unless you have some way of telling whether you're actually making progress, you may end up like Sisyphus, who was eternally condemned to push a rock to the top of a tall mountain, only to have it roll down in the night. You need some way of telling whether you're making net progress, and some idea of which direction to go.

To build robust *composite* objects, you first have to decide *which parts* go with *what whole*. This is the main problem in composition: deciding what to put together and what to separate. The following rules won't give you hard-and-fast, step-by-step instructions for doing that, but they will help you tell whether you're going in the right direction.

> *Iteration—trying out a design, noting its deficiencies, and then building a better model—is an essential component of object-oriented modeling.*

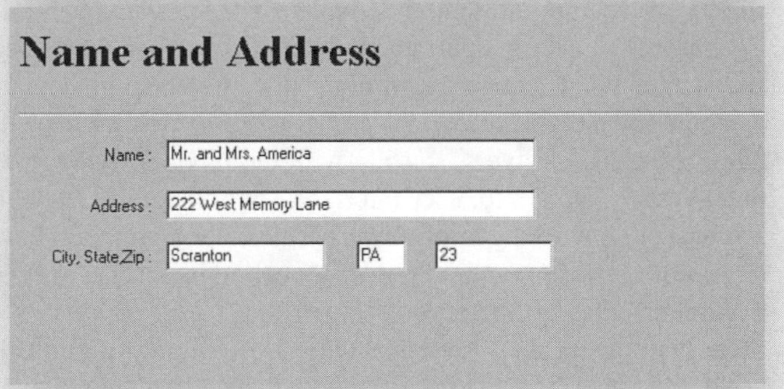

FIGURE 8.2
Running the
LTextFieldUser
applet in a Web browser

Name and Address

Name : Mr. and Mrs. America

Address : 222 West Memory Lane

City, State,Zip : Scranton   PA   23

LOCALIZE MESSAGE TRAFFIC

The first place to start looking for composite objects is to find out what objects already "hang out" together. Like teenage best friends, objects with high-frequency communication between them generally belong in the same subsystem. Objects with less communication belong in separate subsystems or modules. Of course, if the individual subsystems you develop have no communication between them—if they're perfectly decomposable instead of nearly so—you wouldn't have a system, but merely a collection of autonomous agents. The closer you can get to a collection of independent modules working in concert, the more stable and maintainable your system will be.

Begin looking for communication links by identifying the frequency of message traffic between your objects. If you've already identified the associations in your system with the related messages, you've already done this. After you identify parts with a high frequency of interaction between them, you have candidates for a composite class.

Arthur Riel, in his book *Object-Oriented Design Heuristics*, proposes a pair of similar rules that use frequency of communication as a design rule. He suggests that if a class contains objects of another class, the container should be sending messages to the contained objects. Furthermore, most of the methods defined in the class should be using most of the data members most of the time. These rules will help you determine which objects should be eliminated as candidates for composite classes.

AVOID MIXING DOMAINS

A second criterion for grouping objects together revolves around functionality or domains. A king's domain is the land where he rules. In software development, a subsystem's domain is the area of functionality for which the subsystem is responsible. Think of an automobile assembly line, for instance. The machine that welds the bumpers is specialized for that job, and it also doesn't try to adjust the brakes or install the engine; those jobs are outside its domain. Processes, like the assembly line, that can be broken into individual domains are said to be *layered*.

Layering—breaking apart an application based on common functionality—is a time-tested method of grouping similar code together. In telecommunications, the Open Systems Interconnection (OSI) model is a good example of this. It specifies seven different domains or layers, starting with the physical (electrical) specification and moving all the way up to user-interface specifications. Each layer provides a general service for networking applications. This clear distinction between each domain makes it possible to write applications that work together, because each layer or part refrains from interfering with another.

One natural form of layering, which you should definitely consider whenever you build software, is to separate the user-interface, data storage, and business logic portions of your programs into different layers. Most computer applications require you to process some information, store the information, and present the information to users. By keeping the data-storage logic out of your user-interface classes, you make it much less likely that changes to your input screens will affect the integrity of your data, or that switching database vendors will require you to rewrite your user interface.

For systems of any size, you'll also want to consider partitioning the business-logic portion of your program along functional lines. For instance, although you might find it tempting to build a unified, do-it-all program that neatly integrates order entry, shipping, inventory, and billing, you'll be better served by breaking each of these functional parts into its own subsystem, and then defining a set of clearly defined interfaces to facilitate communication between them.

The separation of domains is closely related to the principle of cohesion. In procedural programming, the principle of cohesion states that a function should do only one thing. In OOD, a corresponding rule says that a class should model only a single abstraction. When combining classes into subsystems, you should look for areas that can be logically partitioned. By clearly separating the domains of inventory control and invoicing, for example, and by providing a formal interface between them, you avoid the problems that occur when a bug in the invoicing system brings down your inventory program as well.

ISOLATE THE CHANGEABLE

A third criterion for composition is to group objects by their *stability*, their tendency to change. If you can, identify those portions of your system likely to change, and put those parts together. Then, combine the relatively unchangeable parts into separate subsystems. That way, when the inevitable change comes, rather than make changes scattered throughout 10 subsystems, you can concentrate on only one or two.

A pleasant side effect of grouping changeable parts is that developers spend more time with the most changeable code and thus get to know it better. When changes are scattered throughout the system, much of the cost of change is associated with the overhead required to simply understand the surrounding code.

CREATE SIMPLE INTERFACES

Whereas composite objects should have high-frequency internal communication (that is, most of the methods should use most of the objects most of the time), communication between the "outside" world and the object should have lower frequency. This corresponds to the procedural idea of loose coupling between functions. One way to facilitate this is to create simple interfaces.

To see how this works, look back at the LTextField class presented in the first half of this chapter. If you were to "decompose" the LTextField class, you could get (roughly) the same effect by creating a Label, setting its size based on your desired width, resizing the component, and then creating a TextField and manipulating it. For instance, to replace the two lines that create the LTextField object labeled "Name" in the LTextFieldUser applet in Listing 8.2, you'd have to do this:

```
Label nameLabel = new Label("Name : ", Label.RIGHT);
add(nameLabel);
Dimension d = nameLabel.getPreferredSize();
FontMetrics fm = nameLabel.getFontMetrics(nameLabel.getFont());
```

```
int pixPerCol = fm.charWidth('o');
nameLabel.setSize(15 * pixPerCol, d.height);
TextField nameTextField = new TextField(40);
add(nameTextField);
```

By using `LTextField` objects, all this communication is hidden inside the class. Users of `LTextField` objects use only the constructor and the methods that allow them to change the `Label` text or retrieve the information from the `TextField`. Figure 8.3 illustrates how composition, with a simple interface, separates high-frequency communication from low-frequency, inter-object communication.

One consequence of using composition in this way is that users of `LTextField` objects can't do all the things that they might do with the component parts. You may instinctively recoil at these restrictions and set about making sure that `LTextFields` have at least as rich an interface as the `TextField` and `Label` objects. You should, however, resist this impulse. The strength of composition lies in its capability to bring structure to complexity. Just as the simpler interface of the steering wheel, gas pedal, and brake harnesses the complexity of the automobile, so too you should use composition to build ease-of-use into your objects. For those times when all the gears and levers need to be visible, such as the cockpit of a jetliner, inheritance rather than composition is the better choice.

FIGURE 8.3

Composition isolates high-frequency communication behind a simpler interface

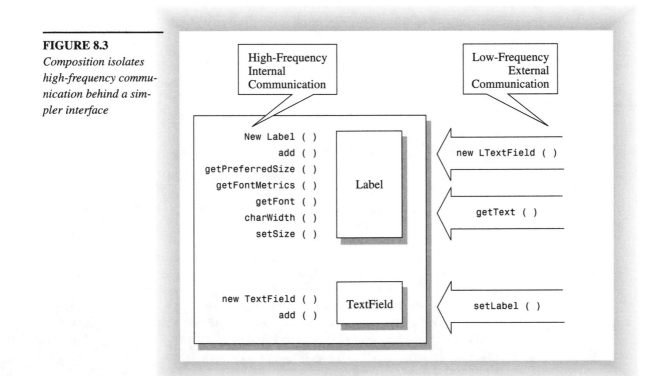

GENERALIZE WHEN POSSIBLE, SPECIALIZE WHEN NECESSARY

Another problem you'll encounter when creating composite objects is deciding how general or specific each part should be. By making very specific parts—parts specialized to do only a single task—you reduce the effort that a user needs to expend in using your part. On the other hand, if you create only specialized parts, you'll soon be drowning in classes.

For instance, rather than create the LTextField class, you could have created specialized classes for storing names, addresses, cities, and zip codes. As you can imagine, if you carry this to the extreme, you could have a separate class for every input field object in your system!

A better solution is to specialize only when necessary. A ZipCode field may have specialized requirements that can't be met by the regular LTextField class; for example, it may check the code against a list of valid postal codes or provide handy formatting services. It's unlikely that the name, address, and city fields would require identical treatment, however. You might, therefore, decide to create a specialized ZipCode field for the zip code, and leave the others as LTextFields. Another alternative is to create a general solution by adding input validation to the LTextField class itself. Of course, that may lead to feature creep and defeat the whole advantage of having a minimal interface in the first place. That's a decision you'll have to make on a case-by-case basis.

As mentioned earlier in the chapter, stable complex systems tend to be composed of a few simple parts, arranged in different ways. If you want your system to be maximally stable, create generalized parts whenever you can.

PREFER A TREE TO A FOREST

The last and most common design decision you'll have to make when creating composite objects is sometimes called the *forest and the trees* problem. Simply stated, should your composite objects be shallow or deep?

In a *shallow containment hierarchy* (forest), most composite objects have many fields, and the fields are composed of relatively basic types. (These basic types aren't necessarily the Java's primitive types, but could be AWT components, strings, or other "built-in" objects.) As the previous section mentioned, building a system in this way— from only a few parts—tends to promote stability.

In a *deep containment hierarchy* (tree), your system is composed of more vertical layers. This is similar to what we observe in biological systems. Your body, for instance, has a circulatory and a digestive system. Rather than be a "shallow" system, the circulatory system is, itself, broken down into subsystems: the blood, the vascular system, the heart, and the lungs. Each of these systems can be further broken down. This is a "deep" hierarchy.

The main argument in favor of deep hierarchies is that, as humans, our short-term memory can handle only a limited amount of information. (This number is generally agreed to be between three and eight discrete pieces of information.) To handle greater amounts of information, we combine related pieces together into chunks. When you create a deep hierarchy, you limit the amount of information you need to absorb at any one level, effectively increasing your processing capability.

On the other hand, as you'll see when you study inheritance in Chapters 9 and 10, deep hierarchies have their own problems, because understanding the hierarchy itself may require you to search the contained classes to learn important information about how they work. Because the interface of a class limits what you can actually do with the class, this is less often a problem with containment than it is with inheritance.

Given these tradeoffs, deep hierarchies generally have an advantage over wide, shallow hierarchies. When writing procedural programs, you might create a series of functions that help clarify a higher-level piece of code. Deep hierarchies bring the same abstraction benefit to composite objects.

Object Notation Revisited

As you saw in Chapter 5, "Designing Classes and Objects," object-oriented design methodologies grew out of the adoption of object-oriented programming languages in the 1980s and 1990s, much like structured design techniques grew out of the use of structured programming languages in the 1960s and 1970s. And, as was true with the earlier structured methodologies, several different processes, graphical notations, and heuristics were adopted and promoted by several different groups.

In late 1994, three of the most successful object-oriented methodologists—Grady Booch, Jim Rumbaugh, and Ivar Jacobson—decided to join forces and create a standard set of graphical notations for object-oriented design. The result was the *Unified Modeling Language* (UML), which is currently going through a standardization process with the Object Management Group. Although not all of the major methodologists have jumped on board, UML seems poised to become a commonly understood notation for describing object-oriented systems.

Although this book isn't a handbook on UML—we recommend Martin Fowler's excellent *UML Distilled* as an accessible introduction to the notation—knowing how to read the major UML diagrams will certainly help you communicate with other object-oriented designers, because it provides a common language.

CLASS DIAGRAMS: DESCRIBING RELATIONSHIPS

UML uses the class diagram to describe both object (association) relationships and class (inheritance) relationships. Class diagrams can be drawn to represent several different viewpoints—from the very high-level conceptual diagrams on down to implementation diagrams. Normally, any system will have several different diagram levels, but there's no formal method for "leveling" the individual drawings. Indeed, only by looking at an individual diagram can you infer which level is being represented.

The main difference between levels is in the amount of detail presented. A class may be represented on a diagram simply by enclosing its name inside a rectangle. You might use this type of diagram to show connections between classes. Figure 8.4 shows a simple representation of the `LineItem` class (used in the `SalesInvoice` application), along with a more detailed representation. A class may be represented by listing important attributes and methods. Generally, only those methods and attributes important to the diagram are shown. It's important to realize that the class may actually be much more complex than shown. The more detailed representation of the `LineItem` class displays the public methods (`getTotal()`), the messages that the class sends (`updateTotals()`), and some private fields that may help you understand the `LineItem` abstraction. Still, almost all the implementation detail is ignored.

ASSOCIATIONS

Associations are represented in UML by simply connecting two classes with a straight line. As you can see in Figure 8.5, the `LineItem` class is associated (in some way) with a class called `LineItems`. Such simple association notation may be fine on a very high-level, conceptual diagram, but it certainly fails to convey the *full* meaning of the relationship between the two classes.

As you'll recall from Chapter 7, capturing the semantic relationships in an association requires that you identify the cardinality of the association—that is, how many members participate in the association. UML also allows you to limit the traversal of an association by adding a navigability arrow to the link connecting the classes. Figure 8.6 shows several possible variations of the `LineItem-LineItems` relationship.

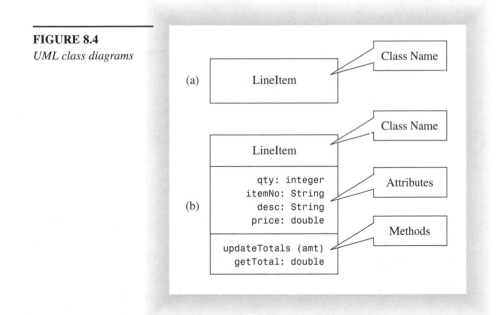

FIGURE 8.4
UML class diagrams

FIGURE 8.5

Simple association in UML

First, this figure shows a `1..5` relationship, where one `LineItems` object is associated with between one and five `LineItems` objects. Because the lower bounds is 1, the relationship is mandatory. Because there are no navigation arrows, you can assume the relationship is bi-directional. Next, the figure shows how you would represent the relationship if you decided that every `LineItems` object should associate with *exactly* five `LineItem` objects, even if all of them were not used. Finally, the figure shows how the relationship would be represented if you wanted to allow an unlimited number of `LineItem` objects per `LineItems` object.

FIGURE 8.6

Cardinality and UML associations

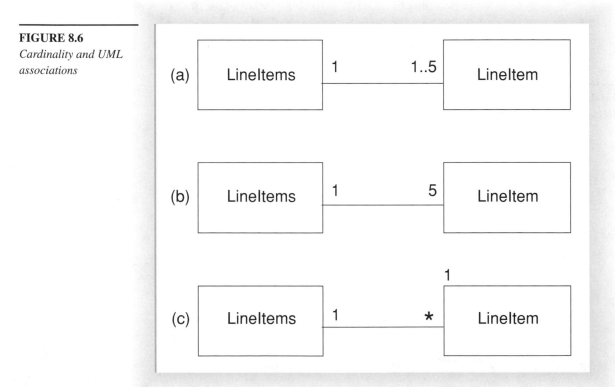

COMPOSITION AND UML

UML provides three different ways of representing composition. In Jim Rumbaugh's *Object Modeling Technique* (*OMT*), a distinction was made between simple aggregation and composition. Some other methodologists have ignored Rumbaugh's distinction and others have defined it differently. To accommodate as many methodologies as reasonable, UML has notations to support both aggregation and composition. You must be careful when communicating with other designers to make you understand what they mean if they show this distinction in their UML diagrams. Both notations connect the *whole* class with a small diamond symbol, as you can see in Figure 8.7. To specify the stronger form of composition, the diamond is filled in. Many diagramming tools, even when they support UML, don't make this distinction and simply use the hollow diamond. Another UML way of depicting composition is by enclosing the symbol for one class within that for the other. Figure 8.7 shows the relationship between the LineItem class and the TextField class used to create the LineItem user interface.

FIGURE 8.7
The LineItem-TextField association

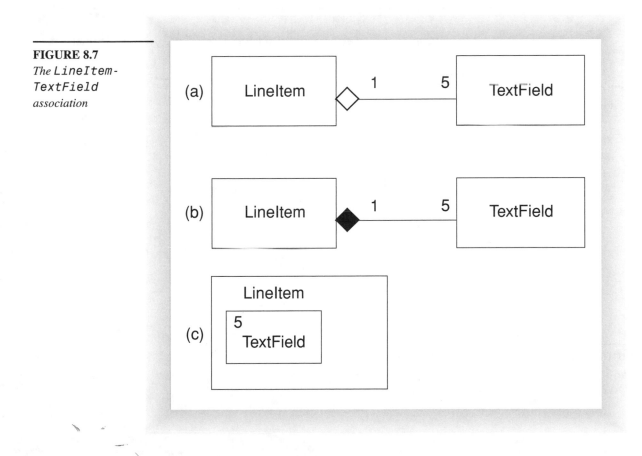

The `LineItem` class contains attributes that represent the quantity, description, and price of an ordered item. But `LineItem` is also a composite object that contains its own user interface in the form of a set of `TextField`s. Figure 8.7 says that every `LineItem` contains five `TextField` objects as part of its state.

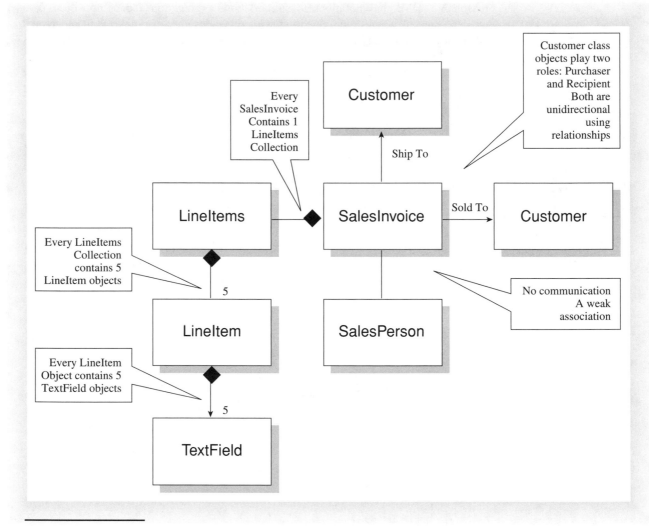

FIGURE 8.8
The `SalesInvoice`
class diagram

THE `SalesInvoice` CLASS DIAGRAMS

The addition of composition notation allows you to create a set of `SalesInvoice` diagrams that are semantically richer than the simple associations you used in Chapter 7. Figure 8.8 shows an annotated class diagram for the `SalesInvoice` application. Note that both the `LineItem-TextField` and `LineItems-LineItem` relationships are specified in terms of composition. This means that every `LineItem` object can appear only inside a single `LineItems` object, and that when the `LineItems` object is destroyed, its individual `LineItem` objects are destroyed as well.

Looking at the `LineItem` Class

> *" In Java, you create multivalued relationships by using collections. "*

Let's look at another application of composition by returning to the `SalesInvoice` application from Chapter 7. Although you wouldn't have noticed unless you looked at the code on the CD-ROM, the `LineItems` class is actually composed of several `LineItem` (notice the singular) objects. The `LineItem` objects are contained inside the `LineItems` object and aren't visible outside the `LineItems` class. Your `SalesInvoice` object sends messages to its single `LineItems` object, and that `LineItems` object then sends messages to each of its individual `LineItem` objects. Thus, the `LineItems`-`LineItem` association is a *uses* relationship, similar to that between `SalesInvoice` and `Customer` (because messages are being passed), but really, it's much more than that. `LineItem` objects are actually part of the `LineItems` object; thus, they have a whole-part or composition relationship.

`LineItems`: IMPLEMENTING COLLECTIONS AND MULTIVALUED RELATIONSHIPS

Like the `LineItem` class, the `LineItems` class includes a number of parts. If you look at the class diagram for the `LineItem-TextField` relationship, you'll see that the cardinality is `1..5`. Likewise, you see a `1..5` relationship with `LineItems-LineItem` association. But even though the diagrams for these relationships look identical, in practice these two relationships are very different.

Unlike the `LineItem` class, where you want different behavior for the `uQty` field and the `uDesc` field, in `LineItems` you want all the parts to act the same, because they really are multiple instances of the same type. Such repeating relationships are called *multivalued*. In Java, you create multivalued relationships by using *collections*. Collections resemble composite objects. The major difference is that there is no whole-part relationship like there is for a composite object. For instance, a car is composed of its engine, body, and wheels; together they cooperate to give a car its "carness." By contrast, a used car lot is a collection of cars. The operation of the lot would not be very much different if it were selling pumpkins instead of cars. In the case of the car, the various elements are of different types. In the case of the used car lot, which models a collection, the elements are all of the same type—each is a car.

The most basic type of collection in Java is the *array*. Listing 8.4 shows the implementation of the LineItems class, using an array. After you've had a chance to look through the listing, let's look at how you use arrays in Java.

Listing 8.4 LineItems.java

```java
// LineItems.java
//
// The LineItems class is a collection of LineItem objects
//
import java.awt.*;

public class LineItems
{
  // ==========================================
  //        CONSTRUCTORS
  // ==========================================
  public LineItems( int size, SalesInvoice owner )
  {
    items = new LineItem[ size ];
    nItems = size;
    for ( int i = 0; i < size; i++ )
    {
      items[i] = new LineItem(this);
    }
    this.owner = owner;
  }


  // ==========================================
  //        PUBLIC INTERFACE
  // ==========================================

  /*  --Mutators---------------------- */
  public void updateTotals()
  {
    owner.updateTotals();
  }

  /*  --Accessors--------------------- */
  public double getTotal()
  {
    double total = 0.0;
    for ( int i = 0; i < nItems; i++ )
    {
      total += items[ i ].getTotal();
    }
    return total;
  }


  // ==========================================
  //        INPUT AND OUTPUT
  // ==========================================
  public void buildUI( Container c )
  {
    // 1. Create a panel to hold all of the LineItems
    Panel p1 = new Panel();
    p1.setLayout( new GridLayout( 0, 1, 2, 2 ) );
```

```
    // 2. Create a panel to hold the column headers
    Panel p2 = new Panel();
    p2.setLayout( new GridLayout( 1, 6 ) );

    p2.add( new Label( "Qty.",        Label.CENTER ));
    p2.add( new Label( "ID." ,        Label.CENTER ));
    p2.add( new Label( "Description", Label.RIGHT ));
    p2.add( new Label( "",            Label.LEFT )); // Filler
    p2.add( new Label( "Price",       Label.CENTER ));
    p2.add( new Label( "Amount",      Label.CENTER ));
    p1.add( p2 );

    // 3. Add each of the LineItem objects
    for ( int i = 0; i < items.length; i++ )
    {
      Panel p = new Panel();
      p.setLayout( new FlowLayout() );
      items[i].buildUI( p );
      p1.add( p );
    }

    // Add the whole panel to the component
    c.add( p1 );
  }

  // =========================================
  //     CLASS AND OBJECT ATTRIBUTES
  // =========================================
  private LineItem[]    items;
  private int           nItems;
  private SalesInvoice  owner;
}
```

UNDERSTANDING THE `LineItems` CLASS

The `LineItems` class is perhaps simpler than any of the other classes in the `SalesInvoice` application. It contains only three fields: an array of `LineItem` objects, called `items`; an `int` containing the number of `LineItem` objects that the `LineItems` object holds; and a referential attribute to the `SalesInvoice` object that contains the `LineItems` object.

The behavior of the `LineItems` object is likewise simple. In a way, it acts as a go-between or mediator between the `SalesInvoice` object and the `LineItem` objects that do the actual work. And, in a way, that's a very apt analogy because most collection relationships involve general management to some degree. The only things that a `LineItems` object does are to:

- Construct the array of `LineItem` objects in its constructor.

- Notify its `SalesInvoice` owner whenever one of its `LineItem` objects changes its value, so the `SalesInvoice` object can update its totals and subtotals.

◈ Provide an accessor method, getTotal(), that allows an interested party to find out the total dollar amount sold on this LineItems object. The getTotal() method works by simply asking each embedded LineItem object for its own total and then simply returning the sum to the caller.

USING ARRAYS IN JAVA

In Java, as in most other high-level computer languages, *arrays* are an ordered collection of data elements, where each element is a reference to an individual object. To create an array, you have to specify the element type that you want to store in the array, and then follow the type with a pair of empty brackets([ ]):

```
Button aButton;            // aButton refers to a single Button object
Button [] buttonArray;     // buttonArray refers to an array of Buttons
```

In this example, both aButton and buttonArray are references that hold the special value null. You use the new operator to give each a value:

```
aButton = new Button( "A Button" );
buttonArray = new Button[100];
```

Now, rather than refer to the null value, aButton refers to the Button object whose caption is "*A Button*," and buttonArray refers to an array of 100 Button references. The size of the array, 100, is fixed when you allocate the array by using the new operator. Note also that brackets ([ ]) are used when allocating an array, unlike the parentheses used when constructing the single Button.

To use the individual objects in an array, simply use the array name—here, it is buttonArray—and an integer subscript (or index) value, enclosed in brackets. To change the text on aButton and the third Button in buttonArray, you would write

```
aButton.setLabel( "A Single Button");
buttonArray[2].setLabel( "The Third Button" );
```

Notice that the third Button in the array is addressed by using the subscript value 2. The valid subscript values for buttonArray start at 0 (which is the first element in the array) and go to 99. For any array of size n, the last element is at position n-1. If you come from another language where array elements are numbered from 1, you may find this numbering scheme—the same as that used in C—annoying. One consolation is that unlike C arrays, Java array references are automatically checked before the referenced element is accessed; attempting to read or write elem[100] in an array that has only 100 elements will cause an exception to be thrown.

If you attempted to type in and run the line of code where buttonArray[2] is given a caption, you might be surprised to find that it doesn't yet work. Even though buttonArray now refers to an array of Button references, each individual Button reference still contains the null value, the default initial value for fields that reference objects. To actually use buttonArray, you have to attach Button objects to each reference you want to use. This is both good news and bad news. The good news is that large arrays with many unused elements don't take up as much storage as if arrays were automatically initialized. The bad news is that you have to remember to initialize the individual elements of an array before you use them. To initialize only the third element of buttonArray, you'd write

```
buttonArray[2] = new Button("");
```

Now you can send the setLabel() method to buttonArray[2], and it works correctly. If you wanted to use all the elements of buttonArray, you could initialize them in a loop:

```
for (int i = 0; i < buttonArray.length; i++)
{
    buttonArray[i] = new Button( "I'm Button # " + i );
}
```

You should notice several things about this code. First, the index variable i is declared inside the initializer expression of the for loop. When you do this, the scope of i is limited to the body of the loop. Second, rather than the test expression i < 100, buttonArray's public attribute, length, is used. Whenever you want to process all the elements in an array, use the array's built-in length field rather than hard-code the size of the array. (Strings have a similar facility, but they provide a length() method rather than a public field.) Finally, notice that the index variable i is combined with the text "I'm Button # " by using the String concatenation operator (+). When used with numeric types, the addition operator (+) adds the numbers together, but when the expression on the left of the operator is a String, the number or object on the right is converted to a String and pasted onto the end of the String on the left.

In addition to objects, arrays can also be used to store primitive types. An array of primitive types stores values rather than references, just as ordinary primitive variables do. Thus, when initializing an array of primitives, you don't have to use the new operator to initialize each array element, although you do have to use the new operator to create the array itself.

Remember

To declare an array, you must specify the type of object you want to store, followed by brackets ([]) and the name of the array:

```
Label []  labelArray;
int []    intArray;
```

To initialize an array, use the new operator with the type of the object to store, followed by the number of elements enclosed in brackets:

```
labelArray = new Label[ 100 ];
intArray   = new int[ 100 ];
```

Before using any of the array elements, you must initialize them:

```
labelArray[2] = new Label( "Label # 2" );
intArray[2] = 100;
```

Summary

Objects can be related to each other in three ways. Objects may be formally related yet not interact: this is a weak association. Objects may send messages to each other; this is a *uses* relationship. Objects may contain other objects; this is known, variously, as a containment, aggregation, composition, or whole-part relationship. Unlike the other two forms of association, composition brings with it an ability to impose a simplifying structure on an object-oriented design.

A primary goal of object-oriented design is to build stable systems—systems that continue to function when the environment changes. Research into stable complex systems suggests that most such systems share four common characteristics. First, they are arranged in the form of a containment hierarchy, where more complex subsystems are built from simpler parts. Second, the system as a whole is nearly decomposable, meaning that you can identify the subsystems and the interactions among those subsystems. In a stable system, the frequency of interaction within each subsystem is greater than the frequency of communication between subsystems. Third, almost all stable complex systems are composed of relatively few parts, arranged in different ways. Finally, complex stable systems that work have almost always developed from simpler systems that work.

Composition relationships are used whenever one object is built from other objects, or when one object represents a logical whole composed of smaller parts. Unlike other forms of association, each part in a composition relationship belongs to only a single whole, and it lives and dies with the whole. When a composite object is created, its parts are likewise created. When a composite object is destroyed, its parts are destroyed.

You can use several rules of thumb for designing composite relationships. First, you should look for high-frequency communications between objects, and put those objects in a common subsystem. Second, you should look for common functionality, partitioning your system into separate domains. Third, you should try to isolate those areas that can change from those that won't, easing the long-term maintenance of your system. Fourth, you should take advantage of encapsulation to hide the complexity of your composite classes behind simpler interfaces. Fifth, you should try to strike a balance between composite classes that are too general and thus susceptible to "featuritis," and those that are too specific, thus leading to an exponential growth in the number of classes in your system. Finally, you should try to hide as much detail as possible, preferring deep hierarchies rather than shallow.

The Unified Modeling Language is an attempt to bring together several disparate notations used by different object-oriented methodologies. It provides several ways to create diagrams that communicate a wealth of semantic information. Depending on the level of your diagram, though, not all information will be included.

You can use Java's inner classes to encapsulate the definition of a class inside another class. This hides the embedded class name inside the enclosing class. When creating composite relationships, the inner class is given access to the data environment of the enclosing class, thus increasing the coupling between the enclosed class and its container. To model multivalued associations, Java has several facilities, the most basic of which is the array.

Questions

1. A composite or aggregate object is one in which other objects are _____ as the composite object's fields.

2. The advantages of composition include which of the following?

   a. Complexity is hidden behind a simpler interface.

   b. A composite object has lower coupling with its parts than if the relationship was a *uses* relationship.

   c. Composition provides a method to structure an object-oriented program.

   d. Composite objects are generally easier to use than trying to use all the parts that make them up.

3. True or false. When creating composite objects, you'll usually increase the coupling between the parts contained in the composite object and the containing object.

4. What are two main differences between a composition relationship and a *uses* relationship?

5. True or false. Every composition relationship is also a *uses* relationship.

6. The main disadvantage of creating very general composite classes is that

   a. The parts are all private.

   b. The interface may become crowded with features, making the class harder to use and understand.

   c. If too many details are hidden, the class may not do what you want.

   d. Composition increases the coupling between the program and its objects.

7. Discuss the pros and cons of dividing your classes up into discrete layers.

8. True or false. You should usually prefer deeper containment hierarchies rather than shallower ones.

9. Multivalued relationships can be best implemented in Java by using the

   a. Inner class syntax

   b. Either arrays or `Vectors`

   c. An anonymous inner class

   d. Individual user interface fields

10. Discuss the pros and cons of making the `LineItems-SalesInvoice` relationship a composition rather than a *uses* relationship. Is there ever any reason you'd want `LineItem` objects to stick around, even if the `SalesInvoice` was gone?

Exercises

1. Print out the listing of the LineItem (note singular) class from the CD-ROM. Draw a set of UML diagrams that depict the association and composition relationships you find there. Draw a set of UML diagrams that present an alternative design that separates the user-interface domain from the business logic domain. Can you implement your design?

2. **Coding Challenge I:** The LineItems class currently uses an array to represent the collect of LineItems it stores. Can you change the program to use Java's Vector class instead? If possible, allow an unlimited number of LineItems for each SalesInvoice. You might want to look into the new Java 1.1 ScrollPane class when you implement your interface.

3. **Coding Challenge II:** Modify the LineItem class so that it uses a "deeper" hierarchy. Create an InvoiceHeader class and an InvoiceUI class that encapsulates the details of sizing the column headers and the columns themselves.

4. **Design Challenge I:** Create a set of high-level (conceptual) diagrams for an automated library system. Identify all the classes and the association relationships between them, but don't be overly concerned with the individual attributes or methods of the classes.

5. **Design Challenge II:** Create a set of high-level (conceptual) diagrams for a "space-war" type video game. What classes can you come up with? Concentrate specifically on how composite or compound objects can make your design easier to understand.

To Learn More

Herbert Simon's pioneering article on the nature of complexity has been reprinted as Chapter 7 in his book *The Sciences of the Artificial*, published by MIT Press. Since his 1962 article, complex systems have become a "hot" topic, even serving as the backdrop for Michael Crichton's dinosaur novels, *Jurassic Park* and *The Lost World*. For an accessible and fascinating introduction to complex systems, you'll want to read M. Michael Waldrop's book, *Complexity: The Emerging Science at the Edge of Order and Chaos* (Touchstone Books). You may never look at software the same again.

For a concise introduction to the Unified Modeling Language, one that we suspect will still be valuable when the market is flooded with books on the subject, you should get Martin Fowler and Kendall Scott's, *UML Distilled: Applying the Standard Modeling Language* (Addison-Wesley). Some of the examples even use Java!

Finally, Mark Priestley's *Practical Object-Oriented Design* from McGraw-Hill offers a wealth of advice (especially on modeling associations) that can help you separate the essential from the peripheral when you start object-oriented modeling in earnest. Although the book uses C++ rather than Java and is based (loosely) on Jim Rumbaugh's Object Modeling Technique, the practical focus of the book extends its usefulness far beyond its immediate context.

9

Implementing Class Relationships: Inheritance and Interfaces

"In the Olympic Games, Greeks ran races, hurled the biscuits, and threw the java," according to the students of Richard Lederer, an English teacher and the author of a best-selling compilation of similar misunderstandings called *Anguished English*.

Whether we can attribute the development of java-hurling to the ancient Greeks is questionable, but many of us, like Mr. Lederer's students, have shared the experience of using the right word in the wrong way. This is especially true when learning a programming language. As a beginner, you may have spent weeks or months learning the correct Java syntax, relying on the `javac` compiler to tell you the error of your ways, only to discover that a syntactically correct program doesn't always do what you meant it to do. The real difficulty lies in writing programs that "say what you mean."

In no place is that difficulty more apparent than when first dealing with inheritance, interfaces, and abstract classes. Java provides all these mechanisms for expressing relationships between classes. But how do you know which one to use, and where to use it? At first glance, each of them seems to do, roughly, the same thing. When writing a new class, you can derive it from an existing class, thus using inheritance, or you can use composition, as you saw in Chapter 8, "Object Relationships: Compositions and Collections." In both cases, you are basing your design on an existing class.

Which of these is better? Should you make an abstract class, or use abstract methods? Or maybe you should forget inheritance, and implement an interface instead. Are there any rules that will help you to decide what to do?

Yes, there are. Each reuse mechanism provided by Java—inheritance, abstract classes, and interfaces—carries with it a specific meaning and is intended to model a particular class relationship. For instance, when you use inheritance to create a new class, you are saying that the new class is a "kind of" an existing class. If you disregard this meaning, using inheritance to create a new class simply because you want to reuse some of the functionality in an existing class, you may create a syntactically correct program, but the program won't "say what you mean." To select the correct method for the job at hand, you must first understand what that mechanism means, and then understand how to apply it to your situation.

In this chapter, you will study different ways you can implement relationships between classes. You will learn:

- About the three different types of inheritance relationships between classes: simple extension, specification, and polymorphic inheritance

- How to create new classes by using Java's inheritance mechanism, for purposes of generalization and specialization

- How to use Java interfaces to create new classes for purposes of specification

- How to use abstract classes and methods to create hierarchies that combine default behavior as well as mandatory specification

- When to use each different inheritance mechanism, as well as the drawbacks and pitfalls of using an inappropriate mechanism

From Encapsulation to Inheritance

Classification is one of the primary mechanisms that we use to understand the natural world around us. Starting as infants we begin to recognize the difference between categories like food, toys, pets, and people. As we mature, we learn to divide these general categories or classes into subcategories like siblings and parents, vegetables and dessert. When faced with a new object, we try to understand it by fitting it into the categories with which we're acquainted: Does it taste good? Perhaps it's dessert. Is it soft and fuzzy? Maybe it's a pet. Otherwise, it's most certainly a toy of some sort!

Encapsulation—the specification of attributes and behavior as a single entity—allows us to build on this understanding of the natural world as we create software. By creating classes and objects that model categories in the "real world," we have confidence that our software solutions closely track the problems we are trying to solve. Rather than think in terms of computer files and variables, our programs can be expressed in terms of `Customers`, `Invoices`, and `Products`.

Inheritance adds to encapsulation the ability to express relationships between classes. Think back to the categories "desserts" and "vegetables." Cherry pie and

> *" Classification is one of the primary mechanisms that we use to understand the natural world around us. "*

broccoli are both, at least arguably, edible items; for humans, they belong to the food class. Yet most of us recognize that, in addition to belonging to the food class, cherry pie is a kind of dessert, whereas broccoli is a kind of vegetable. If you ponder this for a second, you'll realize that you can draw three conclusions:

- Although both cherry pie and broccoli are kinds of food, the food class itself consists of, thankfully, more than just these two items. Cherry pie and broccoli are just two small subsets of all possible food types. Thus, the relationship between the food class and the cherry pie class is one of superset (food) and subset (cherry pie). In object-oriented terminology, we call this the *superclass-subclass* relationship.

- Superclasses and subclasses can be arranged in a hierarchy, with one superclass divided into numerous subclasses, and each subclass divided into more specialized kinds of subclasses. That's what we find with the food class. It can be divided into desserts, vegetables, soups, salads, and entrees. Each category can be further divided into more specialized kinds of food.

- A classification hierarchy represents an organization based on *generalization* and *specialization*. The superclasses in such a hierarchy are very general, and their attributes few; the only thing that a class must do to qualify as food, for instance, is to provide nutrients. As you move down the hierarchy, the subclasses become more specialized, and their attributes and behavior become more specific. Thus, although broccoli qualifies as food (it is, after all, digestible), it lacks the necessary qualifications to make it into the dessert class.

THE VALUE OF INHERITANCE: REUSE AND ORGANIZATION

In object-oriented programming, inheritance gives you a way of taking existing classes and using them to make new and different classes. Rather than build a `BeveledPanel` class from scratch, for instance, you can use the `Panel` class you already have and just write code for the aspects that are different. Your new `BeveledPanel` class will silently and invisibly inherit all the fields and methods from its superclass, `Panel`; you don't have to do any extra work at all.

In addition to giving you the ability to reuse the classes you've already written, inheritance gives you a basis for organizing your classes into class hierarchies, much like procedures gave C and Pascal programmers a tool for creating code libraries.

THREE KINDS OF INHERITANCE RELATIONSHIPS

Inheritance means that you can take an existing class and create a more specialized subclass based on the existing class. When you do this, the new class *is a kind of* the existing class, as you can see in Figure 9.1. Here, the `CoffeeMachine` class is-a-kind-of `VendingMachine`. Informally, this is often called the *isA* relationship, because every subclass *isA* subset of the superclass.

When you begin to actually design inheritance hierarchies, however, you'll quickly discover that there's not just one, but three forms of this *isA* relationship:

- **An extension relationship.** A subclass may *extend* an existing class, so that all the data members and all the methods of the superclass are left intact, and only new methods or fields are added. This extension or *strict-subtype* relationship involves the inheritance of the interface (or public methods) of the superclass, as well as its implementation.

- **A specification relationship.** In contrast to the extension relationship, a superclass may specify a set of responsibilities that a subclass must fulfill, but not provide any actual implementation. In this case, the only thing inherited is the interface from the superclass.

- **A combination of extension and specification.** The final form of inheritance, and by far the most common, combines the first two. In this form, the subclass inherits the interface of the superclass, as it does in specification, but it also inherits a default implementation of, at least, some of its methods. The subclass may override an inherited method to provide specialized behavior, or it may be required to provide an implementation for a particular method, which could not be provided in the superclass. We'll call this form *polymorphic inheritance*, because its principal value lies in its ability to provide specialized behavior in response to the same messages.

FIGURE 9.1

Inheritance and special-ization

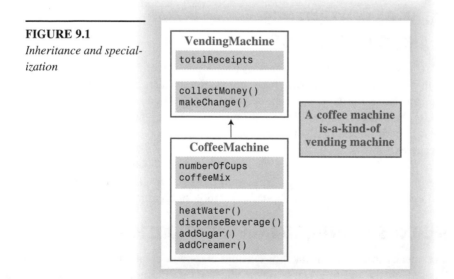

DISCOVERING INHERITANCE RELATIONSHIPS

After you decide on the classes and objects in your system, and after you decide which objects cooperate together to form association relationships, you are ready to begin looking at the class relationships in your system. As with most design activities, you can go about this task in several ways.

You may discover that many objects in your system share data or behavior, leading you to start at the bottom of your system and work up. Or you may start with your more general classes and find that you need more specialized instances in certain cases, finding yourself working from the more abstract to the more concrete. In most systems, however, you'll need to do both: Your inheritance hierarchy will evolve from iterative rounds of top-down specialization and bottom-up generalization.

Specialization

Specialization is what we normally mean when we say that one class *is-a-kind-of* another class. In specialization, every class can inherit both data and methods from its parent—its superclass. As you saw in Figure 9.1, the CoffeeMachine class is a specialized form of the more general VendingMachine class. Notice, however, that the data fields and methods specified in the VendingMachine class aren't redefined inside the CoffeeMachine class. Nevertheless, those fields and methods exist as inherited (albeit implicit) members of the new class. Figure 9.2 shows how the CoffeeMachine class really contains both a totalReceipts field—defined only in the VendingMachine class—as well as a collectMoney() and makeChange() method.

Substitutability and Subtyping

When you decide that one class is a specialization of another, you need to see whether it's a subtype. Having one class as a subtype of another means that you can use the new, more specialized type anywhere an object of the original type would appear.

This test—called the *Liskov Substitution Principle*, after Barbara Liskov who originally proposed it—is especially important when you're designing class hierarchies. Nothing in the Java language prohibits you from creating a subclass that redefines every method defined in its superclass. Thus, theoretically, you could have a class with two methods—add() and subtract()—defined like this:

```
public class SuperClass
{
  public int add(int a, int b) { return a + b; }
  public int subtract(int a, int b) { return a - b; }
}
```

You would then be free to create a subclass and override those methods like this:

```
public class SubClass extends SuperClass
{
  public int add(int a, int b) { return a - b; }
  public int subtract(int a, int b) { return a + b; }
}
```

FIGURE 9.2

*Inheritance of data
and methods*

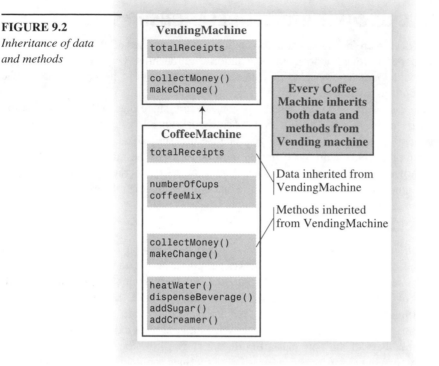

Even though the Java language doesn't prohibit this, it's a violation of the *meaning* of inheritance and specialization. If every SubClass object is, indeed, a SuperClass object, the SubClass must uphold the implied contract that the SuperClass creates. That contract means that every instance of SuperClass *and all its subclasses* will add when told to add(), and not do something else.

In strict subtyping, you have the additional requirement that not only does every subclass have to carry out the meaning of the interface defined in the superclass, but it must also rely on the methods already defined in the superclass to do so. The new class isn't free to redefine superclass methods at all; it can only add to them. Later in the chapter, you'll see how this works.

Generalization

Sometimes when working on an inheritance hierarchy, you'll notice that several classes have data and methods in common. If you've worked in a procedural language, you might see this as an opportunity to create a new function, or perhaps even a module. However, in the object-oriented world, this is a clue to look for generalization.

Generalization is not a different kind of inheritance—it is just the "flip-side" of specialization. When looking at the superclass in a such a relationship, you can call it a generalization. When looking from the other direction, it's a specialization. The only difference is in the way the relationship is originally discovered. If you were writing a

Java application for a catering company, you might find yourself creating classes for CoffeeMachines, SodaMachines, and CandyMachines. Later in your design, you might notice that those classes had some common factors, and you could use those factors to create a new, generalized superclass that encapsulated the shared information, as you can see in Figure 9.3.

Specification

Specialization and generalization allow you to design classes that share both an interface and an implementation. Sometimes, however, that doesn't really provide all the expressive power you need to really "say what you mean." Sometimes, you know exactly *what* a subclass should do, but you simply have no idea *how* it should do it. In this case, you want to *specify* what the subclass should do, and then let the compiler make sure that each subclass complies.

If you were writing a BoardGame class, for instance, you might have some code that looks something like this:

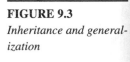

> *Sometimes, you know exactly* **what** *a subclass should do, but you simply have no idea* **how** *it should do it.*

```
public class BoardGame
{
  // Fields and other methods
  public play()
  {
    while (! finished())
    {
      currentPlayer.move();
      currentPlayer = nextPlayer();
    }
  }
}
```

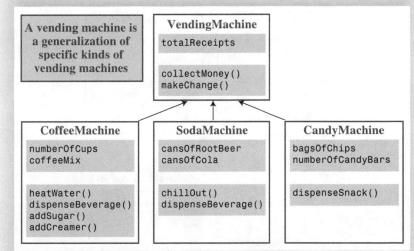

FIGURE 9.3

Inheritance and generalization

A vending machine is a generalization of specific kinds of vending machines

VendingMachine

totalReceipts

collectMoney()
makeChange()

CoffeeMachine

numberOfCups
coffeeMix

heatWater()
dispenseBeverage()
addSugar()
addCreamer()

SodaMachine

cansOfRootBeer
cansOfCola

chillOut()
dispenseBeverage()

CandyMachine

bagsOfChips
numberOfCandyBars

dispenseSnack()

You could then use this class to create classes like ChessGame, Checkers, Parcheesi, and so on. All your subclasses would inherit the code for play() from BoardGame. The currentPlayer object used by play() would be an object derived from a subclass of the GamePiece class, such as a ChessPiece or Checker.

At this point, however, things start to break down. You know that every GamePiece object *must* be able to move(). You simply have no idea how it should go about doing it! Obviously, a Checker has very different moves than a Bishop, and a Bishop has different move than a Knight or a Rook. The declaration of the move() method in the GamePiece class is thus a stipulation that all subclasses inherit the move() specification, but no associated implementation.

Specialization and Specification

When you have a class that needs to specify some behavior that a subclass must perform, and yet has some behavior of its own to pass on to its subclasses, you find yourself needing a combination of specialization and specification. In Java, this is accomplished by making the superclass method abstract, as you can see in Figure 9.4.

FIGURE 9.4

Inheritance and abstract methods

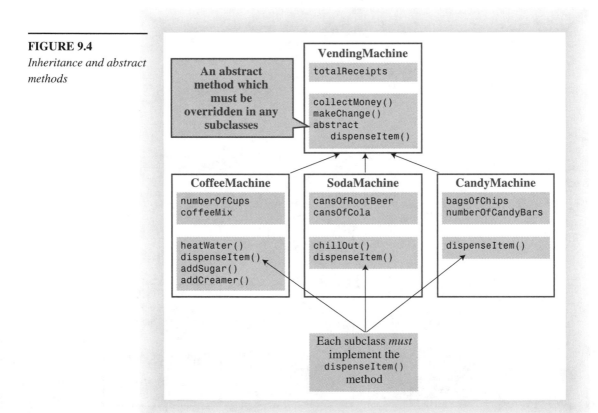

When you "mark" a method as abstract (by adding the `abstract` keyword before the declaration and replacing the method body with a semicolon), you create a requirement that all subclasses must fulfill. In Figure 9.4, the `VendingMachine` class creates a requirement that any subclass *must* supply a `dispenseItem()` method.

Because the actual mechanisms for dispensing candy vary considerably from those required for brewing java, the `VendingMachine` class is obviously in no position to provide any sort of implementation at all. On the other hand, by writing code that uses references to `VendingMachine` objects, programmers can simplify their code considerably; they're freed from the necessity of treating `CoffeeMachines` differently than `CandyMachines`. When a programmer tells a `VendingMachine` object to `dispenseItem()`, the actual object—a `CandyMachine` or `CoffeeMachine`—"knows" how to take the appropriate actions.

Pure Specification

After taking care of specialization, generalization, and specification, you may find remaining places where you want to factor out common behavior. The problem is that the objects sharing that common behavior are otherwise unrelated. When this happens, Java has a facility for writing *pure specifications*: the Java interface.

The interface mechanism differs from the forms of inheritance we have discussed so far in three important ways:

- When a class implements an interface, it doesn't receive any method implementations or nonfinal fields from the interface. Interfaces *can* be used to define inherited constants, but they can't be used to define nonconstant data. Any fields defined within an interface are implicitly `final`.

- Unlike inheritance, a class may implement several `interfaces`. This facility can be used to simulate multiple inheritance, where a subclass inherits behavior from each of several superclasses. This is the only way to model this kind of relationship in Java, which supports only single inheritance (every class other than `Object` has exactly one direct ancestor).

- Classes that implement the same interface don't need to be substitutable in the Liskov sense, except with respect to the interface they implement. Thus, if a class implements the `Runnable` interface, it *isA* `Runnable` object, and it can be used anywhere a `Runnable` object is expected. `Runnable` objects don't have to be otherwise related, however. Because they implement `Runnable`, they must have a `start()` method and a `run()` method; otherwise their class wouldn't have compiled. There's no guarantee they'll have any other methods or fields in common.

Inheritance of Implementation: Contraction

You should be aware of one last form of inheritance, although you should avoid using it in your designs. For an exaggerated example, suppose you have a class that models a

" Contraction is an especially easy trap to fall into when you begin maintaining an existing system. "

virtual automobile called, perhaps, `Cadillac`. This class has an exceptionally fine stereo system, which required a lot of effort to implement and of which you're especially proud. Now you discover that you need to create a `BoomBox` class, for sale over the Web. Because you've already gone to all the work of creating the `Cadillac` class, why not just create a new subclass, and then eliminate all the methods that have nothing to do with playing CDs, transforming the car into a mere sound system?

This practice, called *contraction*, is an especially easy trap to fall into when you begin maintaining an existing system. Because the class hierarchy is already in place, you may feel a lot of pressure not to "tear things up." So, in an effort to reuse the code you've already written, you replace `drive()`, `accelerate()`, and all the other methods from the `Cadillac` class with empty braces. In traditional computer-science terms, you replace them with a `NOP` (No OPeration). You should avoid doing this in your designs for two reasons:

- Because you're violating the substitutability rule, you will undoubtedly break some code that relied on all `Cadillac` objects carrying out a certain set of operations. Because, according to your new hierarchy, a `BoomBox` *isA* `Cadillac`, you are obligated by the `Cadillac` "contract" to perform those operations.

- It's more work than doing the right thing! If you really want to use a `Cadillac` object as a super sound system, simply use composition: Add a `Cadillac` object as one of the fields in your `BoomBox` class. Now you not only have avoided the semantic pitfalls of saying one thing and doing another, you've also saved yourself the work of overriding all those useless methods.

You might find yourself tempted to use contraction in one last place—when you have misidentified an *isA* relationship and don't want to go back to square one. Scott Meyers, in his excellent book *Effective C++*, calls this the

```
All Birds Can Fly
Penguins are Birds
Penguins can fl—·   Uhhoh!
```

problem. Meyers offers no quick fix however. In Java, as in C++, the only solution is to go back to the drawing board and revise the class relationships.

JAVA'S INHERITANCE MECHANISMS

Learning which of these three relationships—extension, specification, or polymorphic inheritance—is the best one to use in a particular situation is a skill that takes years of practice and is, still, more an art than a science. Along with learning to distinguish between specification and extension relationships, you'll also have to learn how to implement those relationships in Java; fortunately, the latter is considerably easier than the former. Java has several different mechanisms that can be used, alone and in combination, to model each of the three forms of the *isA* relationship. Matching up these inheritance relationships with Java's inheritance mechanisms is, thankfully, fairly straightforward. Nevertheless, the similarities between each mechanism can lead to easily avoided design mistakes.

To make sure that you understand the correct application of each of Java's inheritance mechanisms, we'll give you at the end of this chapter a simple checklist that you can follow to help you decide which mechanism is most appropriate. And as we go through the code examples, we'll point out which mechanism was chosen for each example, and why. But for right now, let's take a quick look at each basic form of the *isA* relationship, and how you can use Java's language features to implement it.

Simple Extension

To implement a simple extension relationship in Java, you use the `extends` keyword to create your new subclass. Also, all the methods in the superclass should be marked `final`. You'll use an extension relationship when you want to allow extension to your existing class but don't want the base class implementation changed in any way.

A simple extension relationship is an assertion that, although more functionality can be added to an existing class, the implementation that exists must remain invariant. Simple extension is the inheritance of a mandatory interface as well as a mandatory implementation.

> " *Simple extension is the inheritance of a mandatory interface as well as a mandatory implementation.* "

Specification

To implement a specification relationship between classes, you use the `interface/implements` mechanism. When a class declares that it `implements` a particular interface, it's promising to implement all the methods contained in the interface. The interface itself provides no implementation but provides method signatures that the subclass must implement. If a subclass fails to implement a required method, the compiler will catch the omission.

Polymorphic Inheritance

Polymorphic inheritance is implemented by using the `extends` keyword, as with extension. You can also use the `final` and `abstract` keywords, along with `extends`, to explicitly define which parts of the extended class *may* be further modified, which parts *must* be modified, and which parts *cannot* be modified. In polymorphic inheritance

- Some methods may be invariant, as with simple extension. These methods should be marked `final`. The subclass inherits both a *mandatory* interface and a *mandatory* implementation.

- Some methods may be overridden, allowing subclass objects to behave in a specialized manner. Because subclasses may redefine these methods, these methods should *not* be marked as `final`. Of course, a subclass doesn't have to override a method defined in its superclass—most of the time it won't, but will, instead, use the method that it has inherited. Nonfinal methods in a superclass mean that a subclass inherits a *mandatory* interface and an *optional* implementation.

> Some methods may be specified in the superclass yet have no default implementation defined there. To do this, you include the `abstract` keyword as the first word of the method declaration (in the superclass), and then end the declaration with a semicolon rather than a method body. When a subclass is created, the subclass *must* implement the method. For these methods, the subclass inherits only a *mandatory* interface; no default implementation is provided.

Implementing Inheritance: Extending the `Panel` Class

> *Extending the built-in user-interface components makes it easy for you to see the effects of inheritance.*

Java's Abstract Window Toolkit makes extensive use of inheritance in its design. More than that, the AWT gives you an excellent place to start using inheritance in your own designs. Extending the built-in user-interface components makes it easy for you to see the effects of inheritance. Let's try this out by developing a 3D-style `Panel`, using the AWT's built-in `Panel` class.

The first step in designing any object is deciding what you'd like it to do. Start with the simplest and most fundamental requirements first, and then you can refine your design as you iterate through succeeding generations. The requirements for a `BevelPanel` are fairly simple:

> It should do everything that a regular `Panel` should do, and you should be able to use it any place you would normally use a regular `Panel`.

> The `BevelPanel` varies from the built-in `Panel` because it adds a 3D-Border around its perimeter, which allows it to appear to stand out or sink into the surface on which it's placed.

> The same class should be used to create both sunken and raised `BevelPanel`s.

CHOOSING AN IMPLEMENTATION MECHANISM

Should you use inheritance to implement the `BevelPanel` class, and, if so, what form is appropriate? To answer this question, you first look at your requirements, and then ask the following questions:

1. Is the new class a subtype of an existing class? Can you use the new class anywhere you would have used the previous one, without making any changes? If so—if the new class is substitutable for the existing class—you should use inheritance. The `BevelPanel` class meets this test, because it should be capable of being used in place of a `Panel`.

2. Do you want your new class to inherit behavior, or only an interface, from the existing class? Because BevelPanel will get most of its behavior from its superclass, Panel, inheritance (that is, extension) is called for, rather than the interface mechanism.

3. Will the existing behavior be modified, or are you just adding new behavior? Answering this question is a little more difficult. It helps to know that most of the time, a subclass will make some change to the behavior of its superclass. Even if you don't plan on making such a modification at first, you may choose to make one in the future. Thus, in almost all cases that call for inheritance, you'll want to use polymorphic inheritance rather than simple extension. Because the built-in Panel class already has a display method (paint()), your BevelPanel class can override this method to implement its new behavior.

WRITING THE BevelPanel CLASS

Now that you know what you want your BevelPanel class to do (requirements) and have decided on an implementation strategy based on those requirements, it's time to implement the design in Java. Take a moment to read through the source code for BevelPanel.java in Listing 9.1, and then we'll take a little closer look.

Listing 9.1 BevelPanel.java

```java
// A BeveledPanel
import java.awt.*;

public class BevelPanel extends Panel
{
  private boolean raised  = true;
  private int     thick   = 2;

  public BevelPanel(boolean raised)
  {
    this.raised = raised;
    setBackground(SystemColor.control);
    setForeground(SystemColor.controlText);
  }

  public BevelPanel()
  {
    this(true);
  }

  public void paint(Graphics g)
  {
    super.paint(g);

    int w = getSize().width  - 1;
    int h = getSize().height - 1;

    if (raised) g.setColor(SystemColor.controlLtHighlight);
```

```
        else          g.setColor(SystemColor.controlDkShadow);

        for(int i = 0; i < thick; i++)
        {
          g.drawLine(i, i, w-i, i);
          g.drawLine(i, i, i, h-i);
        }

        if (!raised)  g.setColor(SystemColor.controlLtHighlight);
        else          g.setColor(SystemColor.controlDkShadow);

        for(int i = 0; i < thick; i++)
        {
          g.drawLine(w-i, i, w-i, h-i);
          g.drawLine(i, h-i, w-i, h-i);
        }
      }
    }
```

Understanding the `BevelPanel` Class

The `BevelPanel` class begins by importing the `java.awt` package. Why? Well, if you go through the source code, you'll notice that `BevelPanel` uses several `Graphics` methods to draw its 3D bevel effect, and so you might (correctly) conclude that the `java.awt` package is required. But that's not the only reason. Even if you were to remove all the code, except for the following class declaration

```
public class BevelPanel extends Panel { }
```

you would still need to `import` the `java.awt` package, because that's where the super-class you are extending (`Panel`) is defined. As a general rule, then, when you extend a class, you need to begin by importing the package that includes the superclass you're using.

The `BevelPanel` class has two private fields: the `boolean` field called `raised`, which will be used to decide whether to draw a sunken or raised border, and the `int` field named `thick`, which is used to decide how wide the surrounding border should be.

Inheritance and Constructors The class has two constructors: a default constructor that takes no arguments and a working constructor that allows you to specify whether the `BevelPanel` object you are creating should be raised or sunken. If you create a `BevelPanel` by using the default constructor, it simply calls the working constructor— using the `this()` method and passing `true`—thus creating a raised panel as the default.

The working constructor simply sets the value of the field named `raised` and then sets the background and foreground colors of the `BevelPanel` object. The Java 1.1 `SystemColor` class is used to determine the colors so that your new panel will blend in with the colors used by your specific platform, whether you use Windows, UNIX, or a Mac. By using `SystemColor.control` and `SystemColor.controlText`, the default colors for your `BevelPanel` will be the same as the native controls on your system. The system colors, SystemColor.controlLtHighlight and SystemColor.controlDkShadow, are also used when it comes time to draw the 3D bevel effect.

Even though you only see two constructors in BevelPanel.java, it's important that you realize that an invisible constructor lurks on the premises—the constructor for the Panel class. Whenever you use inheritance, the constructor for your new subclass calls the constructor for its superclass before it begins executing its own statements.

"Wait," you say. "I don't see any call to any constructor, other than the call to this(). Where is the call to the Panel constructor? Or are my eyes deceiving me?" Rest easy, your eyes haven't gone out. The call to the superclass constructor is done automatically as the first line of your subclass constructor. Of course, if you like, you may explicitly choose to call a specific superclass constructor. To do this, you must do the following:

> *Whenever you use inheritance, the constructor for your new subclass calls the constructor for its superclass before it begins executing its own statements.*

- Call the constructor by using the super() method, passing the arguments necessary to select the constructor you want to use.

- Call the super() method only as the first line of your subclass constructor. It won't work anywhere else.

If, for instance, you wanted to have BeveledPanel objects default to using a FlowLayout layout manager, rather than the Panel's default BorderLayout, you could add the following line to the beginning of your BevelPanel constructor:

```
super(new FlowLayout());
```

Inheritance and Overridden Methods   The last method in BevelPanel is paint(), which overrides the paint() method in the Panel class. *Overriding* means that when the paint() method is invoked on a BevelPanel object, your new method is called instead of the original paint() method contained in the Panel class. For this to work correctly, you have to pay special attention to two issues:

- To override an inherited method, you must declare your method in exactly the same manner as the superclass method. That means you must be especially careful to declare exactly the same number and type of arguments, as well as the same return type. If you use different arguments, you are overloading (extending the class by adding a new method) instead of overriding the existing method. If you were to write your new method in BevelPanel as

```
public void paint(Graphics g, int raised){ . . . }
```

the javac compiler wouldn't give you an error, but you also wouldn't see any difference between the built-in Panel and a BevelPanel. When the AWT invoked paint() on your BevelPanel objects, the original inherited method would be used instead of your new method.

- You also must be aware of whether you want your new, overridden method to entirely replace the inherited method, or simply augment it. If you want to replace the behavior of your superclass wholesale, you don't have to do anything special. More often, however, because a subclass is really a special kind of its superclass, the superclass behavior needs only to be extended rather than replaced. You can use the super object (not to be confused with the super() method, which can be used only in a constructor) to invoke a superclass method in such cases. For most AWT components that you extend, for instance, you'll want to invoke the method

```
super.paint(g);
```

as the first line of any paint() method you override. This makes sure that any important processing done in the superclass gets accomplished. If you neglected to include the keyword super, the paint() method would call itself recursively, over and over. The keyword super causes Java to invoke the paint() method of the superclass, even though there's an overriding definition of paint() within the subclass.

" To override an inherited method, you must declare your method in exactly the same manner as the superclass method. "

The paint() method in the BevelPanel class first calls its superclass, Panel, and then uses the inherited method getSize() to compute the height and width it should use for drawing its bevel. Note that getSize() doesn't appear in the source code for BevelPanel. You can use it because it was inherited from one of BevelPanel's ancestor classes. You don't need to qualify the method call by specifying the superclass where the method was actually defined, because Java will search BevelPanel's ancestors until the definition of the method is found. Because BevelPanel doesn't override the getSize() method, you don't need to include the super keyword when calling getSize().

The bevel is drawn by setting the appropriate colors, based on whether the object should be raised or sunken, and then drawing the top and left bevel by using the Graphics method drawLine() in a loop. Then, after switching the colors, the same process is repeated for the bottom and right last margins.

Testing the BevelPanel Class

The BPApplet program, shown in Listing 9.2, uses several features of the BevelPanel class. Notice that you can substitute a BevelPanel for a Panel, but not vice versa. Thus, each of the following lines would work identically:

```
Panel      p  = new BevelPanel(false);
BevelPanel p2 = new BevelPanel(true);
```

These work because a BevelPanel object is also a Panel object. The opposite isn't true, however. Thus, the following code would be illegal:

```
BevelPanel p3 = new Panel();
```

In this case, p3 refers to a BevelPanel object, but it's given a value that's only a Panel. Remember, every BevelPanel is a Panel, but not every Panel is necessarily a BevelPanel.

Listing 9.2 BPApplet.java

```java
//  Test the BevelPanel class
import java.awt.*;
import java.applet.*;

public class BPApplet extends Applet
{
  public void init()
  {
    setLayout(new BorderLayout());
    Panel p = new BevelPanel(); // A BevelPanel isA Panel
    p.add(new Label("A Raised BevelPanel"));
    add(p, "South");

    p = new BevelPanel(false);
    p.setLayout(new FlowLayout(FlowLayout.RIGHT));
    p.add(new Label("A Sunken BevelPanel"));
    add(p, "North");

    p = new Panel();
    p.setBackground(SystemColor.control);
    p.setLayout(new GridLayout(3, 3, 4, 4));
    for(int i = 0; i < 3 * 3; i++)
      p.add(new BevelPanel(((i * i) % 2) == 0));
    add(p, "Center");
  }
}
```

You can use Listing 9.3, BPApplet.html, to display this applet in either the applet viewer or your Web browser. Figure 9.5 shows BPApplet running inside a Web browser.

Listing 9.3 BPApplet.html

```html
<HTML>
<HEAD>
<TITLE>Testing the BevelPanel class</TITL>
</HEAD>
<BODY>
<H1>The BevelPanel class</H1>
<HR>
<APPLET CODE=BPApplet WIDTH=600 HEIGHT=350>
</APPLET>
</BODY>
</HTML>
```

Writing and Using Interfaces

Extension, or *inheritance*, means that a subclass is a kind of its superclass—that the subclass is a more specialized form of its more general superclass. By contrast, the interface mechanism is used to model a relationship between classes that share a specific set of behaviors (an interface) but don't need to be otherwise related. Because of this, implementing an interface is sometimes called *inheritance of specification*.

FIGURE 9.5
Testing the
BevelPanel class

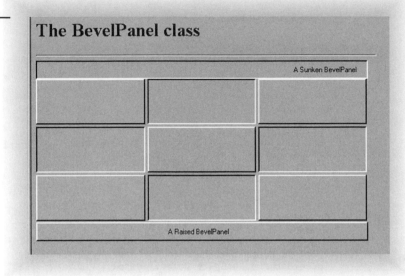

Working with interfaces involves two separate tasks: writing the interface and implementing it. When you write an interface, you design a *specification*—a set of mandatory methods that every class using the interface must implement. When you implement an interface (a much more common occurrence), you write methods for every method that it declares. Let's look at an example.

> " *Implementing an interface is sometimes called inheritance of specification.* "

IMPLEMENTING AN INTERFACE: `CloseableFrame`

Java's AWT `Frame` class is roughly analogous to the window class used in most GUI frameworks. When you want to build a GUI application (as opposed to an applet that relies on your Web browser to provide its window), you'll need to use a `Frame` to "host" your application. A `Frame` has a title bar with controls for minimizing, maximizing, and closing the window, and an area for putting controls or displaying information. It also can generally be resized and moved. It does, however, have a few little peculiarities:

- When created, a `Frame` is zero pixels high and zero pixels wide. No matter how small your application is, this will likely prove too small to hold it.

- `Frame`s are invisible when created.

- A `Frame` uses the `BorderLayout` as its default layout manager, rather than the `FlowLayout` used by an applet. Although there's nothing wrong with this, it does make going back and forth between writing applets and applications difficult. It would certainly be nicer if both classes used the same default! After all, you can always specify a different layout manager if you prefer.

Having different defaults, however, is just one more piece of arcane and unnecessary piece of information for you to remember.

Surprisingly, Frames don't respond well to being closed—actually, they don't respond at all. Even though the title bar of a Frame will usually contain a close box of some sort (an X under Windows 95), programmers new to the Frame class are understandably frustrated when they discover that the control just doesn't work. To "hook it up," you have to tell your class to "listen" for the window to close and then take the appropriate action when that event occurs. You do this by implementing the WindowListener interface.

Listing 9.4, CloseableFrame.java, is a subclass of Frame. CloseableFrame objects act just like regular Frame objects, with three differences:

Unlike a built-in Frame, a CloseableFrame has a default size set in its constructor to 400×300 pixels.

To make moving between applications and applets a bit simpler, the CloseableFrame class installs a FlowLayout object as the default layout manager. Although this won't solve all your layout difficulties, it will reduce the number of times you have to ask yourself, "Which version of add() should I use here?"

The CloseableFrame class implements the WindowListener interface, allowing you to close down your CloseableFrame-hosted application without resorting to heroic measures. (Actually, the measures necessary for closing a nonclosing Frame-based application aren't all that heroic. You can generally shut down the application by switching to the console window where you launched the application and pressing Ctrl+C.)

Listing 9.4 CloseableFrame.java

```
//  A CloseableFrame
import java.awt.*;
import java.awt.event.*;

public class CloseableFrame extends Frame
                            implements WindowListener
{
  public CloseableFrame()
  {
    this("CloseableFrame");
  }

  public CloseableFrame(String title)
  {
    super(title);
    setLayout(new FlowLayout());
    addWindowListener(this);
    setSize(400, 300);
  }
```

```
public void windowOpened(WindowEvent we)      { }
public void windowClosed(WindowEvent we)      { }
public void windowIconified(WindowEvent we)   { }
public void windowDeiconified(WindowEvent we) { }
public void windowActivated(WindowEvent we)   { }
public void windowDeactivated(WindowEvent we) { }
public void windowClosing(WindowEvent we)
{
  quitApplication();
}

protected void quitApplication()
{
  setVisible(false);
  dispose();
  System.exit(0);
}
}
```

IMPLEMENTING WindowListener

The WindowListener interface consists of seven methods: windowOpened(), windowClosed(), windowIconified(), windowDeiconified(), windowActivated(), windowDeactivated(), and windowClosing(). To become a WindowListener, a class must do three things:

- It must add the phrase implements WindowListener to the class declaration. This is similar to the way you use the extends keyword to specify a superclass. With inheritance, however, you may extend only one class; your subclass can have only one immediate superclass. However, a class may implement any number of interfaces. Interfaces also can be combined with regular inheritance. Thus, the CloseableFrame class, which uses both, is both a Frame and a WindowListener.

- You must write implementations for each method declared in the interface. This is different than inheritance. With inheritance, you may implement a new method defined in your superclass, but if you don't, you can use the superclass implementation. With an interface, you must write each method because the interface provides no default behavior. If you want to take action only on some particular method, you still have to include empty methods that satisfy the interface requirements. Notice that this isn't the same thing as contraction: The empty methods don't override behavior defined in the interface because interfaces never implement actual behavior. In the CloseableFrame class, only the windowClosing() method takes any meaningful action. All the others are simply empty stubs.

- The preceding two operations are all you'll normally need to implement an interface. To get your CloseableFrame to actually work, however, you have to take one more step. To receive WindowEvents from the Java runtime environment, your `CloseableFrame` must "subscribe" to them. You do this by first making sure your `CloseableFrame` class imports `java.awt.event.*`. After that, you get things started by adding the following line to the `CloseableFrame` constructor:

```
addWindowListener(this);
```

The `addWindowListener()` method is defined by the `Window` class, an ancestor of `Frame`, the parent class of `CloseableFrame`.

Now you can use the `CloseableFrame` class as the base class for the applications you write, just as you use the `Applet` class as the foundation for your `applets`. Use Listing 9.5, `CFApplication.java`, as a simple model for building GUI applications in Java. The `CFApplication` class extends `CloseableFrame`, meaning that you don't have to implement the `WindowListener` interface in `CFApplication`—`CloseableFrame` has done it for you. Furthermore, if you decide you want to change some of the behavior in one of the other `WindowListener` methods, you can now just override that method directly without re-implementing the interface.

Listing 9.5 CFApplication.java

```java
//   CFApplication.java
//   Extending the CloseableFrame class
import java.awt.*;

public class CFApplication extends CloseableFrame
{
  public CFApplication(String title)
  {
    super(title);
  }

  public static void main(String[] args)
  {
    Frame cf = new CFApplication("Extending CloseableFrame");
    cf.show();
  }
}
```

You can see `CFApplication` at work in Figure 9.6.

ImageButtons: An Extended Inheritance Example

Now that you've seen an example of both inheritance and interfaces at work, let's apply what you've learned to a more extensive example, building an `ImageButton` class that can be used to create toolbars, those palettes of little iconic `Buttons` used in modern graphical interfaces to avoid "menu-pulldown cramp."

FIGURE 9.6
CFApplication: a simple GUI framework

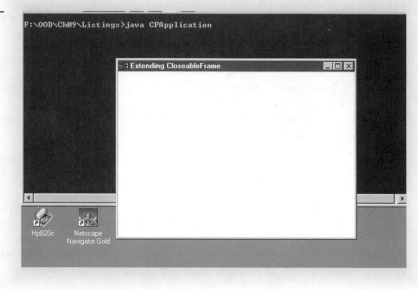

Java's AWT has classes for both `Buttons` and `Images`. So which should you use? Do you think an `ImageButton` is a `Button` that contains an `Image`, or a `Clickable Image`? Or, perhaps, something else entirely? There's no hard-and-fast rule for making these decisions, but you should start by asking yourself, "Is an `ImageButton` a special kind of `Button`?" If your answer is yes, you should probably use inheritance and extend the `Button` class. If you do this, remember the following:

- Everything a `Button` does, an `ImageButton` should do as well. After all, your design asserts that an `ImageButton` *isA* `Button`.

- Anywhere you have a reference to a `Button` object, you should be able to refer to an `ImageButton`. The `ImageButton` should be perfectly substitutable for the built-in AWT `Button`, and clients—that is, programs that use the `Button` objects—should be unaware that any substitution has been made.

- The `ImageButton` may extend the data or behavior of the `Button` class, but it shouldn't attempt to "remove" methods from the `Button` class by overriding them with empty methods. If you do this, you're saying that the `ImageButton` is not really a `Button` after all, but just has some behavior that you find attractive.

You might, after looking at the problem, decide that `ImageButtons` aren't really `Buttons`, but are instead special kinds of `Clickable Image` objects. If you feel that this is a more correct statement of your design, you'll want to create a `Clickable` interface and have your new `ImageButton` class implement that interface. You might then choose to use the `Canvas` or `Panel` class as the superclass on which to base your design. Remember, when you implement an interface, you are saying that

⬦ Your class can perform a certain action or behavior, and it may share this capability with other classes, but it's not necessarily related to those other classes.

⬦ There's no default behavior (implementation) or data that your new class should (or can) inherit. Only the specification—the public description of its behavior—is inherited.

For our ImageButton class, we'd like to create Buttons that act and look like regular Buttons, with the exception that they also contain an Image. That makes inheritance the logical choice. However, when you substitute your ImageButton for one of the built-in Buttons, you certainly want the Image to appear. That means you'll have to override the default implementation that displays the built-in Button's appearance. As you recall, when you want to use inheritance but have subclass objects exhibit specialized behavior, polymorphic inheritance is the design choice you should make. If, instead, you chose simple extension, you wouldn't be able to override the paint() method to display the Image, making your exercise a little pointless.

ImageButton1: A FIRST-DRAFT DESIGN

Let's start by looking at a "first-draft" design that gets the ImageButton class "off the ground," so to speak. After you look at whether the whole idea makes sense at all, we'll come back, round-trip, and see whether there's any way the whole thing can be improved. After all, you may find that the AWT's built-in Button class won't allow you to do what you want, in which case you'll have to go back to square one.

To create a Button that displays Images, you'll have to do only three things:

1. Load the Image and store a reference to it as a private data member inside the ImageButton class.

2. Display the Image in the correct location whenever the Button needs to be repainted. Rather than redraw the entire Button (although you can do that as well, if you want), you can let the Button superclass take care of drawing the actual Button shape, and then just add code to render the image on top of it.

3. Resize the ImageButton based on the size of the Image. Because a Button, by default, is sized according to the text it contains, you'll have to override this behavior to make sure that the ImageButtons you create have room to hold their Images on their surface.

Let's look at how each of these items can be implemented. Listing 9.6 shows the code for ImageButton1.java, which follows this design.

```
Listing 9.6 ImageButton1.java
//  A Button class with images
//  Version 1
import java.awt.*;

public class ImageButton1 extends Button
{
```

```
// Constructors
public ImageButton1(String imageName)
{
  super();
  theImage = tk.getImage(imageName);
  MediaTracker tracker = new MediaTracker(this);
  tracker.addImage(theImage, 0);
  try { tracker.waitForID(0); }
  catch (Exception e) { ; }

  imgWidth  = theImage.getWidth(this);
  imgHeight = theImage.getHeight(this);
  width  = imgWidth + 6;
  height = imgHeight + 6;
  System.out.println("w, h ="+width +", "+height);
}

public Dimension getPreferredSize()
{
  return new Dimension(width, height);
}

public void paint(Graphics g)
{
  super.paint(g);
  g.drawImage(theImage, 3, 3, getSize().width-6,
              getSize().height-6, this);
}

public void update(Graphics g) { paint(g); }

//  ImageButton1 object and class data
private Image theImage;
private int height, width, imgHeight, imgWidth;
private static Toolkit tk = Toolkit.getDefaultToolkit();
}
```

ImageButton1: Loading the Images

The ImageButton1 class uses three different objects to help it load the Image it uses. The first object is a reference to the Image itself. This is stored as a private field called theImage.

The second object used is an instance of a Toolkit object. Because each platform that Java operates on has different requirements for loading Images, the Toolkit class provides a factory for supplying the necessary Toolkit object, which knows how to load Images on that platform. The Toolkit object used by ImageButton1 is named tk, and it's also stored as a private field, which is initialized by calling the static method Toolkit.getDefaultToolkit(). Because every ImageButton object can share the same Toolkit object, the tk field itself is also made static.

The third object enlisted to help ImageButton load its Image is a MediaTracker object, which is created in the ImageButton constructor as a local object named tracker. The `MediaTracker` object is used to monitor the state of the `Image` as it's loaded. A Java program that uses `Images` doesn't typically store those `Images` as part of the compiled byte code that makes up the finished application. Instead, `Image` files are stored as plain graphics files (Java "understands" both the CompuServe GIF format and the ubiquitous JPEG format by default), which may be located locally (on the application user's hard disk) or remotely (somewhere on the Internet).

Because of this, the designers of Java decided to load `Images` *asynchronously*. Thus, when you tell your `Toolkit` object to `getImage("Somefile.gif")`, it creates a `Thread` object to carry out your wish and allows your program to continue. What that means for you, however, is that you won't know when the `Image` has actually arrived, unless you make a special effort to find out. That's what the `MediaTracker` object does—it allows you to make sure that your `Image` object is completely loaded before your program continues.

The `ImageButton` constructor takes care of loading the `Image` that you specify by passing the name of a file to use. After first calling `super()` to make sure that the superclass `Button` constructor is called, it goes on to do the following:

1. Ask the `Toolkit` object (`tk`) to fetch the `Image` from the file that you specified in `imageName`:

```
theImage = tk.getImage(imageName);
```

2. Create a `MediaTracker` object named `tracker` and add the `Image` you just fetched to `tracker`'s monitor list. It then just sits back and waits for `tracker` to report that `theImage` has arrived:

```
MediaTracker tracker = new MediaTracker(this);
tracker.addImage(theImage, 0);
try { tracker.waitForID(0); }
catch (Exception e) { ; }
```

ImageButton1: Sizing the Button

After the `Image` is loaded, the constructor's task is almost done. The only thing that remains is to set the `height` and `width` fields that will be used when your new `ImageButton` is asked how big to make itself.

The constructor should initialize the `height` and `width` fields to the height and width of `theImage`, plus a little extra for the border. To do this, it must wait for `tracker` to inform it that `theImage` has arrived, after which it can ask for `theImage`'s size by sending it the `getWidth()` and `getHeight()` messages. As an exercise, try commenting out the `MediaTracker` code you added previously and see what prints on the console. (The `System.out.println()` code in the constructor is debugging code for use during development, allowing you to double-check that `height` and `width` have reasonable values before proceeding.) As you can see, if you want to get a sensible size back from `getWidth()` or `getHeight()`, you must wait for the `Image` to actually arrive. The value

6 added to both the height and width is used when you paint your Image, to provide a border for the superclass Button to show through:

```
imgWidth  = theImage.getWidth(this);
imgHeight = theImage.getHeight(this);
width  = imgWidth + 6;
height = imgHeight + 6;
System.out.println("w, h ="+width +", "+height);
```

To actually cause your ImageButton to use the values you've set in height and width, you have to override the method that the AWT uses to decide how big to make any Component—the getPreferredSize() method. This method returns a Dimension object, representing the width and height that the object wants to be when laid out. To override getPreferredSize(), just create a new Dimension object, using the height and width fields that you set in the constructor, and return it from the method. Your method should look like this:

```
public Dimension getPreferredSize()
{
  return new Dimension(width, height);
}
```

You should be aware of one small detail when overriding getPreferredSize(). You may want to override getMinimumSize() as well, to increase your chance of getting good-looking Buttons in various situations when space is "tight." To make the minimum size the same as the preferred size, just have getMinimumSize() return getPreferredSize().

ImageButton1: Rendering the Image

When your Image is loaded and your size is all set, it's time to draw your Image. To do that, you have to override two methods: paint() and update().

In the paint() method, you first call super.paint(), passing the Graphics object you've received. This makes sure that the superclass Button has a chance to draw its borders. Then leave a small border around the image by drawing its upper-left corner at the point (3,3) and sizing it to allow the same 3-pixel border on all sides. This calculation ensures that your Image appears in the center of the Button, even if the layout manager swells your Button up like a balloon.

Finally, you'll want to override the update(Graphics) method to simply call paint(). If you fail to override update(), the paint() method may inexplicably erase the work that the super.paint() method has already done. This doesn't happen all the time, but simply overriding update() makes sure that it doesn't happen at all.

Your paint() and update() methods should look like this:

```
public void paint(Graphics g)
  {
    super.paint(g);
    g.drawImage(theImage, 3, 3, getSize().width-6,
            getSize().height-6, this);
}

public void update(Graphics g) { paint(g); }
```

Trying Out `ImageButton1`: The `IB1` Application

Let's write a couple of applications that show how easy it is to use your new `ImageButton` class in place of the built-in `Button` class. The programs `IB1.java` (shown in Listing 9.7) and `IB2.java` (included on the CD-ROM but not listed here) show you how to use your `ImageButtons`.

Listing 9.7 IB1.java

```java
//  ImageButton1 Test
import java.awt.*;
import java.awt.event.*;

public class IB1   extends CloseableFrame
                   implements ActionListener
{
  Button b1, b2, b3;

  public IB1()
  {
    super("Testing the ImageButton1 class");
    b1 = new ImageButton1("chili.gif");
    b2 = new ImageButton1("skisor.gif");
    b3 = new ImageButton1("virtual.gif");

    b1.addActionListener(this);
    b2.addActionListener(this);
    b3.addActionListener(this);

    add(b1);
    add(b2);
    add(b3);

  }

  public void actionPerformed(ActionEvent ae)
  {
    if (ae.getSource() == b2) quitApplication();
    System.out.println("Button: " + (Button)ae.getSource());
  }

  public static void main(String[] args)
  {
    IB1 theApp = new IB1();
    theApp.show();
  }
}
```

`IB1.java` is a test program that simply creates three `ImageButton` objects, adds `ActionListeners` to each, and then adds them to the surface of the application, which itself extends `CloseableFrame`. Notice the following:

🔹 The fields b1, b2, and b3 are all declared to be `Button` objects, yet you can make them refer to `ImageButton` objects. Because an `ImageButton` is a `Button`, it can be used any place a `Button` can be used.

⬥ You didn't have to do any work to implement the addActionListener() method—it was inherited from the Button superclass. Nor did you do anything special to make your application accept your ImageButton when you tried to add it to its Frame. Again, because you derived your subclass from Button, the Frame object treats it just as though it were a Button, which, of course, it is!

You can see IB1.java at work in Figure 9.7. Each ImageButton is attractively sized and inherits from its superclass the ability to respond to ActionEvents.

As mentioned, most layout managers resize your components based on the space available. To see how the ImageButton1 class holds up under that treatment, look at IB2.java in Figure 9.8. Because the code for IB2.java is almost identical to that of IB1.java—except for the addition of a BorderLayout() layout manager—it's not included here. You can find it in the CD-ROM's Listings directory for this chapter if you like.

ImageButton2: Adding Abstract Classes

Although there's nothing wrong with ImageButton1 as it stands, it does have one limitation: You can create ImageButtons only in Java applications, not in applets. If you

FIGURE 9.7

The IB1 application: testing the ImageButton1 *class*

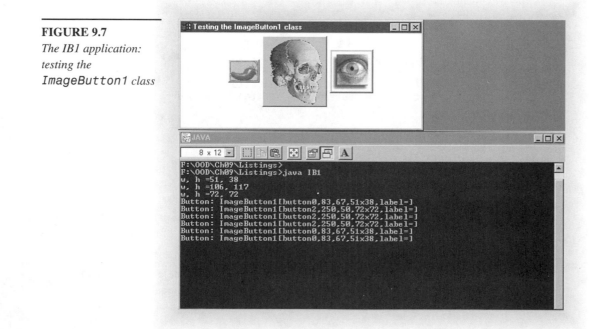

FIGURE 9.8

The IB2 *application:* ImageButton1 *objects, and* BorderLayout

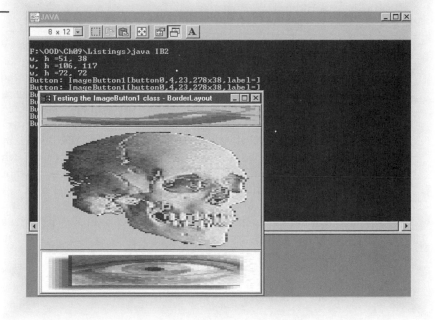

> *Java applets can load images and sounds only from the same host that launched the applet.*

take IB1.java and turn it into an applet, post it on a Web site, and try to access it via your Web browser, you'll quickly discover that your browser reports a security violation. That's because Java applets can load images and sounds only from the same host that launched the applet. After all, you don't want applets you access on the Web to go rummaging around on your hard disk, do you?

That's not to say that applets *can't* load Images or use the ImageButton class, however; they simply have to go about it differently than applications. Actually, it's somewhat easier to load Images from an applet than from an application. The Applet class has a handy getImage() method built in, so you don't even need to create a Toolkit object. The Applet version of getImage() takes two arguments: a URL where the image can be found and a String with the name of the file. The applet method getDocumentBase() will helpfully return the URL of the directory containing the applet. If you put the GIF files for the ImageButton in the same directory, you can use getDocumentBase() to create the necessary URL. So, to revise ImageButton1 for use in an applet, all you have to do is get rid of the Toolkit object, add getDocumentBase() to each getImage() call, and you're all set. Or are you?

What happens now when you want to use your ImageButtons inside an application? Oops! Whereas the applet version doesn't need a Toolkit object, the application requires one; it can't load an image without it. But—and here's the rub—the applet version can't use the Toolkit. It seems that you can have an applet ImageButton or an application ImageButton, but not a single class that works in either type of program. Is there any good solution? Yes.

INTRODUCING THE `ImageSource` CLASS

If you think about the problem you're trying to solve, you realize that the `ImageButton` class itself would work fine in either an application or an applet, if only you could get the `Image` loaded. In other words, you don't need two versions of the `ImageButton` class, you need two different classes for loading `Images`: one to load `Images` in applications and one to load `Images` in applets. But if you write two classes to load `Images`, your `ImageButton` class will have to decide to use one of them, and you'll find yourself right back where you started: You'll have an `AppletImageButton` class and an `ApplicationImageButton` class. That's not really what you want.

The problem is that neither class really seems to have anything in common. But if you step back and think about the problem for a second, you'll realize that they really do. Each has to load an `Image`. Of course, each will go about it in a different way, but the requirement is the same. It sounds like a job for an `abstract` class. Listing 9.8 shows such a class, `ImageSource`.

Listing 9.8 ImageSource.java

```
import java.awt.*;
import java.applet.*;

public abstract class ImageSource
{
  public abstract Image getImage(String s);
}
```

`ImageSource` is an abstract class. By defining the `abstract` method `getImage()`, `ImageSource` specifies the behavior that the `ImageButton` class needs an `ImageSource` to perform. Because the `ImageSource` class doesn't provide any functionality, you could just as easily have used an interface here.

EXTENDING `ImageSource`

By itself, of course, the `ImageSource` class is useless. Like all `abstract` classes, you can't even create an `ImageSource` object; you must create subclasses that actually carry out the work that an `ImageSource` object will be expected to do. It's important to note, however, that `ImageButton` objects won't know that there are different `ImageSource` subclasses for applets and applications. As far as `ImageButton` objects are concerned, all `ImageSource` objects are created equal.

Listing 9.9 shows the code for `ApplicationImageSource.java`, which extends the `ImageSource` class and fulfills the `ImageSource` contract for applications. Note that it contains a `static` `Toolkit` object and uses that `Toolkit` object to fetch `Images` by using `Toolkit.getImage(String)`.

Listing 9.9 ApplicationImageSource.java

```
//  The ImageSource for applications
import java.awt.*;

public class ApplicationImageSource extends ImageSource
```

```
{
  private static Toolkit tk = Toolkit.getDefaultToolkit();

  public Image getImage(String s)
  {
    return tk.getImage(s);
  }
}
```

Listing 9.10 shows the similar code for AppletImageSource.java, which performs the same function when an ImageButton is created inside an applet. Because an AppletImageSource relies on the applet that contains it for its getImage() method, you have to pass in an Applet object when creating a new AppletImageSource object. Normally you'll do this in your applet by passing this. This extra code makes the AppletImageSource class slightly more complex than ApplicationImageSource.

Listing 9.10 AppletImageSource.java

```
//  An ImageSource for Applets
import java.awt.*;
import java.applet.*;

public class AppletImageSource extends ImageSource
{
  private static Applet owner = null;

  public AppletImageSource(Applet owner)
  {
    this.owner = owner;
  }

  public Image getImage(String s)
  {
    return owner.getImage(owner.getDocumentBase(), s);
  }
}
```

MORE ABSTRACTION: `ImageButtonFactory`

Now that you have AppletImageSource and ApplicationImageSource, you can simply retrieve an Image and pass it on to your ImageButton class where it can be displayed. But if you remember, that was one of the charms of the ImageButton class to begin with. You didn't have to be concerned with loading the Image. You simply passed in a String naming the Image you wanted to use, and the ImageButton class took care of retrieving it. Now, by requiring you to create an ImageSource object and use that object to retrieve Images, it seems that you've taken several steps backward.

How about this, then? You have to create an ImageSource object, no matter what you do. That's really not any more difficult that what you did before. Why don't you hand your ImageSource object to your ImageButton class, and then the ImageButton can be responsible for loading its own Images, just like before.

The only complication is deciding how you should pass the ImageSource. The straightforward way is to pass an ImageSource along with the String selecting the

Image file every time you create an ImageButton. The disadvantage of this method is that it clutters up your code, making it more complex. What you'd really like is to make the ImageSource a static field inside the ImageButton class, so you have to pass it only once. You can do this by creating a special "factory" class, a form of the Factory design pattern, which you'll study more fully in Chapter 11, "Patterns: Proven Designs."

Listing 9.11 shows the revised class that puts these ideas into effect. In every class where you want to use ImageButtons, you create a single, static instance of the ImageButtonFactory class, passing it either an AppletImageSource object or an ApplicationImageSource object. The ImageButtonFactory will then produce ImageButton objects for you whenever you invoke its getImage(String) method.

Listing 9.11 ImageButtonFactory.java

```java
// A class for making ImageButtons
import java.awt.*;

public class ImageButtonFactory
{
  protected class ImageButton extends Button
  {
    protected ImageButton(String imageFile)
    {
      super();
      theImage = theSource.getImage(imageFile);
      MediaTracker tracker = new MediaTracker(this);
      tracker.addImage(theImage, 0);
      try { tracker.waitForID(0); }
      catch (Exception e) { ; }

      imgWidth  = theImage.getWidth(this);
      imgHeight = theImage.getHeight(this);
      width  = imgWidth + 6;
      height = imgHeight + 6;
    }

    public Dimension getPreferredSize()
    {
      return new Dimension(width, height);
    }

    public void paint(Graphics g)
    {
      super.paint(g);
      g.drawImage(theImage, 3, 3, getSize().width-6,
                  getSize().height-6, this);
    }

    public void update(Graphics g) { paint(g); }

    //  ImageButton object and class data
    private Image theImage;
```

> *[A] protected interface creates a contract with class extenders, just like [a] public interface creates a contract with class users.*

```
    private int height, width, imgHeight, imgWidth;
  }

  public ImageButton getButton(String s)
  {
    return new ImageButton(s);
  }

  public ImageButtonFactory(ImageSource src)
  {
    theSource = src;
  }

  protected static ImageSource theSource = null;
}
```

Notice that inside ImageButtonFactory, the ImageButton class itself is defined as a protected inner class. By making the ImageButton class protected, you prohibit the general public from creating ImageButton objects without going through the Factory, but you allow those who want to extend the ImageButton class to do so. This protected interface creates a contract with class extenders, just like the public interface creates a contract with class users, as Figure 9.9 illustrates.

FIGURE 9.9
Three contracts of a class

USING THE `ImageButtonFactory`

To use the new `ImageButtonFactory`, you only need to follow these three steps:

1. Create an `ImageSource` object in your program. You need create only one.

2. Create an `ImageButtonFactory` object, passing the `ImageSource` to its constructor. You also need only one of these.

3. Call the `ImageButtonFactory.getButton()` method to construct your `ImageButton` objects. Remember, because every `ImageButton` *isA* `Button`, you don't need to store the `ImageButton` you get back in an `ImageButton` reference—a regular `Button` will do just as well.

Listing 9.12, `TestIBF.java`, shows a program that can be run as either an application or an applet.

Listing 9.12 TestIBF.java

```java
// Test ImageButtonFactory
import java.awt.*;
import java.applet.*;

public class TestIBF extends Applet
{
  private ImageButtonFactory bf = null;
  private Container mainWin     = null;

  public void init()
  {
    if (mainWin == null)
      mainWin = this;
    if (bf == null)
      bf = new ImageButtonFactory(new AppletImageSource(this));
    mainWin.setLayout(new BorderLayout());
    Panel p = new BevelPanel(true);
    p.setLayout(new FlowLayout(FlowLayout.RIGHT));

    p.add(bf.getButton("btar_lft.gif"));
    p.add(bf.getButton("btar_up.gif"));
    p.add(bf.getButton("btar_dn.gif"));
    p.add(bf.getButton("btar_rgt.gif"));
    mainWin.add(p, "North");

    mainWin.add(bf.getButton("cupj.gif"), "Center");
  }

  public static void main(String[] args)
  {
    TestIBF app = new TestIBF();
    CloseableFrame f = new CloseableFrame("Application Buttons");
    f.setLayout(new FlowLayout());
    app.bf = new ImageButtonFactory(new ApplicationImageSource());
    app.mainWin = f;
    app.init();
    f.setVisible(true);
  }
}
```

If you run this program as an application, using the java interpreter, the main() method creates a new CloseableFrame and an ApplicationImageSource, which it uses to construct an ImageButtonFactory before calling init(). In the init() method (which is the *first* thing called if the program is run as an applet), an AppletImageSource is constructed if the class ImageSource object is null. In either case, the various Buttons are loaded and displayed in the window. Use Listing 9.13, TestIBF.html, to view the applet in your Web browser.

Listing 9.13 TestIBF.html

```
<HTML>
<HEAD>
<TITLE>Testing ImageButtonFactory</TITLE>
</HEAD>
<BODY>
<H1>The ImageButtonFactory Class</H1>
<HR>
<APPLET CODE=TestIBF HEIGHT=300 WIDTH=500>
</APPLET>
</BODY>
</HTML>
```

Figure 9.10 shows TestIBF.java running in both a Web browser and as an application. By using abstract classes, you were able to write an ImageButton class that worked, unchanged, in both.

FIGURE 9.10

Running TestIBF.java as an application and as an applet

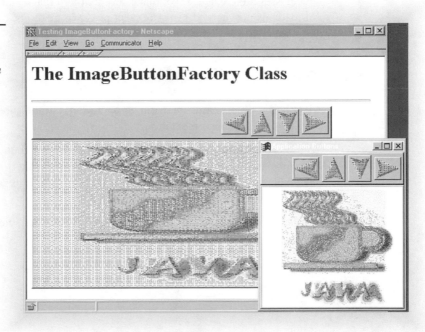

An Inheritance Checklist

How do you decide which inheritance mechanism to use where? When should you use extension, polymorphism, or interfaces? What about abstract classes, abstract methods, final methods, final classes, and overridden methods? Use this handy checklist to make sure what you wrote says what you mean.

USE `final` CLASSES WHEN...

- Your class should not be extended. You can preclude extension by marking the *entire class* as `final`. If you don't make your class `final`, you're saying that it may be extended.

USE `final` METHODS WHEN...

- You want to model a strict subtype relationship between two classes. When you mark a method as `final` (thus preventing subclasses from implementing different behavior), you're saying that the method represents an invariant implementation for all subclasses of this class. If you fail to mark a method as `final`, you're saying that the behavior isn't invariant.

- A method performs an operation in some way that must not change when new classes are created. If so, make sure that you mark that method as `final`. All methods not marked `final` (except `private` methods, of course) are fair game for re-implementation.

USE abstract METHODS WHEN...

- All subclass objects must perform an operation, but the superclass can't provide a default implementation.

- You intend to write code in terms of superclass objects but, in fact, will use only subclass objects. A board game may be written in terms of `BoardPiece` objects, instructing them to `move()`, even though a `BoardPiece` has no default method for implementing that behavior.

- You want to force a subclass to implement a certain behavior, such as initialization.

USE OVERRIDDEN METHODS WHEN...

- A superclass can define some reasonable default action for a method.

- More than one subclass can make use of the default behavior. If only one subclass uses the default behavior, it's not really a superclass method and should be abstract.

- Subclass objects will perform the same operation in different ways, yet make use of some common behavior to carry out that operation. If more than one subclass can use the default operation unchanged, use an overridden method. If all subclasses need to add to or extend the method, place the common code in a protected helper method in the superclass, and make the overridden method an abstract method. If you don't do this, authors of subclasses are likely to forget that they must override the method. By making the overridden method abstract, the compiler will bring it to mind.

USE PURELY abstract CLASSES WHEN...

- You can define a common data member in the superclass, even though you can define no methods.

- You're designing a hierarchy that's expected to model closely related classes.

USE interfaces WHEN...

- You're designing a set of classes that share a common behavior yet aren't otherwise related.

- There's no common implementation you want to inherit, but you want to impose a mandatory interface on all subclasses.

- You need to combine several behaviors, simulating multiple inheritance.

Summary

Encapsulation allows you to organize your software by combining data and the methods that process that data into classes that contain similar characteristics. Inheritance gives you the mechanism to further organize your classes into hierarchies of related classes. The fundamental class relationship is the superclass-subclass relationship. Given a very general class—like food, for instance—you can subdivide that class into more specialized kinds of classes. These specialized classes form a subset of the more general class and thus are called *subclasses*.

Inheritance means that the subclass *is-a-kind-of* the superclass (commonly shortened to say that a subclass *isA* superclass). We can identify three distinct kinds of *isA* relationships. A class may extend another class, adding either data or methods, but making no changes to the behavior of the existing class. Such an *extension relationship* ensures that the new subclass is entirely substitutable for an object of the original class.

In some situations, however, you may be able to create a superclass that captures a general abstraction—such as a `Shape`—but doesn't have enough information to create actual objects. You may specify that all `Shape` objects know how to `draw()` themselves, but you can't provide a default method for them to do so. In this *specification relationship*, subclasses of `Shape` (`Circle`, `Rectangle`, and so forth) inherit their interface from `Shape` but not their implementation.

In the third kind of class relationship, *polymorphic inheritance*, a class inherits some combination of methods. Some will have no implementation; the class inherits only an interface. Some can have a default implementation; the class may override those but doesn't have to. Some can be marked as mandatory methods; the subclass must use the implementation provided by the superclass.

Java provides several different language and syntax mechanisms for expressing these three kinds of class relationships. To create a simple extension (or strict subtype) relationship, you make all the methods in the original class into `final` methods. To create a pure specification relationship between two classes, you can use either the `interface`/`implements` mechanism or a pure `abstract` class. If the relationship between two classes is one of polymorphic inheritance, you use extension and then distinguish between the methods that must not change (which are marked `final`), the methods that may change, and the methods for which no implementation is provided. These last are created as `abstract` methods.

Questions

1. True or false. If you've written a class containing methods that must not be extended, you can use the `final` keyword to make the method unchangeable while leaving the rest of the class extensible.

2. When writing a `BoardGame` class, you have extended the `GamePiece` class that requires you to write a `move()` method. In the superclass, `GamePiece`, the `move()` method must be a _____ method.

   a. `final`

   b. `private`

   c. `abstract`

   d. `derived`

   e. `interface`

3. In Java, you can create two classes that share a similar behavior, even if they aren't otherwise related, by having them both _____ the same _____.

4. In Java, if you have two classes that are both specialized versions of a more general class, you can have both classes _____ the same _____.

5. True or false. One good use for inheritance is to remove extraneous operations from a superclass by simply overriding the inherited method by using a set of empty braces.

6. In a correctly written program, any method that uses an object of the superclass `Animal` should be able to replace that object with an object of `Animal`'s subclass, `Rhinoceros`. This is called the _____ principle.

7. True or false. If `Student` is a subclass of `Person` and every `Student` has a non-inherited method called `study()`, you should be able to send a `study()` message to a `Person` object as well.

8. If you want to create a new class that uses an existing class as a superclass and want to override only one of several methods declared in the superclass, which inheritance mechanism would be most appropriate?

   a. Simple extension

   b. Polymorphic inheritance

   c. Implementing an interface

   d. A final class

   e. Polysyllabic implementation

9. When creating a new subclass from an existing class, you can use the _____ access modifier to allow subclasses access to your data, but prohibit modification by objects of your class.

10. True or false. When overriding a method in a superclass to provide specialized behavior, you are free to add new arguments to the method to help you implement that behavior.

Exercises

1. Modify the `BevelPanel` class by adding a constructor that allows you to change the thickness of the border, and another that allows you to specify which layout manager should be used.

2. Modify the `CloseableFrame` class by implementing code for each `WindowListener` event. Start by using `System.out.println()` to display a message to the console whenever the event occurs. Do some events never occur? Why do you think that happens? What could you do about it?

Implement a `HideableFrame` class that doesn't quit the application when the window closes, and then create an application based on `CloseableFrame` that creates and hides some `HideableFrame` objects.

3. Modify the `ImageButton` class to allow a caption as well as an `Image`. To do this, you'll have to change the constructors that the `ImageButton` uses so that you can add text to the `Button`. When you override the `getPreferredSize()` method in your `ImageButton`, you can call `super.getPreferredSize()` to find out how big the `Button` "wants" to be, and then add the necessary space for your `Image` before returning. When you `paint()` the `Image`, you'll have to adjust the location so that it doesn't overwrite the text drawn by `Button`. Add some static final constants that allow a user to specify whether the `Image` should be drawn above, below, to the left, or to the right of the caption.

4. Combine the `ImageButtonFactory` and `BevelPanel` classes to create a `ToolBar` class. A `ToolBar` should hold multiple `ImageButtons`. (*Hint:* Use an array.) Discuss the advantages and disadvantages of constructing the `ImageButtons` and passing them to the `ToolBar` versus just passing in the names of the graphic files you want to use. Can you think of a good way to hook up an `ActionListener` to your `ToolBar` objects? How should your `ToolBar` report which `Button` was pressed?

To Learn More

Several books have been written that contain useful advice on modeling the inheritance relationship. Few of them are specific to Java. Two of the most valuable are as follows:

- Addison-Wesley's *Effective C++* by Scott Meyers, now in it's second printing, offers 50 ways to improve your C++ programs. Although most of the book is understandably specific to C++, the chapter on "Inheritance and Object-Oriented Design" should be required reading for any object-oriented developer. Although the *way* that you implement inheritance of interface and implementation is different in Java than in C++, the necessity of distinguishing between them is still very important. Meyers will get you thinking in that direction.

- The father of Java, James Gosling (along with Ken Arnold), in *The Java Programming Language* from Addison-Wesley, has a chapter called "Extending Classes." Although most of the book focuses, naturally, on the syntax of Java, this chapter offers abundant advice on how and when you should extend your classes, as well as a section on designing a class to be extended.

10

Designing with Inheritance and Interfaces:

A Case Study

Once upon a time, there was a king who wisely left his affairs in the hands of a capable advisor, who served him well for many years. Eventually, however, the aged advisor passed on, forcing the king to seek a replacement. The king advertised throughout his kingdom and soon scores of wise men and women were arriving daily at the palace gate, certain they would become the king's new advisor.

Mindful of the good advice he had received from his former advisor, the king was concerned to discover which of the many would-be advisors was the most capable. At the king's order, a series of contests was held, and two candidates were selected to compete for the office. One was a computer programmer and the other was a fishmonger. As the final test, the king showed the two candidates a bright metal cube with a glass door, a dial, and a set of on/off buttons. "What do you think this is?" asked the king.

The fishmonger answered first: "It's a microwave oven, your Grace. It makes breakfast."

"Well, then," asked the king, "how do you use it?"

"Simple," replied the fishmonger. "You put your smoked salmon on a bagel, put them both in the oven, close the door, turn the dial a bit to the right, and press the *on* button. When the machine stops whirring, you open the door and eat your breakfast. Here, I'll show you."

A few seconds later, the king and the two candidates were enjoying a deliciously warm breakfast.

"Very impressive," observed the king. Turning to the computer programmer, he challenged him to top the fishmonger's performance: "And what do *you* think this gadget is?" he asked.

"Your majesty," began the computer programmer, "the fishmonger's answer is right, as far as it goes. But it does not go nearly far enough. Microwave ovens don't merely warm lox and bagels, they warm waffles, pizza, even buffalo wings. This unit is actually a food preparation system and, though it meets your subjects' present requirements, I'm concerned that the changing environment will soon compel them to seek a more complete solution to their needs."

"But this breakfast the fishmonger took from the machine is marvelous," protested the king. "How could any of my subjects wish for more?"

"Majesty," began the computer programmer, "recall how the fishmonger was required to open the bag of bagels, place the bagel on the dish, and then place the salmon atop the bagel. When I become your advisor and your subjects view the works I'll commission in your behalf, they will spend vastly more of their time contemplating your greatness and will have less time for meals. Consequently, the unit must do more than simply warm the food. Your subjects will need a system that can cook sausage, fry bacon, cook their eggs the way they like them, and make waffles and pancakes as well."

"I begin to see your point," the king mused, intrigued by the prospect of becoming even more admired by his subjects. "Please continue."

"Well," said the programmer, "first we must create an abstract class of breakfast foods. It need implement only the most essential nutrients; the remainder can be supplied by the concrete classes derived from it. Then, we must apply generalization/specialization to identify a series of subclasses that encompasses a broad range of breakfast foods: meats, dairy products, and grains. We must then recursively apply this technique to specialize the meats into pork and poultry, and do the same for the dairy products and grains. Dairy products can be divided into food and beverages. The foods include butter and cream cheese; the beverages include milk and buttermilk. Cream has both food and beverage properties, so foods and beverages should be defined as interfaces, rather than regular classes.

"Now," continued the programmer, "using the object-oriented principle of polymorphism, each breakfast item should implement a cook() method, so that each can prepare itself to order based on receipt of a single parameterized message. We must also consider the cardinality of relationships between the various classes. For example, some of your subjects prefer two pancakes in their pancake sandwich, whereas others prefer three. We must be careful to make allowance for both possibilities.

"Of course, in order to be able to deploy the system across the kingdom's intranet, it must be implemented in Java. And, we'll need an Andromeda V Web Server to host the pages and applets. This, of course, assumes your subjects are using the NicNac II browser; otherwise, we'll have to deploy the system as a suite of applications, using push technology of some sort, possibly CostALot. And, we'll have to upgrade all the client PCs…"

The king wisely had the computer programmer beheaded and made the fishmonger his new advisor. They all, except of course the computer programmer, lived happily ever after.

Object-oriented technology is not child's play. It's altogether too easy to get caught up in the details, missing the forest for the trees. This chapter is intended to help you avoid the fate of the erstwhile advisor, or whatever equivalent fate is permissible under the laws of your state of residence and the human relations policies of your employer.

Chapter 9, "Implementing Class Relationships: Inheritance and Interfaces," explained the principles of inheritance, abstract classes, and interfaces. This chapter demonstrates how inheritance can improve your software designs. First, you'll learn how to draw class diagrams that depict inheritance relationships. The class diagram is your primary tool for coping with design complexity, because it helps you use the principle of abstraction to present only relevant aspects of your design. After learning more about class diagrams, you'll embark on an extended case study that will help you see how inheritance fits into the software design process.

Class Diagrams

As you've learned, class diagrams are an important design tool. Because they're less detailed and complex than actual code, you can use them to quickly communicate important aspects of a design to other designers, to programmers, and even to users. Moreover, class diagrams can help you think through a design before actually coding it, improving the chances that your program design will be sound.

Although the class diagrams you've used up to this point have not included inheritance relationships, it's simple to add this information. Figure 10.1 shows a class diagram that includes inheritance relationships. The class `MyApplet` and the class `Applet` are related, as indicated by the solid line joining them. The triangle at the end of the line near the `Applet` class indicates that the relationship is an inheritance relationship, and that the class `MyApplet` extends the class `Applet`. (If it seems to you that the triangles are pointing the "wrong" way, you're not alone—many others have voiced the same complaint. Remember though, a notation is a method for communicating with others, and that requires using an accepted notation.)

" Because [class diagrams are] less detailed and complex than actual code, you can use them to quickly communicate important aspects of a design to other designers, to programmers, and even to users. "

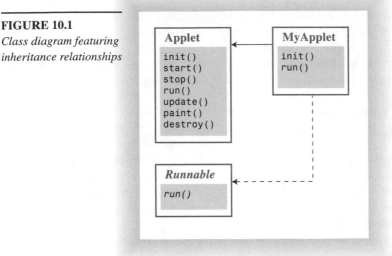

The `Runnable` "class" is actually an interface. (Recall from Chapter 9 that an interface represents specification; it defines methods but provides no implementation.) To indicate this, the class name is italicized in the diagram. Finally, the interface `Runnable` and the class `MyApplet` are related, as indicated by the line joining them. The line is dotted to indicate that it represents an `implements` relationship rather than an `extends` relationship. The triangle near the `Runnable` interface indicates that the `MyApplet` class implements the `Runnable` interface.

Abstract classes can be shown in class diagrams in the same way that interfaces are shown, by italicizing the class name. Because an abstract class can provide both default method implementations (called *concrete* methods) and methods that are only specified (*abstract* methods), you'll need to differentiate between them on your diagrams. The names of concrete methods can appear in non-italicized type and names of abstract methods can appear in italicized type. In the figure, the name of the `run()` method is italicized, indicating that `MyApplet` will not inherit an implementation of the `run()` method from the `Runnable` interface.

A more detailed class diagram featuring inheritance is shown in Figure 10.2. This diagram shows a base class, `Employee`, and two derived classes, `SalariedEmployee` and `HourlyEmployee`. An additional class, `Department`, is related to both `SalariedEmployee` and `HourlyEmployee`.

The relationship between `HourlyEmployee` and `Department` is one in which the `HourlyEmployee` plays the *role* of "Worker." The cardinality notations show that each `Department` may have an indefinite (*) number of Workers, and that each Worker is associated with only a single (1) department.

FIGURE 10.2
Detailed class diagram

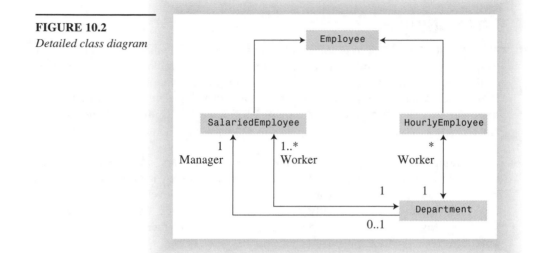

The relationship between `SalariedEmployee` and `Department` is more complex. In fact, there are two distinct relationships between these two classes. In one relationship, the `SalariedEmployee` plays the role of "Worker." This relationship is much like that between `HourlyEmployee` and `Department`. However, each `Department` must have at least one (1..*) `SalariedEmployee`, even though it need not have any (*) `HourlyEmployees`.

In the second relationship between `SalariedEmployee` and `Department`, the `SalariedEmployee` plays the role of "Manager." A given `SalariedEmployee` may or may not (0..1) participate in this relationship, because not every `SalariedEmployee` is the manager of a `Department`. However, each `Department` must have exactly one (1) `SalariedEmployee` designated as its manager.

Also notice the navigability arrowheads, which show that it's possible to navigate from a `Department` to the `Department`'s manager, but not the reverse. This means a `Department` object knows who its `Manager` is, but a `Manager` object doesn't know which `Department` it manages. (After all, designers strive to design object-oriented systems that model the real world.) The remaining relationships with `Department` are both bi-directional. Notice that no navigability arrowheads are included on the lines denoting the inheritance relationships.

When you draw a class diagram, remember that it's counterproductive to include *all* information. So that the diagram can be quickly and easily understood, you should include only the relevant information. Navigability, cardinality, and role notations sometimes make a class diagram clearer and easier to understand. Don't, however, needlessly clutter a diagram with these notations. Unless they make an important point, omit them.

" When you draw a class diagram, remember that it's counter-productive to include all information. So that the diagram can be quickly and easily understood, you should include only the relevant information."

Case Study

Now that you know how to read class diagrams that illustrate inheritance, you're ready to see for yourself how inheritance can lead to better software designs. As an example of design using inheritance, let's design and implement a simple arcade-style game. Rather than design and implement the entire game in a single step, we'll take an iterative approach similar to that typical of object-oriented software development. This way, you'll be able to see for yourself why some design alternatives are better than others.

The Bumpers game simulates amusement park bumper cars, which zoom around a rectangular play field. When one bumper car strikes another, it disables it. In a real bumper car ride, the disabled car can soon run again. However, to make a game of this, the program will permanently disable a car that is struck. The goal of the game will be to drive your car into the other cars, disabling all of them before they disable you.

First Contact: The Bumpers01 Applet

To create a bumper car game, you immediately come face-to-face with two fundamental problems: how do you animate the cars, and how do you handle the ricochet when a bumper car strikes an edge? To get started attacking those problems, let's create a simple applet, named Bumpers01, that displays a group of bumper cars and moves them around randomly. Figure 10.3 shows the applet at play, er, work!

FIGURE 10.3

Running the Bumpers01 applet

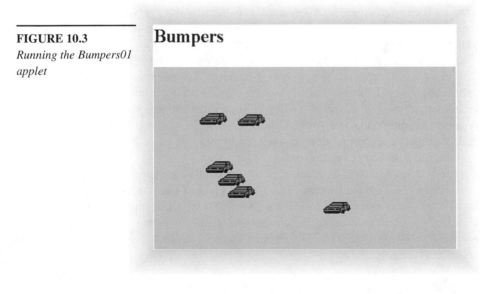

Bumpers

LISTING THE REQUIREMENTS

Because the applet must have a single playing field and several bumper cars, let's create two classes. One class, the applet itself, represents the playing field. A bumper car game with only a single bumper car isn't much fun, so you'll use the other class, representing a bumper car, to create multiple objects. Figure 10.4 shows a class diagram of the Bumpers01 applet. As you can see, the Bumpers01 class extends the Applet class and implements the Runnable interface. Each Bumpers01 object is associated with an indefinite number of FastCar objects.

Each FastCar object has an image, which is painted on the applet surface to represent it. Each FastCar also has a size, a position, and a velocity, given by the remaining fields. FastCars know how to return their size or position, update their position, and paint themselves.

IMPLEMENTING THE PLAYING FIELD

To see how the program is implemented, let's start by looking at the fields used in the Bumpers01 applet, which you can see in Listing 10.1. In order to produce smooth animation, the applet has to update its screen every 33 milliseconds; this value is stored in the SLEEP_TIME field. The number of bumper cars is specified by the CARS field, which is set to 6. The actual cars themselves are stored in the array of FastCar objects named theCar.

FIGURE 10.4

Class diagram of the Bumpers01 applet

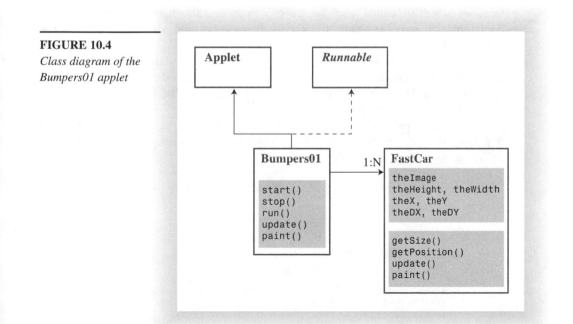

> *In order to produce smooth animation, the applet has to update its screen every 33 milliseconds…*

```
Listing 10.1 Fields of the Bumpers01 Applet
import java.applet.*;
import java.awt.*;
import java.awt.event.*;
import java.net.URL;

public class Bumpers01 extends Applet implements Runnable
{
  public static final int SLEEP_TIME = 33;
  public static final int CARS       = 6;

  Graphics  theGraphics;
  Dimension theSize;
  Image     theImage;
  Thread    theThread;
  boolean   isRunning;
  FastCar[] theCar;

  Image       theFastImage;
  AudioClip theMusic;

  // Methods shown below
}
```

STARTING TO PLAY

After you have the fields for your applet laid out, you'll need some way of getting things started. In an applet, the ideal place to do that is in the `start()` and `stop()` methods, which are called when the browser enters and leaves (respectively) the page containing the applet. Listing 10.2 shows the `start()` and `stop()` methods of the Bumpers01 applet.

The `start()` method first acquires the image used to represent a bumper car and an audio clip used as background music. It then creates the specified number of bumper cars, placing a reference to each in the array `theCar`. Finally, it starts a new thread used to animate the bumper cars.

The `stop()` method sets a flag that terminates execution of the animation thread whenever the user leaves the page with the bumper car applet. As a good citizen, it also stops the background music.

```
Listing 10.2 The start() and stop() Methods of Bumpers01
  public void start( )
  {
    try
    {
      theFastImage = getAppletContext().getImage(
        new URL(getDocumentBase( ), "FastCar.GIF"));

      theMusic = getAppletContext( ).getAudioClip(
        new URL(getDocumentBase( ), "Music.au"));
      theMusic.loop( );
    }
    catch (Exception e)
    {
      System.out.println(e);
```

```
  }
  setBackground(Color.lightGray);

  theCar = new FastCar[CARS];
  for (int i = 0; i < CARS; i++)
  {
    theCar[i] = new FastCar(theFastImage, 500, 300);
  }

  theThread = new Thread(this);
  isRunning = true;
  theThread.start( );
}

public void stop( )
{
  theMusic.stop( );
  isRunning = false;
}
```

RUNNING SMOOTHLY

Now that the cars are loaded and the music is playing, it's time to start the cars running around the screen. What better place to do that than in the run() method?

The Bumpers01 run() method, shown in Listing 10.3, executes in its own thread. Its while loop terminates when the stop() method sets the field isRunning to false. After the while loop is done, the method is exited and the thread is destroyed. This technique is preferred to using the Thread.stop() method, which may leave data in an inconsistent state.

The body of the while loop simply asks each car in the array to update itself, using the Thread.sleep() method to delay each iteration of the loop. As long as the loop is executed at least 20 or so times per second, the animation appears smooth. Animating the bumper cars requires two operations: updating the position of each car and repainting the screen. The cars themselves are each responsible for moving themselves and rendering themselves on the display.

Listing 10.3 The run() Method of Bumpers01

```
public void run( )
{
  while (isRunning)
  {
    try
    {
      Thread.sleep(SLEEP_TIME);
    }
    catch (InterruptedException e) { ; }
    Dimension d = getSize( );
    for (int i = 0; i < CARS; i++)
    {
      theCar[i].update(d.width, d.height);
    }
    repaint( );
  }
}
```

DISPLAYING THE PLAYING FIELD

The last line in the `run()` method simply sends a `repaint()` message to the applet itself. When the applet gets the message, it performs a `paint()` operation by first calling the applet's `update()` method, and then invoking its `paint()` method. Listing 10.4 shows the `update()` and `paint()` methods of the Bumpers01 applet.

To reduce flicker, the applet uses a technique known as double buffering. Instead of drawing directly to a `Graphics` object associated with the screen, the applet draws to an identically sized `Graphics` object associated with an `Image` resident in memory. When it's done drawing, the applet draws the `Image` to the screen in a single operation. In order to make sure the `Image` resident in memory is the same size as the applet, the `update()` method compares their sizes and creates a new `Image` object and a new `Graphics` object if necessary.

When it comes to actually drawing the playing field, the task performed by the `paint()` method, only two steps are required. First, the method erases the screen by repainting it in the background color. Then, it requests each bumper car to paint itself.

Listing 10.4 The update() and paint() Methods of Bumpers01

```
public final synchronized void update(Graphics g)
{
  if (theSize == null
    || theSize.width  != getSize( ).width
    || theSize.height != getSize( ).height)
  {
    theSize = getSize( );
    theImage = createImage(theSize.width, theSize.height);
    theGraphics = theImage.getGraphics( );
  }
  paint(theGraphics);
  g.drawImage(theImage, 0, 0, null);
}

public void paint(Graphics g)
{
  g.setColor(getBackground( ));
  g.fillRect(0, 0, getSize( ).width, getSize( ).height);
  for (int i = 0; i < CARS; i++)
  {
    theCar[i].paint(g);
  }
}
}
```

LOOKING AT `FastCar`

Now that you've seen how the Bumpers01 applet works, it's time to turn your attention to the other class: `FastCar`. Listing 10.5 shows the fields and constructor of the `FastCar` class.

When a `FastCar` is created, (in the constructor `FastCar()`), its image is saved; then it's given a random position (`theX` and `theY`) and velocity (`theDX` and `theDY`). To generate the random values, the method uses `Math.random()`, which returns a `double` value greater than or equal to 0.0 and less than 1.0.

Listing 10.5 Fields and Constructor of the FastCar Class

```
class FastCar
{
  Image theImage;
  int    theWidth  = 50;
  int    theHeight = 25;
  int    theX;
  int    theY;
  float theDX;
  float theDY;

  private static final float MAX_V = 20;

  public FastCar(Image img, int max_x, int max_y)
  {
    theImage = img;
    theX = (int) (Math.random( ) * max_x);
    theY = (int) (Math.random( ) * max_y);
    theDX = MAX_V - 2.0F * (float) Math.random( ) * MAX_V;
    theDY = MAX_V - 2.0F * (float) Math.random( ) * MAX_V;
  }

  // Methods shown below
}
```

Listing 10.6 shows the methods of the `FastCar` class. The accessor methods `getSize()` and `getPosition()` simply return the size and position, respectively, of a `FastCar`. The `update()` method updates the position of a `FastCar`, based on its velocity. If the new position places the `FastCar` outside the playing field, the position and velocity of the `FastCar` are adjusted to produce a ricochet effect. The `paint()` method simply draws the image that represents the `FastCar`, at the appropriate position within the applet surface.

Listing 10.6 Methods of the FastCar Class

```
public final synchronized Dimension getSize( )
  { return new Dimension(theWidth, theHeight); }

public final synchronized Point   getPosition( )
  { return new Point(theX, theY); }

public synchronized void update(int max_x, int max_y)
{
  theX += theDX;
  theY += theDY;
  if (theX < 0)
  {
```

```
      theX = 0;
      theDX = Math.abs(theDX);
    }
    if (theX + theWidth > max_x)
    {
      theX = max_x - theWidth;
      theDX = -1.0F * Math.abs(theDX);
    }
    if (theY < 0)
    {
      theY = 0;
      theDY = Math.abs(theDY);
    }
    if (theY + theHeight > max_y)
    {
      theY = max_y - theHeight;
      theDY = -1.0F * Math.abs(theDY);
    }
  }

  public void paint(Graphics g)
  {
    g.drawImage(theImage, theX, theY, theWidth, theHeight, null);
  }
}
```

TAKING YOUR `FastCar` FOR A RIDE

The HTML file used to run Bumpers01 is shown in Listing 10.7. Before moving on, take a break by watching the Bumpers01 applet run. But, be sure to stop before highway hypnosis sets in.

Listing 10.7 The HTML File for the Bumpers01 Applet

```
<HTML>
<HEAD>
<TITLE>Bumpers</TITLE>
</HEAD>
<BODY>
<H1>Bumpers</H1>
<BR>
<APPLET CODE=Bumpers01 WIDTH=500 HEIGHT=500>
</APPLET>
</BODY>
</HTML>
```

Bumpers02: Adding Collisions

Watching all the cars go careening off the edge of your screen is fun, but, it's time to add even more action. As the next iteration toward implementing the complete game, let's deal with collisions between the bumper cars. The question you face is "Who should handle collisions?"

The work of checking for collisions could be handled either by the applet or by the bumper car class. This is your first major design alternative. Before reading on, spend a few minutes thinking about how you would decide the issue.

Because the game will eventually include multiple types of bumper cars (one type driven by the player and at least one other type driven by the computer), it's best to handle collisions within the applet. Why? The appropriate response to a collision may depend on the types of bumper cars involved. Making every type of bumper car aware of every other type would strongly couple (tie) the various types together. For example, if you created a new type of bumper car, you'd have to modify every existing type to deal with the new type.

Your program is more maintainable if the applet handles collisions. That way, each type of bumper car is coupled to the applet, but not to the other types of bumper cars. Adding a new type of bumper car may necessitate changes to the applet, but not to the existing bumper car types.

THE BUMPERS02 CLASS DIAGRAMS

Figure 10.5 shows the class diagram for the Bumpers02 applet. You'll notice that there are new methods in both the `Bumpers02` class as well as in the `FastCar` class. The `Bumpers02` class now has the ability to check for collisions with the new `checkCollisions()` method. The new `FastCar` class gains the ability to set its state to reflect its drivability with the `setCrunched()` and `isCrunched()` methods.

The `setCrunched()` method is a mutator method—a method that changes the state of an object. The `setCrunched()` method is used to set the value of the field `isCrunched` to `true`. The `isCrunched()` method is an accessor method that returns the value of the `isCrunched` field.

IMPLEMENTING THE BUMPERS02 DESIGN

Listing 10.8 shows the revised applet, named Bumpers02. Because you've added the ability to detect collisions, you'll need some way to communicate to the users that a collision has occurred. To this end, a field named `theBang` has been added to hold a new audio clip that is played when a collision occurs.

To facilitate the new collision features, the following changes have been made:

- The `start()` method has several new statements that acquire the audio clip.

- The `run()` method now invokes a new utility method, `checkCollisions()`, which detects and handles collisions.

FIGURE 10.5

*Class diagram of the
Bumpers02 applet*

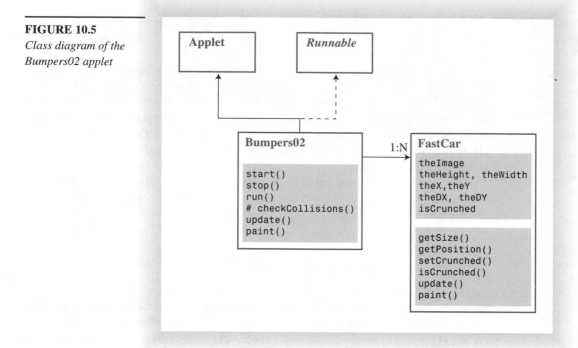

Listing 10.8 The Bumpers02 Class (Partial)

```java
import java.applet.*;
import java.awt.*;
import java.awt.event.*;
import java.net.URL;

public class Bumpers02 extends Applet implements Runnable
{
  public static final int SLEEP_TIME = 33;
  public static final int CARS = 6;

  Graphics  theGraphics;
  Dimension theSize;
  Image     theImage;
  Thread theThread;
  boolean isRunning;
  FastCar [] theCar;

  Image     theFastImage;
  AudioClip theMusic;
  AudioClip theBang;

  public void start( )
  {
    try
    {
```

```
      theFastImage = getAppletContext().getImage(
        new URL(getDocumentBase( ), "FastCar.GIF"));

      theMusic = getAppletContext( ).getAudioClip(
        new URL(getDocumentBase( ), "Music.au"));
      theMusic.loop( );

      theBang = getAppletContext( ).getAudioClip(
        new URL(getDocumentBase( ), "Bang.au"));
      theBang.play( );
    }
    catch (Exception e)
    {
      System.out.println(e);
    }
    setBackground(Color.lightGray);

    theCar = new FastCar[CARS];
    for (int i = 0; i < CARS; i++)
    {
      theCar[i] = new FastCar(theFastImage, 500, 300);
    }

    theThread = new Thread(this);
    isRunning = true;
    theThread.start( );
  }

  public void run( )
  {
    while (isRunning)
    {
      try
      {
        Thread.sleep(SLEEP_TIME);
      }
      catch (InterruptedException e) { ; }
      Dimension d = getSize( );
      for (int i = 0; i < CARS; i++)
      {
        theCar[i].update(d.width, d.height);
        checkCollisions( );
      }

      repaint( );
    }
  }

  // Remaining methods shown separately
}
```

CHECKING FOR COLLISIONS

Let's take a look at the details necessary to actually check whether two cars have collided. Listing 10.9 shows the checkCollisions() method.

This method uses a nested pair of loops to check each bumper car for a possible collision with every other bumper car. To improve play, a bumper car that collides with a disabled car is not disabled. The loops check for this possibility and execute a continue when appropriate.

Listing 10.9 The checkCollisions( ) Method of the Bumpers02 Class

```
protected void checkCollisions( )
{
  for (int i = 0; i < CARS - 1; i++)
  {
    if (theCar[i].isCrunched( )) continue;

    Point     p1 = theCar[i].getPosition( );
    Dimension d1 = theCar[i].getSize( );
    Rectangle r1 = new Rectangle(p1, d1);
    r1.translate(p1.x / 8, p1.y / 8);
    r1.grow(-1 * d1.width / 4, -1 * d1.height / 4);

    for (int j = i + 1; j < CARS; j++)
    {
      if (theCar[j].isCrunched()) continue;
      Point     p2 = theCar[j].getPosition( );
      Dimension d2 = theCar[j].getSize( );
      Rectangle r2 = new Rectangle(p2, d2);
      r2.translate(p2.x / 8, p2.y / 8);
      r2.grow(-1 * d2.width / 4, -1 * d2.height / 4);

      if (r1.intersects(r2))
      {
        theBang.play( );
        if (p1.y < p2.y)
          theCar[j].setCrunched( );
        else
          theCar[i].setCrunched( );
      }
    }
  }
}
```

To create realistic collisions, there are several details that you must consider. Every bumper car has a *bounding rectangle* that represents the smallest rectangle that can completely enclose a FastCar image. You can obtain this bounding rectangle by calling the getSize() method. After you have the rectangles for two cars, you can see if they have collided by using the Rectangle class intersect() method. The only difficulty with this method is that the car images are irregular and don't actually fill up their bounding rectangle. To compensate for this, and to add a realistic feel to the collision, the bounding rectangle is downsized to 3/4 of its actual size, and centered by offsetting it by 1/8 its size, relative to the position returned by getPosition().

The `checkCollision()` code is just about complete. Only one issue remains to be settled: when two cars collide, who's the winner? In the real world, that's settled by the principles of mass and acceleration; in the bumper car world you'll make an executive decision. When a collision is detected, the bumper car higher on the screen (the one with the lower y coordinate) is deemed the winner. It usually requires some experience in the game for a player to discover this policy; figuring out how the game works is part of the fun of playing it. The losing car gets disabled by means of its `setCrunched()` method.

The `stop()`, `update()`, and `paint()` methods of the `Bumpers02` class are identical to those in the `Bumpers01` class. Therefore, they are not shown here; they are included in the source files contained on the CD-ROM.

THE NEW `FastCar` CLASS

Listing 10.10 shows the revised `FastCar` class, which now knows how to respond to an accident—truly a useful quality. Where would we all be if our cars went through a collision unscathed? The new field, `isCrunched`, and its accessor and mutator methods, `setCrunched()` and `isCrunched()`, have been added. The `update()` method now simply returns if the bumper car has been disabled, because a disabled car can no longer move.

```
Listing 10.10 The FastCar Class
class FastCar
{
  Image theImage;
  int    theWidth  = 50;
  int    theHeight = 25;
  int    theX;
  int    theY;
  float theDX;
  float theDY;
  boolean isCrunched = false;

  private static final float MAX_V = 20;

  public FastCar(Image img, int max_x, int max_y)
  {
    theImage = img;
    theX = (int) (Math.random( ) * max_x);
    theY = (int) (Math.random( ) * max_y);
    theDX = MAX_V - 2.0F * (float) Math.random( ) * MAX_V;
    theDY = MAX_V - 2.0F * (float) Math.random( ) * MAX_V;
  }

  public final void setCrunched( )
  {
    isCrunched = true;
  }

  public final boolean isCrunched( )
  {
```

```
      return isCrunched;
  }

  public synchronized void update(int max_x, int max_y)
  {
    if (isCrunched) return;

    theX += theDX;
    theY += theDY;
    if (theX < 0)
    {
      theX = 0;
      theDX = Math.abs(theDX);
    }
    if (theX + theWidth > max_x)
    {
      theX = max_x - theWidth;
      theDX = -1.0F * Math.abs(theDX);
    }
    if (theY < 0)
    {
      theY = 0;
      theDY = Math.abs(theDY);
    }
    if (theY + theHeight > max_y)
    {
      theY = max_y - theHeight;
      theDY = -1.0F * Math.abs(theDY);
    }
  }

  // Methods identical to those in Bumpers01 omitted
}
```

The `getSize()`, `getPosition()`, and `paint()` methods of the `FastCar` class are identical to those in the version of the `FastCar` class included within the `Bumpers01` class. Therefore, they are not shown here; they are included in the source files contained on the CD-ROM.

User-Driven Cars: The Next Iteration

Now that your cars can move around the screen and collide with each other, let's add some real excitement. Let's face it, the attraction of bumper cars is bumping into other cars, not avoiding them. Obviously, the next step is to let the player steer one of the cars around, instead of simply watching.

Let's add a new class that represents a user-driven car to the Bumpers applet. The user-driven car has its own image, distinct from that of the other bumper cars. When the user clicks the mouse button, the user-driven car moves toward the location of the click. By clicking judiciously, the user can steer the car into, or away from, other cars. Figure 10.6 shows the new Bumpers03 applet.

FIGURE 10.6

Running the Bumpers03 applet

FIGURE 10.6

Running the Bumpers03 applet

THE BUMPERS03 CLASS DIAGRAM

> *" In principle, design proceeds top-down, from goals to means. Often, however, the need to figure out how to do something compels departure from the ideal. "*

Figure 10.7 shows the class diagram for the Bumpers03 class. The revised program features a new class, DrivenCar, representing the user-driven car. Notice that DrivenCar has much in common with FastCar. In the next version of the applet, Bumpers04, we'll re-factor the design using inheritance, deriving DrivenCar and FastCar from a common superclass. However, at this point in the design process it's not certain which fields and methods should be inherited from a superclass and which should be implemented separately.

Rather than attempt to resolve the issue now, let's figure out how to make the user-driven car work. In principle, design proceeds top-down, from goals to means. Often, however, the need to figure out how to do something compels departure from the ideal. Here, it's important to see how to make the DrivenCar respond to mouse events before returning to more general design issues.

As the class diagram shows, the DrivenCar uses a MouseHandler, which is derived from MouseAdapter. Notice that the line joining MouseHandler and DrivenCar includes an arrowhead that points from MouseHandler to DrivenCar. This indicates that MouseHandler is invoking methods of DrivenCar, whereas DrivenCar is not invoking methods of MouseHandler. When you look at the implementing code, you'll see why this is.

FIGURE 10.7

Class diagram of the Bumpers03 applet

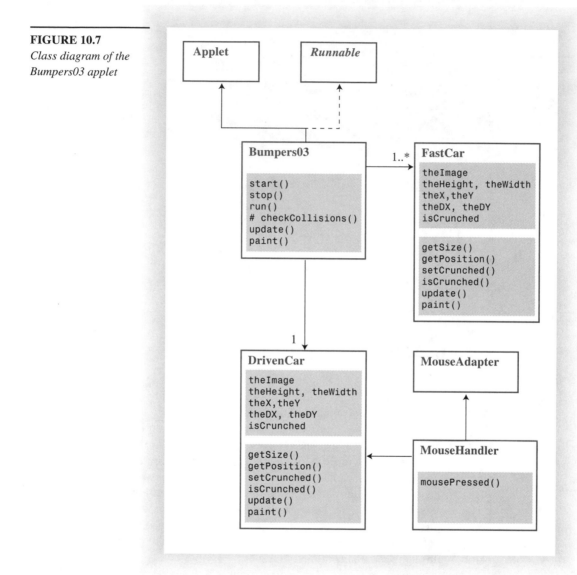

STARTING AND RUNNING BUMPERS03

The Bumpers03 class requires a few changes. First, there are two new fields that are necessary to support the new `DrivenCar` class. These fields are defined as follows:

```
DrivenCar   theDrivenCar;
Image       theDrivenImage;
```

Also, the start(), run(), checkCollisions(), and paint() methods are slightly different than those in the Bumpers02 class. Listing 10.11 shows the revised start() method, which now fetches an image used to represent the user-driven car. The method also instantiates a DrivenCar object and a MouseHandler object. The MouseHandler is added as a listener of mouse messages.

Listing 10.11 The start() Method of the Bumpers03 Class

```
public void start( )
{
  try
  {
    theFastImage = getAppletContext().getImage(
      new URL(getDocumentBase( ), "FastCar.GIF"));

    theDrivenImage = getAppletContext().getImage(
      new URL(getDocumentBase( ), "DrivenCar.GIF"));

    theMusic = getAppletContext( ).getAudioClip(
      new URL(getDocumentBase( ), "Music.au"));
    theMusic.loop( );

    theBang = getAppletContext( ).getAudioClip(
      new URL(getDocumentBase( ), "Bang.au"));
    theBang.play( );
  }
  catch (Exception e)
  {
    System.out.println(e);
  }
  setBackground(Color.lightGray);

  theDrivenCar = new DrivenCar(theDrivenImage);
  addMouseListener(new MouseHandler(theDrivenCar));

  theCar = new FastCar[CARS];
  for (int i = 0; i < CARS; i++)
  {
    theCar[i] = new FastCar(theFastImage, 500, 300);
  }

  theThread = new Thread(this);
  isRunning = true;
  theThread.start( );
}
```

RUNNING THE BUMPERS03 APPLET

The Bumpers03 run() method, shown in Listing 10.12, now instructs the DrivenCar object to update its position. It also checks whether the DrivenCar has been disabled; if so, it terminates, ending the animation.

Listing 10.12 The run() Method of the Bumpers03 Class

```
public void run( )
{
  while (isRunning)
  {
    try
    {
      Thread.sleep(SLEEP_TIME);
    }
    catch (InterruptedException e) { ; }
    Dimension d = getSize( );
    theDrivenCar.update(d.width, d.height);
    for (int i = 0; i < CARS; i++)
    {
      theCar[i].update(d.width, d.height);
      checkCollisions( );
    }
    if (theDrivenCar.isCrunched()) stop();
    repaint( );
  }
}
```

CHECKING FOR COLLISIONS

As shown in Listing 10.13, the checkCollisions() method is now simpler and faster than before. It no longer needs to look for collisions between FastCars; instead, it looks only for collisions between the DrivenCar and a FastCar.

Listing 10.13 The checkCollisions() Method of the Bumpers03 Class

```
protected void checkCollisions( )
{
  Point     p1 = theDrivenCar.getPosition( );
  Dimension d1 = theDrivenCar.getSize( );
  Rectangle r1 = new Rectangle(p1, d1);
  r1.translate(p1.x / 8, p1.y / 8);
  r1.grow(-1 * d1.width / 4, -1 * d1.height / 4);

  for (int i = 0; i < CARS - 1; i++)
  {
    if (theCar[i].isCrunched( )) continue;

    Point     p2 = theCar[i].getPosition( );
    Dimension d2 = theCar[i].getSize( );
    Rectangle r2 = new Rectangle(p2, d2);
    r2.translate(p2.x / 8, p2.y / 8);
    r2.grow(-1 * d2.width / 4, -1 * d2.height / 4);

    if (r1.intersects(r2))
    {
      theBang.play( );
      if (p1.y < p2.y)
        theCar[i].setCrunched( );
```

```
        else
            theDrivenCar.setCrunched( );
      }
   }
}
```

PAINTING THE APPLET

The paint() method, shown in Listing 10.14, now instructs the DrivenCar object to paint itself. Otherwise, it is unchanged.

Listing 10.14 The paint() Method of the Bumpers03 Class

```
  public void paint(Graphics g)
  {
    g.setColor(getBackground( ));
    g.fillRect(0, 0, getSize( ).width, getSize( ).height);
    theDrivenCar.paint(g);
    for (int i = 0; i < CARS; i++)
    {
      theCar[i].paint(g);
    }
  }
```

The stop() and update() methods of the Bumpers03 class are identical to those of the Bumpers02 class. Therefore, they are not shown here; they are included in the source files contained on the CD-ROM. Similarly, the FastCar class is unchanged.

INTRODUCING THE DrivenCar CLASS

The DrivenCar class, a new class, is shown in Listing 10.15. It is very similar to the FastCar class. One difference is that DrivenCar objects are initialized with a fixed position (theX=5, theY=5) rather than a random position. They also start motionless (theDX=0.0F, theDY=0.0F) rather than with a random velocity.

Listing 10.15 The DrivenCar Class

```
class DrivenCar
{
  Image theImage;
  int    theWidth  = 50;
  int    theHeight = 25;
  int    theX      = 5;
  int    theY      = 5;
  float  theDX     = 0.0F;
  float  theDY     = 0.0F;
  boolean isCrunched = false;

  private static final float V = 5.0F;

  public DrivenCar(Image img)
  {
```

```
    theImage = img;
  }

  public final synchronized Dimension getSize( )
    { return new Dimension(theWidth, theHeight); }

  public final synchronized Point   getPosition( )
    { return new Point(theX, theY); }

  public final void setCrunched( )
  {
    isCrunched = true;
  }

  public final boolean isCrunched( )
  {
    return isCrunched;
  }

  public synchronized void update(int max_x, int max_y)
  {
    if (isCrunched) return;

    theX += theDX;
    theY += theDY;
    if (theX < 0)
    {
      theX = 0;
      theDX = Math.abs(theDX);
    }
    if (theX + theWidth > max_x)
    {
      theX = max_x - theWidth;
      theDX = -1.0F * Math.abs(theDX);
    }
    if (theY < 0)
    {
      theY = 0;
      theDY = Math.abs(theDY);
    }
    if (theY + theHeight > max_y)
    {
      theY = max_y - theHeight;
      theDY = -1.0F * Math.abs(theDY);
    }
  }

  public void paint(Graphics g)
  {
    g.drawImage(theImage, theX, theY, theWidth, theHeight, null);
  }

  public synchronized void mouseClicked(int x, int y)
  {
    int a = x - theX;
    int b = y - theY;
    double theta = Math.atan2(a, b);
```

```
      theDX = V * (float) Math.sin(theta);
      theDY = V * (float) Math.cos(theta);
    }
  }
```

EXAMINING DrivenCar

When a `DrivenCar` receives a `mouseClicked` message, it begins moving with a fixed velocity toward the location at which the click occurred. The velocity is slow enough that successfully piloting the car is a significant challenge. Because the car doesn't respond immediately to your clicks, you might find the effect similar to that encountered when driving a motor boat for the first time. Like the novice motor-sailor, you'll have to be careful to avoid over-steering.

Listing 10.16 shows the `MouseHandler` class, which was established by the `Bumpers03.start()` method as a listener of mouse messages. The constructor saves its parameter, a reference to the `DrivenCar`, and uses it to forward a `mouseClicked()` message to the `DrivenCar` whenever the mouse button is clicked.

```
Listing 10.16 The MouseHandler Class
class MouseHandler extends MouseAdapter
{
  DrivenCar theDrivenCar;

  public MouseHandler(DrivenCar dc)
  {
    theDrivenCar = dc;
  }

  public void mousePressed(MouseEvent e)
  {

    theDrivenCar.mouseClicked(e.getX( ), e.getY( ));
  }
}
```

Generalization: Putting Inheritance to Work

Now, as promised, it's time to re-factor the program to gain the benefits of inheritance. The `DrivenCar` class and the `FastCar` class share many common fields and methods. Now that it's clear exactly what these must do, it's a simple matter to change the design structure. As you'll see, the result is a smaller, clearer, more maintainable program.

Figure 10.8 shows the revised class diagram. A new class, `Car`, has been added; `DrivenCar` and `FastCar` are now derived from it. `FastCar` doesn't override any methods inherited from `Car`. `DrivenCar` overrides `paint()` to implement a new policy: when the `DrivenCar` is disabled, it disappears from the screen. `DrivenCar` also supplies a new method, `mouseClicked()`, used to handle mouse events forwarded by the `MouseHandler`.

FIGURE 10.8

Class diagram of the Bumpers04 applet

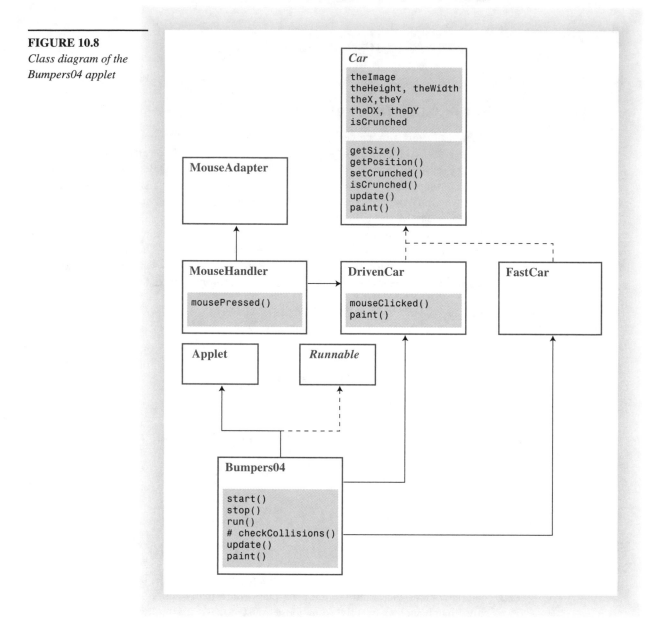

Notice that Car is an abstract class, indicated by the italic font in which its name appears and the dotted lines joining it to DrivenCar and FastCar. Car could have been implemented as a concrete class. But, there is never a need to instantiate a Car; only DrivenCars and FastCars are instantiated. Making Car an abstract class eliminates the possibility of mistakenly instantiating a Car, which would turn out to be a useless act.

Car could have been made an interface rather than an abstract class. But, by implementing it as an abstract class, it's possible to provide concrete implementations of its methods, including getSize(), getPosition, and so on. Recall that an interface cannot provide implementations for its methods; making Car an abstract class is clearly the better choice.

THE BUMPERS04 IMPLEMENTATION

Listing 10.17 shows the implementation of the Bumpers04 class. It is little changed from previous versions, except that now the DrivenCar and the FastCars can all inhabit the same array, an array of type Car named theCar; deriving both classes from the same superclass, Car, allows you to simplify your design. Rather than having separate arrays, you need only one. A reference to the DrivenCar is stored in element 0 of the array, and references to the FastCars are stored in the remaining elements.

Listing 10.17 The Bumpers04 Class

```java
import java.applet.*;
import java.awt.*;
import java.awt.event.*;
import java.net.URL;

public class Bumpers04 extends Applet implements Runnable
{
  public static final int SLEEP TIME = 33;
  public static final int CARS = 6;

  Graphics  theGraphics;
  Dimension theSize;
  Image     theImage;
  Thread theThread;
  boolean isRunning;
  Car [] theCar;

  Image theFastImage;
  Image theDrivenImage;
  AudioClip theMusic;
  AudioClip theBang;

  public void start()
  {
    try
    {
      theFastImage = getAppletContext().getImage(
        new URL(getDocumentBase( ), "FastCar.GIF"));

      theDrivenImage = getAppletContext().getImage(
        new URL(getDocumentBase( ), "DrivenCar.GIF"));

      theMusic = getAppletContext( ).getAudioClip(
        new URL(getDocumentBase( ), "Music.au"));
      theMusic.loop( );

      theBang = getAppletContext( ).getAudioClip(
        new URL(getDocumentBase( ), "Bang.au"));
```

```java
      theBang.play( );
    }
    catch (Exception e)
    {
      System.out.println(e);
    }
    setBackground(Color.lightGray);

    theCar = new Car[CARS];

    DrivenCar dc = new DrivenCar(theDrivenImage);
    addMouseListener(new MouseHandler(dc));
    theCar[0] = dc;

    for (int i = 1; i < CARS; i++)
    {
      theCar[i] = new FastCar(theFastImage, 500, 300);
    }

    theThread = new Thread(this);
    isRunning = true;
    theThread.start();
  }

  public void stop()
  {
    theMusic.stop();
    isRunning = false;
  }

  public void run()
  {
    while (isRunning)
    {
      try
      {
        Thread.sleep(SLEEP_TIME);
      }
      catch (InterruptedException e) { ; }
      Dimension d = getSize();
      for (int i = 0; i < CARS; i++)
      {
        theCar[i].update(d.width, d.height);
        checkCollisions();
      }
      if (theCar[0].isCrunched()) stop();
      repaint();
    }
  }

  protected void checkCollisions( )
  {
    Point     p1 = theCar[0].getPosition( );
    Dimension d1 = theCar[0].getSize( );
    Rectangle r1 = new Rectangle(p1, d1);
```

```
    r1.translate(p1.x / 8, p1.y / 8);
    r1.grow(-1 * d1.width / 4, -1 * d1.height / 4);

    for (int i = 1; i < CARS; i++)
    {
      if (theCar[i].isCrunched( )) continue;

      Point     p2 = theCar[i].getPosition( );
      Dimension d2 = theCar[i].getSize( );
      Rectangle r2 = new Rectangle(p2, d2);
      r2.translate(p2.x / 8, p2.y / 8);
      r2.grow(-1 * d2.width / 4, -1 * d2.height / 4);

      if (r1.intersects(r2))
      {
        theBang.play( );
        if (p1.y < p2.y)
          theCar[i].setCrunched( );
        else
          theCar[0].setCrunched( );
      }
    }
  }

  public final synchronized void update(Graphics g)
  {
    if (theSize == null
      || theSize.width  != getSize( ).width
      || theSize.height != getSize( ).height)
    {
      theSize = getSize( );
      theImage = createImage(theSize.width, theSize.height);
      theGraphics = theImage.getGraphics( );
    }
    paint(theGraphics);
    g.drawImage(theImage, 0, 0, null);
  }

  public void paint(Graphics g)
  {
    g.setColor(getBackground( ));
    g.fillRect(0, 0, getSize( ).width, getSize( ).height);
    for (int i = 0; i < CARS; i++)
    {
      theCar[i].paint(g);
    }
  }
}
```

CARS: IMPLEMENTING AN INHERITANCE HIERARCHY

Listing 10.18 shows the Car class, which closely resembles the FastCar class of Bumpers03. The Car class provides a default implementation of every method required by a FastCar. However, it has no constructor. The getSize() and getPosition()

accessor methods are declared to be `final`. It's unlikely that a child class would need to override either method, and they execute somewhat faster because they're `final`. Testing whether the latter is true for your compiler, by the way, is a simple yet interesting experiment you should try.

```
Listing 10.18 The Car Class
abstract class Car
{
  Image theImage;
  int   theWidth  = 50;
  int   theHeight = 25;
  int   theX      = 5;
  int   theY      = 5;
  float theDX     = 0.0F;
  float theDY     = 0.0F;
  boolean isCrunched = false;

  public final synchronized Dimension getSize()
    { return new Dimension(theWidth, theHeight); }

  public final synchronized Point   getPosition()
    { return new Point(theX, theY); }

  public synchronized void update(int max_x, int max_y)
  {
    if (isCrunched) return;

    theX += theDX;
    theY += theDY;
    if (theX < 0)
    {
      theX = 0;
      theDX = Math.abs(theDX);
    }
    if (theX + theWidth > max_x)
    {
      theX = max_x - theWidth;
      theDX = -1.0F * Math.abs(theDX);
    }
    if (theY < 0)
    {
      theY = 0;
      theDY = Math.abs(theDY);
    }
    if (theY + theHeight > max_y)
    {
      theY = max_y - theHeight;
      theDY = -1.0F * Math.abs(theDY);
    }
  }

  public final void setCrunched()
  {
```

```
      isCrunched = true;
    }

    public final boolean isCrunched()
    {
      return isCrunched;
    }

    public void paint(Graphics g)
    {
      g.drawImage(theImage, theX, theY, theWidth, theHeight, null);
    }
}
```

FastCar AND DrivenCar: IMPLEMENTING SUBCLASSES

Listing 10.19 shows the revised FastCar class. Note how simple it is in comparison to the previous version, consisting only of a constructor, which provides a reference to the image used to represent the FastCar and the boundaries of the playing field. The latter are used merely to establish a suitable initial random position for the FastCar.

Listing 10.19 The FastCar Class

```
class FastCar extends Car
{
  private static final float MAX_V = 20;

  public FastCar(Image img, int max_x, int max_y)
  {
    theImage = img;
    theX = (int) (Math.random() * max_x);
    theY = (int) (Math.random() * max_y);
    theDX = MAX_V - 2.0F * (float) Math.random() * MAX_V;
    theDY = MAX_V - 2.0F * (float) Math.random() * MAX_V;
  }
}
```

Listing 10.20 shows the DrivenCar class, which is also much simpler than before. It includes a constructor, which initializes the DrivenCar motionless at a fixed position. It also includes an overriding implementation of the paint() method. This causes the DrivenCar to disappear when it is disabled, signaling the end of the game. Finally, the class includes a mouseClicked() method used to handle messages received from the MouseHandler, just as in previous versions.

Listing 10.20 The DrivenCar Class

```
class DrivenCar extends Car
{
  private static final float V = 5.0F;

  public DrivenCar(Image img)
  {
```

```
      theImage = img;
      theX = 5;
      theY = 5;
      theDX = 0.0F;
      theDY = 0.0F;
    }

    public synchronized void mouseClicked(int x, int y)
    {
      int a = x - theX;
      int b = y - theY;
      double theta = Math.atan2(a, b);
      theDX = V * (float) Math.sin(theta);
      theDY = V * (float) Math.cos(theta);
    }

    public void paint(Graphics g)
    {
      if (!isCrunched()) super.paint(g);
    }
  }
```

The `MouseHandler` class is identical to that included in `Bumpers03`. It is not shown here, but is included on the CD-ROM.

Specialization: Adding a New Car Type

As a further demonstration of the power of inheritance, let's add a new car type, a `SlowCar`, to the game. Having some slower cars will encourage the novice, who might be unable to score a victory against the more formidable `FastCars`. So it's not *too* easy to pick them off, the `SlowCars` will move somewhat erratically. As you'll see, the abstract class `Car` makes it virtually child's play to add the new car type. Figure 10.9 shows the new applet, named `Bumpers05`.

Figure 10.10 shows the class diagram of the new applet, which includes the new `SlowCar` class. The `SlowCar` class overrides the `update()` method of `Car` to provide new movement policies. Otherwise, the class diagram is unchanged.

Apart from increasing the number of cars created, the only change made relative to `Bumpers04` is the loop used to create the bumper cars. It now reads:

```
      for (int i = 1; i < CARS; i++)
      {
        switch (i % 2)
        {
          case 0:
            theCar[i] = new SlowCar(theSlowImage, 500, 300);
            break;
          default:
            theCar[i] = new FastCar(theFastImage, 500, 300);
        }
      }
```

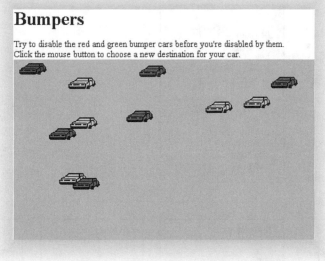

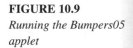

FIGURE 10.9

Running the Bumpers05 applet

Half the created Cars are SlowCars and half are FastCars. The FastCar, DrivenCar, and MouseHandler classes are, of course, entirely unchanged.

Listing 10.21 shows the new SlowCar class. The maximum velocity (MAX_V) of a SlowCar is set to 2; the corresponding value of a FastCar is 6, so SlowCars are indeed slow.

Listing 10.21 The SlowCar Class

```
class SlowCar extends Car
{
  private static final float MAX_V = 2;
  private static final float JUMP = 4.0F;

  public SlowCar(Image img, int max_x, int max_y)
  {
    theImage = img;
    theX = (int) (Math.random() * max_x);
    theY = (int) (Math.random() * max_y);
    theDX = MAX_V - 2.0F * (float) Math.random() * MAX_V;
    theDY = MAX_V - 2.0F * (float) Math.random() * MAX_V;
  }

  public synchronized void update(int max_x, int max_y)
  {
    if (Math.random() < 0.05F)
    {
      theDX = MAX_V - 2.0F * (float) Math.random() * MAX_V;
      theDY = MAX_V - 2.0F * (float) Math.random() * MAX_V;
    }
    super.update(max_x, max_y);
  }
}
```

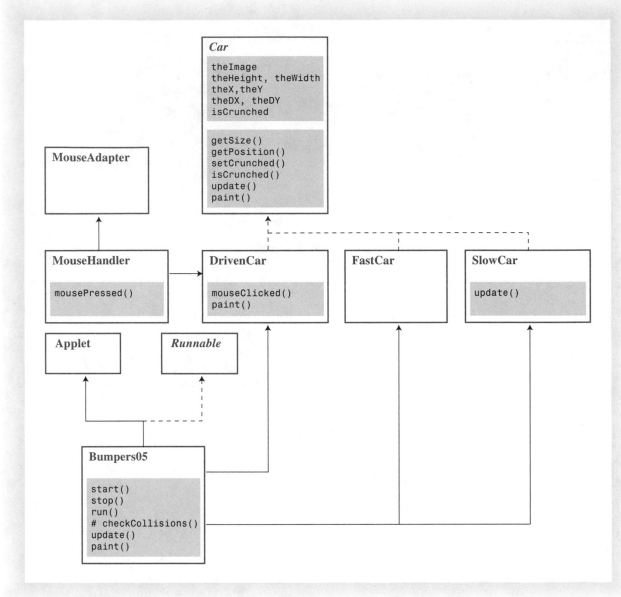

FIGURE 10.10

Class diagram of the Bumpers05 applet

The update() method generates and tests a random number. About 95 percent of the time, the body of the if is skipped. But, the remaining 5 percent of the time (about 5 times in 3 seconds) the velocity of the SlowCar is randomly perturbed, making it a little harder to catch.

Summary

Class diagrams can depict inheritance relationships. Inheritance of implementation is indicated by a solid line, terminated by a triangle attached to the base class. Inheritance of specification is indicated by a dashed line.

An abstract class or interface is shown using an italicized name. An abstract method is shown using an italicized name.

Class diagrams help reduce complexity by abstracting away unimportant details. A class diagram should include only those details and notations important to communicating a good understanding of the design.

Seldom does a first try at design produce a satisfactory result. Instead, the process of object-oriented design is iterative. It's common to re-factor a design, changing its structure. A particularly common sort of re-factoring involves identification of a base class that can provide common fields and methods to a family of child classes.

Questions

For multiple-choice items, indicate all correct responses.

1. To depict an inheritance relationship in a class diagram, you use a line terminated by

   a. an arrowhead

   b. a diamond

   c. a solid dot

   d. a triangle

2. To depict an abstract class or interface in a class diagram, you _____ the name of the "class."

3. In a class diagram, a line indicating an `implements` relationship is

   a. colored

   b. curved

   c. dotted

   d. solid

4. In a class diagram, a line indicating an inheritance relationship is never decorated with a navigability arrowhead (true/false).

5. The symbol that identifies a line as indicating an inheritance relationship is placed neared the

   a. abstract class

   b. interface

   c. subclass

   d. superclass

6. When depicting an abstract class on a class diagram, italicized method names indicate methods that

   a. are abstract

   b. are concrete

   c. are inherited from a base class

   d. return no value

7. Restructuring a set of classes so that common elements can reside in a base class is called _____.

Exercises

1. Extend the Bumpers applet by adding an additional type of car, one that regularly disappears and then reappears at a random location.

2. Extend the Bumpers applet by adding an additional type of car, one that emits a sound when it's involved in a collision.

To Learn More

The following books will help you learn more about using inheritance to design classes.

The first book of a series that will present Unified Modeling Language (UML), an important *de facto* standardization of notations for modeling object-oriented software, is:

> Fowler, Martin, with Kendall Scott. *UML Distilled: Applying the Standard Object Modeling Language.* Reading, Massachusetts: Addison-Wesley, 1997.

These books present the approach to object-oriented analysis and design developed by Grady Booch:

> Booch, Grady. *Object-Oriented Analysis and Design with Applications, 2nd ed.* Redwood City, California: Benjamin/Cummings, 1994.

> White, Iseult. *Using the Booch Method: A Rational Approach.* Redwood City, California: Benjamin/Cummings, 1994.

11
Patterns: Proven Designs

How do you learn to program? Well, how did you learn to ride a bicycle or a surfboard, or drive a car? If you're like most people, you learned by imitation. "Here, do it like this," your father, or your best friend, or your teacher would say, before giving you a demonstration. Watching carefully, and with a little practice, you learned to distill the essential parts from their example: step on the brake to stop, press the gas pedal to go, turn the steering wheel to change directions. These "essential parts" form a *pattern* for driving.

In the late 1970s, the architect Christopher Alexander wrote a series of influential books describing the recurring themes found in buildings and towns throughout the ages. In *A Pattern Language* and *A Timeless Way of Building*, Alexander argued that it was possible to objectively determine which of these themes produced habitable dwellings and which produced ugly, unlivable monstrosities. He called these recurring themes *patterns*. Whereas Vitruvius proposed goals of firmness, commodity, and delight, Alexander measured architectural success by the livability of the structures he studied, what he called "the quality without a name." The architectural patterns he describes are an attempt to provide concrete guidance for producing such structures.

More recently, a number of software visionaries applied a similar perspective to their study of object-oriented software systems. They found that object-oriented software developers often found themselves up against similar problems, and often found similar solutions to them. These visionaries realized that, by publishing descriptions of these patterns, they could provide an important service to the software community. Thus, *object-oriented design patterns*, as they're called, were born.

Design patterns are useful in design the same way that data structures are useful in programming. Each helps you avoid "re-inventing the wheel." Design patterns describe a design in terms of the participating objects and classes, the roles they take on, and the problem the design solves.

In this chapter you will learn:

- What design patterns are

- How to read class diagrams depicting design patterns

- Where design patterns have been used in the Java Application Programming Interfaces (APIs)

- How a design pattern can be implemented in Java

- How several popular and useful design patterns work

What Are Patterns?

What is the difference between a Chess grandmaster and the rest of us? In the early 1960s, researchers looking into this question started with the hypothesis that the grandmaster had a form of "photographic" memory, because the grandmaster could easily reconstruct a complex chessboard after looking at it for only a few seconds. The famous experiments by Adriaan de Groot, however, showed that this just wasn't so. When the pieces on the chessboard were arranged *at random*, the grandmasters had no greater recall than the rest of us. The facility that first seemed to be super-human recall turned out to be something else entirely: the grandmasters had recognized patterns.

Learning about design patterns is an important part of object-oriented design. A design pattern is simply a problem-solution pair that occurs repeatedly. Gamma, Helm, Johnson, and Vlissides, in their acclaimed book *Design Patterns*, identify four essential elements of a design pattern:

- The *design pattern name* identifies the pattern. These names are not mere jargon. Naming things helps us to think about them more effectively. By learning the names of several of the most common patterns, you extend your ability to think about designs at a new, higher level of abstraction. Instead of seeing a maze of unrelated details, you can look at a design and see *Factories*, *Decorators*, and *Singletons*. And, having access to a common, higher-level, vocabulary facilitates communicating with others about your designs.

- The *problem* describes the situations to which the design pattern applies. It helps you know when the design pattern might be useful, just like word problems, however painful, show you how calculus might actually be used.

- The *solution* describes the elements (classes and objects), and the relationships between the elements (composition, inheritance, and

" *A design pattern is simply a problem-solution pair that occurs repeatedly.* "

instantiation), that solve the problem. The solution is described in general terms, rather than highly specific terms, because each real-world problem is a little different from others. Solutions typically must be tweaked here and there before they can be successfully applied to a given problem.

The *consequences* help you understand the ramifications of applying the solution. As usual in design, your choice of a solution involves tradeoffs. The consequences help you to decide which alternative, among the range of available alternatives, best fits your needs.

AN EXAMPLE PATTERN

Table 11.1 shows an example pattern, one that is used throughout Java's API.

TABLE 11.1
THE DECORATOR PATTERN

Pattern name	Decorator, wrapper, or filter
Problem	How can the capabilities of an object be extended at runtime?
Solution	Create an object that contains (that is, decorates or wraps around) the existing object. The containing object can forward messages to the original object, preserving the original object's capabilities. It can also respond to messages not implemented by the original object, extending the original object's capabilities.
Consequences	Extending an object's capabilities at runtime is more flexible than extending the object's class, which must be done at compile time.
	The decorator pattern lets you add capability dynamically in small increments.
	Systems that support the decorator pattern can be highly flexible.

Notice that the pattern has several names. This, unfortunately, is common. It's useful, therefore, to become familiar with each of the names given so that you can communicate with others who know the pattern by one name, but not by the others. For the sake of consistency, we'll refer to each pattern by the name preferred by the authors of *Design Patterns.* This is admittedly awkward in cases where a particular Java class implements a given pattern, because Java programmers are apt not to know the pattern name, even if they're familiar with the Java class. We'll alert you of such instances, but we'll try to be consistent in using the *Design Patterns* name, because it has status as a *de facto* standard.

Figure 11.1 shows how the `java.io` package uses the Decorator pattern to allow customization of the capabilities of input streams.

To implement this design pattern in Java, you'd write something like this:

```
DataInputStream in
  = new DataInputStream(new BufferedInputStream(
      new FileInputStream("data.txt")));
```

FIGURE 11.1

*The java.io package
and the decorator pat-
tern*

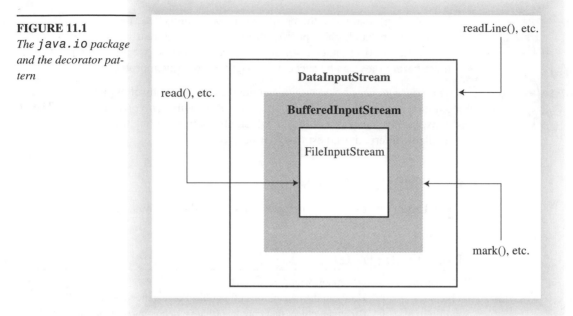

A FileInputStream object implements the read() method and several other methods, but neither performs buffering nor implements the mark() or readLine() methods. By wrapping the FileInputStream object inside a BufferedInputStream, its
performance is improved by the addition of buffering. It also becomes capable of
responding to the mark() message and several others (see the API documentation of
the BufferedInputStream class for details).

In the example, this operation is repeated, wrapping the BufferedInputStream
inside a DataInputStream, further increasing its capabilities. The original
FileInputStream object is now capable of responding to readLine() and other messages not handled by either a FileInputStream or BufferedInputStream.

These operations are possible because the designers of the java.io package provided constructors that allow a BufferedInputStream to be instantiated from a
FileInputStream, and a DataInputStream to be instantiated from a
BufferedInputStream. They did this by using another design pattern, one so simple
and common that it's nameless. Many classes of java.io have constructors that accept
any subclass of the abstract class InputStream as a parameter. This allows you to wrap
descendants of InputStream inside one another in a variety of ways. If you've done
much work with Java files, you're experienced in doing this, even if you were
unaware of the full implications.

Other Essential Patterns

If you're a programmer, most likely there are one or two books that you always keep within easy reach. If you can't remember the exact details of the Boyer-Moore string matching algorithm, for example, you reach for your copy of Sedgewick or Knuth. One of the goals of the "patterns movement" is to provide a catalogue of common, higher-level, problem-solution pairs that can be used as a reference just like a standard book of algorithms is now.

Advocates of design patterns have identified dozens of other patterns besides Decorator. Because it's not possible to present all of them here, the next several subsections examine four of the most common and useful patterns in detail:

" One of the goals of the 'patterns movement' is to provide a catalogue of common, higher-level, problem-solution pairs that can be used as a reference just like a standard book of algorithms is now. "

- Factory Method
- Singleton
- Iterator, also known as Enumeration
- Command

After that, you'll get a quick fly-by showing you some patterns that are embedded in Java's APIs. These aren't presented in detail, because the Java API documents tell you all you need to know.

THE FACTORY METHOD DESIGN PATTERN

Suppose you want to build a class that has responsibility for making meals. Thinking about the problem, you realize that an important subtask is making the entree. For breakfast, your class might make scrambled eggs and ham, for lunch it might make a grilled cheese sandwich, and for dinner it might make pot roast. Putting the logic for all three meals in a single class might create some confusion: grilled chicken sounds okay, but a scrambled cheese sandwich sounds positively frightening. So, on second thought, it seems better to have a separate class for each meal.

A good approach would be to create a base class called `Entree` and subclass it to create a `BreakfastEntree` class, a `LunchEntree` class, and a `DinnerEntree` class. The base class can have a `createEntree` method that each subclass can override to make the appropriate type of entree.

But now, your meal-making class has become complicated. If it's preparing lunch, it needs to prepare a lunch entree, a lunch beverage, a lunch dessert, and so on. But, if it's preparing dinner, it needs to prepare a dinner appetizer, a dinner salad, a dinner beverage, and so on. Again, rather than tangling the logic for the three kinds of meals together, you'd prefer to keep it separate and simple. But, you'd still like to have that single class that can do breakfast, lunch, or dinner. How?

This is the problem the Factory Method design pattern addresses. Figure 11.2 shows the Factory Method design pattern as it's implemented by the `FactoryTest` class, which you'll meet shortly.

FIGURE 11.2
The Factory Method pattern

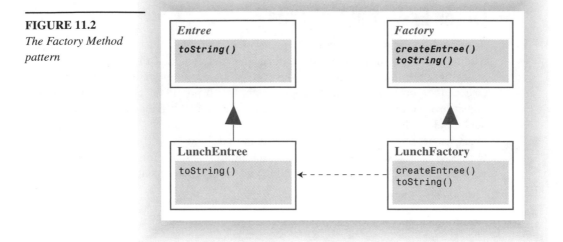

NOTATION REFRESHER

Before you go on, take a second to recall the notations used in class diagrams like Figure 11.2. The rectangles, you remember, represent classes and objects. This diagram doesn't distinguish classes from objects (although class diagrams can make that distinction); instead, it represents an object by a rectangle labeled with the name of the class it belongs to. Abstract classes are those with bold, italic names. Concrete classes and objects have names in regular type. The methods of a class may be shown above a horizontal line through the middle of the class; fields may be shown below the line.

The vertical line decorated with a triangle means that the lower class extends the upper class. If you find this confusing, just remember that the triangle points toward the super or parent class. The horizontal dashed line shown in the diagram indicates that one class instantiates (or makes an object from) another (the one at which the arrow points).

Reading Figure 11.2 tells you that the abstract class `Factory` is extended by the concrete class `LunchFactory`. (Breakfast and dinner work the same. For the sake of simplicity, they're not shown.) The `LunchFactory` class instantiates a `LunchEntree` object. The `LunchFactory` class is a concrete subclass of the abstract class `Factory`.

The beauty of the Factory Method design pattern is that once you've instantiated the proper kind of `Factory` for the meal at hand, your program can deal with any kind of meal the same way. Each new meal subclasses `Factory`, so each has a `createEntree()` method (for example) that returns an `Entree` object, which could be a `BreakfastEntree`, a `LunchEntree`, or a `DinnerEntree`. Each type of `Entree` knows how to respond appropriately to every message an `Entree` is responsible for, so a client program doesn't have to remember that it should scramble the eggs but not the cheese sandwich.

Testing the Factory Method

To see how the design pattern can be implemented in Java, take a look at Listing 11.1, which shows the `FactoryTest` applet. `FactoryTest` has a single `Factory` object that can refer to either a `LunchFactory` or a `DinnerFactory` by clicking the Change Shift button.

After the proper subtype of `Factory` has been created, nothing in `FactoryTest` treats lunch differently than dinner. All the complications of each type of meal are handled in the meal's respective class. The applet would be considerably more complicated if it had to include selection logic to keep the different types of meals straight. Using the Factory Method makes it easy to add a `MidnightSnack`, too: all that's needed is an instantiation of the new subtype of `Factory`.

Listing 11.1 The FactoryTest Class

```java
// FactoryTest.java
//
import java.awt.*;
import java.awt.event.*;
import java.applet.*;

public class FactoryTest extends Applet
{
  public void init()
  {
    setLayout(new BorderLayout());

    Panel topPanel   = new Panel();
    Button nextShift = new Button("Next Shift");
    Button serveMeal = new Button("Get Your Meal");
    topPanel.add(shift);
    topPanel.add(nextShift);
    topPanel.add(serveMeal);
    add(topPanel, "North");

    center.setBackground(Color.cyan);
    center.setLayout(new FlowLayout());
    add(center, "Center");

    nextShift.addActionListener(shiftChanger);
    serveMeal.addActionListener(mealServer);
  }

  protected Panel center = new Panel();
  protected Factory fred = new LunchFactory();
  protected Label shift  = new Label("11:00 am - Lunch Time!!!");
  protected boolean isLunch = true;

  private ActionListener shiftChanger = new ActionListener()
  {
    public void actionPerformed(ActionEvent ae)
    {
      if (isLunch)
      {
        shift.setText("4:15 pm - Dinner Time!!!");
```

```
          fred = new DinnerFactory();
          isLunch = false;
        }
        else
        {
          shift.setText("11:00 am - Lunch Time!!!");
          fred = new LunchFactory();
          isLunch = true;
        }
      }
    };

    private ActionListener mealServer = new ActionListener()
    {
      public void actionPerformed(ActionEvent ae)
      {
        Entree theEntree = fred.createEntree();
        center.add(theEntree);
        center.invalidate();
        center.validate();
      }
    };
}
```

The FactoryTest applet has six fields:

◖ The Panel, center, is a handy place to set your meals after they are served. The embedded ActionListener object, mealServer, will take care of that chore.

◖ The Factory object, fred (think of him as the experienced cook who keeps Eddie's Diner running behind the scenes), is initially set up to refer to a LunchFactory object.

◖ The Label, shift, and the boolean field, isLunch, are used to let you know what shift is at work at Eddie's All Automatic Food Factory.

◖ The ActionListener object, shiftChanger, is constructed inline as a named inner class. ActionListener objects, recall, handle ActionEvents. The shiftChanger object will be "hooked-up" to the Change Shift button when you initialize your applet. By using an inner class to construct shiftChanger, its actionPerformed() method is able to check the isLunch field inside FactoryTest and construct a new DinnerFactory or LunchFactory, whichever is appropriate.

◖ The last field, also an ActionListener called mealServer, is where all of the real work of the applet is done, yet its actionPerformed() method is the simplest of all. It simply asks the Factory object, fred, to give it an Entree. It then adds the Entree to the surface of the center Panel using add(), and issues an invalidate()-validate() sequence asking center to lay out the new components.

Besides the two `actionPerformed()` methods contained in the embedded `ActionListener` objects, `shiftChanger` and `mealServer`, the `FactoryTest` applet has only a single method, `init()`. The `init()` method is very straightforward. It simply creates two buttons, adds them to the applet, and then hooks them up to `shiftChanger` and `mealServer`, who actually get things rolling when the buttons are pressed.

Looking Inside the Factories

Because the real magic of the Factory design pattern is done inside the `Factory` class and its subclasses, you'll want to take a look at them. They're shown in Listing 11.2.

Listing 11.2 The Factory Class and Its Subclasses

```
abstract class Factory
{
  public abstract Entree createEntree();
}

class LunchFactory extends Factory
{
  public Entree createEntree() { return new LunchEntree(); }
}

class DinnerFactory extends Factory
{
  public Entree createEntree() { return new DinnerEntree(); }
}
```

`Factory` is defined as an abstract class. Its subclasses must, at a minimum, implement the `createEntree()` method. Of course, this fails to account for the full range of responsibilities of a meal factory: what about dessert, for example? Any additional methods, `createDessert()` among them, could be added to `Factory`. `Factory` has been kept as simple as possible here, so the main idea of the Factory Method design pattern stands out.

Each of `Factory`'s subclasses, `LunchFactory` and `DinnerFactory`, implements the required method, `createEntree()`, established by `Factory`. The Java compiler enforces this rule. If a subclass such as `LunchFactory` failed to implement even one required method, it would then itself be an abstract class rather than a concrete class. If you tried to create an object from the class, Java would issue an error, because abstract classes cannot be instantiated.

Preparing the Entree

The work of preparing the entree is performed by the `Entree` abstract class and the classes that extend it, shown in Listing 11.3. Because the `Entree` class extends the `Button` class (so you'll have something to see on the screen when dinner is served), it cannot be implemented as an interface instead of as an abstract class. The only important difference between an abstract class and an interface is that an abstract class can provide implementations for some of its methods; an interface cannot. Because

Factory does not provide any default behavior, it could have been implemented as either an abstract class or an interface. The Entree class, through its superclass Button, does have a considerable amount of default behavior. It usually makes sense to use an abstract class when there is default behavior that can be implemented in the parent class, and use an interface otherwise. But, if you prefer otherwise, you can have it your own way.

Listing 11.3 The Entree Abstract Class and Its Concrete Classes

```
abstract class Entree extends Button
{
  public Entree(String s) { super(s); }
}

class DinnerEntree extends Entree
{
  public DinnerEntree()
  {
    super("Pot Roast");
    setFont(new Font("Helvetica", Font.BOLD, 24));
  }
}

class LunchEntree extends Entree
{
  public LunchEntree()
  {
    super("Cheese Sandwich");
    setFont(new Font("TimesRoman", Font.ITALIC, 14));
  }
}
```

You can use Listing 11.4, FactoryTest.html, to try out the FactoryTest applet for yourself.

Listing 11.4 FactoryTest.html

```
<HTML>
<HEAD>
<TITLE>Eddie's Food Factory</TITLE>
</HEAD>
<BODY>
<H1>Welcome to Eddie's</H1>
<HR>
At Eddie's Food Factory (tm), everything is automatic.<BR>
When you change the shift, your applet delivers the appropriate meal.<BR>
The thing is, the applet doesn't know what the appropriate meal is!<BR>
It just asks fred the Factory object for the correct Entree and lets
fred take care of the rest.
</HR>
<APPLET CODE=FactoryTest HEIGHT=400 WIDTH=600>
</APPLET>
</BODY>
</HTML>
```

Figure 11.3 shows the FactoryTest applet at work. Notice that when you change shifts, the meal server button delivers the appropriate entree to you, even though it has no knowledge of either the time of day, or the type of meal it's serving of up.

USING THE FACTORY METHOD PATTERN

When it's time to build your next Java application, most likely you won't be building an automated diner serving cheese sandwiches and pot roast. Nevertheless, you'll probably find the Factory Method a useful design pattern in the real, industrial strength software you do build. Consider a few examples:

- Suppose you want to be able to handle multiple "look and feel" styles of user interface. You want to write an application that uses buttons, but you want the buttons to appear as Mac buttons on a Macintosh, and Windows buttons on a Windows machine. Hmmmm. Sounds a lot like Java doesn't it? Well, it is Java. It's also an application of the Factory design pattern. If you build your applications to get buttons from a ButtonFactory, you can then change the type of buttons used in your application simply by changing a single ButtonFactory object.

- How would you write an application that handles different types of documents? Suppose you were to write a Java word processor that can read files produced by Microsoft Word, WordPerfect, and Lotus WordPro. One way to proceed is to litter your code with switch statements, handling each document according to its own peculiarities. The smart way, however, is to create a single abstract Document class, with subclasses for each of the

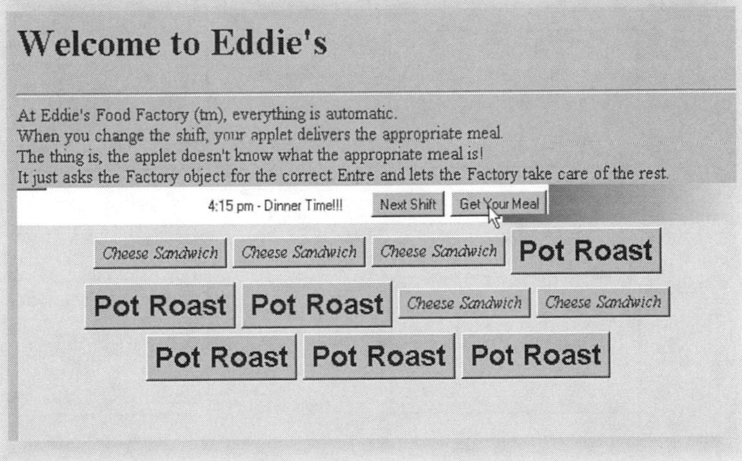

FIGURE 11.3
Running the FactoryTest applet

Welcome to Eddie's

At Eddie's Food Factory (tm), everything is automatic.
When you change the shift, your applet delivers the appropriate meal.
The thing is, the applet doesn't know what the appropriate meal is!
It just asks the Factory object for the correct Entre and lets the Factory take care of the rest.

4:15 pm - Dinner Time!!!   Next Shift   Get Your Meal

Cheese Sandwich   Cheese Sandwich   Cheese Sandwich   **Pot Roast**

Pot Roast   **Pot Roast**   Cheese Sandwich   Cheese Sandwich

Pot Roast   **Pot Roast**   **Pot Roast**

particular file types. Then, by getting all of your documents from a
`DocumentFactory`, your main code doesn't have to know about the
differences between documents at all.

⬗ Consider the lowly desktop interface. Your new all-Java replacement for the
Windows Explorer or the Mac Finder will succeed only if you solve one
fundamental design problem: how to make your desktop extensible. You may
have supplied it with a wealth of handy objects—phone dialers and notepads
and nifty, time-wasting games. But what about the objects you haven't
thought of? How about the accessories that haven't been invented yet? The
Factory Method design pattern was born to handle this problem. By creating
a new subclass for each new accessory as it's created, your main desktop
doesn't even have to know that it's not working with the same familiar
objects it's always dealt with.

Figure 11.4 shows the general form of the Factory Method pattern. In it, the partici-
pating classes are given general names, rather than specific names like `LunchFactory`.
See if you can match the class names in Figure 11.4 to the class names in Figure 11.2.
The figures are laid out the same to make this easier for you.

An important extension of the Factory Method design pattern is the Abstract Factory
design pattern. In Factory Method, there is only one Product class. In Abstract Factory,
there is an entire set of Products. In Abstract Factory, sending the proper message to
the ConcreteCreator causes it to create not one object, but an entire set of objects. If
the FactoryTest applet had fully solved the problem—creating not merely an entree,
but a beverage, a dessert, and so on—it would have been an instance of Abstract
Factory rather than Factory Method.

FIGURE 11.4

*The Factory Method
pattern (general form)*

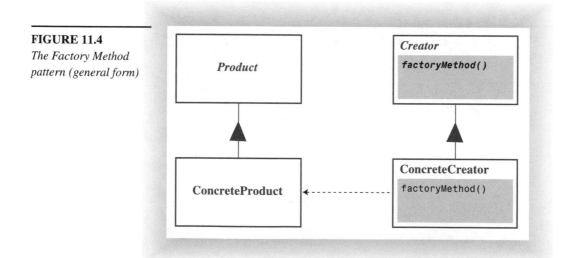

Factory Method is used by the java.util package as well as the java.awt package. In java.util, for example, the Vector.elements() method returns an Enumeration object, as do Hashtable.elements() and Dictionary.elements(). Enumeration is actually an interface, not a class. So the true nature and complexity of the returned object is hidden from the client for whom it was created.

Table 11.2 summarizes the key features of the Factory Method design pattern.

TABLE 11.2
THE FACTORY METHOD PATTERN

Pattern name	Factory Method, Virtual Constructor.
Problem	Given an object containing a method that returns a new instance of some class, how can subclasses of the object return new instances of some other type?
Solution	Allow subclasses to override the method; each returning a different type of object, all of which implement a common interface.
Consequences	The Factory Method allows its client objects to work only with the Product interface, keeping most of the complexity in the ConcreteProduct classes.

THE SINGLETON DESIGN PATTERN

A second common design pattern is Singleton. Singleton is useful when you want to constrain a class to having a single, unique instance. There's a straightforward way to enforce this uniqueness using static members. For example, the following code will do the job:

```
public class OneInstance
{
    public static OneInstance getInstance() { return theInstance; }
    protected OneInstance() { ; }
    private static final theInstance = new OneInstance();
}
```

Notice that the constructor is protected, preventing clients from directly instantiating OneInstance objects. Instead, they must use the class method getInstance(), which returns a reference to the unique instance created when the class is loaded by the static final field, theInstance.

The rub, however, is that you can't easily subclass OneInstance. Each subclass would have to re-implement the behavior that constrains the class to a single instance. The Singleton design pattern solves this problem. To see how, take a look at Figure 11.5, which shows the Singleton pattern as it will be used in the example program, SingletonTest, and in its general form.

FIGURE 11.5

The Singleton pattern

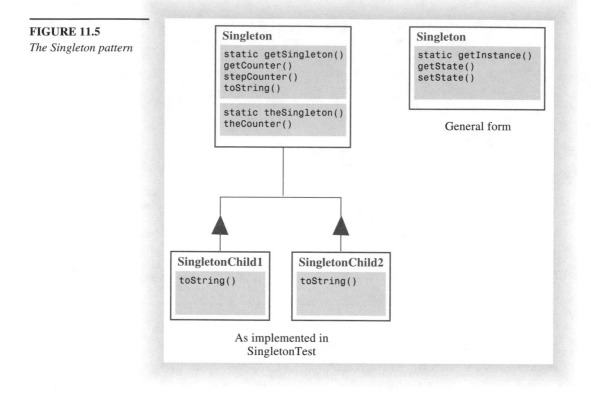

From the figure, you can see that `Singleton` implements a `getSingleton()` method, which a client can use to get a reference to the singleton instance. It also implements several methods (`getCounter()`, `stepCounter()`, and `toString()`) that get or change the state of the singleton, which consists of a `static` reference to the unique instance (`theSingleton`) and an `int` that serves as a counter (`theCounter`). The child classes, `SingletonChild1` and `SingletonChild2`, override the `toString()` method of their parent.

To see how `Singleton` is implemented, see Listing 11.5.

```
Listing 11.5 The Singleton Class
public class Singleton
{
    public static Singleton getSingleton(int type)
    {
        if (theSingleton == null)
        {
            if (type == 1) theSingleton = new SingletonChild1();
            else if (type == 2) theSingleton = new SingletonChild2();
        }
        return theSingleton;
    }
```

```
    public int getCounter()
    {
        return theSingleton.theCounter;
    }

    public void stepCounter()
    {
        theSingleton.theCounter++;
    }

    public String toString()
    {
        return "theCounter=" + getCounter();
    }

    protected Singleton()
    {
        System.out.println("Constructor executed ...\n");
    }

    private static Singleton theSingleton = null;
    private int theCounter = 0;
}
```

Notice that, as in the OneInstance class, the Singleton's constructor is protected. Unlike OneInstance, however, Singleton declares the field holding the unique reference (theSingleton) as static, rather than static final.

The reason is found within the getSingleton() method. When a client invokes getSingleton(), the client sends along an int parameter specifying whether a SingletonChild1 or a SingletonChild2 instance of Singleton is desired. The getSingleton() method checks whether a unique instance has been established by storing its reference in the field theSingleton. If not, it creates a child class object of the requested type, stores its reference in theSingleton, and returns the reference to the client.

Subsequent calls to getSingleton() will return this same reference. If a client erroneously (or maliciously) provides a parameter value unlike the one used to initialize the Singleton, no problem results. The parameter is only tested when initializing the Singleton.

Listing 11.6 shows the child classes of Singleton. Each simply overrides the toString() method of the parent. The revised method returns a result that discloses the type of the child.

```
Listing 11.6 Child Classes of the Singleton Class
class SingletonChild1 extends Singleton
{
    public String toString()
    {
        return "Child1: " + super.toString();
    }
}

class SingletonChild2 extends Singleton
```

```
{
    public String toString()
    {
        return "Child2: " + super.toString();
    }
}
```

Listing 11.7 shows the `SingletonTest` class, which functions as a client that demonstrates the operation of the `Singleton` class. Notice that the client cannot instantiate a Singleton instance using the `new` operator. The constructor is hidden (that is, `protected`), so Java flags any attempt to use it as an error. Instead, the client must use the `getSingleton()` method.

The method returns a reference, which the client uses to print and update the state of the object. Next, a second variable, `s2`, is declared and initialized using `getSingleton()`. By printing the value of the `Singleton`'s counter, the client demonstrates that the instance is unique, as desired. Both references refer to the same object. Check the output in Figure 11.6 to see for yourself.

Listing 11.7 The SingletonTest Class

```
public class SingletonTest
{
    public static void main(String [] args)
    {
        //Singleton s1 = new Singleton();  <-- error: no matching
                                            //constructor
        Singleton s1 = Singleton.getSingleton(1);
        System.out.println(s1);
        s1.stepCounter();
        System.out.println(s1);
        System.out.println();

        Singleton s2 = Singleton.getSingleton(2);
        System.out.println(s2);
        System.out.println();

        try
        {
            System.out.println("\nPress RETURN/ENTER to continue ...");
            System.in.read();
        }
        catch (Exception e) { ; }
    }
}
```

Java's `java.awt` package creates its unique `Toolkit` object using the `Singleton` package. You can view the JDK source code to see this. Look under the directory in which you installed the JDK for the file `src/java/awt/Toolkit.java`.

Ed Shea shared an important observation with visitors to the Portland Pattern Repository (`http://c2.com/ppr/`). In Java, when the only remaining reference to a singleton is the one in the singleton class itself, the Java garbage collector may collect the instance and unload the class. The solution is to register singleton instances in a system-wide table, thus protecting them from garbage collection. If you use a

FIGURE 11.6
Output of the
`SingletonTest`
application

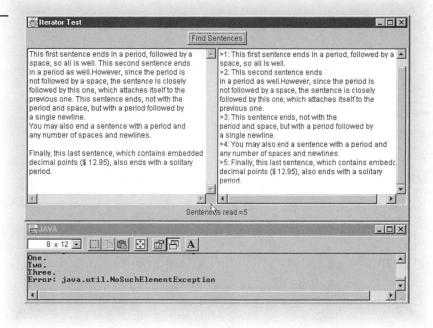

`Hashtable` for this purpose, you can assign each singleton a name and then conveniently access your singletons by name, using the `get()` method.

Table 11.3 summarizes the Singleton design pattern. The class diagram for the Singleton design pattern appears in Figure 11.5.

TABLE 11.3
THE SINGLETON PATTERN

Pattern name	Singleton
Problem	How can you ensure that a class has only one instance and yet not have to make the class `final`?
Solution	Forbid access to the constructor and implement an accessor that returns a reference to the unique instance.
Consequences	Control over access to the unique instance.
	Solution generalizes well to n instances.

THE ITERATOR DESIGN PATTERN

As a Java programmer, you'll frequently deal with collections of objects rather than individual objects. Collections allow you to perform the same operations on several elements, without repeating the same code over and over again. In Chapters 7 and 8, when you built the `SalesInvoice` application, you were able to use a collection of `LineItem` objects to store the quantities and descriptions of each item which you'd sold. Without a collection, you would have to duplicate your code for each line item, or, at the very best, make method calls for each line item like this:

```
double total = 0.0;
total = total + item1.getTotal() + item2.getTotal() + item3.getTotal();
```

By using an array to hold a collection of items, however, you could write this instead:

```
double total = 0.0;
for (int i = 0; i < nItems; i++ )
{
   total += items[ i ].getTotal();
}
```

While the first method might seem simpler for three items, you can easily imagine how unmanageable it would become at 50 or 100 items.

Rather than dealing with each item individually, a collection lets you simply loop over each of its items, performing the same processing for every element. In such a case, using an array is a vast improvement—it's just not as flexible as it could be. If you decide at a later date that another method of storage would be more appropriate—a `Vector` or a `Hashtable`, for instance—you'll have to go back and write code to correctly visit each element in its new data structure. Using the Iterator design pattern allows you to avoid this effort, and to build flexibility into your collections from the very start.

The Enumeration Interface

The Iterator design pattern (which is known to Java programmers by the alternative names Enumerator or Enumeration) is a very important pattern used, as mentioned earlier, in the `java.util` package. There, the `elements()` method of the collection classes `Vector`, `Hashtable`, and `Dictionary` return an `Enumeration` object that lets a client move serially through the elements of a collection. Such an operation is called a *traversal* and the client is said to *traverse* the collection. You can think of such traversal as being equivalent to looping through the elements of an array, without being bound to the array structure. Several other classes provide the same, or a similar, method.

`Enumeration` is an interface. To implement the interface you have to write two methods: `nextElement()` and `hasMoreElements()`. The former returns the next element during traversal of the collection; the latter returns a `boolean` value that tells you whether untraversed elements remain to be visited.

By using an interface rather than a superclass, each collection class is able to organize its elements differently. When you write programs that use the `Enumeration` interface, you really don't want to depend on the way that a collection implements the `hasMoreElements()` and `nextElement()` methods. By avoiding this, your programs won't be affected by changes to the implementation of the collection. You may even be able to substitute a better collection class when one becomes available, changing only the statement that creates the collection.

By interposing the Enumeration interface between your classes and the collection classes that hold your objects, you are able to use the services of the collection without knowledge of its implementation. This is precisely the kind of thing the interface feature of the Java language was designed to support.

An Iterator Example

Let's take a look at an example that uses the Iterator design pattern. Suppose you were writing a Java word processor. One of the design decisions you'd have to make would be how to store the actual text that your application processes: an array, a linked list, or just one giant String. No matter how you store a document, however, your program still must deal with the individual pieces that are the stock-in-trade of a word processor: characters, words, sentences, and paragraphs. By separating these objects from the data structures used to store them, you are free to try out different storage mechanisms without changing the central logic of your word processor. The Iterator design pattern gives you that separation.

Figure 11.7 shows the Iterator pattern used in the IteratorTest example program. IteratorTest shows you how to write your own iterators to traverse collection classes you, or others, have written. To use an array of ints, you first create the array and then loop through it using an index, as you saw above. By using Iterators, you can step through the logical pieces of your collections, such as the words and sentences, as easily as an array allows you to step through a collection of ints. To do this,

FIGURE 11.7

The Iterator pattern

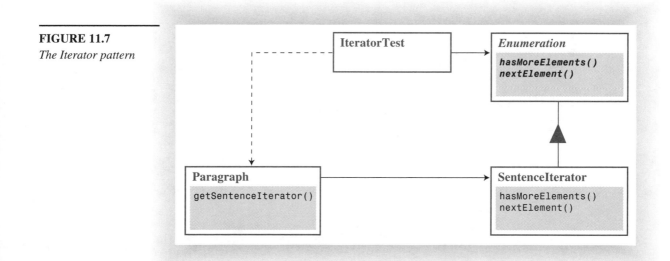

IteratorTest uses the Paragraph class, which implements the Enumeration interface. Using Paragraph along with the Iterator class SentenceIterator enables you to walk through your Paragraph sentence by sentence, instead of stepping through it character by character.

Before looking at the SentenceIterator class itself, take a look at Listing 11.8, which shows the client class (the class that *uses* the SentenceIterator), IteratorTest.

Listing 11.8 The IteratorTest Class

```
//   Test the SentenceIterator class

import java.awt.*;
import java.util.*;
import java.awt.event.*;

public class IteratorTest extends Frame
                          implements ActionListener
{
  Button    iterate = new Button("Find Sentences");
  TextArea  input   = new TextArea(15, 30);
  TextArea  output  = new TextArea(15, 30);
  Label     report  = new Label("", Label.CENTER);

  public IteratorTest()
  {
    super("Iterator Test");

    setLayout(new BorderLayout());
    setBackground(Color.lightGray);

    Panel p = new Panel();
    p.add(iterate);
    add(p, "North");
    add(report, "South");

    p = new Panel();
    p.setLayout(new GridLayout(1, 2, 5, 5));
    p.add(input);
    p.add(output);
    add(p, "Center");

    addWindowListener(new WindowAdapter()
    {
      public void windowClosing(WindowEvent we)
      {
        setVisible(false);
        dispose();
        System.exit(0);
      }
    });

    iterate.addActionListener(this);
    pack();
    show();
```

```
    }

    public void actionPerformed(ActionEvent ae)
    {
      Paragraph    p = new Paragraph(input.getText());
      Enumeration e = p.getSentences();

      output.setText("");
      int nSentences = 0;
      while (e.hasMoreElements())
      {
        Sentence s = (Sentence) e.nextElement();
        nSentences++;
        output.append("\n>" + nSentences + ": " + s);
      }
      report.setText("Sentences read =" + nSentences);

      // Demonstrate Enumeration exception
      try
      {
        p = new Paragraph("One. Two. Three.");
        e = p.getSentences();
        while (true)
        {
          Sentence s = (Sentence) e.nextElement();
          System.out.println(s);
        }
      }
      catch (NoSuchElementException nsee)
      {
        System.out.println("Error: " + nsee);
      }
    }

    public static void main(String [] args)
    {
      new IteratorTest();
    }
  }
```

Inside the `IterateTest` Client IterateTest is an application with two TextAreas—input and output—a Button named iterate, and a Label named report. In its constructor, IterateTest() creates a user interface by placing the two TextAreas side-by-side in the center of the application, adding the Button on the top, and the Label on the bottom. To run the application, type some sentences into the input TextArea on the left, and click the iterate Button. The actionPerformed() method will count the number of sentences in the input TextArea and move them to the output TextArea.

IteratorTest creates a Paragraph by using a constructor that takes a String as its parameter. It then obtains an Enumeration object (that is, an iterator) by calling Paragraph.getSentences():

```
Paragraph    p = new Paragraph(input.getText());
Enumeration e = p.getSentences();
```

The `Enumeration.hasMoreElements()` and `Enumeration.nextElement()` methods are then used in a `while` loop to perform a traversal of the `Paragraph`, adding each element (sentence) to the output `TextArea` as it is traversed:

```java
int nSentences = 0;
while (e.hasMoreElements())
{
  Sentence s = (Sentence) e.nextElement();
  nSentences++;
  output.append("\n>" + nSentences + ": " + s);
}
```

The `nextElement()` method returns an `Object`, as required by the `Enumeration` interface. The `IteratorTest` application simply casts the `Object` to a `Sentence` and implicitly invokes the `Sentence`'s `toString()` method by using `String` concatenation to paste together the number of the `Sentence` before passing it on to `output`. Finally, the number of `Sentences` actually read is reported on using the `Label` named `report`:

```java
report.setText("Sentences read =" + nSentences);
```

An important property of Java's `Enumeration` class is that it throws a `NoSuchElementException` if a client object tries to traverse a collection that has no remaining elements. The next several statements of `IteratorTest` demonstrate this by intentionally over-traversing a `Paragraph`. Figure 11.8 shows the output of the `IteratorTest` application.

FIGURE 11.8

Output of the
IteratorTest
application

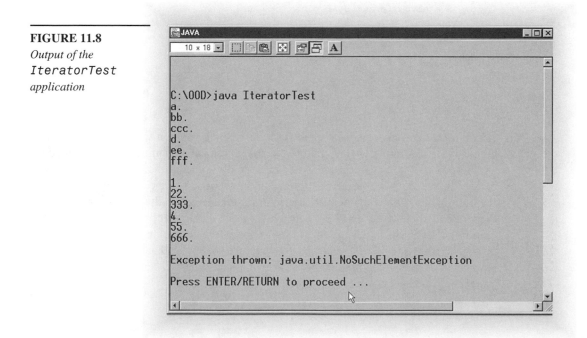

> *An important property of Java's* `Enumeration` *class is that it throws a* `NoSuchElement-Exception` *if a client object tries to traverse a collection that has no remaining elements.*

Looking at Paragraphs and Sentences   Listing 11.9 shows the collection class, `Paragraph`, used by `IteratorTest`. The class constructor simply stores the `String` passed to it. The lone method, `getSentences()`, instantiates a `SentenceIterator` and returns it to the client object.

Listing 11.9 The Paragraph Class

```
class Paragraph
{
  public Enumeration getSentences()
  {
    return new SentenceIterator(theText);
  }

  public Paragraph(String text)
  {
    theText = text;
  }

  private String theText;
}
```

Recall from `IteratorTest` that the `Object` returned by the `Enumeration` provided by `Paragraph.getSentences()` is a `Sentence`. The `Sentence` class, shown in Listing 11.10, encapsulates a `String` of text, providing a `toString()` method that returns the `String`. Nothing fancy here.

Listing 11.10 The Sentence Class

```
class Sentence
{
  public String toString()
  {
    return theText;
  }

  public Sentence(String text)
  {
    theText = text;
  }

  private String theText;
}
```

The Iterator Workhorse: `SentenceIterator`   The real work is done by the `SentenceIterator` class, shown in Listing 11.11. As required, the class implements the `Enumeration` interface, providing concrete implementations for the methods `hasMoreElements()` and `nextElement()`.

Listing 11.11 The SentenceIterator Class

```
class SentenceIterator implements Enumeration
{
  // -------------------------------------------------
  //   hasMoreElements() returns true if:
```

```
//    a. There are any more sentences past the cursor
//    b. This means the last sentence (if not ended
//       by a period and a space) will not count.
// ----------------------------------------------
public boolean hasMoreElements()
{
  return (nextSentencePos > 0);
}

public Object nextElement() throws NoSuchElementException
{
  //  1. Check that there are elements left
  if (! hasMoreElements()) throw new NoSuchElementException();

  //  2. Extract the substring representing this Sentence
  nextSentencePos++;  // Include the period
  String next = theText.substring(theCursor, nextSentencePos);

  //  3. Set theCursor to point at next character
  theCursor = nextSentencePos;

  //  4. Set the nextSentencePos to point to the next period
  nextSentencePos = findEnd();

  //  5. Strip whitespace from front of String, next
  int i=0;
  char ch;
  while ( (ch = next.charAt(i)) == ' ' || ch == '\n' || ch == '\t')
    i++;

  //  6. Return the Sentence
  return new Sentence(next.substring(i));
}

private int findEnd()
{
  int posNL, posSP;

  posSP = theText.indexOf(". ", theCursor);
  posNL = theText.indexOf(".\n", theCursor);
  if ( posNL > 0 && posSP > 0)
    return  (posNL > posSP ? posSP : posNL);
  if ( posNL > 0) return posNL;
  if ( posSP > 0) return posSP;
  return -1;
}

public SentenceIterator(String text)
{
  theText = text;
  theCursor = 0;
  nextSentencePos = findEnd();
}

private String   theText;
private int      theCursor;
private int      nextSentencePos;
}
```

To support its responsibilities, the class defines three fields:

- A `String`, `theText` holds a reference to the text being traversed.

- An `int`, `theCursor` holds a moving index into the text. This holds the position where the current `Sentence` starts. Such an index is called a *cursor*.

- An `int`, `nextSentencePos` holds the position of the end of the current `Sentence`.

The constructor for the `SentenceIterator` class accepts a reference to the text it is to step through and stores that reference in the field `theText`. It then initializes the cursor with the index of the first character of the text (which is at position 0), and finally, calls the private method, `findEnd()`, to locate the end of the first sentence. It stores this information in the field, `nextSentencePos`.

The `SentenceIterator` class assumes that a sentence starts with a non-blank character and is ended by either a period and a newline (".\n") or a period and a space (". "). This allows you to embed dollar amounts or make other uses of the period, but is still a rather naive definition of a sentence. It doesn't consider sentences that end in question marks or exclamation points. A little more sophisticated logic can overcome this flaw, but at the cost of obscuring the point of the example. To find the end of the current sentence, the `findEnd()` method follows these steps:

1. It uses the `String` class' built-in method `indexOf()` to find the location of both period-newline and period-space character pairs (because a paragraph could contain some sentences that end with one and some that end with the other).

2. If both pairs are found, the one that is nearer the beginning of the `String` must end the current sentence, and so it is returned.

3. If only one type of ending is found, it is returned by checking the value of each instance against zero.

4. If none of these cases is found, then `findEnd()` returns −1 to signal that the current sentence doesn't end.

A complication that can arise in implementing any Iterator class is the possibility that the collection may be changed during a traversal. Imagine, if you will, an Iterator that skips through the records of a database. After it has iterated through half the records, someone could add a record to the first half of the list (the part already iterated). Thus the element would not be counted in the traversal. A user could also move an element from the first half to the second half. Thus Ms. Bauer, who just got married and chose to take her husband's name of Zemekis, would get counted twice if the database was updated during the traversal.

While this example may seem contrived, such possibilities are very real in a multi-threaded programming environment like Java. However, because the `SentenceIterator` class deals with Java `Strings`, and because `Strings` are immutable, this cannot happen here.

`SentenceIterator`'s `hasMoreElements()` method simply checks whether the `nextSentencePos` field is greater than zero. It returns `true` if so and `false` if not.

The `nextElement()` method implements the traversal. It first checks whether there are any elements left to return. It does this by calling its own `hasMoreElements()` method. If there are no more elements (that is, if `nextSentencePos` is < 0) then `nextElement()` throws a `NoSuchElementException`, which causes the method to be exited. Otherwise, it uses the `String substring()` method to extract the `String` between `theCursor` and `nextSentencePos`. Both fields are then updated in anticipation of the next call to `nextElement()`. Finally, any white space characters (spaces, tabs, or newlines) are removed from the current `String` before the method ends, returning a new `Sentence` that contains the characters it collected.

Iterator: The General Form

Figure 11.9 shows the general form of the Iterator design pattern.

If you compare the structure of IteratorText with Figure 11.9 you'll note that IteratorText simplifies one aspect of the Iterator pattern. It works directly with the concrete collection class (called a ConcreteAggregate in the figure, following the terminology of the *Design Patterns* book) rather than with the abstract collection class. This is a common simplification of the design pattern. The advantage of following the general design pattern more literally is that client objects that use your iterators won't even be aware of the true type of the collection. This allows you to change the type of the collection without revising the client object. Often, this presents little practical advantage and so the simplification adopted by IteratorText is widespread.

Table 11.4 summarizes the characteristics of the Iterator design pattern.

FIGURE 11.9

The Iterator pattern (general form)

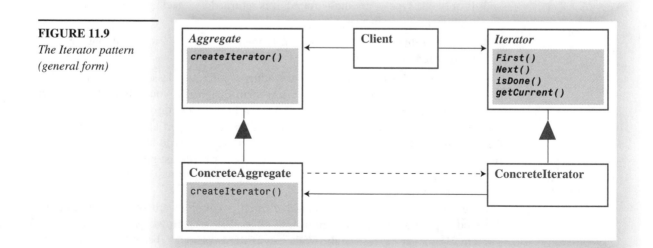

TABLE 11.4
THE ITERATOR PATTERN

Pattern name	Cursor, Enumerator
Problem	How can the elements of a collection be accessed sequentially without exposing its implementation?
Solution	Provide a go-between object that's aware of the implementation of the collection, but that can be used by client objects without exposing the implementation.
Consequences	Support for variation in traversal, eliminate need for traversal interface in the collection (making it simpler), allow multiple pending traversals.

THE COMMAND DESIGN PATTERN

The Command design pattern, the last one you'll study in detail in this chapter, lets you create *command objects*. A command object represents a message and its receiver. By creating a command object you give the users of your class the ability to send messages to receivers any time they want, simply by notifying the command object.

Because objects already have the ability to respond to messages, you might be wondering just what you can do with a command object that you can't easily do with a regular object. Because a command object encapsulates *both* the message and receiver into one object, it lends itself to many practical applications. For example, you can build queues that hold messages waiting to be processed, handling them in a prioritized order. You can create a log of all the messages sent by (or sent to) a particular object or class of objects. You can create a facility that lets the user undo operations by keeping track of the messages sent to an object and restoring it to some previous state.

The most common use of the Command design pattern, however, is somewhat less flashy. Because a command object encapsulates both a message and its receiver, and because these relationships are established at runtime, the Command pattern enables you to *decouple* objects that generate messages from the messages they generate and the objects that receive the messages. Let's consider a specific case.

A Design Problem

Toolbars, those small buttons that appear at the top of most modern GUI applications, are one of the great advances in user-interface design since mice and windows took over the desktop. Early GUIs limited themselves to menu commands that frequently required several steps to accomplish even a simple task. With the advent of the toolbar, common, repetitive actions were put within easy reach. As noted interface designer Alan Cooper points out, menus may make it easy to learn a program, but toolbars make a program easy to continue using.

Both toolbars and menus share a common design problem however: how should you hook up the user-interface object—the toolbar button or the menu selection—with the code that actually carries out the action? One common solution is to direct all menu

> *Because a command object encapsulates both a message and its receiver, and because these relationships are established at runtime, the Command pattern enables you to decouple objects that generate messages from the messages they generate and the objects that receive the messages.*

selections and button clicks to a common handler routine that finds out which button or menu item triggered the event, and then acts accordingly. This sort of code was common in early Microsoft Windows programs, and was even given a name—"the switch statement from hell"—so dubbed because of its tendency to grow to dozens of pages.

The object-oriented reaction to this sort of code was to apply the principle of encapsulation to the problem, and put the code that responds to the button press inside a new subclass of the Button class itself. But, there are two problems with this inheritance-based solution. First, because each interface element becomes a subclass, there is a proliferation of classes. Second, this solution tightly ties each interface element to a particular action. Even worse, if several elements are needed to generate the same action, you have several subclasses with essentially the same code.

The Command design pattern addresses the shortcomings of both of these solutions. By encapsulating a message and its receiver in an object, client objects can connect objects to receivers without being aware of the nature of the message or of the receiver. That way, the client object is less likely to require change when a message needs to be handled differently or a different type of message needs to be added.

Scratcher: A Command Pattern Example

Let's take a look at how you can implement the Command design pattern in Java. If you've ever eaten at a fast-food restaurant or purchased groceries from a supermarket, you're probably familiar with *scratchers*. A scratcher is a small card on which is printed a number of figures or numbers. These figures are covered with a soft, silvery metallic film that can be scratched off using a coin, revealing the figure underneath—hence the name scratcher. In some variations of the game you are only allowed to scratch off 3 of 5 positions, for instance. If you match three figures, you may win a hamburger or a soda.

The Scratcher applet, which you can see running in Figure 11.10, works in a similar manner.

FIGURE 11.10
The Scratcher applet

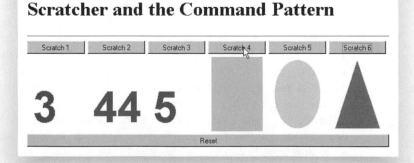

The applet presents the user with a screen containing six "silvered" squares. Because using a coin to scratch the silver coating wouldn't do your monitor any good, a separate button is provided for each square. Click a button, and either a red triangle, a green oval, or a blue number (between 1 and 52) will be revealed. A *reset* button spanning the bottom of the applet enables you to start over. As written, the applet does no scoring. Rather than being a deficiency, this is actually a feature. You can play "match four of six," make the triangles act as wild cards, or otherwise amuse yourself for hours. Before you set off to do that, however, you'll want to spend a little time getting acquainted with `Scratcher.java` and the way it implements the Command design pattern.

The Command Pattern Architecture The Command design pattern works by apportioning the responsibilities for issuing, routing, and responding to commands among different classes. In `Scratcher.java`, these responsibilities fall on the shoulders of the following classes:

- The abstract `Command` class (and its concrete subclasses, `TriangleCommand`, `CircleCommand`, and `NumberCommand`) carry out the actual work of drawing triangles, circles, and numbers on a `Component` object. This object—the receiver of the action—can be dynamically determined at runtime.

- The `CmdButton` class, which holds a reference to a `Command` object, and which, when clicked, delegates the performance of its command to its `Command` object. The `CmdButton` class doesn't really know (nor can it know) what the `Command` object is going to do; it just tells the `Command` object, "Perform your action!"

- The client class, `Scratcher`, which creates the actual `scratcher` panels (simple `Canvas` objects), and then connects the `CmdButton` objects to the `Command` objects and associates each `Command` object with a `scratcher` panel.

- A factory class, `CommandFactory`, which provides `Command` objects by using a random number generator. Although using the Factory design pattern is not really part of the Command pattern, using the factory class shows that the client class—which implements the user interface—is completely uncoupled from the actual `Commands` that are executed. Likewise, the `CmdButton` objects are uncoupled from the `Commands` that they execute.

Figure 11.11 shows a graphical representation of each of the major elements in the Scratcher applet.

The Scratcher Class After you understand the architecture of the Command design pattern, you're ready to start looking at the actual code that implements it. Let's start by looking at the client class, `Scratcher.java`, in Listing 11.12.

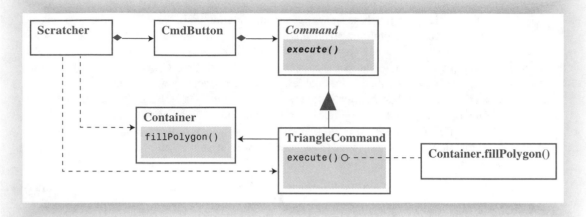

FIGURE 11.11

The Command design pattern used in the Scratcher applet

Listing 11.12 The Scratcher Class

```java
//  Scratcher.java
//  Uses the Command design pattern
import java.awt.*;
import java.awt.event.*;
import java.applet.*;
import java.util.*;

public class Scratcher extends Applet
                       implements ActionListener
{
  public void init()
  {
    //  1. Set the color and layout manager
    setBackground(Color.white);
    setLayout(new BorderLayout());

    //  2. Add the CmdButtons to the top
    Panel p = new Panel();
    p.setLayout(new GridLayout(1, 6, 5, 5));
    for (int i = 0; i < 6; i++)
    {
      buttons[i] = new CmdButton("Scratch "+(i+1));
      p.add(buttons[i]);
    }
    add(p, "North");

    //  3. Add the "Reset" button to the south
    add(reset, "South");
    reset.addActionListener(this);

    //  4. Add the "scratcher" Canvases to the center
    p = new Panel();
    p.setLayout(new GridLayout(1, 6, 5, 5));
    for (int i = 0; i < 6; i++)
    {
      scratchers[i] = new Canvas();
```

```
      p.add(scratchers[i]);
    }
    add(p, "Center");
  }

  // -------------------------------------------------
  //  The reset button
  //    For each command object
  //       Asks the CommandFactory for a Command object
  //       Sets its receiver to the current scratcher
  //       Assigns the Command to a CmdButton
  //    Each scratcher is then "blanked out"
  //
  public void actionPerformed(ActionEvent ae)
  {
    for (int i = 0; i < 6; i++)
    {
      Command cmd = CommandFactory.getCommand();
      cmd.setReceiver(scratchers[i]);
      buttons[i].setCommand(cmd);

      Dimension d = scratchers[i].getSize();
      Graphics g = scratchers[i].getGraphics();
      g.setColor(Color.lightGray);
      g.fillRect(5, 5, d.width-10, d.height-10);
      g.dispose();
    }
  }

  //   --Class and object fields----------------------
  Command[]    commands   = new Command[6];
  Canvas[]     scratchers = new Canvas[6];
  CmdButton[]  buttons    = new CmdButton[6];

  Button       reset      = new Button("Reset");
}
```

The Scratcher class contains four fields:

- An array of six Command objects named commands

- An array of six Canvas objects named scratchers

- An array of six CmdButton objects named buttons

- A single regular Button, named reset

To put these four fields to work, the applet also has two methods, init() and actionPerformed(). The init() method builds the user interface by:

1. Setting the background color to white and installing a BorderLayout object as the layout manager.

2. Adding each of the CmdButtons in the buttons array to a Panel object that acts as a toolbar at the top of the applet. This requires the use of a loop to create each of the CmdButton objects and add them to the Panel. After the Panel is completed, it is added to the top of the applet.

3. Adding the reset Button to the bottom of the applet. The applet signs up to listen for ActionEvents generated by reset Button by passing this to the Button's addActionListener() method.

4. Adding each of the Canvas objects in the scratchers array to the center of the applet. Like the CmdButtons, this requires a loop to create and add each Canvas object to an intermediate panel, which is then added to the center of the applet.

The second method in the Scratcher applet is the actionPerformed() method, which is triggered when the reset Button is pressed. The actionPerformed() method loops through each of the three arrays (buttons, scratchers, commands) and carries out these actions on each element:

1. It gets a Command object from the CommandFactory class. The Scratcher applet doesn't know what kind of Command it will get.

2. The Command object is then told to associate itself with one of the Canvas objects, using its setReceiver() method.

3. A CmdButton is then associated with the Command object by using the CmdButton.setCommand() method.

4. Finally, each of the scratcher Canvases is repainted to give each Canvas that silver, covered over, look.

The important thing to notice about this applet is that it has no idea what the Command objects are going to do, or even what kind of Command objects it receives. Note also that the CmdButton objects, which trigger the Commands, also have no idea of what kind of actions they'll start rolling. Finally, notice that the Command object is associated with the scratcher Canvases at runtime. The Command object itself isn't aware that the Scratcher applet with its Canvas objects even exist. It just gets a receiver and paints on it.

The Command design pattern is often used in user interfaces to decouple the interface from the actions it controls.

The Command Class   The Command design pattern is often used in user interfaces to decouple the interface from the actions it controls. For example, you could associate each item of a menu with a specific Command object representing the proper message and receiver. When the user selects a menu item, the user interface code would simply invoke the execute() method of the Command object associated with the menu item. Like magic, the proper action would occur. Changing the nature of the action would not normally require any change to the user interface.

Listing 11.13 shows the abstract Command, and the three concrete classes used in Scratcher.java.

Listing 11.13 The Command, TriangleCommand, CircleCommand, and NumberCommand Classes

```
// ====================================================
//  Command and Concrete Commands
// ====================================================
abstract class Command
```

```java
{
  abstract public void execute();

  public void setReceiver(Component c)
  {
    receiver = c;
  }
 Component receiver;
}
// ----------------------------------------------------
//  Draws a Red Triangle on the receiver
// ----------------------------------------------------
class TriangleCommand extends Command
{
  public void execute()
  {
    Graphics g = receiver.getGraphics();
    Dimension d = receiver.getSize();

    g.setColor(Color.white);
    g.fillRect(5, 5, d.width-10, d.height-10);

    g.setColor(Color.red);
    int[] xPoints = {10, d.width/2, d.width-10};
    int[] yPoints = {d.height-10, 10, d.height-10};
    g.fillPolygon( xPoints, yPoints, 3);
    g.dispose();
  }
}
// ----------------------------------------------------
//  Draws a Green Circle on the receiver
// ----------------------------------------------------
class CircleCommand extends Command
{
  public void execute()
  {
    Graphics g = receiver.getGraphics();
    Dimension d = receiver.getSize();

    g.setColor(Color.white);
    g.fillRect(5, 5, d.width-10, d.height-10);

    g.setColor(Color.green);
    g.fillOval(10, 10, d.width-20, d.height-20);
    g.dispose();
  }
}
// ----------------------------------------------------
//  Draws a blue number on the receiver
// ----------------------------------------------------
class NumberCommand extends Command
{
  public NumberCommand(int value)
  {
    super();
    this.value = value;
  }
```

```
  public void execute()
  {
    Graphics g = receiver.getGraphics();
    Dimension d = receiver.getSize();

    g.setColor(Color.white);
    g.fillRect(5, 5, d.width-10, d.height-10);

    g.setColor(Color.blue);
    g.setFont(new Font("Helvetica", Font.BOLD, 72));
    g.drawString(""+value, d.width / 10, (int)(d.height * .85));
    g.dispose();
  }
  private int value;
}
```

The abstract class `Command` has a single field, `receiver`, which is used to store a reference to the `Component` that acts as the receiver of the actions performed by `Command`'s concrete subclasses. The non-abstract method, `setReceiver()`, can be used with any `Command` object to associate it with any `Component`. Although all of the concrete `Command` classes developed here paint on the surface of the receiver `Component`, you are not limited to such actions.

The real magic of the Command pattern occurs, however, because of the final method in the Command class: the abstract method `execute()`. Because this is an `abstract` method, all of `Command`'s subclasses must implement it. Each of the three concrete classes illustrated above implement `execute()` in much the same way. First, the concrete `Command` object obtains a `Graphics` object from it's `receiver` field by calling the `getGraphics()` method. Then the color or the font used by the `Graphics` context is manipulated. Finally, either a geometric figure or some numeric value is painted on the surface of the `receiver`, depending on the actual `Command` object that is instantiated.

The **CmdButton** *Class* Because the client objects of `Command` deal not with concrete objects like `CircleCommand`, but with references to the abstract `Command` class, they only have to send the `execute()` method to any `Command` object to have it perform its magic. That is exactly what the `CmdButton` class, shown in Listing 11.14, does.

Listing 11.14 The CmdButton Class

```
// =====================================================
//  CmdButton: Listens to itself and calls execute()
// =====================================================
class CmdButton extends Button
{
  public CmdButton(String s)
  {
    super(s);
    addActionListener(al);
  }

  public void setCommand(Command c)
  {
    cmd = c;
```

```
  }

  protected Command cmd;

  ActionListener al = new ActionListener()
  {
    public void actionPerformed(ActionEvent ae)
    {
      System.out.println("CmdButton called:" +this);
      if (cmd != null) { cmd.execute(); }
    }
  };
}
```

The `CmdButton` class is derived from `Button`. It contains a field, `cmd`, which is a `Command` object. Every `CmdButton` object can be dynamically set to perform an entirely different set of actions by simply using its `setCommand()` method to wire it up to another `Command`.

In addition to the field `cmd`, all `CmdButtons` have an `ActionListener` field, `al`, which is defined using a named inner class. Although you can attach ActionListeners to `CmdButtons` the same way you would with regular `Buttons`, this really isn't necessary because they are hooked up to their internal `ActionListener` object when they are created. `CmdButtons` thus "listen to themselves;" they are entirely self-contained. When a `CmdButton` object is pressed, its internal `actionPerformed()` method sends an `execute()` message to its contained `Command` object. When using `CmdButtons`, you don't have to worry about adding `ActionListeners` or writing `actionPerformed()` methods. Just drop one in your applet, use `setCommand()` to associate it with a `Command` object, and it will work.

The `CommandFactory` Class   The final class in `Scratcher.java` is the `CommandFactory` class, shown in Listing 11.15. As previously mentioned, the `CommandFactory` is not an integral part of the Command design pattern, but is included here to show how completely the Command pattern allows you to separate the generator, performer, and receiver of an action from each other.

Listing 11.15 The CommandFactory Class

```
// ====================================================
//  CommandFactory: Produces Random Command objects
// ====================================================
class CommandFactory
{
  static Random randomizer = new Random();
  static public Command getCommand()
  {
    int index = Math.abs(randomizer.nextInt() % 52);
    switch (index)
    {
      case  7:
      case 11: return new CircleCommand();
      case  1:
      case  9:
      case 18:
```

```
        case 36: return new TriangleCommand();
        default: return new NumberCommand(index);
      }
    }
  }
```

Command Pattern: The General Form

Figure 11.12 shows the general form of the Command design pattern, and Table 11.5 summarizes it, using the terms from the *Design Patterns* book.

A variation of the Command design pattern is used by the AWT's event system. `ActionEvents`, for example, are generated by user-interface components, queued up, and dispatched to receivers. In the AWT, receiver information is not encapsulated within the message object because the message receiver is not unique. Many objects can register to receive `ActionEvents` from a single component. Therefore, references to registered objects are stored in a separate data structure. However, the spirit of the Command design pattern is evident.

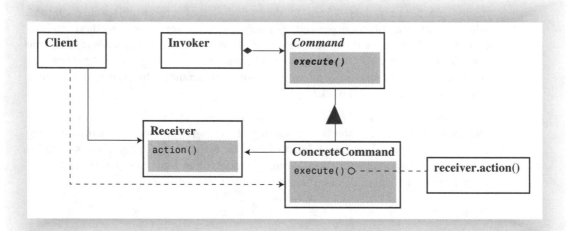

FIGURE 11.12

The Command pattern (general form)

TABLE 11.5
THE COMMAND PATTERN

Pattern name	Action, Transaction
Problem	How can a message be encapsulated as an object that can be stored or passed as an argument, allowing queues, message logging, undoable operations, and so on?
Solution	Create a set of objects, representing the range of possible actions, that implement a common interface. Store the target (that is, the receiver of the message) as a field of the concrete implementation.
Consequences	Decouples the identity of an operation from details of its performance.
	Commands are first-class objects (that is, objects that can be passed as parameters, manipulated, and so on).
	Commands can be inserted into a collection class to form macros.
	It's easy to add new commands.

OTHER DESIGN PATTERNS IN THE JAVA APIS

Several other design patterns are found in the Java APIs. Because you can look them up in the API documentation, they're not described in detail here. You would probably find it instructive to learn more about how they work and then draw class diagrams describing these additional design patterns.

The AWT organizes windows by using Containers (Applets, Frames, and Panels among them) to hold Components. The handy part is that every Container is also a Component. This means that a Container can hold other Containers, which in turn hold other Containers or Components. This design pattern is called *Composite*.

Another AWT design pattern is *Strategy*, which generalizes Command. Rather than encapsulating a single message, Strategy encapsulates a whole family of algorithms. The AWT LayoutManagers use the Strategy design pattern to give Containers the ability to regulate their layout. Just as Command lets a message vary without affecting Command's, Strategy lets a set of algorithms vary without affecting its client Containers.

A design pattern called *Adapter* plays an important role in AWT event handling. Each type of AWT event, such as the MouseMotion event, is associated with an interface that identifies the messages sent to event listeners. For the MouseMotion event, these include mouseClicked(), mouseEntered(), mouseExited(), mousePressed(), and mouseReleased(). If a class wishes to subscribe to MouseMotion events, it must implement methods to handle each of these messages. An adapter class eases this burden by providing a default implementation, that does nothing, for each message. By subclassing the proper adapter and overriding only the method(s) of interest, a listener can be spared the effort of implementing each of the five MouseMotion messages.

" A design pattern called Adapter plays an important role in AWT event handling. "

You'll meet one more design pattern, *Observer*, in Chapter 12, "Designing Concurrent Objects." The Observer design patterns solves the common problem of keeping a set of client objects aware of the current status of a server object.

Summary

Design patterns are proven solutions to problems that come up again and again in the design of object-oriented software. By familiarizing yourself with a range of design patterns, you can learn a great deal about designing object-oriented software.

The design patterns described in this chapter are Decorator, Factory Method, Singleton, Iterator, and Command. Several other patterns were mentioned. Many design patterns appear within the Java APIs, though the related classes are often called by names different than those most commonly used by people who study patterns.

Questions

For multiple-choice items, indicate all correct responses.

1. A design pattern may be described by giving its

   a. Name

   b. Problem

   c. Solution

   d. Consequences

2. Another name for the Decorator design pattern is _____.

3. The Decorator design pattern appears frequently in what Java package?

   a. `java.awt`

   b. `java.io`

   c. `java.lang`

   d. `java.util`

4. The Factory Method design pattern is useful when a client must create objects having different _____.

5. The _____ design pattern limits the number of instances a class can create.

6. The Iterator design pattern is known to Java programmers as _____, because of the corresponding interface of the `java.util` package.

7. Iterators are useful when dealing with _____ classes.

   a. Dynamic

   b. Collection

    c. Singleton

    d. Small

8. The two methods required by the `Enumeration` interface are

    a. `firstElement()`

    b. `hasMoreElements()`

    c. `nextElement()`

    d. `traverse()`

9. The Command design pattern _____ a message and its receiver in an object.

10. A(n) _____ class makes it easier to create a class that receives events representing AWT actions.

    a. Adapter

    b. Converter

    c. Mediator

    c. Transformer

Exercises

1. Write a class that uses a `Hashtable` to encapsulate references to singletons, so that they won't be garbage collected. Your class should include methods that let the client register a singleton using a `String` as a key and later fetch the singleton by presenting the same key.

2. Write a graphical application that includes menu bars and that uses the Command design pattern to decouple the user interface from the related actions. Your menu bar can include any menu items you choose, but it should include at least three items.

3. Modify the Scratcher applet to add scoring and the ability to collect secure micropayments from the Net. Set it up on your Web page and forward a portion of your earnings to the authors. As with all such enterprises, if you lose money, you're on your own.

4. Create an `Enumeration` object that iterates over the words of a text file. Do not use `StreamTokenizer` or `StringTokenizer` in your object. You may, however, consult the Java API documentation related to them.

5. Study the Java API documentation for the `LayoutManager` interface and the classes that implement it. Draw a class diagram that shows their interaction with `Containers`. When you're done, try to identify the pattern by picking out the parts of the diagram that might be reusable in some other context.

To Learn More

The following books will help you learn more about design patterns:

- Gamma, Erich, et al. *Design Patterns: Elements of Reusable Object-Oriented Software.* Reading, Massachusetts: Addison-Wesley, 1995.

  This is the book that has most widely disseminated the idea of design patterns—the seminal catalog by Eric Gamma, Richard Helm, Ralph Johnson, and John Vlissides. This is one of the first, and one of the best, books on design patterns. The examples are mostly in C++, but should be easily translated by an average Java programmer.

- Pree, Wolfgang. *Design Patterns for Object-Oriented Software Development.* New York, New York: ACM Press Books, 1995.

  This is a book that attempts to provide an overview of different approaches to design patterns within the object-oriented software development community. Pree argues for even higher-level abstractions, which he calls meta-patterns, and he presents seven of them. This book is denser and requires much more study than Gamma's book.

- Gabriel, Richard P. *Patterns of Software: Tales from the Software Community.* New York, New York: Oxford University Press, 1996.

  If you are interested in the philosophy behind design patterns, or if you just want to read a really interesting book by a really great writer, this book is highly recommended. Not technical in the same way that the previously mentioned books are, Gabriel's book is a combination of memoir, opinion, and insightful essay.

12

Designing Concurrent Objects

Did you ever have a boss who seemed more concerned about your use of time than his or her own? You know, the kind of boss who checks your time sheet 50 times before signing it, the kind who wonders why you made so little progress on the Alpha project last week—the week you worked 25 hours of overtime helping rescue the Zed project. "So, what's the problem?" such a boss asks, "Can't you do two things at once?"

Well, of course, you can't. But, by working rapidly and switching regularly from one task to another, you can create the illusion of simultaneously working on multiple tasks. This illusion comes unraveled, however, when you have so much to do that there simply aren't enough hours in a 24-hour day.

Modern computers are similar. Most of them can create the illusion of working on multiple tasks at the same time, even though they're not really capable of that feat. A few so-called multiprocessor systems actually do have multiple CPUs and therefore can make the illusion come true. But, so far, multiprocessor systems account for only a small minority of computers in use.

Still, whether it's illusion or reality, the ability to seem to do multiple things at once is useful. You want your computer to be able to display an animated GIF file and play a sound clip while you download your e-mail, don't you? Only, don't be like your boss and complain that the computer is too slow merely because it takes a little longer to download your e-mail with all the razzle-dazzle multimedia going on. Or, if the delay annoys you, upgrade your system.

In this chapter you will learn:

- How the Java API supports programming with threads

- How threads can help you write better programs

- How to draw interaction diagrams that show how threads interact

- How to design programs to avoid special problems that can affect threaded programs

- How to use the `Observable` class and the `Observer` interface to coordinate actions between, or among, objects

- How to generalize the `Observable`/`Observer` pattern to include concurrency

Introduction to Concurrency

Java and its Application Programming Interfaces (APIs) provide high-quality support for *concurrent programs*, programs that work simultaneously on multiple tasks, or that appear to do so. Many object-oriented languages, including C++, lack built-in support for concurrent programming. This is unfortunate because concurrent programming helps you model the real world more accurately. After all, real objects don't always take turns interacting with one another; they act *asynchronously*. Walk onto a kindergarten playground and you'll see simultaneous, asynchronous action all around you. But don't think such action is limited to active, young children; this same sort of action is characteristic of a business office or a stock exchange.

Why would anyone design an object-oriented language without facilities for writing concurrent programs? There are many possible reasons, some of them technical. But, recall that one way we deal with complexity is by simplification. The synchronous perspective—in which activity is controlled and directed—is simpler than the asynchronous perspective—in which all the participants act independently. That's why we have air traffic control systems and symphony orchestra leaders. Putting someone in charge makes it easier for everyone's efforts to fit together.

But, just as there is jazz music, there are patterns of collaboration that do not depend upon the efforts of an "orchestra leader." This is not to say that such processes are chaotic, though to the ears of some they might be. Instead, leadership in such processes is dynamic, rather than static. First the guitarist picks up the theme, and the other players hang back. Soon the guitarist tires, and the drummer picks up the theme, and so on. Rather than following a rigid orchestral score, the musicians yield to, and express, their moods as they play.

If you prepared an object model of a musical group, would you limit the model to representing only orchestral patterns of music, or would you want the model to be capable of representing the more general case? Java lets you have it either way.

REASONS FOR USING THREADS

Java supports concurrent programs in two ways. First, you can write separate programs and run them simultaneously as separate processes. Under Microsoft Windows, for example, you can open two command windows and use the Java interpreter to run a different Java program in each. The two programs can even communicate with one another by using files, pipes, or other means. This kind of concurrent programming is provided by almost every programming language.

A second way that Java supports concurrent programs is through the facilities of the `java.lang.Thread` class, which allows the programmer to create and control *threads*. You can think of a thread as a program counter that, like a finger on a program listing, points to the next instruction to be executed within some method of some object. A thread is a flow of control within a program.

Processes, too, have program counters. What then, you ask, is the difference between a process and a thread? Whereas two processes each have distinct address spaces and resources, two threads can share them. Say you have a Java object and two distinct threads are executing statements within its methods. Each thread has access to the fields of the object and can get their values, set their values, or send them messages (the latter only if they're objects, of course). Local variables are not shared; each thread gets its own copy of the local variables of any method it executes.

Because threads share fields, threads can easily exchange information. They often need no external means of communication such as a file or pipe. Threads can be asynchronous, but still be conveniently "in touch." So, when necessary, they can synchronize with one another. The drummer object won't keep banging out the tempo when the other musician objects long ago called it a day. Figure 12.1 illustrates the distinction between processes and threads.

As mentioned, threads are handy when you're writing a program that needs to do, or seem to do, several things at once. Here are some more specific reasons for using threads:

- **Improved response to events:** By assigning a thread to each event source or task, and prioritizing the threads, you might be able to make your programs more responsive because low-priority tasks will yield to high-priority tasks.

- **Control of thread execution:** Java's APIs give you considerable control over thread execution. You can change the execution priority of a thread, suspend it, resume it, stop it, and so on.

- **Parallel computing:** If you're among the lucky few who use multiprocessor computers, you can use Java's threads to keep all your CPUs busy, thereby earning a greater return on your hardware investment.

- **Inherent concurrency in Java itself:** Many of Java's objects, particularly the Abstract Window Toolkit (AWT) objects, use threads. Even if you're not interested in writing threaded programs, most Java programs you write will probably be threaded.

" You can think of a thread as a program counter that, like a finger on a program listing, points to the next instruction to be executed."

FIGURE 12.1
Processes and threads distinguished

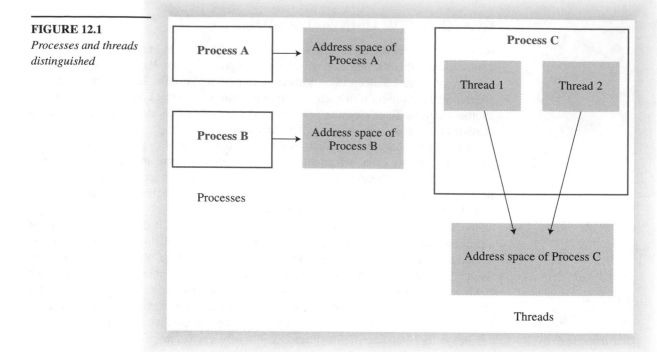

ISSUES IN USING THREADS

The old saying that "you can't get something for nothing" seems true more often than not. Certainly, it's true of using threads in your Java programs. Threaded programs let you write programs containing bugs of several sorts that you'll never see in a non-threaded program. If logic errors and off-by-one-errors were the ubiquitous programming errors of the 20th century, thread-related errors might well turn out to be the programming errors of the 21st century. (Let's hope that we soon succeed in significantly reducing the number of 20th-century bugs in our programs, lest we find ourselves with all disadvantages of both sorts of bugs.)

Among the issues raised by writing threaded programs are the following:

- **Safety:** Just like cars careening down the turnpike, threads can "collide" and attempt to simultaneously access or modify a field. Without due attention to program design, one or the other thread can get (or often worse, set) an invalid value.

- **Liveness:** Ever have the experience of waiting for a friend to call you, only to find out later that your friend was waiting for you to call? This can happen to threads as well. Again, careful design can reduce the likelihood that this will occur.

> *Threaded programs let you write programs containing bugs of several sorts that you'll never see in a non-threaded program.*

🔹 **Nondeterminism:** When you run a nonthreaded program over and over, things happen in exactly the same order each time. Not so for a threaded program. Java makes no guarantees concerning the order of execution of *unsynchronized* threads. (You'll read more about synchronization later in this chapter.) If your program's results depend on the order in which its threads execute, the results can be different each time you run the program. This can greatly complicate troubleshooting.

🔹 **Performance:** You might have decided to write your program as a threaded program because you hoped to maximize performance. Using threads, however, does not automatically improve performance. As the saying goes, "your mileage may vary." The performance of a threaded program might be poorer than that of a nonthreaded program, due to the overhead involved in creating threads, switching context between threads, synchronizing threads, and so on.

JAVA'S SUPPORT FOR THREADS

This chapter focuses on design issues related to threads. A familiarity with the Java API facilities that support threads is helpful for understanding these issues; unfortunately, it is not possible to present such an introduction in this chapter without compromising the attention paid to design issues. Here are the parts of the Java API that concern the designer and programmer of threaded programs:

🔹 The `java.lang.Thread` class

🔹 The `java.lang.Runnable` interface

🔹 The Java language keywords `synchronized` and `volatile`

🔹 The `wait()`, `notify()`, and `notifyAll()` methods of the `java.lang.Object` class

To learn more about these facilities, you can consult the online documentation that accompanies the JDK. Alternatively, you might take a look at Chapter 16 of our book *Object-Oriented Programming in Java* (The Waite Group Press, 1997), which provides such an introduction, or at *The Java Language Specification* by James Gosling, Bill Joy, and Guy Steele (Addison-Wesley, 1996), which covers Java's thread facilities comprehensively.

THE `CipherServer` SAMPLE PROGRAM

The `CipherServer` program shows how a Java program can use threads to improve response time. `CipherServer` is a simple network-based server that echoes text sent to it over a TCP/IP socket connection. Of course, with an application named `CipherServer` you'd expect some sort of cryptographic translation of the message sent to the server. As written however, `CipherServer` uses the simplest code of all, plain text. Obviously, that's not very secure. However, the program is easily modified to accommodate more sophisticated cipher algorithms. For greater security, you might want to shift any lowercase letters in the message text to uppercase, and vice versa. Or, you can substitute that character *1* for the letter *a*, the character *2* for the letter *b*, and so on. The security of your cipher is limited only by your imagination.

The `CipherServer` Class

The `CipherServer` class is shown in Listing 12.1. Its `main()` method, which is a `static` method, creates a `CipherServer` instance and sends it the `start()` message. One of Java's little peculiarities is that invoking the `start()` message on an object that extends the `Thread` class (or that implements the `Runnable` interface) causes execution of the `run()` method of the object as a new thread. The similarly named `Applet.start()` method, by the way, has nothing to do with `Thread.start()`. They simply share the same name.

When a `CipherServer` instance starts up, it opens a `ServerSocket` (designated by a port number) on which it will listen for requests from clients. Sending an `accept()` message to the `ServerSocket` initiates listening. The thread blocks (that is, it suspends execution) until the `ServerSocket`'s `accept()` method returns, indicating that a client request has been received. When the method returns, it provides a `Socket` object, which the server and client use to hold a private conversation. That way, their conversation won't get in the way of other clients who want to make requests of the server.

Setting aside a socket for the client/server conversation profits nothing, however, unless the server is threaded. Until another `accept()` message is sent to the `ServerSocket`, further client requests will not be handled. `CipherServer`, therefore, immediately uses the `Socket` to create a `Connection` object, which runs as a thread that handles further business between the client and server. It then loops and sends the `accept()` method, rapidly preparing itself to handle another client request.

```
Listing 12.1 The CipherServer Class
//  CipherServer.java

import java.net.*;
import java.io.*;

public class CipherServer
{
  //  ==========================================
  //       MAIN METHOD
  //  ==========================================
  public static void main(String args[])
  {
    new CipherServer().run();
  }

  //  ==========================================
  //          CONSTRUCTORS
```

```
//   ===========================================
public CipherServer()
{
  try
  {
    theServerSocket  = new ServerSocket(thePort);
  }
  catch (IOException io)
  {
    System.err.println("Socket error:  terminating");
    System.exit(1);
  }
}

//   ===========================================
//        IMPLEMENT RUNNABLE
//   ===========================================
public void run()
{
  try
  {
    System.out.println("CipherServer is open for business.");

    while (true)
    {
      Socket theSocket = theServerSocket.accept();
      System.out.println("A client has requested service.");
      Connection connection = new Connection(theSocket);
    }
  }
  catch (IOException io)
  {
    System.err.println("Socket error:  terminating");
    System.exit(1);
  }
}

//   ===========================================
//        CLASS AND OBJECT ATTRIBUTES
//   ===========================================
private final static int thePort = 1234;
private ServerSocket theServerSocket;
}
```

The Connection Class

Listing 12.2 shows the Connection class, which responds to requests sent by a client that has established a connection with the server. Its first task is to create a BufferedReader and a PrintWriter that are used, respectively, to read data from the client and write data to the client, via the socket passed by the CipherServer object to the Connection constructor. These statements are executed in the same thread that sends the accept() message.

Listing 12.2 The Connection Class

```java
class Connection extends Thread
{
  //  =============================================
  //          CONSTRUCTORS
  //  =============================================
  public Connection(Socket socket)
  {
    try
    {
      theSocket = socket;

      in  = new BufferedReader(
              new InputStreamReader(
                  theSocket.getInputStream())));

      out = new PrintWriter(
              new OutputStreamWriter(
                  theSocket.getOutputStream()), true);
      start();
    }
    catch (IOException io)
    {
      System.err.println("Socket error:  terminating");
      System.exit(1);
    }
  }

  //  =============================================
  //          IMPLEMENT RUNNABLE
  //  =============================================
  public void run()
  {
    int port = 0;
    try
    {
      port = theSocket.getPort();

      System.out.println("Client assigned to port "+port+".");
      out.println("Server ready.");

      while (true)
      {
        String line = in.readLine();
        if (line == null)
          break;

        System.out.println("port "+ port +" sent "+ line +".");
        out.println("You sent " + line + ".");
      }

      in.close();
      out.close();
      theSocket.close();
    }
    catch (IOException io)
    {
```

```
        System.err.println("Client on port " + port +
                            " has disconnected.");
    }
}

//  ============================================
//      CLASS AND OBJECT ATTRIBUTES
//  ============================================
private Socket          theSocket;
private BufferedReader  in;
private PrintWriter     out;

}
```

The run() method of the Connection class includes the statements executed as part of the special thread allocated to a Connection instance. Apart from some statements that report progress (to aid in troubleshooting network connection problems), the main work of the run() method is done in an endless while loop. This loop simply reads lines of data (terminated by a platform-dependent end-of-line sequence) from the client and writes them back. It is here that you should insert some additional code that increases the limited protection afforded by this dumbest-of-all ciphers.

The loop continues until the readLine() method returns null, indicating that the client has closed the connection or has otherwise been disconnected. When this occurs, the Reader and Writer are closed, along with the Socket, and the thread terminates.

The significant thing about CipherServer, apart from its incredibly poor encryption, is its use of a distinct thread for each client connection. This enables CipherServer to quickly re-issue the important accept() message that readies it to handle the next client requesting a connection.

> *" The significant thing about CipherServer, apart from its incredibly poor encryption, is its use of a distinct thread for each client connection. "*

The CipherClient Class

To see how things look from the client's side of the conversation, take a look at Listing 12.3, which shows the CipherClient class. Whereas CipherServer is written as an application, because it has little need for a graphical user interface, CipherClient is written as an applet. Much of the code included in CipherClient is devoted to handling user input, which is passed to CipherServer, and output returned by CipherServer, which is displayed to the user.

```
Listing 12.3 The CipherClient Class
//  CipherClient.java

import java.awt.*;
import java.awt.event.*;
import java.applet.*;
import java.net.*;
import java.io.*;

public class CipherClient extends Applet
{
```

```
//   ============================================
//        APPLET METHODS
//   ============================================

/*  --Initialization---------------- */
public void init()
{
  try
  {
    setLayout(new BorderLayout());

    add( theField, "North" );
    add( theArea,  "Center" );
    theArea.setEditable(false);
    setVisible(true);

    theSource = new StreamSource(theField);
    theSink   = new StreamSink(theArea);

    String host = getCodeBase().getHost();
    theSocket   = new Socket( host, thePort );

    theReader  = new BufferedReader(
                   new InputStreamReader(
                     theSocket.getInputStream ()));
    theWriter  = new PrintWriter(
                   new OutputStreamWriter(
                     theSocket.getOutputStream()), true);

    theInputCoupler  = new StreamCoupler(
                         new BufferedReader(theSource),
                           theWriter);
    theOutputCoupler = new StreamCoupler(theReader,
                         new PrintWriter(theSink));

    theInputCoupler. start();
    theOutputCoupler.start();
  }
  catch (IOException io) { ; }
}

/*  --Starting and Stopping---------- */
public void stop()
{
  try
  {
    theSource.close();
    theSink.close();
    theReader.close();
    theWriter.close();
    theSocket.close();
  }
  catch (IOException io) { ; }
}

//   ============================================
//        CLASS AND OBJECT ATTRIBUTES
```

```
    //  ============================================

    private TextField      theField  = new TextField();
    private TextArea       theArea   = new TextArea();

    private StreamSource   theSource = null;
    private StreamSink      theSink   = null;

    private int            thePort   = 1234;
    private Socket         theSocket = null;
    private BufferedReader theReader = null;
    private PrintWriter    theWriter = null;

    private StreamCoupler  theInputCoupler  = null;
    private StreamCoupler  theOutputCoupler = null;
}
```

Some special classes are used to facilitate the input and output. A `StreamSource` object presents information typed by the user into a `TextField` as a `Reader`. This `Reader` is used by `CipherClient` as its input source. A `StreamSink` object presents information written to its `Writer` as lines of text within a `TextArea`. This `Writer` is used by `CipherClient` as its output sink (that is, `CipherClient` writes to the `Writer`). Two `StreamCouplers` are used, one to couple the output typed by the user and fed through the `StreamSource` to the server (via the `Socket`), and another to couple the input received from the server to the `StreamSink`, so it can be viewed by the user. Figure 12.2 shows how this arrangement works.

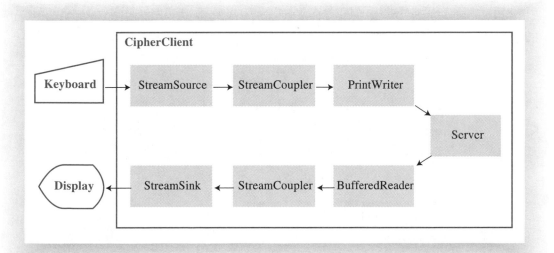

FIGURE 12.2

Data flow in the
CipherClient applet

The `StreamSource` and `StreamSink` Classes

Listing 12.4 shows the `StreamSource` class, which presents data keyed by the user into a `TextField` as a `Reader`. The class uses a `Pipe` as a buffer to store data entered via the `TextField` but not yet requested from the `Reader`. The functions provided by the `StreamSource` class are general and are therefore potentially reusable; hence they were encapsulated within a separate class, rather than included with `CipherClient`.

```java
Listing 12.4 The StreamSource Class

// StreamSource.java

import java.io.*;
import java.awt.*;
import java.awt.event.*;

public class StreamSource extends      Reader
                          implements  ActionListener
{
  // ==========================================
  //        CONSTRUCTORS
  // ==========================================
  public StreamSource(TextField textfield) throws IOException
  {
    theTextField = textfield;
    theInputPipe.connect(theOutputPipe);
    theTextField.addActionListener(this);
  }


  // ==========================================
  //        PUBLIC INTERFACE
  // ==========================================

  /* --Mutators--------------------- */
  public synchronized int read( char[] buffer,
                                int offset,
                                int len) throws IOException
  {
    int avail = theInputPipe.available();
    if (avail == 0)
      return 0;
    if (avail > len)
      avail = len;

    for (int i = 0; i < avail; i++)
    {
      char c = (char) theInputPipe.read();
      buffer[offset] = c;
      //System.out.println("Read " + c + " from pipe");
      offset++;
    }
    return avail;
  }

  public synchronized void close() throws IOException
  {
```

```
      theTextField.removeActionListener(this);
      theTextField.setEnabled(false);

      theInputPipe. close();
      theOutputPipe.close();
    }

    // ==========================================
    //        IMPLEMENTS ACTIONLISTENER
    // ==========================================
    public void actionPerformed(ActionEvent event)
    {
      try
      {
        String  line = theTextField.getText();
        theTextField.setText("");

        int     len  = line.length();
        byte [] bytes = line.getBytes();

        theOutputPipe.write(bytes, 0, len);
        theOutputPipe.write('\n');
        //System.out.println("Wrote data to pipe");
      }
      catch (IOException io) { ; }
    }

    // ==========================================
    //        CLASS AND OBJECT ATTRIBUTES
    // ==========================================
    private TextField         theTextField;
    private PipedInputStream   theInputPipe =
                                  new PipedInputStream();
    private PipedOutputStream theOutputPipe =
                                  new PipedOutputStream();
}
```

Listing 12.5 shows StreamSink, which is functionally the mirror image of the StreamSource class. StreamSink, however, is much simpler because output can be written immediately when provided—there is no need to buffer it as input from StreamSource's TextField had to be.

Listing 12.5 The StreamSink Class

```
import java.io.*;
import java.awt.*;
import java.awt.event.*;

public class StreamSink extends Writer
{
  // ==========================================
  //        CONSTRUCTORS
  // ==========================================
  public StreamSink(TextArea textarea)
  {
```

```
    theTextArea = textarea;
  }

  //   ==========================================
  //        PUBLIC INTERFACE
  //   ==========================================

  /*   --Mutators---------------------- */
  public synchronized void write( char[] chars,
                                  int offset,
                                  int len) throws IOException
  {
    theTextArea.append(new String(chars, offset, len));
  }

  public synchronized void flush() throws IOException
  {
    // null
  }

  public synchronized void close() throws IOException
  {
    theTextArea.setEnabled(false);
  }

  //   ==========================================
  //        CLASS AND OBJECT ATTRIBUTES
  //   ==========================================
  private TextArea theTextArea;

}
```

The `StreamCoupler` Class

Listing 12.6 shows the `StreamCoupler` class, which is also a potentially reusable class.
A `StreamCoupler` object runs as a thread, continually trying to read its input. When
input arrives, it is immediately written to the `StreamCoupler`'s output, and the process
repeats.

```
Listing 12.6 The StreamCoupler Class
//  StreamCoupler.java

import java.io.*;

public class StreamCoupler extends Thread
{
  //   ==========================================
  //        CONSTRUCTORS
  //   ==========================================
  public StreamCoupler(BufferedReader in, PrintWriter out)
  {
    theInput  = in;
    theOutput = out;
  }

  //   ==========================================
```

```
//      IMPLEMENT RUNNABLE
// ==========================================
public void run()
{
  try
  {
    while (true)
    {
      String line = theInput.readLine();
      if (line == null)
        break;
      //System.out.println("Coupler read " + line);

      theOutput.println(line);
    }
    System.out.println("Coupler found EOF");
    theInput .close();
    theOutput.close();
  }
  catch (IOException io) { System.out.println(io); }
}

// ==========================================
//      CLASS AND OBJECT ATTRIBUTES
// ==========================================
private BufferedReader theInput;
private PrintWriter    theOutput;
}
```

One aspect of StreamCoupler's design handicaps its reuse within new programs. As
you see, the input-output statements within its run() method can throw
IOExceptions. Ideally these would be passed on to the client, who could handle them
in a way appropriate to the problem domain. This would be done by eliminating the
try-catch block and revising the method header to read:

```
public void run() throws IOException
```

This however, cannot be done, because the Thread.run() method in
StreamCoupler's superclass does not throw IOExceptions. Consequently,
StreamCoupler.run() is not allowed to throw them and must handle them itself,
rather than deferring to its client. In the case of the CipherClient program, error handling is not important. So, the run() method simply returns, terminating the thread
when an error occurs. Chapter 17, "Designing with Class Libraries," revisits error handling within reusable classes in a more general context.

Listing 12.7 shows the HTML file used to execute the CipherClient applet.

Listing 12.7 Cipher.html

```
<HTML>

<HEAD>
<TITLE>Cipher.html</TITLE>
</HEAD>

<BODY>
```

```
<APPLET CODE=CipherClient HEIGHT=100 WIDTH=200>
</APPLET>

<APPLET CODE=CipherClient HEIGHT=100 WIDTH=200>
</APPLET>

</BODY>
</HTML>
```

Figure 12.3 shows the execution of the CipherServer application.

Figure 12.4 shows the execution of the CipherClient applet. When running the program, CipherServer should be started before CipherClient. To stop CipherServer, just press Ctrl+C in the window used to run it.

Notations for Concurrent Objects

Diagrams are one of the most helpful tools during design. Just as your designs model the real world, diagrams model your design. By representing a design in simpler, diagrammatic form, applying the principle of abstraction, you're able to focus on relevant issues and, at least for the moment, ignore the rest. Moreover, it's easier, faster, and cheaper to change a diagram than to change a completed software program. Or, at least, it should be.

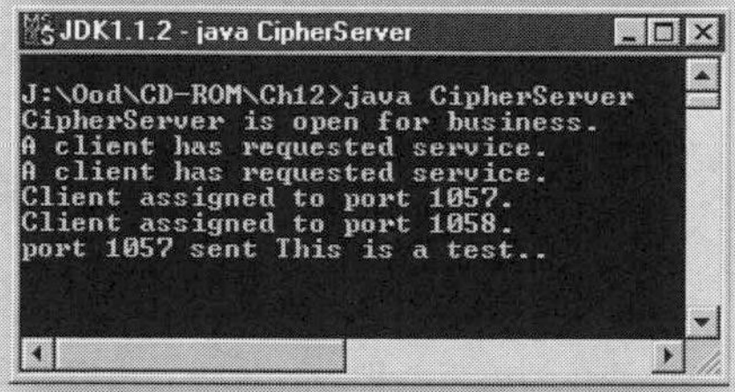

FIGURE 12.3
Starting the
CipherServer
application

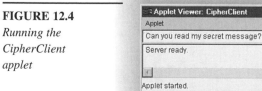

FIGURE 12.4
Running the
CipherClient
applet

" Just as your designs model the real world, diagrams model your design. "

Some designers seem to believe that "if a little is good, a lot is better." Creating too many diagrams and spending too much time making them too "pretty" can undercut your whole purpose in using them: to quickly, efficiently, and adequately design a system. One problem that afflicts many of the computer-aided design tools available is that they don't make the job easier; they simply make the output look better.

THE ADVANTAGE OF SIMPLICITY

If you're working with an automated design tool and find yourself spending hour after hour tweaking diagram after diagram, try working with pencil and paper or, better yet, with a large whiteboard. You might find—surprise—that it takes less time to do the job manually. If your boss insists that you use the tool, you can enter the diagrams once your sketches have reached the point that you don't expect any remaining changes to be a burden. Meanwhile, survey the Web for alternative tools that you might find easier to use. Also, check out the programs on the CD-ROM included with this book.

" One problem that afflicts many of the computer-aided design tools available is that they don't make the job easier; they simply make the output look better. "

An important diagram for designs involving threads is the interaction diagram. Figure 12.5 shows an interaction diagram, drawn in a style resembling that recommended by Grady Booch in his book, *Object-Oriented Analysis and Design with Applications, 2nd Ed.* (Benjamin/Cummings, 1994).

The diagram depicts the interactions among the objects of the `Cipher` program. Each object is drawn at the head of a column. The `CipherServer` object, drawn at the upper left of the page, initiates the interactions by sending a `ServerSocket()` constructor message to the `ServerSocket` class. When the constructor completes its work, the `CipherServer` then sends an `accept()` message to the newborn `ServerSocket`. Again, the `CipherSever` blocks, pending completion of the message handling. This, as described earlier, occurs when a client requests service. In response, the `CipherServer` sends a `Connection()` constructor message to the `Connection` class.

The `Connection` object sends constructor messages to the `BufferedReader` and `PrintWriter` classes. It's important to notice that all this is done in the same thread (that is, the same flow of control) that originally sent the `accept()` message to the `ServerSocket`.

Things change at this point, however. The `Connection` next sends a `start()` message to itself. This causes the statements of `Connection.run()` to commence execution in a new thread, even as the original thread returns control to the `ServerSocket` object, which issues a new `accept()`. The remaining part of the diagram presents no special problems of interpretation.

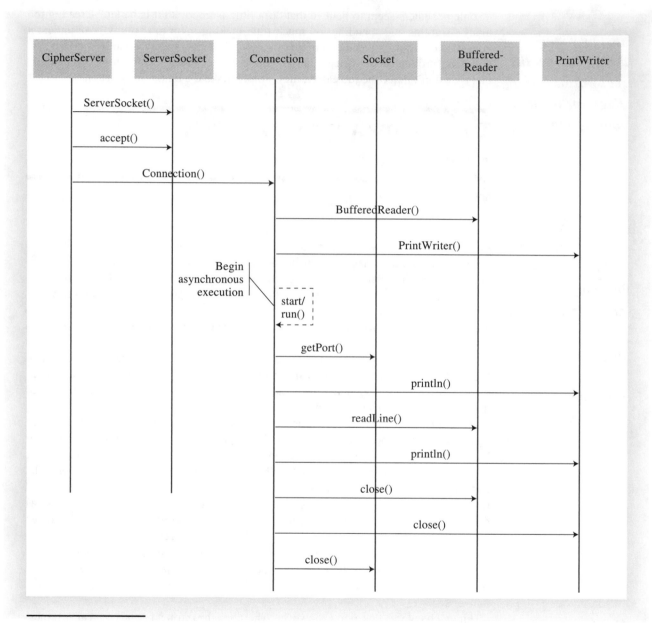

FIGURE 12.5

Booch-style interaction diagram

Another form of the Booch-style interaction diagram, shown in Figure 12.6, widens each vertical line during intervals in which the corresponding object is active. This can make the distinction between nonthreaded and threaded execution easier to discern: In nonthreaded execution no two objects will have wide (active) lines at the same time (that is, at the same vertical distance from the top of the diagram). Threaded programs, in contrast, can have two or more objects that are simultaneously active. The lines of their bars will all be wide at the same time.

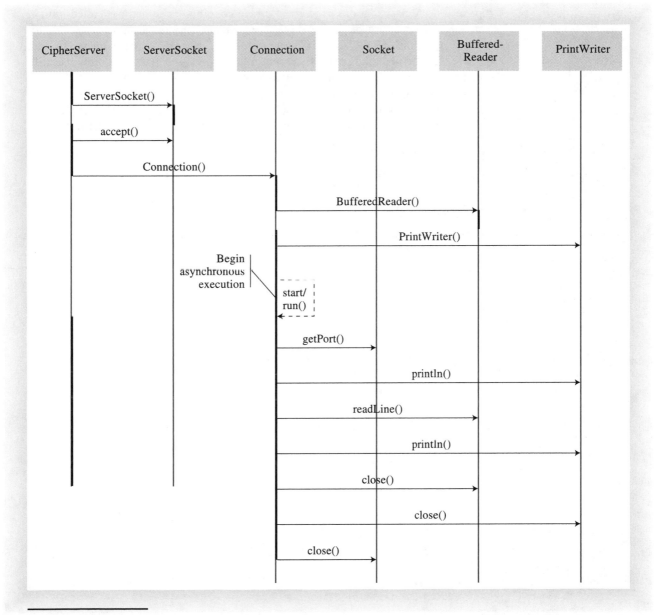

FIGURE 12.6

Alternative style interaction diagram

Races Violate Safety

As previously mentioned, using threads creates whole new categories of bugs that can infest your program. Programs that run concurrently can experience so-called race conditions that corrupt the fields of methods or cause accessor methods to return corrupt results. A class that can experience a race condition is sometimes called *unsafe*. You might have heard of device drivers or software programs that are not *thread-safe*. Sadly, some JDBC drivers written for use by Java programmers are not thread-safe. The potential result is a program that reports incorrect data or, worse still, one that writes incorrect data to the database.

To see how this can happen, take a look at Listing 12.8, which shows the HensTeeth class. HensTeeth is an applet that creates a ShapeShifter object and then continually and asynchronously probes the new object, querying its species and number of teeth.

Listing 12.8 The HensTeeth Class

```
//  HensTeeth.java

import java.applet.*;
import java.awt.*;

public class HensTeeth extends Applet implements Runnable
{
  //  =========================================
  //         APPLET METHODS
  //  =========================================
  /*  --Initialization---------------- */
  public void init()
  {
    setLayout(new BorderLayout());
    add(theArea, "Center");
    theArea.setEditable(false);
  }

  /*  --Starting and Stopping---------- */
  public void start()
  {
    new Thread(this).start();
  }

  public void stop()
  {
    System.out.println("Done ...");
  }

  //  =========================================
  //         IMPLEMENT RUNNABLE
  //  =========================================
  public void run()
  {
    theShifter.start();
    System.out.println("Searching ...");
```

```
    while (true)
    {
      if (theShifter.getSpecies() == theShifter.HEN
          && theShifter.getNumberOfTeeth() > 0)
      {
        System.out.println("Hens really DO have teeth!");
        theArea.append("Hens really DO have teeth!\n");
      }
    }
  }

  // ==========================================
  //       CLASS AND OBJECT ATTRIBUTES
  // ==========================================
  private ShapeShifter theShifter = new ShapeShifter();
  private TextArea theArea = new TextArea(10, 32);
}
```

Listing 12.9 shows the `ShaperShifter` class, which uses a thread to shift its species continually from horse to hen, and back again. As the `ShapeShifter` changes species, it also changes its number of teeth accordingly. Horses, on average, have about 38 teeth, but hens have no teeth at all.

Listing 12.9 The ShapeShifter Class

```
class ShapeShifter extends Thread
{
  // ------------------------------------------
  //       PUBLIC INTERFACE
  // ==========================================

  /* --Accessors-------------------- */
  public int getSpecies()
  {
    return theSpecies;
  }

  public int getNumberOfTeeth()
  {
    return theNumberOfTeeth;
  }

  // ==========================================
  //       IMPLEMENT RUNNABLE
  // ==========================================
  public void run()
  {
    while (true)
    {
      switch (theSpecies)
      {
        case HORSE:
          theSpecies = HEN;
```

```
                theNumberOfTeeth = HEN_TEETH;
                break;

            case HEN:
                theSpecies = HORSE;
                theNumberOfTeeth = HORSE_TEETH;
                break;
        }
      }
    }

    // =========================================
    //      CLASS AND OBJECT ATTRIBUTES
    // =========================================
    private int theSpecies = HORSE;
    private int theNumberOfTeeth = HORSE_TEETH;

    private static final int HORSE_TEETH = 38;
    private static final int HEN_TEETH   = 0;
    private static final int DELAY = 100;

    public static final int HORSE = 1;
    public static final int HEN   = 2;
}
```

You might expect the loop in `HensTeeth` to iterate forever, which it will do unless it discovers a toothed hen. Use the HTML file shown in Listing 12.10 and run the applet, or look ahead to Figure 12.7 to see what actually happens.

Listing 12.10 HensTeeth.html

```
<HTML>

<HEAD>
<TITLE>HensTeeth.html</TITLE>
</HEAD>

<BODY>
<H1>Do Hens Have Teeth? </H1>
<APPLET CODE=HensTeeth HEIGHT=100 WIDTH=300>
</APPLET>

</BODY>
</HTML>
```

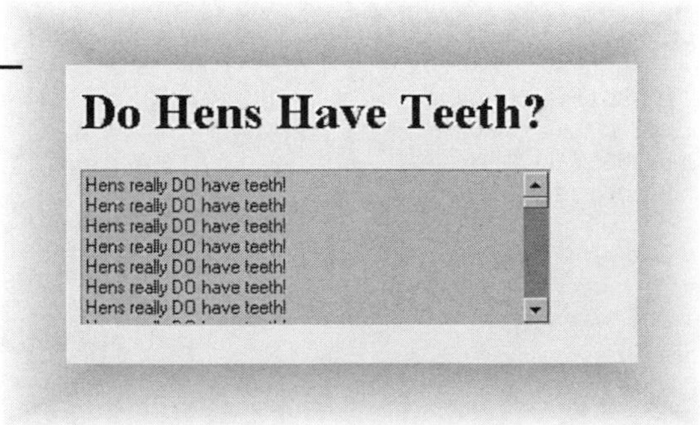

FIGURE 12.7
Running the HensTeeth applet

Do Hens Have Teeth?

Hens really DO have teeth!
Hens really DO have teeth!
Hens really DO have teeth!
Hens really DO have teeth!
Hens really DO have teeth!
Hens really DO have teeth!
Hens really DO have teeth!

Surprised? It appears that hens really *do* have teeth. How does this occur? The problem is that the ShapeShifter changes its state *non-atomically*—that is, in two distinct operations: first the species and then the number of teeth. It's possible, therefore, for the HensTeeth applet to access ShapeShifter's state information just after the species has been changed, but before the corresponding change is made to the number of teeth. The result: hen's teeth.

Now, your computer might not duplicate the results shown above. Variations in the speed at which instructions are executed and in the way the operating system schedules thread execution can affect the result. But, you *do* want your program to run on anyone's computer, not just your own, don't you? The window during which the data is inconsistent is a tiny one: Two adjacent statements change the state. If your computer seems to run the program fine, just put a call to Thread.sleep() between each pair of statements that updates the state, like this:

```
case HORSE:
    theSpecies = HEN;
    Thread.sleep(1000);
    theNumberOfTeeth = HEN_TEETH;
    break;

case HEN:
    theSpecies = HORSE;
    Thread.sleep(1000);
    theNumberOfTeeth = HORSE_TEETH;
    break;
```

You'll soon be seeing hen's teeth.

Strategies for Avoiding Race Conditions

Hopefully, you're convinced that avoiding race conditions is a worthwhile pursuit. If so, this section will provide some help toward that end.

The race condition in ShapeShifter occurs because of a non-atomic update. Most Java operations are atomic—they cannot be interrupted in midstream. You don't have to worry that someone will read the high-order byte of an int while your program is setting the low-order byte. But, notice the very important word *most*. A major exception is any operation on a long or a double; operations on these types are *not* guaranteed to be atomic and can result in hen's teeth. The more common way that race conditions arise, however, is through multistatement updates, like those of ShapeShifter. Whenever a partially complete multistatement update leaves an object (or class) in a state that does not satisfy the class invariants, the potential for a race condition exists.

How can you design and write programs that cannot be victimized by race conditions? Well, an equally fair question is, "How do you design and write programs that are free of logic errors?" Or, more generally, "How do you avoid mistakes?"

> *Just as there is no patented formula for avoiding mistakes, there is no guaranteed way to avoid race conditions.*

> *Unfortunately, other things being equal, the more methods that are* `synchronized`, *the greater is the chance of a deadlock.*

Just as there is no patented formula for avoiding mistakes, there is no guaranteed way to avoid race conditions. However, there are some useful strategies:

- **Avoid change:** Some methods don't really need to change an object's state at all. Every place you avoid changing state is one fewer potential source of race conditions. Where you can, use local copies of values to avoid changing the fields of an object or class.

- **Dynamically ensure exclusive access:** You can't write every method in a way that avoids changing fields. Sometimes, methods *must* update the state of the containing object. There, you can use the `synchronized` keyword to prevent multiple threads from accessing a method, or critical section of a method, simultaneously. The next section shows you how to use `synchronized` methods and `synchronized` statements. The downside of using `synchronized` is that, by using it, you trade one problem (safety, due to race conditions) for another (deadlocks and other problems, due to liveness failures). You'll learn about deadlocks in a subsequent section.

- **Structurally ensure exclusive access:** An extreme measure that can sometimes be useful is to tag *every* method of a class with the keyword `synchronized`. Then, as long as the class contains no fields that can be directly accessed without using accessor or mutator methods, race conditions are ruled out. Unfortunately, other things being equal, the more methods and statements that are `synchronized`, the greater is the chance of a deadlock.

Synchronized Methods and Statements

Java's `synchronized` keyword can be used in either of two ways: to synchronize a statement or to synchronize an entire method. The simpler alternative is to synchronize an entire method. To synchronize a method, you simply add the keyword `synchronized` as part of the method header, just before the return data type, like this:

```
public synchronized void theMethod()
{
    // statements of method
}
```

A synchronized method can be executed by only a single thread at a time. If a thread is executing the method, any other thread needing to execute the method will simply wait its turn.

How does this work? Each Java object has an invisible one-bit field known as its "monitor." The monitor controls access to the object: It is set whenever a synchronized method is executing. Once it is set, other synchronized methods of the object must wait until the bit has been reset before they can execute. The monitor is said to be "unavailable" (set) or "available" (reset). When the monitor is unavailable a thread must wait before executing a synchronized method. When the monitor becomes available, the thread can proceed. But first, it sets the monitor to unavailable so that other threads attempting to access the method will be blocked. When the thread has finished executing the method, it resets the monitor to available.

Several methods for working with an object's monitor are provided by the `Object` class. These are summarized in Table 12.1.

TABLE 12.1
KEY THREAD-RELATED METHODS OF THE `Object` CLASS

Method Header	Function
`void notify()`	Wakes up a single thread waiting on the `Object`'s monitor
`void notifyAll()`	Wakes up all threads waiting on the `Object`'s monitor
`void wait(long mills)`	Waits to be notified of a change in the `Object`'s status, for not longer than the specified number of milliseconds
`void wait()`	Waits indefinitely to be notified of a change in the `Object`'s status

Synchronizing a statement is a more sophisticated way of controlling concurrency than synchronizing a method and provides finer control. To synchronize a single statement, you prefix the statement with the `synchronized` keyword and an expression that refers to an object (or array because a Java array is represented as an object):

```
synchronized (object-expression) statement
```

The statement will be executed only if the monitor of the object identified by `object-expression` is available. The statement can, and usually does, take the form of a compound statement enclosed within curly braces. The code contained in the statement is called *critical* code because it is protected against simultaneous execution by multiple threads. Here's an example:

```
synchronized (theObject)
{
    // do something here
    theObject.notifyAll();
}
```

Why does the example include a call to `notifyAll()`? A thread that finds itself unable to proceed can invoke the `wait()` method, which puts it to sleep until some other thread calls `notify()` or `notifyAll()` on the synchronized object. The `notify()` method wakes the first thread that called `wait()` on the synchronized object. The `notifyAll()` method wakes *every* thread that has called `wait()` on the object; access to the CPU goes to the highest priority thread among them. By calling notifyAll(), the example code makes sure that, if there are waiting threads, they are notified that they should wake up and re-attempt to access the synchronized object. Of course, only one of them will succeed, because the synchronized keyword guarantees that threads will execute the statement one at a time.

Deadlocks and Other Liveness Problems

As you've learned, race conditions are easily prevented through liberal use of the synchronized keyword. Your program, however, might then exhibit either of the following symptoms:

- **Starvation:** One or more threads might not get their "fair share" of access to the CPU. Consequently, the tasks assigned to them might not get accomplished.

- **Deadlock:** Two or more threads might be mutually waiting on one another, none of them able to proceed. Such a condition can continue indefinitely, seen as a "hung" program or system.

How do you avoid such liveness problems? Well, one answer is to remove all the synchronized keywords from your program. Of course, that's not the answer you want to hear, because that throws you right back into the arms of safety problems. Moreover, in a few odd cases, removing the synchronized keyword might actually *create* a liveness problem. You might run into this if you boldly hack the source code for an AWT class supplied by Sun and include the result in your program (not normally a recommended practice, of course).

The better answer is that you must selectively remove (or sometimes, insert) synchronized keywords from your methods. How can you know when it is safe to do so? Here are some guidelines.

For accessor methods, you can safely remove the synchronized keyword if

- The value returned by the accessor method never transiently takes on an invalid value during execution of any mutator methods.

- The value is atomically assignable (that is, assignable in a single operation). Note that this precludes removing synchronized from accessor methods that return a long or double.

For mutator methods, you can safely remove the synchronized keyword if

- All the conditions given above for accessor methods hold for the mutator method.

- Values of any variable assigned by the mutator are valid at all times for all possible execution sequences of accessor and mutator methods.

- The method requires no special synchronized actions in response to special states of variables it accesses (for example, semaphore variables).

Note that, generally, it is not possible to remove the `synchronized` keyword from a mutator method because its variables are rarely valid at all times.

How, then, can you have your cake and eat it too? How can you synchronize methods and at the same time minimize the possibility of liveness failures? The answer is the guarded method.

A *guarded* method is one that tests a condition when the method is initially entered. If the condition is true, the method proceeds. However, if the condition is false, the guarded method waits for the condition to become true before it proceeds. By careful choice of the condition tested, you can avoid a safety failure yet minimize the likelihood of a liveness failure.

How do you code a guarded method? One time-honored technique, certainly honored for no other reason, is the so-called busy wait. Here's an example:

```
void busyWait()
{
    while(! condition )
        Thread.currentThread().yield();
    // remaining statements of method
}
```

> *"A guarded method is one that tests a condition when the method is initially entered."*

As long as the condition remains false, the remaining statements of the method will not be executed. Thus, it's possible, by means of a wisely chosen condition, to avoid safety problems. But the busy wait has serious drawbacks. Chief among these is the fact that the loop can consume unbounded (as in *enormous*) amounts of CPU time. Moreover, deadlocks can result if, for example, a low-priority thread has responsibility for changing the condition to true. The `yield()` will not yield control to a lower-priority process and so the condition might never change.

A better approach is the so-called guarded wait:

```
protected synchronized void guard ()

{
    while (! condition )
    {
        try
        {
            wait();
        }
        catch (InterruptedException ex) { ; }
    }
}

public synchronized void guardedMethod()
{
    guard();
    // state-changing actions
}

// Note: call notifyAll() after any state change that
// might allow a waiting method to run.
```

Here, a `guard()` method is defined so that several guarded methods can invoke its services, avoiding needless duplication of code. The `guardedMethod()` uses `guard()` to check whether it can proceed. If the condition tested by the guard is true, execution can proceed. Otherwise, the guard() method executes a wait(), which suspends and queues the thread. Inside any method that changes state in a way that might allow a queued thread to proceed, you should call notifyAll() after the completion of the change of state. This wakes all the queued threads, which again check their conditions, one at a time (remember that the guard() method is synchronized). If the condition has become true for a given thread, it will be allowed to proceed.

How is this different from the busy wait? The suspended threads consume no CPU time except when they are periodically awakened to check a potentially significant change of state. Moreover, unlike the busy wait, this technique will yield control even to low-priority threads.

The guarded method technique is not the only option for achieving synchronization without risking liveness. Another simple technique is to ensure that resources are acquired, using synchronization, in a standard order. Perhaps surprisingly, it can be demonstrated that this is a sufficient condition for avoiding deadlocks. It is also most inconvenient, however, and not always possible to apply.

Other possible options include timeouts, which attempt to detect, and recover from, possible deadlock situations by monitoring thread activity; and balks, which simply report an error if an expected condition is not met.

Design Patterns for Concurrency

A popular means of synchronizing the activities of asynchronous objects is Java's Observable class and Observer interface, which are used as a team. Smalltalkers (that is, Smalltalk programmers) know this design pattern as Model-View-Controller (MVC).

The MVC pattern features an object known as the Observable (or subject) whose state changes regularly. Client objects, known as Observers, can register with the Observable to receive a message every time the state of the Observable changes. In Java, this message is the update() message, and client objects must implement the Observer interface in order to advertise their ability to handle the update() message, which is the lone method defined by that interface.

THE MVC APPLET

Listing 12.11 shows the MVC applet, which demonstrates the use of the Observable-Observer design pattern.

```
Listing 12.11 The MVC Class
//  MVC.java

import java.applet.*;
import java.awt.*;
import java.awt.event.*;

public class MVC extends Applet
{
```

```
//   =========================================
//         APPLET METHODS
//   =========================================

/*  --Initialization---------------- */
public void init()
{
  setLayout(new GridLayout(2, 1));

  theBarChart = new BarChart(theTrack);
  thePieChart = new PieChart(theTrack);

  Panel south = new Panel();
  south.setLayout(new GridLayout(1, 2));
  south.add(theBarChart);
  south.add(thePieChart);

  add(theTrack);
  add(south);
}

//   =========================================
//         CLASS AND OBJECT ATTRIBUTES
//   =========================================
private Trackball theTrack    = new Trackball( );
private Applet    theBarChart;
private Applet    thePieChart;
}
```

Figure 12.8 shows the execution of the applet, which displays a simulated trackball in the upper half of its window. By dragging the trackball using the mouse, you change its state, given by its x-y position relative to the window boundaries, expressed as a percentage ranging from 0 to 100. The current relative x-position is displayed by a bar chart at the lower left of the window, and the current relative y-position is displayed by a pie chart at the lower right of the window.

FIGURE 12.8
Running the MVC applet

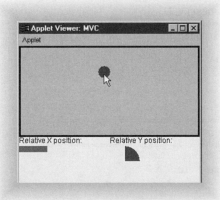

The `BarChart` class, shown in Listing 12.12, and the `PieChart` class, shown in Listing 12.13, are similar, differing only in their `paint()` methods. The `BarChart`, as you might expect, paints a filled rectangle and the `PieChart` paints a filled arc.

Listing 12.12 The BarChart Class

```java
//  BarChart.java

import java.applet.*;
import java.awt.*;
import java.util.*;

public class BarChart extends     Applet
                      implements  Observer
{
  // ========================================
  //        CONSTRUCTORS
  // ========================================
  public BarChart(Subject subject)
  {
    subject.addObserver(this);
  }

  // ========================================
  //        APPLET METHODS
  // ========================================

  /*  --Painting---------------------- */
  public void paint( Graphics g )
  {
    super.paint(g);

    g.setColor(Color.black);
    g.drawString("Relative X position:", 0, 10);
    g.setColor(Color.red);
    g.fillRect(0, 15, theSize, 10);
  }

  // ========================================
  //        IMPLEMENT OBSERVER
  // ========================================
  public void update(Observable subject, Object arg)
  {
    Point p = (Point) arg;
    theSize = p.x;
    repaint( );
  }

  // ========================================
  //        CLASS AND OBJECT ATTRIBUTES
  // ========================================

  private int theSize = 10;

}
```

Listing 12.13 The PieChart Class

```java
//  PieChart.java

import java.applet.*;
import java.awt.*;
import java.util.*;

public class PieChart extends     Applet
                      implements  Observer
{
  //  ==========================================
  //       CONSTRUCTORS
  //  ==========================================
  public PieChart(Subject subject)
  {
    subject.addObserver(this);
  }

  //  ==========================================
  //       APPLET METHODS
  //  ==========================================

  /*  --Painting--------------------- */
  public void paint(Graphics g)
  {
    g.setColor(Color.black);
    g.drawString("Relative Y position:", 0, 10);
    g.setColor(Color.blue);
    g.fillArc(0, 15, 50, 50, 0, 360*theSize/100);
  }

  //  ==========================================
  //       IMPLEMENT OBSERVER
  //  ==========================================
  public void update(Observable subject, Object arg)
  {
    Point p = (Point) arg;
    theSize = p.y;
    repaint( );
  }

  //  ==========================================
  //       CLASS AND OBJECT ATTRIBUTES
  //  ==========================================
  private int theSize = 10;

}
```

Each uses a constructor parameter, which specifies a Subject, to register itself as an Observer. And, each receives update() messages whenever the state of the Subject changes.

The Subject interface is shown in Listing 12.14. The promise made by a Subject is simply that it can handle the addObserver() method.

Listing 12.14 The Subject Interface

```java
import java.util.Observer;

public interface Subject
{
    public void addObserver(Observer o);
}
```

Another small unit of code, the OwnedSubject class, is shown in Listing 12.15. An OwnedSubject combines the properties of an Observable, the class it extends, and a Subject, the interface it implements. You'll see the need for the Subject and OwnedSubject in a moment.

Listing 12.15 The OwnedSubject Class

```java
//  OwnedSubject.java

import java.util.Observable;

public class OwnedSubject extends     Observable
                          implements  Subject
{

  //  ==========================================
  //      IMPLEMENTS SUBJECT
  //  ==========================================
  public void setChanged()
  {
    super.setChanged();
  }
}
```

The Trackball class, shown in Listing 12.16, implements a trackball object that informs clients of its relative x-y position within its bounds. The Trackball class extends the Canvas class, inheriting a wealth of state and behavior as a consequence. Of course, the Trackball also needs the state and behavior of an Observable. Because Java does not allow multiple inheritance, the Trackball creates a captive Observable object, which will do its bidding, and then implements the Subject interface, which advertises its willingness to handle addObserver() messages from clients. The Subject interface could also include other Observable methods, such as deleteObserver(). These were not needed in this program, however, and it was deemed simpler to ignore them.

Listing 12.16 The TrackBall Class

```java
//  Trackball.java

import java.awt.*;
import java.awt.event.*;
import java.util.*;

public class Trackball  extends     Canvas
                        implements  Subject,
```

```
                                        MouseListener,
                                        MouseMotionListener
{
  //  ==========================================
  //         CONSTRUCTORS
  //  ==========================================
  public Trackball()
  {
    setBackground(Color.lightGray);
    addMouseMotionListener(this);
  }


  //  ==========================================
  //         PUBLIC INTERFACE
  //  ==========================================

  /*  --Accessors--------------------- */
  public Point getState()
  {
    int width  = getSize().width;
    int height = getSize().height;

    int relx = (int) (100.0 * (double) theX /
                ((double) width  - DIAMETER) + 0.5);

    int rely = (int) (100.0 * (double) theY /
                ((double) height - DIAMETER) + 0.5);

    return new Point(relx, rely);
  }

  /*  --Common Interface-------------- */
  public void paint(Graphics g)
  {
    g.setColor(Color.black);
    g.drawRect(0, 0, getSize().width - 1, getSize().height - 1);
    g.drawRect(1, 1, getSize().width - 3, getSize().height - 3);
    g.drawRect(2, 2, getSize().width - 5, getSize().height - 5);
    g.setColor(Color.darkGray);
    g.fillOval(theX, theY, DIAMETER, DIAMETER);
  }


  //  ==========================================
  //       IMPLEMENTS SUBJECT
  //  ==========================================
  public void addObserver(Observer o)
  {
    theSubject.addObserver(o);
  }


  //  ==========================================
  //       IMPLEMENTS MOUSEMOTIONLISTENER
  //  ==========================================
  public void mouseDragged (MouseEvent event)
  {
    int x = theX + DIAMETER/2;
    int y = theY + DIAMETER/2;

    int px = event.getX();
    int py = event.getY();
```

```
      int d = (int) Math.sqrt((x - px)*(x - px) +
                              (y - py)*(y - py));

    if (isDragging ¦¦ d < DIAMETER/2)
    {
      isDragging = true;

      theX = px - DIAMETER/2;
      theY = py - DIAMETER/2;

      int width  = getSize().width;
      int height = getSize().height;

      if (theX < 0) theX = 0;
      if (theY < 0) theY = 0;
      if (theX > width  - DIAMETER)
        theX = width  - DIAMETER;
      if (theY > height - DIAMETER)
        theY = height - DIAMETER;

      theSubject.setChanged();
      theSubject.notifyObservers(getState());

      repaint( );
    }
  }

  public void mouseMoved   (MouseEvent event) { ; }

  // =============================================
  //      IMPLEMENTS MOUSELISTENER
  // =============================================
  public void mouseReleased(MouseEvent event)
  {
    isDragging = false;
  }

  public void mouseClicked (MouseEvent event) { ; }
  public void mouseEntered (MouseEvent event) { ; }
  public void mouseExited   (MouseEvent event) { ; }
  public void mousePressed (MouseEvent event) { ; }

  // =============================================
  //      CLASS AND OBJECT ATTRIBUTES
  // =============================================
  private OwnedSubject theSubject = new OwnedSubject();
  private static final int DIAMETER = 20;
  private int theX = DIAMETER;
  private int theY = DIAMETER;
  private boolean isDragging = false;

}
```

The Trackball also implements the MouseListener and MouseMotionListener interfaces, advertising its ability to handle messages that inform it of the current state and position of the mouse. It uses these to discern when the mouse is "dragging" the circle painted by the Trackball, which is not an object at all and, therefore, cannot actually be dragged. This feat is accomplished by checking whether the mouse is positioned over the circle while the left button is down, indicating that a drag is in progress. Even on fast computers, the mouse tends to get ahead of the circle, so once a drag has begun, the Trackball continues processing the drag until the mouse button is released, regardless of the mouse position.

During a drag, the Trackball reports its position to all registered Observers by calling setChanged(), followed by notifyObservers(). Each registered Observer then receives an update() message. Although the JDK documentation provides scant information on the setChanged() method, study of the source code for the Observable class shows you that the update() messages are only sent if setChanged() is called. In the same manner, you can also learn an important fact about the way notification is accomplished: It is synchronous notification, performed by a single thread, that sends messages one-by-one to each registered Observer. The next example program shows how to overcome that limitation, providing potentially greater throughput and availability.

Listing 12.17 shows the HTML file used to execute the MVC applet. If you haven't run the applet, do so now. You'll probably find that it's fun to use. Don't get so caught up, however, that you neglect to finish the chapter.

```
Listing 12.17 MVC.html
<HTML>

<HEAD>
<TITLE>MVC.html</TITLE>
</HEAD>

<BODY>
<H1>Observable/Observer Pattern </H1>
<APPLET CODE=MVC HEIGHT=300 WIDTH=300>
</APPLET>

</BODY>
</HTML>
```

THE ConcurrentMonitor APPLICATION

As you just learned, the standard Java Observer-Observable pattern synchronously notifies client Observers of changes to the subject Observable. In this section, you'll learn how to create a threaded version of this pattern.

Listing 12.18 shows the ConcurrentSubject class, which performs the functions of a multithreaded Observable. Rather than using a private Observable object, it registers Observers (more accurately, ConcurrentObservers) using a Vector. Returning a non-atomic long value as its state, it defines a getState() accessor method and a setState() mutator method. The setState() method accomplished the asynchronous notification by using a helper class named Notifier.

Listing 12.18 The ConcurrentSubject Class

```java
// ConcurrentSubject.java

import java.util.Vector;
import java.util.Enumeration;

public class ConcurrentSubject
{
  //   ==========================================
  //         CONSTRUCTORS
  //   ==========================================
  public ConcurrentSubject(long state)
  {
    theState = state;
  }

  //   ==========================================
  //         PUBLIC INTERFACE
  //   ==========================================

  /*   --Mutators---------------------- */
  public synchronized void addObserver(ConcurrentObserver o)
  {
    theObservers.addElement(o);
  }

  public synchronized void deleteObserver(ConcurrentObserver o)
  {
    theObservers.removeElement(o);
  }

  public synchronized void setState(long state)
  {
    theState = state;

    Enumeration e = theObservers.elements();
    while (e.hasMoreElements())
    {
      ConcurrentObserver o =
          (ConcurrentObserver) (e.nextElement());

      new Thread(new Notifier(this, o)).start();
    }
  }

  /*   --Accessors---------------------- */
  public synchronized long getState()
  {
    return theState;
  }

  //   ==========================================
  //         CLASS AND OBJECT ATTRIBUTES
  //   ==========================================
  protected long    theState;
  protected Vector theObservers = new Vector();

}
```

The `Notifier` class, shown in Listing 12.19, does the work of notifying registered clients of a change in the subject's state. Implementing the `Runnable` interface, each `Notifier` runs as a separate thread, quickly putting all client objects on notice of any change, even if some require some time to handle the change. These might otherwise "starve" other client objects, delaying their notification. The technique shown in `Notifier` works best on operating systems that perform so-called round robin scheduling, time slicing the execution of threads within each priority level so that every thread gets a share of available CPU time. Microsoft Windows 95 and Windows NT are among those that do so.

Listing 12.19 The Notifier Class

```
class Notifier implements Runnable
{

  //   ==========================================
  //        CONSTRUCTORS
  //   ==========================================
  Notifier(ConcurrentSubject s, ConcurrentObserver o)
  {
    theSubject = s;
    theObserver = o;
  }

  //   ==========================================
  //        IMPLEMENT RUNNABLE
  //   ==========================================
  public void run()
  {
    theObserver.update(theSubject);
  }

  //   ==========================================
  //        CLASS AND OBJECT ATTRIBUTES
  //   ==========================================
  private ConcurrentSubject  theSubject;
  private ConcurrentObserver theObserver;
}
```

Listing 12.20 shows the `ConcurrentObserver` class, which registers to receive updates and reports them as they are received. A real-world application would likely perform more extensive processing in response to `update()` messages.

Listing 12.20 The ConcurrentObserver Class

```
//  ConcurrentObserver.java

public class ConcurrentObserver
{
  //   ==========================================
  //        CONSTRUCTORS
  //   ==========================================
  public ConcurrentObserver(ConcurrentSubject s)
  {
```

```java
    theID = theNextID;
    theNextID++;

    theSubject  = s;
    theState    = s.getState();
    s.addObserver(this);
  }

  //   =========================================
  //          PUBLIC INTERFACE
  //   =========================================

  /*   --Mutators---------------------- */
  public synchronized void update(ConcurrentSubject s)
  {
    if (s != theSubject)
      throw new Error(
        "Concurrent Observer supports only a single subject");

    long last_state = theState;
    theState        = theSubject.getState();

    if (theState != last_state)
      showState();
  }

  /*   --Accessors--------------------- */
  public void showState()
  {
    System.out.println( "Observer " + theID +
                        " reports " + theState);
  }

  //   =========================================
  //        CLASS AND OBJECT ATTRIBUTES
  //   =========================================
  protected static int theNextID = 1;
  protected int theID;
  protected long theState;
  protected ConcurrentSubject theSubject;

}
```

The ConcurrentMonitor class, shown in Listing 12.21, is simply a test bench that you can use to execute the classes that make up the concurrent Observable-Observer pattern. It creates instances of the relevant objects and then enters a timed loop that regularly changes the state of the ConcurrentSubject object.

Listing 12.21 The ConcurrentMonitor Class

```java
//  ConcurrentMonitor.java

public class ConcurrentMonitor extends Thread
{

  //   =========================================
```

```
//          MAIN METHOD
//   ==========================================
public static void main(String args[])
{
  new ConcurrentMonitor().start();
}


//   ==========================================
//          CONSTRUCTORS
//   ==========================================
public ConcurrentMonitor()
{
  theSubject = new ConcurrentSubject(0);
  theObservers = new ConcurrentObserver [OBSERVER_COUNT];

  for (int i = 0; i < OBSERVER_COUNT; i++)
  {
    theObservers[i] = new ConcurrentObserver(theSubject);
  }
}


//   ==========================================
//          IMPLEMENT RUNNABLE
//   ==========================================
public void run()
{
  System.out.println("Running ...");

  while (true)
  {
    System.out.println("State=" + theSubject.getState());
    theSubject.setState(theSubject.getState() + 1);

    try
    {
      Thread.sleep(DELAY);
    }
    catch (InterruptedException e) { ; }
  }
}


//   ==========================================
//          CLASS AND OBJECT ATTRIBUTES
//   ==========================================
private static final int OBSERVER_COUNT = 2;
private static final int DELAY = 1000;
private ConcurrentSubject theSubject;
private ConcurrentObserver [] theObservers;
}
```

Figure 12.9 shows the execution of the ConcurrentMonitor class. Figure 12.10 shows an interaction diagram for the concurrent Observable-Observer pattern. Notice how the asynchronous start()/run() permits the update() and getState() methods to execute in separate threads.

FIGURE 12.9
Running the
`Concurrent-`
`Monitor`
application

FIGURE 12.10
*Interaction diagram for
the concurrent*
`Observer-`
`Observable` *pattern*

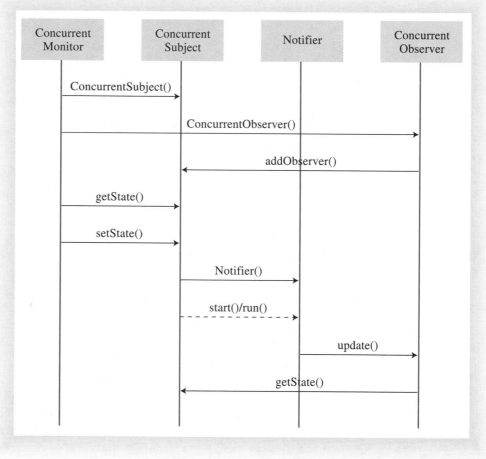

Summary

Java's facilities for creating and controlling threads allow your programs to include concurrent objects that execute, or appear to execute, simultaneously. Threads can help programs perform better, making them more responsive to events.

However, threaded programs are subject to several kinds of bugs that do not affect nonthreaded programs. Race conditions, owing to lack of proper synchronization, can corrupt the states of objects and classes. Liveness failures, owing to improper synchronization, can result in sluggish performance or hung programs or systems.

Guarded methods using Java's synchronized and wait keywords can help the programmer achieve synchronization at a reasonable price. The concurrent version of the Observable-Observer design pattern can also assist in coordinating the actions of concurrent objects.

" Java's facilities for creating and controlling threads allow your programs to include concurrent objects that execute, or appear to execute, simultaneously. "

Questions

For multiple-choice items, indicate all correct responses.

1. True or False. All object-oriented languages, including Java, provide support for concurrent programming.

2. Some reasons for using threads in your program include which of the following.
    a. Improved response to events.
    b. Race conditions.
    c. Support for parallel computing on multiprocessor systems.
    d. LaGrange multiplication.

3. One potential drawback of using threads is the possibility of program deadlock due to failure to satisfy _____ conditions.

4. A thread is initiated by using the _____ method, which causes the _____ method of the thread to execute.

5. Ways of creating threads in Java include which of the following:
    a. Extending the Thread class.
    b. Implementing the Runnable interface.
    c. Using direct access to native threads.
    d. Passing an object reference to the Object.createThread() method.

6. The run() method of a thread can/cannot throw an IOException.

7. The Booch-style interaction diagram shows objects and classes along the
_____ edge of the diagram.

8. Non-atomic updates may jeopardize the ability of a program to satisfy
_____ conditions:

   a. invariant

   b. busy wait

   c. observable

   d. safety

9. The two Java data types for which atomic updates are not guaranteed are
_____ and _____.

10. The guarded wait typically consumes more/fewer CPU cycles than the busy
wait.

Exercises

1. Using the `Observable-Observer` pattern, design a software distribution
system. Clients wishing to execute a program can use the system to determine
if an updated version of the program is available, and download it. The server
should be capable of handling up to 10 simultaneous clients.

2. Study Java's APIs for threads and prepare a set of tables, one for each class
or interface, that describe the constructors, constants, and public methods of
the class or interface. Also prepare a set of example code sections that
demonstrate the use of the Java language keywords related to threads.

3. Design a scheduling system that provides round robin scheduling of threaded
objects for use on systems that do not provide such scheduling in their
implementation of Java. Round robin scheduling prevents a thread from
running indefinitely if other threads of the same priority are ready to run. It is
implemented, in its most basic form, using a *time slice*, which specifies the
maximum length of time a process can use the CPU when other equal-
priority processes are ready to run.

4. Choose a program that includes a graphical user interface that allows the user
to execute any of a number of functions. Design a new version of the
program that allows several such functions to execute simultaneously. Pay
careful attention to the possibility of conflict, which might compel you to
forbid certain functions from executing concurrently. But, strive to provide as

much concurrency as possible. Also show how adding concurrency will change the user interface.

To Learn More

The following books will help you learn more about designing concurrent objects:

- Gilbert, Stephen, and Bill McCarty. *Object-Oriented Programming in Java.* Corte Madera, California: The Waite Group Press, 1997.

  Chapter 16 of the authors' book on object-oriented programming presents an introduction to Java's APIs for thread programming.

- Lea, Doug. *Concurrent Programming in Java: Design Principles and Patterns.* Reading, Massachusetts: Addison-Wesley, 1997.

  This is an excellent book on threads and concurrent programming, written for Java programmers.

- Gosling, James; Bill Joy; and Guy Steele. *The Java Language Specification.* Reading, Massachusetts: Addison-Wesley, 1996.

  Java's facilities for thread programming are thoroughly covered in this book.

- Booch, Grady. *Object-Oriented Analysis and Design with Applications, 2nd Ed.* Redwood City, California: Benjamin/Cummings, 1994.

  Further techniques and hints for designing concurrent programs are found in this title.

- Hoare, C.A.R. *Communicating Sequential Processes.* New York: Prentice Hall, 1985.

  The foundation theories of concurrent programming are set forth in this book.

13

Designing Remote Objects

From the time of Marco Polo in the middle ages, and even before, trade between communities has been one of the driving forces in civilization. As a result of trade, you can go to your local grocery store and purchase Spanish olives, Hawaiian pineapples, Swiss cheese, and Italian salami. As Adam Smith pointed out in *The Wealth of Nations*, trade allows people to concentrate on their "core competencies" and ultimately leaves everyone better off.

Object-oriented programs are communities of objects and, like human communities, they benefit from specialization and "trade." If you've done graphics programming involving fractals or ray tracing, or written programs involving complex calculation, you've probably wished you could "hand off" some of the work to an object running on a Cray supercomputer, rather than sitting around waiting for your 166 megahertz Pentium to finish. What if, instead of just the processing power of the machine setting on your desktop, you could harness the power of any machine on the network? Imagine the possibilities. This is the promise of using remote objects.

In Chapter 12, "Designing Concurrent Objects," you saw how objects on separate computers could communicate with one another via sockets. With sockets, the client process running on your machine sends a stream of bytes to a server machine running somewhere on the network, telling the server what operation you want it to perform. The server handles your request and returns a response by sending you back another stream of bytes.

You may have wished that things were simpler, that you could send messages to objects living on remote servers in the same way you send messages to local objects: by simply invoking a method. The problem is that, to invoke a message, you must have a reference to an object. How can you get a reference to an object running inside the Java Virtual Machine of a computer tens, or even tens of thousands, of miles away? This task is the job of Java's Remote Method Invocation (RMI) facility, which solves this problem along with several important related problems.

RMI, however, is not the only way, and possibly not the best way, to access remote objects. This chapter focuses on RMI because RMI is included in the Java Developer's Kit. You can download RMI and experiment with it without tapping your bank account. To give you some information about alternatives to RMI, this chapter also includes a tour that will acquaint you with the most prominent options. When you're done, you'll understand the basics of accessing remote objects and be prepared to shell out some of your earnings to explore some of the more commodious, but more expensive, alternatives.

In this chapter you will learn:

- What remote objects are, and how they work.

- What advantages and disadvantages are posed by various ways of accessing remote objects.

- How to implement remote objects using RMI.

Remote Objects

Not so long ago, high-speed computer networks were among the exotica of computing, the property only of the prosperous few organizations that could afford the enormous costs of telecommunications equipment and line charges necessary to link remote sites. Today, all that has changed; even consumer operating systems like Windows 95 include support for local area networking, and many individuals use Ethernet networks to link computers in their homes.

Once your computer is joined to a network, the notion that your Java objects should talk only to one another, and never to Java objects on other computers, might strike you as idiosyncratic as wooden false teeth. "The network *is* the computer," a famous marketing slogan of Sun Microsystems, Inc., makes its point well. When computers cooperate, the whole can be greater than the sum of the parts.

REMOTE PROCEDURE CALLS

How can you convince your computers to cooperate with each other? One approach is to use a technology called Remote Procedure Call (RPC). RPC allows a program running on one computer to call a procedure that executes on another computer. If this sounds to you like a non-object-oriented approach, you're right. RPC inhabits the world of structured programs, where encapsulation of related data and behavior is unknown. But, if you know a little about how RPC works, you'll quickly grasp how today's more sophisticated object-oriented facilities work.

Figure 13.1 shows two processes communicating via RPC.

In RPC, a network connection to a remote computer is first made by using sockets, the standard way of communicating over a TCP/IP network. After a socket connection

FIGURE 13.1

Two processes communicating via RPC

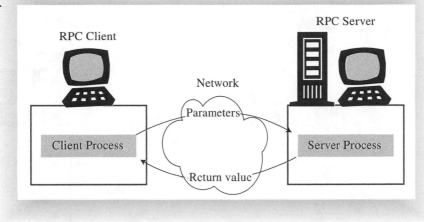

Using RPC is much more convenient than using sockets alone.

is made with the server computer, you can invoke a function on the remote machine, much like you would if you were starting a program using a telnet connection. Calling a function, though, is a little different than just running a program. When you call a function, you usually need to pass arguments to the function and generally want to get some results back. RPC establishes a standard method for sending your arguments via a socket to the function residing on the server, and for sending the return value via a socket back to your machine. This process is termed *parameter marshaling,* and is performed automatically by RPC.

Using RPC is much more convenient than using sockets alone. When writing a pure socket-based client or server, you must marshal the parameters yourself. If, like the CipherServer example program in Chapter 12, you have only one or two kinds of messages, this may not be too tedious. But, coding the logic to handle dozens of messages is not only boring, but error-prone. Using RPC to make remote procedure calls allows you to work at a higher level of abstraction than the byte stream used for pure socket programming, so it's less complex.

Whereas RPC solves the problem of calling procedures located on different machines, it doesn't allow you to call object or class methods, which is what you need to get your objects communicating. But, assuming you *had* a mechanism like RPC that would marshal the parameters of a method call to a remote server object, what *else* would you need before your client could access the remote object? You'd need a reference to the object on the remote server, of course. But, this presents an interesting chicken-and-egg problem.

In general, when a client needs a service, it asks a server. When your Web browser wants a Web page, it sends out an HTTP request to a Web server. In a like manner, you'd expect that the way to get a reference to an object on a remote server is to simply ask a server for it. But, there are two problems with this. First, what server should you ask? Second, how should you make your request? Figure 13.2 shows how the first part of this problem is solved.

FIGURE 13.2
*Finding a remote
object's server*

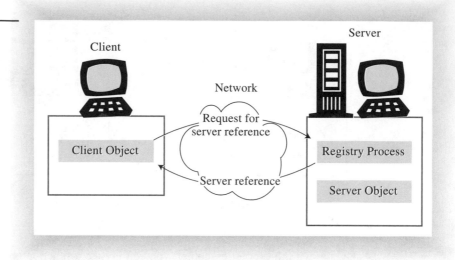

When working with remote objects, the computer that houses the object you want to use runs a special *registry service*. This registry service is a program that listens for client requests on a designated port, in much the same way that a Web server listens for HTTP requests or a mail server listens for SMTP requests. And, just as with the Web server and mail server, all you need to know to access the registry is the name of the host machine. Your program then combines the remote host name and the port to form the socket address of the registry service to which you simply open a connection. Once the connection is open, your program asks the remote registry to give you a reference to the remote object you want to use, and the registry complies. Problem solved.

OBJECT REQUEST BROKERS

" ORBs make remote clients and servers much easier to program, because they do most of the hard work for you. "

Sometimes, even if you know how something works, it's easier to hand off the work to an expert. Many people sell their homes themselves, but most use the services of a real estate broker. Likewise, when it comes to love and marriage, you might prefer the do-it-yourself method, but that doesn't stop your friends from fixing you up on Saturday night.

Fixing up your objects to connect with a suitable mate on a remote machine can similarly be done behind the scenes by special software running on the client and the server. Software of this sort is called an *object request broker* (*ORB*). ORBs make remote clients and servers much easier to program, because they do most of the hard work for you.

Figure 13.3 shows how a typical ORB works. The ORB includes parts running on both the client and the server.

FIGURE 13.3

How an Object Request Broker (ORB) works

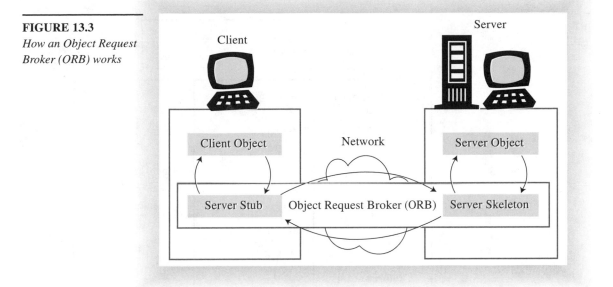

On the client side (your local machine), the ORB creates an object known as a *server stub*. Your program treats this stub, which runs in the same Java Virtual Machine (JVM) as your program, as a "stand-in" for the object that lives on the remote server. When you send a message to this stand-in object, the stub gathers up all the parameters and marshals them over the network, where it hands them over to a *server skeleton*.

The server skeleton is an object running on the remote server that acts as a stand-in for your local object. The skeleton unmarshals the parameters that you've sent and then invokes the requested method. As soon as the method finishes running on the remote machine, the skeleton takes the results provided by the method, marshals them, and transmits them back to the server stub running on your machine. The stub then unmarshals the parameters and hands them over to your client object, completing the method call.

If this seems unnecessarily complex, you might want to look at Figure 13.4, which shows an object interaction diagram that summarizes the process. The beauty of using an ORB, however, is that you can use it even if you don't understand exactly how it works!

The special stub and skeleton objects used by an ORB are known generically as *proxies*, because each "stands in" for the client or server during a remote method invocation. Their purpose is to present a simpler interface to the client and server. The client, for example, communicates with the stub, using it as a stand-in for the server. Because the stub runs in the same JVM as the client, the client sees the server (through the stub proxy) as if it were a local object running on the same JVM. The complexities of remote object invocation are, therefore, hidden from the client. The skeleton provides the corresponding service to the server, which sees the client as if it were a local object.

FIGURE 13.4

Object interaction within an ORB

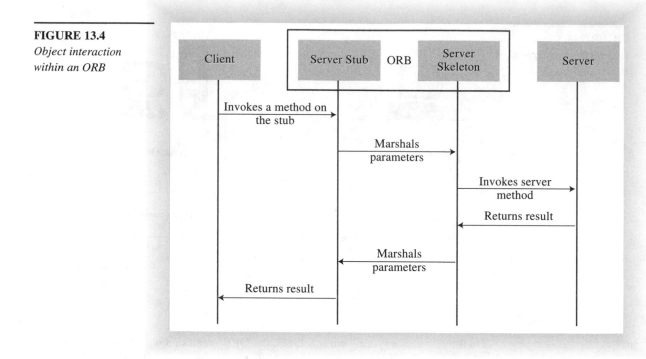

At the most basic level, the functions provided by an ORB include establishing an object registry and providing transparent local/remote access to objects. A typical ORB, however, may provide services beyond these. For example, several ORBs provide built-in support for security and transactions.

Remote Computing Alternatives

RPC and ORBs are *generic* solutions to the problems of accessing remote objects. By now you're probably ready for more specific details. In Java, if your application needs to access remote objects, there's no shortage of ways this can be done. This section examines five remote computing alternatives for Java software:

- Sockets
- Common Gateway Interface (CGI)
- Common Object Request Broker Architecture (CORBA)
- Remote Method Invocation (RMI)
- Distributed Component Object Model (DCOM)

SOCKETS

You met sockets in Chapter 12, "Designing Concurrent Objects," where they were used to build a simple client-server application. While flexible, using sockets to communicate between client and server can be cumbersome because of all the details you have to handle yourself. To create a simple client-side connection using sockets, you must do the following:

- Locate the remote server and open a socket connection to it.

- Marshal the parameters to be transmitted, including a value that identifies the service you're requesting.

- Transmit the parameters.

- Listen for, and receive, the response from the server.

- Decode the response from the server, unmarshaling its components if necessary.

The most complex part of all this is sending and receiving parameters. If the parameters you're sending to the server, and the value it returns, are primitive (that is, non-object) values, the process is fairly straightforward. If, however, you want to send an object as a parameter, or receive one as a return value, things get more exciting. To send objects via a socket connection, you must first extract each of the object's attributes, then marshal and transmit them. Of course, if any attribute of your object is itself an object, you must apply this technique recursively—only primitive values can be sent across the socket stream.

Implementing the server-side of this connection is no easier than implementing a client. The server object must unmarshal any parameters it receives, decode the value telling it what service to perform, and so on.

All of this marshaling and unmarshaling might lead you to wish that Java included an RPC facility, which would at least help you pack and unpack your arguments. Rather than just RPC, however, Java provides the Remote Method Invocation (RMI) facility, which goes RPC one better. You'll learn more about RMI in a subsequent section. But for right now you might wonder why you might choose to use sockets to communicate with remote objects when RMI is available? Here are two possible reasons:

- **To communicate with non-Java objects and programs:** Not all software on networks is written in Java—at least, not yet. Until it is, from time to time you'll need to interface a Java program with a non-Java program. Sockets are a good way to do this, because data transmitted over a socket is reduced to its lowest common denominator: a stream of bytes. A program written in almost any language, running on almost any platform, can deal with a stream of bytes.

⚫ **To communicate as efficiently as possible:** The convenience of RPC, RMI, and other facilities extracts a price in the form of processing overhead. A well-designed socket interface between programs can outperform one based on such higher-level facilities. If your server must handle large volumes of requests, this may be important to you.

As usual, deciding whether to use sockets, RMI, CORBA, or some other facility involves a design tradeoff. A program written using sockets is larger and more complex than one written using RMI, yet may perform better. This choice is analogous to the choice of programming languages: a program written in assembly language can, in principle, outperform one written in C or Java. But an assembly program is much harder to write, is likely to contain more errors, and is more difficult to maintain than a program written in a high-level language.

" As usual, deciding whether to use sockets, RMI, CORBA, or some other facility involves a design tradeoff. "

COMMON GATEWAY INTERFACE (CGI)

A second, very popular way of communicating over a computer network (possibly the most popular way), is via the Common Gateway Interface, or CGI. CGI is a way to program your Web server so that it can offer more than the static form of HTML documents. When a client requests a CGI page, the server runs a program (identified by a special form of URL) that builds an HTML page on the fly. The server then transmits this dynamically constructed page back to the client. The CGI program that builds the page can perform a simple computation, access a database, access another host, or do almost anything necessary to acquire the data it includes in the requested page. Figure 13.5 illustrates the operation of CGI.

FIGURE 13.5
The operation of the Common Gateway Interface (CGI)

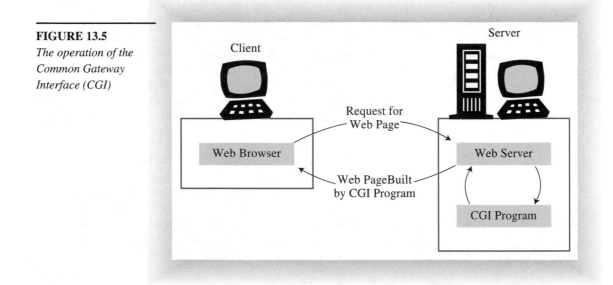

The handy thing about CGI is that it's supported by every Web browser and essentially every Web server. Even a Java applet or application can easily access a CGI page by using:

```
new java.net.URL(theURL).getConnection().getContent()
```

where *theURL* specifies the URL of the CGI page.

Limitations of CGI

Despite its ease of use and popularity, however, CGI has some serious drawbacks:

- **CGI is slow.** Tests reported by Orfali and Harkey, leading authorities on client-server computing, show that CGI is about 200 times slower than IIOP, a popular inter-object protocol.

- **CGI can compromise server security.** CGI is a jerrybuilt extension to Web servers. Many sites have been compromised by hackers who have exploited weaknesses arising from the inadequate integration between a Web server and the CGI programs it spawns.

- **CGI cannot store state information.** Hypertext transfer protocol (HTTP), the protocol used by Web servers, is a *stateless protocol*. This means that Web browsers (and other HTTP clients) are connected to Web servers only for the duration of a single request. A browser cannot ask the server to remember who it is, or anything about its previous requests. The client must store this information and re-transmit it with any request that needs it.

The Servlet Alternative

The limitations of the CGI architecture led Sun to introduce its own alternative based on Java, the JavaServer architecture. JavaServer introduces the *servlet*, which is a Java program that in many ways resembles an applet, but that runs on the server rather than on the client. Clients can request that servlets be started and can obtain results produced by servlets. Like client-side applets, servlets run under control of a security manager that monitors their activities, preventing them from performing actions that might threaten system security. Moreover, servlets, though they are written in Java (an interpreted language), run more efficiently than CGI scripts.

Because servlets are written in Java, they can invoke any of Java's APIs or facilities. Thus, for example, a servlet could use RMI to communicate with a second remote server, or with the originally requesting client. This chameleon characteristic makes it difficult to anticipate the typical ways in which servlets may someday come to be used, if they gain a permanent foothold in the computing marketplace.

When might you choose to use CGI as a means of communicating with a remote server? If performance is not a major concern and you're concerned with providing access to a wide variety of clients (for example, the public), then CGI has important strengths. If, on the other hand, you are creating applications that will be confined to your own organization, some other approach will probably serve you better. Servlets are an interesting alternative because they provide the same strength as CGI (compatibility with virtually every browser) with fewer drawbacks.

COMMON OBJECT REQUEST BROKER ARCHITECTURE (CORBA)

The third remote computing alternative available to you is the Common Object Request Broker Architecture, or CORBA. Despite its name, CORBA is not an ORB. CORBA is a document, a standard developed, and agreed to, by the over 700 members of the Object Management Group (OMG). The standard was developed to make sure that ORBs created by one vendor would work (interoperate) with ORBs created by another. After all, what's the point in having distributed objects if all the machines have to be running the same ORB? It would be like having the World Wide Web divided up into fiefdoms where those running Microsoft's browsers could only contact sites that use Microsoft's servers, and Netscape's browsers were limited to accessing only Netscape-controlled sites. The beauty of HTTP and the Web is that it makes no difference which browser or server you are using; they can all interoperate by following the standards. What HTTP does for the World Wide Web, CORBA attempts to do for distributed objects.

> *" What HTTP does for the World Wide Web, CORBA attempts to do for distributed objects. "*

The CORBA standard has three main elements:

- 🌐 The Internet Inter-ORB Protocol
- 🌐 The Interface Definition Language
- 🌐 System services and facilities

The Internet Inter-ORB Protocol (IIOP) enables your objects to interact across a network, using an ORB. IIOP forms an *object bus* that can link your objects and ORBs into systems, much the same way that the hardware bus in your personal computer links the RAM memory, the CPU, and the expansion cards. IIOP is analogous to HTTP.

The Interface Definition Language (IDL) allows you to describe the interface of an object, regardless of its implementation language. By using IDL to describe the interface of an object and then plugging that object into the object bus with IIOP, you can make your object's methods available to any other object on the bus. You can also use IDL to encapsulate (or wrap) a non-object–oriented legacy system, so that its data and behavior can be made available via the object bus. Even database stored procedures can be described using IDL.

The CORBA system services and common facilities provide general-purpose functionality to objects traveling on CORBA's IIOP bus. One example is the *interface repository*, implemented as a distributed database, that contains IDL descriptions of all the objects on the bus. Using the repository, your objects can discover and use servers without being aware of the servers' locations at runtime. CORBA provides many other services and facilities, including a security service that supports authentication and access control lists.

CORBA and Java

While the OMG has yet to issue official Java bindings for CORBA (that is, specifications that allow Java systems to access, and be accessed by, other CORBA software), several vendors have already brought to market products that allow Java programs to access CORBA ORBs. Appendix C includes information about some of the offerings that were available at the time of writing.

Evaluating CORBA

Why would you choose to use CORBA over some other method of communicating with remote objects? CORBA has a number of advantages:

- It's much easier to use than sockets.

- It enables access to software, including so-called legacy systems, running on a variety of platforms.

- It is an open standard, supported by many vendors and many products.

- It scales well, enabling the construction of large systems.

Well, if CORBA's so great, why would you choose to use some other method, instead of CORBA? The most likely reason would be cost. Sockets, RMI, and DCOM are free, but acquiring an ORB will cost you a bit. The cost is not high, however, relative to the labor costs of software construction. Whereas the cost of an ORB might tip the balance against CORBA for your own experimentation, it is less likely to be a factor in deciding whether to use CORBA to implement a "real" information system.

REMOTE METHOD INVOCATION (RMI)

" RMI helps with the two hardest problems in implementing remote objects: getting references to remote objects and passing messages to and from them. "

Your fourth choice for creating remote-object systems is the Remote Method Invocation (RMI) facility that is built into the 1.1 version of JDK. You might think of RMI as a poor man's CORBA. It helps with the two hardest problems in implementing remote objects: getting references to remote objects and passing messages to and from them. Despite its attractiveness, however, RMI lacks support for many of the useful services provided by CORBA, including CORBA's interface repository and security facilities. With RMI, you'll either have to do without these, or write them yourself, which might turn out to be more than you bargained for.

Another thing you should consider when evaluating RMI is its status as a proprietary Sun technology, rather than an open standard. Furthermore, RMI is a Java-only technology, and won't give you any help with non-Java programs. So, RMI's base of support and scope of application are both significantly narrower than CORBA's. These factors are significant disadvantages.

If that's the down side, then what's the up side? Why might you choose to use RMI? Well, for one thing, because RMI is part of the JDK, it's free! That's the main reason the upcoming example in this chapter uses RMI. You can run it yourself without first purchasing an ORB.

In addition to an unbeatable price, however, RMI does provide one important capability you won't get with CORBA: RMI makes it easy to download Java classes and stubs so that object behaviors, not just object data, can be sent over the network. Because it's a multi-platform standard, CORBA doesn't address software portability of the sort Java delivers. After all, why bother transmitting C++ object code over the network when the receiving host may well have a different hardware architecture and, therefore, not be able to execute the code anyway?

Of course, a CORBA program could use IIOP to transfer Java bytecodes from one host to another. So, it's not that CORBA *can't* handle software portability; it's merely that it doesn't directly support it. But the same thing, of course, could be said of CORBA services and facilities not supported by RMI. It's not, for example, that RMI *can't* handle security; it's merely that it doesn't directly support it.

DISTRIBUTED COMPONENT OBJECT MODEL (DCOM)

A final alternative approach to remote computing is Microsoft's Distributed Component Object Model (DCOM). You may have heard of ActiveX components even if you've not heard of DCOM; an ActiveX component is simply another word for a DCOM object.

What are the advantages and disadvantages of using DCOM technology? Like RMI, DCOM is a closed standard. Unlike RMI, however, DCOM is only supported on Microsoft Windows systems. DCOM also has its share of warts. For one thing it is hard to configure. Orfali and Harkey describe DCOM as "the configuration from hell."

As another example, DCOM does not support garbage collection. It is the responsibility of a client to notify a server when an object is no longer needed. This arrangement may be satisfactory within the context of a single computer, but it is entirely unsatisfactory within the context of remote objects, where network connections come and go. A disconnected client can saddle a server with a redundant object, one that will not disappear until the server is restarted, continuing to hold resources (such as memory) in the meantime. An overabundance of such objects would seriously compromise server performance.

Are there any situations where DCOM might be the distributed architecture of choice? Yes. If you're only interested in using Microsoft Windows-based clients and servers and you want the tightest possible integration between your applications and the Windows application programming interface (API), then DCOM may be exactly your ticket. However, for those who embrace the Java vision of open and portable computing, DCOM is simply not an option.

WEIGHING YOUR REMOTE COMPUTING ALTERNATIVES

Table 13.1 summarizes the key advantages and disadvantages of each of the alternative approaches to implementing remote objects. As you can see, the clear winner, except for a handful of specialized cases, is CORBA.

In the table, "scope of services" refers to the range and power of facilities and services provided by the technology; "scope of application" refers to the range of platforms, products, and vendors embracing the technology.

TABLE 13.1
SUMMARY OF REMOTE COMPUTING ALTERNATIVES

Technology	Cost	Ease of use	Scope of services	Scope of application
Sockets	Low	Low	Low	High
CGI	Low	Low	Low	High
CORBA	High	High	High	High
RMI	Low	High	Low	Low
DCOM	Low	Low	Low	Low

A Hands-On Look at RMI

If you're a Java programmer and have read this far, you're doubtless in the thralls of code withdrawal. Good news, relief is on its way. In this section, you'll get an up-close look at a remote server and a remote client, each implemented using RMI. As explained, RMI was chosen as the technology because you can run the example yourself, using packages included in the standard JDK.

The example program consists of a client applet that presents a list of names. To use the applet, first select one or more of the names from the list; then click the Set Meeting button. When you call for a meeting, the applet will use RMI to transmit the names of the participants you've chosen to the server program (which must be running concurrently). A method in the server object schedules the meeting, determines an appropriate time and place, and then sends the information back to your applet, which displays your new appointment on the screen.

It sounds simple, doesn't it? Let's take a look and see how you'd implement this using RMI. Then we'll come back and see how you'd do the same thing using CORBA.

IMPLEMENTING THE SERVER

As you learned in Chapter 4, "Encapsulation: Classes and Methods," design starts by looking at a problem from the client's point of view. Even though you're going to be writing a server, you want to start by defining how that server will appear to the client objects that use it. If you look at Listing 13.1, you'll see the VenueInterface, which is an interface that defines the server's attributes and methods as seen and used by the client object.

" Design starts by looking at a problem from the client's point of view. "

VenueInterface is a very simple interface; it contains only a single method named setMeeting(), which returns a Venue object describing a meeting. From the point of view of those who use the server, that is all it does. The client software calls setMeeting() and the server takes care of the rest.

There are several implementation details you should pay attention to. The first is that the setMeeting() method can possibly throw a RemoteException. Almost all methods that can be invoked on a remote machine can throw this exception. You can also see that the VenueInterface extends Remote, which is a class defined in the java.rmi package. Thus, you have to make sure you import java.rmi.*. This too is characteristic of all remote objects.

Listing 13.1 The VenueInterface Interface

```
// VenueInterface.java

import java.rmi.*;

public interface VenueInterface extends Remote
{
  public Venue setMeeting(String [] names)
              throws RemoteException;
}
```

The next listing you'll want to look at is the definition for the Venue class, shown in Listing 13.2. When your client program calls VenueInterface.setMeeting(), it gets back a Venue object. The Venue object contains all the information necessary to carry out a meeting: who, where, and when.

Listing 13.2 The Venue Class

```
// Venue.java

import java.io.Serializable;

public class Venue implements Serializable
{
  // ==========================================
  //        CONSTRUCTORS
  // ==========================================
  public Venue( String [] names,    // Who?
                String place,       // Where?
                String time         // When?
              )
  {
    theParticipants = names;
    thePlace        = place;
    theTime         = time;
  }


  // ==========================================
  //        PUBLIC INTERFACE
  // ==========================================

  /*  --Common Interface-------------- */
```

```java
public String toString()
{
  // 1. Build a String with all participants except the last
  String result = "";
  for (int i = 0; i < theParticipants.length - 1; i++)
  {
    if (i > 0)
      result += ", ";
    result += theParticipants[i];
  }

  // 2. Add the last participant
  if (theParticipants.length > 1)
    result += " and ";

  result += theParticipants[theParticipants.length - 1];

  // 3. Add the place and time, and return the result
  result += " will meet in " + thePlace + " at " + theTime;
  return result;
}

//   ==========================================
//       CLASS AND OBJECT ATTRIBUTES
//   ==========================================
String [] theParticipants;
String thePlace;
String theTime;

}
```

Before you turn your attention to the details of the implementation of Venue, notice the class header, which specifies that Venue implements the Serializable interface (accessed by importing java.io.serializable). This is the "magic" that allows Venue objects to be reduced to a stream of bytes and transmitted over the network. Better yet, the Serializable interface does not require you to implement any methods; all the necessary behavior is included within the Object class.

The Venue class includes a single constructor that requires you to pass the participants (as a String array), and the place and time of the meeting as individual String arguments. These values are stored by the constructor in the corresponding fields of the object. The only method in the Venue class is the toString() method, which formats the attributes of the object into a String suitable for printed or displayed output.

The last task left for you to accomplish is to define the VenueServer class, which you can see in Listing 13.3. When you create an instance of VenueServer, you'll have a running remote-object server. Following the listing there is a discussion of the implementation, which you'll want to browse, because VenueServer introduces several classes and facilities you have yet to meet.

Listing 13.3 The VenueServer Class

```java
// VenueServer.java

import java.rmi.*;
import java.rmi.server.*;
```

```java
public class VenueServer  extends     UnicastRemoteObject
                          implements  VenueInterface
{
  // ==========================================
  //         CONSTRUCTORS
  // ==========================================
  public VenueServer() throws RemoteException
  {
    ; // Dummy constructor defined so that
      // the throws clause can be specified
  }


  // ==========================================
  //         PUBLIC INTERFACE
  // ==========================================
  public Venue setMeeting(String [] names)
              throws RemoteException
  {
    String [] places =
      new String [] {"London", "Paris", "Rome"};

    int placeno = (int) (places.length * Math.random());

    int hour  = (int) (24 * Math.random() + 1.0);
    int min   = (int) (60 * Math.random() + 1.0);

    String zero = "";
    if (min < 10)
      zero = "0";

    String ampm = "a.m.";
    if (hour > 12)
    {
      ampm = "p.m.";
      hour = hour - 12;
    }

    String time = "" + hour + ":" + zero + min + " " + ampm;

    return new Venue(names, places[placeno], "" + time);
  }


  // ==========================================
  //         MAIN METHOD (CONSOLE APP)
  // ==========================================
  public static void main(String [] args)
                    throws RemoteException
  {
    System.setSecurityManager(new RMISecurityManager());

    try
    {
      VenueServer vs = new VenueServer();
      Naming.rebind("oodexample", vs);
      System.out.println(
        "Server is ready (press Ctrl-C to end).");
    }
    catch (Exception e)
```

```
  {
    System.err.println(e);
  }
 }
}
```

There are three implementation details to consider before you delve into VenueServer's code.

- First, notice that the VenueServer class implements the VenuInterface that you previously wrote. This means, of course, that it must implement the setMeeting() method.

- Next, notice that VenueServer extends the class UnicastRemoteObject. Unless you've done previous work with RMI, you won't have used this class as a superclass before. This class provides important behavior necessary for remote objects.

- Finally, notice that the lone constructor for the class is a no-argument constructor that, oddly, contains no executable statements. You must explicitly define an empty constructor like this in order that the throws RemoteException clause may be included. As mentioned, every method (or constructor) of a remote object must be specified as a potential source of RemoteExceptions, which are thrown in response to a network problem.

With that out of the way, you can turn your attention to the implementation of the VenueServer class. The VenueServer class has two methods. The main() method starts up the server and gets things rolling. Your clients call the setMeeting() method remotely. Let's look a little deeper into both these methods.

To start up the server, the main() method performs four tasks:

1. First, the main() method calls the System.setSecurityManager() method to ensure that a security manager object is in place. The security manager ensures that downloaded stubs keep their proper place, lest some hacker substitute a stub with a Trojan horse version intended to penetrate the security of your application or system.

2. Once the security manager is in place, the main() method then creates an instance of a VenueServer object.

3. The static rebind() method of the java.rmi.Naming class is used to enter a reference to the new server into the registry of its host computer. This enables clients to get a reference to the server object so that they can send it messages. Notice that for purposes of the RMI registry, the name of the object is "oodexample," not VenueServer. This demonstrates that the name in the registry does not have to be the same as the name of the Java class.

4. Finally, the main() method prints a message to the console window, letting the console operator know that the server is up and running. If you run this application as a local process, you'll see this message in the MS-DOS window you use to start the server.

Note also that the last three tasks are carried out in a `try-catch` block, which simply prints to the console window any unusual conditions that cause your server to fail.

The `setMeeting()` method is required by the `VenueInterface` interface, and is invoked remotely by your client program. For demonstration purposes, this implementation of `setMeeting()` simply returns a randomly chosen time and place for the requested meeting. A more realistic implementation of the method would involve accessing a database of some sort, containing the schedules of potential meeting participants. This could be done using the JDBC facility described in Chapter 14, "Designing Persistent Objects: Database Design and Implementation."

LOOKING AT THE CLIENT

Listing 13.4 shows the client program that works with the VenueServer application: the `VenueClient` class. As you can see, `VenueClient` looks pretty much like an ordinary applet. The only early cue that something is different is the presence of the two `import` statements for RMI packages.

Listing 13.4 The VenueClient Class

```
// VenueClient.java

import java.applet.*;
import java.awt.*;
import java.awt.event.*;
import java.rmi.*;
import java.rmi.server.*;


public class VenueClient  extends Applet
                            implements ActionListener
{
  //  ==========================================
  //        APPLET METHODS
  //  ==========================================
  /*  --Initialization----------------- */
  public void init()
  {
    theList.add("Agnes");
    theList.add("Bob");
    theList.add("Cindy");
    theList.add("David");
    theList.add("Eleanor");
    theText.setEditable(false);
    setLayout(new BorderLayout());

    Panel north = new Panel();
    north.setLayout(new GridLayout(2, 1));
    north.add(new Label("Choose Participants:"));
    north.add(theList);

    Panel center = new Panel();
    center.setLayout(new BorderLayout());
    center.add(new Label("Results:"), "North");
    center.add(theText, "Center");
```

```
      add(north, "North");
      add(center, "Center");
      add(theButton, "South");
      theButton.addActionListener(this);
   }

   //  =========================================
   //      IMPLEMENT ACTIONLISTENER
   //  =========================================
   public void actionPerformed(ActionEvent event)
   {
     String [] names = theList.getSelectedItems();
     if (names.length == 0)
       return;

     try
     {
       // 1. Assign the registered name to a String
       String url = "rmi://localhost/oodexample";

       // 2. Look up the name in the registry
       VenueInterface vi = (VenueInterface) Naming.lookup(url);

       // 3. Use the remote object to get the Venue
       Venue v = vi.setMeeting(names);

       // 4. Use Venue.toString to print it out
       theText.append(v.toString() + "\n");
     }
     catch (Exception e)
     {
       theText.setText(e.toString());
       e.printStackTrace();
     }
   }

   //  =========================================
   //      CLASS AND OBJECT ATTRIBUTES
   //  =========================================
   private Button   theButton = new Button("Set meeting");
   private List     theList   = new List(3, true);
   private TextArea theText   = new TextArea(5, 16);
}
```

The `VenueClient` class contains only two methods, `init()` and `actionPerformed()`. The `init()` method—as usual for applets—builds the user interface. It contains nothing unusual. The `actionPerformed()` method is where all the action is; it is invoked when you click the Set Meeting button. This causes the applet to send a request to the server.

To execute the remote method invocation, you use your `VenueClient` object to carry out these four steps:

1. First you obtain a reference to a `VenueInterface` object living out on the server. You obtain this reference by creating a `String` that forms a URL that includes the host name of the server and the name ("oodexample") under which the server object registered itself. Notice that the protocol used in forming the URL `String` is `rmi://`.

2. This registered name is passed to the `static` method `Naming.lookup()`, which returns a remote object. To use this remote object, you first need to cast it to a `VenueInterface` (not a `VenueServer`).

3. Once you have your `VenueInterface` object, you use it to call the remote `setMeeting()` method, just as if the object were a local object.

4. Finally, you can use the result returned by your remote method invocation like any result. Here, it is displayed in the applet's `TextArea` named `theText`.

The one final piece you'll need to get this all running is an HTML file to allow you to access the applet through appletviewer. (As of this writing, some of the popular browser programs don't yet support RMI, so don't point your browser toward this file. You'll learn how to run the applet in just a bit.) Listing 13.5 shows the HTML file used to execute the client.

" Getting an RMI application running is a little more complicated than the steps you normally go through to run a Java applet or application."

Listing 13.5 The VenueClient.html File

```
<HTML>
<HEAD>
<TITLE>VenueClient.html </TITLE>
</HEAD>

<BODY>
<APPLET Code=VenueClient Width=500 Height=300>
</APPLET>

</BODY>
</HTML>
```

STARTING AND RUNNING THE EXAMPLE

If you've made it this far, stick around a little longer to find out how to actually run this application. It is a little more complicated than the steps you normally go through to run a Java applet or application. Listing 13.6 shows the DOS commands required to start the server. To run this program, you must have TCP/IP support installed. You can run the client and server on the same computer, or run them on separate computers joined by a TCP/IP network.

Listing 13.6 Running the Server

```
C:\> start /min rmiregistry

C:\> javac VenueInterface.java
C:\> javac VenueServer.java

C:\> rmic VenueServer

C:\> start /min java VenueServer
```

If you don't have a permanent connection to a TCP/IP network, you can install the Windows 95 Dial-Up Networking facility, or Windows NT Remote Access Service

(RAS). See your Windows help files for information on installing and configuring these services.

The first step in starting your server is to get the RMI registry program (rmiregistry) going. The registry will run asynchronously in its own minimized window. Next, you need to compile both the interface and server source files. Then you run the rmic utility. This generates the special stub and skeleton files required to make RMI work. To do this, rmic uses the VenueServer.class file, so make sure you compile VenueServer.java first. (Don't include the .class extension when you run rmic). Finally, you can start the server program itself, which runs asynchronously in its own window, after announcing its presence.

To run the client half of this example, you'll have to jump through a similar set of hoops. Listing 13.7 shows the steps necessary to run the client applet. You must first compile the source code for both VenueInterface and VenueClient. Of course, if you're running the client and server on the same machine, you may have already compiled VenueInterface; it won't hurt to compile it a second time. Likewise, the client needs access to the stub (but not the skeleton) file generated by rmic. It's safe to run rmic a second time, so running client and server on the same machine presents no special problem. Finally, run appletviewer and take the client applet out for a spin.

Listing 13.7 Running the Client

```
javac VenueInterface.java
javac VenueClient.java

rmic VenueServer

appletviewer VenueClient
```

Figure 13.6 shows how the VenueClient looks when it runs. Notice that the applet has a preference for meetings in three tourist-friendly European capitals. Substitute names of your co-workers for those hard-coded in the client and see if you can convince your boss to give your new conference scheduling system a try—especially if you've never been to Rome.

Moving to CORBA

Even if you don't have the money to purchase a CORBA compliant ORB, it's interesting to see what changes you'd need to make to port your program from RMI to CORBA. The code required to implement the example program as a typical CORBA program is not that different from the RMI version. The example is based on Visigenic's Visibroker for Java, but other CORBA ORBs work pretty much the same. Start by looking at the VenueInterface definition, which you can see in Listing 13.8.

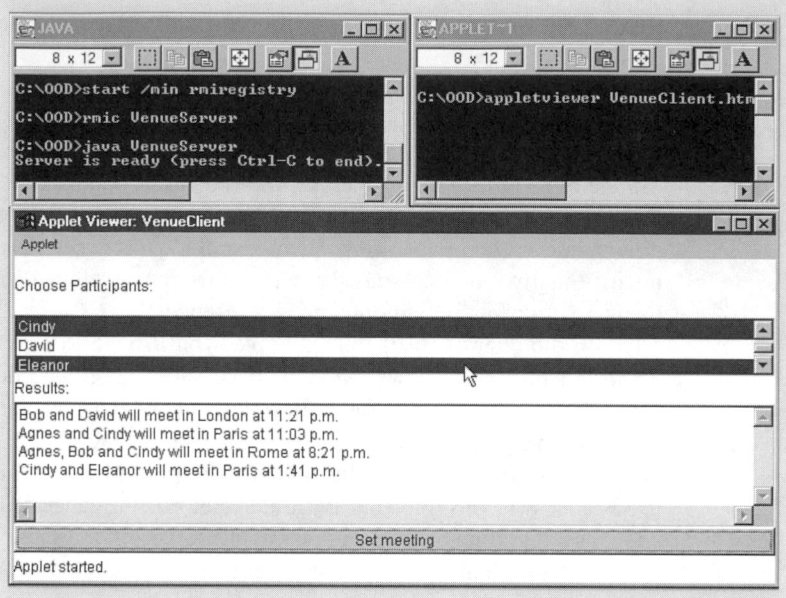

FIGURE 13.6

The VenueClient applet

Listing 13.8 The VenueInterface Interface: CORBA Version

```
public interface VenueInterface extends CORBA.Object
{
    public Venue setMeeting(String [] names) throwsCORBA.SystemException;
}
```

Notice that all you have to change is the name of the interface extended by VenueInterface, and the name of the exception thrown by the setMeeting() method.

THE CORBA SERVER

The server class, too, needs little change. The CORBA version is shown in Listing 13.9.

Listing 13.9 The VenueServer Class: CORBA Version

```
//  VenueServer.java (CORBA edition)

public class VenueServer  extends      _sk_VenueInterface
                          implements  VenueInterface
{
    //  =========================================
    //          CONSTRUCTORS
    //  =========================================
    public VenueServer(String name)
    {
        super(name);      // Give the server a name
    }
```

```
//   ==========================================
//         PUBLIC INTERFACE
//   ==========================================
public Venue setMeeting(String [] names)
               throws CORBA.SystemException
{
  // Code unchanges
}


//   ==========================================
//         MAIN METHOD (CONSOLE APP)
//   ==========================================
public static void main(String [] args)
{
  System.setSecurityManager(new RMISecurityManager());

  try
  {
    CORBA.ORB orb = CORBA.ORB.init();   // initialize the ORB
    CORBA.BOA orb = orb.BOA_init();     // initialize basic object
                                        // adapter
    VenueServer vs = new VenueServer("oodexample");
    boa.obj_is_ready(vs);               // export the server to the ORB
    boa.impl_is_ready();                // begin servicing requests
    System.out.println("Server is ready (press Ctrl-C to end).");
  }
  catch (Exception e)
  {
    System.err.println(e);
  }
}
}
```

The first thing you'll notice is that the class has been changed to extend sk_VenueInterface, which is a skeleton class generated by the Visibroker idl2java utility. Also note that the constructor no longer throws an exception, but it has been changed to include a single argument, a String identifying the server.

The initialization of the ORB, performed by the main() method, requires several changes to move from RMI to CORBA. The revised method creates an ORB object and a BOA (Basic Object Adapter) object. The latter is an adapter object that provides behaviors needed by CORBA server objects. It is sent a reference to the server object and then signaled to begin servicing clients' requests.

A CORBA CLIENT

The client applet, shown in Listing 13.10, is even simpler to change than the server. The only change required is to the statements that invoke the setMeeting() method on the server, which are located in the actionPerformed() method. First, an ORB is created and initialized. Then, a method from the client-side stub, bind(), is used to obtain a reference to the server. After that, everything proceeds as before.

Listing 13.10 The VenueClient Class: CORBA Version

```
public class VenueClient   extends Applet
                           implements ActionListener
{
  //  ==========================================
  //        APPLET METHODS
  //  ==========================================
  /*  --Initialization---------------- */
  public void init()
  {
    // Code unchanged
  }


  //  ==========================================
  //       IMPLEMENT ACTIONLISTENER
  //  ==========================================
  public void actionPerformed(ActionEvent event)
  {
    String [] names = theList.getSelectedItems();
    if (names.length == 0)
      return;

    try
    {
      CORBA.ORB orb = CORBA.ORB.init();  // initialize the ORB
      VenueInterface vi = VenueInterface_var.bind("oodexample");
      Venue v = vi.setMeeting(names);
      theText.append(v.toString() + "\n");
    }
    catch (Exception e)
    {
      theText.setText(e.toString());
      e.printStackTrace();
    }
  }


  //  ==========================================
  //       CLASS AND OBJECT ATTRIBUTES
  //  ==========================================
  private Button    theButton = new Button("Set meeting");
  private List      theList   = new List(3, true);
  private TextArea theText    = new TextArea(5, 16);
}
```

Notations for Remote Objects

Two sorts of diagrams are particularly useful in designing systems that include remote objects. The first is the object interaction diagram described in Chapter 12, "Designing Concurrent Objects." Refer to Figure 13.4 to see how object interaction diagrams can be used to describe how stubs and skeletons interact with clients and servers to perform remote method invocations.

You may also find informal diagrams of the sort used in Figures 13.1, 13.2, 13.3, and 13.5 useful when you need to describe systems that include remote objects. These diagrams let your readers focus on the broad pattern of interaction among objects. Then, you can use object interaction diagrams where necessary to communicate the details of specific interactions.

Design Tips for Remote Objects

The best single piece of advice for working with remote objects is to work at the highest level of abstraction you possibly can. Unless cost or performance considerations dictate some other choice, you should design systems around CORBA rather than one of the alternative architectures.

Design based around CORBA ORBs will be particularly attractive once versions of browsers that include built-in ORBs become available. If you implement your remote clients as applets, you'll find it easy to keep up-to-date versions available to your users, who will receive fresh copies every time they access the Web pages that host your applets. Larger programs can be implemented as applications, but you'll then have to provide some suitable mechanism for updating the .class files when they become outdated.

CORBA is particularly useful for encapsulating data and behavior contained in legacy systems. By using CORBA IDL to create object-oriented wrappers, you can make the functionality of these older systems available in a more modern, user-friendly package. By moving as much functionality as possible to CORBA, you relieve yourself of the responsibility of developing and maintaining programs that provide that functionality. You also free yourself from dependence on a single vendor, because the CORBA market includes a wide range of products from established vendors and small startup companies.

Summary

Remote objects are objects that exist in separate Java Virtual Machines on separate computers. Passing data from a client to a remote server poses several problems, including obtaining a reference to the remote object, marshaling method parameters over the network to the server, and marshaling a return value back to the client.

CORBA provides useful mechanisms and services for implementing remote objects. CORBA is an open standard, for which there are multiple products that run on a variety of computing platforms. CORBA ORBs are simpler to use than sockets and perform better than CGI.

Other technologies for implementing remote objects include sockets, CGI, RMI, and DCOM. The leading alternative to CORBA is DCOM, a Microsoft standard that runs only on Windows platforms.

Questions

For multiple-choice items, indicate all correct responses.

1. True or false. Remote Procedure Call (RPC) allows object-oriented programs to exchange messages.

2. The restructuring of parameters for transmission over a byte stream is called _____.

3. Two significant problems of remote computing are:

   a. Obtaining references to remote objects

   b. The high cost of multiprocessor systems

   c. Getting parameters to, and returning values from, remote objects

   d. Choosing a reliable object request broker

4. The part of an object request broker that runs on the client system is known as a (skeleton/stub) and the part that runs on the server system is known as the (skeleton/stub).

5. Options for implementing remote objects include:

   a. Sockets

   b. CGI

   c. RMI

   d. CORBA

6. The chief advantage of implementing a system using _____ is high performance.

7. Which of the following are *not* open technologies:

   a. CGI

   b. RMI

   c. CORBA

   d. DCOM

8. The principle advantage of RMI is that it's _____.

9. The technology offering the greatest range of facilities and services for remote computing is _____.

10. The program run to establish an object registry for RMI servers is:

   a. `rmidirectory`

   b. `rmiregister`

   c. `rmiregistry`

   d. `rmisearch`

Exercises

1. Using RMI, write a remote server that echoes text, like the `CipherServer` example of the previous chapter. Write an applet client that tests the server.

2. Using RMI, write a remote server and an applet client that allow users to send text to one another ("chat") via the applets. The applet's user interface should include a `TextField` for input and a `TextArea` for output.

3. Using RMI, write a remote server that functions as a simple Web proxy server for client applets. An applet can send a `String` that specifies a URL to the server, which uses the `URLConnection` class to fetch the document. It then transmits it back to the client applet, which displays it in the browser window using `showDocument()`. By operating on special ports, such an arrangement can be used to allow selective access across an Internet firewall.

To Learn More

There are several books that will help you learn more about designing remote objects.
The following book includes a comprehensive analysis of alternative technologies for remote computing. It also includes thorough coverage of CORBA as it relates to Java:

- Orfali, Robert, and Dan Harkey. *Client/Server Programming with Java and CORBA*. New York: John Wiley & Sons, 1997.

The following books deal with CORBA generally:

- Otte, Randy, Paul Patrick, and Mark Roy. *Understanding CORBA: The Common Object Request Broker Architecture*. Upper Saddle River, New Jersey: Prentice Hall, 1996.

- Siegel, Jon. *CORBA: Fundamentals and Programming*. New York: John Wiley & Sons, 1996.

14

Designing Persistent Objects: Database Design and Implementation

Persistence is a virtue—not only for people, but also for objects. What, you ask, is a persistent object? A *persistent object* retains its attributes even after the program running it terminates. In fact, most business programs would be useless without persistent objects. Suppose that you've automated your entire catalog business by using the latest, state-of-the-art Java applets and applications with, unfortunately, one little omission: you've made no provision for persistence.

On a stifling hot July day, the businesses in your town are all running their air conditioning at maximum, hoping to keep their workers and customers comfortable. Meanwhile, somewhere in the south central U.S., a power plant fails. Of course, all the other plants connected to the power grid immediately step up output to offset the drop in power production, but some of them also fail under the increased strain. The remaining plants find it harder to keep up with the demand for power, and shutdowns spread across the country like a tsunami.

> *" For business programs, persistence is not only useful, it's essential. "*

When the rolling wave hits the plant that supplies power to your business district, its generators shut down, attempting to protect themselves from overexertion. Your lights flicker and, for a few tens of milliseconds, all computing ceases. Fortunately, the outage is brief. Power is restored in less than a minute, and your computers are again happily humming and clicking in under five minutes.

But while all your computers are back at work, all the objects in all your programs have lost the state they had before the power failure—all of them, that is, that still exist. Most have simply disappeared, as there are now no references to them. How, you wonder, are you to match up Ms. Mertz's order with the 1,100 shipments being processed? Was it chocolates she ordered, or bath soap? And what about Mr. Munster, Ms. Stevens, and the other 1,100 customers with pending orders?

For business programs, persistence is not only useful, it's essential.

In this chapter you will learn:

- How to design relational databases that can be used to give your objects persistence.

- How to use entity/relationship (E/R) modeling to assist you in database design.

- How to design normalized databases that help avoid inconsistent and corrupted data.

> *" Both tables and classes represent patterns for storing information about a single kind of entity. "*

Types of Persistence

Persistence can be achieved in many different ways. For most of the history of computing, persistence has been achieved through the use of files stored on magnetic tape or, more recently, on magnetic disk drives. Today, however, the most common way to make your objects persistent is to use a relational database, which arranges and manages the storage of your data.

Using a relational database isn't the only way to achieve object persistence. There are also object-oriented databases, although these aren't yet as widely used as relational databases. Chapter 16, "Designing with Components," presents another way of achieving persistence—one that uses the `Serializable` interface provided by the Java Application Programming Interface (API).

Relational Database Concepts and Terms

A relational database stores data in *tables,* like those depicted in Figure 14.1.

Tables are much like spreadsheets, consisting of *rows* and *columns*. Each table of a database stores information about a single type of entity. For example, the Book table stores information about books, and the Author table stores information about authors.

Each row of a database table stores information about a single instance of the related entity. For example, the first row of the Book table stores information about book #2453, titled *Java is Easy.*

Publishing Database

Book Table			
BookID	Title	SeriesID	Price
2453	Java is Easy	9716	$49.95
2567	Java is Fun	9716	$39.95
2773	SmallTalk Rules	9719	$149.95
2899	Java for Everyone	9716	$13.95

Customer Table		
CustomerID	Customer Name	City
1002	Smith, Sam	Ada, OK
1005	Smith, Louise	Ada, OK
1006	Adams, Adam	Paradise, CA
1007	Yantos, Juan	Washington, DC

Author Table		
AuthorID	AuthorName	City
101	Ackerman, Richard	Chicago, IL
102	Yantos, Juan	Washington, DC
104	Agram, Anne	Los Angeles, CA
110	Muny, E.Z.	Dallas, TX

Series Table	
SeriesID	Series Title
9716	Java Programming
9719	Small Antics

FIGURE 14.1

A relational database

Each column of a database table stores information about a particular attribute of the related entity. For example, the second column of the Book table stores book titles. Within a given row of the Book table, the value in the second column (the Title column) gives the book's title.

If a database is especially large, its tables may be grouped into units called *catalogs,* much the same way that Java classes can be grouped into packages. In fact, as shown in Table 14.1, there's considerable similarity between terms used to describe databases and terms used to describe object-oriented programs. Don't try to press these analogies too far—a table and a class aren't the same thing. The most obvious difference between them is that a table doesn't encapsulate behavior along with its data, whereas a class or object does. But tables and classes do represent patterns for storing information about a single kind of entity.

TABLE 14.1
ANALOGIES BETWEEN DATABASE TERMS AND OBJECT-ORIENTED TERMS

Database Term	Object-Oriented Term
Catalog	Package
Table	Class
Row (or record)	Object
Column (or attribute)	Field (or attribute)

Creating and Manipulating Databases and Tables

To create a Java program, you need a text editor and compiler (or an IDE that combines their functions). Similarly, to create or manipulate a database, you need some tools. Even if you're just designing a database, you'll find it helpful to have these tools because you then can try out your design.

THE DATABASE SERVER

First, you need the database engine (also known as a *database server*). A modern database engine understands some dialect of Structured Query Language (SQL). When your program sends SQL commands describing a set of table rows to the database engine, the engine returns the actual rows.

Most database engines include utilities that let you create databases and tables. You can also create tables by using SQL. Some popular database engines are

- Borland Interbase
- IBM DB2
- Informix Universal Server, Online Workgroup Server, and others
- Microsoft Access and SQL Server
- Oracle Server 7
- Sybase SQL Anywhere and SQL Server

DATABASE DRIVERS

To access your database with a Java program, you'll also need a driver class. You can use the JDBC-ODBC bridge included in the Java Developer's Kit (JDK), but the bridge offers limited functionality. (JDBC stands for *Java Database Connectivity* and is part of the JDK. ODBC stands for *Open Database Connectivity* and is a standard developed by Microsoft for accessing a wide variety of different database servers.)

For serious database development, you'll probably want to investigate the various commercial database drivers available. You may also want to investigate middleware servers, which can provide access to multiple database engines by using a single driver class. Information on drivers and middleware servers is available on Sun's Java Web site at `http://java.sun.com/products/jdbc/index.html`. You can also read more about how database servers and drivers work together in Chapter 18, "Architectures: Design-In-the-Huge."

THE JDBC API

When your database engine and driver are in place, you use the classes and interfaces of the `java.sql` package that comprise the so-called JDBC facility to send commands to the engine and obtain the results it sends back. The details of writing Java programs that use JDBC and SQL are beyond the scope of this chapter.

Database Design

Traditional software development included the activities of systems analysis and system design. Systems analysis focused on the system from the user's perspective, whereas system design focused on the system from the technical perspective. A logical/physical boundary separated the two activities. The user was interested in *what* the system would do, not *how* the system would do it. The former is a logical, conceptual viewpoint, whereas the latter is a physical, concrete viewpoint.

Object-oriented technology broke down the barrier—or at least much of the barrier—between systems analysis and system design by making it possible to build working software structures (classes and objects) that had counterparts in the real world of the user. The logical and physical viewpoints were brought into close correspondence.

Relational database design is more like traditional software development than object-oriented software development in that it consists of two discrete activities: logical database design and physical database design. The logical database design activity focuses on the user's data needs. The physical database design activity focuses on choosing a concrete database structure that supports the logical design and balances additional criteria such as performance and reliability.

The relational database design process includes these steps:

1. Perform logical database design.

2. Perform physical database design.

3. Assign data types to columns.

4. Prototype the database.

Logical database design is usually performed by using a technique known as *entity/relationship* (*E/R*) *modeling*. The model database that results is then structurally transformed during physical design, using a technique known as *database normalization*, to minimize the likelihood of database anomalies. (A *database anomaly* is a situation where data is lost or inaccurately stored.) Finally, a data type is chosen for each column of the database, which is then prototyped and revised as needed.

Design Quality

You might wonder why you should bother with database design—what's the purpose? By going through the process of database design, you'll improve your programs in three specific ways. When you design a database, using the process of database design, you'll create a database structure that

- Controls data redundancy
- Ensures data integrity
- Accommodates ad hoc queries

An important potential benefit of a database is that it helps you control the amount of *redundant data*. Think, for example, of the files of a typical organization and ask yourself, "In how many places would the name of a worker be stored?" You'll probably think of such places as the payroll file, the benefits file, and the telephone directory. But there are other, less obvious, places as well. What about parking spaces, lockers, the office door, the e-mail directory, and so on?

> *"One chief potential benefit of a database is that it helps you control the amount of redundant data."*

Now consider what's necessary when Fred Gonner marries Ima Gladde and she elects to change her name to Mrs. Gonner. All those places that used to say "Ima Gladde" must be changed to say "Ima Gonner." Even in an efficiently run organization, it may require several months to hunt down and destroy every reference to Ima Gladde.

The problem is that Ima's name is stored redundantly—that is, in many places. Redundant data in computer files wastes storage space and requires excess processing time to revise. Potentially worse, errors can result when the "correction police" haven't yet caught up with all the redundant instances.

> *"Database normalization is the key to controlling data redundancy within a database."*

As you'll see, database normalization is the key to controlling data redundancy within a database. Normalizing a database is also one important step toward ensuring *database integrity*. Organizations often spend large sums creating and maintaining databases. To protect this investment, it's important for the database design to address data integrity.

An *ad hoc database query* is an unplanned request for information. An e-mail directory system may regularly provide the e-mail address of a worker to someone who knows the worker's name. But can the supporting database also provide a worker's name, given the worker's e-mail address? It's simply not possible at design time to anticipate every possible question that will ever be asked. Nevertheless, it's important to provide the flexibility to handle unanticipated queries. The main step you can take to facilitate handling of ad hoc queries is database normalization.

If you're beginning to think that database normalization is the answer to the world's problems, you're catching on. Database normalization won't cure the hiccups, but it's an excellent prescription for improving database performance and reliability.

Are there any drawbacks to using a database for object persistence? Not really. You may have heard that early relational databases were known for poor performance. Although there are recent cases of failure in the application of relational database technology to very-large-scale databases, modern relational databases are much improved over their ancestors. Moreover, it's not at all clear that the recent failures you may have read about are the result of failed technology.

In cooking, it's axiomatic that the ingredients count. But you'll never hear an accomplished chef avoiding the blame for a mediocre ceviche by blaming the ingredients. The wise chef doesn't prepare ceviche except on days when ingredients of the proper quality are available. Similarly, a failure in application of relational technology must be laid, in at least some degree, at the feet of the analysts and designers, and not solely blamed on "inadequate technology."

" Database normalization won't cure the hiccups, but it's an excellent prescription for improving database performance and reliability. "

Entity/Relationship (E/R) Modeling

The first step in database design is creating a logical database model, using a technique called entity/relationship (E/R) modeling. Before learning how to *perform* E/R modeling, though, you'll learn how to *read* an E/R diagram. Figure 14.2 shows an E/R diagram for the same database that was shown in Figure 14.1. Review the database in Figure 14.1 before moving on to study Figure 14.2.

The E/R diagram consists of rectangles and lines. Each rectangle contains a name, and each line is labeled with a phrase. Each end of a line is labeled with the digit *1* or the letter *N*. You'll learn about the labels in a bit; for now, focus on the rectangles and the lines.

The rectangles correspond to the database tables shown in Figure 14.1: Author, Book, Customer, and Series. That's easy. But what do the lines correspond to? They tell you which tables are related, much like the lines connecting two associations in the

FIGURE 14.2
An entity/relationship diagram

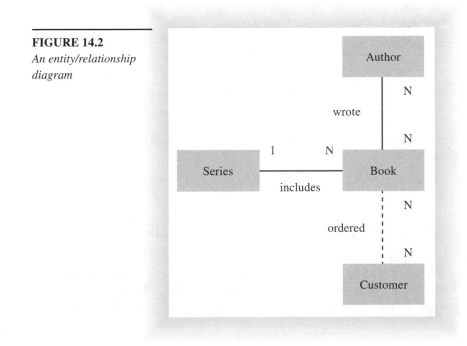

class diagrams you studied in Chapters 7 and 8. Notice the two types of lines: the line between Book and Customer (the *sold to* line) is dotted, whereas all the other lines are solid.

ENTITIES AND RELATIONSHIPS

In an E/R diagram, the rectangles are referred to as *entities,* and the lines are referred to as *relationships*. That's, of course, how the E/R diagram got its name: it depicts entities and the relationships that join them together. But what exactly is the essential difference between an entity and a relationship?

An *entity* represents a thing or a concept. An entity is usually

> *" An entity represents a thing or a concept. In contrast, a relationship represents an association between entities. "*

- **A person**—A bank teller or the President of the U.S.

- **A place**—Conference room 3 or Liberty Hall

- **A real-world object**—A deposit slip or the U.S. Constitution

- **An event**—Making a deposit or the signing of the Declaration of Independence

- **A concept**—An account or troop strength

In contrast, a *relationship* represents an association between entities. Sometimes the relationship represents an event that links the entities; other times it's merely a logical affinity between them:

- **A logical affinity**—Being present in Liberty Hall (relationship between a person and a place)

- **A logical affinity**—Being a descendent of George Washington (a relationship between two people)

- **An event**: Making a deposit or the signing of the Declaration of Independence

Notice that an event may be either an entity or a relationship. This ambiguity will be resolved shortly.

OPTIONAL RELATIONSHIPS AND CARDINALITY

Recall that the lines in the E/R diagram show which entities are related to each other. You can see that Author is related to Book, Book is related to Series, and Book is related to Customer. Remember also that the line connecting Book with Customer is dotted but the others are solid. This is because it represents an *optional* relationship, whereas the other lines represent *required* relationships. Every book has an author and every book is part of some series. Not every book has a customer, however—the book may be so new that it hasn't yet arrived at the warehouse and therefore can't have been sold.

The phrase that labels each line identifies the relationship that the line represents. The line from Author to Book is labeled *wrote* because the line tells which Author wrote which book. Or, if you prefer, it tells which book was written by which author. If you're partial to the latter, you might prefer the label *written by*, which is perfectly okay. Some designers actually label every line twice. Such a designer might have labeled the line from Author to Book as *wrote/written by*. This isn't a major point, so draw your E/R diagrams to suit yourself—as long as your boss doesn't object.

The 1's and N's haven't slipped through the cracks—you'll come to them shortly. Hold your curiosity concerning them for just another moment.

DATABASE RELATIONSHIPS AND RELATIONSHIP TABLES

You've seen how relationships are represented in the E/R diagram as lines. But how are relationships actually represented in a database? Let's look at an example by using the database in Figure 14.1.

One important relationship in the publishing industry is that between a book and its series. Can you use Figure 14.1 to determine what series includes the book *Java is Easy*? It's easy: *Java is Easy* is the book described by the first row of the Book table. You can see that it's part of series #9716. After moving to the Series table, you can see that series #9716 is titled Java Programming. Thus, you can use the series number you derived from the Book table, #9716, as a kind of *key* to unlock the Series table and extract the information you want. Such keys are the—well...—key to implementing database relationships.

Okay, here's a harder one. Can you use Figure 14.1 to determine who wrote the book *Java is Easy*? No, you can't; the information isn't present in the database. How might you add this information? Figure 14.3 shows you.

Two new tables have appeared: Authorship and Sales. The former tells which author wrote what book, the latter tells which customer has ordered what book. See if you can use Figure 14.3 to learn who wrote *Java is Easy*. The book has two authors: Ackerman and Muny. Now, see if you can learn what book was ordered by Sam Smith. You should find that he ordered *SmallTalk Rules* on July 2.

How would an E/R diagram based on the revised database look? Figure 14.4 shows you.

Publishing Database

Book Table

BookID	Title	SeriesID	Price
2453	Java is Easy	9716	$49.95
2567	Java is Fun	9716	$39.95
2773	SmallTalk Rules	9719	$149.95
2899	Java for Everyone	9716	$13.95

Customer Table

CustomerID	Customer Name	City
1002	Smith, Sam	Ada, OK
1005	Smith, Louise	Ada, OK
1006	Adams, Adam	Paradise, CA
1007	Yantos, Juan	Washington, DC

Series Table

SeriesID	Series Title
9716	Java Programming
9719	Small Antics

Authorship Table

BookID	AuthorID
2453	101
2453	110
2773	102
2899	101
2899	104

Sales Table

BookID	CustomerID	Date Shipped
2453	1005	June 12
2587	1005	June 13
2773	1002	July 2
2899	1005	January 4

Author Table

AuthorID	AuthorName	City
101	Ackerman, Richard	Chicago, IL
102	Yantos, Juan	Washington, DC
104	Agram, Anne	Los Angeles, CA
110	Muny, E.Z.	Dallas, TX

FIGURE 14.3

The revised database

Notice that the Authorship and Sales tables appear as diamonds in the E/R diagram. As you know, these tables represent relationships. For example, the Authorship table describes a relationship between a Book and its Author. The diamond reminds you of this. It tells you that you can read the lines that pass into the diamond as though they passed *through* it, joining a pair of rectangles.

Note that the relationship between a Book and its Series isn't represented by a diamond. A mere line joins the rectangle for Book with that of Series. Why? Recall that the Book-Series relationship was explicit in the database of Figure 14.1, which you could use to find which books were part of which series.

Diamonds represent relationships that require a database table of their own, like Authorship and Sales. You might say that such relationships are so powerful they're transformed into entities, becoming shapes rather than mere lines.

FIGURE 14.4

*The revised entity/
relationship diagram*

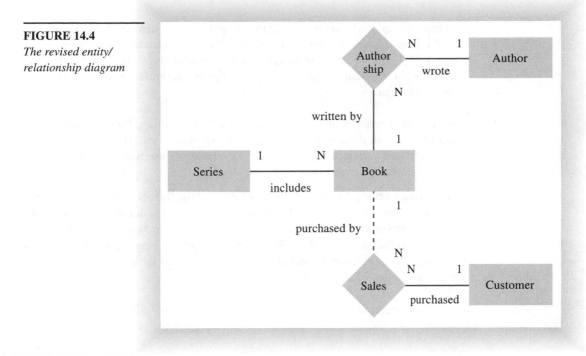

It really shouldn't surprise you that a relational database represents entities and relationship as tables, although they are different things. After all, *everything* in a relational database is represented as a table or as part of a table. There simply aren't any other options.

CARDINALITY

It's finally time to learn about the notations 1 and N on the lines of the E/R diagram. These represent the *cardinality* of each relationship, which refers to the relative number of participants from each entity that's part of the relationship. *Cardinality*, then, is merely a sesquepedalian way of saying *number*. If you look at any line that joins two entities, you'll encounter a number at each end of the line:

- **The number *1* and the letter *N* (in either order).** This is called a *1:N relationship*. (If you like to be contrary, you might call it an *N:1* relationship.) An example is the relationship shown in Figure 14.2 between the Book entity and the Series entity. In this 1:N relationship, each book belongs to exactly one series, although a series can include an arbitrary number (*N*) of books.

- **The letters *N* and *N*.** This is called an *N:N relationship*. Figure 14.2 showed two such relationships: that between Author and Book, and that between Book and Customer. Taking the former as an example, a book might have multiple (*N*) authors, and a given author might have written multiple (*N*) books. Note that these are the very relationships that became diamonds in Figure 14.4. During database design, every N:N relationship is converted to a pair of 1:N relationships. No N:N relationships are permitted to appear in a finished design.

 The numbers *1* and *1*. This is called a *1:1 relationship*. You actually don't find any of these in Figure 14.2 or Figure 14.4. Most 1:1 relationships are eliminated during database design. Occasionally, some are allowed to remain, as you'll see shortly.

You may have wondered why E/R diagrams don't show the columns of the database tables. Some experts recommend that you include the columns, drawing them as ovals, connected by lines with the entity that contains them. If your database design is even moderately complex, however, the E/R diagram is likely to become so cluttered that it's unreadable. If you're concerned about keeping track of table columns, list them elsewhere, not on the E/R diagram.

Remember

Restated, the principle of abstraction says, "Less is more." Abstraction is the designer's friend, helping the designer combat complexity.

> *" A conference room is a better workplace for your team than an office, because it reduces the likelihood that you'll be interrupted. "*

Preparing E/R Diagrams

Now that you can read E/R diagrams like an expert, you're ready to learn how to prepare them. Your first step in database design is to assemble a team. Database design isn't a job for a lone ranger; you'll need the assistance of a team that includes several members who know the problem domain well.

A conference room is a better workplace for your team than an office, because it reduces the likelihood that you'll be interrupted. A conference room may offer a whiteboard or flip charts, either of which is helpful. You might also find an overhead projector with a stack of blank transparency sheets and a handful of colored markers helpful, as well as a large blank wall and a package of sticky notes. While you're at it, coffee would be nice too; doughnuts would be even better. (By the way, Uncle Sam may pick up part of your donut bills for such meetings—consult your tax advisor. Use your savings to buy additional copies of this book for your friends and family.)

Recall that, as always, design is an iterative process. Although it's described here in linear fashion, that's because it's easier to explain it and understand it in linear fashion. But design isn't linear—at least, *good design* usually isn't. (The occasional burst of genius might allow you to create a great design in a single sitting, but it's rare.)

STEP 1: IDENTIFY THE COLUMNS

Although the database columns (attributes) don't appear in the E/R diagram, they're an important part of your database design. They're also a good starting place because they're concrete and familiar to the users who participate on your design team. Spend time brainstorming the question, "What attributes or characteristics do we need to keep track of?" List the candidates on the whiteboard so that every team member can see them. Use only half of the whiteboard, reserving the remainder for step 2.

It's also possible to start by identifying entities (tables) rather than columns. But this often leads to quick decisions by the team, at a time when further exploration and discussion is generally warranted. If you're pressed for time, you may find it helpful to begin by identifying entities; otherwise, you're better advised to focus on columns first.

Once the team seems to have identified all the candidate columns, and before moving on to identifying the entities and relationships, you should clean up your list of candidate columns. It's likely that several of the candidate columns are synonyms: different names for the same thing. Identify any synonyms and eliminate the unnecessary entries.

If your organization uses a standard way of naming column attributes, you should revise your list of candidate columns, giving each entry a name that conforms to your organization's standard. Such standards usually govern use of uppercase and lowercase letters and special characters within names. In an organization that writes Java programs, the standards will probably look a great deal like the informal conventions used by Java programmers. Standards often allow the same name, or nearly the same name, to be used by users, designers, and programmers.

Discussion may disclose that some of the candidates aren't attributes or characteristics at all. Some of them may actually be candidate entities and should be moved to a list, perhaps at the other end of the whiteboard, in preparation for the next design step. Others are simply irrelevant and can be discarded.

STEP 2: IDENTIFY THE ENTITIES

Now that you've identified the columns, it's time to identify the entities. Begin by grouping the columns under implied subjects. For example, Name, Phone number, and E-mail may point to an entity named Worker. Give each candidate entity an appropriate name, and write the candidate entities and their columns on the remaining half of the whiteboard, reserved during step 1.

You might experience some difficulties with similar entities. For example, should the entities Worker and Manager be combined into a single Employee entity, or should they remain separate? Ideally, you would show Worker and Manager as subtypes of Employee, but the relational database model isn't object-oriented and doesn't allow you to construct inheritance relationships. Make your best guess at this point, but don't hesitate to reconsider your decision as the need arises. If you do decide to combine the entities, you may need to add a column to contain a type code that will enable you to distinguish them. For example, you might add an EmployeeType column that takes the value 'M' for a Manager and 'W' for a Worker.

When all the entities have been transferred, you can erase the half of the board used in step 1. Then begin an E/R diagram by drawing a rectangle for each entity.

STEP 3: IDENTIFY DATABASE PRIMARY KEYS

Each table of a relational database should include a column, or combination of columns, that can be used to *uniquely* identify every row of the table. This column, or combination of columns, is called the *primary key* of the table.

In assigning a primary key, you have three options:

- Use an existing column as the primary key.
- Use a combination of existing columns as the primary key, called a *composite* primary key.
- Construct an artificial key.

Primary Keys for Entity Tables

Most of the time, your best option is to construct an artificial key. To understand why, consider first the possibility of using an existing column as the primary key.

Suppose that you're designing a payroll system and trying to decide what primary key to use to identify rows in the Employees table. Your first thought may be to use Social Security Number, which is listed as a column in the Employees Table. This may work just fine until you find that your system has to support a subsidiary based in Toronto, where the employees don't have Social Security Numbers. Or, however unlikely, you may find employees that have the same Social Security Number. (This, of course, is the result of an error somewhere—perhaps at the Social Security Administration.) Do you tell the employees that they can't get paid until the Social Security Administration corrects the error? This probably isn't a reasonable choice.

Failure to recognize that supposedly unique keys are sometimes not unique is a common error. Several states have experienced problems with their motor vehicle records because designers made this faulty assumption.

Similar problems attend the use of a combination of fields as a primary key. What appears to be unique might not actually, and always, be unique. By using an artificial key, one that your organization constructs, you can avoid this problem. Your payroll department can assign each new employee a number, which you can use as the primary key of the Employees table. If two employees are somehow erroneously assigned the same number, folks in the payroll department can fix the problem themselves. (Of course, your payroll department may not be a lot more responsive than the Social Security Administration.)

Primary Keys for Relationship Tables

An exception to this advice applies when the table in question represents a relationship. In this case, it's usual to form the primary key of the table from the combination of columns that are primary keys of the related tables. For example, the Authorship table in Figure 14.4 might take as its primary key the combination of AuthorID, which is the primary key of the Author table, and ISBN, which is the primary key of the Book table.

The same technique won't work, however, for the Sales table. You might try defining its primary key as the combination of ISBN and CustomerID. To see what's wrong with this, consider what would happen when a customer orders a book and likes it so much she decides to order another copy for a friend. There are two sales, but each would have the same value of the primary key.

How do you fix this? One approach would be to add a third column to the key, DateShipped. This, too, presents problems, because it's possible for a customer to order multiple copies that end up being shipped the same day. A better solution is to construct an artificial key, call it SalesID, and assign it a value by sequentially numbering each sale.

Why wasn't this necessary for the Author-Book relationship? Although a customer can place any number of orders for the same book, an author is listed only once on the cover of a book. For a given book and author, there will be only a single row within the Authorship table; but for a given book and customer, there may be any number of rows within the Sales table.

> *The primary key **must** never include an optional column.*

 Remember

When assigning primary keys, an artificial key is usually best. A possible exception is when the table defines a single-instance relationship between two tables.

Primary Keys and Optional Columns

When choosing a primary key, make sure that you don't include any optional columns as part of the primary key. Most databases allow you to add rows to a table, even if you don't know the values of all the columns. The database will use a placeholder value, called *null*, as the value of any omitted fields. As a database designer, you can decide which columns should enjoy this courtesy and which must always be supplied before a table row is added. The primary key, however, must *never* include an optional column.

Once you've decided on the primary key for a table, make a note of it, either with the list of columns or on the E/R diagram itself. It doesn't matter which; just be consistent.

STEP 4: IDENTIFY AND MANAGE THE RELATIONSHIPS

Now that you have the entities, attributes, and primary keys defined, you're ready to identify the relationships between the entities in your database. Here is how you do that.

Start by considering, one at a time, each pair of entities. If the pair is related, join them with a line and label the line with a phrase describing the relationship. Then label the line with the cardinality of the relationship: 1:1; 1:N, or N:N. Your line should be solid for a required relationship and dotted or dashed for an optional relationship. Look back to Figure 14.2 to see how this is done.

Occasionally, you may find an entity that's related to itself in some way. For example, parts in a Parts table may be related because they're components in the same assembly. These are called *self* relationships. Scan your entities to identify any self relationships and include these on your E/R diagram by drawing a loop that begins, and ends, with the same entity. Figure 14.5 shows how this is done.

Evaluating and Transforming Relationships

Some types of relationships are forbidden to appear in a finished database design. Each of these that appears in your database design must be converted to another type. Other types need no special treatment. Here's what should be down for each type of relationship:

- **1:N relationships.** These should be the mainstay of your database design and need no special treatment. Sometimes such relationships are termed *master-detail* relationships, because each entry in the master table (the 1 side of the relationship) may be related to a set of entries in the detail table (the N side of the relationship).

FIGURE 14.5

A self relationship

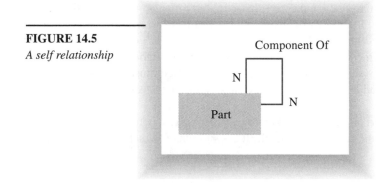

- **1:1 relationships.** Often, a *1:1* relationship points to a database design problem. The question you should ask is, "Should these entities be combined into a single entity?" If so, combine them. If not, accept the 1:1 relationship.

- **N:N relationships.** All N:N relationships must be removed from your database design. You accomplish this by replacing each N:N relationship with a pair of 1:N relationships. You may need to add a new entity, represented as a diamond on the E/R diagram, to perform this conversion. Make sure that any entities you add are included in the list of entities.

Identifying Foreign Keys

A foreign key is simply a table column that takes as its value the primary key of another table.

The final task in managing the relationships is identifying any *foreign keys* within your database tables. What, you ask, is a foreign key? Well, foreign keys have nothing to do with making sure that your application works throughout the countries of the Pacific rim. A foreign key is simply a table column that takes as its value the primary key of another table.

A foreign key is used to establish a relationship between database tables. For example, consider the Book-Series relationship shown in Figure 14.4. Each row of the Book table includes a column that contains the SeriesID of the book. SeriesID is the primary key of the Series table and is a foreign key of the Book table. It's said to *point* to the Series table, linking a book with the series that includes it.

Although a table must have only one primary key, it may have one, none, or many foreign keys. For example, the Authorship table in Figure 14.4 might take as its primary key the combination of AuthorID and ISBN. In this case, its foreign keys would be AuthorID, pointing to the Author table, and ISBN, pointing to the Book table.

Even if you create an artificial key as the primary key of the Authorship table, AuthorID and BookID will still be foreign keys within it. Any column that points into another table must be identified as a foreign key.

In the same place you identified the primary keys, note the names of any foreign keys included in each table. Make sure that it's clear whether a given column is a primary key or foreign key. A good way to do this is to put the letters *PK* next to the primary key and the letters *FK* next to any foreign keys.

STEP 5: REITERATE

Don't settle for satisfactory when excellent may require only a little more diligence.

Hopefully, you've felt free to iterate within and among the four steps presented so far. If not, this step is included as a reminder that you can, and should, do so. Go back, check your work, rethink your earlier decisions in the light of additional knowledge, and change what needs changing. Don't settle for satisfactory when excellent may require only a little more diligence.

Understanding Database Anomalies

Thus far, the database design process has led you through creation of an E/R diagram, a list of columns for each table, and a list of primary keys and foreign keys for each table. The next database design step is normalization. Before you learn *how* to normalize a database design, it's good to understand *why* database designs need to be normalized.

One primary reason to normalize your database is to eliminate the possibility of the following kinds of database corruption:

- The insert anomaly

- The update anomaly

- The delete anomaly

So that you can see how these occur, Figure 14.6 shows an example of an unnormalized database. As you'll soon see, *unnormalized* translates to *bad*.

The database in Figure 14.6 is intended to store information on book sales. Notice that no single column of the table can uniquely identify each row of the table. Assume, therefore, that the combination of all four fields will be used as the primary key.

What happens, then, when you attempt to add a new store to the table—say, store #1205 in Cincinnati? Everything's fine as long as that store has already placed an order. If not, what value should you use for the BookID? Because BookID is part of the primary key, which can't include any optional columns, you must supply a value for BookID. Because you don't have one, you can't add the row to the table. This is called the *insert anomaly*.

FIGURE 14.6

An unnormalized database

BookSales Table			
BookID	City	StoreID	Quantity
2453	Boston	1201	15
2567	Boston	1201	15
2453	Los Angeles	1202	15
2567	Chicago	1203	12
2773	Chicago	1203	12
2899	Chicago	1203	12
2773	New York	1204	2
2899	New York	1204	2

“It’s easy to update the normalized database without tripping over any anomalies.”

You’ll run into the second type of anomaly, the *delete anomaly*, when you discover that the shipment sent to store #1202 was really meant for store #1203. If you delete the erroneous shipment (recorded in the third row of the table), you’ll also delete your only record showing that store #1202 is located in Los Angeles.

The final type of anomaly, the *update anomaly*, occurs when you find out that store #1203 has moved from Chicago to Denver. You’re forced to look through the entire database and change every record that pertains to store #1203 to reflect the move. The example database has only several such records. But consider that in the general case, hundreds, thousands, or even millions of records could need to be changed.

The problem, in each case, is that the table has too many columns. Several tables should have been used to store this information, not just one. Figure 14.7 shows how the single table should be divided into several.

It’s easy to update the normalized database without tripping over any anomalies. You can add a store without mangling the orders or delete an order without losing track of a store. You can even change the location of a store by updating a single table row.

“Normalizing a database involves checking its tables to see whether each conforms to three simple rules.”

Normalization

Now that you see the benefits of normalization, you’re probably eager to learn how to normalize a database. Good news: normalization is straightforward and easy. Normalizing a database involves checking its tables to see whether each conforms to three simple rules. If it does, you’re done. If it doesn’t, you must restructure the database so that each table conforms to the rules.

FIGURE 14.7
The same database, normalized

Store Table	
StoreID	City
1201	Boston
1202	Los Angeles
1203	Chicago
1204	New York

Sales Table		
BookID	StoreID	Quantity
2453	1201	15
2567	1201	15
2453	1202	15
2567	1203	12
2773	1203	12
2899	1203	12
2773	1204	2
2899	1204	2

The key to database normalization is understanding the term *normal form*. Each rule mentioned in the preceding paragraph calls for tables in your database to conform to a particular form. If all your tables conform to rule 1, your database is said to be in *first normal form* (1NF). Likewise, if all your tables conform to rule 2, your database is in *second normal form* (2NF). As you might expect, a database is in *third normal form* (3NF) when all its tables conform to rule 3.

The normal forms are arranged in a hierarchy. You can't reach second normal form without going through first normal form, and you can't reach third normal form without satisfying the rules for first normal form and second normal form. As Figure 14.8 shows, the rules for third normal form guarantee that you've satisfied the lesser requirements of the other forms.

Some database experts have defined additional normal forms beyond third normal form. In practice, most real databases that satisfy the rules for third normal form also satisfy the rules for these higher levels of normalization. Consequently, only the first three normal forms are presented in this section.

FIRST NORMAL FORM: ONLY ATOMIC VALUES

Because a database that's in third normal form is also in first and second normal form, you might not want to bother learning about first and second normal form. Why not simply go straight to third normal form and be done with it? As is usual in design, doing everything at once isn't the most efficient or effective way of getting to your goal.

A database table in first normal formal form is one in which each column is atomic— that is, there are no repeating groups or *arrays* of columns. Surprisingly, this is one of the most common mistakes that beginning database designers make.

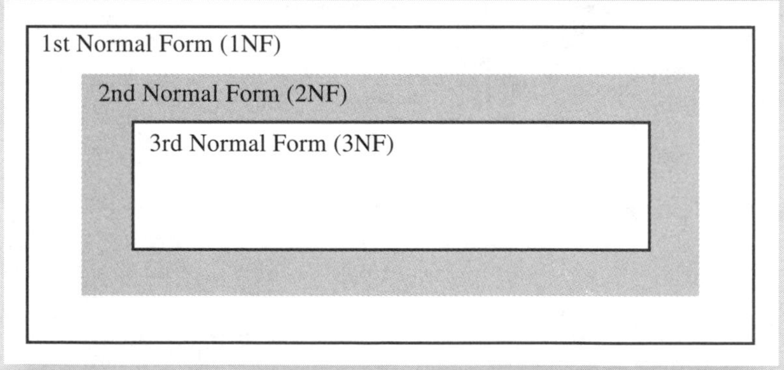

FIGURE 14.8

A database in third normal form is also in first and second normal form

1st Normal Form (1NF)

    2nd Normal Form (2NF)

        3rd Normal Form (3NF)

No Repeating Groups

Let's see how you might end up with repeating groups in your database. Suppose that you decide that the publishing database of Figure 14.3 could be improved. Why not make things easier by restructuring the Authorship table so that all the authors of a book could be listed in a single table row, allowing room for up to three authors? The identifiers for the authors of the book *Java is Easy*, author #101 and author #110, would be stored in a single row like this:

```
BookID       Author #1      Author #2       Author #3
2453         101            110             null
```

Now whenever you look up a book ID, you no longer have to go looking through different records to find the coauthors. All the data is right at your fingertips. What could be better? Well, stop and think for a second. What will you do when a book has more than three authors? Will the fourth and subsequent authors simply be ignored?

The identifiers for the authors really belong in a separate table, just as Figure 14.3 shows. That way, the database is in first normal form and there is no arbitrary upper limit on the number of authors a book may have.

Remember

A table in first normal form must have no repeating groups. If you discover an attribute that looks like an array, you probably have a repeating group.

No Compound Values

Strictly speaking, a table in first normal form must also satisfy a second condition: It must contain no columns that have *compound values*. A compound value exists whenever a single column contains several distinct pieces of information. For example, the AuthorName column of the Author table contains each author's first name and last name. The AuthorName column has a compound value and, thus, the Author table isn't in first normal form.

This can be easily fixed by using separate columns, called AuthorFirstName and AuthorLastName, to hold the information. This has the benefit of making it simpler to write a form letter to each author. A program can now easily access the AuthorFirstName and write "Dear Sam," for example. Otherwise, the program would need to search the AuthorName value for the comma that separates the first name from the last name.

Often, minor violations of this part of the first rule are overlooked. A business might assign identifying codes to products or locations in a structured way so that each part of the code has some meaning. As long as the code is never disassembled, with one part stored in one table and another part stored in another table, this infraction may not provoke a serious penalty. But it's best to avoid such problems at the outset.

Remember

When a value has multiple parts, define each as a distinct column. Don't violate the rule for first normal form by compounding the parts.

SECOND NORMAL FORM: ALL COLUMNS MUST DEPEND ON THE ENTIRE PRIMARY KEY

The rule for second normal form is easy to apply because it typically affects only a minority of database tables—only those with a *composite* primary key. Other tables are automatically in second normal form.

Recall that a composite primary key is one made up of a combination of database columns. It's not the same as the compound column forbidden by first normal form, which is a single *column* that contains multiple *parts*.

The rule for second normal form is that every non-key column within the table must depend on the primary key. Assume that you have a composite primary key consisting of two columns: City and State. Note that these are two separate columns, not a single compound column.

Assume that the data in the table gives the city and state tax rate. The city tax rate correctly depends on the city and the state. The state tax rate, however, depends only on the state. The table isn't in second normal form.

When you discover a table that's not in second normal form, the remedy is simple. Move any columns that don't depend on the entire primary key to a table that has as its primary key just the part of the key the column depends on. You may have to create a new table to accomplish this. In the example, you'd create a new table having State as its primary key, and move the state tax rate to it.

THIRD NORMAL FORM: ALL COLUMNS MUST DEPEND ONLY ON THE PRIMARY KEY

The third normal form extends the principle of second normal form to all tables, not merely those that have composite primary keys. A table is in third normal form if it has no non-key columns that depend on anything other than the primary key of the table. In this context, the word *depend* refers to values that determine other values.

For example, suppose you decide to add the series title as a new column of the Book table, shown in the database of Figure 14.3. The Book table would now include series ID and series title. Series title depends on series ID in the sense that, if you know one, you know the other. Series title, then, depends on a column other than the primary key—the table isn't in third normal form.

The close relationship between second and third normal form should help you anticipate the way a violation of third normal form is repaired. Just as before, you move the offending item to a more appropriate table. In our example, you'd move the series title back to the Series table, where it was initially—and quite correctly—stored.

NORMAL FORMS SUMMARIZED

William Kent, a prominent database expert, wrote that the whole of database normalization comes to this: *every non-key column must provide a fact about the primary key, the whole primary key, and nothing but the primary key.* This wise, bird's-eye view of normalization can help keep you from getting so caught up in the mechanics of the rules of normalization that you lose sight of your goal. Remember that the rules don't give you a way to prove that your database *is* in third normal form; they only point out ways in which your database may fall short.

Insight and understanding are necessary to proper database normalization. Although some tools claim that they can normalize your data, be careful in using them. The computer doesn't understand your data as well as you should. If you don't understand it as well as you should, the remedy isn't a more sophisticated software tool—it's spending the time necessary to adequately understand the problem domain. Getting the continual help of those who understand the problem domain isn't merely helpful, it's essential.

Choosing Data Types

Now that your database is normalized, it's time to turn your attention away from entities and relationships and back to individual columns. You face two decisions for each column:

- Should the column be required or optional?
- What should the data type for the column be?

If the column is part of the primary key of its table, it *must* be required. Otherwise, you have a choice.

How do you decide whether a non-primary-key column should be required or optional? Start by looking at the *availability* of the column data and the *need* for the column data. If the column data may not be available when a new row is added to your table, you have to ask whether the information is immediately needed. If the data isn't immediately needed, you probably should consider the column an optional column. Otherwise, you have a case for making the column a required column. You should clearly designate any required columns on your list of tables and columns. You may want to use the letters *NN* (not null) to designate required columns.

Various databases support a variety of different data types. Furthermore, because databases are designed to work with many different programming languages, your database may support a different set of data types than your programming language does. Most databases, however, support each of the following in some form:

- Character (that is, text) data
- Whole (that is, integer) numbers
- Decimal (that is, floating point) numbers
- Dates and times
- Binary data

You should choose one of these data types for each column and note it on your list, next to the name of the column. In most cases, the choice will be a clear one.

One area where you might have difficulty is deciding between using a whole number data type and a decimal number data type. Ordinarily, we distinguish between the two types by saying that whole numbers don't have fractions, although decimal numbers do. But when it comes to computer languages and database programs, things get a little more complex.

Some computer languages—for example, COBOL—have a fixed-point decimal data type specifically designed for working with dollars and cents. Others, C and Java among them, use floating-point decimal numbers instead. If your database has a currency type—that is, a fixed-point decimal data type intended for working with money—and your programming language doesn't, the DBMS driver software will have to translate between the two types, sometimes resulting in loss of precision.

One solution to this translation problem is to manipulate currency amounts as whole numbers (that is, as cents rather than dollars and cents) when programming in a language that doesn't support fixed-point decimal arithmetic. Although prices expressed in fractional dollars typically have two decimal places, multiplying such a price by 100 converts it to a whole number, which can then be stored in a whole number column or a decimal number column.

Generally, the most salient difference between whole numbers and floating-point numbers is that arithmetic performed with whole numbers is exact, whereas arithmetic performed with floating-point decimal numbers is approximate. When you're content with an approximate answer, the floating-point decimal number is the correct choice. When your answer must be exact, the whole number is the correct choice.

Occasionally, you may need to work with very large numbers or very small numbers. In such a case, approximate computation may be the only choice because the range of whole numbers is typically smaller than the range of decimal numbers.

Prototyping the Database Design

The final step in designing a database is to prototype it and evaluate the prototype's performance. To do this, you'll need the tools and utilities that work with your database. You may also need the assistance of your organization's database administrator. In any case, don't neglect this opportunity to iterate a little closer to the ideal.

Your main concern in database prototyping will be the performance of the database. Can it complete any time-critical operations within the allowable time limits? If not, you may need to alter the structure of the database. This is largely a trial-and-error process, one that requires deep knowledge of the internals of your database engine to be applied effectively. Typically, your experimentation will revolve around indexing choices: what tables will be indexed in what ways? Many database systems use indexes to speed performance, but unnecessary indexes can bring insert, update, and delete performance to a standstill. Consult available documentation on your database for clues on how to proceed. Good luck!

Summary

Relational databases store data in tables. Information in a given table pertains to a single entity type and is stored in rows and columns. Each row identifies and describes an instance of the entity; each column gives the value of an attribute of the entity.

Database design includes logical database design, physical database design, selecting data types for columns, and prototyping. Logical database design is performed by using entity/relationship (E/R) diagrams, which illustrate entities and the relationships between them.

The cardinality of a relationship, which refers to the number of instances of each participating entity involved in a single instance of the relationship, can be 1:1, 1:N, or N:N. Any N:N relationships are removed from the database design and replaced with a pair of 1:N relationships.

Database anomalies can arise as a result of a non-normalized database design. Normalization is the process of applying three rules to all the tables in your database. The first rule says that there can be no columns with repeating values or no compound keys. Such a database is in first normal form. Second normal form requires that all columns rely on every part of a composite key. All columns in a table in third normal form rely only on data in the primary key. Database normalization says, in essence, that every non-key column of a table must give a fact about the key, the whole key, and nothing but the key.

After the database design is normalized, a data type is chosen for each column of each table of the database. The database can then be prototyped and studied to assess its performance.

Questions

For multiple-choice items, indicate all correct responses.

1. A database table stores information about a single _____.

    a. row

    b. type

    c. object

    d. entity

2. A database table _____ contains values for a single attribute of an entity.

3. Match each item in the left column with an analogous item in the right column.

    a. Package   1. Table

    b. Class   2. Row

    c. Object   3. Catalog

    d. Field   4. Column

4. On an E/R diagram, the rectangles represent _____.

5. On an E/R diagram, the lines represent _____.

6. The _____ of a relationship refers to the number of instances of the related entities that participate in an instance of the relationship.

7. Any _____ relationships in the E/R diagram must be replaced by a pair of 1:N relationships.

8. A _____ database is less likely to be subject to a database anomaly.
   a. relational
   b. object-oriented
   c. normalized
   d. congruent

9. If a database table is in third normal form, every non-key column of the table depends on no other column except that/those of the _____.

10. Database _____ helps determine whether database performance will be acceptable.

Exercises

1. Draw an E/R diagram that represents the data needed by the meeting scheduling system of Chapter 6.

2. Draw an E/R diagram for a database, intended to support an employee information system, that includes the following entities: employee, department, skill, and job class. The system should track each employee's work assignment, which may include multiple departments. The system should also track the identity of the manager of each department.

3. Draw an E/R diagram that describes the database a public library might need to track items borrowed by patrons. The system should allow library workers to search a catalog of items by item ID, title, author, and subject. The library loans 7-day books, 21-day books, video tapes, and cassette tapes. Borrowers with an overdue item or an unpaid fine may not borrow additional items.

4. Extend the meeting scheduling system of Chapter 6 to allow scheduling of meeting by department, skill, or rank. For example, rather than require John Coder, a programmer, to attend the meeting, the user can ask that some programmer, chosen by the system on the basis of availability, be scheduled to attend the meeting. Draw an E/R diagram that represents the revised system.

To Learn More

The following books will help you learn more about designing databases:

- Hernandez, Michael J. *Database Design for Mere Mortals: A Hands-On Guide to Relational Database Design.* Reading, Massachusetts: Addison-Wesley, 1997.

  This is a good source for additional practical advice on database design.

- Date, C.J. *An Introduction to Database Systems,* 6th. ed. Reading, Massachusetts: Addison-Wesley, 1995.

  This standard textbook on database theory is written by one of the architects of the relational database revolution.

- Bruce, Thomas A. *Designing Quality Databases with IDEF1X Information Methods.* New York: Dorset House, 1992.

  This book presents the widely used IDEF1X standard for data modeling.

User Interface Design and Implementation

Slowly and warily, the three men move among the tombstones, which await the outcome of the desert showdown with indifference. Instinctively forming an irregular circle, the men dance—not with one another, but with fear itself. Each knows that the briefest misstep will be fatal. Unholstered and ready for action, their pistols seek the moment of advantage. The rays of the high-noon sun reflect off the gun barrels, blinding first one man and then another. The men squint, struggling to keep the others in view.

Sergio Leone's 1966 Italian-Spanish film, *The Good, the Bad, and the Ugly*, and its three central characters, are a metaphor for many of the user interfaces common in today's software. The man with no name (played by Clint Eastwood), although the hero of the film, still falls short of our moral expectations. He is good enough to comfort a dying soldier with a last cigarette, but bad enough to kill in order to satisfy his greed. Like much of today's software, he both delights and disappoints us. By contrast, the villain (played by Lee Van Cleef) does not disappoint us. He is *all* bad, mercilessly killing anyone who stands between him and the lost gold. Many user interfaces are similarly "merciless," making a user's job harder rather than easier. Finally, the character played by Eli Wallach is neither good enough to be a hero nor bad enough to be a villain: He is simply ugly. Computer users see more than their share of ugly user interfaces, software that not only lacks commodity, but which also lacks even a redeeming modicum of beauty.

Today, software programs are more than just a tool that you occasionally pick up and then discard when you are finished with that odd job. Instead, for many of us, computers have become the environment in which we work and interact with others. You might spend hours each day "living inside" your spreadsheet, word processor, or your Web browser. And, although you might be able to tolerate an ugly or unusable program when you must face it only once in a blue moon, you probably feel a lot differently about software you use every day.

Chapter 1, "What Is Design and Why Is It Needed?," cited the wisdom of the architect Vitruvius, whose words challenge us to design for commodity, firmness, and delight. Although commodity—being a benefit to the user—and firmness—operating in an efficient manner in a range of circumstances—are both important qualities, Vitruvius recognized that this was not enough. A program should also be pleasant to use; it should delight the user.

What is required to create a delightful user interface? What, exactly, does *delight* mean in this context? Creating a user interface that is a pleasure to use requires you to consider three different areas:

- **Visual design:** The purpose of a user interface is to convey information. The first section of this chapter teaches you some enduring principles that will help you to recognize and build designs that look attractive and which communicate effectively.

- **Usability:** Your interface not only displays information, it also interacts with the user. The techniques you'll learn in the second section of this chapter will help you build user interfaces that not only look attractive, but are simple and convenient to use as well.

- **Style:** Besides the general principles of visual design and usability, you'll also have to deal with the details of user interface design. The last section of this chapter presents specific rules of thumb that you can use as a checklist when designing your Java applications.

In this chapter, you will learn:

- How to recognize and apply the principles of clarity, coherence, symmetry, and elegance to evaluate the software interfaces you build.

- How to use the grid system to build interfaces that look good, even if you lack "artistic talent."

- How to build Java custom layout managers, which help you to implement the grid system.

- How to design software that works to advance the user's goals, and to avoid getting mired in solutions that focus on technology or the user's tasks.

- How to get the most out of the AWT by using specific rules of thumb for colors, layout, fonts, windows, components, messages, and help.

Visual Design: Conveying Information

" What is the purpose of your user interface? In a word, communica-tion. "

What is the purpose of your user interface? In a word, communication. The notion of communication stands at the very heart of visual interface design. If you create a well-designed visual interface, your users will quickly and easily understand what you are trying to convey. A poorly designed visual interface will leave them confused and frustrated.

In addition to being easily understood, you also want to make sure that your interface conveys your intentions accurately. The interface that succeeds is one that removes ambiguity and occasions for misunderstanding. A good visual design can ensure that the message your users receive is the one you intended.

How do you go about designing interfaces that are visually effective? A search of your computer book store will turn up several books on designing graphical user interfaces, but only a few that concentrate on the specific principles of visual design for interfaces. The best of these is Kevin Mullet and Darrell Sano's volume from SunSoft press, *Designing Visual Interfaces.*

According to Mullet and Sano, four characteristics are shared by every well-designed visual interface: clarity, coherence, symmetry, and elegance. By examining these concepts, training yourself to look for and recognize them, and by learning how to apply them to your own designs, you'll be well on your way to making your interface "say what you mean."

CLARITY

As an interface designer one of the hardest things to do is to make your software clear. After all, you have an advantage that your user doesn't: You can see inside your program; you know what routine is executed when the button on the bottom of that dialog box is pressed. Your user, on the other hand, can see only what you choose to put on the surface; your user sees only your interface. Clarity is the extent to which you succeed in conveying your intentions to your user—the extent to which you let your user know what will happen when that button is pressed.

How do you accomplish that? What can you do to bring clarity to your software? To paraphrase Edward Tufte, one of the most important writers on the subject of visual communication, clarity is achieved *when differences make a difference.*

When designing your user interface, a whole palette of raw materials is at your disposal. You have fonts, buttons, color, and layout. Each of your visual interface components can differ in shape, size, color, texture, position, or orientation. If you create a dialog box using four different fonts, each in a different size, your users are going to wonder about the significance of the different sizes and fonts. "Is the big type more important?" they'll wonder. "Why is this word in red?"

When such differences are accidental, the visual interface is confusing and difficult for the user to interpret. When such differences are used to highlight important information or to otherwise direct the attention of the user, clarity is enhanced. A warning dialog box that uses a large stop-sign icon is conveying important information, and conveying it clearly. Using different icons simply as a decorative touch conveys no information at all.

The Squint Test

One way to pre-test your visual interface for clarity is to apply the "squint test." Simply close one eye completely and almost close the other, squinting at your visual interface. Squinting enables you to quickly see which elements stand out in your design. Take careful note of the things that you can easily see; those are the things that will be apparent to your busy users. Are they the elements you want to stress? Are they the most important parts of your interface? As you practice the technique, you'll discover that certain kinds of contrasts are evident when squinting. These are the contrasts most evident to your users.

For example, consider the layout of the OK and Cancel buttons on the left side of Figure 15.1. When scanning the layout, your users will quickly notice the contrasting sizes of the buttons and will wonder what the contrast signifies. Unfortunately, the contrast is accidental, signifying nothing. Such a meaningless contrast makes the visual interface more difficult for the user to interpret. Now consider the two buttons shown on the right side of Figure 15.1. There, both buttons have the same size and shape, and so your user's attention is drawn to the significant difference: one says Cancel and one says OK. Eliminating the unnecessary contrast in sizes helps make your interface clearer.

Accidental Differences in Java

Because you're using Java's AWT components in your visual design, you face several challenges as you try to eliminate accidental differences in your layouts. The first difficulty arises from Java's cross-platform nature.

When you create a user interface in Java, the actual interface the user sees will depend on the computer system on which your program runs. Java's AWT uses the native platform on each system to construct a different "look and feel." This means a Mac user gets an interface that looks like a Mac interface and a Windows user gets a Windows-flavored interface. Unfortunately, this makes it difficult for you as a designer to eliminate accidental differences that might arise as your application is run in different environments.

FIGURE 15.1

Contrasting component sizes

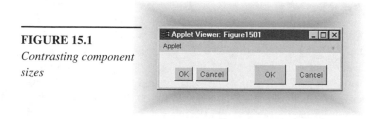

Another, related difficulty is the way in which AWT components tend to size themselves according to the size of their associated text. This is particularly true when they are placed within a container controlled by a FlowLayout layout manager. Buttons, for example, size themselves according to the size of the Button label. Principles of good visual interface design call for the elimination of such meaningless contrasts.

Designers coming from a platform-specific visual development environment, such as Visual Basic or Delphi, usually begin their search for a solution by attempting to express their designs in terms of absolute positioning. You can accomplish this in Java simply by using a null layout manager like this:

```
Panel p = new Panel();
p.setLayout(null);
```

After you've done this, you can size and position every component as you want.

However, despite the apparent attractiveness of this solution you should avoid it because it creates more problems than it solves. (Even in platform-specific user interface design, absolute pixel positioning causes problems. This is why Microsoft uses dialog-units rather than pixels in its user-interface library.)

How do you solve this problem, then? The answer is easy: Learn to use the various layout managers provided by the AWT. For example, if you create your Buttons using this code, you'll end up with Buttons that are arbitrarily sized:

```
Panel p = new Panel();
p.setLayout(new FlowLayout());
p.add(new Button("OK")),
p.add(new Button("Cancel"));
```

Instead, by learning to use the GridLayout layout manager, as shown in the following code, you can eliminate the accidental complexity and guide your users to concentrate on what your Buttons say, not on how they look:

```
Panel p = new Panel();
p.setLayout(new GridLayout(1, 2, 15, 15));
p.add(new Button("OK"));
p.add(new Button("Cancel"));
```

" If the key to clarity is making different things different, then the key to coherence is making similar things similar. "

COHERENCE

If the key to clarity is making different things different, then the key to coherence is making similar things similar. In a newspaper or magazine, headlines, subheads, illustrations, and articles are all combined together for a particular purpose. Likewise, the elements of a visual interface must be combined into a coherent whole. Just as the headlines and subheads in a newspaper article help the reader understand its subject, the organization and structure of your visual interface should help your users understand how its parts relate to the whole.

To accomplish this, you should group the related elements of your visual interface together so that your users can readily see that they are related. In a similar manner, you should establish a hierarchy of importance between the groups and elements so that your user's attention is quickly directed to the most important parts of your display.

You can use two techniques to group related elements together. The first, and most important, is to put related items close to each other and generously use whitespace to separate them from unrelated elements. You can emphasize this grouping by aligning related components along the horizontal or vertical axis. The second grouping technique, which is not as effective as spatial grouping, is to use grouping elements such as borders and boxes. These are especially useful when you're grouping relatively small, similar components such as radio buttons or check boxes.

You can test the effectiveness of your layout by using the same squint test described earlier in this chapter. Your alignment and use of whitespace will be readily perceived by your users, even though they're likely to be busy concentrating on their jobs and not on your layout. Just as variations in alignment will attract the attention of your users, who will wonder what they signify, so too, lack of differentiation will make it difficult for your users to appreciate the significance of a control. Interspersing a button that formats the user's hard disk with buttons that pick up and send email would be a poor design decision. Before you automatically respond that this is a ridiculous example, ask yourself how many times you've accidentally closed a window you meant to minimize or maximize, simply because all three controls look almost alike and sit right next to each other under Windows 95.

Mullet and Sano, mentioned earlier in this chapter, suggest these guidelines for aligning your visual interface components:

1. First, identify the major groups of components in the layout. Unless you know which parts go together and which parts are separate, you won't be able to communicate that information to your users. Then, look for ways to move elements that belong to the same group into alignment with each other, making the groups even more evident.

2. Look for components that nearly align with one another. Eliminate such accidental contrasts by moving or resizing the related components so that they're in alignment (if they're related to each other) or clearly differentiated.

3. Look for "maverick" components and align them with something else on the display.

4. If a component is not related to anything else, then relate it to the layout as a whole by positioning it to correspond to a regular division of space. For example, center the component, or put it in one of the corners rather than place it randomly.

Because spatial grouping is the primary means you'll use to create coherence, your use of whitespace is very important. You should observe two important points:

⬥ Generously use whitespace to separate independent elements. Whitespace is not wasted space; it helps the user understand which elements belong together and which elements are distinct. It has the added advantage of allowing the eye to rest.

- Whitespace also works to emphasize important elements. When an element is surrounded by whitespace, your user's attention will naturally be drawn to that element.

SYMMETRY

In addition to being concerned about the size, position, and alignment of your elements, you'll also have to think about the sizes and positions of *groups* of elements: the overall look of your design. Variations in group size and position can send signals to your users; signals that either help or confound their attempts to understand your visual interface. By placing groups in regularly occurring patterns, you'll make your interface more understandable and, in general, more aesthetically pleasing.

If you feel that such considerations are a little too pretentious for such a utilitarian artifact as a software program, remember that the effectiveness of your program can depend on how your users feel about using it. A technically correct program that is visually discordant will not be as successful as one whose design is attractive and pleasing. Even if you are not artistically gifted, you can make your programs more visually pleasing simply by employing a regular layout.

Again, Mullet and Sano suggest some techniques that will help you regularize your visual interface, including these:

- Use regular geometric forms, simplified contours, and muted colors. Even at Christmas time, a program that uses a bright red background and green text is not going to be appreciated.

- Make similar elements identical in size, shape, color, texture, line weight, orientation, alignment, and spacing. Your goal is to develop a consistent, regular style, just as a magazine uses the same basic layout in different combinations throughout each issue. Buttons used by your application, for example, should be the same size and position from screen to screen. They should not be at the top one time and in the lower right the next.

- Limit variation in typography to a few sizes of only one or two type families. (A type family, or *typeface*, is a group of related fonts. In Java, for example, SanSerif is one type family that comes in several different styles—bold, italic, and so on—and sizes.)

- Do not regularize the critical elements of the design. By making them larger, for example, they attract your user's attention.

The Grid Method: Layout Made Easy

Unless you've worked on a newspaper or magazine, you might be unfamiliar with the idea of a *layout grid*. During production, layout artists traditionally arrange the finished type and illustrations for their publications on a specially ruled sheet of layout board. This is a sheet of heavy cardboard, broken into regular divisions and lined with non-reproducing ink. Of course, today, such layout boards are virtual, having been replaced by programs like Adobe's PageMaker and QuarkXpress. Nevertheless, even in these programs, the layout grid and its rulings remain. You can see this in Figure 15.2, which shows Adobe's newsletter script, which creates a three-column layout grid that can be used to build several different page layouts.

If you've worked with a visual development environment like Visual Basic or a drawing program like Visio, you're already familiar with the idea of a grid, which helps you to visually align components. The layout grid, however, is a little different than the grid used in those tools. For one thing, a layout grid is not just a series of evenly spaced lines like graph paper; instead, it provides guidance for the consistent placement of elements throughout the publication.

A layout grid typically includes ruling lines for margins (so each page has identical whitespace around it) and columns, along with their corresponding gutters (whitespace between columns). The layout grid is used to enforce a consistent look across the entire publication, yet not every page necessarily has the same number of columns. Instead, the layout grid is developed using a base layout that includes a regular spacing of three, five, or seven columns. Then, every actual element is laid out by using some combination of these column measurements. An individual element is free to span several columns, but "splitting" a column is forbidden. This promotes symmetry and yet allows variety.

FIGURE 15.2

A page layout grid in Adobe PageMaker

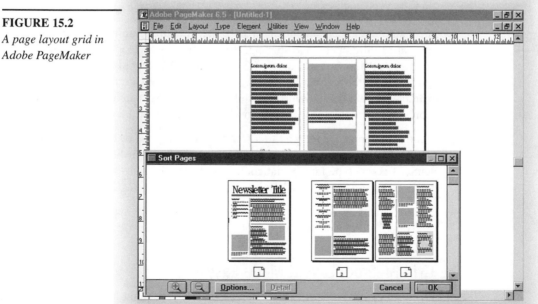

Layout Grids in Java

Of course, Java doesn't have a `LayoutGrid` object, but it has something almost as good: layout managers. You can use layout managers to enforce consistency and produce a pleasingly regular design, in much the same way that print publications have for years.

Figure 15.3 shows a canonical (that is, standardized or regular) grid that provides one-, two-, three-, four-, and six-column layouts. Notice that, within a row of the grid, each column has the same size. Notice also how the two- and three-column grids are regularly subdivided to produce each of the other grids, apart from the one-column grid.

Using a grid is one of the quickest ways to make your user interfaces look better, all with very little effort. To use a grid, start by placing your components so that they precisely line up with the grid. Usually, you base your grid patterns on either the two-column grid or the three-column grid, along with subdivisions of the main grid. In addition to the grid columns, a left column (which is not counted as one of the grid elements) is usually designated to hold labels. Figure 15.4 shows an example of a visual interface designed using a two-column grid.

If you're convinced that using a grid to lay out your designs is a wise decision, you're probably wondering which layout manager you should use to implement it. Unfortunately, in Java, achieving such a regular layout by using the layout managers included with the AWT is not simple. You can use the GridLayout layout manager to divide a panel into rows, but getting the columns to line up properly is difficult. If the left column contains labels for each row, getting the labels to line up with the rows might be difficult. The more sophisticated GridbagLayout layout manager solves these

> *Using a grid is one of the quickest ways to make your user interfaces look better, all with very little effort.*

FIGURE 15.3

A canonical grid

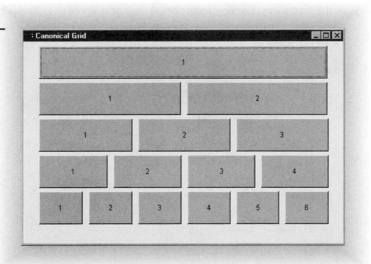

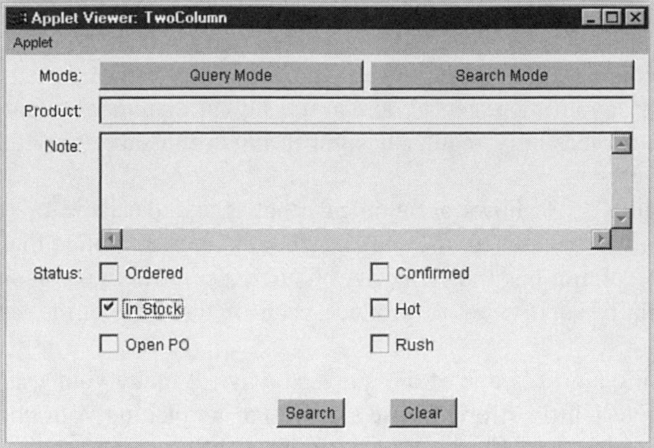

FIGURE 15.4

*A visual interface based
on the two-column grid*

problems but introduces another. Its rows and columns line up fine, but there's no simple way to obtain columns of equal width. The solution? A custom layout manager: the RowLayout class.

Using the RowLayout Layout Manager

Before looking at the layout manager itself, here's an example showing how it can be used. The TestRowLayout applet, shown in Listing 15.1, creates a layout that includes five rows and five columns. The RowLayout layout manager assumes that the left column will be used for labels, so this is actually an instance of a four-column grid. Each of the five rows contains from two to five buttons of various sizes.

```
Listing 15.1 The TestRowLayout Applet
import java.applet.*;
import java.awt.*;

public class TestRowLayout extends Applet
{
  public int [][] pattern =
  {
    { 5, 1, 1, 1, 1, 1 },
    { 5, 1, 1, 1, 2, 0 },
    { 5, 1, 2, 0, 1, 1 },
    { 5, 1, 2, 0, 2, 0 },
    { 5, 1, 4, 0, 0, 0 }
  };

  public void init()
  {
    setLayout(new RowLayout());

    int buttons = 0;
```

```
int rows = pattern.length;
for (int i = 0; i < rows; i ++)
{
  int cols = pattern[i][0];
  int cum = 0;
  for (int j = 0; j < pattern[i].length - 1; j++)
  {
    int width = pattern[i][j+1];
    if (width == 0) continue;
    add(new Button("" + ++buttons),
    new RowLayoutConstraint(i, j, width,
    RowLayoutConstraint.FILL_BOTH));
  }
}
}
}
```

You can see what this applet looks like in Figure 15.5. Notice that the left column, assumed by the layout manager to contain labels, is right justified. This means that the labels appearing in that column will be aligned to the right so they are close to the components that each label describes. The left column is sized to fit its contents; the other columns evenly divide the remaining width of the layout.

Examining *TestRowLayout*

At the of the TestRowLayout applet, you'll find an array named pattern defined like this:

```
public int [][] pattern =
{
  { 5, 1, 1, 1, 1, 1 },
  { 5, 1, 1, 1, 2, 0 },
  { 5, 1, 2, 0, 1, 1 },
  { 5, 1, 2, 0, 2, 0 },
  { 5, 1, 4, 0, 0, 0 }
};
```

This array is used to specify how the components are treated by the layout manager. The array contains one row for each row of the display. Within each row, the first element specifies the number of columns in the row. Notice that this is fixed as five. The

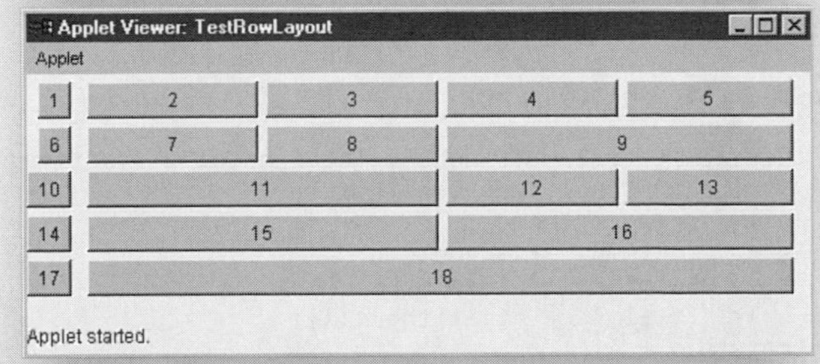

FIGURE 15.5

Output of the TestRowLayout applet

remaining elements specify the relative width of each of the components, and their sum must add up to five. Because the total width was specified as five, one or more elements can have their width set to zero.

The *RowLayoutConstraint* Class

The RowLayout layout manager is used much the same way that GridbagLayout is used. Like GridbagLayout, RowLayout is unable to accomplish its work alone; instead, it relies on a helper class to control the placement of individual components. Whenever you add a component to a container controlled by RowLayout, you also must specify a *constraint* object. This constraint specifies the following:

- **Row:** The vertical position of the component, relative to zero.

- **Column:** The horizontal position of the component, relative to zero.

- **Width:** The width (horizontal size) of the component.

- **Fill:** Specifies whether the component should expand to fill its grid position.

You can read the class definition for the RowLayoutConstraint class in Listing 15.2. The class simply encapsulates the constraint data, providing some static final fields used to specify fill, a constructor, and a toString() method.

Listing 15.2 The RowLayoutConstraint Class

```
public class RowLayoutConstraint
{
  public static final int FILL_NONE       = 0;
  public static final int FILL_HORIZONTAL = 1;
  public static final int FILL_VERTICAL   = 2;
  public static final int FILL_BOTH       = 3;

  public int theRow    = 0;
  public int theColumn = 0;
  public int theWidth  = 1;
  public int theFill   = FILL_NONE;

  public RowLayoutConstraint(int row, int column, int width, int fill)
  {
    theRow    = row;
    theColumn = column;
    theWidth  = width;
    theFill   = fill;
  }

  public String toString()
  {
    String [] fill = { "none", "horizontal", "vertical", "both" };
    String s = "RowLayoutConstraint[";
    s += "row=" + theRow;
    s += ",column=" + theColumn;
    s += ",width="  + theWidth;
    s += ",fill="   + fill[theFill];
    return s + "]";
  }
}
```

The `RowLayout` Class: Fields and Constructors

Although it relies on the help of the constraint class, the layout manager itself does the real work. As mentioned in Chapter 11, "Patterns: Proven Designs," a layout manager uses the Strategy design pattern, encapsulating an algorithm or method for convenient reuse.

To see how the `RowLayout` class actually lays out your components, begin by looking at the class fields and constructors, which you can see in Listing 15.3. When you construct a `RowLayout` object, you can specify the horizontal and vertical gaps (in pixels) that you'd like to separate layout elements, as well as the size of the horizontal and vertical margins (gutter) separating the layout from its container. These values are stored in fields for later use.

In addition to the fields used to store the margins and gutters, two `Hashtable` objects are used to look up the constraint associated with each component. A default constructor is also provided. The class implements the `LayoutManager2` interface (defined in the AWT, for the implementation of custom layout managers), which requires implementation of a variety of methods, shown later.

```
Listing 15.3 Fields and Constructors of the RowLayout Class
import java.awt.*;
import java.util.*;

public class RowLayout implements LayoutManager2
{
  int theHGap;
  int theVGap;
  int theHGutter;
  int theVGutter;

  Hashtable theComponents = new Hashtable();
  Hashtable theByAddress  = new Hashtable();


  public RowLayout()
  {
    this(5, 5, 5, 5);
  }

  public RowLayout(int hgap, int vgap, int hgutter, int vgutter)
  {
    theHGap = hgap;
    theVGap = vgap;
    theHGutter = hgutter;
    theVGutter = vgutter;
  }
```

Adding and Removing Components

To implement the `LayoutManager2` interface, you must write methods that allow a container to associate your layout manager with the components it contains. Listing 15.4 shows these methods, `addLayoutComponent()` and `removeLayoutComponent()`.

The addLayoutComponent() method is called by a container whenever a component is added to the container. The component and its associated constraint object are added to two Hashtable objects, one keyed by the component reference and the other keyed by the row and column position of the component. The Hashtable objects make it easy to retrieve this information when the container is being laid out.

The second version of the addLayoutComponent() method, which takes a String as parameter, is implemented to satisfy the requirements of the LayoutManager2 interface, but its implementation is null, as is that of the removeLayoutComponent() method.

Listing 15.4 The addLayoutComponent() and removeLayoutComponent() Methods

```
// Adds the specified component to the layout, using the specified
// constraint object.

// Parameters:
// comp - the component to be added
// constraints - where/how the component is added to the layout.

public void addLayoutComponent(Component comp, Object constraints)
{
  theComponents.put(comp, constraints);
  RowLayoutConstraint rc = (RowLayoutConstraint) constraints;
  String address = "" + rc.theRow + "," + rc.theColumn;
  theByAddress.put(address, comp);
}

public void addLayoutComponent(String name, Component comp)
{
  // null implementation
}

public void removeLayoutComponent(Component comp)
{
  // null implementation
}
```

Arranging the Components

Now that you've constructed your layout manager and added the components, it's time to see how the RowLayout class actually accomplishes its work. When a container wants its layout manager to arrange the components it contains, it sends it a layoutContainer() message. You can see how the RowLayout class responds by looking through the layoutContainer() method, shown in Listing 15.5. Immediately following the listing, you can find an analysis of the layout manager's strategy.

Listing 15.5 The layoutContainer() Method

```
public void layoutContainer(Container parent)
  {
    //  Step 1: Determine the size of the container and
    //          number of components it holds, as well as
```

```
//            the size of its parent
int components  = theComponents.size();
Dimension psize = parent.getSize();
Insets pinsets  = parent.getInsets();

//  Step 2: Determine the number of rows and columns
//          of the layout by checking the row and column
//          number of each component.
int cols = 0;
int rows = 0;
RowLayoutConstraint rc;
Enumeration constraints = theComponents.elements();

while (constraints.hasMoreElements())
{
  rc = (RowLayoutConstraint) constraints.nextElement();
  if (rc.theColumn > cols) cols = rc.theColumn;
  if (rc.theRow    > rows) rows = rc.theRow;
}
cols++;
rows++;

//  Step 3: Determine the width of column 1 (which will
//          be used to hold the labels) and the minimum
//          row height
int vgap   = (rows - 1) * theVGap;
int width  = psize.width - 3 * theHGutter;
int height = psize.height - 2 * theVGutter;
    height -= height % rows;

int c1width  = 0;
int rheight[] = new int[rows];

for (int i = 0; i < rows; i++)
  rheight[i] = 0;

Enumeration comps = theComponents.keys();
Component c;
while (comps.hasMoreElements())
{
  c = (Component) comps.nextElement();
  int cheight = c.getPreferredSize().height;
  int cwidth  = c.getPreferredSize().width;
  rc = (RowLayoutConstraint) theComponents.get(c);
  if (cheight > rheight[rc.theRow])
    rheight[rc.theRow] = cheight;
  if (rc.theColumn == 0 && cwidth > c1width)
    c1width = cwidth;
}

//  Step 4: Determine the width of the remaining columns
int c2width = width - c1width;
int cwidth  = c2width - (theHGap * (cols - 1));
    cwidth  = cwidth / (cols - 1);

//  Step 5: Place each component at the proper position
//          within the container and set its size according
//          to the value of the fill parameter specified.
int x,  y;
```

```java
        int dx, dy;
        y = theVGutter;

        for (int i = 0; i < rows; i++)
        {
          for (int j = 0; j < cols; j++)
          {
            String address = "" + i + "," + j;
            c = (Component) theByAddress.get(address);
            if (c == null)
              continue;

            rc = (RowLayoutConstraint) theComponents.get(c);
            Dimension csize;
            if (j == 0)
            {
              csize = c.getMinimumSize();
              x   = c1width - csize.width;
              dx = csize.width;
              dy = csize.height;
            }
            else
            {
              x = theHGutter +  (c1width  - cwidth) + j   *
                                (cwidth + theHGap);
              dx = cwidth * rc.theWidth;

              if (rc.theWidth > 1)
                dx += (rc.theWidth - 1) * theHGap;

              csize = c.getPreferredSize();
              dy    = rheight[i];

              switch(rc.theFill)
              {
                case RowLayoutConstraint.FILL_NONE:
                  dx = csize.width;
                  dy = csize.height;
                  break;

                case RowLayoutConstraint.FILL_HORIZONTAL:
                  dy = csize.height;
                  break;

                case RowLayoutConstraint.FILL_VERTICAL:
                  dx = csize.width;
                  break;

                case RowLayoutConstraint.FILL_BOTH:
                  break;
              }
            }
            c.setBounds(x, y, dx, dy);
          }
          y += rheight[i] + theVGap;
        }
      }
```

Although this method is certainly large, and might seem complex, in reality it consists of five simple steps:

1. Determine the size of the container and the number of components it holds.

2. Determine the number of rows and columns of the layout by checking the row and column number of each component.

3. Determine the width of column 1 (the first column, which holds the labels) and the minimum height of each row.

4. Determine the width of columns 2–n.

5. Place each component at the proper position within the container and set its size according to the value of the `fill` parameter specified.

Additional Methods

In addition to the methods you've already seen, the `RowLayout` class contains several other methods that are required by the `LayoutManager2` interface:

- Methods used to calculate the size of the layout. Because the `RowLayout` class adapts the layout to the current size of the container, whatever it might be, these methods simply return the size of the parent container.

```
public Dimension preferredLayoutSize(Container target)
{
  return target.getSize();
}

public Dimension minimumLayoutSize(Container target)
{
  return target.getSize();
}

public Dimension maximumLayoutSize(Container target)
{
  return target.getSize();
}
```

- Methods that determine how components should be aligned. These methods have no real effect; as far as the container knows, there is no surrounding whitespace within which the layout should be aligned.

```
public float getLayoutAlignmentX(Container target)
{ return 0.0F; }

public float getLayoutAlignmentY(Container target)
{ return 0.0F;}
```

- The `invalidateLayout()` method, which is unused by the `RowLayout` class because `RowLayout` does not cache any layout information. If a layout manager saves results of the `layoutContainer()` method as part of its state, this method can be used to reset the state.

```
public void invalidateLayout(Container target)
{
  // null implementation
}
```

Putting `RowLayout` to Work

"Notice how the use of a regular grid provides a pleasing symmetry to the layout. Nothing looks out of place or haphazard."

There's no question that implementing a custom layout manager requires a considerable amount of code. Nevertheless, when it comes to your user interface, you'll find the effort worthwhile. Figure 15.6 shows how you can use the `RowLayout` class to implement a contact manager application, based on a three-column layout.

You can find the source code for the ThreeColumn applet on the CD-ROM. Note how the labels in the left column neatly line up with the row that each label describes. Also, notice how individual elements can consist of either a single column—the phone and fax numbers for example, as well as the Home, Office, and Other buttons—or can span two or more columns as the Name and City fields do.

Finally, notice how the use of a regular grid provides a pleasing symmetry to the layout. Nothing looks out of place or haphazard. Of course, you can use the `RowLayout` class for four- and five-column layouts with equally satisfactory results. Figure 15.7 shows the FourColumn applet, whose source code you can also find on the CD-ROM.

When looking at the illustrations, you might be wondering why the command buttons along the bottom are not aligned with the other elements on the screen. This is an application of the principle of clarity: make different things different. Because the command buttons are not part of the dialog box itself, they shouldn't be treated as part of the regular layout group. Of course, between themselves, their relationship should, indeed, be regularized.

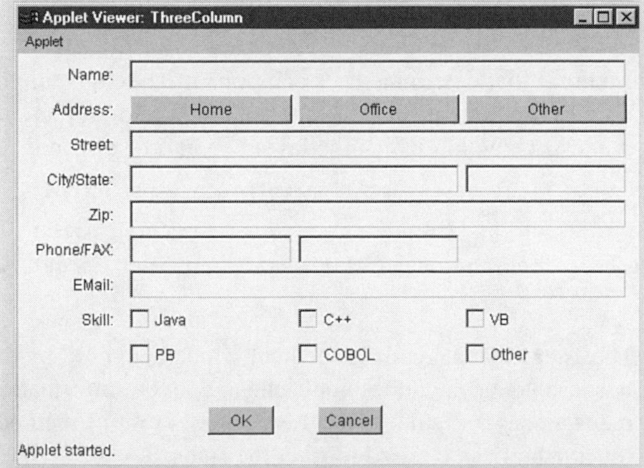

FIGURE 15.6
A three-column layout

FIGURE 15.7
A four-column layout

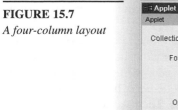

ELEGANCE

What comes to mind when you hear the word *elegance*? Refinement? Gracefulness? Good taste? Perhaps even luxury and wealth? Certainly those are all elements encompassed by the popular notion of elegance. However, when it comes to visual design, elegance has less to do with richness and elaboration than it does with the following qualities:

- Novelty
- Simplicity
- Economy
- Effectiveness

As a programmer, you're probably already familiar with this use of the word elegance. Perhaps, after struggling with a particularly complicated section of code, a co-worker has shown you a straightforward way to accomplish the same thing in half the code. Or maybe, on your commute home at the end of a long and tiring day, you've found yourself turning your class hierarchy on its head, eliminating half your methods, and seeing things in an entirely different light. Although quantifying the quality of elegance can be difficult, like art, you'll know it when you see it.

What Makes an Elegant Design?

One thing that characterizes an elegant design is its novelty, a novelty that results from looking at a problem in a new light or through a different lens. Of course, it's important to remember that just because most elegant designs are novel, it doesn't follow that novel designs are necessarily elegant; simple difference, like random genetic mutation, is seldom beneficial. Instead, a truly elegant design causes you to ask, "Why didn't I think of that? It's so obvious!" Simple novelty provokes the opposite question: "Why would anyone do that?"

An elegant design is simple, not in the sense of being plain or ordinary, but in the sense that it contains no unnecessary ornamentation or embellishment. After the end of the first world war in Germany, a group of designers under the leadership of architect Walter Gropius formed a design institute called the *Bauhaus*, which was dedicated to the principles of simplicity, economy, and effectiveness. Their world-renowned chairs, for example, combined a novel simplicity with an unerring grace.

The Bauhaus ideas about design were widely accepted, influencing designers in fields as diverse as architecture, industrial design, furniture making, typography, and the graphic arts. The most famous aphorism to come out of the movement was "form follows function." That simply means that the form of an object should be dictated by its purpose. The Bauhaus designers refused to separate the utility or effectiveness of an object from its aesthetic component. Thus, a "beautiful" chair that you couldn't comfortably sit in was seen as a design flaw. True beauty flows from artifacts that fulfill their intended purpose.

Creating Elegant Designs

Being able to recognize an elegant design certainly is a good thing, but being able to create an elegant design is even better. How do you go about it? The key is to master subtraction.

A sculptor was once asked how he created such realistic figures from lifeless blocks of marble. "It is very, very simple," he replied. "If I am going to sculpt a horse, I simply remove everything that is not a horse!" Like the sculptor, to create an elegant user interface, you must be willing to remove the parts that don't belong. When looking at your visual design, you must be willing to look at every element and ask the following:

- Does it contribute to the purpose of my design? Do I really need those borders around each element? Do I have components that duplicate the work of other components? Do I have gratuitous information displayed? Does everything work together?

- After you've made sure that everything works together, you must put your visual design on a diet. Look at each element and ask yourself, "What happens if I remove this? Does the design still work?" If the answer is yes, remove the item. You must edit your visual designs in much the same way a newspaper copy editor reduces the overactive prose of her reporters.

- Finally, you must ask yourself if the elements you are using are the best ones for the job. Don't be afraid to try a different method. Ask yourself if a choice control would be more appropriate than a slew of radio buttons, or if a dozen text fields could be replaced by a single text area. Adopt "form follows function" as your personal design motto, and you'll be well on your way to creating more elegant designs.

Usability Principles

Choosing an appropriate visual design for a user interface is only half of your job. A good user interface must not only look good, it must work well: in addition to having a pleasing form, it should actually function.

As a user-interface designer you'll find yourself wearing two hats as you switch between designing the *look* of your application and its *feel*. When designing the visual elements, you're concerned with clarity, coherence, and elegance. In the words of Vitruvius, you focus on the quality of delight. When it comes to designing the usability of your interface, however, you must switch gears and concentrate on the quality of commodity: making sure your interface works well in its intended role. In a way, your job is very much like the producer of a play: you not only must have a nice-looking set, but you must get the actors to say all their lines at the right time. To be successful, you require both.

How do you go about designing a user interface that works? In considering usability, user interface designers tend to focus on one of three aspects of their job:

- ◖ The user interface technology
- ◖ The user's task
- ◖ The user's goals

Of these three alternatives, only one is appropriate. Can you guess which? The next three sections examine each of the alternatives in turn.

> *"A good user interface design focuses on providing useful capabilities to the user, not merely extending access to every capability of the underlying system."*

FOCUS ON TECHNOLOGY

There's no doubt about it—technology is neat. Many an interface designer has become enamored of the latest user-interface gadgets: exploding windows, 3D widgets, sounds, animations, designer fades, and color effects. All too often, however, a designer who focuses on technology fails to produce a design that meets the user's actual needs. Often such a design incorporates the latest gadgets, but equally often the user interface is cumbersome to use. Lacking both commodity and firmness, such a user interface is the archetypal bad user interface. Unless the designer understands the user's needs and takes full account of them in making each design decision, the design is at risk.

Remember the word *interface* in the phrase *user interface*. A user interface is not merely the point of contact between a user and a system. Like the interface of a Java object, the user interface of a system defines the user's view of the system. As one human-computer interaction researcher put it, "To the user, the user interface *is* the system."

A good user interface design focuses on providing useful capabilities to the user, not merely extending access to every capability of the underlying system. Do you remember the hypothetical household robot from Chapter 4, "Encapsulation: Classes and Methods"? The robot's initial design—a design rooted in technology—included user interface functions such as the following:

- Start

- Stop

- Move forward

- Move backward

- Turn left

- Turn right

The problem with this interface is that, for a household robot, it ignores the needs of the users. With an interface like this, you might find vacuuming your home using an ordinary vacuum easier than putting this "labor-saving" device to work at the task. At least, by sidelining the device, you wouldn't have to worry about accidentally demolishing your costly big-screen TV.

The ideal design, employing the principle of abstraction, would include only functions that correspond to the tasks the user is trying to accomplish:

- Vacuum the house.

- Do the laundry.

- Cook dinner.

Now, when you tell your robot to vacuum the house, it begins its job without further instruction, vacuuming around obstacles without your advice or assistance. You're free to enjoy your big-screen TV while your robot—let's call it the Model 110HR—does its work. If you get a phone call or friends drop by, you can switch the unit off. No more user interface functions are needed.

Of course, the first version of the vacuum is easier to implement. You might find the second version not simply harder, but impossibly hard. However, you'll never know until you try. This is one reason why design tends to be iterative. Striving for excellence can occasionally lead you to attempt things that turn out to be impossible. If you fail to accept this challenge, you'll retrace your steps less often, but you'll also turn out mediocre designs.

FOCUS ON THE USER'S TASK

If focusing on the technology is wrong, focusing on the user's task might seem to be a step in the right direction. To see why this is not adequate, consider again the Model 110HR household robot. Focusing on the task might lead you to define the following user interface functions in place of a single "Vacuum the house" instruction:

- Vacuum on.

- Vacuum off.

- Vacuum an open area.

- Vacuum around a rectangular object.

- Vacuum around a circular object.

- Vacuum under the couch.

Certainly, this approach is better than focusing on the underlying technology. At least you can catch a few irregular moments of TV while your 110HR finishes a task. However, just as you're about to find out "who dunnit" on your favorite drama, your robot is likely to need further instructions. Again, you want a user interface that provides a higher level of abstraction.

Focusing on the user's task often leads to ineffective use of technology. Too many computer systems work exactly the way some ancient labor-intensive process worked, except that the work is now done by a computer rather than by an army of clerks. Although the computer might be faster and more accurate than its human predecessors, different ways of structuring the work can make even better use of its potential.

FOCUS ON THE USER'S GOALS

" Good design focuses neither on technology nor task, but on the user's goals. Its mission is to make the user more effective. "

Good design focuses neither on technology nor task, but on the user's goals. Its mission is to make the user more effective. How do you go about creating such a design? There is only one way: You must talk to your users to see how they actually use your software.

Applying this principle is often difficult for designers and other technical workers. For them, technology takes center stage. To combat this tendency, it's important to talk with prospective system users. Better still, if possible, ask permission to quietly and unobtrusively observe them at work. As Yogi Berra quipped, "You can see a lot just by observing."

What you find might surprise you. You'll probably discover system features that provoke user frustration. You might find users employing awkward procedures (called *workarounds*) because your system doesn't do what they need done. You might find system features that virtually ensure that mistakes are made. Take careful note of these and vow never again to impose similar burdens on users of systems that you design.

GUIDELINES FOR DESIGNING USABLE INTERFACES

When you adopt the proper perspective for user interface design—maximizing the effectiveness of system users—your design decisions are likely to be good ones. But, you might find that working through every design decision from first principles is time consuming. Fortunately, some shortcuts can help you make design decisions more quickly.

Put the User in Control

An important characteristic of a good user interface is that it puts the user in control. The user should be able to decide what is done and when it is done.

Some designers understand user interfaces as though they are a dialog between the user and the computer. Certainly, information flows between the user and the computer, so this model is at least partly valid. However, the designer who employs this model risks falling victim to the master-genie syndrome. To see the master-genie syndrome in action, consider the following user-interface dialog:

- Master: I'd like a chocolate ice cream cone.

- Genie: I take it that you're hungry, master?

- Master: Yes, I'm hungry. I'd like a chocolate ice cream cone.

- Genie: Would you like to see a menu?

- Master: No, I just want a chocolate ice cream cone.

- Genie: I'm sorry, master, but you must order from the menu. Would you like to see the menu?

- Master: Oh, all right. Let me see the menu.

- Genie: Well, master, do you see anything you like?

- Master: Yes, I want a chocolate ice cream cone.

- Genie: Ice cream. An excellent choice, master. And what sort of ice cream would you like? May I show you the menu?

- Master: Like I said, I want chocolate ice cream. In a cone.

- Genie: I'm sorry, master, but you must order from the menu. May I show you the menu?

- Master: No. I give up. I'll make it myself.

A user interface like this is termed *modal*. It defines a number of modes that limit the user's options. Such a user interface is cumbersome to use because, even if you know exactly what you want, you're forced to navigate a tortuous, multi-step dialog. You can avoid the master-genie syndrome by streamlining your user-interface dialogs, or, if possible, eliminating dialogs all together.

Be Predictable

Imagine a Web-based form several pages long. You work your way through the form, filling in text boxes and checking options, taking several minutes to arrive at the bottom of the form. There you find two buttons, one marked Press Me and See What Happens and the other marked No, Press Me Instead. What do you do? If you press the wrong button, you might have to re-enter all the data. How do you decide which button to press?

Many real user interfaces are not far removed from this hypothetical example. They lack predictability. A good user interface helps the user understand the consequences of pushing a button or manipulating a control. The user is not really in control unless the user knows what's going to happen. Strive to make your user interfaces predictable.

Give Feedback

Not knowing what will happen is scary, but not knowing what has happened is even scarier. A good user interface provides users with feedback telling them what has happened. If an operation is time consuming, it tells them what is going on and helps them estimate how much longer it will take. Remember to give your users feedback for every operation.

Forgive Errors

Unless your users are superhuman, they will make errors from time to time. A good user interface anticipates this possibility and provides an "undo" or other mechanism that helps the user cope with the consequences of a bad choice. Be sure your user interfaces require no more than human competency for correct operation.

Allow Customization

Not all users are the same. A user interface designed for beginners can provide special helps and prompts that lead the beginner through complex operations. An advanced user who doesn't need the helps and prompts might find this same interface too cumbersome for effective use.

A good user interface accommodates users of all levels, providing the beginning user with special helps and prompts but providing the advanced user with shortcuts that permit efficient operation. A good design will allow the advanced user to disable the menus and wizards that the novice user finds so helpful. You should strive to design systems that let users choose an interaction model that suits their particular needs.

In addition to allowing customization of the user interaction model, a good design will let your users adapt your software to their preferred working environments. You might have a 20-inch monitor and prefer using a small typeface. Your users, with less lofty equipment, might prefer larger type. For example, you should use the Java `SystemColor` class rather than hard-coding the colors your program uses. That way, those who prefer a muted gray to the nice teal that you selected can "have it their way." If you use function keys in your application, you can let your users select which key gets assigned to which function.

For every feature, ask yourself, "Will my users want to change this?," and, if the answer is "Yes," enable them to customize that feature.

Anticipate Portability

Particularly when designing systems to be implemented in Java, you should anticipate that the system will be used on multiple platforms. Java's controls adopt the look and feel of each platform. A text field has one look on Microsoft Windows 95 and another on X Window Motif. Become familiar with the idiosyncrasies of each platform so you can anticipate how the system will behave on each.

Style Guidelines: User Interface Elements

General principles of the type given in the last section are helpful, but the new designer often seeks more specific advice as well. This section aims to meet that need by surveying Java's graphical user interface elements and offering concise suggestions for their use. The material is grouped into five subsections:

- Basic elements, which looks at colors and fonts
- Windows, which looks at dialog boxes and menus
- Components, which looks at Java's principal user-interface components
- Messages, which gives suggestions for presenting various types of messages
- Special operations, which looks at cut and paste, drag and drop, and online help

" Color attracts the user's attention and should be used sparingly so that the user is not overwhelmed by competing centers of attention."

BASIC ELEMENTS: COLOR AND FONTS

Color attracts the user's attention and should be used sparingly so that the user is not overwhelmed by competing centers of attention. Use color to direct the user's attention to important parts of the user interface.

Using Color

There are a few guidelines to remember when using color:

- Use only a few colors (not more than four) per screen.
- Remember that some users might have monochrome monitors or suffer from red-green color blindness: do not rely exclusively on color to distinguish the meaning of user interface elements. Make sure that elements that are really different are distinguished by grouping, size, or position, as well.
- Java 1.1 provides the class `java.awt.SystemColor`, which lets you determine the color of GUI objects on a system. Because most systems enable the user to customize the color of GUI objects, using this class in your programs will enable users to customize the color of your programs' text and components. This helps make your program more adaptable to hardware limitations and personal preferences.

Using Fonts

Using different fonts in your applets and applications can help make your programs more attractive and can also increase the clarity of your interface. Overuse and misuse of fonts, however, is also one of the quickest ways to make your interface totally illegible.

Although the terms *font* and *typeface* are sometimes used interchangeably, they do not mean exactly the same thing. In traditional graphic design, a typeface is a particular "family" of related fonts. For example, Times Roman is a typeface, and it includes bold and italic variations. To further confuse matters, a font is, technically, a given typeface in a particular variation and size. Thus, when you create a Font object in your Java program, you specify not only the typeface, but its style and size as well.

Java adds one additional wrinkle to this subject, because of the way in which it specifies typefaces. Because Java programs are designed to run on different platforms where a given typeface might not be installed, Java created several "generic" typefaces, which are really type categories rather than specific typefaces. When you use these type categories (SansSerif, Serif, and Monospaced) the Java runtime will substitute the closest actual typeface available on your user's machine.

Here are some specific guidelines to make your use of type more effective:

- Sans serif fonts, such as the Java font SansSerif, are more readable on video monitors than serif fonts, which have horizontal strokes at the base of most letters. These horizontal strokes are not clearly rendered at the typical 72 dpi resolution of computer monitors, resulting in text that is hard to read.

- Limit the number of font families appearing on a screen. Try to use only a single font family, if possible.

- Use fonts consistently in all screens of a single program. If you use SansSerif on one screen and Serif on another, your users will notice, if only subconsciously, and wonder what the difference signifies.

- Use a bold font rather than color to emphasize text. You can use several font sizes on a screen, but do not use font size for emphasis. It seldom has sufficient impact for this purpose.

- Avoid using ALL CAPITALIZED MESSAGES. It makes your text hard to read, and it looks like you're SHOUTING. Instead, as with color, use a bold font to emphasize your messages.

- Avoid using italic type in small sizes, and your users will bless you. Italics can be effective on screen only in large sizes. As with the Serif type family, the screen resolution of even the best monitor is just too coarse to make italic text readable.

The Fonts applet shown in Figure 15.8 illustrates the legibility of different typefaces and styles. You can find the source code on the CD-ROM.

FIGURE 15.8

Guildelines for using type—the Fonts applet

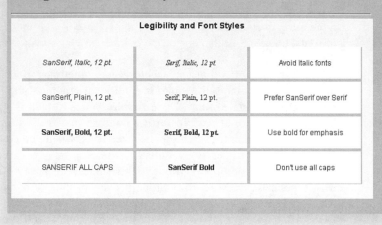

Using Fonts Effectively

Legibility and Font Styles		
SanSerif, Italic, 12 pt.	*Serif, Italic, 12 pt.*	Avoid italic fonts
SanSerif, Plain, 12 pt.	Serif, Plain, 12 pt.	Prefer SanSerif over Serif
SanSerif, Bold, 12 pt.	**Serif, Bold, 12 pt.**	Use bold for emphasis
SANSERIF ALL CAPS	**SanSerif Bold**	Don't use all caps

WINDOWS

To the user interface designer, windows and dialog boxes act as natural containers for related information. For a small program—one with only a single window—your main task will be to arrange the layout in a pleasing and efficient manner. But, for real-world applications, those involving multiple screens and dialog boxes, you'll also need to coordinate the appearance and responsibilities of each of your windows. Here are some guidelines that can help you.

Using Windows

- Try to design screens so that horizontal scrolling is not necessary. Use a larger window or separate the information and place it in multiple windows.

- Use layout managers that realign components appropriately when the window is resized. Resist the temptation to use a `null` layout manager with absolute positioning. When you give in, your code no longer is portable.

Using Dialog Boxes

- Never use a modal dialog box, which prevents the user from accessing the application until the dialog box is closed, if you can reasonably avoid it. Modal dialog boxes are best for small tasks; they can lead to the master-genie syndrome if used inappropriately.

⚫ Use the `FileDialog` class to create dialog boxes that open or save files. `FileDialogs` enable your users to interact with the file system on their computer in the manner with which they are accustomed and free you from the dangers of writing platform-specific code that relies on the characteristics of a particular file system.

Using Menus

⚫ Carefully choose the labels of menu items so that users can predict what will happen when an item is selected.

⚫ Position menu items consistently throughout the screens of a program. Put the most frequently selected items near the top of a menu and use separator bars to group related items. Of course, you can't always accurately predict which items will be used most frequently; instead, you must make some reasonable assumptions or, better yet, take some time to observe your users. If you've done a good job of talking to your users, you should have a good idea of which operations are done frequently and which are accessed only occasionally.

⚫ Define keyboard shortcuts that facilitate access to frequently used menu items.

COMPONENTS

Components are the basic building blocks of the modern user interface. Just as a builder works with lumber, bricks, and mortar, the user interface designer bolts together buttons, labels, lists, and check boxes. Like the builder, you also face two critical questions: What component should you use, and where should you use it? Most of the decisions you'll make when using components involve selecting the correct component for the job and then using that component correctly. The following are some guidelines to help you.

Using Button Controls

⚫ Use buttons sparingly, and only for frequent or critical functions. Moving other functions to a menu will free screen space for better uses.

⚫ Choose button labels so that the user clearly understands what each button does.

⚫ Group related buttons and set them off from other components. They should be placed consistently in all the screens of a single program. This is especially true for command buttons. These are the normal buttons that are used to accept or reject the changes in a dialog box. Make sure you choose a location for these buttons and stick to it.

> *" Components are the basic building blocks of the modern user interface. Just as a builder works with lumber, bricks, and mortar, the user interface designer bolts together buttons, labels, lists, and check boxes."*

Using Check Box and Radio Button Controls

Using a check box when you should use a radio button, or vice versa, can make your interface counter-intuitive and difficult to use. Make sure you understand the semantic differences between each type of control:

- Use check boxes when the user can choose one or more options. Figure 15.9, the Pizza applet (available on the CD-ROM), shows an appropriate use of check boxes for choosing toppings on a pizza, because you might want both pepperoni and pineapple.

- Use radio buttons when the user must choose only one option from a list of options. In the Pizza applet, radio buttons are used for the Sizes Available group of choices, because a single pizza cannot be both small and large. In Java, you create radio buttons by associating check boxes with a CheckboxGroup object, like this:

```
CheckboxGroup sizeGroup = new CheckboxGroup();
add(new Checkbox("Small", false, sizeGroup));
add(new Checkbox("Medium", false, sizeGroup));
add(new Checkbox("Large", false, sizeGroup));
add(new Checkbox("Family", true, sizeGroup));
```

- Check boxes and radio buttons should be grouped and labeled so that their function is clearly understandable.

- Check boxes or radio buttons within a group should be ordered. Order them by frequency of use or logical order if possible; use alphabetical order if you can find no better alternative.

FIGURE 15.9

Effective use of check boxes and radio buttons

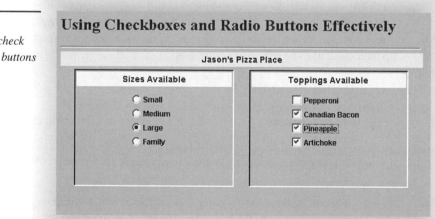

Using List and Choice Controls

> *"A list box or choice box (also known as a drop-down list box) should be used in place of a large group of radio buttons."*

A list box or choice box (also known as a *drop-down list box*) should be used in place of a large group of radio buttons. Either is also useful when the list of items changes during program execution. Changing the labels of a check box or radio button might compel changing the layout of the screen to accommodate a longer label; this is less often a problem with a list box or choice. Here are some guidelines for using these components:

- If your users must select one item from a group, you really have three options: the radio button, the list box, and the choice. If the number of options from which to select is more than 10, you should almost always use either a choice or a list box instead of radio buttons, simply to reduce the amount of screen clutter. Figure 15.10, the States applet, shows how much more effective a list box or a choice can be.
- The choice box, which until selected shows only the currently chosen item, takes up less room on the screen. However, because it must be selected before being used, it costs the user an extra step. It should be used when most users will select the first item in the list.
- You should clearly label each list box or choice box, which should display no more than five to ten items.
- If a list box or choice box includes more than 30 items, you should provide some type of filter option that enables the user to view its contents one group at a time.

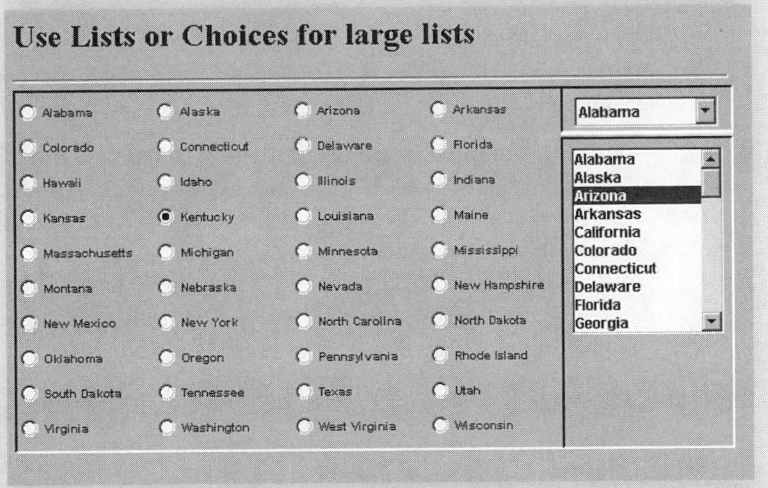
Use Lists or Choices for large lists
Alabama
Alaska
Arizona
Arkansas
Colorado
Connecticut
Delaware
Florida
Hawaii
Idaho
Illinois
Indiana
Kansas
Kentucky
Louisiana
Maine
Massachusetts
Michigan
Minnesota
Mississippi
Montana
Nebraska
Nevada
New Hampshire
New Mexico
New York
North Carolina
North Dakota
Oklahoma
Oregon
Pennsylvania
Rhode Island
South Dakota
Tennessee
Texas
Utah
Virginia
Washington
West Virginia
Wisconsin
Alabama
Alabama
Alaska
Arizona
Arkansas
California
Colorado
Connecticut
Delaware
Florida
Georgia

FIGURE 15.10
The States applet: radio buttons, list boxes, and choice controls

🜨 List boxes can be configured to allow multiple selections, allowing a list box to replace a large group of check boxes. However, novice users often do not know how to operate a multiple-selection list box, so you should include brief instructions on the screen.

🜨 It's frequently helpful to use a pair of list boxes, one containing items eligible to be chosen and one containing items that have been chosen. This makes it easier for the user to quickly see exactly what items have been chosen.

Using Scrollbars and Labels

🜨 Scrollbars are useful for increasing and decreasing continuous values, such as color values. They are most useful when the number of data values is large.

🜨 When you use a scrollbar, you should associate it with a text field that displays the exact current value and allows direct entry so that a user who knows the exact value needed can input it rather than use the scrollbar.

🜨 Labels should be used to display data that cannot be changed. Text fields and text areas should be used to display data that can be changed.

🜨 If data is temporarily not to be changed, you can set the `Editable` property of the component to `false`.

🜨 Group related text fields and label them to their left, placing a colon after the label. The colon should be aligned right, so the colons for all of the labels line up.

MESSAGES

Messages provide feedback to the user. In the user's mind, messages are the voice of the computer; to the extent that your program has a personality, it will be displayed through your messages. There are three types of messages:

🜨 **Feedback messages:** Feedback messages are used to tell users about a result or provide feedback when a lengthy (more than five-second) operation is in progress. Feedback messages should tell the user what has been done and whether the operation was successful. If the operation is still in progress, the message should help the user estimate how much longer it will take. The Message1 applet, shown in Figure 15.11, illustrates several of these principles. Using the `ProgressBar` class from Chapter 4, it keeps the user informed about the status of a lengthy download over the Web. The user is told which file is being transferred, where the file is going, and how much of the transfer has been completed. In addition, Cancel and Pause buttons put the user in control of the process.

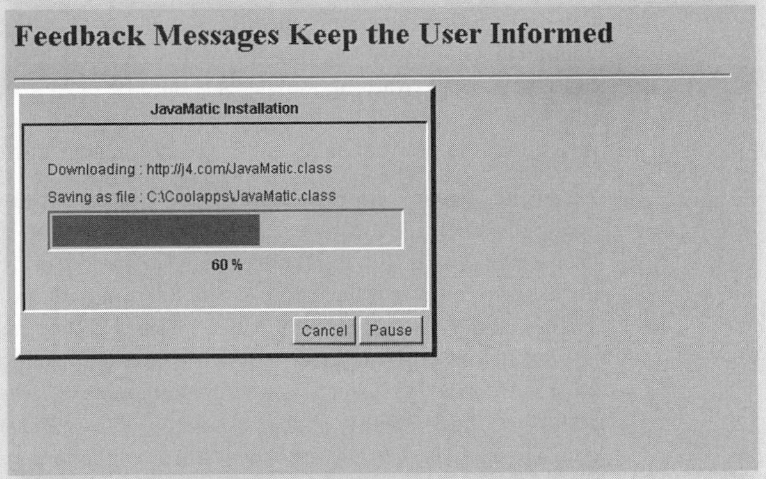

FIGURE 15.11
Feedback messages keep the user informed

Feedback Messages Keep the User Informed

JavaMatic Installation

Downloading : http://J4.com/JavaMatic.class
Saving as file : C:\Coolapps\JavaMatic.class

60 %

Cancel | Pause

🔹 **Warning messages:** Warning messages are used to request confirmation of a potentially irreversible operation. Successful warning messages are both unambiguous and enable the user to do something meaningful. Figure 15.12, the Message2 applet, in keeping with the theme of the chapter, shows some good, bad, and ugly warning messages. Warning messages should always enable the user to take meaningful action; requiring the user to click OK

FIGURE 15.12
Warning messages should be clear and enable the user to take meaningful action

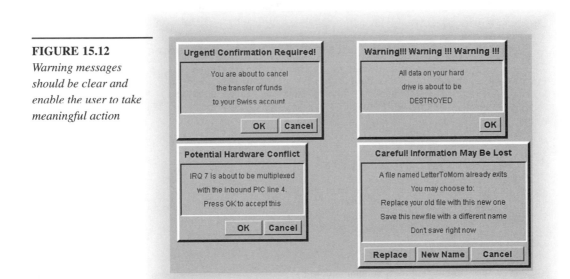

Urgent! Confirmation Required!

You are about to cancel
the transfer of funds
to your Swiss account

OK | Cancel

Warning!!! Warning !!! Warning !!!

All data on your hard
drive is about to be
DESTROYED

OK

Potential Hardware Conflict

IRQ 7 is about to be multiplexed
with the inbound PIC line 4.
Press OK to accept this

OK | Cancel

Careful! Information May Be Lost

A file named LetterToMom already exits
You may choose to:
Replace your old file with this new one
Save this new file with a different name
Don't save right now

Replace | New Name | Cancel

when destroying data is not meaningful action. Warning messages should be unambiguous. Should the user click OK or Cancel to stop the funds transfer in Figure 15.12? Warning messages should be clear. You might know what PIC line 4 is, but will your users? The best warning messages clearly explain the actions the user can take and the consequences of those actions.

Error messages: Error messages are used when a user or system error has occurred. When the message results from a user error, it should remind the user what the user did, tell the user why it was not correct, and help the user decide how to correct the error. Avoid "blaming" the user for the problem. The users of your program don't like being told they made a mistake any more than you do. Your error messages should concentrate on how to perform an action correctly; instead of saying `User Error: Invalid Filename`, you could say, `There was a problem saving file. Filenames cannot contain spaces or any of the following characters`.

SPECIAL OPERATIONS

Special operations include cut and paste, drag and drop, and online help. Most users of graphical user interfaces are accustomed to using standard cut-and-paste operations, so it is important to provide these in your Java programs. Although this was originally difficult to do in Java, JDK 1.1 has added support for clipboard operations.

Listing 15.6 shows the Cutter applet, which demonstrates how to perform cut and paste operations in Java. The applet uses the `getSystemClipboard()` method, which is a privileged operation. The applet must run in appletviewer or a browser configured to permit access to the system clipboard. Recall that applications are not subject to such restrictions; implementing clipboard access in an application presents no special problems.

Listing 15.6 The Cutter Applet (partial listing)

```
// Access to the system clipboard is a privileged
// operation. This applet must run in appletviewer
// or in a browser configured to allow local applets
// unrestricted access.

import java.applet.*;
import java.awt.*;
import java.awt.event.*;
import java.awt.datatransfer.*;

public class Cutter extends Applet
  implements ActionListener, ClipboardOwner
{
  TextArea theText = new TextArea();

  public void init()
  {
    setLayout(new BorderLayout());

    Panel p = new Panel();
```

```
      add(theText, "Center");
      add(p,       "South");

      p.setLayout(new GridLayout(1, 0, 15, 15));
      Button b;
      p.add(b = new Button("Copy"));
      b.addActionListener(this);
      p.add(b = new Button("Cut"));
      b.addActionListener(this);
      p.add(b = new Button("Paste"));
      b.addActionListener(this);
      p.add(b = new Button("Clear"));
      b.addActionListener(this);
   }

   public void lostOwnership(Clipboard c,
      Transferable t)
   {
      ; // null implementation
   }

   public void actionPerformed(ActionEvent event)
   {
      String cmd = event.getActionCommand();

      if    (cmd.equals("Copy"))  copy();
      else if (cmd.equals("Cut"))   cut();
      else if (cmd.equals("Paste"))  paste();
      else if (cmd.equals("Clear"))  clear();
   }
```

If you're content to access a private clipboard that can be used only by your Java application, you can use the `Clipboard()` constructor to create your own clipboard. The important thing about `getSystemClipboard()` is that it permits applications to exchange data with other, non-Java programs.

The Cutter applet creates a user interface that includes two text areas and a series of buttons for copying and cutting selected data from one clipboard and pasting it into the other. Listing 15.7 shows the `copy()` method from the Cutter applet. Copying text is a straightforward operation:

1. Use the `getSelectionStart()` and `getSelectionEnd()` methods to find out which text has been marked by the user. If no text has been marked, then the `copy()` method simply beeps.

2. Retrieve the text from the `TextArea` control, `theText`, using the `getText()` method.

3. Make a copy of the selected text by using the `StringSelection()` constructor. Remember, in Java, `Strings` are immutable. If you want to send text to the clipboard, you must make a copy.

4. You retrieve the system clipboard by using the `Toolkit` object, and the text is transferred to the clipboard using the `setContent()` method. This erases any previous contents that the clipboard might have held.

Listing 15.7 The copy() Method of the Cutter Applet

```
void copy()
{
  int  start = theText.getSelectionStart();
  int  end   = theText.getSelectionEnd();
  String text  = theText.getText();
  if (start != end)
  {
    StringSelection ss =
      new StringSelection(
      text.substring(start, end));
    getToolkit().getSystemClipboard().
      setContents(ss, this);
  }
  else
  {
    getToolkit().beep();
  }

}
```

The cut() method, shown in Listing 15.8, is similar to the copy() method, except that the selected text is removed from the TextArea control, theText. To remove the text, a new String is created by concatenating the substring starting at the beginning of the text up to the beginning of the selection, with a second substring, which starts where the selection area ends. Note how the method checks for a selection that starts at position 0. After the new String is constructed, it is placed back into theText using the setText()method.

Listing 15.8 The cut() Method of the Cutter Applet

```
void cut()
{
  int  start = theText.getSelectionStart();
  int  end   = theText.getSelectionEnd();
  String text  = theText.getText();
  if (start != end)
  {
    StringSelection ss =
      new StringSelection(
      text.substring(start, end));
    getToolkit().getSystemClipboard().
      setContents(ss, this);

    String x = "";
    if (start >= 0)
      x += text.substring(0, start);
    x += text.substring(end);

    theText.setText(x);
  }
  else
  {
    getToolkit().beep();
  }
}
```

The paste() and clear() methods are shown in Listing 15.9. The clear() method is simplicity itself, because you don't need to transfer the data to the clipboard, nor do you need to worry about a particular selection. It simply sets the text in the TextArea to the empty String, "".

The code for pasting is a little more complex, but not overly so. To paste what is in the clipboard you must do the following:

1. Create a Clipboard object and initialize it by retrieving the system clipboard via the Toolkit, as you did for copy() and paste().

2. Create a Transferable object by using the clipboard's getContents() method. Because the clipboard might contain information that is not text, the Transferable class is used to represent any kind of object that can be stored there.

3. Turn the Transferable object you retrieved in step 2 into a String. This is done by using the Transferable method, getTransferData(), passing it DataFlavor.stringFlavor and casting the returned object to a String. All this is put inside a try-catch block to handle any problems that might arise.

4. After you've converted the data on the clipboard into a String, pasting it into your document is fairly straightforward. You first determine whether a selection area exists because, if so, you want to replace the selection area with the new text. You'll also need to retrieve the *caret* position (the caret is another name for the text cursor that shows you where your typing will take place). When you know where the data should go (and what, if any, data should be deleted), you only must create a new String, using concatenation, just as you did for the cut()method.

Listing 15.9 The paste() and clear() Methods of the Cutter Applet

```
void paste()
{
  Clipboard clip = getToolkit().
    getSystemClipboard();
  Transferable t = clip.getContents(this);
  try
  {
    String s = (String) t.getTransferData(
      DataFlavor.stringFlavor);

    int  start = theText.getSelectionStart();
    int  end   = theText.getSelectionEnd();
    int  cur   = theText.getCaretPosition();
    String text = theText.getText();
    int  len   = text.length();

    if (start == end)
    {
      start = cur;
      end   = cur;
    }
```

```
      String x = "";
      if (start >= 0)
        x += text.substring(0, start);
      x += s;
      if (end <= len)
        x += text.substring(end);

      theText.setText(x);
    }
    catch (Exception e)
    {
      getToolkit().beep();
    }
  }

  void clear()
  {
    theText.setText("");
  }
}
```

Figure 15.13 shows how the applet looks in operation.

Java 1.1 does not support drag-and-drop operations, but these are expected to be a part of Java 1.2. Drag-and-drop operations are very convenient for users; you should consider incorporating them into your applications as soon as Java supports this important capability.

Java likewise provides no direct support for online help, an important user aid. You can work around this deficiency in either of two ways. First, you might consider building help files as HTML documents that can be accessed using a standard Web browser. If your program is implemented as an applet, you can use the `AppletContext.showDocument()` method to access the HTML pages. If your program is implemented as an application, you can use `Runtime.exec()` to launch a browser that can display your help files.

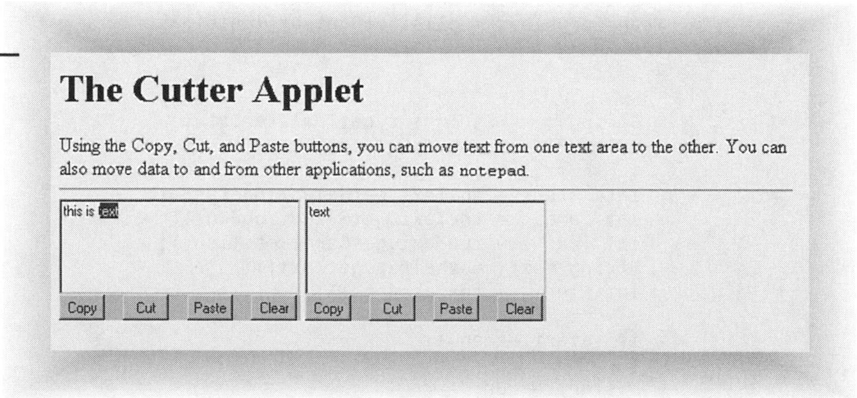

FIGURE 15.13

The output of the Cutter applet

The Cutter Applet

Using the Copy, Cut, and Paste buttons, you can move text from one text area to the other. You can also move data to and from other applications, such as notepad.

this is text

text

| Copy | Cut | Paste | Clear | Copy | Cut | Paste | Clear |

Alternatively, you can seek out a commercial Java package, such as Sun's *JavaHelp*, that provides access to online help. Several such packages exist at the time of writing. Of course, you can always write your own online help package, but a full-functioned help system is a significant piece of software. You can save yourself significant time and trouble by buying a solution off the shelf.

Summary

Designing a good user interface requires attention to the visual design of the interface and to its usability. A high-quality visual interface is characterized by clarity, coherence, symmetry, and elegance.

Clarity is the extent to which the designer's intentions are understood by the user. Clarity is achieved by making sure different things look different. Coherence is the extent to which the interface seems to be a complete whole. Coherence helps the user pick out related elements of the user interface, and is achieved by making sure that things that are the same appear the same. Symmetry, achieved by using a grid to align components, improves the aesthetic appeal of a visual interface. A custom layout manager is a helpful means of improving the symmetry of screens built using Java's Abstract Window Toolkit. Elegance is achieved when a visual interface solves its problem in a simple and novel, but highly effective manner.

Designing a usable interface involves focusing on the user's goals rather than the user's task or the available technologies. A highly usable interface uses the design principle of abstraction to present the user with an appropriate range of functions, instead of merely exposing the capabilities of the system. In addition, a highly usable interface puts the user in control, acts in a predictable manner, provides feedback, forgives errors, allows customization, and anticipates portable use.

Questions

For multiple-choice items, indicate all correct responses.

1. A well-designed visual interface is characterized by _____.

   a. Clarity

   b. Coherence

   c. Elegance

   d. Productivity

   e. Symmetry

2. Clarity is achieved when differences make a _____.

   a. Advantage

   b. Difference

   c. Contrast

   d. Grid

3. The _____ test is a good way to assess the clarity of a visual interface.

4. True or false. You should generously use whitespace to separate independent elements.

5. True or false. The layout managers of Java's Abstract Window Toolkit are well-suited to building screens based on a canonical grid.

6. When designing for usability, the designer should focus first on _____.

   a. Elegance

   b. The available technologies

   c. The user's goals

   d. The user's task

7. True or false. An important characteristic of a usable interface is that it tells the user what to do.

8. True or false. A highly usable interface uses as many colors as possible.

9. To emphasize text, you should _____.

   a. Use a bold font

   b. Use a sans serif font

   c. Use colored text

   d. Use large letters

10. Java _____ might have difficulty accessing the system clipboard.

    a. Applets

    b. Applications

    c. Programs

    d. Systems

Exercises

1. Choose a familiar application program and study its user interface. List no fewer than 10 ways in which it could be improved.

2. Design a user interface that could be used to control a VCR. Include capability to record programs based on the channel and time.

3. Using a text area, a menu, and the code from the Cutter applet, write a program that can edit text files. Pay special attention to the design of the menus, striving to make them as usable as possible.

4. Design a user interface that could be used to edit, compile, and execute Java applets and applications.

5. Using the results of exercise 3 and exercise 4, write a program that you can use to edit, compile, and execute Java applets and applications. Your program should invoke `javac` to compile programs and `javac` or `appletviewer`, as appropriate, to run them.

To Learn More

The following books will help you learn more about designing user interfaces:

- Mullet, Kevin, and Darrell Sano. *Designing Visual Interfaces*. Englewood Cliffs, New Jersey: SunSoft Press, 1995.

  Few books deal thoroughly with the principles of graphic design relevant to the design of visual interfaces. Fortunately, Mullet and Sano have written an excellent introduction to the subject.

- Cooper, Alan. *About Face: The Essentials of User Interface Design*. Foster City, California: Programmers Press, 1995.

  This title is a good source for additional information on user interface design.

- Norman, Donald. *The Design of Everyday Things*. New York: Doubleday, 1990.

  Although it does not deal primarily with user interface design, this a delightful book that contains much of interest and relevance to the designer of user interfaces.

- Borenstein, Nathaniel. *Programming as if People Mattered*. Princeton, New Jersey: Princeton University Press, 1991.

- Rubinstein, Richard, and Harry Hersh. *The Human Factor: Designing Computer Systems for People*. Bedford, Massachusetts: Digital Press, 1984.

  The previous two books deal well with the topic of design for usability.

- Manasi, Mark. *Secrets of Effective GUI Design*. Alameda, California: Sybex, 1994.

  This is a simple and clear book that includes many useful hints for user interface design.

- Microsoft Press. *The Windows Interface Guidelines for Software Design*. Redmond, Washington: 1995.

  This is an important book that gives specific guidelines for user interface design for Microsoft Windows 95.

16

Designing with Components

It's 11:15 p.m., and you've just arrived home. For the umpteenth time, you say to yourself, "I'm really getting much too old for this." Pulling a soda out of the refrigerator, you pop the top, settle back in your recliner, and press the button on your remote control, hoping to catch the highlights of the game on the late news. Instead, you're greeted with a pop, a hiss, and a thin column of smoke rising from the back of your ten-year-old TV set. "Just great," you say to yourself. "As if I didn't have enough to do. Now I have to build a new TV!"

As the old question goes, "What's wrong with this picture?" Today, unless you're a hobbyist, it's unlikely that you'll build your own television set from individual electronic components. Furthermore, it's also unlikely that you'll hire a skilled TV craftsman to build your television for you. Instead, you'll head on down to Sears or K-Mart, pick out the nice 27-inch special that's on sale, bring it home, plug it in, and expect it to work.

Two things make it possible for you to do this. First, you have standard electrical outlets throughout your house that can power different kinds of appliances. Provided you have the right kind of plug, it doesn't matter whether you plug in your juicer, your popcorn machine, or your TV; they all work. Second, this standard way of plugging in items has facilitated a market in prebuilt appliances. Both these circumstances are necessary: Without an electrical standard, most folks won't buy a television; without appliances you can use, why bother getting electricity?

In the past five years, the market for software components—prebuilt pieces of software functionality—has mushroomed, creating a fledgling market in prepackaged software parts that can be bolted together to create applications. These parts have enabled a new generation of programmers to write sophisticated applications that previously would have been beyond their capability. Now, version 1.1 of the Java Developer's Kit adds support for writing software components in Java. Of course, because this is Java, a catchy name is inevitable. Rather than write boring old Java components, you'll have the pleasure of working with Java beans!

Beans are objects that are intended to be written once but used many times. As you'll see, a bean can have special capabilities that set it apart from ordinary objects. In comparison to a bean, a regular object resembles a clumsy job interviewee who is unable to respond when asked the inevitable "Tell me about yourself." Beans know how to speak up. They have elaborate networks of social connections and know how to fit in well.

Many believe that Java's future depends on the development of a substantial market for prewritten beans. It's important, therefore, to know how beans work and how to use them. This chapter teaches you that and also about how to write simple beans.

In this chapter you will learn:

- What components are and why they're important

- What Java beans are

- How beans are used

- What main facilities and features beans offer

- How to integrate beans within your program

Introduction to Components

In 1798...Eli Whitney introduced an innovation [the interchangeable part] that revolutionized manufacturing forever. Today a similar innovation is under way that promises to do much the same thing for software.

—*Dr. Brad Cox,* Object-Oriented Programming

From the time in the early 1980s that Dr. Cox wrote this, the shining promise of object-oriented technology has been to bring to software developers the same tool that has eased the work of generations of mechanical and electrical engineers: the component. Modern electrical engineers, for example, do not design systems using transistors, resistors, capacitors, and inductors. Instead, they use integrated circuits (IC)—standardized off-the-shelf parts that encapsulate the majority of functions needed in a typical design. Rather than build their own integrated circuits, they just order them out of a catalogue or pick them up at ICs-R-Us.

If you open up your computer and take a look at the system motherboard, you'll see a few resistors or capacitors here and there, but most of the work is done by ICs, which contain the equivalent of hundreds of thousands of transistors and other parts. Because all this complexity is encapsulated into standardized parts, the computer designer's job is much easier. Because the power, speed, and capabilities of these ICs double roughly every year and a half, the computer on your desk that cost a week's salary has greater processing power than the multimillion dollar corporate mainframes of a decade ago. You might have heard the comparison, "If automobiles had advanced at the same rate as computers, today you could buy a Rolls-Royce for a dollar, and it would get a million miles to the gallon." (You might have also heard the rejoinder: "And once a year your car would blow up, killing all aboard.")

Until the introduction of object-oriented technology, software developers had nothing similar to ICs to help them work at a higher level of abstraction. Like the computer hardware engineers in the 1940s and early 1950s, software developers have continued building programs piece by piece, one at a time. If personal computers were still built using this part-by-part approach, we'd all have 50-foot-long motherboards running at 0.5 MHz and failing every four hours of operation—if we could even afford a computer at all.

COMPONENTS AND STANDARDS

> *" Unfortunately, object-oriented technology, which was supposed to bring software construction into the industrial era, has failed to live up to its promise. "*

Unfortunately, object-oriented technology, which was supposed to bring software construction into the industrial era, has failed to live up to its promise. Why? Although there are several factors contributing to this failure, the one critical factor is the absence of a widely agreed-upon standard governing the interaction of objects. Perhaps you remember the VHS/Betamax controversy of the 1970s? These two competing standards for home video cassette recorders (VCRs) delayed the wide acceptance of home video tape. If you bought a Betamax machine, you couldn't exchange tapes or rent movies in the VHS format, and vice versa. Until the VHS standard won out, the home video market didn't really take off.

A similar situation exists in the market for plug-in software components. It's not that such standards do not exist. There are several such standards, all actively trying to gain the upper hand in the marketplace. For you, the software developer, that spells trouble. Like the unfortunate Betamax owner, if you have the wrong player, you may not be able to find the component you want to use.

While object-oriented programming was promising components, an unexpected event made component-built software a reality, at least on a limited scale. The introduction of Visual Basic for Windows, which used special precompiled dynamic link libraries called VBX controls, introduced a whole new generation to programming. Rather than construct applications line by line, Visual Basic programmers were able to regularly build entire applications from a handful of VBX controls, using some code to define a user interface and using a little more code to glue everything together. The ease with which this could be done made application programming accessible to a much wider and larger audience, and this larger audience, in turn, created a thriving market in custom Visual Basic controls.

The success of Visual Basic controls opened the eyes of many software developers to the possibilities of component-based software construction. Notwithstanding their success in the market, however, VBX controls proved short-lived. Because VBX controls were closely tied to the 16-bit Windows 3.1 architecture, VBX controls were not really an enterprisewide solution. With the advent of 32-bit Windows, Microsoft introduced a new architecture based on its Object Linking and Embedding (OLE) technology. These components were called OCX controls, though lately Microsoft has changed the nomenclature, referring to the Component Object Model (COM), instead of OLE, and rechristening OCX controls as ActiveX.

Although Visual Basic controls in all their incarnations have been the dominant example of component-based software, other models do exist. Borland's Delphi product has its own component standard, called the Visual Component Library or VCL, which has created a market for those controls. Thus far, other component models, such as OpenDoc and LiveConnect, have failed to achieve the market status of Microsoft's OLE/COM/ActiveX. However, the arrival of Java beans may herald a sea change because beans work not only on Windows machines but also on any machine that can run Java.

TYPES OF COMPONENTS

At a consumer electronics store like Circuit City, you can purchase household components that range from stereos to computers to waffle makers to washing machines. What type of software component will you be able to purchase after component-based development becomes more widespread? If you plan to produce components, where are the opportunities? Where is the component market headed?

There are two types of components you can expect to find. The first consists of small and general components that can find their way into a variety of applications. You could call these *fine-grained* or *general-purpose* components. The second sort consists of larger, more specific components that have narrower application. Call these *large-grained* or *domain-specific* components.

For instance, a fine-grained component that displays itself on the screen and enables the user to pick out a time interval, say, for booking appointments, could be used in applications ranging from dental office scheduling to shop floor workflow planning. On the other hand, a large-grained component that values a commodities option using the Black-Scholes model would obviously contain more functionality and have a more limited application. Such a component could be widely used in building financial systems but would not find much use outside that domain.

COMPONENT ENVIRONMENTS
AND CHARACTERISTICS

Components are not, by themselves, very useful. If you remove your TV from the power grid and disconnect the antenna, it serves, at best, as a rather large end table. Likewise, for a component to be useful, it must live inside an application or framework that provides an environment for it to perform in.

Component environments come in two varieties. When you build an application using an environment that supports component-based development, each component has a design-time persona. In this design environment, most components present themselves visually as a widget or gadget on a toolbar or palette. To use a component, you click it or drag it onto a form (typically an application window) where you can visually manipulate it and arrange for it to send messages or respond to events. Currently, Visual Basic is the most popular host application, but component-based design environments also exist for Microsoft Office and Netscape Navigator and include such popular products as Sybase's PowerBuilder and Borland's Delphi and C++Builder.

Although most components present themselves visibly in their design environment, when the application is finally deployed, things are different. During runtime, a great many components make up the user interface. Buttons, labels, text input areas, scrollbars—all these are visible. Other components, however, such as the hypothetical model that values a stock option, live behind the scenes. The important thing to realize is that the runtime environment and the design-time environment of a component may be different.

Not every piece of software is suitable for use as a component. To be useful, a component must be self-contained. If it depends too much on the existence of a particular environment or set of conditions, there won't be much opportunity to reuse it. In addition, a useful component must also have a well-defined interface so that it's convenient to use.

Meet the Beans

The Java bean component model isn't that different from alternative models, except that it is based on Java. Of course, that's a big *except* because Java has many unique capabilities, chief among them being the portability of Java programs. The notion of components that not only can be reused but also can be reused on a variety of host platforms is extremely attractive. This gives Java beans a wider runtime environment to perform in.

Sun's vision for Java beans transcends even this expansive horizon. Rather than just make it possible for beans to run on any platform with a Java Virtual Machine, Sun has made it possible (by means of a special software bridge) for beans to function within an ActiveX environment. You have the best of both worlds! Put yourself in the place of a developer hoping to bring to market a component that, say, facilitates access to an object-oriented database. Would you prefer to write an ActiveX component that runs only under Windows or write a bean that can run not only on Windows but also on any Java-capable platform? Sun and many market analysts see the latter as the more reasonable, and hence more likely, choice. If Sun is right, beans will soon become a key technology, one that every software developer needs to understand.

THE BEANS DEVELOPMENT ENVIRONMENT

Sun's official definition of a Java bean is a "reusable software component that can be manipulated visually in a builder tool." If you're familiar with a rapid application development (RAD) tool such as Borland's Delphi or JBuilder, Microsoft's Visual Basic, or Symantec's Visual Café for Java, you understand what's meant by visual manipulation.

RAD tools let you program by dragging components (that is, controls) from a palette onto a workspace that depicts the user interface of your application. You can move the components around the workspace and can resize them. By using the mouse or a function key, you can also call up a properties sheet for any control on the workspace. The properties sheet lets you view and set component properties. The particular properties vary from component to component but typically include things such as the foreground color, background color, font, and so on. Sophisticated components, such as a text box tied to a database column, may enable you to specify the name of the database being accessed and a query string used to select the relevant table and row. Figure 16.1 shows the property sheet associated with a button component in Borland's JBuilder environment.

Some Java beans are simple GUI elements such as buttons and sliders. Other Java beans are sophisticated visual software components such as database viewers, or data feeds. Some Java beans have no GUI appearance of their own but can still be

FIGURE 16.1

Components in a RAD tool

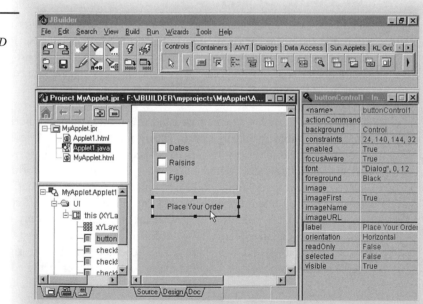

employed visually using an application builder. The beans API is intended to support the construction of large beans and nonvisual beans but is geared primarily to support the more common small- and medium-sized visual components.

Because Sun's definition anticipates that most beans will be manipulated visually, much of the beans application programming interface (API) is designed to support such manipulation. Taking a more detailed perspective, here are some characteristics (most are provided by the beans API) common to beans:

- Support for properties, which can be accessed and set during programming, perhaps using a properties sheet, and at runtime, using method calls

- Support for events, which enable the bean to interface with other beans and objects in a manner similar to that of Abstract Window Toolkit (AWT) objects

- Support for *introspection,* an API that enables a RAD tool to look inside a bean and discover what properties should be displayed on its properties sheet, as well as other useful information

- Support for *serialization,* an API that enables the state of a bean to be saved by writing it to a data stream, such as a disk file

- Support for customization, so a RAD tool can enable the programmer to customize the appearance and behavior of a bean

RECOGNIZING A BEAN

> *" Applets are easy to spot because every applet extends the class* `Applet`*. Recognizing a bean isn't as easy."*

Applets are easy to spot because every applet extends the class `Applet`. Recognizing a bean isn't as easy. The difficulty in pinning down exactly what is, or is not, a bean arises because beans are not required to extend any particular class, nor do they consistently implement any particular interface. Beans intended to be added to AWT `Containers` must, of course, extend `java.awt.Component`, but not every bean has a visual runtime representation. Your super-duper option-pricing bean, for example, would probably depend on some other object, possibly another bean, to establish its runtime visual representation. That way, you could select any of a variety of representations.

It's worth mentioning that not all objects should be implemented as beans. Unless your component is to be manipulated visually or customized in some way, there's little point in wiring the component as a bean. Beans are intended to present a friendly interface to useful functionality, which can be implemented within the bean or elsewhere.

A case in point is the Java Database Connectivity (JDBC) API, which Sun implemented as a class library rather than as a bean. Sun explains this choice by pointing out that the JDBC classes and objects are intended for programmatic, not visual, manipulation. Of course, you can write a bean that packages state and functionality of the JDBC API and presents it to the user for visual manipulation. In fact, that's exactly what tools like Symantec's Visual Café for Java (Database Development Edition) and Borland's JBuilder do: They include database components that you can visually manipulate, using a property sheet. Figure 16.2 illustrates this multilayered approach to component design.

How Beans Are Used

In the days before components, it was easy to tell the programmers from the civilians (so to speak). Programmers were people who designed and built software, but they frequently weren't the people who used that software. Traditionally, there has been a divide between the technical staff on one hand—concerned with bytes and cycles and throughput and protocols—and the user community on the other hand—wanting applications that help get their jobs done faster and easier.

Today, thanks to components, programming is no longer restricted to an elite technical priesthood. It's not unusual to find that business applications are being built by domain-experts—programmers whose expertise is not technical computer know-how

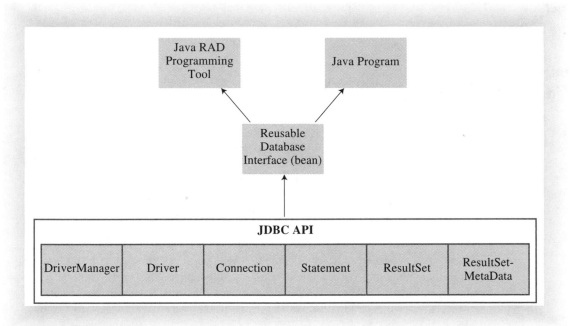

FIGURE 16.2

A multilayered approach
to component design

but skill in accounting, stock options, finance, or real estate. Components are what make this possible.

Three kinds of programmers use Java beans, each calling on different bean features:

- Tool builders, who write the RAD tools that programmers use to construct applications

- Bean builders, who write beans that can be loaded into a RAD tool and included by programmers in applications they write

- Bean users, programmers who write applications that include beans

Let's take a look at each group and see how the Java beans API makes its job easier.

TOOL BUILDERS

Imagine that you have just bought a new high-tech desk, all black and chrome and glass. How would you feel if the first time you set your trusty stapler on the corner, it jumped off onto the floor? When you call technical support (this is, after all, a really high-tech desk), they tell you, "I'm sorry, your stapler isn't compatible with that desk. You'll have to buy the AZ2000 model stapler." Then, after you've bought the AZ2000, which does indeed stay put, you find out that your desk won't let you add the new video-conference phone system your company has just purchased. "We'll be releasing a desk that can hold a video-conference phone in the first quarter of next year," they say when you call. "As a loyal customer, you'll qualify for special upgrade pricing."

This is a ridiculous scenario, right? No matter how high-tech the desk, you expect to be able to pile anything you please on top and have it stay put.

Tool builders face a similar challenge. They want to build tools that are easy for programmers to use and that have a lot of features, but they also want their tools to readily accept beans created by third-party developers, because beans help make an application programmer more productive.

The task faced by the tool builder is to build in extensibility. Given the class file for a bean—a bean written by someone other than the tool builder—the tool builder wants to be able to figure out what it should look like on the RAD tool's palette and user-interface worksheet, what properties should be included in its property sheet, what kinds of values these properties can take, and so on. After the user has tweaked the bean's properties, the tool builder wants to be able to save the values of the properties so that the application generated by the tool can load and initialize the bean according to the application programmer's choices.

Therefore, the bean API features that are of greatest interest to the tool builder are the following:

- **Introspection**—The ability to find the properties, methods, and events when given a class file

- **Customization**—The ability to construct custom design-time interface mechanisms for a wide variety of beans

🔹 **Serialization**—The ability to store the persistent state of the beans the user has designed

Tool builders are also concerned with bean properties and events because the code generated by their RAD tools must be able to access and set bean properties and properly wire together beans and other objects by using events.

Tool builders require, and receive, a lot of support from the bean API, and much of the bean API is of interest *only* to tool builders.

BEAN BUILDERS

It's unlikely that you will soon build your own RAD tool, so many of the API facilities that help tool builders will be of only minimal interest to you. On the other hand, the features that help bean builders (as opposed to tool builders) also have broad application in the realm of everyday applications. Bean builders are those who design and implement beans, making them available (sometimes for free, sometimes at a price) to application programmers who incorporate beans in their applications. Bean builders don't need to know as much about the bean API as do tool builders. They do, however, need to know how to structure their code to facilitate the job of the tool builder, who wants to build tools that efficiently discover how to use an unfamiliar bean.

In addition to the code for the component itself, bean builders sometimes implement special methods that help tool builders set complex bean properties. For example, a bean builder might provide a graphical color picker to spare bean users the need to type colors into a property sheet as RGB values. The bean builder must know how to tell a tool about the color picker so that the tool can permit this special visual manipulation.

In general, however, the bean builder is mainly concerned with the operation of the bean inside an application program. So, the focus of the bean builder is on the properties and events of the bean. However, the bean builder must also know something about introspection and customization so that the tool builder's requirements can be met.

BEAN USERS

Bean users are by far the largest of the three groups. Bean users want to build applications, and if beans make that easier or faster, they want lots of beans.

Bean users have the lightest burden of the three groups, in terms of familiarity with the beans API. Bean users need to understand bean properties and events. More importantly, though, they need to understand each specific bean: the meaning of each of its properties, what events it fires and when, and for which events (if any) it should listen. Bean users are not normally much concerned with introspection, customization, or serialization; these matters are handled by tool builders and bean builders acting on behalf of bean users. Bean users focus on the runtime operation of a bean and can take a bean's design-time operation for granted.

In this chapter, you'll learn enough to write some simple beans, but there isn't sufficient space to tell you all there is to know. Instead, this chapter focuses on the needs of bean users. If your main interest is in designing components, rather than using them, you should consult the references given at the end of this chapter.

INTER-BEAN COOPERATION THROUGH PUBLISH/SUBSCRIBE

As you've learned, a successful reusable component must be self-contained. If a component requires too specific an environment, it will have limited potential for reuse. Imagine a stereo system, like that in Figure 16.3, in which the CD player, the tuner, the amplifier, and the speakers are all contained in a single box. What happens when the tuner fails? You must throw away the entire stereo because the working components cannot be reused.

Figure 16.4, by contrast, shows a modular stereo system. Here, the components connect via plugs and jacks rather than directly. If a component fails, perhaps the tuner, the other components can be reused. You just plug in a new tuner to replace the old one.

Similarly, software components can be either *tightly coupled* or *loosely coupled* with other components. If any of your components directly call the methods of another component, those components are tightly coupled; all the components must be present in order for any one of them to be used. This inhibits reuse.

"Wait," you say. "I thought that the way objects communicated was by sending messages to each other. Are beans different from regular objects?" Well, yes and no. Beans are just regular objects, but, because of their need for independence, a modular approach to inter-object communication is better that the direct approach.

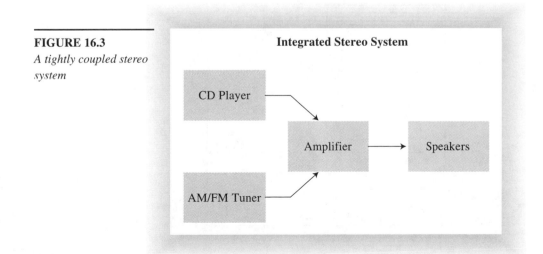

FIGURE 16.3

A tightly coupled stereo system

FIGURE 16.4

A modular stereo system

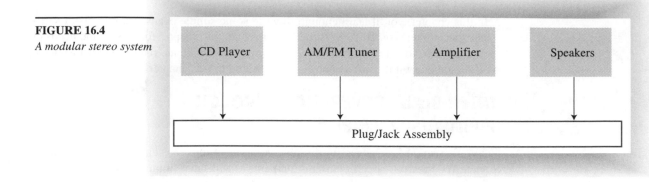

Rather than have your bean directly call the methods of another object, you should arrange to have it fire events instead. Then, those objects that are interested in your bean can subscribe to receive events sent by your component. Your component maintains a list of its subscribers. When it wants to contact them, it publishes an event by sending it to each subscriber in turn.

Figure 16.5 shows how this publish/subscribe design pattern works. In the figure, Component A is the publisher and Components B and C are subscribers. Publish/

FIGURE 16.5

The publish/subscribe design pattern

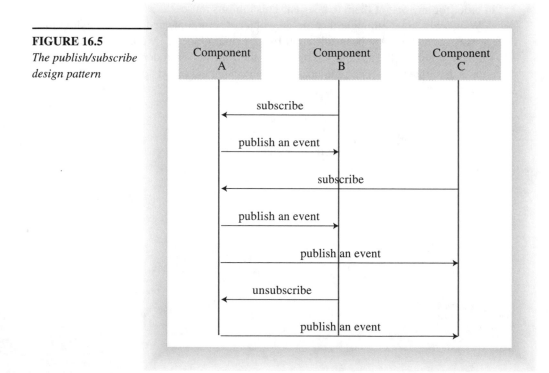

subscribe is just another name for the observer/observable pattern, which you met in Chapter 12, "Designing Concurrent Objects." It deserves a special name because of the extra support the beans API lends it, as you'll see in the next section.

Bean Properties, Methods, and Events

" The interface exposed by a bean includes the methods it makes available to other objects and the events it fires. "

Now that you have a basic grounding in components, you're ready to learn more about beans and how to use them. The interface exposed by a bean includes the methods it makes available to other objects and the events it fires. A bean's methods usually include accessor and mutator methods for bean properties, as well as methods that perform processing at higher levels of abstraction.

A RAD tool may handle a bean's properties, methods, and events for you. In such a case, you may not normally need to be aware of them. However, RAD tools are not infallible. Many a programmer could have been spared a long evening of debugging by knowing more about the faulty code the RAD tool generated.

PROPERTIES AND METHODS

What are properties? Bean properties are similar to ordinary object attributes, with a few subtle differences:

- Bean properties are available and visible to component users at design time. Regular object attributes (fields) are not. When used inside a RAD tool, a bean with a `title` property would normally display the `title` inside a property sheet (a visual dialog box) and give the user the opportunity to interactively modify its value.

- Bean properties store object state, much like object attributes do, yet the underlying storage implementation remains hidden from the user. This means that there need not be a one-to-one correspondence between bean properties and the object attributes used to store the state of the property. You may have a `weight` property, for instance, without having a corresponding attribute called `weight`. At design time, the `weight` property would show up in the builder tool and enable you to modify it there, but underneath the hood, the actual `weight` state (unfortunate pun intended) could be stored as a combination of fields named `density` and `area`.

- Bean properties can cause appropriate events to fire when the component user changes a property value. Setting the background color attribute for a regular object will not cause the object to reflect the change; it is up to the user to repaint the component. By contrast, methods that handle bean properties can be written to repaint the bean whenever the property value is changed.

Although this list gives you a good idea of the difference between a property and an attribute, it doesn't answer the question "How do you define a bean property?" Unlike what you might expect, there is no new property keyword to learn. Instead, you define a property by adding `public` methods to your class that use a special set of naming conventions. Sun calls these naming conventions *design patterns*, but they are quite different from the design patterns you were introduced to in Chapter 12.

RAD tools look for methods using these special naming conventions when they make bean properties available for editing at design time. The good news is that these same naming conventions make it easy for you to use beans, even if you're not using a RAD tool. The conventions identify four types of properties and specify the name and form of accessor and mutator methods for each type of property.

Simple and Boolean Properties

The first type of property is called a *simple property*. A simple property consists of a single value, which can have a primitive type or an object type. If your bean has a simple property called `weight`, you would write the accessor and mutator methods for the `weight` property like this:

```
public PropertyType getWeight();              // simple accessor
public void setWeight(PropertyType value); // simple mutator
```

`PropertyType` stands for the data type of the simple property. Of course, the parameter doesn't need to be named `value`; you can name the parameter as you choose. You must, however, use the method names `getWeight` and `setWeight`, if the name of the property is `weight`. That is how the bean API identifies `weight` as a property. As mentioned before, the `weight` property doesn't have to correspond to an actual field called `weight`. Whereas to the user of your bean, these seem to be simple accessor and mutator methods, the actual storage type or method of retrieval is never revealed to the user.

As you'll see shortly, the Java API was extended to include a mechanism that lets you programmatically analyze a `.class` file to determine what public methods it supports. By naming accessor and mutator methods according to the recommended convention, you make it possible for a tool builder to write code that finds bean properties. If you are a bean user, this same pattern helps you determine what the properties of a bean are and how to get and set them.

The second type of property is called a *Boolean property* because it is always either `true` or `false`. To create accessor and mutator methods for a Boolean property named `home`, you'd write

```
public boolean isHome();           // Boolean accessor
public void setHome(boolean m);   // Boolean mutator
```

Again, the name of the parameter (here, `m`) could be any name you choose, but the methods must be named `isHome()` and `setHome()`.

Indexed and Customized Properties

The third of the four property types the conventions identify is the *indexed property*. An indexed property represents a one-dimensional array of property values, though the values need not be stored in an array. They might, for example, be stored in a `Vector` or a `List`. The important thing is that each property value is associated with a numerical index that ranges from 0 to one less than the number of property values. To define an indexed property named `passenger`, you'd write

```
public PropertyType getPassenger (int index);            // indexed
                                                         // accessor
public void setPassenger (PropertyType values[]);        // array
                                                         // accessor
public void setPassenger(int index, PropertyType value); // indexed
                                                         // mutator
public PropertyType[] getPassenger ();                   // array mutator
```

As before, `PropertyType` denotes the property type, and the parameter names (`index`, `value`, and `values`) are not fixed; they can be anything you like.

For indexed properties, you may define four methods instead of the usual two. One pair deals with individual property values, and each member of the pair requires a parameter specifying an index. The other pair gets, or sets, the entire array of property values.

The final type of property is the *customized property*. This includes any type of property that doesn't belong in the other three categories. The beans API provides a sophisticated mechanism for describing customized properties. The bean must implement the `BeanInfo` interface, which identifies a series of methods that interrogate the bean and return information about its properties, methods, and events. A complete discussion of the `BeanInfo` interface is beyond the scope of this chapter because the interface is of interest primarily to bean builders and tool builders. You can consult the JDK documentation or the books listed at the end of this chapter for further information on `BeanInfo`.

INTTEXTFIELD: A SIMPLE BEAN

Let's take a look at a simple class that implements a few properties. Listing 16.1, `IntField.java`, extends the `TextField` class by restricting its input to integers. By intercepting keystrokes as they are typed, using an inner-class derived from `KeyAdapter`, and by implementing the `TextListener` interface, `IntField` objects spare the programmer the trouble of manually extracting integer values and checking for errors from `TextField`s designed for numeric input. Throughout the rest of this chapter, you'll examine this simple class as it's promoted to a full-featured Java bean.

```
Listing 16.1 Intfield.java
//  IntTextField.java
//
import java.awt.*;
import java.awt.event.*;
import java.text.*;

public class IntTextField extends     TextField
                          implements TextListener
{
  // Default constructor: required for Beans
  public IntTextField()
```

```java
  {
    this( 0, DEF_WIDTH );
  }

  //  Working constructor: pass both a value and a width
  public IntTextField( int val, int width )
  {
    super( width );
    setText("" + val);
    value = val;
    lastText = getText();

    addKeyListener( intValidator );
    addTextListener( this );
  }

  //  Implements the TextListener interface ----------
  public void textValueChanged(TextEvent te)
  {
    int oldValue = value;

    if (getText().equals(""))
    {
      setText("0");
      selectAll();
    }
    try
    {
      setValue(Integer.parseInt( getText() ));
      lastText = getText();
    }
    catch (NumberFormatException e)
    {
      setValue(oldValue);
    }
  }

  //  Bean Properties--------------------------------
  public int  getValue() { return value; }
  public void setValue( int val )
  {
    String newText = ""+val;
    value = val;

    if (! newText.equals(getText()))
    {
      int pos = getCaretPosition();
      setText(newText);
      setCaretPosition(pos-1);
    }
  }


  //  Object fields ---------------------------------
  public static final int DEF_WIDTH = 12;
  private int      value;
  private String   lastText = "";

  //  Intercepts keystrokes, filtering invalid characters
```

```
    private KeyAdapter intValidator = new KeyAdapter()
    {
      public void keyPressed(KeyEvent ke)
      {
        char      keyChar = ke.getKeyChar();

        if ( (keyChar >= '0' && keyChar <= '9' )   ||
              keyChar == ke.VK_BACK_SPACE          ||
              keyChar == ke.VK_TAB                 ||
              keyChar == ke.VK_DELETE              ||
              ke.isActionKey()
           )
          ; // All is OK, let it be
        else
          ke.consume();
      }
    };
}
```

The `IntTextField` class has one simple property, called `value`. It is both a readable property, accessed through the `getValue()` method, and a writable property, accessed through the `setValue()` method. The `getValue()` method returns the contents of the private field named `value`. The `setValue()` mutator, however, updates the text contained in the component. Recall that the use of these special names is what enables a Java RAD tool to discover and provide visual editing capabilities for your Java bean.

In addition to the `get` and `set` methods that define the `IntTextField`'s lone property, the class also has two constructors. The default, or no-arg, constructor, initializes each `IntTextField` object to hold the value `0` and uses the default width, specified by the static final constant, `DEF_WIDTH`. Every Java bean *must* have a public no-arg constructor. The working constructor, which the no-arg constructor calls, accepts arguments for both `value` and `width`. The working constructor first sets the `value` field, and the `TextField` display itself, to the current value specified in the argument list. It then adds both a `KeyListener` and a `TextListener` to handle the keystroke events.

The `KeyListener` duties are assumed by a private data field called `theValidator`, which subclasses `KeyAdapter`. This class is implemented as a named inner class. The validator object examines each keystroke that goes by, passing only the digit characters (`'0'` to `'9'`), the Backspace, Tab, and Delete keys to the `TextField`. The cursor arrow keys are activated by including the `isActionKey()` method along with the other allowable key events. All other keystrokes are eaten by calling `KeyEvent.consume()`.

The actual text contained in the component doesn't change until `theValidator` has finished its work. Each keystroke is either passed on to the native peer object or is consumed. Thus, the `textValueChanged()` method is implemented to convert the text value stored in the component into an `int`, by using the `Integer.parseInt()` method. This method also handles the case when a `KeyEvent` deletes the last character in the `TextField`. In that case, the `value` field is reset to `0`, and the input area is selected. Finally, the `textValueChanged()` method must deal with the case of an integer that is too large, which it does by means of a `try-catch` block. If the input area is too large to be stored, the component reverts to its previous value.

Listings 16.2, `IntTextFieldTest.java`, and 16.3, `IntTextFieldTest.html`, create a simple applet that lets you try out and compare both an `IntTextField` and a regular `TextField` component.

Listing 16.2 IntTextFieldTest.java

```java
//  IntTextFieldTest.java

import java.awt.*;
import java.applet.*;

public class IntTextFieldTest extends Applet
{
  public void init()
  {
    add( new Label("Regular text field:"));
    add( new TextField( 10 ));
    add( new Label("The IntTextField:"));
    add( new IntTextField( 100, 10 ));
  }
}
```

Listing 16.3 IntTextFieldTest.html

```html
<HTML>
<HEAD>
<TITLE>Testing the IntTextField class</TITLE>
</HEAD>
<BODY>
<H1>The IntTextField class</H1>
<HR>
<UL>
<LI>
The IntTextField class prevents a user from
putting invalid characters into a field meant
to be used for numeric input.
<LI>
The digits 0 to 9 are accepted, as well as the
backspace, delete, and tab characters.
<LI>
If backspace or delete is used to erase the entire
field, the value is set to zero, and the
entire field is selected.
<LI>
The applet below displays a regular text field and
an IntTextField
</UL>
<HR>
<APPLET CODE=IntTextFieldTest HEIGHT=150 WIDTH=100>
</APPLET>
</BODY>
</HTML>
```

Figure 16.6 shows the applet at work in a browser.

The IntTextField class

- The IntTextField class prevents a user from putting invalid characters into a field meant to be used for numeric input.
- The digits 0 to 9 are accepted, as well as the backspace, delete, and tab characters.
- If backspace or delete is used to erase the entire field, then the value is set to zero, and the entire field is selected.
- The applet below displays a regular text field and an IntTextField

Regular text field:

The IntTextField:

12345

BUT IS IT A BEAN?

"The BeanBox is not a full-fledged RAD tool for building Java bean–enabled applications.... Like appletviewer, however, the BeanBox is an invaluable tool for getting quick feedback on your efforts."

You might have a hard time believing it, but the IntTextField class really is a bean that can be manipulated in a RAD tool. Because such tools are not yet widespread, however, Sun has created a mini-testing environment called the *BeanBox*. The BeanBox is not a full-fledged RAD tool for building Java bean–enabled applications, any more than the appletviewer is a tool for deploying applets. Like appletviewer, however, the BeanBox is an invaluable tool for getting quick feedback on your efforts.

The BeanBox is part of Sun's Bean Developer Kit (BDK), which, like the JDK, is freely available from the JavaSoft Web site. Downloading and installing the BDK is straightforward and easily accomplished by following the instructions on the Web page. After you've completed the installation, there are a few short steps you need to follow to try out your new bean.

A bean that you want to run in the BeanBox first needs to be packaged as a Java archive file, or jar. (You'll read more about these later in the chapter.) To create a jar file for IntTextField.java and use the resulting bean in the BeanBox, follow these steps:

1. Create a new directory and copy the file IntTextField.java into the directory.

2. Compile IntTextField.java, using the javac compiler. You will find two new classes afterward. One of these is the inner class defined inside the IntTextField class.

3. Create the jar file by typing

   ```
   jar cfM itf.jar *.class
   ```

   (The c means to create a new archive, the f means to use the filename specified [itf.jar], and the M means to skip creating a manifest file, an advanced option some bean builders may use. Later in the chapter you can learn about the rest of the jar utility's options.)

4. Copy the resulting file (itf.jar) to the jars subdirectory where you installed the BDK.

5. Go to the BeanBox subdirectory and type run. You'll see your new bean in the list of installed beans on the ToolBox window. Click on IntTextField, and when the cursor changes to a crosshair, click inside the BeanBox frame itself. Voilà, you're visually manipulating a bean!

Figure 16.7 shows the BeanBox with two IntTextField beans hooked up to Sun's Juggler bean. Note the property sheet for the bottom IntTextField bean on the right of the screen. Even though you didn't specify properties for such things as the font used for the display and the number of columns, those properties are also exposed in the tool because of the common naming convention. If you change the value property in the property sheet at the right, the two new properties you created will be activated.

For more information on using the BeanBox to hook up and test components, browse the BeanBox.html file in the doc subdirectory of your BDK installation.

EVENTS

Apart from knowing the properties and methods of a bean, a skilled bean user needs to know about the events the bean publishes. The whole point of bean events is to let subscribed objects know whenever a bean property changes. Of course, your objects

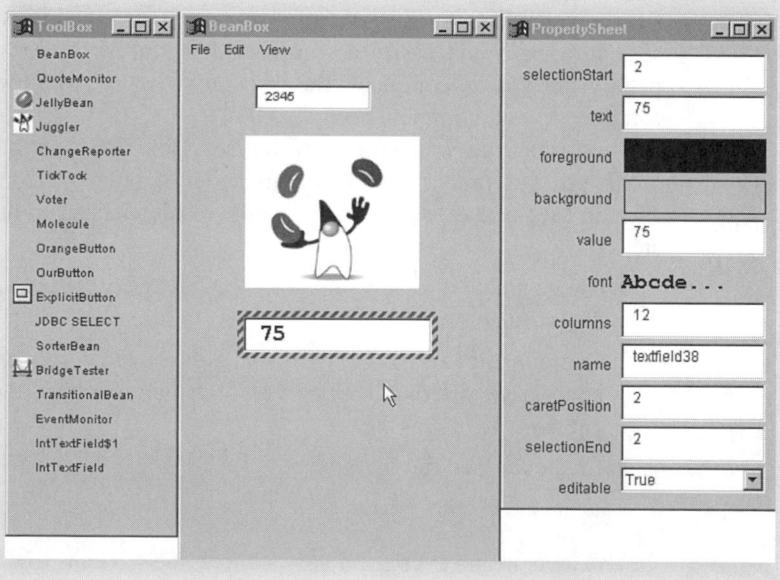

FIGURE 16.7

Working with
IntTextFields
in the BeanBox

could regularly poll the bean, using accessor methods to determine its current state, but that is a waste of valuable processor cycles. It's much more efficient for your objects to go about their business, waiting for the bean to notify them when something of possible interest occurs.

The bean API includes a pair of mechanisms for implementing the publish/subscribe pattern used to connect beans and objects. The first mechanism establishes what's called a *bound property*, a property that automatically notifies its subscribers whenever its value changes. The second mechanism establishes what's called a *constrained property*, one that must get approval from its subscribers before changing its value. When a subscriber is notified of a pending change to a constrained property, the subscriber can disallow the change by notifying the constrained property. This is called a *veto*.

For a property to be a constrained property, it must also be a bound property. There is no way to constrain a property that doesn't notify its subscribers. Remember, too, that only properties can be bound and constrained, and only beans have properties. Ordinary classes cannot use these mechanisms to communicate with each other. Figure 16.8 illustrates the publication of changes to bound and constrained properties. Notice that Java doesn't guarantee a subscriber will be notified when a change event occurs if a particular subscriber vetoes a change. The constrained property in Figure 16.8 has already notified Subscriber A that a change has occurred, but because of Subscriber B's veto, Subscriber C is never informed.

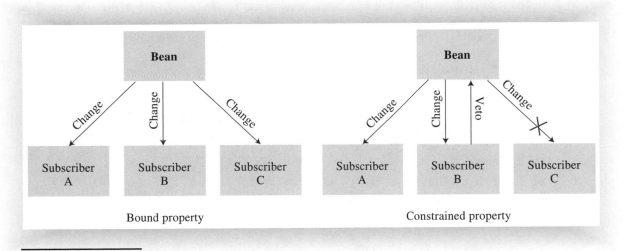

FIGURE 16.8

The publication of bound and constrained properties

Notice that, in the event that a change to a constrained property is vetoed, some subscribers may have already been notified of the pending change. Some subscribers may want to be notified only if a change actually occurs. To provide for this, a bean can implement both bound and constrained notification for a single property. That way, subscribers are notified of the pending change by the constrained property change event. If no subscriber vetoes the change, the bean can then publish a bound property change event. Subscribers may request notification of bound property change events, constrained property change events, or both.

A BOUND AND CONSTRAINED BEAN

Although the `IntTextField` class is useful just as it is, it could be even more useful if its `Value` property were bound and constrained. Do you recall the `SalesInvoice` example of Chapter 7 and 8? One goal of that application was to have a set of `LineItem` objects that behaved independently. The difficulty, however, lay in having the `SalesInvoice` object recalculate the total amount of merchandise sold whenever one `LineItem` amount changed. The solution used in Chapter 8—implementing a two-way association between the `LineItem` object and the `SalesInvoice` object—was less than ideal because it introduced unnecessary coupling between the classes. Because every `LineItem` object had to have a communication link back to its `SalesInvoice` container, you were effectively prohibited from dropping `LineItem` objects into any other class, no matter how useful they might be.

Implementing bound and constrained properties breaks the undesirable coupling used in the `SalesInvoice` application. Unlike that application, an object that implements a bound field doesn't have to be aware of who is subscribing to its events. If `LineItems` could have fired events, the `SalesInvoice` object could have subscribed to them without any cooperation or awareness on the part of the `LineItems` themselves. Even if you don't intend to develop your own beans, these techniques belong in your design arsenal.

Listing 16.4 shows the `BCIntTextField` class, which is derived from `IntTextField` and implements `Value` as a bound and constrained property. As you'll see, this enables your applications to subscribe to any changes made to a `BCIntTextField` object and even to veto those changes.

```
Listing 16.4 BCIntTextField.java
//  BCIntTextField.java
//
//  This is a Bound and Constrained version of
//  the IntTextField class
import java.awt.event.*;
import java.beans.*;

public class BCIntTextField extends IntTextField
{
  // --Override setValue() to fire events------------------
  public void setValue( int val )
  {
```

```
  Integer oldVal = new Integer(getValue());
  Integer newVal = new Integer(val);

  try
  {
    vcSupport.fireVetoableChange("Value", oldVal, newVal);
    super.setValue( newVal.intValue());
    pcSupport.firePropertyChange("Value", oldVal, newVal);
  }
  catch (PropertyVetoException pve)
  {
    super.setValue(oldVal.intValue());
  }
}

// --------------------------------------------------------
//  Add and remove PropertyChangeListeners
// --------------------------------------------------------
public void
  addPropertyChangeListener(PropertyChangeListener pcl)
{
  pcSupport.addPropertyChangeListener(pcl);
}

public void
  removePropertyChangeListener(PropertyChangeListener pcl)
{
  pcSupport.removePropertyChangeListener(pcl);
}

// --------------------------------------------------------
//  Add and remove VetoableChangeListeners
// --------------------------------------------------------
public void
  addVetoableChangeListener(VetoableChangeListener vcl)
{
  vcSupport.addVetoableChangeListener(vcl);
}
public void
  removeVetoableChangeListener(VetoableChangeListener vcl)
{
  vcSupport.removeVetoableChangeListener(vcl);
}

// --------------------------------------------------------
//  ChangeSupport fields
// --------------------------------------------------------
private PropertyChangeSupport pcSupport =
              new PropertyChangeSupport(this);

private VetoableChangeSupport vcSupport =
              new VetoableChangeSupport(this);
}
```

Dissecting the `BCIntTextField`

Although at first glance adding bound and constrained properties seems to add considerable complexity, you'll find, in fact, that most of the code is boilerplate code that appears in every class that implements bound and constrained behavior. Let's take a quick look at the pieces:

1. The first step in implementing support for bound and constrained properties is to import the classes from the `java.beans` package.

2. Next, you add a `PropertyChangeSupport` object and a `VetoableChangeSupport` object as fields within your class. These are both classes that handle much of the detail work required to notify property subscribers of changes and to notify property publishers when one subscriber has vetoed a change. Of course, if you are only going to make your property a constrained property, you don't need to add the `VetoableChangeSupport` object. When you construct these fields, pass `this` as the argument to the constructors like so:

```
private PropertyChangeSupport pcSupport =
                new PropertyChangeSupport(this);
private VetoableChangeSupport vcSupport =
                new VetoableChangeSupport(this);
```

3. The `PropertyChangeSupport` and `VetoableChangeSupport` fields provide support for adding and removing subscribers from your bean. All you have to do is implement a pair of methods for each support class. For the `PropertyChangeSupport` object, you'll add an `addPropertyChangeListener()` method and a `removePropertyChangeListener()` method. For the `VetoableChangeSupport` object, you'll write `addVetoableChangeListener()` and `removeVetoableChangeListener()` methods. Each of these methods takes a `PropertyChangeListener` (or `VetoableChangeListener`) object and passes it on to the embedded `PropertyChangeSupport` (or `VetoableChangeSupport`) object. Remember, this is boilerplate code. It will be the same in every bean you write.

4. The final step in implementing bound and constrained properties is to actually fire the events themselves. You do this by writing (or in this case, overriding) the mutator method for your property. For the `BCIntTextField` class, you'll override the `setValue()` method. The new `setValue()` method is conceptually simple. Whenever you change the property, you send the `firePropertyChange()` message to the embedded `PropertyChangeSupport` object. Along with the message, you send three pieces of information:

   🔹 The name of the property, passed as a `String`.

   🔹 The old value of the property before it was changed.

> *The new value of the property. By sending both old and new values, you allow subscribers to decide whether they want to take an action when both the old and new values are identical.*

Firing VetoableChange events is similar in concept but needs to take into consideration the fact that the change may be vetoed by a subscriber, in which case your bean must be prepared to revert to its previous value. You send the fireVetoableChange message to the VetoableChangeSupport object that you created earlier. The object that wants to veto a change throws a PropertyVetoException. Your bean must be prepared to catch that exception when it notifies subscribers of a change to a constrained property. In BCIntTextField the code looks like this:

```
try
{
  vcSupport.fireVetoableChange("Value", oldVal, newVal);
  super.setValue( newVal.intValue());
  pcSupport.firePropertyChange("Value", oldVal, newVal);
}
catch (PropertyVetoException pve)
{
  super.setValue(oldVal.intValue());
}
```

First, the VetoableChangeSupport object vcSupport is asked to send out a VetoableChange event to all subscribers. This message is placed inside a try-catch block. If a subscriber actually vetoes the change, the subscriber throws a PropertyVetoException, and the catch block sets the Value property back as it was. If the change isn't vetoed, the Value property is set to its new value, and all the bound property subscribers are notified via the firePropertyChange() method.

Two details deserve further explanation. First, the notification methods used to fire events work only with objects, not with primitive types. Thus, to get BCIntTextField to fire when its Value property changed, the int, Value, had to be wrapped in an Integer object. Second, notice that the BCIntTextField class changes its property before it fires the PropertyChange event. For the BCIntTextField, this is helpful, but for other classes, it might make more sense to fire the PropertyChange event first; it all depends on whether you want your bean to broadcast the message "I've changed!" or whether you want it to say, "I'm about to change."

Using BCIntTextFields

To actually work with an object that implements bound and constrained properties, you must implement the appropriate interface and include the corresponding method. To receive PropertyChange events, your class must implement the PropertyChangeListener interface that entails writing a PropertyChange() method. Likewise, to receive VetoableChange events, you must implement the VetoableChangeListener interface and include the VetoableChange method.

Listing 16.5 shows the BCIntTextFieldTest applet, which uses several BCIntTextField objects. This applet uses its BCIntTextField objects to keep a running total and to keep inattentive employees from offering discounts greater than 10%.

Listing 16.5 BCIntTextFieldTest.java

```java
//  BCIntTextFieldTest.java
//
//  Test the PropertyChange and VetoableChange support
//   in the BCIntTextField class

import java.awt.*;
import java.applet.*;
import java.text.*;
import java.awt.event.*;
import java.beans.*;

public class BCIntTextFieldTest extends Applet
                                implements PropertyChangeListener,
                                           VetoableChangeListener
{
  // --Build a user interface---------------------------------
  public void init()
  {
    Panel p = new Panel( new GridLayout(4, 1, 5, 5));
    p.add(new Label("Quantity: ",          Label.RIGHT));
    p.add(new Label("Price: ",             Label.RIGHT));
    p.add(new Label("Discount% (<10): ",   Label.RIGHT));
    p.add(new Label("Total: ",             Label.RIGHT));
    add(p, "West");

    p = new Panel( new GridLayout(4, 1, 5, 5));
    p.add(qty);
    p.add(price);
    p.add(disc);
    p.add(total);
    add(p, "Center");

    qty.addPropertyChangeListener(this);
    price.addPropertyChangeListener(this);
    disc.addVetoableChangeListener(this);
    disc.addPropertyChangeListener(this);
  }

  // --Handle Bound Fields (qty, price, disc)--------------------
  public void propertyChange(PropertyChangeEvent pce)
  {
    // 1. When property is changed, first get each value
    double dQty   = qty.getValue();
    double dPrice = price.getValue();
    double dDisc  = disc.getValue() / 100.0;

    // 2. Then compute the total and discount
    double dTotal = dQty * dPrice;

    if (dDisc > 0.0)
      dTotal = dTotal - ( dTotal * dDisc );

    // 3. Then format the output
    DecimalFormat df = new DecimalFormat("###,###,##0.00");
    total.setText( df.format(dTotal));
  }

  // --Handle Constrained Field (disc)------------------------
```

```
public void vetoableChange(PropertyChangeEvent pce)
          throws PropertyVetoException
{
  // 1. If the discount is greater than 10%, then Veto change
  Integer newVal = (Integer) pce.getNewValue();
  if ( newVal.intValue() > 10 )
  {
    throw new PropertyVetoException("Invalid discount", pce);
  }
}

// --Object fields----------------------------------------
private BCIntTextField qty    = new BCIntTextField();
private BCIntTextField price  = new BCIntTextField();
private BCIntTextField disc   = new BCIntTextField();
private Label          total  = new Label("", Label.RIGHT);
}
```

The `BCIntTextFieldTest` applet contains three `BCIntTextFields` named `qty`, `price`, and `disc`, which represent, naturally enough, quantity, price, and discount. A regular `Label`, named `total`, is used for output.

The `init()` method of the applet constructs the user interface. First, a set of `Labels` is added to the applet, defining each field. Next, the four fields are added to the applet. A pair of `Panels`, each using a `GridLayout`, is used to line up all the components attractively. The last section of the `init()` method sends the `addPropertyChangeListener()` message to each of the three `BCIntTextField` objects. In addition, the `addVetoableChangeListener()` message is sent to the `disc` field. In all cases, `this` is passed as the argument. You are, in effect, telling each object to notify you when its state changes. That way you don't have to check up on them.

The last task in using bound and constrained properties is to handle the messages to which you've subscribed. You do this by writing `propertyChange()` and `vetoableChange()` methods. The `propertyChange()` method in `BCIntTextFieldTest` first retrieves the values from `qty`, `price`, and `disc`, then computes the new total amount, and finally formats and displays the amount using the `amount` field.

The `vetoableChange()` method is even less complex. It simply retrieves the value from the `disc` field. If it is greater than 10%, it throws a `PropertyVetoException`. The mechanism you've already built into the `BCIntTextField` class takes care of rolling the value back to its previous state. Listing 16.6, `BCIntTextFieldTest.html`, gives you the opportunity to try out the bound and constrained properties.

Listing 16.6 BCIntTextFieldTest.html

```
<HTML>
<HEAD>
<TITLE>The BCIntTextFieldTest Applet</TITLE>
</HEAD>
<BODY>
<H1>Bound and Constrained</H1>
The applet below uses bound and constrained fields<BR>
All three textfields send a PropertyChange event whenever
their value changes. This is used to update the total amount.<BR>
The constrained field, Discount, sends a VetoableChange event
if you attempt to enter a discount greater than 10%
```

```
<HR>
<APPLET CODE=BCIntTextFieldTest HEIGHT=300 WIDTH=300>
</APPLET>
</BODY>
</HTML>
```

Figure 16.9 shows the BCIntTextFieldTest applet running in a browser.

"Reflection is the capability of a class to discover the methods and fields of another class."

The Reflection API

In addition to support for properties and events, the new Java beans API adds support for reflection. Reflection is the capability of a class to discover the methods and fields of another class. It was added to the beans API to enable tool builders to create RAD environments that easily accommodate any bean that adheres to the property and event naming conventions.

To see the power of Java's reflection API, take a look at Listing 16.7, which shows the `Reflector` class.

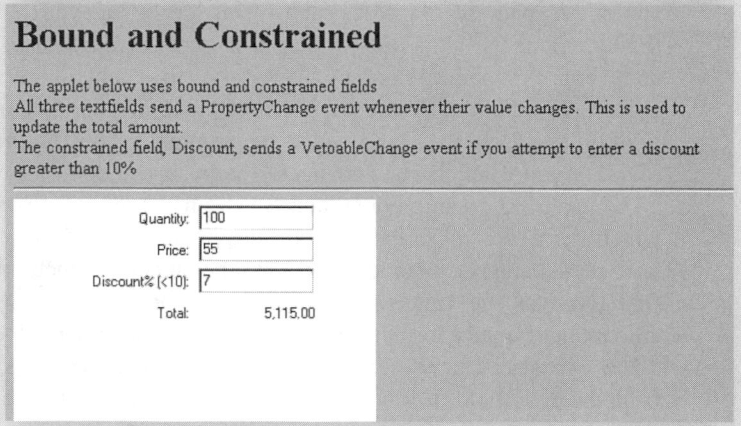
Bound and Constrained
The applet below uses bound and constrained fields
All three textfields send a PropertyChange event whenever their value changes. This is used to update the total amount.
The constrained field, Discount, sends a VetoableChange event if you attempt to enter a discount greater than 10%
Quantity: 100
Price: 55
Discount% (<10): 7
Total: 5,115.00

FIGURE 16.9
Running the BCIntTextFieldTest applet

Listing 16.7 The Reflector Class

```java
//  Reflector.java
import java.awt.*;
import java.lang.reflect.*;

public class Reflector
{
  public static String reflect( String s )
  {
    String ret = "";
    try
    {

      ret = "Analyzing class " +  s + "...\n";

      Class c = Class.forName(s);

      ret += "\nPublic Methods:\n====================\n";
      Method [] meth = c.getMethods();
      for (int i = 0; i < meth.length; i++)
      {
        ret += "   " + meth[i] + ";\n";
      }

      ret += "\nPublic Fields:\n====================\n";
      Field [] fld = c.getFields();
      for (int i = 0; i < fld.length; i++)
      {
        ret += "   " + fld[i] + ";\n";
      }

      ret +="\nPublic Constructors:\n====================\n";
      Constructor [] con = c.getConstructors();
      for (int i = 0; i < con.length; i++)
      {
        ret += "   " + con[i] + ";\n";
      }
    }
    catch (Exception e)
    {
      ret += "\n*** Can only analyze .class files ***\n";
      ret += "   " + s + " is not a .class file\n";
    }
    return ret;
  }
}
```

The Reflector class has a single static method called reflect() that takes a String argument representing the name of the class you want to decode. The reflect() method uses the static forName() method of Class to obtain an object that represents the class defined in the .class file. The Class class defines a number of useful methods, several of which reflect() proceeds to call. You can check your JDK documentation to learn about others.

The methods called by `reflect()` include `getMethods()`, `getFields()`, and `getConstructors()`. Each of these methods returns an array, so `reflect()` includes loops that iterate over the results they return. The `Method`, `Field`, and `Constructor` objects each include useful `toString()` methods that enable them to be concatenated with the `String ret`, which is returned as the output.

You can use the `reflect()` method to create applets and applications that investigate and decode the methods and fields of any class, even without the source code. Listings 16.8, `ReflectApplet.java`, and 16.9, `ReflectApplet.html`, show one demonstration of this capability. The CD-ROM contains both a console-mode, command-line application, `Reflect.java`, as well as a GUI standalone application, `ReflectApp.java`.

Listing 16.8 ReflectApplet.java

```java
//  ReflectApplet.java
import java.awt.*;
import java.applet.*;
import java.awt.event.*;
import java.lang.reflect.*;

public class ReflectApplet extends Applet
                           implements ActionListener
{
  TextField theInput  = new TextField();
  TextArea  theOutput = new TextArea( 25, 80 );

  public void init()
  {
    setLayout(new BorderLayout());
    setBackground(Color.lightGray);

    add(theOutput, "Center");
    add(theInput, "North");

    theInput.addActionListener(this);
  }

  public void actionPerformed(ActionEvent ae)
  {
    String theFile = theInput.getText();
    if ( theFile != null )
      theOutput.append(Reflector.reflect(theFile));
  }
}
```

Listing 16.9 ReflectApplet.html

```html
<HTML>
<HEAD>
<TITLE>The Reflection Applet</TITLE>
</HEAD>
<BODY>
<H2>Type a class name in the text field below. The
    Reflection API will show you the public fields
    and methods.
</H2>
</HR>
```

```
<APPLET CODE=ReflectApplet HEIGHT=450 WIDTH=550>
</APPLET>
</BODY>
</HTML>
```

Figure 16.10 shows the result of running `ReflectApplet` on the `Applet` class itself. When you enter a class filename, be sure you don't add the `.class` extension, because that is assumed by the `Reflector` class. .

You might find it fun to run the `ReflectApplet` program on unfamiliar classes. If you experiment thoroughly, you may find that certain types of methods, fields, and constructors sometimes are not reported by `Reflector`. This is a feature of Java's reflection API, not a bug. Reflection uses the Java `SecurityManager` to decide what's okay and what's not. If you download the `ReflectApplet` from a Web server, you'll find that its capabilities have been greatly restricted.

As a Java application developer, however, is there any reason for you to learn about the reflection API, other than sheer curiosity? Yes, there is. Although reflection is certainly necessary for tool builders, it also makes possible several programming techniques that should be in the toolbox of every application programmer.

One such technique made possible by reflection is the ability to create dynamic classes, classes that interpret user input, and act accordingly. Because the reflection API gives you the ability to extract a `Method` object from a class by using its name, you can then invoke the `Method` object you get back from `getMethods()`. This technique, clearly explained by Paul Tremblett in the January 1998 issue of *Dr. Dobb's Journal*, is a very easy way for you to add a macro or scripting capability to your programs.

FIGURE 16.10

Output of the
`ReflectApplet`

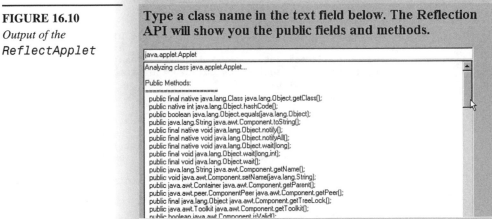

Persistence and Packaging

Two other important bean-related technologies that can be useful to application programmers are *object persistence* and *packaging*. Object persistence enables an object's state to be written to a file so that it can be stored and retrieved. Such an object is said to have been *serialized*. Packaging enables several .class files, as well as graphics and property files, to be combined into a single file and compressed for efficient transmission across a network.

SERIALIZABLE INTERFACE

Listing 16.10 contains the SerialBean class, which shows how a bean's state can be stored and retrieved. The class implements the Serializable interface of the java.io package. (*Serialization* means that an object can be converted to a stream of bytes and either sent to a file or transferred over a network connection.) This unusual interface includes no methods; a class that implements the interface is simply signaling its willingness to be serialized. The serialization itself is handled by the Java API.

```
Listing 16.10 The SerialBean Class
import java.io.*;

public class SerialBean implements Serializable
{
    public static void main(String [] args)
    {
        try
        {
            SerialBean b1 = new SerialBean();

            b1.theClassState = 2;
            b1.theObjectState = 3;
            b1.theTransientState = 4;
            System.out.println("Original object:   " + b1);

            FileOutputStream out  = new FileOutputStream("tmp");
            ObjectOutput     sout = new ObjectOutputStream(out);
            sout.writeObject(b1);
            sout.close();

            FileInputStream in   = new FileInputStream("tmp");
            ObjectInputStream sin = new ObjectInputStream(in);
            SerialBean b2 = (SerialBean) sin.readObject();
            System.out.println("Serialized object: " + b2);

            System.out.println("\nPress ENTER/RETURN to continue ...");
            System.in.read();
        }
        catch (Exception e)
        {
            System.err.println(e);
            e.printStackTrace();
        }
    }
}
```

```java
public String toString()
{
    return "ClassState="      + theClassState  + " " +
           "ObjectState="     + theObjectState + " " +
           "TransientState=" + theTransientState;
}

public static    int theClassState     = 1;
public           int theObjectState     = 1;
public transient int theTransientState = 1;
}
```

> *The* **transient** *keyword is used to mark fields that need not be saved when an object is serialized. This makes serialization more efficient by reducing processing time and storage space.*

The `SerialBean` class defines three public fields: One is `public static`, another is `public`, and the third is `public transient`. The `transient` keyword is used to mark fields that need not be saved when an object is serialized. This makes serialization more efficient by reducing processing time and storage space.

To see how serialization works, take a look at the `main()` method. First, it creates an object to be serialized, naming it `b1`. Next, it sets the fields of `b1` to values other than their initial values so that it will later be possible to see that the serialization worked properly.

To serialize the object, an `ObjectOutputStream` is wrapped around a `FileOutputStream`, and the `writeObject()` message is sent to the result, with the `b1` object as a parameter. The `ObjectOutputStream` is then closed, completing the serialization.

To retrieve the object, an `ObjectInputStream` is wrapped around a `FileInputStream`. The `readObject()` method returns the retrieved object, which is typecast to a `SerialBean`. Implicitly invoking its `toString()` method by using it in a `println()` produces the output shown in Figure 16.11. The output demonstrates that both nontransient fields were correctly restored.

JARS

Packaging the `.class` files of an applet in a Java archive (JAR) can speed their transmission over a network, owing to data compression and a single `HTTP get` request,

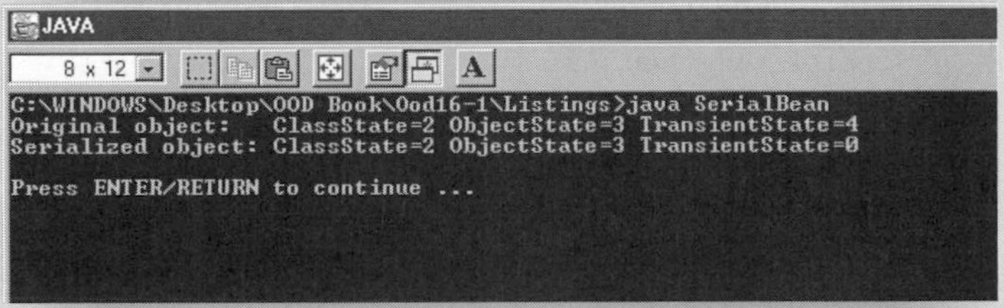

FIGURE 16.11

Running the `SerialBean` *application*

instead of one request for each file. The jar command is used to create JAR files. Its syntax is as follows:

```
jar [ options ] [manifest] destination input-file [input-files]
```

The manifest file in this command line describes the contents of the JAR that contains it. A manifest can be prepared or revised manually, but if you don't specify a manifest, the JAR will create one for you. The manifest file can be used by a RAD tool to help it load the beans contained in the jar file. You don't need the manifest file to use the jar file, however, and you omit it by using the M option. The options that can appear are patterned after those used by the UNIX tar command. They are shown in Table 16.1.

TABLE 16.1
OPTIONS OF THE jar COMMAND

Option	Meaning
c	Creates a new archive.
t	Lists the table of contents of an archive.
x file	Extracts all files (if none are named), or just the named files, from the archive.
f	Specifies the JAR filename.
0	Store only; use no ZIP compression. Make sure that you use this option if you are creating a jar file that can be put in your CLASSPATH.
M	Do not create a manifest file for the entries.
v	Generates verbose output.

A typical example of creating a JAR file is

```
jar cf jarfile *.class
```

which stores every .class file in the current directory in a JAR file named jarfile. A manifest file is automatically generated. If any file is a directory, it is processed recursively.

When an applet and its associated files (if any) are placed in a JAR file, the JAR file can be specified in the applet's HTML file like this:

```
<applet code=myapplet.class
  archive="myjar.jar"
  width=460 height=160>
</applet>
```

The applet is named myapplet, and the JAR file is named myjar.jar. Several JAR files can be specified by separating them with commas. The Web server searches all files on the list for the applet and any files it needs.

Summary

Components are objects that are designed for reuse, making it easier, faster, and cheaper to develop applications. Java beans are Sun's answer to the need for components. Because they're written in Java, beans can run on a variety of platforms. Emulators enable beans to operate within other component frameworks, such as Microsoft's ActiveX/COM.

Beans, like other components, are designed for use inside rapid application development (RAD) tools and other sorts of tools. Programmers can include a bean in a program and visually manipulate it to customize its state and behavior. Tool builders, bean builders, and bean users are concerned with different aspects of beans and the beans API.

The Java beans architecture consists of both properties and events. Properties contain the state of an object, much as object attributes do, but properties can be visually manipulated in a RAD tool. Beans communicate with other objects by sending them events and using a publish/subscribe pattern based on the observer/observable pattern.

Bean properties can be simple, Boolean, indexed, or customized. The related accessor and mutator methods should be named according to a recommendation that facilitates identifying a bean's characteristics at design time.

Bean properties can be bound, meaning that subscribers are notified of changes, or constrained, meaning that a subscriber may veto a pending change. A single property can be both bound and constrained, but it cannot be constrained without being bound.

The reflection API lets objects determine the members of other objects. The persistence API uses serialization to enable the storage and retrieval of objects. The jar utility can be used to package classes and serialized objects for efficient network transmission.

Questions

1. The idea of components is to enable the _____ of software across many applications.
   a. Reuse
   b. Networking
   c. Concurrency
   d. Productivity

2. The failure of software components to achieve the goal mentioned in question 1 is primarily due to the lack of a _____.

3. The most successful component model today is found in _____.
   a. Java
   b. Visual Basic

    c. Smalltalk

    d. Eiffel

4. A bean is a component that can be manipulated _____ in a builder tool.

5. The facility that enables a tool to discover the members of a bean is _____.

6. The facility that enables the state of a bean to be saved is _____.

7. (Bound/Constrained) properties cause subscribers to be notified when their value is changed.

8. (Bound/Constrained) properties cause subscribers to be notified when a change to their value is pending, enabling a subscriber to veto the change.

9. Properties with values that take the form of arrays are known as _____ properties.

10. The name of a method that gets the value of a simple property named `lost` should be _____.

Exercises

1. Study a Java RAD tool, such as Visual Café for Java or JBuilder, and identify the types of components and beans it supports. Learn how new components and beans are added to the tool. Write a simple bean or use one of the beans of this chapter, and add it to the tool's inventory.

2. Write a bean that serves as an interface to the encryption server of Chapter 12. Show how the bean interface makes the server easier to access and enables transparent change of the networking technology used by the server. If you have a Java RAD tool, add the bean to the tool's inventory.

3. Using the reflection API, create a GUI class browser that lets you study a class, scrolling through its members. The browser should let you easily browse classes that represent types of method return values, method and constructor parameters, and fields.

4. Use the `jar` utility to package an applet, along with some images (GIFs or JPEGs), the more and the larger the better. Create an HTML file that loads the applet from the JAR and another that loads the individual files. Compare your browser's performance in loading the HTML files from your local hard drive. If you have access to a Web server, repeat the experiment, downloading the files from the server instead of your local hard drive. Note: You'll need to disable your browser's cache to get accurate results. You can reset the cache when you're done.

To Learn More

The following books will help you learn more about designing with components and Java beans, in particular.

The indisputable father of the software component, and the originator of the phrase *Software IC*, is Dr. Brad Cox. His book, *Object-Oriented Programming: An Evolutionary Approach* (with Andrew Novobilski: Addison-Wesley, 1986, 1991) deals with the language he pioneered, Objective-C, but the Java programmer interested in components will find much to learn. His articles, "Planning the Software Industrial Revolution" (*IEEE Software* magazine) and "There Is a Silver Bullet" (*Byte* magazine), expand on his ideas that widespread use of components and OOP will introduce an entirely new programming age.

The difficulties and issues surrounding effective component design can be summed up in one question: "How do you write reusable software?" A book that addresses this particular issue is Martin Carroll and Margaret Ellis's work, *Designing and Coding Reusable C++* (Addison-Wesley, 1995). Although less philosophical than Cox's work and more focused on C++, it still raises essential issues with which the Java component developer should be concerned.

A well-written and well-illustrated book dealing with components generally is *The Essential Distributed Objects Survival Guide*, by Robert Orfali, Dan Harkey, and Jeri Edwards (New York: John Wiley & Sons, 1996).

The following books deal with Java beans, primarily from the perspective of the bean builder:

- Englander, Robert. *Developing Java Beans*. Sebastopol, California: O'Reilly, 1997.

- Feghhi, Jalal. *Web Developer's Guide to Java Beans*. Albany, New York: Coriolis Group, 1997.

- Sridharan, Prashant. *Java Beans Developer's Resource*. Upper Saddle River, New Jersey: Prentice Hall, 1997.

Designing with Class Libraries

Can you juggle? Early in their careers, most programmers learn how—not with balls, soda cans, or technical manuals, of course, but with tasks. "How's that new object for the sales system coming?" asks the boss, not more than five minutes after he asks, "Hey, did you fix that bug in the purchasing system yet?" If you're having trouble coping with all that's on your plate—and what programmer isn't—perhaps the software library known as JGL (pronounced *juggle*) can help you juggle your software overload.

JGL is the Java Generic Library, patterned after the C++ STL (Software Template Library) and written by ObjectSpace, Inc. Several vendors, including Borland and Symantec, have licensed JGL for inclusion in their Java IDEs (interactive development environments). This is good news. Even better news is that you don't have to buy a costly IDE to gain access to JGL. You can download JGL, including class files and sources, and use it for personal and commercial purposes without charge. You can find JGL at `http://www.objectspace.com`.

The Java Generic Library, like the C++ STL, is a library of collections and algorithms. *Collections* (sometimes called *containers*) are classes whose objects are designed to hold objects of other classes. Java's built-in arrays are a form of collection, as are the `Vector`, `Hashtable`, and `Dictionary` classes from the standard Java utility package, `java.util`. *Algorithm*, of course, is a general term that refers to the specific actions a method performs to accomplish its task. When used to refer to a generic class library like JGL or the STL, however, *algorithm* refers to classes that perform generic operations. Algorithms are usually designed to work on the objects contained in one of the library's collection classes. Common algorithms include classes for sorting and searching, which work just the same whether you're sorting messages in a mail system or invoices in an accounting system.

In this chapter, you will learn:

- How to use JGL containers, including `Sequence`, `Set`, `Map`, `Queue`, and `Stack`, to improve your programming productivity

- How to override `Object.clone()` to perform a deep or shallow copy

- How to override `Object.hashCode()` to properly order elements of a sorted collection

- How to use JGL algorithms, predicates, and functions to process data held in your containers

- How to use JGL iterators to traverse containers, sparing you the need to write complicated loops

- How design principles and design patterns were applied in the development of JGL

Software Reuse

Every era has its quest. In the 16th century, explorers such as Juan Ponce de León sought the legendary Fountain of Youth, hoping to become immortal by bathing in its waters. In the 17th and 18th centuries, sea captains and mainland explorers sought a way around or across the North American continent, hoping to reach the Orient and its riches.

More recently, in the 20th century, software designers and programmers have sought to reduce software development costs and increase software quality by finding the key to software reuse. Just as ancestral explorers before them, these modern explorers have experienced more failure than success. Generic libraries are designed to change that.

WHAT IS SOFTWARE REUSE?

An unknown wag once insisted that only one computer program has ever been written. According to the story, the second computer program contained snippets of code from the first program, copied by a programmer who wisely preferred to reuse rather than rewrite. Allegedly, the same is true of all subsequent programs, which have shared code much the way that asexually reproducing bacteria share DNA.

This so-called *code salvaging*, popular though it is, isn't true software reuse, although it has the same intention. Code salvagers correctly recognize that some tasks are done by more than one program. By reusing code instead of writing new code, they become more productive.

True software reuse is *planned* reuse rather than merely opportunistic reuse. By planning for software reuse, designers and programmers can increase the amount of code actually reused, thereby boosting productivity above the level achievable merely by means of code salvaging. Moreover, planned software reuse can decrease the effort involved in adapting code for reuse and increase the likelihood that reused code will function properly. Software reuse aims at

- Making it easy to find code that might be reusable

- Making it easy to understand reusable code, so that reuse is less difficult

- Testing reusable code thoroughly so that no unexpected bugs surface when the code is reused

- Decoupling reusable code from the code that contains it, so that the reusable code requires no changes when it's used in a new context

SOFTWARE REUSE MYTHS

Like any technical innovation, software reuse has had fans who've hyped its benefits beyond all reality. Among the myths they've spawned are these:

- Software reuse will solve all our software problems.

- All code should be built for possible reuse.

- Object-oriented design and programming make software reuse easy.

As Frederick Brooks points out in his article, "No Silver Bullet," user expectations tend to rise to meet our technical capabilities. Even if software reuse were to improve software development productivity and software quality tenfold, users would soon come to expect—and demand—performance at twice that level. Software reuse can improve our ability to develop software, but it won't forever solve our software problems.

Making it easy to reuse code requires effort. It's senseless to expend the effort to make a given software unit reusable unless there's a reasonable prospect the unit will be reused. Of course, many software units unexpectedly become candidates for reuse. So you shouldn't be hasty in ruling out the possibility that a given software unit may be reused.

Although object-oriented design and programming make creating reusable software easier, software reuse is seldom easy. Considerable skill and hard work—and maybe even a little good luck—are required to create reusable software.

SOFTWARE REUSE OBSTACLES

Martin Carroll and Margaret Ellis, in their book *Designing and Coding Reusable C++*, summarize a number of obstacles that constrain the practice of software reuse or reduce the benefits achieved. Among the obstacles they mention are these:

- The original programmer of a software unit must recognize that it's potentially reusable; otherwise, the programmer won't plan for the unit's reuse.

🔹 The original programmer must expect a reward for making the unit reusable because of the extra effort required. Unless there's some incentive, it's unlikely that the effort will be expended.

🔹 Someone must accept responsibility for maintaining the reusable software unit. Often, the reusable unit will contain errors that will be discovered only after its initial application. Someone must correct these errors and make corrected software available to those who've reused the unit.

🔹 The reusing programmer must be able to find, acquire, and use the software unit.

🔹 The reusing programmer must expect a reward for reusing the software unit. Some programmers are evaluated based on the number of lines of code they write in a given period. A programmer working under such a regime has an incentive to rewrite code rather than reuse it.

🔹 Possible use contexts are unknown to the original programmer and continually change. This greatly complicates writing truly reusable code. Java's cross-platform capabilities do ease this burden considerably, in comparison to platform-dependent languages such as C++.

🔹 Reusing programmers often have conflicting requirements. There is an old saying: "He who trims himself to please everyone will soon find himself whittled away." The opposite tends to be true of reusable software: trying to please everyone results in fat, complex software. No one likes to work with fat, complex software, so software that tries to please everyone may end up pleasing no one.

LIBRARY DESIGN PRINCIPLES

One important form of software reuse is creating reusable components, such as the Java beans described in the previous chapter. However, as pointed out in that chapter, beans are intended for visual manipulation. Software components intended for programmatic manipulation aren't usually implemented as beans. Instead, they're implemented as libraries. For example, Java's Abstract Window Toolkit (AWT) and the Java Database Connectivity (JDBC) application programming interface are both implemented as libraries.

Libraries are often designed so that the functions they provide can be extended. The object-oriented principle of inheritance is the most common means of extending the capabilities of library members. Anticipating the desires of users is one of the most challenging tasks faced by the designer of a class library.

Another important property of a well-designed class library is interface consistency. When the functions of a class library must be used sometimes in one way and sometimes in another, it makes it much more difficult for programmers to become proficient in using the library. For example, if a container library requires you to add() an element to one type of container but put() it to another, you may find it difficult to remember when to add() and when to put(). If the inconsistencies are too many or too annoying, you may even choose to write new code rather than use the library.

Obviously, a class library won't be used unless its performance is acceptable. But, as William Wulf observed, "More computing sins are committed in the name of efficiency (without necessarily achieving it) than for any other single reason—including blind stupidity." Balancing concern for proper performance against reusability and other concerns is another significant challenge for the class library designer.

A final crucial issue in class library design is the library's error-handling mechanisms. Only the application programmer knows the true significance of an error. Therefore, the application programmer—not the library designer—must decide the application's error strategy. Some class library implementations violate this principle, hamstringing the application programmer by constraining the error-handling options. Fortunately, Java's exception mechanism provides a way for library designers to signal that an error has occurred, without reducing the options available to the application programmer.

The Java Generic Library

The Java Generic Library (JGL) is an example of a generally well-designed class library. The remainder of this chapter examines the structure and mechanisms of JGL in some detail. By studying the design of JGL, you can learn much about how class library design should be done. Moreover, your knowledge of JGL will provide additional practical benefit because you'll know how to tap its power for reuse in your own programs.

JGL, like other class libraries, does much to overcome limitations of its host language (Java). Beyond arrays, Java provides little help in organizing collections of data. The java.util package includes the Vector, Hashtable, and Stack classes and the Enumeration interface, but that's about the size of it. Of course, in its youth, C++ was no better. In fact, it was worse, providing only arrays. But C++ has matured by adopting the Standard Template Library as part of its language standard.

Good news: You don't have to wait for Java to grow up to gain access to a variety of useful objects that let you build and manipulate collections. JGL provides the following:

- 11 powerful and flexible types of collections

- Adapter classes that let you use Java arrays and Vectors as though they were JGL collections

- More than 50 algorithms and function objects that let you transform data held in JGL collections

The ability to work with distributed collections and algorithms, when used with ObjectSpace Voyager—which is also free for the download.

Because JGL supports version 1.1 of the Java Developer's Kit, you can serialize collections and iterators transparently. This lets you work with collections at runtime and then save them to nonvolatile storage (for example, a disk file) when you're done. That way, they'll still be there when the proverbial rainy day arrives. In return for a little programming effort, JGL gives you much of the power of an object-oriented database management system at less than 0.1 percent of the cost (because, of course, JGL is *free!*).

To run the JGL examples in this chapter, you must download and install the JGL class library from `http://www.objectspace.com`, where you'll find detailed installation instructions. After you install the JGL libraries, you need to modify your `CLASSPATH` to include the JGL libraries. If you've installed JGL in a directory called JGL on your C:\ drive, for instance, you would add

```
C:\JGL\lib\jgl3.0.0.jar
```

to your current `CLASSPATH`. Of course, the actual name of the file you point to depends on the version of JGL you download. JGL 3.0 is designed for use with JDK 1.1, but you can still get version 2, which also works with earlier versions of the JDK, if, for instance, you're writing applets that need to work in a wide variety of browsers.

THE Container FAMILY

Figure 17.1 shows several collection interfaces provided by JGL, each of which extends the root interface `Container`. Each subinterface is itself extended, as you'll soon see. By the time grandchild and great-grandchild interfaces are tallied, the prolific `Container` interface sires 11 collection interfaces and 10 wrapper interfaces—one for each of the eight Java primitive types, one for `Object`, and one for `Vector`.

FIGURE 17.1
The JGL Container interface

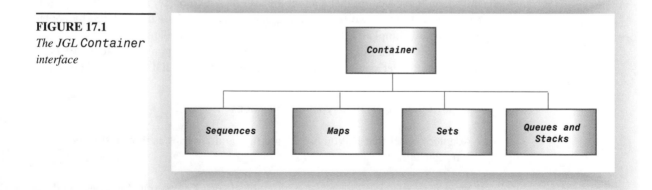

COLLECTIONS BY ANY OTHER NAME

It's unfortunate that the authors of JGL chose the name Container for the root interface of all collections because confusion with the java.awt.Container class is inevitable. If you use JGL to write a program that also uses the java.awt.Container class, even the Java compiler can become confused. The way to cope with this is to fully qualify the name Container: always write java.awt.Container or COM.objectspace.jgl.Container, whichever you mean. Fortunately, most programs seldom directly refer to either sort of Container; each Container lets its children do most of the work.

To help avoid confusion, we'll refer to collections rather than containers, except when we refer to the specific JGL interface or AWT class.

Table 17.1 shows the methods included within the Container interface. Every JGL collection class is responsible for handling these methods.

TABLE 17.1
METHODS OF THE JGL Container INTERFACE

Method	Function
add()	Adds an element to the Container
clear()	Removes every element from the Container
clone()	Returns a copy of the Container
elements()	Returns an Enumeration positioned at the start of the Container
equals()	Returns true if the contents of the Container match those of a specified Container
finish()	Returns an iterator positioned at the finish of the Container
isEmpty()	Returns true if the Container contains no elements
maxSize()	Returns the maximum number of elements in the Container
remove()	Removes the element(s) represented by Enumerations
size()	Returns the current number of elements in the Container
start()	Returns an iterator positioned at the start of the Container
toString()	Returns a string that describes the Container

Most of the methods and their functions in Table 17.1 should be familiar to you, because they resemble the sort of methods defined by the JDK's Vector class. For now, you can think of an iterator as a specialized form of Enumeration. Iterators, like Enumerations, let you traverse a collection, viewing or manipulating its elements one by one. You'll learn more about JGL's iterators later in this chapter.

REFERENCE VERSUS VALUE SEMANTICS

All JGL container classes hold objects. Although this might seem to be a restatement of an obvious fact, when applied to container classes, it brings up an important question: When you put an object into a collection, do you want to store a copy of the object or a reference to the original object itself?

A program designed to go through your employee database, updating everyone's salary according to the latest contract, would want to make sure that it was dealing with the actual employee object themselves. It would want to hold references to objects; this is called *reference semantics*. On the other hand, if you were writing a "what-if" program that tried to ascertain the financial effect on your company of slashing every employee's salary by 50 percent, you'd be better advised to have your program make a copy of each employee object rather than work with references; this is called *value semantics*.

Unfortunately, this simple distinction is further complicated by the *copy semantics* of the objects you're storing. If you use a collection that dutifully makes a copy of each object as you add it, you have to find out what the object itself means when you ask it to make a copy. Although you might think that every copy is the same, that's not entirely correct; an object may be copied by using a deep copy or a shallow copy. A *shallow copy* simply means that a class adopts reference semantics as its copy semantic. When the class makes a copy of an object, it copies only the reference to the actual object rather than make a duplicate of the actual object itself. A class that makes *deep copies* works just the opposite; when you make a copy of such an object, the object returns a duplicate of itself, not simply a reference.

When designing classes destined to be used inside a collection, you control the type of copy semantics that the class uses by overriding its `clone()` method.

CLONES: DEEP COPY AND SHALLOW COPY

You might be unfamiliar with the `clone()` method, which certainly presents some important subtleties worthy of digression. You may recall that the `Object` class supports a `clone()` method, but you may not know exactly what the method is for or how it works. You may have tried invoking it, in which case your program probably terminated with a `CloneNotSupportedException`. Before calling for increases in the AFDC (Aid to Families with Dependent Clones) program, it would be good to learn a little more about the problem.

Like the `Serializable` interface that tells a client whether the objects of a class are willing to be serialized, the `Cloneable` class tells a client whether the objects of a class are willing to be cloned—that is, copied. If you want a class to be cloneable, your class should implement the `Cloneable` interface and override the `Object.clone()` method. The former is easy because, like `Serializable`, the `Cloneable` class requires no methods or fields. The latter, however, presents some complications.

You might have suspected that copying things isn't entirely straightforward. After all, if it were, the `Object` class would implement a `clone()` method that did something more useful than throwing a `CloneNotSupportedException`, right? The complication is one of choosing between the two ways of copying an object: shallow copying and deep copying. Java's designers couldn't know in advance which way would be appropriate for your objects, so they took the easy way out: they left not only the decision, but also the implementation, up to you.

To see how to copy an object, look at Listing 17.1, which shows the CopyTest class.

Listing 17.1 The CopyTest Class

```java
import java.applet.*;
import java.awt.*;
import java.awt.event.*;

public class CopyTest extends Applet implements ActionListener
{
  LittlePig theLittlePig, theShallowClone;
  BigPig   theBigPig,   theDeepClone;

  Button  theSpeakButton  = new Button("Speak");
  Button  theModifyButton = new Button("Morph to Dog");

  Panel[]   thePigPanel = new Panel[4];

  public void init()
  {
    theLittlePig = new LittlePig();
    theShallowClone = (LittlePig) theLittlePig.clone();

    theBigPig = new BigPig();
    theDeepClone = (BigPig) theBigPig.clone();

    for (int i = 0; i < thePigPanel.length; i++)
    {
      thePigPanel[i] = new Panel();
      thePigPanel[i].setLayout(new BorderLayout());
    }

    setLayout(new GridLayout(2, 3));
    add(thePigPanel[0]);
    add(thePigPanel[1]);
    add(theModifyButton);
    add(thePigPanel[2]);
    add(thePigPanel[3]);
    add(theSpeakButton);

    thePigPanel[0].add(new Label("Little Pig:"), "North");
    thePigPanel[0].add(theLittlePig, "Center");

    thePigPanel[1].add(new Label("Big Pig:"), "North");
    thePigPanel[1].add(theBigPig, "Center");

    thePigPanel[2].add(new Label("Shallow Clone:"), "North");
    thePigPanel[2].add(theShallowClone, "Center");

    thePigPanel[3].add(new Label("Deep Clone:"), "North");
    thePigPanel[3].add(theDeepClone, "Center");

    theModifyButton.addActionListener(this);
    theSpeakButton.addActionListener(this);
```

```
      theSpeakButton.setEnabled(false);
    }

    public void actionPerformed(ActionEvent event)
    {
      Object source = event.getSource();
      if (source == theSpeakButton)
      {
        theLittlePig.speak();
        theShallowClone.speak();
        theBigPig.speak();
        theDeepClone.speak();
        theSpeakButton.setEnabled(false);
      }
      else if (source == theModifyButton)
      {
        theLittlePig.setTalk("Arf!");
        theBigPig.setTalk("Arf!");
        theModifyButton.setEnabled(false);
        theSpeakButton.setEnabled(true);
      }
    }
  }
```

CopyTest creates two different kinds of objects: a LittlePig and a BigPig. A LittlePig, as you'll see in a moment, responds to a clone() message by returning a shallow copy of itself. A BigPig responds to the same message by returning a deep copy of itself.

Figure 17.2 shows the output of the applet, which highlights the difference between a shallow copy and a deep copy. Looking back to the init() method of CopyTest, you can see that for each type of Pig, it performs the following steps:

1. Creates an object.

2. Clones the object.

3. Adds the object to the applet window.

When the user clicks the Speak button, a speak() message is sent to each original object or clone. When the user clicks the Morph to Dog button, a setTalk() message is sent to each original object; no message is sent to either clone. The setTalk() message causes an object to say "Arf" in response to a speak() message. Though neither clone object receives the setTalk() message, the shallow clone object says "Arf" along with its original, the LittlePig object. The LittlePig object and its shallow clone share data, so changes to one can affect the other. Figure 17.2 shows this result.

The deep clone of the BigPig object continues to say "O-o-o-o-oink!" as a pig should. To see why this happens, look at Listing 17.2, the LittlePig class.

Listing 17.2 The LittlePig Class

```
class LittlePig extends Canvas
{
  public Object clone()
  {
    return new LittlePig(thePigTalk);
  }
```

```
    public void setTalk(String text)
    {
      thePigTalk.setTalk(text);
      repaint();
    }

    public void speak()
    {
      repaint();
    }

    public void paint(Graphics g)
    {
      g.drawString(thePigTalk.getTalk(), 10, 10);
    }

    public LittlePig()
    {
      thePigTalk = new PigTalk("Oink!");
    }

    public LittlePig(PigTalk talk)
    {
      thePigTalk = talk;
    }

    private PigTalk thePigTalk;
}
```

A `LittlePig` object contains a `private` field named `thePigTalk`, a `PigTalk` object. When a `LittlePig` is constructed by using the default constructor, the `PigTalk` is initialized by using the `String` "Oink!" If the client provides a reference to a `PigTalk`, a second constructor builds the `LittlePig` and stuffs the reference into the `LittlePig`'s field.

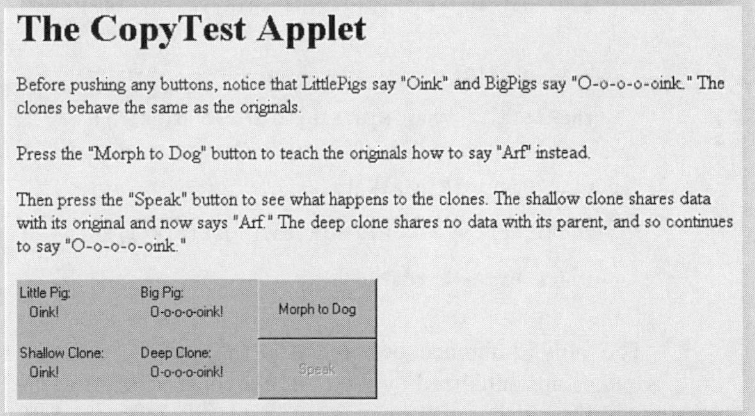

FIGURE 17.2

Output of the CopyTest applet

The CopyTest Applet

Before pushing any buttons, notice that LittlePigs say "Oink" and BigPigs say "O-o-o-o-oink." The clones behave the same as the originals.

Press the "Morph to Dog" button to teach the originals how to say "Arf" instead.

Then press the "Speak" button to see what happens to the clones. The shallow clone shares data with its original and now says "Arf." The deep clone shares no data with its parent, and so continues to say "O-o-o-o-oink."

Little Pig: Oink!	Big Pig: O-o-o-o-oink!	Morph to Dog
Shallow Clone: Oink!	Deep Clone: O-o-o-o-oink!	Speak

The clone() method is short and sweet: it uses the one-argument constructor to return a new LittlePig that has the same PigTalk reference in its field thePigTalk as the original.

Did you catch that? Not a reference to a PigTalk with the same value, but a reference to the *same* PigTalk. That's the essence of a shallow copy, and that's what causes the pig clone to begin sounding like a dog.

The setTalk() method alters the value of a LittlePig's PigTalk object. When a shallow copy is used to clone a LittlePig, the original and the clone share a reference to a single PigTalk object. When the original LittlePig receives a message that causes it to change the value of the PigTalk object, the original and the clone are affected because they "share" references to a single PigTalk. Figure 17.3 illustrates this situation.

To see how BigPig performs its deep copy, look at Listing 17.3.

Listing 17.3 The BigPig Class

```
class BigPig extends Canvas
{
  public Object clone()
  {
    return new BigPig(thePigTalk);
  }

  public void setTalk(String text)
  {
    thePigTalk.setTalk(text);
    repaint();
  }

  public void speak()
  {
    repaint();
  }

  public void paint(Graphics g)
  {
    g.drawString(thePigTalk.getTalk(), 10, 10);
  }

  public BigPig()
  {
    thePigTalk = new PigTalk("O-o-o-o-oink!");
  }

  public BigPig(PigTalk talk)
  {
    thePigTalk = new PigTalk(talk.getTalk());
  }
  private PigTalk thePigTalk;
}
```

The only difference between BigPigs and LittlePigs (other than the fact that BigPigs are initialized by their default constructor to say "O-o-o-o-oink!" rather than "Oink!") is their implementation of the clone() method. If you examine the methods, you'll find them identical. But each calls the one-argument constructor of its class, and

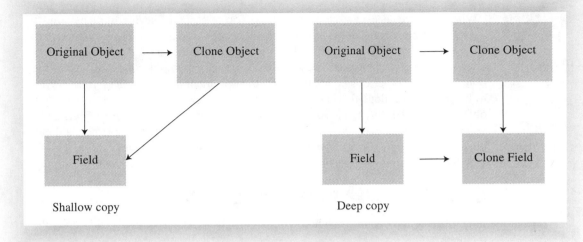

FIGURE 17.3

Shallow versus deep copy

these constructors are slightly different. Look at the one-argument constructor of `BigPig`, which, as you recall, performs a deep copy. Rather than return a clone sharing a reference to the same `PigTalk` as the original, `BigPig`'s one-argument constructor creates a new `PigTalk`. The original and the clone have their own `PigTalk`, so changes to the one don't affect the other. Figure 17.3 shows how the deep copy works.

To see the rest of the applet, look at Listing 17.4, the `PigTalk` class. You shouldn't find anything surprising there. The class simply encapsulates a string of text, providing accessor and mutator methods for use by clients `LittlePigs` and `BigPigs`.

```
Listing 17.4 The PigTalk Class
class PigTalk
{
  public String getTalk()
  {
    return theText;
  }

  public void setTalk(String text)
  {
    theText = text;
  }

  public PigTalk(String text)
  {
    setTalk(text);
  }

  private String theText;
}
```

When you create a new cloneable class, you're responsible for implementing the clone() method. You can implement a shallow copy, which is quick and efficient, or a deep copy, which avoids commingling of data. To implement a deep copy, you must create new instances of each field that has an object type. Of course, if any of these objects contain other objects, you'll need to copy them as well, unless you're willing to have them co-mingled. This process should continue to the children of the original object, its grandchildren, and so on (that is, recursively). You can stop, of course, when you reach the root class Object or when you reach an object that has no fields with object types. Don't forget, however, to handle the "siblings" of such an object—they may have any number of generations of descendants that must be cloned.

COLLECTION OPERATIONS AND ERRORS

In addition to the clone() method, you may want your objects to override these three methods:

- equals()
- hashCode()
- toString()

If you don't understand what the equals() method is used for and why you may need to override it, or what the toString() method is about, review Chapter 3, "Teach Yourself Java in 21 Minutes." The hashCode() method is less often used; you'll see why it can be important in the section on Maps.

Keep in mind that JGL's collection classes store Objects. You can subclass a collection so that it accepts only objects of a specific type—Integers, for example. But there's no way that the Java compiler can flag source code statements that attempt to load a Float into your Integer-only collection. Your subclass can check the type of each element as it's inserted, but this will occur at runtime, not at compile time. This is one weakness of Java in comparison to C++, which comes equipped with templates that can provide compile-time checking of element types.

If you add a type-specific collection, your collection should throw an Exception of the proper type when its type is violated. Table 17.2 shows the Exceptions thrown by JGL. The IllegalArgumentException is the Exception your class should throw. Every Exception thrown by JGL is a subclass of RuntimeException, a Java class that, along with Error, represents *unchecked* exceptions. All that really means is that you aren't *required* to add a try-catch or throws to methods that may throw one. (If you're interested in the design rationale behind checked and unchecked exceptions, be sure to read Appendix B in James Gosling's book, *The Java Programming Language,* where he strongly argues against allowing unchecked exceptions in your code.)

TABLE 17.2
JGL Exceptions

Exception	Meaning
InvalidOperationException	An invalid operation was attempted.
IllegalArgumentException	An illegal argument was supplied to a method.
IndexOutOfBoundsException	An illegal index was supplied to an operation.
NullPointerException	An attempt was made to add a null key or value.

Sequences: BETTER Vectors

In the same way that Java's Vectors improve on arrays, JGL's Sequences improve on Java's Vectors. Like a Vector, a Sequence is a collection whose elements are accessed by using an index and which automatically expands to make room for new elements. JGL includes five different kinds of Sequences:

- Arrays, the plain vanilla variety of Sequence

- Deques, a variety of Sequence optimized for fast insertion at the beginning or end

- SLists, a variety of Sequence optimized for even faster insertion at the beginning or end than a Deque, but which provides slower traversal

- DLists, a variety of Sequences optimized for fast insertion at any point, but which provides slow traversal

- Array Adapters, a variety of Sequence that makes it possible to use JGL's Container methods on arrays of Java primitives or objects and on Java Vectors

Figure 17.4 shows JGL's Sequence classes and their relationships. All of them support the methods shown in Table 17.3.

Creating a Sequence is simple. For example, to create an Array, you can write:

```
Array theArray = new Array();
```

JGL's array adapters make it easy for you to work with arrays of Java primitives or objects, or Java Vectors. When you read *adapter*, you may think of the Adapter design pattern mentioned in Chapter 11, "Patterns: Proven Designs." However, JGL's array adapters really work like the wrappers of the Decorator design pattern. You use a wrapper to add Sequence behavior to a Java array or Vector. For example, to work with an array of ints by using the Sequence methods, you can write:

```
int [] theInts = { -1, 0, 1, 2, 3, 4 };
IntArray theIntArray = new IntArray(theInts);
```

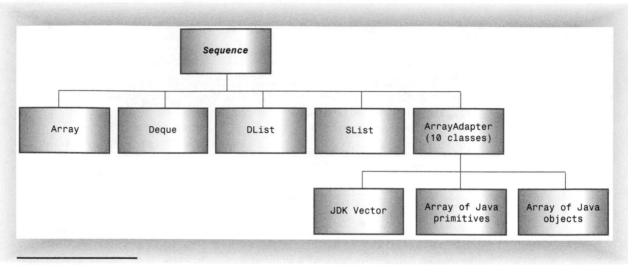

FIGURE 17.4
*JGL's Sequence
classes*

TABLE 17.3
THE JGL SEQUENCE INTERFACE

Method	Function
at()	Returns the item at a specified index
back()	Returns the last item
contains()	Returns true if a particular element is present
count()	Counts the number of matching elements
front()	Returns the first item
indexOf()	Returns the index of a particular element
remove()	Removes a particular value
replace()	Replaces one value with another
popBack()	Removes and returns the item at the end
popFront()	Removes and returns the item at the beginning
pushBack()	Inserts an item at the end
pushFront()	Inserts an item at the beginning
put()	Replaces the item at a specified index

Table 17.4 gives the name of the JGL array adapter for each type of Java array. In addition to the wrappers shown in Table 17.4, you can use the VectorArray class to add Sequence behavior to a Java Vector.

TABLE 17.4
ARRAY ADAPTER CLASSES

Java Type	Adapter Class	Element Type
boolean[]	BooleanArray	Boolean
byte[]	ByteArray	Integer
char[]	CharArray	Character
double[]	DoubleArray	Double
float[]	FloatArray	Float
int[]	IntArray	Integer
long[]	LongArray	Long
Object[]	ObjectArray	Not applicable
short[]	ShortArray	Integer

> " *Just as JGL's Sequences improve on Java's Vectors, JGL's* Maps *improve on Java's* Hashtables. *Maps allow you to store key-value pairs and rapidly retrieve the value associated with a key.* "

Maps: BETTER HASHTABLES

Just as JGL's Sequences improve on Java's Vectors, JGL's Maps improve on Java's Hashtables. Maps allow you to store key-value pairs and rapidly retrieve the value associated with a key. JGL's Maps include the following:

- HashMap, which performs better than Java's Hashtables

- OrderedMap, a variety of Map that allows you to retrieve its elements in sequence

- HashMultiMap, a variety of HashMap that allows you to put() multiple key-value pairs having the same key value

- OrderedMultiMap, a variety of OrderedMap that allows you to put() multiple key-value pairs having the same key value

Figure 17.5 shows JGL's Map classes and their relationships. Maps support the methods shown in Table 17.5.

You never directly instantiate a HashMultiMap or OrderedMultiMap. If you provide the argument true to a HashMap or OrderedMap constructor, JGL will construct a HashMultiMap or OrderedMultiMap, as appropriate:

```
HashMap DupsNo = new HashMap();
HashMap DupsOK = new HashMap(true);
```

As you may recall, this is an application of the Factory Method design pattern. Notice that the get() method always returns the first key-value pair, if any, having the specified key value. You can put() multiple key-value pairs with the same key value to a HashMultiMap or a OrderedMultiMap, but only the most recently put() value is accessible. Notice that the remove() method removes *all* key-value pairs with a given key value.

FIGURE 17.5
The JGL Map methods

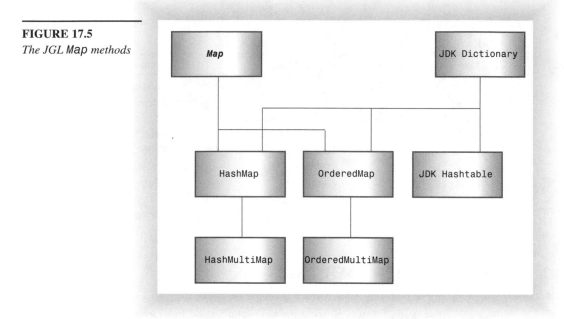

TABLE 17.5
THE JGL Map METHODS

Method	Function
add()	If the key doesn't exist or duplicates are allowed, associate the value with the key and return null; otherwise, don't modify the map and return the current value associated with the key.
elements/keys()	Returns a JDK Enumeration over the container's values/keys.
get()	Returns the first value associated with a particular key.
put()	If the key doesn't exist, associate the value with the key and return null; otherwise, replace the first value associated with the key and return the old value.
remove()	Removes all the key-value pairs with a particular key.

A peculiarity of the OrderedMap is that it uses the hashCode() method, not the key value, to order stored elements. If you think about it, this makes sense. OrderedMap needs some way of knowing whether one element is greater than, less than, or equal to another. For some types of elements—Strings and Integers, for example—the desired behavior is intuitively obvious. But how should OrderedMap compare two instances of your Wonk class?

The answer is that you must override the default implementation of the Object.hashCode() method so that the values returned produce the ordering you desire. Neglecting this step is one of the most common errors in using Maps. The HashTest class, shown in Listing 17.5, demonstrates what happens when you fail to override the method. It also demonstrates some interesting behavior of the default implementation of Object.equals().

Listing 17.5 The HashTest Class

```java
import java.applet.*;
import java.awt.*;
import COM.objectspace.jgl.*;
import java.util.Enumeration;

public class HashTest extends Applet
{
  TextArea [] theText = new TextArea[3];
  TextArea    theCurrentText;
  String []   theType = { "Hash", "Smart Hash", "Genius Hash" };

  public void init()
  {
    setLayout(new GridLayout(1, 3));
    setFont(new Font("Monospaced", Font.PLAIN, 10));

    int n = 0;
    for (int i = HashFactory.HASH; i <= HashFactory.GENIUS_HASH; i++)
    {
      theText[n] = new TextArea();
      add(theText[n]);
      theCurrentText = theText[n];
      writeText(theType[n]);
      writeText("");
      n++;

      Hash   h1 = HashFactory.createHash(i, 2);
      Hash   h2 = HashFactory.createHash(i, 1);
      Hash   h3 = HashFactory.createHash(i, 1);

      writeText("Element values and hashcodes");
      writeText("");
      writeText("h1: " + h1);
      writeText("h2: " + h2);
      writeText("h3: " + h3);
      writeText("");
      writeText("");

      writeText("Equality and identity:");
      writeText("");
      if (h3.equals(h2))
        writeText("h3.equals(h2)");
      else
        writeText("!h3.equals(h2)");
      if (h3.hashCode() == h2.hashCode())
      {
        writeText("h3.hashCode() == ");
        writeText("  h2.hashCode()");
      }
      else
      {
```

```
            writeText("h3.hashCode() != ");
            writeText("  h2.hashCode()");
         }
         writeText("");
         writeText("");

         COM.objectspace.jgl.OrderedMap map =
           new COM.objectspace.jgl.OrderedMap();

         map.put(h1, "1");
         map.put(h2, "2");
         map.put(h3, "3");

         writeText("Number of entries: " + map.size());
         writeText("");
         Enumeration e = map.keys();
         while (e.hasMoreElements())
         {
           writeText(e.nextElement().toString());
         }
         writeText("");
         writeText("");
      }
   }

   public void writeText(String text)
   {
     theCurrentText.append(text);
     theCurrentText.append("\n");
   }
}
```

> *" The default implementation of* `equals()` *works like the* `==` *operator: It returns* `true` *if two references refer to the same object (as determined by their hash codes) and* `false` *otherwise. "*

HashTest uses a factory method, `HashFactory.createHash()`, to create three Hash objects and puts them to an `OrderedMap`. It uses a loop to perform this experiment three times, once for each of three varieties of Hash object. You can see its output in Figure 17.6.

The three varieties of Hash are Hash, SmartHash, and GeniusHash. As you can see, applying the `equals()` method to two Hashes with the same contents doesn't necessarily return `true`. Also, neither Hash nor SmartHash is properly ordered by the OrderedMap; only the GeniusHash is properly treated.

To see what went wrong and what went right, begin by looking at Listing 17.6, the Hash class. Hash is the base class for SmartHash and GeniusHash. It provides a constructor and a `toString()` accessor; its state is represented by an Integer. From the Object class, it inherits default implementations of `equals()` and `hashCode()`. The default implementation of `hashCode()` uses an object's reference as its result. The default implementation of `equals()` works like the `==` operator: It returns `true` if two references refer to the same object (as determined by their hash codes) and `false` otherwise. That's why the Hash object misbehaves inside HashTest. Even if two Hashes have the same value, they're considered to be unequal.

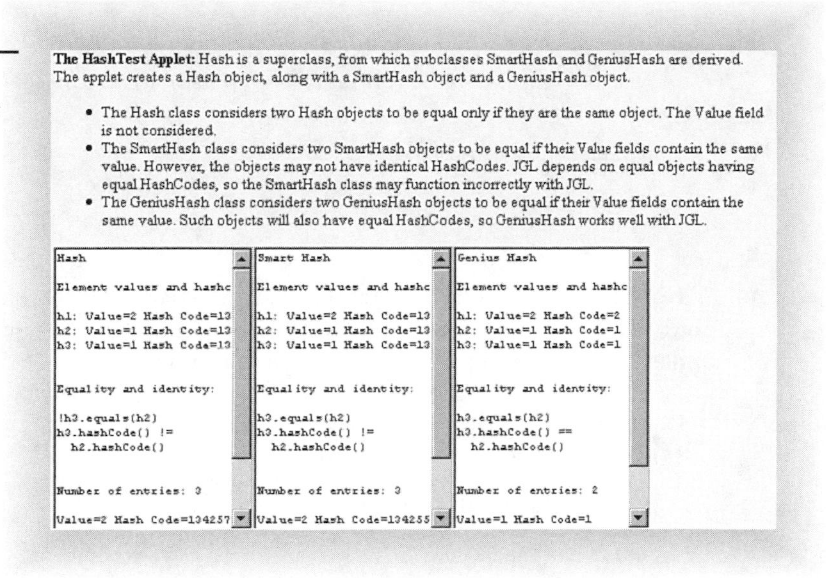

FIGURE 17.6

Output of the HashTest applet

The HashTest Applet: Hash is a superclass, from which subclasses SmartHash and GeniusHash are derived. The applet creates a Hash object, along with a SmartHash object and a GeniusHash object.

- The Hash class considers two Hash objects to be equal only if they are the same object. The Value field is not considered.
- The SmartHash class considers two SmartHash objects to be equal if their Value fields contain the same value. However, the objects may not have identical HashCodes. JGL depends on equal objects having equal HashCodes, so the SmartHash class may function incorrectly with JGL.
- The GeniusHash class considers two GeniusHash objects to be equal if their Value fields contain the same value. Such objects will also have equal HashCodes, so GeniusHash works well with JGL.

Listing 17.6 The Hash Class

```
class Hash
{
  // inherits equals() from Object

  // inherits hashCode() from Object

  public String toString()
  {
    return "Value=" + theInteger + " Hash Code=" + hashCode();
  }

  public Hash(int n)
  {
    theInteger = new Integer(n);
  }

  public Integer theInteger;
}
```

To improve on the behavior of the Hash class, the SmartHash class (shown in Listing 17.7) provides an improved implementation of the equals() method. The improved method looks at the state of the Hash classes and returns true if both have the same state. They don't need to be the same object, as long as they have the same value.

Listing 17.7 The SmartHash Class

```
class SmartHash extends Hash
{
  // inherits hashCode() from Object

  public boolean equals(Object h)
  {
```

```
      if (! (h instanceof Hash)) return false;
      return theInteger.intValue() == ((Hash) h).theInteger.intValue();
    }

  public SmartHash(int n)
  {
    super(n);
  }
}
```

Notice in Figure 17.6 that the two SmartHashes, like the Hashes, are improperly ordered by the OrderedMap. To fix this flaw, the GeniusHash class implements an improved hashCode() method, as shown in Listing 17.8.

Listing 17.8 The GeniusHash Class

```
class GeniusHash extends SmartHash
{
  // inherits equals() from SmartHash

  public int hashCode()
  {
    return theInteger.hashCode();
  }

  public GeniusHash(int n)
  {
    super(n);
  }
}
```

To make things simple for itself, GeniusHash.hashCode() simply sends the hashCode() message to its Integer field and returns the result to the caller. The implementation of hashCode() provided by the Integer class returns the value of the encapsulated int as its result. Therefore, two GeniusHashes that hold the same value not only test as equal (using the equals() method), they also have hash codes that reflect their proper relative places in a numerical ordering. Look back at Figure 17.6 to verify that GeniusHash works as advertised.

To complete the picture, Listing 17.9 shows the HashFactory class. Recall that its createHash() method was used by HashTest to create a Hash, SmartHash, or GeniusHash, depending on the value of the argument supplied.

Listing 17.9 The HashFactory Class

```
class HashFactory
{
  public static Hash createHash(int type, int value)
  {
    Hash result = null;
    switch (type)
    {
      case HASH:
        result = new Hash(value);
        break;
      case SMART_HASH:
        result = new SmartHash(value);
```

```
        break;
      case GENIUS_HASH:
        result = new GeniusHash(value);
        break;
    }
    return result;
  }

  public static final int HASH = 1;
  public static final int SMART_HASH  = 2;
  public static final int GENIUS_HASH = 3;
}
```

Sets: WHAT THE JDK NEVER GAVE YOU

Have you ever wanted to find out what elements are in one collection but not in another? Or have you ever wanted to combine the elements of two containers, discarding any duplicates? Nothing in the JDK helps you perform such common operations, but the JGL Set interface, and its implementing classes HashSet and OrderedSet, are exactly what you need.

Figure 17.7 shows the Set classes and the relationships between them. Table 17.6 shows the methods of the Set interface.

You may wonder why you don't see methods implementing set intersection, set union, and so forth in the table. That's because they're implemented within a special algorithm class named SetOperations. Algorithms are the subject of an upcoming section.

FIGURE 17.7
The JGL Set classes

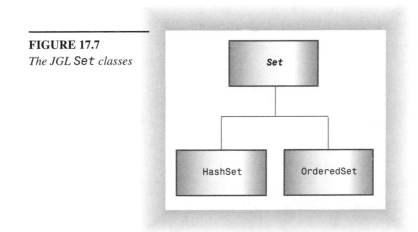

TABLE 17.6
THE JGL SET INTERFACE

Method	Function
`put()`	Replaces the first matching object or adds it if none exists
`get()`	Returns the first matching object
`count()`	Returns the number of key/value pairs that match a particular key
`remove()`	Removes all matching objects

Queues AND Stacks: SPECIALIZED COLLECTIONS

The `Stack`, `Queue`, and `PriorityQueue` classes add `push()` and `pop()` methods to the methods of the `Container` interface. `Stack` resembles Java's `java.util.Stack` but has superior performance. It's a last-in, first-out (LIFO) collection. The similar `Queue` is a first-in, first-out (FIFO) collection and works the way lines at the grocery market work: the customer first in line is the one served first. The `PriorityQueue` extends the `Queue` by allowing each element to be tagged with a priority. Elements with a high priority are popped off the queue ahead of other elements, regardless of the order in which they arrived. Figure 17.8 shows these special classes.

  Listing 17.10 shows the `PriorityTest` class, a simple demonstration of the `PriorityQueue`. `PriorityTest` does the following:

1. Creates an `int` array.

2. Creates a `PriorityQueue`.

3. Pushes the elements of the `int` array onto the `PriorityQueue`, one by one.
   The hash value of each element becomes its priority.

4. Pops the elements off the `PriorityQueue` and prints them.

FIGURE 17.8
The JGL `Stack`,
`Queue`, *and*
`PriorityQueue`
classes

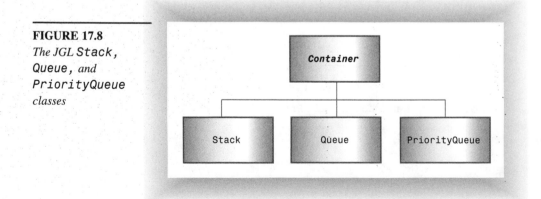

Listing 17.10 The `PriorityTest` Class

```
import java.applet.*;
import java.awt.*;
import COM.objectspace.jgl.*;

public class PriorityTest extends Applet
{
  TextArea theInputText  = new TextArea();
  TextArea theOutputText = new TextArea();

  public void init()
  {
    setLayout(new GridLayout(1, 2));
    add(theInputText);
    add(theOutputText);

    int [] inputs = { 1, 2, 3, 3, 1, 2 };

    writeText(theInputText, "Input values:");
    writeText(theInputText, "");
    for (int i = 0; i < inputs.length; i++)
    {
      writeText(theInputText, "" + inputs[i]);
    }

    PriorityQueue q = new PriorityQueue();

    for (int i = 0; i < inputs.length; i++)
    {
      q.push(new Integer(inputs[i]));
    }

    writeText(theOutputText, "Output values:");
    writeText(theOutputText, "");

    while (! q.isEmpty())
    {
      writeText(theOutputText, q.pop().toString());
    }
  }

  public void writeText(TextArea area, String text)
  {
    area.append(text);
    area.append(System.getProperty("line.separator"));
  }
}
```

Figure 17.9 shows the output of the applet. Notice that the elements are printed in numerical order, according to their priority.

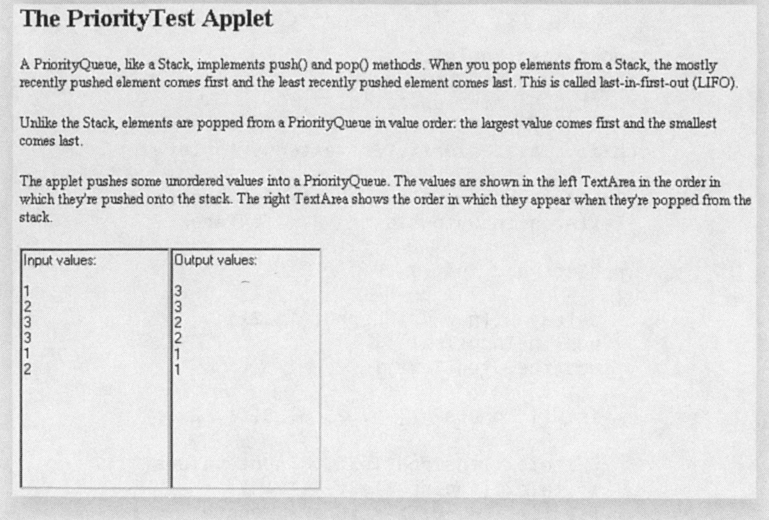

FIGURE 17.9

Output of the
PriorityTest applet

The PriorityTest Applet

A PriorityQueue, like a Stack, implements push() and pop() methods. When you pop elements from a Stack, the mostly recently pushed element comes first and the least recently pushed element comes last. This is called last-in-first-out (LIFO).

Unlike the Stack, elements are popped from a PriorityQueue in value order: the largest value comes first and the smallest comes last.

The applet pushes some unordered values into a PriorityQueue. The values are shown in the left TextArea in the order in which they're pushed onto the stack. The right TextArea shows the order in which they appear when they're popped from the stack.

Input values:	Output values:
1	3
2	3
3	2
3	2
1	1
2	1

FIGURE 17.9

Output of the
PriorityTest applet

Algorithms: Who Has the Loops?

> **" JGL includes a rich repertoire of more than 40 algorithms, implemented as a set of classes. "**

JGL includes a rich repertoire of more than 40 algorithms, implemented as a set of classes. You might wonder why the algorithms are separately implemented from the data on which they operate, recalling the warnings against "spectral classes" earlier in the book. You might feel that JGL's design isn't entirely in keeping with the object-oriented notion of encapsulation. In JGL, the Sort class knows how to sort an Array, but an Array doesn't know how to sort itself. Doesn't this seem kind of backward?

Well, you're not alone in noticing this. Noted computer scientist Tim Budd remarked on this aspect of the C++ Standard Template Library when he wrote that it seems almost "anti-object oriented." Budd doesn't necessarily see that as a bad thing, however. And if you think about the alternative—requiring every container class to re-implement generic operations, like sorting and searching—you'll realize that the approach taken by the JGL (and STL) designers makes a whole lot of sense. Rather than think about generic algorithms and generic containers as a compromise to object-oriented principles, recognize them as a very specific and particular exception.

Table 17.7 shows various JGL algorithm classes and the methods they implement. Most of the methods are static and can be called without creating an object.

The JGL's algorithm classes are useful and powerful. They let you accomplish—with a single message—operations that would otherwise require loops or even nested loops. Using these algorithms can make your loopy programs much more straightforward. As a demonstration, consider Listing 17.11, which shows the ApplyTest class.

TABLE 17.7
THE JGL ALGORITHMS

Class	Algorithms
Applying	forEach(), inject()
Comparing	equal(), lexicographicalCompare(), median(), mismatch()
Copying	copy(), copyBackward()
Counting	accumulate(), adjacentDifference(), count(), countIf()
Filling	fill(), fillN()
Filtering	reject(), select(), unique(), uniqueCopy()
Finding	adjacentFind(), detect(), every(), find(), findIf(), some()
Heap	makeHeap(), popHeap(), pushHeap(), sortHeap()
MinMax	minElement(), maxElement()
Permuting	nextPermutation(), prevPermutation()
Printing	print(), println(), toString()
Removing	remove(), removeCopy(), removeCopyIf(), removeIf()
Replacing	replace(), replaceCopy(), replaceIf()
Reversing	reverse(), reverseCopy()
Rotating	rotate(), rotateCopy()
SetOperations	includes(), setDifference(), setIntersection(), setSymmetricDifference(), setUnion()
Shuffling	randomShuffle()
Sorting	sort()
Swapping	iterSwap(), swapRanges()
Transforming	collect(), transform()

Listing 17.11 The ApplyTest Class

```java
import java.applet.*;
import java.awt.*;
import COM.objectspace.jgl.*;

public class ApplyTest extends Applet
{
  TextArea theInputText  = new TextArea();
  TextArea theOutputText = new TextArea();

  public void init()
  {
    setLayout(new GridLayout(2, 1));
    add(theInputText);
    add(theOutputText);

    Array a = new Array();
    a.add(new Employee("Adam",    20000.0f));
    a.add(new Employee("Betty",   30000.0f));
    a.add(new Employee("Charles", 25000.0f));
```

```
        writeText(theInputText, "Input values:");
        writeText(theInputText, a.toString());

        Applying.forEach(a, new SalaryRaise(0.05f));
        writeText(theOutputText, "Output values:");
        writeText(theOutputText, a.toString());
    }

    public void writeText(TextArea area, String text)
    {
      area.append(text);
      area.append("\n");
    }
}
```

This applet creates an `Array` that holds `Employee` objects. Each `Employee` object includes a name and a salary. By sending the `forEach()` message to the `Applying` class and passing the `Array` and a function object (you'll learn about those in just a moment), the salary of each employee is updated without so much as a `while`, `do-while`, or `for`. Figure 17.10 shows the output of the applet.

Listing 17.12 shows the `Employee` class, which encapsulates a name and salary along with some accessor and mutator methods. The key method is the `stepSalary()` mutator, which is used to give an employee a raise (or possibly a cut) in pay.

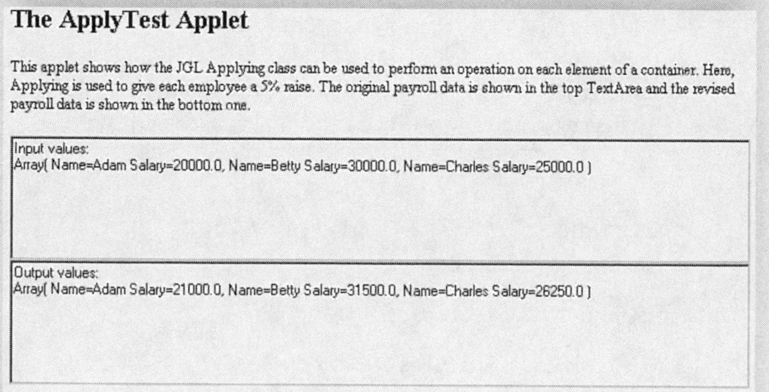

FIGURE 17.10

Output of the ApplyTest applet

The ApplyTest Applet

This applet shows how the JGL Applying class can be used to perform an operation on each element of a container. Here, Applying is used to give each employee a 5% raise. The original payroll data is shown in the top TextArea and the revised payroll data is shown in the bottom one.

```
Input values:
Array( Name=Adam Salary=20000.0, Name=Betty Salary=30000.0, Name=Charles Salary=25000.0 )
```

```
Output values:
Array( Name=Adam Salary=21000.0, Name=Betty Salary=31500.0, Name=Charles Salary=26250.0 )
```

Listing 17.12 The Employee Class
```
class Employee
{
  public String getName()
  {
    return theName;
```

```
  }

  public float getSalary()
  {
    return theSalary;
  }

  public void setSalary(float salary)
  {
    theSalary = salary;
  }

  public void stepSalary(float raise)
  {
    setSalary((1.0f + raise) * getSalary());
  }

  public String toString()
  {
    return "Name=" + theName + " Salary=" + theSalary;
  }

  public Employee(String name, float salary)
  {
    theName = name;
    setSalary(salary);
  }

  private String theName;
  private float  theSalary;
}
```

Listing 17.13 shows the function object used in `ApplyTest`. Function objects are a variation on the Command design pattern. They encapsulate an operation but don't encapsulate a specific target for the operation. The `SalaryRaise` class implements the `UnaryFunction` interface. JGL also provides a similar `BinaryFunction` interface. The built-in function classes provided by JGL are the topic of the next section.

Listing 17.13 The SalaryRaise Class

```
class SalaryRaise implements UnaryFunction
{
  public Object execute(Object o)
  {
    if (! (o instanceof Employee))
      throw new IllegalArgumentException("That's no employee!");
    Employee e = (Employee) o;
    e.stepSalary(theRaise);
    return e;
  }

  public SalaryRaise(float raise)
  {
    theRaise = raise;
```

```
    }

  private float theRaise;
}
```

Function Objects: Frozen Algorithms

Just as objects of the Command design pattern represent *frozen* (that is, encapsulated) commands, function objects represent frozen functions. By freezing a function as a function object, you can send it to objects as an argument. Thus, if you write a method—say, animate()—that takes a function object as a parameter, you can actually pass the method used to perform the animation operations as an argument. This is particularly useful with algorithmic methods like apply(), which can be used to apply the frozen function to each element of a collection.

JGL includes more than 40 predicate functions (that is, functions that return true or false) and almost 20 other functions. You also can define your own function objects by subclassing UnaryFunction or BinaryFunction. JGL's predicate functions are used mainly to modify the way an algorithm works. Not every algorithm accepts predicates. Consult the JGL documentation to determine what functions are available and whether an algorithm you're interested in can use predicate functions.

As an example of function use, Listing 17.14 shows the TransformTest class.

Listing 17.14 The TransformTest Class

```java
import java.applet.*;
import java.awt.*;
import COM.objectspace.jgl.*;

public class TransformTest extends Applet
{
  TextArea theText  = new TextArea();

  public void init()
  {
    setLayout(new BorderLayout());
    add(theText, "Center");

    Array saturday = new Array();
    saturday.add(new Integer(100));
    saturday.add(new Integer(150));

    writeText("Sales:");
    writeText("");
    writeText(saturday.toString());

    Array sunday  = new Array();
    sunday.add(new Integer(25));
    sunday.add(new Integer(35));
    writeText(sunday.toString());
```

```
    Array total = new Array();

    Transforming.transform(
      saturday,
      sunday,
      total,
      new PlusNumber());

    writeText("");
    writeText("");
    writeText("Summary:");
    writeText("");
    writeText("Product totals=" + total);

    Integer grand = (Integer) Applying.inject(total, new Integer(0), new
    ➥PlusNumber());
    writeText("Grand total=" + grand);
  }

  public void writeText(String text)
  {
    theText.append(text);
    //area.append(System.getProperty("line.separator"));
    theText.append("\n");
  }
}
```

The `TransformTest` class uses the `Transforming.transform()` method and the `PlusNumber()` unary function to add weekend sales by product at the Bug Boutique. It also uses the `Applying.inject()` method to determine the grand total sales of all products over the weekend.

Saturday's sales of 100 units of one product and 150 units of another are stored in one `Array`. Sunday's sales of 25 units of the first product and 35 units of the other are stored in another `Array`. A third `Array` is used to hold the total sales by product, which the `transform()` method computes. Notice that the program is loopless—iteration is implicit in the methods invoked, not explicit in the client program.

The `inject()` method works somewhat unusually. The function specified as its third argument is first applied to its second argument and the first element of the collection give as its first argument. Here, the `PlusNumber()` method, which simply adds two integers, is applied to 0 and the first element of the collection. The result, of course, is the value of the first element of the collection.

What's interesting is what comes next: the `PlusNumber()` method is now applied to the current result and to the second element of the collection. The result is the sum of the first and second elements of the collection. This process is then repeated until all elements of the collection are processed. When the smoke clears, you're left with the sum of the elements of the collection. This probably seems roundabout; it does trade one sort of complexity (the use of loops) for another sort of complexity (iterative application of a function). If you're more comfortable using loops, by all means do so. The object is to write a clear, nearly bug-free program, not to use the latest technology. Figure 17.11 shows the output of the applet.

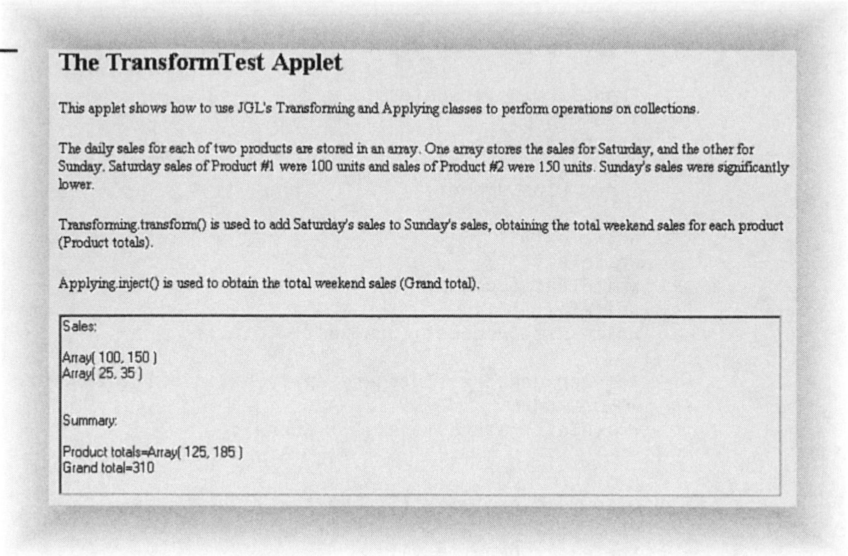

FIGURE 17.11

*Ouput of the
TransformTest applet*

The TransformTest Applet

This applet shows how to use JGL's Transforming and Applying classes to perform operations on collections.

The daily sales for each of two products are stored in an array. One array stores the sales for Saturday, and the other for Sunday. Saturday sales of Product #1 were 100 units and sales of Product #2 were 150 units. Sunday's sales were significantly lower.

Transforming.transform() is used to add Saturday's sales to Sunday's sales, obtaining the total weekend sales for each product (Product totals).

Applying.inject() is used to obtain the total weekend sales (Grand total).

```
Sales:

Array( 100, 150 )
Array( 25, 35 )

Summary:

Product totals=Array( 125, 185 )
Grand total=310
```

Iterators: Progress and Regress

If you often find yourself running forward and backward and expect your programs to do the same, you'll greet JGL's iterators with enthusiasm. Iterators are nothing more than industrial-strength `Enumerations`. In fact, JGL's iterators implement the `Enumeration` interface. But, as any fan of TV infomercials will tell you, the phrase *industrial-strength* makes all the difference in the world.

JGL supports five different types of iterators, as shown in Table 17.8.

TABLE 17.8
JGL'S `Iterator` INTERFACES

Interface	Description
`InputIterator`	Can read one item at a time, in a forward direction only
`OutputIterator`	Can write one item at a time, in a forward direction only
`ForwardIterator`	Combines characteristics of input and output iterators
`BidirectionalIterator`	Like `ForwardIterator`, plus the capability to move backward
`RandomAccessIterator`	Like `BidirectionalIterator`, plus the capability to jump by an arbitrary distance

Table 17.9 shows the methods supported by the various iterators. Notice that, in contrast to Enumerations, which provide only single-step forward movement, JGL's iterators provide multistep forward and backward movement. JGL also provides an OutputIterator that you can use to put elements into a collection, and a RandomAccessIterator that lets you retrieve elements by means of an index.

TABLE 17.9
JGL'S Iterator METHODS

Method	Function
advance()	Advances by one element
advance(int)	Advances by a specified number of elements
atBegin()	Returns true if positioned at the first item of the input stream
atEnd()	Returns true if positioned after the last item in the input stream
clone()	Returns a clone of the iterator
distance(ForwardIterator)	Returns the distance from one iterator to another (ForwardIterators only)
get()	Returns the object at the current position
index()	Returns the index of the current position (RandomAccessIterators only)
less(RandomAccessIterator)	Returns true if the iterator is before a specified iterator (RandomAccessIterators only)
put(Object)	Sets the object at the current position to a specified value (OutputIterators only)
retreat()	Retreats by one element (BidirectionalIterators only)
retreat(int)	Retreats by a specified number of elements (BidirectionalIterators only)

Most JGL collections support the most general iterator interface—the RandomAccessIterator. Table 17.10 shows the concrete iterator class returned by each collection class and the iterator interface that the returned class implements.

TABLE 17.10
JGL'S CONTAINER-ITERATOR RELATIONSHIPS

Container	Associated Iterator	Iterator Interface
Array	ArrayIterator	RandomAccessIterator
BooleanArray	BooleanIterator	RandomAccessIterator
ByteArray	ByteIterator	RandomAccessIterator
CharArray	CharIterator	RandomAccessIterator
Deque	DequeIterator	RandomAccessIterator
DoubleArray	DoubleIterator	RandomAccessIterator
FloatArray	FloatIterator	RandomAccessIterator
IntArray	IntIterator	RandomAccessIterator
DList	DListIterator	BidirectionalIterator
HashMap	HashMapIterator	ForwardIterator
ObjectArray	ObjectIterator	RandomAccessIterator
OrderedMap	OrderedMapIterator	BidirectionalIterator
OrderedSet	OrderedSetIterator	BidirectionalIterator
PriorityQueue	ArrayIterator	RandomAccessIterator
Queue	Same as underlying sequence	Same as underlying sequence
HashSet	HashSetIterator	ForwardIterator
ShortArray	ShortIterator	RandomAccessIterator
SList	SListIterator	ForwardIterator
Stack	Same as underlying sequence	Same as underlying sequence
VectorArray	VectorIterator	RandomAccessIterator

> *Although the designers of JGL have made your job much easier by implementing common data structures, chances are that someday you'll have to implement a class library of your own.*

Design Hints

Although the designers of JGL have made your job much easier by implementing common data structures, chances are that someday you'll have to implement a class library of your own. You may never have to write your own Vector class, but you may find yourself writing a framework for banking, real estate, or aardvark farming. When you do, you'll want to keep some things in mind:

- **Use consistent names**. JGL classes and interfaces follow a consistent naming pattern. For example, the names of each iterator end in Iterator, making it much easier for you to learn where things are and how things work. You should follow this example in your library.

🔹 **Use clear, reasonable names**. The designers of JGL weren't afraid to use long names when doing so contributed to clarity. They could have given all the iterators names ending in `It`. But by giving each iterator a name that tells you what it is, they made it easy for you to extrapolate from what you know. When you design your library, you should do likewise.

🔹 **Use consistent mechanisms**. Throughout JGL, you use the `get()` method to retrieve an element of a collection. You use the `elements()` method to get an `Enumeration` over the elements of a collection and so forth. Things work consistently throughout the library. This is due, in large part, to the use of interfaces, which impose a common mechanism on classes that implement them. You should use interfaces to establish consistent mechanisms in any library you design.

🔹 **Use consistent error handling**. JGL defines an error policy consisting of a set of `Exceptions` and the circumstances under which they're thrown. Every method adheres to the policy, so you know what you'll get, even when things go wrong. You should emulate this example in your own libraries.

Summary

Software reuse can increase software development productivity and software quality. JGL is a free Java library that provides many useful collection classes, along with algorithms and functions that operate on them. JGL's main collection types include `Sequences`, `Maps`, `Sets`, `Queues` and `Stacks`. `Sequences` resemble Java's arrays and `Vectors`. `Maps` resemble `Hashtables`. `Sets` make it easy to perform common set operations like intersection and union. `Queues` are like Java's `Stacks`, except that they are first-in, first-out (FIFO) rather than last-in, first-out (LIFO).

Shallow copying results in clone objects that share references to underlying fields. Deep copying instantiates new objects so that the clone and the original reference distinct fields.

JGL's `OrderedMap` classes depend on an object's hash code to determine the proper ordering of elements. You must override the `Object.hashCode()` method so that it returns a value consistent with the desired ordering of your collection.

Algorithms let you iterate over the elements of a container without using explicit loops. This can make your programs more or less clear, depending on your point of view. Function objects encapsulate an algorithm in a manner similar to that of the Command design pattern.

JGL provides several powerful iterators that extend the capabilities of the JDK `Enumeration` class.

Questions

For multiple-choice items, indicate all correct responses.

1. The root interface implemented by JGL's collections is
   a. `Collection`
   b. `Container`
   c. `Enumeration`
   d. `Vector`

2. A _____ copy results in shared references, but a _____ copy instantiates new objects so that there are no shared references.

3. The methods required by the `Cloneable` interface include
   a. `clone()`
   b. `copy()`
   c. `deepCopy()`
   d. none of the above

4. JGL's `Sequence` classes resemble the JDK class
   a. `Array`
   b. `Enumeration`
   c. `Hashtable`
   d. `Vector`

5. An `OrderedMap` orders its elements by the return value of the _____ method.

6. The `equals()` method
   a. Is defined in the `Object` class
   b. Shouldn't be used to compare objects
   c. Tests whether two objects have the same state
   d. Tests whether two references refer to the same object

7. The set operation methods that manipulate `Set` objects are defined in the class
   a. `Algorithm`
   b. `BinaryFunction`
   c. `Set`
   d. `SetOperations`

8. The `Stack`, `Queue`, and `PriorityQueue` classes add the _____ and _____ methods to those defined by the `Container` interface.

9. JGL's _____ are closely related to the JDK's `Enumerations`.

10. An important principle of library design is to use _____ names, mechanisms, and error handling.

Exercises

1. Write a JGL class that can read lines of text from a disk file, alphabetize the lines, and write the result to a disk file.

2. By using JGL classes, write a simple employee database browser. The browser should let you traverse forward and backward through a collection of employee elements, search for employee elements by name or employee number, add new employees, and change existing employees. Employees should be characterized by name, address, telephone number, email, and salary. Your program should be able to save the collection to a disk file, restore the collection from a disk file, and print the collection.

3. Write a program that tests JGL classes, comparing their performance to that of similar JDK classes. Your program should test various operations, including gets, puts, and traversals. Use the Factory Method design pattern to parameterize the choice of JGL and JDK classes.

4. Write a class that uses a JGL collection of your choice to store serialized objects, represented by `byte` arrays. Include some methods that let a client serialize and store an object in a single call, making the class easy to use. Your class should be capable of serializing itself, saving its elements to a disk file.

To Learn More

The following books will help you learn more about designing with class libraries:

- Horstmann, Cay. *Practical Object-Oriented Development in C++ and Java.* New York: John Wiley & Sons, 1997. This book gives some good advice on designing your own class libraries in C++ and Java. Most of the material deals with C++, but the book includes many useful hints and tips for designing Java class libraries.

- Carrol, Martin, and Margaret A. Ellis. *Designing and Coding Reusable C++.* Reading, Massachusetts: Addison-Wesley, 1995. This book deals exclusively with writing reusable C++ libraries, but many of the principles apply equally well to Java libraries.

- Budd, Timothy. *Data Structures in C++ Using the Standard Template Library.* Reading Massachusetts: Addison-Wesley, 1998. Although there are no specific books on using the Java Generic Libraries, several books will help you use the C++ Standard Template Libraries, on which JGL is modeled. One of the best is this introductory computer science text by Tim Budd.

For an introduction to the general subject of data structures in Java, several texts have recently appeared. Although these books don't deal with container class libraries specifically, the will help you understand how and where to use the fundamental data structures that such libraries contain:

- Lafore, Robert. *Data Structures In Java*. Corte Madera, California: Waite Group Press, 1998.

- Standish, Thomas. *Data Structures in Java*. Reading, Massachusetts: Addison-Wesley, 1997.

- Weiss, Mark Allen. *Data Structures and Problem Solving Using Java*. Reading, Massachusetts: Addison-Wesley, 1998.

The Weiss and Standish books are academic texts aimed at a sophomore-level computer science data structures course, as is Budd's book. By contrast, Lafore's text is aimed at a more general audience, suitable for programming professionals and self-study.

18

Architectures: Design-in-the-Huge

What makes a good design? Well, that depends. Whether a design is good or not depends a lot on whether it "fits" into the world around it. At the end of Michael Crichton's best-selling novel *Jurassic Park*, the recently revived inhabitants of the ancient world found our modern version a very good fit indeed, as they began to eat their way across the jungles of Central America. Truly a frightening thought. But, think for a second about a very different type of creature: the microbe. Although the threat of catching a common cold pales when compared to being pursued by a Tyrannosaurus Rex or a pride of raptors, in many ways, the design of the microbe is better than that of the dinosaur. The microbe has been able to change and adapt to its environment, but the dinosaur has not. Like it or not, the flu that laid you up last winter is better adapted to the modern world than is Tyrannosaurus Rex.

In this chapter, you'll study the design of a different type of dinosaur: information system architectures. Architectures are to designs what dinosaurs are to lizards. They represent the upper end in size and scope. Architectural design is sometimes referred to as "design-in-the-huge." Like the 80-foot long brachiosaurus plodding through Jurassic marshes, architectures move relatively slowly. But, also like the brachiosaurus, they are always in danger of extinction as rapid changes in the technological climate overwhelm their capability to adapt.

If you work with computer-based information systems, you know that you must keep up your own skills as well, or likewise fall by the wayside. In this chapter, you will learn:

- What the elements of an information system architecture are.

- How changes in technology have caused major changes in information system architectures.

- How the invention of time sharing and the dumb terminal lead to the first era of information systems: the traditional architecture.

- How the proliferation of the PC led to systems built around a new architecture: file server systems.

- How the widespread acceptance of the relational database led to client/server architectures.

- How Java and the Web are leading the charge toward new types of systems: thin clients and distributed architectures.

- How to choose an information system architecture.

Information System Architectures and Components

Information system (IS) architecture sounds like a very complex and esoteric subject. In fact, an *information system architecture* is simply a design pattern that describes the way in which the various application programs that your company uses are related to each other. Your company might have a payroll system that runs on a mainframe computer while word processing is done on PCs connected to a file server. Your sales and inventory information might be stored in a relational database that you can query through your PC, but which also provides the raw material for your executive reporting system.

The relationship between these various application programs—payroll, word processing, sales, and inventory—is your IS architecture. Most of this book has focused on the relationships between objects. This is different. The IS architecture is the highest, or most general, level at which you'll work as a designer. As you can see from Figure 18.1, when you design an IS architecture, you fit applications together; when you design an application, you fit objects together.

PHYSICAL COMPONENTS

When you learned to design objects, the pieces or components you had to work with were attributes and methods. You arranged these components to create objects that were robust and effective. When you design an IS architecture, there are also some basic parts you focus on. The three main building blocks are:

> *" An information system architecture is simply a design pattern that describes the way in which the various application programs that your company uses are related to each other. "*

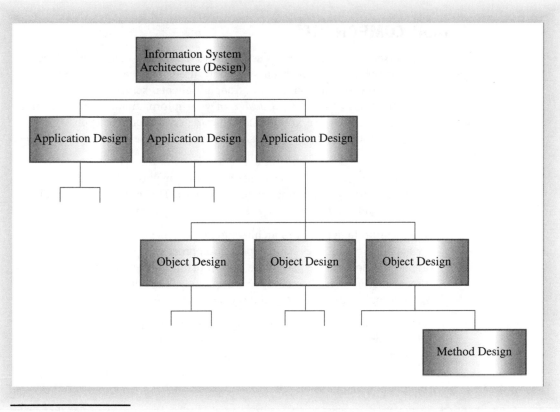

FIGURE 18.1

An information system architecture

● **Clients:** These are devices, usually computers, that let people use your system. A client usually provides the user with a keyboard and video display. Today, modern clients will also normally provide a graphical user interface and a pointing device (mouse). Tomorrow's clients might give their users voice recognition, notepads, or scanners.

● **Servers:** These are the computers that provide services to the client devices. If you have a local area network at work, you might have a server on which you can store your files. Your company might use a database server to store transaction or sales information. If you have a Web page, the HTML files are stored on a Web server.

● **The network:** Clients and servers can't work together unless they have some way to communicate. The network is the hardware (network interface cards and cabling) and software (network operating system) that puts clients in touch with servers. When a client device wants something from a server, it sends its request over the network. The server, which handles each request in turn, then sends the results back to the client who made the request, via the network.

LOGICAL COMPONENTS

As you'll soon see, there are many possible ways you can arrange these three elements. Some arrangements have been so widely used that they are recognized as design patterns. However, in addition to arranging clients, servers, and networks in different configurations—the *physical design* of your information system—designing an IS architecture requires that you consider the *logical* structure of your system as well. To design the logical structure, most applications require you to consider these three types of processing:

- **User interface:** Every system must have some method of getting input from the user and presenting output to the user. This part of your logical design is sometimes called the *presentation* component.

- **Application logic:** In an IS architecture, the application logic is simply "what the program does." If an application processes payroll, the application logic is the part of the system that is concerned with processing the payroll correctly and accurately. The application logic part of your logical design is sometimes called the *business rules* component.

- **Data management:** The data management component of your IS architecture is concerned with storing information for later use and with retrieving that stored information. When you design this part of your architecture you'll make decisions about databases, files, and the distribution and transmission of information.

In Chapter 4, "Encapsulation: Classes and Methods," you saw that one of the marks of a good object-oriented design is that it distributes the processing between different objects. Rather than having one object that does all the work, you give each object its own little piece of responsibility. When you design an IS architecture, you'll face a similar set of design decisions. You have three different physical components and three different logical components; which component should do which portion of the processing, and in what way?

Architectures differ in the way they allocate the required processing among clients and servers. Some architectures place almost all the processing burden on a single server; others place most of the burden on individual clients. Not only must you decide "who gets to do what," but you also must decide how it's going to be done. Different architectures use different technologies to provide the user interface, the application processing, and the data storage component. Now let's take a look at what your choices are.

USER INTERFACE TECHNOLOGY

Several technologies have been used to provide users with an interface (a *user interface*) to computer applications.

Dumb Terminals

A popular early technology that is still sometimes used today is the *dumb terminal*. Dumb terminals usually consist of a video display, a keyboard, and some type of network or serial connection to a server. You don't have to (nor can you) program a dumb terminal. An architecture that uses dumb terminals places all three logical components—interface, logic, and storage—on the server. Dumb terminals fulfill the role of client in many information systems, particularly large systems.

The chief virtue of the dumb terminal is its low cost and simplicity. Its greatest liability is its lack of local processing power and its limited capability. Dumb terminals are equipped with a keyboard, but most lack a pointing device. Dumb terminals can display text, but many cannot display lines or graphics. Rapid changes in technology—the development of inexpensive microprocessors and random access memory—have driven down the cost of more capable clients, however, erasing much of the cost advantage that dumb terminals once held.

X-Terminals

One step up from the dumb terminal (in terms of capability) is the X-terminal. X-terminals are designed to run the X Window graphical user interface, an interface system that dominates the UNIX world.

Like a dumb terminal, the X-terminal is a specialized device rather than a general-purpose computer. But, unlike the dumb terminal, the X-terminal provides an input pointing device and a graphical video display. X-terminals span a wide range of prices. Low-end models cost only several hundred dollars. High-end models with high-resolution color displays can cost more than a well-equipped PC.

Graphical user interfaces, like those provided by the X-terminal, are generally easier for users to learn and use than text-based user interfaces based on dumb terminals. The savings in training costs help offset the higher hardware cost of X-terminals or other graphical user interfaces.

Personal Computers

The dominant user interface technology today, in terms of popularity, is the IBM-compatible personal computer (PC) equipped with Microsoft Windows. PCs are everywhere. Like the X-terminal, a Windows PC is equipped with a pointing device and always provides a graphical video display. Because a PC is a general-purpose computer, you can use software to make it appear as a dumb terminal or as an X-terminal when necessary. This provides your users with two capabilities: They can run general-purpose application software, such as a spreadsheet program or a word processor, and still access your company's *legacy* IS applications (which expect users to connect via dumb terminals), both using a single system.

Another advantage of using PCs as the user interface element of your architecture is that many workers have PCs at home for personal use. They are familiar with the standard ways to access Windows user interface elements and can run the same word processor, for example, at home and at work. Even though an X-terminal can cost less, it can't run shrink-wrapped software that has been written for PCs. If you base the interface component of your IS architecture on X-terminals, you might have to provide your workers with PCs as well as X-terminals so that they can run the productivity applications they'll need to get their jobs done. Of course, if you use PC-based hardware, you could provide your users with an X-terminal software emulator. Either way, though, an X-terminal-based information system generally leads to higher desktop costs than the Windows-based system. Of course, desktop costs are only one component of your information systems architecture. You'll have to weigh all the advantages and disadvantages.

The NC Solution

If you read the news, you can't have missed all the hoopla over *network computers* (NCs). A fourth alternative technology, the Java-enabled network computer, might become the dominant user-interface solution of the next decade. Many people are betting that this will come to pass.

Network computers stand somewhere between X-terminals and PCs in terms of processing power. An X-terminal has more processing power than a dumb terminal, but the only processing that the X-terminal does is to present the user interface. None of the application logic—the real work of your system—can be carried out on the X-terminal; that is still relegated to the server. Like the PC, the network computer is a general-purpose processor. Unlike the PC, however, the NC is designed to be simple, inexpensive, and trouble-free. If you've just spent the last week reinstalling Windows for the umpteenth time, you might be asking, "Where do I sign up?"

Before you put a For Sale sign on your PC, you'll want to ask what you give up by implementing an NC solution. Like the dumb terminal and the X-terminal, NC machines will not run the same desktop applications that users currently use. Because NC machines usually don't have a hard or floppy disk (one reason why they're less expensive) and because they won't necessarily run the Windows operating system, user's can't load Word, Excel, Lotus, or WordPerfect.

On a brighter note, network computers are designed to run Java software, and to run it even better than a standard PC. As soon as Java-based desktop applications are widely used and familiar to computer users, network computers might begin to displace Windows-based PCs as the dominant user interface technology.

Table 18.1 summarizes user interface technologies.

TABLE 18.1
USER INTERFACE TECHNOLOGIES

Technology	Characteristics
Dumb terminals	Low cost, keyboard input, text-based output
X-terminals	Intermediate cost, keyboard and pointing device input, graphical output, specialized software, limited popularity
Windows-based PCs	High cost, keyboard and pointing device input, graphical output, shrink-wrapped software
Network computers	Intermediate cost, keyboard and pointing device input, graphical output, shrink-wrap software promised

APPLICATION TECHNOLOGY

In contrast to the whirlwind changes in user interface technology, technology for application processing has been relatively stagnant. Many information systems in use today were originally designed and implemented during the 1960s, using the COBOL programming language.

There have been many changes in programming languages and tools since then. These new technologies—integrated development environments, application frameworks, rapid-application development (RAD) environments, visual GUI builders—all help you to develop and deploy applications much more quickly than you could using COBOL. But, in terms of affecting the IS architecture—the distribution of application processing between the client and server components of the design—little has changed. When they are deployed, such systems seem no different to your user than those built using COBOL. Unless your new application has a distinctive user interface or runs a little slower or faster, your users won't know anything has changed at all. Remember, to the user, the user interface *is* the system.

Java and related technologies might change that. Java provides entirely new ways to distribute the application processing between client and server components in your design, as well as new ways to deploy applications. Using applets, applications, and Java's capabilities to distribute different parts of the same application remotely across the network (using CORBA and RMI), you can create systems with much greater control over which portions reside on client stations, and which portions reside on the server. You'll learn more about these options later in this chapter.

DATA MANAGEMENT TECHNOLOGY

When you consider the third element of your IS architecture, data storage, you'll find two main alternatives: files and databases. A system based on files uses your operating system's application programming interface (API) to store data in files that are specific to your application. A system based on a database uses the Structured Query Language (SQL) to communicate with a database server that takes care of the details of file storage.

File-Based Systems

Traditionally, information systems have relied on files to store persistent information. A utility company might have a customer file and a billing file, for example. The application that sends out utility bills might use both, whereas the sales reporting application might need only the billing file.

Because files use simpler technology than databases, you might find designing and implementing a file-based system easier than one using a database. However, there are several reasons to consider long and hard before you commit to this decision. Although simplicity—and occasionally, performance—are obvious attractions, the drawbacks of a file-based system include the following:

- **Reduced functionality:** A file-based system often provides less functionality than a system that uses a database. Most operating systems provide only limited support for file sharing. When information is going to be used throughout your company, such issues as file locking, deadlock detection, and control over who is allowed access to which information (data security), all must be addressed by your application rather than by the underlying data storage system.

- **Reduced robustness:** Operating system APIs do not generally address the need to control the redundancy of data stored in files. This means that the same information might be present several times in your files, often in slightly different forms. Such uncontrolled redundancy can result in lost or inaccurate data—a mortal sin for an information system.

- **Lack of scalability:** File-based systems tend to be nonscalable; that is, unable to support large-scale use. You can write a system that works perfectly for your workgroup or office but fails to run correctly and efficiently when you try to deploy it across your entire company or on different hardware. File-based systems also tend to be inflexible, due to the limited support provided by the operating system API and the lack of specialized data management tools.

Database Systems

Although a system based on a database, like those you studied in Chapter 14, "Designing Persistent Objects: Database Design and Implementation," can be harder to design and implement, you'll find that a database management system (DBMS) gives you the necessary tools that your operating system's file API lacks. It's generally easier for you to control data redundancy and provide for application security and integrity using a database than with files. As a result, systems based on a database tend to fare better when moved to different hardware or deployed across the corporation than those based on files.

Another major advantage of using database technology includes modern database support for SQL. Although there are dialectical differences from vendor to vendor, SQL has emerged as a popular universal language for database access. If you base your design on SQL databases, therefore, your architecture will tend to be less idiosyncratic than if you base it on files. The following are other advantages of using a SQL database for the data management portion of your logical architecture:

- SQL databases typically provide a plethora of useful tools and functions that can greatly increase the flexibility of a system.

- SQL databases are capable of handling *ad hoc* requests for information. Using SQL, you can formulate queries that you never considered when you were designing the system. SQL enables you to retrieve your information in a timely manner, without requiring special programming. Most file-based systems are not up to this challenge.

SQL databases support *data independence*, often entirely lacking in file-based systems. Data independence means that the DBMS insulates your application programs from changes to the structure of the data. For example, the simple maintenance task of adding a new field to a file-based system can require extensive reprogramming. If you've based your design on a database, however, your application programs see only those table columns they use. Adding a new table column generally does not affect existing programs; only those programs that use the new column must be modified.

In principle, you could build this same functionality into your file-based system. However, by the time you were finished you would have written the same kind of code that DBMS vendors have already included in their products. This is generally too costly compared to the relatively low cost of a DBMS. By building a system around a database, you gain significant capability at low cost.

Table 18.2 summarizes the differences between file-based systems and systems based on a database.

TABLE 18.2
DATA MANAGEMENT TECHNOLOGIES

Technology	Pros	Cons
Files	Easy to design and implement	Limited support for data sharing Inflexible Nonscalable
Databases	Include useful data management tools Support for SQL Flexible Support for ad hoc queries Scalable Data independence	Harder to design and implement

Designing IS Architectures

Every design activity that you've studied so far has notations and diagrams that help you focus on relevant aspects of the design problem. Designing IS architectures is no exception. You'll find two types of diagrams particularly useful:

Geographical decomposition diagrams

Network connectivity diagrams

GEOGRAPHICAL DECOMPOSITION DIAGRAMS

Geographical decomposition diagrams show how the users of your system are related geographically. These diagrams are simple to understand and easy to prepare. Figure 18.2 shows a sample geographical decomposition diagram for the Bug Boutique, that ever-hopeful group of entrepreneurs you met in Chapter 5, "Designing Classes and Objects."

As you can see, the Bug Boutique's Inventory Control System serves three distribution centers. Only one of the three, the London center, is shown in detail. There are four types of users at the London center:

- The inventory manager
- The shipping clerks
- The buyers
- The key suppliers

The rounded corners of the symbol for the suppliers indicate that they are connected to the system via the London center but are located at a remote site. Their actual location is not given. The symbols for the clerks, the buyers, and the suppliers are replicated, indicating that they represent groups of users rather than an individual user.

There is no standardized form for the geographical decomposition diagram, so you can use other symbols if you prefer. Some designers like to indicate a group by placing an asterisk (*) in the upper-right corner of the corresponding symbol. Another common variation is to use a trapezoid or parallelogram to indicate a remote location, rather than a rounded rectangle.

FIGURE 18.2

A geographical decomposition diagram

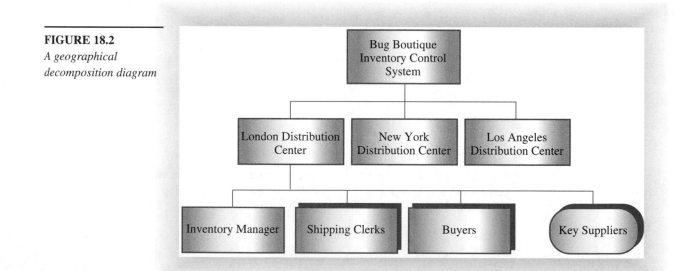

NETWORK CONNECTIVITY DIAGRAMS

> *Whereas the geographical decomposition diagram focuses on users, the network connectivity diagram is used to show the clients and servers that make up your IS architecture.* "

The second diagram that you'll use to describe or design an IS architecture is called the network connectivity diagram. Whereas the geographical decomposition diagram focuses on users, the network connectivity diagram is used to show the clients and servers that make up your IS architecture. Figure 18.3 shows a network connectivity diagram.

The clients and servers are usually shown pictorially but, if you lack access to a drawing program that provides convenient, ready-made symbols, you can draw a network connectivity diagram in schematic form. Figure 18.4 shows a schematic network connectivity diagram.

Often, when drawing a network connectivity diagram, you'll want to include additional information describing the configuration of the *hosts* (a generic term referring to either a client or a server) or the processing they perform. You'll see such diagrams in the next section, which walks you through some of the alternative architectures that other designers have used.

FIGURE 18.3

A network connectivity diagram

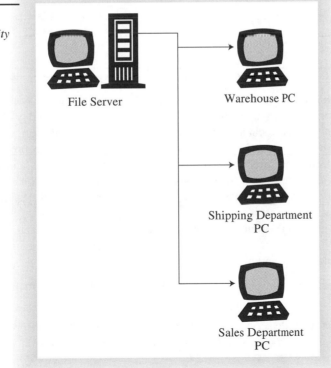

File Server

Warehouse PC

Shipping Department PC

Sales Department PC

FIGURE 18.4

A schematic network connectivity diagram

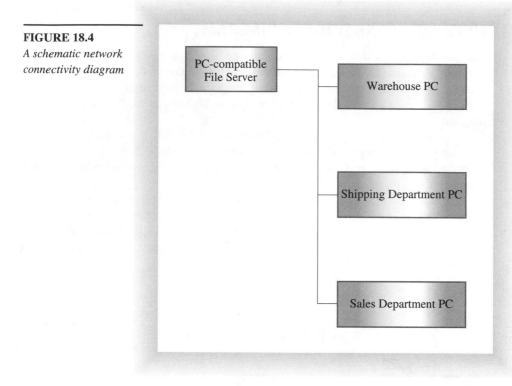

Architectural Alternatives

Now that you have some tools for describing information system architectures, you're ready to learn about some specific architectures in use today. Information system architectures have changed over the years as technological change has enabled designers to try new arrangements. Sometimes new designs have proven impractical and have been abandoned; other designs have proven themselves and often exist side by side with systems that have survived from previous eras. Sometimes, the old infrastructure becomes so frail that a new system entirely replaces it—sort of an urban renewal for computer systems.

Four general IS architectures are in widespread use today. Each of these architectures evolved in response to changes in the technological environment. In order from oldest to youngest, they are:

- The traditional architecture, which developed in the mainframe computer era

- The file server architecture, which followed the widespread introduction of microcomputers and local area networks (LANs)

> 🔹 The client/server architecture, an outgrowth of the development of relational databases

> 🔹 The distributed architecture, based on the adoption of ubiquitous telecommunications and networking

Although each of these architectures was prevalent during a particular era, you don't need to slavishly submit to the current architectural fad. As you design the IS architecture for your system, you might find yourself using ideas from several of these different computing paradigms.

THE TRADITIONAL ARCHITECTURE

> *"The first computers, built at the end of the 1940s, processed information in* **batch** *mode. Users provided input in the form of punched cards and received their output on printed listings."*

The first computers, built at the end of the 1940s, processed information in *batch* mode. Users provided input in the form of punched cards and received their output on printed listings. Users seldom had direct contact with the computer. Instead, they used pencil and paper, completing forms that were sent to a keypunch group where the data was transcribed from the forms to punched cards.

These early computers were "single-tasking" machines; they ran only a single job at a time. Usually a single computer operator was responsible for "feeding" the machine. Even these crude machines, however, had voracious appetites, and their handlers were not able to feed them as quickly as they could consume their data. Furthermore, while they were being "fed"—during input and output operations—the central processing unit stood idle, waiting for its data to arrive so it could go to work. Early computers had quite a bit of time on their hands—very, very expensive time. These systems were so primitive they can scarcely be said to have had an architecture.

The development of preemptive multitasking—the capability of the CPU to perform several tasks in parallel, switching between tasks in an attempt to keep the CPU fully occupied—opened the door for more efficient use of the expensive mainframes of the day. The replacement of the punched-card stack with the CRT terminal, or dumb terminal as it's called today, and advances in communication technology opened the doors in the early 1960s to *time sharing* and *online* systems. With time sharing, the CPU time that had previously stood idle waiting for I/O operations to complete was divided up and sold off piecemeal to subscribers. Although each subscriber got only a fraction of the computer's attention, the computer was capable of switching between users so quickly, that each had the illusion of being the only user—at least until the number of subscriptions sold exhausted the computer's idle capacity. With the proper software support, it was possible for the CRT terminal user to type data directly into the computer and view the results almost immediately. A new era in computing had begun, initiated by technological improvement of the user interface.

Figure 18.5 is a network connectivity diagram that shows a typical instance of the traditional information system architecture. Although a dumb terminal contains a small CPU, the traditional (sometimes called *host-based*) architecture places the mainframe on center stage. The mainframe does essentially all the user interface processing, along with application processing and data management.

The traditional architecture of the 1960s was dominated by expensive mainframe computers. Most organizations that could afford a computer at all could afford only one. Application software was also primitive by modern standards. COBOL was the dominant programming language. Building online applications was a more complex and difficult task than building batch-oriented systems such as payroll and billing, and systems support for user-interface technology was weak. Data management was like-wise primitive, and databases were scarce. Operating system support for file sharing was weak. Along with the shortcomings of support for terminals, this made develop-ment of multiuser applications a difficult endeavor.

The high cost of computers, and initially even of dumb terminals, made the tradi-tional architecture a costly step. Many organizations simply could not afford to "go online" and continued batch processing of data into the 1970s and beyond. This was particularly true of organizations that had deployed large, batch-oriented systems. Such systems were too large to be quickly or inexpensively replaced.

The traditional information system architecture was not, however, without certain benefits. Because the information systems group had custody of the data, which was fully contained within the organization's mainframe, they were able to exercise

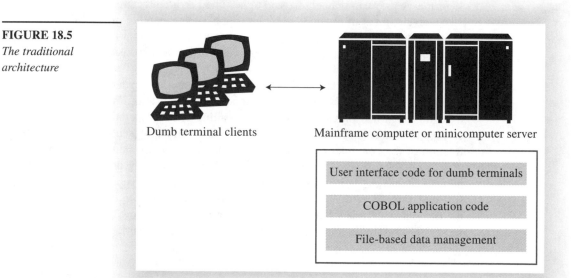

FIGURE 18.5

The traditional architecture

Dumb terminal clients   Mainframe computer or minicomputer server

User interface code for dumb terminals

COBOL application code

File-based data management

considerable control. Data security, therefore, was high. Moreover, such systems were generally as reliable as the technology on which they depended, and were scalable. Many very large systems built using this architecture continue to operate successfully today.

In the 1970s, minicomputers were introduced, leading to a drop in computer prices. However, the hardware cost of systems built using the traditional architecture was not the only cost. Because of the limited support for user interface management and data management provided by operating systems, online systems remained difficult and expensive to develop.

Table 18.3 summarizes the pros and cons of the traditional information system architecture.

> " *The introduction of the microprocessor and the development of inexpensive local area networks (LANs) provoked another evolutionary jump in information system architecture.* "

TABLE 18.3
SUMMARY OF THE TRADITIONAL ARCHITECTURE

Server hardware	Mainframe or minicomputer
Client hardware	Dumb terminals
User interface technology	Keyboard input, text output
Application programming technology	COBOL plus operating system APIs
Data management technology	File system
Cost	Medium (minicomputer) to high (mainframe)
Reliability	High
Security	High
Scalability	High
Flexibility	Low

THE FILE SERVER ARCHITECTURE

The introduction of the microprocessor and the development of inexpensive local area networks (LANs) provoked another evolutionary jump in information system architecture. As PC prices dropped, they began to infiltrate corporate America. Today, of course, it's hard to find a desk in any business that doesn't have at least one computer sitting on it.

With the introduction of the PC, IS managers, who had previously controlled all of the computing resources, tried to make the new machine "fit." Some organizations equipped PCs with terminal emulators so that users could tap into the organization's existing information system, organized using the traditional model.

Some designers, on the other hand, wondered whether the PC could be used to replace the server at the center of the traditional architecture. Because PCs had so much processing power—at least compared to dumb terminals—creating an architecture with PC clients would allow the designer to move much of the processing currently carried out on the server over to the client. Whereas the traditional information system architecture featured a dumb client and a smart server, this new file server architecture featured a smart client and a dumb server. Figure 18.6 illustrates the file server architecture.

FIGURE 18.6
*The file server
architecture*

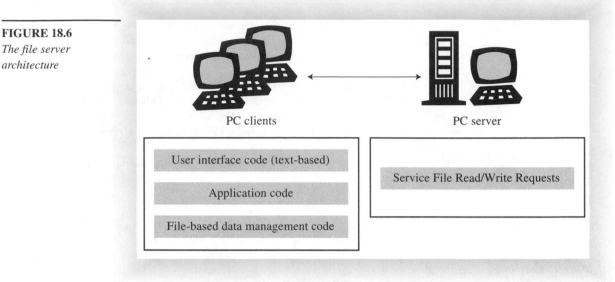

Although it connected the clients to the server using a high-bandwidth local area network (LAN) rather than the lower-speed networks used in the traditional architecture, the file server architecture generally continued to use a text-based, rather than graphical, approach to the user interface. Various programming languages were used, including BASIC, C, and several proprietary data manipulation languages like dBASE III and Paradox.

The server in a file server-based system did little more than transmit to clients the contents of file records they requested, or write to its hard drives the contents of file records transmitted by clients. On most systems, these files appeared just like an extension of the user's local file system. When the user wanted to run an application on such a system—say, a word processor or spreadsheet—the code was transported over the network where it was loaded into memory on the client's machine and executed. File server-based applications executed (or *ran*) on the client machine, not on the server. In effect, the file server acted like a large, external disk drive.

When used to support workgroup productivity applications such as word processing or spreadsheets, file servers were easily capable of supporting hundreds of users. However, for data-intensive information systems, the file server architecture was intrinsically limited. If, for example, the president of The Bug Boutique wanted to find out how many of his one million customers were repeat customers, the file server might have to transmit the entire file over the network to his local machine where it could be processed. The file server operating system was incapable of sorting through the data and sending only the necessary information. As you can imagine, if 10 or 20 of the Bug Boutique's employees asked for such information on a routine basis, the network could easily get bogged down.

The file-system architecture also suffered from several other weaknesses. The two biggest problems were security and reliability:

- Security was often low. When a user logged in to a PC server, the server's files simply appeared as additional local drives attached to the client PC. An unruly user could often access the files using an editor or other program and read them, alter them, or damage them.

- Reliability was also low because the software configuration tended to be fragile. To reduce network traffic, many file server-based applications used index files stored on the file server. However, because the file server did not actually process the data, these indexes had to be maintained on the local, client machines. When an individual machine would crash, perhaps running out of memory when adding a record or building an index, the index files would be corrupted for everyone else using the system on the network. Each client node on the network thus became dependent on the proper operation of all the clients on the network.

Flexibility of the file server architecture was high, however. Such systems were relatively easy to program, in part because really large or complex problems could not be adapted to the architecture. Relative to systems built using the traditional architecture, systems built using the file server architecture provided a high return on the hardware/software investment. Because they were also inexpensive to deploy, many small- and medium-size businesses built such systems.

Table 18.4 summarizes the file server architecture.

TABLE 18.4
SUMMARY OF THE FILE SERVER ARCHITECTURE

Server hardware	PC
Client hardware	PCs
User interface technology	Textual
Application programming technology	Various languages
Data management technology	File system
Cost	Low
Reliability	Low
Security	Low
Scalability	Low
Flexibility	High

CLIENT/SERVER ARCHITECTURES

Two technological changes led to the next step in IS architecture evolution:

- The availability of high-performance relational database management systems (DBMS)

🔷 The acceptance and widespread availability of a common graphical user interface, in this case, Microsoft Windows

Up to this point, the distribution of computing responsibility had been lopsided: the traditional architecture put almost all the responsibility on the server, whereas the file server architecture placed most of the load on the client. The client/server architecture, by contrast, aims for balance; any given type of processing can be allocated to the client or the server, according to whichever is best suited for the role. This configuration has been aptly referred to as a smart-client, smart-server configuration.

In practice, the advantages afforded by a centralized relational database almost always lead designers to allocate data management processing to the server rather than the client. As you'll see in the next section, however, newer architectures have questioned this assumption, with interesting results. Figure 18.7 shows a typical instance of the client/server architecture.

In its simplest form, the client/server architecture simply replaces the PC-based file server of the file server architecture with a PC running a relational database server. Notice that the weakness of the file server-based architecture was not the use of the PC as the server, but, in a sense, its under-use. A general-purpose network operating system (NOS) such as Novell NetWare or Windows NT Server is designed to provide client access to files. A database server, such as Oracle, Informix, or Sybase, which might also run on a PC using a network operating system, is designed to perform significant data processing for clients. And, if the PC hardware itself becomes a

FIGURE 18.7
The client/server architecture

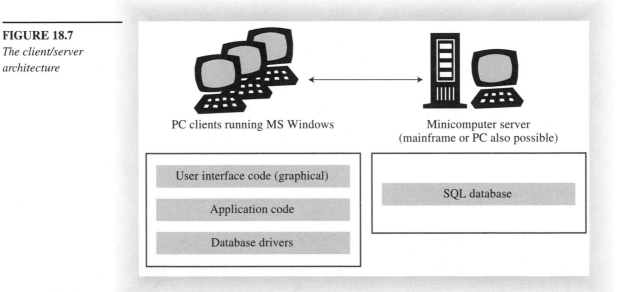

PC clients running MS Windows

Minicomputer server
(mainframe or PC also possible)

User interface code (graphical)

Application code

Database drivers

SQL database

limitation, systems based on a database server can be scaled up to support hundreds or even thousands of users, by simply replacing the server PC with a minicomputer (or even a mainframe).

Using a relational database instead of a set of files significantly increases the security and reliability of the architecture. The relational database also makes it easier to respond to *ad hoc* queries and provides mechanisms for achieving data independence, which enhances system flexibility.

Because they have only recently been developed, and because the client portion of the client/server architecture is almost always a PC running a modern operating system, client/server systems almost always include a graphical user interface rather than the text-based interface of earlier generations. This makes client/server systems much easier for users to learn than traditional or file server systems. And, the still-continuing reign of Microsoft Windows as the *de facto* standard for user interfaces, at home and at work, has helped propel this architecture to the forefront.

The client/server architecture, apart from its use of more advanced technologies for data management and user interface management, benefits from a relaxation of design rigidity inherent in previous architectures, which were all or nothing. In earlier architectures either all the processing was done by the server or (nearly) all was done by the client. Client/server introduced the term *rightsizing* as system designers sought to choose configurations that allocated the right task to the right box (that is, the right size of computer).

Too often, rightsizing was simplistically taken to refer to the practice of replacing an organization's mainframe computer with a less expensive minicomputer, a common practice encouraged by the intense cost pressures on businesses during the client/server era. Although replacing the mainframe computer was often a positive step, the real significance of rightsizing was that the designer had a choice.

Lately, as designers have gained experience by observing the systems they've designed, they have begun using a modified form of the client/server architecture, called the *three-tier* client/server architecture. The original form of client/server architecture split processing responsibility between a client, which usually provided user-interface and business logic, and a server, which took over the data-management tasks. Because of this division, the traditional client/server architecture consequently has become known as the *two-tier* client/server architecture. Figure 18.8 shows a typical instance of the three-tier client/server architecture.

The three-tier client/server architecture tries to solve several problems that hamper two-tier client/server architectures:

- **Driver maintenance:** In a two-tier system, each client system must be equipped with a driver for each database it accesses. Because vendors regularly distribute product updates, information systems staff must continually maintain and configure the drivers.

- **Database costs:** As client/server systems have become more popular, database vendors have begun charging for their products based on the maximum number of concurrent users. Because applications generally hold databases open for the duration of the user session, this constrains the number of clients the two-tier architecture can economically support.

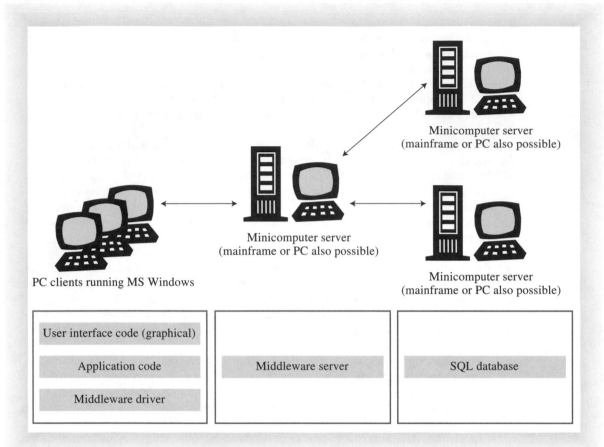

Minicomputer server
(mainframe or PC also possible)

Minicomputer server
(mainframe or PC also possible)

PC clients running MS Windows

Minicomputer server
(mainframe or PC also possible)

| User interface code (graphical) |
| Application code |
| Middleware driver |

| Middleware server |

| SQL database |

FIGURE 18.8

The three-tier client/server architecture

The three-tier architecture attacks these problems by interposing a so-called *middleware* server between the client and the database. In a three-tier architecture, your clients no longer communicate directly with the database. Instead, they communicate with the middleware server and must be equipped only with a relatively simple driver for the middleware server, instead of a driver for each database. In addition to acting as a conduit for connecting to the data-management server, the middle tier has become the ideal place to put the business logic portion of your application. Thus, when you change a business rule used in your application, you need only update the middleware server, and not the hundreds of clients using your program. Clients in three-tier architectures have come to be known as *thin clients* because they are easier to configure and maintain than so-called *fat clients*.

Middleware servers have done their parts well, caching data to improve performance and allowing multiple clients to share a single database connection, thereby reducing database licensing costs. Today, the two-tier and three-tier client/server architectures are those most commonly used for new system development. The client/server architecture is summarized in Table 18.5.

TABLE 18.5
SUMMARY OF THE CLIENT/SERVER ARCHITECTURE

Server hardware	PC
Client hardware	PCs
User interface technology	Graphical
Application programming technology	Various languages
Data management technology	Relational database
Cost`	Low to medium
Reliability	High
Security	High
Scalability	High
Flexibility	High

> " *The central idea of distributed architectures is that a single, centralized database might not be the ideal way to structure your organization's data, particularly if your organization is itself geographically dispersed.* "

DISTRIBUTED ARCHITECTURES

You've seen the traditional architecture, the ruler of the mainframe era; the file server architecture that rode the wave of PCs and local area networks to prominence; and the rise and refinement of two- and three-tier client/server architectures. What then is the fourth architecture: the distributed architecture? The term *distributed architecture* is commonly used to refer to any architecture in which a client accesses more than one server concurrently. Therefore, client/server architectures and distributed architectures overlap to a degree. In many client/server systems, however, a single server does almost all the work. Processing in such systems is not substantially distributed among the participating servers; therefore, they are better seen as client/server systems than as distributed systems.

The central idea of distributed architectures is that a single, centralized database might not be the ideal way to structure your organization's data, particularly if your organization is itself geographically dispersed. Suppose your company has offices in New York, Chicago, and Los Angeles. A nondistributed client/server architecture might consist of a central database located in Chicago and network connections reaching from Chicago to New York and Los Angeles.

This means that data pertaining to the Los Angeles office is stored in Chicago—even data that would be of no interest outside Los Angeles. To process its data, the Los Angeles office must transmit it and receive it across the network linking it with Chicago, possibly incurring costly telecommunications charges. In contrast, a distributed architecture, like that shown in Figure 18.9, attempts to locate data nearer to the point at which it's used most.

Two enabling technologies are key to your successful design and development of a distributed system: CORBA and RMI, which were presented in Chapter 13, "Designing Remote Objects." Before choosing a distributed architecture, be sure that you and your programmers have a solid understanding of one or both of these technologies. CORBA, RMI, and similar technologies let you change the topology of your

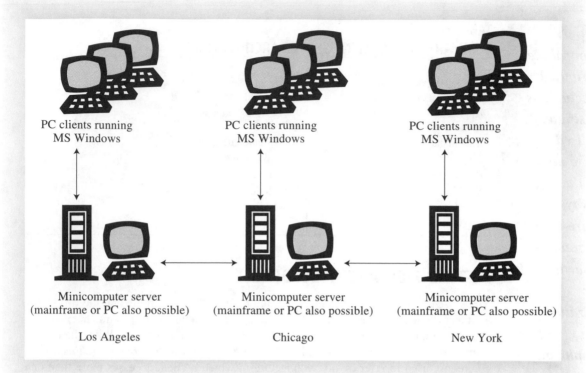

FIGURE 18.9

The distributed architecture

application without changing its classes. This topology independence is analogous to the data independence provided by a database management system and can similarly reduce the effort and cost of maintaining a distributed system.

Most developers, however, have had little or no experience in using CORBA or RMI. Unless you're willing to be exposed to significant risk of failure, your project plan should include education and training in these technologies.

JAVA AND THE WEB

Since the 1950s, user interfaces have gone from punched cards to point-and-click high-resolution displays. Database technologies have gone from reels of magnetic tape to online relational DBMS systems and data warehouses. But application processing technology has gone through no such upheaval—at least until now. Today, of course, there is Java.

The Java language and its APIs provide two key capabilities lacking in other popular languages:

- Portability
- Automatic software distribution

Because Java programs are portable, Java is an ideal language for implementing client software, which can then be run on any platform that offers a Java interpreter. Thus, platform independence can be added to the data independence provided by a relational database and the topology independence provided by an object request broker, such as CORBA or RMI.

In addition to being portable, Java programs are distributable. As shown in Figure 18.10, Java applets are automatically downloaded from a server when accessed, assuring that the user is running the latest (hopefully the most correct) version of the software. Related *push technologies*, such as Marimba's Castanet, allow updates to Java applications to be automatically propagated to client systems. Combined with a thin-client driver that talks to a middleware server, this can greatly reduce requirements for software maintenance of your client computers.

Together, Java and the Web provide you, the designer, with new architectural options. You can use the Web as a part of your telecommunications infrastructure, which can now reach outside your organization into the homes and businesses of millions of people. This opens up opportunities for you to develop new kinds of applications or to retrofit your existing applications for the Web. Even for those organizations with sensitive data best kept isolated from the Web, Java and intranets provide a completely new way to deploy and manage your application portfolio.

FIGURE 18.10
Running a Java applet

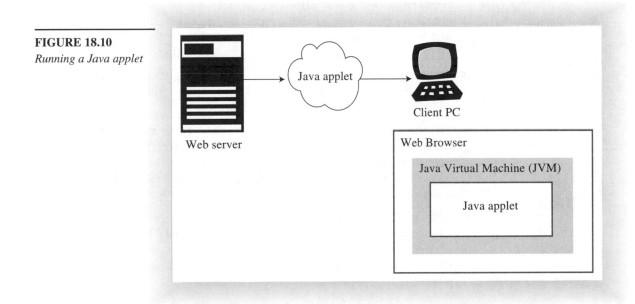

Choosing an Architecture

How should you choose an IS architecture? Well, your choice will be determined largely by the technologies available to you. Choosing which technologies to implement, however, is not really simple. As you ride technological waves from the past, to the present, and on to the future, you can erroneously end up too far ahead of the wave. If you had attempted to implement a client/server system during the early 1960s, for example, you would have faced a Herculean task. But, it's also possible to lag too far behind; this won't often result in complete and abject failure, but your organization will not be getting the best return on dollars invested in information technology, and you might be slowly building a ground-swell of user dissatisfaction.

The contingent, changing nature of information system architectures makes it difficult, and risky, to venture detailed advice. However, you won't go far wrong in following these broad principles:

- Don't get swept up in the latest architecture fad: Fads come and go, but good design abides forever. Recall how the concept of rightsizing became the oversimplified concept of downsizing. Search for, and analyze, the principles that underlie a new architecture before jumping on board.

- Provide users with an interface that is easy to learn and efficient to use. This is not as straightforward as it sounds. Graphical user interfaces are popular and easy to learn. However, applications that are easy to learn are not always easy to use when the user is no longer a novice. Remember, a user will be a novice only once; they'll be a user forever. Consider your users' productivity when you design your user interface.

- Allocate processing to clients and servers according to which can do the job better. Avoid dogmatism like that inherent in the traditional architecture and the file server architecture.

- Stay abreast of middleware products that might reduce the cost of maintaining client configurations and database licenses. Client/server technology changes rapidly. Use your Web browser to bookmark the pages of middleware vendors and regularly check their pages for product updates.

- Consider using distributed computing as a means of reducing telecommunications costs and balancing the processing load. Although telecommunications costs are dropping, they can still be enormous. Distributed computing is one tactic for coping, and poses the added possibility of reducing processor costs as well.

- If you decide to design a distributed system, make sure your programmers and other designers are trained in the use of distributed technologies such as CORBA or RMI. Because they're new, these technologies are not yet well understood by most designers and programmers. Don't learn about them the hard way, by fielding a system that fails. Do your homework before committing to a distributed design.

> *"Like any craft, the only real way to learn is through practice: Listen to your users; strive to accurately and completely understand their wants and needs; keep stocked at all times a full kit of up-to-date technical options."*

The End of the Line

Well, you've finally reached the end of the line, where all readers must disembark. Thanks for your diligent persistence, which we hope is rewarded many times over. Keep reading about design. Keep reviewing the designs of others. And, most of all, keep designing.

Like any craft, the only real way to learn is through practice: Listen to your users; strive to accurately and completely understand their wants and needs; keep stocked at all times a full kit of up-to-date technical options.

Remember, your job as a designer is to act as an agent for those who will use the artifacts you build. Be honest about your own failures. As Henry Ford said, "A mistake is an event, the full benefit of which has not yet been turned to your advantage." Try to see each failure as an opportunity to modify your design, bringing it ever closer to firmness, commodity, and delight.

Summary

An information system architecture is a pattern that describes typical relationships between clients, servers, and the network that joins them. Change in three key technologies has driven change in information system architecture: user interface technology, data management technology, and application processing technology. Over several decades, user interfaces have moved from textual to graphical, and data management has moved from file servers to relational databases accessed via Structured Query Language. With the advent of Java, applications have begun moving to a distributed, network-centered mode.

The traditional information system architecture—sometimes called the dumb-client, smart-server architecture—featured dumb terminals and a mainframe computer. Cheap microprocessors led to the file-sever information systems architecture—the smart-client, dumb-server architecture—featuring PC-based clients and a PC-based file server.

More recently, information systems have been built according to the client/server or distributed computing architectures. These architectures—the smart-client, smart-sever architectures—are more general than early architectures, allocating processing to client or server according to whichever is better suited to the task.

Whereas client/server generally involves a single primary server, distributed computing involves multiple clients and servers that cooperate in storing and processing geographically dispersed data. Technologies like CORBA and RMI, which help decouple an application from its network topology, are key to implementing a distributed information system architecture.

Java and related technologies provide new options for designers, who can avail themselves of platform-independent programs that are automatically downloaded, so that the most current version is the one run. Network-based applications, whether on the Web or an organization's intranet, are rapidly growing in use.

Questions

For multiple-choice items, indicate all correct responses.

1. An information system architecture is nothing more than a design _____.

    a. Document
    b. Pattern
    c. Formula
    d. Heuristic

2. The primary elements of an information system architecture are

    a. Clients
    b. Servers
    c. Networks
    d. Applications

3. The three primary technologies that have driven the evolution of information system architectures are

    a. User interface
    b. Application processing
    c. Programming languages
    d. Data management

4. A _____ is a special PC designed to run Java better than a standard PC.

5. The traditional information system architecture was characterized by low/high cost and low/high flexibility.

6. The file server information system architecture was characterized by low/high cost and low/high flexibility.

7. The client/server information system architecture usually allocates database processing to the _____.

8. The distributed information system architecture is characterized by the use of multiple _____.

9. Thin clients require the use of a _____ server, which requires the client to load only a single driver.

10. The key facilities offered by Java and its APIs, from an architectural standpoint, are

    a. SQL compatibility
    b. Portability
    c. Automatic software distribution
    d. An open standard

Exercises

1. Draw a geographical decomposition diagram and a network connectivity diagram for the customer deposit/withdrawal system of a small bank. Assume the bank has ATMs, branch offices, and a headquarters. Use fictional location names taken from your local community.

2. Using the Web, explore at least three alternative middleware technologies. The JDBC home page on Sun Microsoft's Java site will help you find them. Prepare a summary of their relative strengths and weaknesses, relative to one another and relative to two-tier client/server architectures.

3. Using the Web, explore at least three alternative "push" technologies that can help keep software and data on a client system up to date. Prepare a summary of their relative strengths and weaknesses. Use a search engine to help you find the home pages of companies that offer push technologies.

4. Using the Web or current periodicals, prepare a description of network computer products currently available. Show a network connectivity diagram that illustrates their use in a typical application of your choice.

To Learn More

The following books will help you learn more about information system architectures:

 Watterson, Karen. *Client/Server Technology for Managers*. Reading, Massachusetts: Addison-Wesley, 1995.

 This an excellent introduction to the organizational issues that surround client/server computing.

 Orfali, Robert, and Dan Harkey. *Client/Server Programming with Java and CORBA*. New York: John Wiley & Sons, 1997.

 Several of the references given in Chapter 13 are helpful in understanding how CORBA and RMI shape information system architectures. This title is particularly useful.

 The following books deal with architecture and design conceptually, without reference to specific technologies:

 Rechtin, Eberhardt. *Systems Architecting: Creating and Building Complex Systems*. Englewood Cliffs, New Jersey: Prentice Hall, 1991.

 Witt, Bernard, F. Terry Baker, and Everett Merritt. *Software Architecture and Design: Principles, Models, and Methods*. New York: Van Nostrand Reinhold, 1994.

Glossary

1NF   First normal form. No columns with repeating groups or compound values.

2NF   Second normal form. If the table has a composite key, every column must depend on all of the key.

3NF   Third normal form. No column is allowed to depend on any value except the primary key value.

abstract class   A class that contains one or more abstract methods or is specified as abstract. An abstract class can't be used to instantiate objects, although it can be extended.

abstract method   A method that has no implementation. The enclosing class is implicitly an abstract class.

abstraction   Ignoring the irrelevant so as to focus on the essential.

accessor   A method that doesn't alter the state (attributes) of an object, having the purpose of returning information.

accidental difference   When visual elements appear different but the difference doesn't signify a difference in meaning or purpose.

ActiveX   The current name for controls based on COM. Succeeds OLE/OCX.

ad hoc queries   Requests to retrieve information in ways that weren't anticipated when the data was stored.

adapter   (1) A class designed to make the built-in Java classes act like the classes in a container class library. (2) A class that implements the Adapter pattern.

Adapter pattern   A design pattern that provides a default implementation for a set of messages.

algorithm   The precise instructions used to carry out a task. When used in the context of a collection class library, algorithm refers to generic code to perform operations such as searching or sorting, without regard to the type of collection searched or sorted.

API   Acronym for *application programming interface*, the facilities offered by your operating system or programming language that allow your programs to access its features.

application logic   The processing specific to your application, as compared to generic operations such as user-interface design and data management.

application technology   Different methods for distributing application processing between clients and servers.

association   A uses relationship.

asynchronous interaction   Interaction that doesn't occur according to a prearranged schedule, in which multiple operations are simultaneously ongoing.

attribute   An element of data contained in an object, as specified within the object's class.

AWT   The Abstract Window Toolkit, the Java component that manages graphical user interfaces.

batch mode systems   Programs that primarily process data without interactive user input. The program that prints your payroll check is typically a batch-mode program.

BDK   Sun's Bean Development Kit.

Bean   A software component built according to the JavaBeans architecture.

Bean builder   A programmer who creates Beans, which can be used inside a visual application builder.

Bean event   The mechanism used by Beans to communicate with other Beans. Bean events provide the framework for building component-based applications.

Bean property   The mechanism used in the JavaBeans API to store state information that can be visually manipulated.

Bean user   A programmer who builds Java applications by using Beans inside a RAD environment.

BeanBox   A tool supplied in Sun's Bean Development Kit for testing interaction between Beans.

bi-directional relationship   An association in which objects exchange messages.

Boolean property   A single Boolean value manipulated by using the isXX() and setXX() methods.

bottom-up   An approach to software development that stresses experimentation and adaptation.

bound property   A type of property that accepts subscribers and notifies them when its value changes.

business rules   The logic that determines how your application runs. Another term for *application logic*.

button   A component that normally triggers an action when clicked.

canonical grid   A standardized layout grid that can be used as the basis for several different layouts: two-column, three-column, and so on.

cardinality   (1) The number of objects that may participate in a single instance of an object relationship. (2) The number of rows involved on each side of a database relationship. Key database cardinality relationships are 1:N (one-to-many), 1:1 (one-to-one), and N:N (many to many).

catalog   A database whose tables store information about other databases in an information system.

CGI   Common Gateway Interface, a facility that lets Web servers return the output of a program execution as a document.

checkbox   A component that stores an on/off choice, often used to specify an option. When part of a group of checkboxes, each checkbox can be on or off, allowing users to request combinations of options.

CHI   Acronym for *computer-human interaction*.

choice   A list box control that's activated and "dropped down" when users click a small arrow on the control. A choice control preserves valuable screen real estate by showing only the current choice.

clarity   The extent to which the designer's intentions are conveyed to users by the interface.

class   A combination of data and the operations that can be performed on that data.

class diagram   A design tool that shows the attributes and methods of a class.

class library   A collection of classes designed to work together to perform a particular job. The AWT, the JDBC, and the JGL are all examples of class libraries.

class relationship   A relationship between classes.

client   (1) The person or company who authorizes and pays for construction of your system. (2) An object or module that uses—or makes requests of—another object or module. (3) The desktop computer or terminal used to access a computer-based information system.

client object   An object that sends messages to other (server) objects.

client/server architecture   An information systems architecture in which processing responsibility is shared by the server and the client. Typically, the client performs the user-interface tasks and the server performs the data management tasks.

Clonable interface   Used to mark a class as supporting the clone() method.

COBOL   Acronym for *Common Business Oriented Language*. A computer programming language developed near the end of the 1950s, used primarily for data processing applications.

code salvaging   The practice of using "cut-and-paste" to reuse portions of a previous program in a current program.

coherence   The extent to which similar elements are grouped to form a unified whole, having all the parts work together.

cohesion   A property of an interface that represents a single, whole abstraction.

collaboration   A relationship between two classes, in which one uses services provided by the other (the collaborator) to perform its function.

collaboration diagram   A design tool that shows a single use case.

collection   A class designed to hold objects. Collection classes are also sometimes called *data structures*.

column   Used to store the individual attributes of a database table.

COM   Acronym for *Component Object Model*. Microsoft's architecture for communication between its software components in Windows 95/NT.

Command pattern   A design pattern that allows a message to be encapsulated as an object so that it can be stored, passed as an argument, or manipulated.

commodity   A software product that has the quality of commodity is fit for its intended purpose; it works and is effective.

composite key   The use of several columns to form a key.

Composite pattern   A design pattern that allows one object to contain other (nested) objects.

composition relationship   A relationship that exists when an object is composed of one or more objects.

compound object   An object composed of other objects.

compound value   A single column composed of several separate values.

concurrent program   A program that works simultaneously on multiple tasks.

constrained property   A bound property that also allows its subscribers to prohibit a particular change.

contraction   Overriding a method inherited from a superclass with an empty method.

copy semantics   The method that an object uses (either by reference or by value) to produce a copy of an object. By default, Java uses reference copy semantics for objects and value copy semantics for primitive types. To change the semantics for a class, override `clone()`.

CORBA   Acronym for *Common Object Request Broker*. A set of specifications for creating distributed information systems, using various technologies.

coupling   The relative degree to which a relationship causes participating objects to depend on one another.

CRC card   A design tool prepared by using a 3×5 card that shows the responsibilities and collaborations of a class.

critical code   Statements that execute only if a designated monitor is available.

CRT   Acronym for *cathode ray tube*, the dominant technology used to make computer video displays.

customization   (1) The extent to which users can select an interaction model they prefer, and suppress others. (2) The Java API facility that allows a bean builder to create custom tools that can be invoked to manipulate the bean when it's added to a RAD environment.

customized property   A property that's not simple, Boolean, or indexed. Requires using the BeanInfo interface.

data independence   The ability to change a data source (such as a database table or a file) without affecting the applications that use that data source. Database systems usually exhibit more data independence, whereas file-based systems tend to exhibit less.

data integrity   A software quality factor that indicates low risk of inaccurate or lost data.

data management   The tasks necessary to enable access to a data source. Typically, data management tasks include providing facilities for security and protection of data, for mediating contention, and for controlling data redundancy.

data redundancy   Storing the same information in multiple places in the database. Data redundancy can lead to data corruption if one part of the data is updated and another isn't.

database anomaly   Data corruption or loss, usually as a result of storing data in non-normalized tables.

database driver   Software that allows your application to "talk to" a database management system.

database engine   Synonym for *database management system*.

database management system   Software that provides generic data management facilities (access, security, locking, recovery, and transactions) for a variety of applications.

database normalization   The process of checking your tables to make sure that they conform to certain rules designed to avoid database anomalies. Steps are first normal form (1NF), second normal form (2NF), and third normal form (3NF).

database server   Synonym for *database management system*.

DBMS   Acronym for *database management system*.

DCOM   Acronym for *Distributed Component Object Model*, a Microsoft architecture for distributed computing.

deadlock   A condition in which two or more threads mutually wait for the other(s), with the result that none actually execute.

decomposition   Breaking a complex structure into a set of smaller, simpler structures.

Decorator pattern   A design pattern that allows the capabilities of an object to be extended at runtime.

deep copy   To make a copy of an object, deep copying uses *value semantics* to make an entirely new object.

delete anomaly   May occur when deleting a row of an unnormalized table. The anomaly causes information about a related entity instance to be lost.

delight   A software product that has the quality of delight is attractive and a pleasure to use; it is elegant.

deque   Abbreviation for *double-ended queue* (pronounced "deck"). An array-like container that allows elements to be added at either the front or back.

design   (1) A process of determining the structure and composition of a product, balancing the demands of commodity, firmness, and delight. (2) A software development activity that identifies an appropriate technical solution that satisfies the system requirements.

design pattern   A common design problem and its solutions, described and packaged for ease of application.

design time   Occurring when designing an application—as opposed to when running the finished application. Programmers can visually manipulate Java beans during design time.

distributed architecture   An architecture that distributes additional processing on multiple servers and isn't typically tied to a single database server. Distributed architectures usually include the use of technologies like RMI and CORBA.

DOD   Acronym for the U.S. *Department of Defense*.

downsizing   (1) Taking an application running on a mainframe and putting it on a minicomputer or PC. (2) Corporate staff reductions designed to increase profitability.

DPI or dpi   Acronym for *dots per inch*. Unit of measure for the resolution of video-display terminals and laser or inkjet printers.

dumb terminal   A terminal (keyboard and video CRT display) with no local processing power or storage.

E/R modeling   Entity-relationship modeling. The first step in logical database design.

elegance   A quality of a visual interface that possesses novelty, simplicity, economy, and efficiency.

encapsulation   A technique that separates the interface of a class from its implementation.

entity   Information about a thing or concept. Like objects, entities are usually the nouns in a database design model.

environment   The hardware and software environment in which a program runs.

exception mechanisms   The means by which errors are returned to users of a class library.

Factory pattern   A design pattern that allows construction of an instance of a specified subclass of a given superclass.

feedback   The extent to which your users can tell what happened when they interacted with your interface.

file-based system   An information system based on files unique to that system. A file-system based architecture puts the responsibility for data integrity on each application that accesses the data.

FileDialog class   A Java class that uses the native file-picking dialog to select files.

file-server architecture   An architecture that uses a local area network to provide centralized file storage for a group of PCs. In the file-server architecture, application processing is performed on the client, not the server.

fine-grained components   Components designed for general-purpose use. GUI controls, networking components, and graphics controls are all examples of fine-grained components.

firmness   A software product that has the quality of firmness is fast and small and continues working in a wide range of situations; it's efficient and robust.

first normal form   No columns with repeating groups or compound values.

FK   Acronym for *foreign key*.

flexibility   The ability to have the same application run across several different architectures.

font   A particular size and style of a typeface.

foreign key   A key used to identify rows in another table for purposes of linking two tables in a relationship. A foreign key is the primary key in the foreign table.

forgiveness   The extent to which your interface allows your users to recover from mistakes.

form follows function   Guiding principle of the Bauhaus design movement. Stipulates that the ideal design eschews ornamentation, and instead flows from the functional description of the artifact.

function objects   Algorithms that can be instantiated and passed as objects to other methods.

functionality   The functions or services provided by an object.

generalization   A superclass is a generalization of its subclass.

generic programming   Writing programs and classes that are unconcerned about the type of objects they operate on. The Java Generic Library, for instance, is designed to provide collections and algorithms that operate on many different objects.

geographic decomposition diagram   Shows the location of users in an information system architecture.

goal-oriented design   An interaction methodology that ignores how things are currently accomplished and instead asks, "What does the user want to accomplish?"

guarded method   A method that tests a condition and executes only if the condition is true; otherwise, it waits for the condition to asynchronously change.

GUI   Acronym for *graphical user interface*. Also sometimes called the *WIMP interface* for its chief distinguishing elements: windows, icons, menus, and pointing devices.

hashtable   A collection organized as key-value pairs. The actual implementation of a hashtable may use either a vector or a list.

hierarchy   A pyramidal model that shows how categories are related.

high bandwidth   The ability to move large amounts of data over a network, very quickly.

host   A generic term that can refer to clients and servers (because they can both host applications) but which usually refers only to a server.

host application   The program the supplies the framework in which components operate.

host-based computing   An alternative term for the traditional mainframe-based IS architecture.

IC   Acronym for *integrated circuit*. A prebuilt electronic component used to construct computers.

IDE   Acronym for *integrated development environment*. These programming tools give programmers a single environment for building programs rather than individual editors and debuggers.

IDL   Acronym for *Interface Definition Language*, which allows the interface of an object to be described in a language-independent manner.

IIOP   Acronym for *Internet Inter-ORB Protocol*, which allows objects to interact across a network by using object request brokers.

implementation   (1) The private attributes and methods of a class. (2) The details of how an object accomplishes its services.

incremental development   An approach to software development that divides a system into many pieces, each of which has value to the user, and strives to deliver each piece rapidly.

indexed property   A set of values that can be individually set and retrieved or can be set and retrieved en masse.

information systems architecture   The arrangement and deployment of applications and responsibilities. The IS architecture includes the physical components (clients, servers, and the network) and the logical components (user interface, application logic, and data management).

inheritance   A relation between two classes in which one inherits the attributes and methods of another.

inner class   A Java 1.1 feature that allows one or more classes to be defined within the body of an enclosing class.

insert anomaly   An anomaly associated with an unnormalized table, in which adding a new record causes inconsistent or invalid data.

instance   An individual object of some class.

interaction diagram   A diagram that shows the interactions among the objects of a program.

interface   (1) The publicly available attributes and methods of a class. (2) The services an object provides to client objects. (3) The Java language keyword and construct used to define a pure specification which may be implemented by a class.

interface consistency   An interface is consistent when all the methods use similar naming conventions and similar copy semantics.

interface repository   A CORBA database that describes object services and interfaces for accessing them.

interface technology   Methods of user interaction: menus, buttons, mice, overlapping windows, and so forth.

introspection   The Java API facility that allows a builder tool to inspect the class file of a bean and determine the properties and events that the bean responds to.

iterator   A class that works in concert with a collection class to allow you to traverse the elements in the class.

Iterator pattern   A design pattern that allows the elements of a collection to be sequentially traversed, without exposing the structure of the collection.

JAR file   A Java archive file that allows you to package multiple class, graphic, and property files in a single disk file. Built using the jar utility from the JDK.

JavaBean   Software component built using Java, designed to be used in Java programs and manipulated in a Java GUI builder tool.

JDBC   Acronym for the *Java Database Connectivity* package, which provides Java programs access to SQL and legacy database systems.

JDBC-ODBC bridge   A software program that connects JDBC programs to ODBC-compliant databases.

JGL   The Java Generic Library from ObjectSpace Inc. A freely available class library based on the generic programming ideas developed in the C++ Standard Template Library.

key   A column whose value identifies each row.

LAN   Acronym for *local area network*. A high-speed network between relatively nearby computers (for example, the same office or building).

large-grained component   A component designed to solve a problem in a specific industry or for a particular type of product.

layout grid   Use of symmetrical or regular divisions to arrange your layout.

layout manager   A class used to position and size visual components in a Java program.

list   A linear collection in which elements aren't necessarily contiguous and the next element relationship is explicitly specified by a reference held as part of the element. Lists provide only sequential traversal.

list box   A vertically scrolling list of strings that allows users to select one or several of the strings.

liveness failure   A program failure due to starvation or deadlock.

logical database design   The process of determining which entities and relationships will be required in your database.

logical design   The partitioning of different tasks—user interface, application logic, and data management—among the different physical elements of your IS architecture.

mandatory association   An association that must exist between or among a set of objects.

map   A container class organized as key-value pairs. A dictionary is a type of map.

master-genie syndrome   A method of interaction that requires particular responses be given in a particular order to accomplish a task.

message   Sent to an object, it triggers a behavior.

method   (1) A behavior or operation of an object. (2) A procedure used by an object to respond to a message, as specified within the object's class.

methodology   A prescribed way of using software abstractions that includes a process, notations, and heuristics.

middleware server   A server program that sits between the database server and the client software, which may provide driver or business-logic services.

modal interface   Another name for a master-genie interface.

model   An abstract representation of something real or imaginary.

monitor   An invisible 1-bit field associated with every object, used to synchronize access to the object.

monospaced typeface   A typeface in which every character has the same width, as opposed to a proportional face in which some characters (such as m) are wider than others (such as i). The popular Courier font is a monospaced typeface.

multitasking   The ability of a computer to run several programs apparently simultaneously by switching between them.

mutator   A method that alters the state (attributes) of an object.

MVC pattern   The *model-view-controller pattern* that alerts a client when the state of a server is changed. Implemented in Java by using the `Observable` class and the `Observer` interface.

NC   The *Network Computer*. An inexpensive, Java-based computer with limited local storage but with extensive local processing capabilities.

network   The combination of hardware (cables and network interface cards) and software (network operating system) that allows different computers to communicate and work together, sharing data and applications.

network connectivity diagram   Shows the location of clients and servers in an information system architecture.

null layout manager   Removing the layout manager so you can position and size each component by using absolute pixel measurements.

object   The building block of an object-oriented program, an object possesses identity, data (called state), and behavior.

object bus   A network that links objects by using one or more object request brokers.

object relationship   A relationship between objects.

object-oriented design   A design methodology based on object-oriented programming.

object-oriented programming   Programming that uses classes and objects as the fundamental components of a program.

Observer pattern   A design pattern that keeps client objects advised of changes in the state of a server object.

OCX control   The successor technology to OLE controls.

ODBC   Acronym for the *Open Database Connectivity* standard. A standard method for communicating with different database servers.

OLE control   A control that uses Object Linking and Embedding; Microsoft's original name for its 32-bit software components.

online systems   Applications that provide interactive, instantaneous access to data, rather than process it in large chunks. Your bank's ATM machine is part of an online system.

OOD   Object-oriented design.

operation   (1) The phase during the life of a software system in which it is in actual use. (2) A method or service provided by an object.

optional association   An association that may, but need not, exist between or among a set of objects.

optional relationship   Whether the rows on both sides of a relationship must be present for either to exist.

ORB   Acronym for *object request broker*, which provides references to remote objects and marshals method arguments and return values.

overload   To define a new method with the same name but a different signature (number and types of arguments) as a method in the same class or a superclass.

overloaded constructor   A constructor that exists in several forms, each having a different number or types of arguments.

override   To define a new method with the same name and signature (number and types of arguments) as a method in a superclass.

palette   The visual library of components inside a RAD environment, from which a bean user can select components.

paradigm   A perspective or way of looking at something; a pattern.

parameter marshaling   An RPC facility that automatically sends procedure or function arguments across a network connection.

part-of relationship   A composition relationship.

persistence   The ability to store data on a (semi)permanent medium, such as magnetic tape or disks.

physical database design   The process of translating your logical database model to tables, rows, and columns.

physical design   The architectural choices you'll make in deciding which types of clients, servers, and network your system will use.

PK   Acronym for *primary key*.

polymorphic inheritance   A relationship that holds when a class implements methods specified in an interface or inherited from an abstract superclass, but also overrides one or more methods inherited from a superclass.

polymorphism   The ability of two subclasses of a single superclass to respond differently to an identical message.

predicate functions   Function objects that allow you to query the state of an object in a collection class, and which generally return Boolean results.

predictability   The extent to which your users can tell what will happen when they interact with your interface.

preemptive multitasking   The ability to switch between execution of programs that weren't specially written to allow this. Multitasking that requires special programming is called *cooperative multitasking*.

presentation component   The portion of your information system that presents data to users and with which users interact.

primary key   The non-optional value that uniquely identifies each row in a database table.

priority queue   A queue in which elements are kept in sorted order, so that the item with the highest priority is always at the front of the queue. Items of the same priority are accessed as a regular FIFO queue.

problem summary paragraph   A paragraph that describes a problem to be solved in terms of the characteristics any solution must possess.

procedural decomposition   A structured design technique that attempts to find a series of steps that, performed in sequence, solve a given problem.

procedure   (1) A single step within a process. (2) Within a procedural program, a unit of code larger than a statement.

process   (1) The steps necessary to carry out a task. (2) A separate flow of control within a program, which has its own address space.

programming   The software development activity that produces the program source code.

property support classes　Classes used to manage both bound and constrained properties and which facilitate maintaining lists of subscribers.

property sheet　A dialog box that displays the properties of a component and provides the environment for manipulating those properties.

prototyping　An approach to software development that relies on working models of the system to explore system requirements.

proxy　A server stub or skeleton server.

Publish-subscribe　The design pattern used to describe how beans communicate.

push technologies　The ability to send information to a client without the client first initiating a request.

queue　A sequence in which elements may only be added at the end and removed at the front. A queue is thus a first-in-first-out (FIFO) data structure.

race condition　A computation for which the result varies depending on the order of execution of multiple threads.

RAD　Acronym for *Rapid Application Development*.

RAD tool　A component-based software development tool that relies on programmers visually arranging the interface and manipulating components.

radio button　A component that allows users to make a single selection from many. Works like old-fashioned radio buttons in an automobile.

reference semantics　When adding an element to a container or making a copy of an object, produces a reference to the original object rather than a duplicate object.

referential attribute　A field that refers to an object.

reflection　The Java API facility used to support introspection.

relational database　Collections of files arranged into tables with a formalized structure uniting them. Also refers to the software that manages such collections.

relational DBMS　Database management systems based on E.F. Codd's relational database concepts. Today, almost all DBMS systems are relational.

relationship   Rules governing the connections between different entities. Relationships include the optional/required quality and cardinality.

reliability   A software quality factor that refers to an architecture or system's capability to ensure the integrity of data and availability of access.

repeating groups   When a single column in a single row holds multiple (array-like) values.

requirements analysis   A software development activity that identifies the requirements a system must satisfy to achieve its goal.

responsibility   A service or operation provided by a class.

rightsizing   Partitioning processing among clients and servers to make use of the best qualities of each.

RMI   Acronym for *Remote Method Invocation*, a Java technology used to create distributed systems with Java components. Where not all the components are Java-based, you should use CORBA instead.

row   Instance of an individual entity stored in a table. A row is composed of multiple columns.

RPC   Acronym for *remote procedure call*, a technology that allows programs to invoke functions that run on remote computers.

runtime   The period during which a component-based application is interacting with users. Components have both a runtime and a design-time interface.

runtime exceptions   Exceptions that are part of the built-in Java exception hierarchy and are thrown by the Java virtual machine.

safety failure   A program failure due to a race condition.

sans serif typeface   A type family that doesn't have small filigrees at the ends of each stroke. Popular sans serif faces include Helvetica and Arial.

scalability   An architecture's capability to be moved to larger and more powerful hardware or to be deployed in wider distribution without unwanted deterioration of its performance.

SDLC   Acronym for the Software Development Life Cycle, a division of the task of creating software into a series of activities, performed in phases.

second normal form   If the table has a composite key, every column must depend on all of the key.

security   The ability to manage and control access to data.

self relationship   When a single entity is related to itself, such as the parts in a parts catalog.

sequence   A container in which one element follows (or precedes) another. Sequences include lists and vectors but not trees.

Serializable interface   Used to mark a class to indicate that all the methods and attributes of the class can be made persistent (that is, copied to a file or stream.)

serialization   The Java API facility that allows a bean to convert its state into a stream and then send that stream over the network or save it to a persistent medium.

serif typeface   A type family that includes small filigrees at the ends of each stroke. Originally designed to make stone-carved letters more durable. Serif faces include Times Roman and Century Schoolbook.

server object   An object that responds to messages sent by client objects, by performing actions or returning data.

server stub   A client-side program that acts as a stand-in for a server running on a remote computer.

set   A map that includes the restriction that only unique values can be stored.

shallow copy   To make a copy of an object, shallow copying uses reference semantics to return a new reference to the same object.

signature   The number and types of arguments of a method.

simple extension   A relationship that holds when a subclass adds new fields or methods to those it inherits from its superclass, but doesn't override any superclass methods.

simple property   A property that manipulates a single non-boolean value by using the getXX() and setXX() methods.

single-direction relationship   An association in which an object sends messages to another object, but the second object sends no messages to the first object.

Singleton pattern   A design pattern that ensures that a class has only a single instance.

skeleton server   A server-side program that acts as a stand-in for a client running on a remote computer.

software components   Highly reusable software objects designed to be manipulated in a RAD tool.

software crisis   The prevalence of software that's late, costs too much, or doesn't work as planned.

software reuse   Creating objects and classes that can be "dropped into" a current project, or of creating classes that operate on a wide variety of different objects. The goals of software reuse include reduced software costs and increased software reliability. Generic programming and component software are both methods of software reuse.

spatial grouping   Using white space to put similar visual elements closer to each other and separate disparate elements.

specialization   A subclass is a specialization of its superclass.

specification inheritance   A relationship that holds when a class implements the methods specified in an `interface` or inherited from an `abstract` superclass.

SQL   Acronym for *Structured Query Language*, the standard language for accessing data in the relational databases of a client/server system.

squint test   Viewing a visual design by squinting so that the most noticeable attributes are apparent.

stack   A sequence where elements may only be added at the front and removed from the front. A stack is thus a last-in-first-out (LIFO) data structure.

starvation   A condition in which a thread doesn't get sufficient access to the CPU and therefore can't do its work.

STL   Acronym for the *Standard Template Library*. Part of the Standard C++ Library, which provides generic collections and algorithms.

Strategy pattern   A design pattern that generalizes the Command design pattern, encapsulating an entire family of algorithms.

structured design   A methodology based on structured programming.

software development life cycle   A division of the task of creating software into a series of activities, performed in phases.

structured programming   A technique that simplifies the structure of a program's flow of control.

subclass   A class that inherits the attributes and methods of a superclass.

subtype   A subclass is said to be a subtype of its superclass, because an instance of the subclass may appear wherever an instance of the superclass is allowed.

summary paragraph   A paragraph that describes what a program must do, used as a starting point for design.

superclass   A class that provides its attributes and methods to a subclass.

symmetry   The regular positioning of elements and groups in a visual interface.

`SystemColor` class   A Java class that allows you to specify component colors, which users can change through the operating system utilities.

tables   Information about a single entity in a relational database. Tables are organized as rows and columns.

task-oriented design   An interaction methodology that focuses on automating the manual procedures currently used.

template   A file used as a starting point for writing the source code of a Java class.

testing   A software development activity that attempts to assess and improve the quality of the software.

thin client   An architecture in which the client (desktop) machine is responsible for the user-interface portion of the application.

third normal form   No column is allowed to depend on any value except the primary key value.

thread   A separate flow of control within a program that shares an address space (access to fields) with other threads.

thread-safe   An object whose state remains valid during execution of its methods by multiple threads. By design, a thread-safe object isn't subject to safety or liveness failures.

three-tier client/server   The use of a separate server program that acts as an intermediary between client software and database servers. Such middleware can provide both driver and business logic services.

time-sharing   The use of preemptive multitasking in the traditional architecture to allow multiple clients to simultaneously connect to a single server.

tool builder   A programmer who or organization that creates environments for building applications by using components. Borland, Symantec, and Microsoft are all tool builders.

top-down   An approach to software development that stresses planning, control, and documentation.

traditional IS architecture   The use of dumb terminals and superservers (large-scale servers). In the traditional architecture, all of an application's processing, including user-interface processing, is carried out on the server. This is the traditional mainframe type of application.

transaction   A business event or user request to which a system must record or respond.

two-tier client/server   The processing in a two-tier application is shared between the client and the server machine, with the server usually performing the data-management chores. The client will usually handle the business logic and the user-interface portion of the application.

typeface   A family of type styles, such as Times Roman or Helvetica.

unchecked exceptions   Exceptions that are subclasses of `RuntimeException` or `Error`, and don't require programmers to specify the exceptions that may be thrown by the affected method.

update anomaly   An anomaly, resulting from unnormalized database structure, in which changing the data in a single row causes the data in other rows to become inconsistent.

usability   The extent to which the "feel" of an application helps or hinders users.

use case   A description of a transaction that focuses on the interactions between related objects.

user interface   The part of a computer program that interacts with users.

uses **relationship**   A relationship that exists when an object sends a message to another object.

value semantics   When adding an element to a container or making a copy of an object, value semantics produces a duplicate of the original object, rather than just a reference to the original.

VBX control   A control that uses *Visual Basic Extensions*, software components used in Microsoft's Visual Basic for 16-bit Windows.

VCL control   A control that uses the Visual Component Library, the component model used in Borland's Delphi and C++ Builder development environments.

vector   A collection (data structure) in which elements are arranged in a contiguous, linear order, and which provides random, indexed access to its elements. Similar to an array, the vector is resizable.

veto   The action a subscriber takes when disallowing a change specified by a publisher.

visual manipulation   The ability to directly manipulate—by dragging, dropping, and working with property sheets—the design-time representation of a software component.

waterfall model   An approach to software development that endeavors to treat the software development life cycle activities as phases and to move strictly forward from one phase to the next.

weak association   A relationship that exists when an object depends on another object but never sends messages to or receives messages from the other object.

X-terminal   Specialized terminal hardware for accessing applications based on the UNIX X-Windows system.

Bibliography

Alexander, Christopher. *A Pattern Language: Towns, Buildings, Construction*. New York: Oxford University Press, 1977.

Alexander, Christopher. *A Timeless Way of Building*. New York: Oxford University Press, 1987.

Arnold, Ken, and James Gosling. *The Java Programming Language*. Reading, Massachusetts: Addison-Wesley, 1996.

Booch, Grady. *Object-Oriented Analysis and Design with Applications*, 2nd ed. Redwood City, California: Benjamin/Cummings, 1994.

Borenstein, Nathaniel. *Programming as if People Mattered*. Princeton, New Jersey: Princeton University Press, 1991.

Bruce, Thomas A. *Designing Quality Databases with IDEF1X Information Methods*. New York: Dorset House, 1992.

Budd, Timothy. *Data Structures in C++ Using the Standard Template Library*. Reading, Massachusetts: Addison-Wesley, 1998.

Carrol, Martin, and Margaret A. Ellis. *Designing and Coding Reusable C++*. Reading, Massachusetts: Addison-Wesley, 1995.

Constantine, Larry L. *Constantine on Peopleware*. New Jersey: Hall Computer Books, 1995.

Cooper, Alan. *About Face: The Essentials of User Interface Design*. Foster City, California: Programmers Press, 1995.

Cornell, Gary, and Cay S. Horstmann. *Core Java 1.1: Fundamentals*. Englewood Cliffs, New Jersey: Prentice Hall, 1997.

Cox, Brad. "There Is a Silver Bullet." *Byte*, Oct. 1990, pp. 209-218.

Cox, Brad. "Planning the Software Industrial Revolution," *IEEE Software*, Nov. 1990, pp. 25-33.

Cox, Brad, and Andrew Novobilski. *Object-Oriented Programming: An Evolutionary Approach*. Reading, Massachusetts: Addison-Wesley, 1986.

Date, C.J. *An Introduction to Database Systems*, 6th ed. Reading, Massachusetts: Addison-Wesley, 1995.

Degrace, P., and L. Stahl. *Wicked Problems, Righteous Solutions: A Catalog of Modern Software Engineering Paradigms*. Englewood Cliffs, New Jersey: Yourdon Press, 1990.

DeMarco, Tom and Timothy Lister. *Peopleware: Productive Projects and Teams*. New York: Dorset House Publishing Co., 1987.

DeMarco, Tom and Timothy Lister. *Software State-of-the-Art: Selected Papers*. New York: Dorset House Publishing Co., 1990.

Englander, Robert. *Developing Java Beans*. Sebastopol, California: O'Reilly, 1997.

Feghhi, Jalal. *Web Developer's Guide to Java Beans*. Albany, New York: Coriolis Group, 1997.

Fowler, Martin, with Kendall Scott. *UML Distilled: Applying the Standard Object Modeling Language*. Reading, Massachusetts: Addison-Wesley, 1997.

Gabriel, Richard P. *Patterns of Software: Tales from the Software Community*. New York: Oxford University Press, 1996.

Gamma, Erich, et al. *Design Patterns: Elements of Reusable Object-Oriented Software*. Reading, Massachusetts: Addison-Wesley, 1995.

Gilbert, Stephen, and Bill McCarty. *Object-Oriented Programming in Java*. Corte Madera, California: The Waite Group Press, 1997.

Gosling, James, Bill Joy, and Guy Steele. *The Java Language Specification*. Reading, Massachusetts: Addison-Wesley, 1996.

Hernandez, Michael J. *Database Design for Mere Mortals: A Hands-On Guide to Relational Database Design*. Reading, Massachusetts: Addison-Wesley, 1997.

Hoare, C.A.R. *Communicating Sequential Processes*. New York: Prentice Hall, 1985.

Holub, Alan. *Enough Rope to Shoot Yourself in the Foot: Rules for C and C++ Programming*. New York: McGraw-Hill, 1995.

Horstmann, Cay. *Mastering Object-Oriented Design in C++*. New York: John Wiley & Sons, 1995.

Horstmann, Cay. *Practical Object-Oriented Development in C++ and Java*. New York: John Wiley & Sons, 1997.

Knuth, Donald. *The Art of Computer Programming: Fundamental Algorithms* (vol. 1, 3rd ed.). Reading, Massachusetts: Addison-Wesley, 1997.

Lafore, Robert. *Data Structures In Java*. Corte Madera, California: The Waite Group Press, 1998.

Lea, Doug. *Concurrent Programming in Java: Design Principles and Patterns*. Reading, Massachusetts: Addison-Wesley, 1997.

Lemay, Laura, and Charles Perkins. *Teach Yourself Java 1.1 in 21 Days*. Indianapolis, Indiana: Sams Publishing, 1997.

Lemay, Laura, and Charles Perkins. *Laura Lemay's Java 1.1 Interactive Course*. Corte Madera, California: The Waite Group Press, 1997.

Manasi, Mark. *Secrets of Effective GUI Design*. Alameda, California: Sybex, 1994.

McConnell, Steve. *Code Complete*. Redmond, Washington: Microsoft Press, 1993.

McConnell, Steve. *Rapid Development: Taming Wild Software Schedules*. Redmond, Washington: Microsoft Press, 1996.

McIntosh, Harry, and Lynnzy Orr. *Talk Java to Me : The Interactive Click, Listen, and Learn Guide to Java Programming*. Corte Madera, California: The Waite Group Press, 1996.

Meyers, Scott. *Effective C++: 50 Specific Ways to Improve Your Programs and Designs*. Reading, Massachusetts: Addison-Wesley, 1997.

Microsoft Press. *The Windows Interface Guidelines for Software Design*. Redmond, Washington: 1995.

Mullet, Kevin, and Darrell Sano. *Designing Visual Interfaces*. Englewood Cliffs, New Jersey: SunSoft Press, 1995.

Norman, Donald. *The Design of Everyday Things*. New York: Doubleday, 1990.

Orfali, Robert, and Dan Harkey. *Client/Server Programming With Java And CORBA*. New York: John Wiley & Sons, 1997.

Orfali, Robert, Dan Harkey, and Jeri Edwards. *The Essential Distributed Objects Survival Guide*. New York: John Wiley & Sons, 1996.

Otte, Randy, Paul Patrick, and Mark Roy. *Understanding CORBA: The Common Object Request Broker Architecture*. Upper Saddle River, New Jersey: Prentice Hall, 1996.

Page-Jones, M. *The Practical Guide to Structured Systems Design*. Englewood Cliffs, New Jersey: Yourdon Press, 1988.

Pree, Wolfgang. *Design Patterns for Object-Oriented Software Development*. New York: ACM Press Books, 1995.

Pressman, R. *Software Engineering: A Practitioner's Approach*, 4th ed. New York: McGraw-Hill, 1996.

Priestley, Mark. *Practical Object-Oriented Design*. New York: McGraw-Hill, 1997.

Rechtin, Eberhardt. *Systems Architecting: Creating And Building Complex Systems*. Englewood Cliffs, New Jersey: Prentice Hall, 1991.

Riel, Arthur J. *Object-Oriented Design Heuristics*. Reading, Massachusetts: Addison-Wesley, 1996.

Rubinstein, Richard, and Harry Hersh. *The Human Factor: Designing Computer Systems for People*. Bedford, Massachusetts: Digital Press, 1984.

Rumbaugh, James, et al. *Object-Oriented Modeling and Design*. Englewood Cliffs, New Jersey: Prentice Hall, 1991.

Sedgewick, Robert. *Algorithms in C++*. Reading, Massachusetts: Addison-Wesley, 1992.

Siegel, Jon. *CORBA: Fundamentals and Programming*. New York: John Wiley & Sons, 1996.

Simon, Herbert. *The Sciences of the Artificial*. Cambridge, Massachusetts: MIT Press, 1996.

Sridharan, Prashant. *Java Beans Developer's Resource*. Upper Saddle River, New Jersey: Prentice Hall, 1997.

Standish, Thomas. *Data Structures in Java*. Reading, Massachusetts: Addison-Wesley, 1997.

Watterson, Karen. *Client/Server Technology For Managers*. Reading, Massachusetts: Addison-Wesley, 1995.

White, Iseult. *Using the Booch Method: A Rational Approach*. Redwood City, California: Benjamin/Cummings, 1994.

Wiess, Mark Allen. *Data Structures and Problem Solving Using Java*. Reading, Massachusetts: Addison-Wesley, 1998.

Wilkinson, Nancy. *Using CRC Cards: An Informal Approach to Object-Oriented Development*. New York: SIGS, 1995.

Wirfs-Brock, Rebecca, Brian Wilkerson, and Lauren Wiener. *Designing Object-Oriented Software*. Englewood Cliffs, New Jersey: Prentice Hall, 1990.

Witt, Bernard, F. Terry Baker, and Everett Merritt. *Software Architecture And Design: Principles, Models, and Methods*. New York: Van Nostrand Reinhold, 1994.

Yourdon, Edward, and Larry Constantine. *Structured Design: Fundamentals of a Discipline of Computer Program and System Design*. Englewood Cliffs, New Jersey: Yourdon Press, 1986.

Product Reference

Java Generic Library

The Java Generic Library (JGL) is available from ObjectSpace, Inc. at its Web site http://www.objectspace.com/.

CORBA Products and Information

Sun Microsystems, Inc. maintains a Web page that can help you locate CORBA products at http://jsg.cuesta.com/. Searching for the keyword *CORBA* will access the current list of products.

Another excellent source for information on CORBA products from many vendors is the Web site maintained by Software Technologies Ltd. at http://www.sw-technologies.com/. The site also contains useful information on Java, databases, middleware, and many other topics.

Sun distributes a lightweight CORBA ORB that's compatible with Java 1.1. The product, known as Java IDL, can be downloaded at no cost from http://java.sun.com/ products/jdk/idl/index.html.

IBM, Netscape, Oracle, and Sun have released a joint position paper proposing CORBA extensions to integrate Java beans. Current information on this effort is available on the Object Management Group's Web page (http://www.omg.org/) and the Web sites of the participants.

Visigenic's Visibroker, used as the basis for the CORBA example in Chapter 13, can be found at http://www.visigenic.com/.

Quiz
Answers

Chapter 1

1. A designer approaching a software product from the engineering perspective would most likely be concerned with the quality of **firmness**.

2. When you ignore irrelevant or extraneous details, you are using the process of **abstraction**.

3. A map, a novel, and a blueprint are all examples of a **model** of something real or imaginary.

4. An effective way to understand a complex process is to break it into smaller pieces, using the process called **decomposition**.

5. A software designer who was primarily concerned with creating attractive buttons and screen layouts would be focusing on the design quality of **delight**.

6. b. complex, easily changed, and invisible.

7. A software development methodology uses a **notation** to represent a set of models, and prescribes a **process** for using those models.

8. A designer acts as an agent for the client, designing artifacts that meet the client's needs. Her designs will exhibit the quality of **commodity** if she is successful.

9. The abstraction process of **classification** allows us to tell the difference between a garden hose and a rattlesnake.

10. A primary reason for designing a program before writing it is because it is **less expensive** to make a change to a design than to a shipping program.

Chapter 2

1. The principle of combining, in an object, the data that describes its state and the operations that can be performed on the data is called **encapsulation**.

2. The data and operations of an object that are visible externally comprise its **interface**.

3. The data and operations of an object that are not visible externally comprise its **implementation**.

4. The principle of **inheritance** allows object-oriented designers to classify objects based on similarity of properties.

5. The principle of **polymorphism** allows objects that belong to different classes to respond distinctively to identical messages.

6. The **requirements analysis** activity of the SDLC involves understanding and documenting user requirement.

7. The **design** activity of the SDLC involves choosing a system structure capable of satisfying the Requirements Specification.

8. During the **programming** activity of the SDLC, the software is actually written.

9. The **testing** activity of the SDLC aims at ensuring the software is of suitable quality.

10. A **class** is a pattern, or blueprint, used to construct actual **objects**.

11. A development process that uses experimental software to better understand user requirements is **prototyping**.

Chapter 3

1. The **source** code for a Java program is created by using a text editor, and the **executable** code is created by compiling the source code with the Java compiler, **javac**.

2. A Java program that runs in the context of a Web browser is called an **applet**, whereas a program that runs by using the java interpreter is called an **application**.

3. b. class

4. Every Java source file can contain only one **public** class, but may include other helper classes, provided they are not created with **public** access.

5. The public class JaguarButton must be contained in the file named **JaguarButton.java**.

6. In a class definition, the **fields** describe the attributes of the object, whereas the **methods** define its behavior.

7. Methods and fields can have access specifiers that determine their visibility. If you want to create a field that is only accessible by the methods of the same class, you would use the access **private**.

8. False. Attributes that are declared as static, not those that are declared as final, are shared among all instances of the class. Individual fields are created for all other defined attributes.

9. Two differences between primitive types and objects are an object can store **many values**, whereas a primitive stores a **single value**. Objects are manipulated by using **methods**, whereas primitives use **operators** for the same purpose.

10. False. To support the principle of encapsulation, you will usually make the fields in your class private, while making your methods public.

Chapter 4

1. For any kind of object, one way of looking at it is to describe its **attributes**, whereas another equally valid way is to describe its **behavior**.

2. The **interface** of a well-designed object describes the services that the client of the object wants performed.

3. The **implementation** of an object is the manner or techniques it uses to carry out its functions.

4. When designing classes, abstraction is the process of discovering the essential behavior of an object. These behaviors are used to construct the object's **public interface**.

5. The purpose of a well-designed class is to model an **abstraction** from the user's point of view.

6. The first step in designing a class begins by identifying the class' **environment**, **client objects**, and **functionality**.

7. A **summary paragraph** describes the client's conceptual model in an informal way.

8. Your object's client is anyone or anything that sends your object **messages**.

9. Three common techniques that will help you implement your designs are to begin with a **template**, write a **main()** method that exercises your class, and use **stub** methods to refine your interface before looking at the details.

10. Your class will define three types of attributes: **object attributes (or fields)**, which store the state of each individual object; **class** attributes, which share state among all members of the class; and **constant** class attributes, which store unchanging state.

11. The "Prime Directive" for object attributes is that all state variables should be declared **private**.

12. An object contains both **data** and **methods** that operate on that data. Objects with no **data** are ghosts!

13. The principle of **cohesion** says that every class should model a single abstraction.

14. Using `static final` constants allows you to use your facility for **recognition**, rather than rely on **recall**.

15. When constructing an object, Java gives you the opportunity to decide which superclass constructor should be called first by using the **super()** method.

16. To write all your constructors in terms of the working constructor, you can use the special **this()** method.

17. The most important consideration when writing constructors is to make sure that all fields are **initialized** and that all **invariants** are satisfied.

18. When dealing with errors that occur in your methods, you have the options of doing nothing, stopping the program after testing (by writing an **assert()** method), fixing the mistake (which is called **defensive** programming), or **throwing an exception**, which is the preferred way of dealing with errors in Java.

19. Methods that change the state of an object (called **mutators**) must be very careful to preserve the invariants of the class.

20. Methods that return information to the client without changing the state of the object are called **accessors**.

Chapter 5

1. a. Problem summary
2. CRC cards are used to identify **classes**, responsibilities, and **collaborations**.
3. a. collaborate
4. An object that receives a message has the **responsibility** for handling it.
5. A collaboration diagram depicts the sequence in which objects exchange messages in a single **use-case** scenario.
6. A class diagram specifies the **attributes** and **methods** of a class.
7. To a system user, the user interface is the **system**.
8. b. iterative
9. A good tool for helping the user visualize the user interface is **prototyping**.
10. True.

Chapter 6

1. d. All of the above
2. c. What the software should do, from the user's perspective

3. c. Defining requirements and brainstorming general classes and their responsibilities

4. b. Class Responsibility Collaborations

5. a. Underline nouns in the problem statement, trying to discover candidate classes

6. a. Be conceptual, rather than technically complete

7. c. Class responsibilities

8. d. Build "slack time" into the schedule to provide a buffer against unforeseen circumstances

Chapter 7

1. Experience-based rules that help you decide which relationships to implement and the best way to implement them are called **heuristics**.

2. A relationship where no messages are passed between two objects, yet the relationship cannot be eliminated, is called a **simple** or **weak** association.

3. A **uses** relationship exists between two objects when one object sends messages to another object.

4. d. Composition relationship

5. b. *Uses* relationship

6. False. You can implement a *uses* relationship in several ways.

7. False. Using a referential attribute doesn't imply containment. Containment is determined by whether the object shares a semantic part-of relationship.

8. False. A weak association may be necessary to capture an important relationship, even when the classes do not directly communicate.

9.
```
public class PaintThis extends Applet
{
    public void init()
    {
        // First method--pass an argument
        graphics g = getGraphics();
        paintMe( g );
    }
    public void paintMe( Graphics g )
    {
        // Second method--create an instance
        Graphics g = getGraphics();
        g.setBackground( Color.red );
        repaint();
    }
}
```

10. The term used to describe the mutual dependence of two objects upon each other is **coupling**. All things being equal, **lower** is better than **higher**.

Chapter 8

1. A composite or aggregate object is one in which other objects are **encapsulated** as the composite object's fields.

2. a. Complexity is hidden behind a simpler interface.

   c. Composition provides a method to structure an object-oriented program.

   d. Composite objects are generally easier to use than trying to use all of the parts that make them up.

3. True.

4. In a composition relationship, a part can be contained in only one whole. By contrast, an object may participate in several using relationships.

   In composition, the lifetime of the parts is usually the same as the lifetime of the composite object. The parts of a composite object are created when the composite object is created, and the parts of a composite object are destroyed when the composite object is destroyed. In a uses relationship, the lifetime of individual objects is not dependent on the lifetime of the relationship.

5. True.

6. b. The interface may become crowded with features, making the class harder to use and understand.

7. Con: Too many layers may increase the communication overhead in your program.

   Pro: Layers allow you to change one part without affecting the others.

8. True.

9. b. Either arrays or `Vectors`.

10. By using a composition relationship, the `SalesInvoice` doesn't have to be concerned with the details of each `LineItem` object (or the fields that it contains). You may indeed want to use `LineItem` objects when the invoices are gone, for inventory or sales analysis.

Chapter 9

1. True.

2. c. `abstract`

3. In Java, you can create two classes that share a similar behavior, even if they aren't otherwise related, by having them both **implement** the same **interface**.

4. In Java, if you have two classes that are both specialized versions of a more general class, you can have both classes **extend** the same **superclass**.

5. False. This is contraction and it violates the meaning of inheritance.

6. In a correctly written program, any method that uses an object of the superclass `Animal`, should be able to replace that object with an object of

Animal's subclass, Rhinoceros. This is called the **Substitution (or Substitutability or Liskov Substitutability)** principle.

7. False. A Student *isA* Person. Not every Person *isA* Student.

8. b. Polymorphic inheritance

9. When creating a new subclass from an existing class, you can use the **protected** access modifier to allow subclasses access to your data, but prohibit modification by objects of your class.

10. False. Adding new arguments, or changing the type of existing arguments, overloads the method, thus creating two methods of the same name. The original method isn't overridden.

Chapter 10

1. d. a triangle

2. To depict an abstract class or interface in a class diagram, you **italicize** the name of the "class."

3. c. dotted

4. True.

5. d. superclass

6. a. arc abstract

7. Restructuring a set of classes so that common elements can reside in a base class is called **refactoring**.

Chapter 11

1. a. Name

   b. Problem

   c. Solution

   d. Consequences

2. Another name for the Decorator design pattern is **wrapper/filter**.

3. b. java.io

4. The Factory Method design pattern is useful when a client must create objects having different **types**.

5. The **Singleton** design pattern limits the number of instances a class can create.

6. The Iterator design pattern is known to Java programmers as **Enumerator/Enumeration** because of the corresponding interface of the **java.util** package.

7. b. Collection

8. b. hasMoreElements()

   c. nextElement()

9. The Command design pattern **encapsulates** a message and its receiver in an object.

10. a. Adapter

Chapter 12

1. False. Many of the most popular object-oriented languages do not provide built-in support for concurrent programming.

2. a. Improved response to events

   c. Support for parallel computing on multiprocessor systems

3. One potential drawback of using threads is the possibility of program deadlock due to failure to satisfy **liveness** conditions.

4. A thread is initiated by using the **start()** method, which causes the **run()** method of the thread to execute.

5. a. Extending the **Thread** class

   b. Implementing the **Runnable** interface

6. The **run()** method of a thread can/**cannot** throw an IOException.

7. The Booch-style interaction diagram shows objects and classes along the **top** edge of the diagram.

8. a. invariant

   d. safety

9. The two Java data types for which atomic updates are not guaranteed are **long** and **double**.

10. The guarded wait typically consumes more/**fewer** CPU cycles than the busy wait.

Chapter 13

1. False. RPC does not allow you to call object or class methods.

2. The restructuring of parameters for transmission over a byte stream is called **marshaling**.

3. a. Obtaining references to remote objects

   c. Getting parameters to, and returning values from, remote objects

4. The part of an object request broker that runs on the client system is known as a **stub** and the part that runs on the server system is known as the **skeleton**.

5. a. Sockets

b. CGI

c. RMI

d. CORBA

6. The chief advantage of implementing a system using **sockets** is high performance.

7. b. RMI

d. DCOM

8. The principle advantage of RMI is that it's **free**.

9. The technology offering the greatest range of facilities and services for remote computing is **CORBA**.

10. `rmiregistry`

Chapter 14

1. d. entity

2. A database table **column** contains values for a single attribute of an entity.

3. a. Package, 3. Catalog

b. Class, 1. Table

c. Object, 2. Row

d. Field, 4. Column

4. On an E/R diagram, the rectangles represent **entities**.

5. On an E/R diagram, the lines represent **relationships**.

6. The **cardinality** of a relationship refers to the number of instances of the related entities that participate in an instance of the relationship.

7. Any **N:N** relationships in the E/R diagram must be replaced by a pair of 1:N relationships.

8. c. normalized

9. If a database table is in third normal form, every non-key column of the table depends on no other column except that/those of the **primary key**.

10. Database **prototyping** helps determine whether database performance will be acceptable.

Chapter 15

1. a. clarity
   b. coherence
   c. elegance
   e. symmetry
2. b. difference
3. The **squint** test is a good way to assess the clarity of a visual interface.
4. True.
5. False. To implement a canonical grid, you'll normally need to also implement your own layout manager.
6. c. the user's goals
7. False. A usable interface helps accomplish the user's goals; it doesn't make the user adjust to its idiosyncrasies.
8. False. Using more than a few colors leads to interfaces that are unreadable and unusable.
9. a. use a bold font
10. a. applets

Chapter 16

1. a. reuse
2. The failure of software components to achieve the goal mentioned in question 1 is primarily due to the lack of a **standard**.
3. b. Visual Basic
4. A Bean is a component that can be manipulated **visually** in a builder tool.
5. The facility that allows a tool to discover the members of a Bean is **introspection/reflection**.
6. The facility that allows the state of a Bean to be saved is **persistence/serialization**.
7. **Bound** properties cause subscribers to be notified when their value is changed.
8. **Constrained** properties cause subscribers to be notified when a change to their value is pending, allowing a subscriber to veto the change.
9. Properties with values that take the form of arrays are known as **indexed** properties.
10. The name of a method that gets the value of a simple property named **lost** should be **getLost()**.

Chapter 17

1. b. `Container`
2. A **shallow** copy results in shared references, but a **deep** copy instantiates new objects so that there are no shared references.
3. d. none of the above
4. d. `Vector`
5. An `OrderedMap` orders its elements by the return value of the **hashCode()** method.
6. a. Is defined in the `Object` class.
7. d. `SetOperations`
8. The **Stack**, **Queue**, and **PriorityQueue** classes add the **pop()** and **push()** methods to those defined by the `Container` interface.
9. JGL's **iterators** are closely related to the JDK's `Enumerations`.
10. An important principle of library design is to use **consistent** names, mechanisms, and error handling.

Chapter 18

1. b. pattern
2. a. Clients
   b. Servers
   c. Networks
3. a. user interface
   b. application processing
   d. data management
4. A **network computer** is a special PC designed to run Java better than a standard PC.
5. The traditional information system architecture was characterized by **high** cost and **low** flexibility.
6. The file server information system architecture was characterized by **low** cost and **high** flexibility.
7. The client/server information system architecture usually allocates database processing to the **server**.
8. The distributed information system architecture is characterized by the use of multiple **servers**.
9. Thin clients require the use of a **middleware** server, which requires the client to load only a single driver.
10. b. portability
    c. automatic software distribution

Index

This binary code license ("License") contains rights and restrictions associated with use of the accompanying software and documentation ("Software"). Read the License carefully before installing the Software. By installing the Software you agree to the terms and conditions of this License.

1. Limited License Grant. Sun grants to you ("Licensee") a non-exclusive, non-transferable limited license to use the Software without fee for evaluation of the Software and for development of Java™ compatible applets and applications. Licensee may make one archival copy of the Software. Licensee may not re-distribute the Software in whole or in part, either separately or included with a product. Refer to the Java Runtime Environment Version 1.1 binary code license (http://www.javasoft.com/products/JDK/1.1/index.html) for the availability of runtime code which may be distributed with Java compatible applets and applications.

2. Java Platform Interface. Licensee may not modify the Java Platform Interface ("JPI", identified as classes contained within the "java" package or any subpackages of the "java" package), by creating additional classes within the JPI or otherwise causing the addition to or modification of the classes in the JPI. In the event that Licensee creates any Java-related API and distributes such API to others for applet or application development, Licensee must promptly publish an accurate specification for such API for free use by all developers of Java-based software.

3. Restrictions. Software is confidential copyrighted information of Sun and title to all copies is retained by Sun and/or its licensors. Licensee shall not modify, decompile, disassemble, decrypt, extract, or otherwise reverse engineer Software. Software may not be leased, assigned, or sublicensed, in whole or in part. **Software is not designed or intended for use in on-line control of aircraft, air traffic, aircraft navigation, or aircraft communications; or in the design, construction, operation, or maintenance of any nuclear facility. Licensee warrants that it will not use or redistribute the Software for such purposes.**

4. Trademarks and Logos. This License does not authorize Licensee to use any Sun name, trademark, or logo. Licensee acknowledges that Sun owns the Java trademark and all Java-related trademarks, logos, and icons, including the Coffee Cup and Duke ("Java Marks") and agrees to: (i) comply with the Java Trademark Guidelines at http://java.com/trademarks.html; (ii) not do anything harmful to or inconsistent with Sun's rights in the Java Marks; and (iii) assist Sun in protecting those rights, including assigning to Sun any rights acquired by Licensee in any Java Mark.

5. Disclaimer of Warranty. Software is provided "AS IS," without a warranty of any kind. ALL EXPRESS OR IMPLIED REPRESENTATIONS AND WARRANTIES, INCLUDING ANY IMPLIED WARRANTY OF MERCHANTABILITY, FITNESS FOR A PARTICULAR PURPOSE, OR NON-INFRINGEMENT, ARE HEREBY EXCLUDED.

6. Limitation of Liability. SUN AND ITS LICENSORS SHALL NOT BE LIABLE FOR ANY DAMAGES SUFFERED BY LICENSEE OR ANY THIRD PARTY AS A RESULT OF USING OR DISTRIBUTING SOFT-WARE. IN NO EVENT WILL SUN OR ITS LICENSORS BE LIABLE FOR ANY LOST REVENUE, PROFIT OR DATA, OR FOR DIRECT, INDIRECT, SPECIAL, CONSEQUENTIAL, INCIDENTAL OR PUNITIVE DAMAGES, HOWEVER CAUSED AND REGARDLESS OF THE THEORY OF LIABILITY, ARISING OUT OF THE USE OF OR INABILITY TO USE SOFTWARE, EVEN IF SUN HAS BEEN ADVISED OF THE POSSIBILITY OF SUCH DAMAGES.

7. Termination. Licensee may terminate this License at any time by destroying all copies of Software. This License will terminate immediately without notice from Sun if Licensee fails to comply with any provision of this License. Upon such termination, Licensee must destroy all copies of Software.

8. Export Regulations. Software, including technical data, is subject to U.S. export control laws, including the U.S. Export Administration Act and its associated regulations, and may be subject to export or import regulations in other countries. Licensee agrees to comply strictly with all such regulations and acknowledges that it has the responsibility to obtain licenses to export, re-export, or import Software. Software may not be downloaded, or otherwise exported or re-exported (i) into, or to a national or resident of, Cuba, Iraq, Iran, North Korea, Libya, Sudan, Syria, or any country to which the U.S. has embargoed goods; or (ii) to anyone on the U.S. Treasury Department's list of Specially Designated Nations or the U.S. Commerce Department's Table of Denial Orders.

9. Restricted Rights. Use, duplication, or disclosure by the United States government is subject to the restrictions as set forth in the Rights in Technical Data and Computer Software Clauses in DFARS 252.227-7013(c) (1) (ii) and FAR 52.227-19(c) (2) as applicable.

10. Governing Law. Any action related to this License will be governed by California law and controlling U.S. federal law. No choice of law rules of any jurisdiction will apply.

11. Severability. If any of the above provisions are held to be in violation of applicable law, void, or unenforceable in any jurisdiction, then such provisions are herewith waived to the extent necessary for the License to be otherwise enforceable in such jurisdiction. However, if in Sun's opinion deletion of any provisions of the License by operation of this paragraph unreasonably compromises the rights or increase the liabilities of Sun or its licensors, Sun reserves the right to terminate the License and refund the fee paid by Licensee, if any, as Licensee's sole and exclusive remedy.

SUN MICROSYSTEMS, INC., THROUGH ITS JAVASOFT BUSINESS ("SUN") IS WILLING TO LICENSE THE HOTJAVA BROWSER VERSION 1.1 SOFTWARE AND THE ACCOMPANYING DOCUMENTA-TION INCLUDING AUTHORIZED COPIES OF EACH (THE "SOFTWARE") TO LICENSEE ONLY ON THE CONDITION THAT LICENSEE ACCEPTS ALL OF THE TERMS IN THIS AGREEMENT.

PLEASE READ THE TERMS CAREFULLY BEFORE INSTALLING THE SOFTWARE. BY INSTALLING THE SOFTWARE, LICENSEE ACKNOWLEDGES THAT LICENSEE HAS READ AND UNDERSTANDS THIS AGREEMENT AND AGREES TO BE BOUND BY ITS TERMS AND CONDITIONS.

IF LICENSEE DOES NOT ACCEPT THESE LICENSE TERMS, SUN DOES NOT GRANT ANY LICENSE TO THE SOFTWARE, AND LICENSEE MAY NOT INSTALL THE SOFTWARE.

1. LICENSE GRANT

    (A) License Rights

Licensee is granted a personal, non-exclusive and non-transferable no fee license to install and use the binary Software. Licensee may make one archival copy of the Software, pro-vided that Licensee reproduces all copyright and other proprietary notices that are on the original copy of the Software. Licensee may not distribute the Software to any third party. This license is for individual personal use only. Use of multiple copies of the Software within an organization, whether commercial or non-commercial, shall be subject to a per copy fee. Contact the JavaSoft sales representative at 1-888-THE JAVA, or if outside of the U.S., call JavaSoft in the U.S. 512-434-1591, for further information.

    (B) License Restrictions

The Software is licensed to Licensee only under the terms of this Agreement, and Sun reserves all rights not expressly granted to Licensee. Licensee may not use, copy, modify, or transfer the Software, or any copy thereof, except as expressly authorized in this Agreement. Except as otherwise provided by law for purposes of decompilation of the Software solely for inter-operability, Licensee may not reverse engineer, disassemble, decompile, or translate the Software, or otherwise attempt to derive the source code of the Software. Licensee may not rent, lease, loan, sell, or distribute the Software, or any part of the Software. No right, title, or interest in or to any trademarks, service marks, or trade names of Sun or Sun's licensors is granted hereunder.

(C) Aircraft Product and Nuclear Applications Restriction

SOFTWARE IS NOT DESIGNED OR INTENDED FOR USE IN ON-LINE CONTROL OF AIRCRAFT, AIR TRAFFIC, AIRCRAFT NAVIGATION OR AIRCRAFT COMMUNICATIONS; OR IN THE DESIGN, CONSTRUCTION, OPERATION OR MAINTENANCE OF ANY NUCLEAR FACILITY. SUN DISCLAIMS ANY EXPRESS OR IMPLIED WARRANTY OF FITNESS FOR SUCH USES. LICENSEE REPRESENTS AND WARRANTS THAT IT WILL NOT USE THE SOFTWARE FOR SUCH PURPOSES.

2. CONFIDENTIALITY

The Software is the confidential and proprietary information of Sun and/or its licensors. The Software is protected by United States copyright law and international treaty. Unauthorized reproduction or distribution is subject to civil and criminal penalties. Licensee agrees to take adequate steps to protect the Software from unauthorized disclosure or use.

3. TERM, TERMINATION AND SURVIVAL

(A) The Agreement is effective until terminated.

(B) Licensee may terminate this Agreement at any time by destroying all copies of the Software.

(C) This Agreement will immediately terminate without notice if Licensee fails to comply with any obligation of this Agreement.

(D) Upon termination, Licensee must immediately cease use of and destroy the Software or, upon request from Sun, return the Software to Sun.

(E) The provisions set forth in paragraphs 1 (B), 2, 6, 7, 8, and 9 will survive termination or expiration of this Agreement.

4. NO WARRANTY

THE SOFTWARE IS PROVIDED TO LICENSEE "AS IS". ALL EXPRESS OR IMPLIED CONDITIONS, REPRESENTATIONS, AND WARRANTIES, INCLUDING ANY IMPLIED WARRANTY OF MERCHANTABILITY, SATISFACTORY QUALITY, FITNESS FOR A PARTICULAR PURPOSE, OR NON-INFRINGEMENT, ARE DISCLAIMED, EXCEPT TO THE EXTENT THAT SUCH DISCLAIMERS ARE HELD TO BE LEGALLY INVALID.

5. MAINTENANCE AND SUPPORT

Sun has no obligation to provide maintenance or support for the Software under this Agreement.

6. LIMITATION OF DAMAGES

TO THE EXTENT NOT PROHIBITED BY APPLICABLE LAW, SUN'S AGGREGATE LIABILITY TO LICENSEE OR TO ANY THIRD PARTY FOR CLAIMS RELATING TO THIS AGREEMENT, WHETHER FOR BREACH OR IN TORT, WILL BE LIMITED TO THE FEES PAID BY LICENSEE FOR SOFTWARE WHICH IS THE SUBJECT MATTER OF THE CLAIMS. IN NO EVENT WILL SUN BE LIABLE FOR ANY INDIRECT, PUNITIVE, SPECIAL, INCIDENTAL OR CONSEQUENTIAL DAMAGE IN CONNECTION WITH OR ARISING OUT OF THIS AGREEMENT (INCLUDING LOSS OF BUSINESS, REVENUE, PROFITS, USE, DATA OR OTHER ECONOMIC ADVANTAGE), HOWEVER IT ARISES, WHETHER FOR BREACH OR IN TORT, EVEN IF SUN HAS BEEN PREVIOUSLY ADVISED OF THE POSSIBILITY OF SUCH DAMAGE. LIABILITY FOR DAMAGES WILL BE LIMITED AND EXCLUDED, EVEN IF ANY EXCLUSIVE REMEDY PROVIDED FOR IN THIS AGREEMENT FAILS OF ITS ESSENTIAL PURPOSE.

7. GOVERNMENT USER

Rights in Data: If procured by, or provided to, the U.S. Government, use, duplication, or disclosure of technical data is subject to restrictions as set forth in FAR 52.227-14(g)(2), Rights in Data-General (June 1987); and for computer software and computer software documentation, FAR 52-227-19, Commercial Computer Software-Restricted Rights (June 1987). However, if under DOD, use, duplication, or disclosure of technical data is subject to DFARS 252.227-7015(b), Technical Data-Commercial Items (June 1995); and for computer software and computer software documentation, as specified in the license under which the computer software was procured pursuant to DFARS 227.7202-3(a). Licensee shall not provide Software nor technical data to any third party, including the U.S. Government, unless such third party accepts the same restrictions. Licensee is responsible for ensuring that proper notice is given to al such third parties and that the Software and technical data are properly marked.

8. EXPORT LAW

Licensee acknowledges and agrees that this Software and/or technology is subject to the U.S. Export Administration Laws and Regulations. Diversion of such Software and/or technology contrary to U.S. law is prohibited. Licensee agrees that none of this Software and/or technology, nor any direct product therefrom, is being or will be acquired for, shipped, transferred, or reexported, directly or indirectly, to proscribed or embargoed countries or their nationals, nor be used for nuclear activities, chemical biological weapons, or missile projects unless authorized by the U.S. Government. Proscribed countries are set forth in the U.S. Export Administration Regulations. Countries subject to U.S.

embargo are: Cuba, Iran, Iraq, Libya, North Korea, Syria, and the Sudan. This list is subject to change without further notice from Sun, and Licensee must comply with the list as it exists in fact. Licensee certifies that it is not on the U.S. Department of Commerce's Denied Persons List or affiliated lists or on the U.S. Department of Treasury's Specially Designated Nationals List. Licensee agrees to comply strictly with all U.S. export laws and assumes sole responsibility for obtaining licenses to export or reexport as may be required.

Licensee is responsible for complying with any applicable local laws and regulations, including but not limited to, the export and import laws and regulations of other countries.

9. GOVERNING LAW, JURISDICTION AND VENUE

Any action related to this Agreement shall be governed by California law and controlling U.S. federal law, and choice of law rules of any jurisdiction shall not apply. The parties agree that any action shall be brought in the United States District Court for the Northern District of California or the California superior Court for the County of Santa Clara, as applicable, and the parties hereby submit exclusively to the personal jurisdiction and venue of the United States District Court for the Northern District of California and the California Superior Court of the county of Santa Clara.

10. NO ASSIGNMENT

Neither party may assign or otherwise transfer any of its rights or obligations under this Agreement, without the prior written consent of the other party, except that Sun may assign its right to payment and may assign this Agreement to an affiliated company.

11. OFFICIAL LANGUAGE

The official text of this Agreement is in the English language and any interpretation or construction of this Agreement will be based thereon. In the event that this Agreement or any documents or notices related to it are translated into any other language, the English language version will control.

12. ENTIRE AGREEMENT

This Agreement is the parties' entire agreement relating to the Software. It supersedes all prior or contemporaneous oral or written communications, proposals, warranties, and representations with respect to its subject matter, and will prevail over any conflicting or additional terms of any subsequent quote, order, acknowledgment, or any other communications by or between the parties. No modification to this Agreement will be binding, unless in writing and signed by an authorized representative of each party.

This is a legal agreement between you, the end user and purchaser, and The Waite Group®, Inc., and the authors of the programs contained in the disk. By opening the sealed disk package, you are agreeing to be bound by the terms of this Agreement. If you do not agree with the terms of this Agreement, promptly return the unopened disk package and the accompanying items (including the related book and other written material) to the place you obtained them for a refund.

SOFTWARE LICENSE

1. The Waite Group, Inc. grants you the right to use one copy of the enclosed software programs (the programs) on a single computer system (whether a single CPU, part of a licensed network, or a terminal connected to a single CPU). Each concurrent user of the program must have exclusive use of the related Waite Group, Inc. written materials.

2. The program, including the copyrights in each program, is owned by the respective author and the copyright in the entire work is owned by The Waite Group, Inc. and they are therefore protected under the copyright laws of the United States and other nations, under international treaties. You may make only one copy of the disk containing the programs exclusively for backup or archival purposes, or you may transfer the programs to one hard disk drive, using the original for backup or archival purposes. You may make no other copies of the programs, and you may make no copies of all or any part of the related Waite Group, Inc. written materials.

3. You may not rent or lease the programs, but you may transfer ownership of the programs and related written materials (including any and all updates and earlier versions) if you keep no copies of either, and if you make sure the transferee agrees to the terms of this license.

4. You may not decompile, reverse engineer, disassemble, copy, create a derivative work, or otherwise use the programs except as stated in this Agreement.

GOVERNING LAW

This Agreement is governed by the laws of the State of California.

LIMITED WARRANTY

The following warranties shall be effective for 90 days from the date of purchase: (i) The Waite Group, Inc. warrants the enclosed disk to be free of defects in materials and workmanship under normal use; and (ii) The Waite Group, Inc. warrants that the programs, unless modified by the purchaser, will substantially perform the functions described in the documentation provided by The Waite Group, Inc. when operated on the designated hardware and operating system. The Waite Group, Inc. does not warrant that the programs will meet purchaser's requirements or that operation of a program will be uninterrupted or error-free. The program warranty does not cover any program that has been altered or changed in any way by anyone other than The Waite Group, Inc. The Waite Group, Inc. is not responsible for problems caused by changes in the operating characteristics of computer hardware or computer operating systems that are made after the release of the programs, nor for problems in the interaction of the programs with each other or other software.

THESE WARRANTIES ARE EXCLUSIVE AND IN LIEU OF ALL OTHER WARRANTIES OF MERCHANTABILITY OR FITNESS FOR A PARTICULAR PURPOSE OR OF ANY OTHER WARRANTY, WHETHER EXPRESS OR IMPLIED.

EXCLUSIVE REMEDY

The Waite Group, Inc. will replace any defective disk without charge if the defective disk is returned to The Waite Group, Inc. within 90 days from date of purchase.

This is Purchaser's sole and exclusive remedy for any breach of warranty or claim for contract, tort, or damages.

LIMITATION OF LIABILITY

THE WAITE GROUP, INC. AND THE AUTHORS OF THE PROGRAMS SHALL NOT IN ANY CASE BE LIABLE FOR SPECIAL, INCIDENTAL, CONSEQUENTIAL, INDIRECT, OR OTHER SIMILAR DAMAGES ARISING FROM ANY BREACH OF THESE WARRANTIES EVEN IF THE WAITE GROUP, INC. OR ITS AGENT HAS BEEN ADVISED OF THE POSSIBILITY OF SUCH DAMAGES.

THE LIABILITY FOR DAMAGES OF THE WAITE GROUP, INC. AND THE AUTHORS OF THE PROGRAMS UNDER THIS AGREEMENT SHALL IN NO EVENT EXCEED THE PURCHASE PRICE PAID.

COMPLETE AGREEMENT

This Agreement constitutes the complete agreement between The Waite Group, Inc. and the authors of the programs, and you, the purchaser.

Some states do not allow the exclusion or limitation of implied warranties or liability for incidental or consequential damages, so the above exclusions or limitations may not apply to you. This limited warranty gives you specific legal rights; you may have others, which vary from state to state.

SATISFACTION REPORT CARD

Please fill out this card if you wish to know of future updates to *Object-Oriented Design in Java*, or to receive our catalog.

First Name: _____ **Last Name:** _____

Street Address: _____

City: _____ **State:** _____ **Zip:** _____

Email Address _____

Daytime Telephone: ( )_____

Date product was acquired: **Month** **Day** **Year** **Your Occupation:**

Overall, how would you rate *Object-Oriented Design in Java*?

☐ Excellent ☐ Very Good ☐ Good
☐ Fair ☐ Below Average ☐ Poor

What did you like MOST about this book? _____

_____

_____

What did you like LEAST about this book? _____

_____

Please describe any problems you may have encountered with installing or using the disk: _____

_____

How did you use this book (problem-solver, tutorial, reference...)?

_____

What is your level of computer expertise?

☐ New ☐ Dabbler ☐ Hacker
☐ Power User ☐ Programmer ☐ Experienced Professional

What computer languages are you familiar with? _____

_____

Please describe your computer hardware:

Computer _____ Hard disk _____

5.25" disk drives _____ 3.5" disk drives _____

Video card _____ Monitor _____

Printer _____ Peripherals _____

Sound Board _____ CD-ROM _____

Where did you buy this book?

☐ Bookstore (name): _____
☐ Discount store (name): _____
☐ Computer store (name): _____
☐ Catalog (name): _____
☐ Direct from WGP ☐ Other _____

What price did you pay for this book? _____

What influenced your purchase of this book?

☐ Recommendation ☐ Advertisement
☐ Magazine review ☐ Store display
☐ Mailing ☐ Book's format
☐ Reputation of Waite Group Press ☐ Other

How many computer books do you buy each year? _____

How many other Waite Group books do you own? _____

What is your favorite Waite Group book? _____

_____

Is there any program or subject you would like to see Waite Group Press cover in a similar approach? _____

_____

Additional comments? _____

_____

_____

Please send to: **Waite Group Press**
200 Tamal Plaza
Corte Madera, CA 94925

☐ **Check here for a free Waite Group catalog**

Installing the CD-ROM

Windows 95/NT 4

1. Insert the CD-ROM into your CD-ROM drive.

2. Click the Start button and select Run.

3. Type D:\WSETUP.EXE and click OK. If your CD-ROM drive letter is not D:, replace D: with the drive letter that corresponds to your system.

4. Follow the onscreen instructions.

NOTE: If AutoPlay is enabled, the WSETUP.EXE program starts automatically whenever you insert the disc into your CD-ROM drive.

Solaris 2.4+

1. Log in as root.

2. Insert the CD-ROM into your CD-ROM drive.

3. If Volume Manager is running, kill the process.

4. Type

    ```
    mkdir /cdrom/ood <ENTER>
    ```

5. Mount the CD-ROM to the mountpoint you just created.

6. The file README.TXT contains detailed installation instructions for the contents of the CD-ROM.

BEFORE YOU OPEN THE DISK OR CD-ROM PACKAGE ON THE FACING PAGE, CAREFULLY READ THE LICENSE AGREEMENT.

Opening this package indicates that you agree to abide by the license agreements found in the back of this book. If you do not agree with them, promptly return the unopened disk package (including the related book) to the place you obtained them for a refund.

Borland International TRIAL EDITION SOFTWARE License Statement

YOUR USE OF THE TRIAL EDITION SOFTWARE DISTRIBUTED WITH THIS LICENSE IS SUBJECT TO ALL OF THE TERMS AND CONDITIONS OF THIS LICENSE STATEMENT. IF YOU DO NOT AGREE TO ALL OF THE TERMS AND CONDITIONS OF THIS STATEMENT, DO NOT USE THE SOFTWARE.

1. This Software is protected by copyright law and international copyright treaty. Therefore, you must treat this Software just like a book, except that you may copy it onto a computer to be used and you may make archive copies of the Software for the sole purpose of backing up our Software and protecting your investment from loss. Your use of this software is limited to evaluation and trial use purposes only.

FURTHER, THIS SOFTWARE CONTAINS A TIME-OUT FEATURE THAT DISABLES ITS OPERATION AFTER A CERTAIN PERIOD OF TIME. A TEXT FILE DELIVERED WITH THE SOFTWARE WILL STATE THE TIME PERIOD AND/OR SPECIFIC DATE ("EVALUATION PERI-OD") ON WHICH THE SOFTWARE WILL EXPIRE. Though Borland does not offer technical support for the Software, we welcome your feedback.

If the Software is a Borland development tool, you can write and compile applications for your own personal use on the computer on which you have installed the Software, but you do not have a right to distribute or otherwise share those applications or any files of the Software which may be required to support those applications. APPLICATIONS THAT YOU CREATE MAY REQUIRE THE SOFTWARE IN ORDER TO RUN. UPON EXPIRATION OF THE EVALUATION PERIOD, THOSE APPLICATIONS WILL NO LONGER RUN. You should therefore take precautions to avoid any loss of data that might result.

2. BORLAND MAKES NO REPRESENTATIONS ABOUT THE SUIT-ABILITY OF THIS SOFTWARE OR ABOUT ANY CONTENT OR INFOR-MATION MADE ACCESSIBLE BY THE SOFTWARE, FOR ANY PUR-POSE. THE SOFTWARE IS PROVIDED 'AS IS' WITHOUT EXPRESS OR IMPLIED WARRANTIES, INCLUDING WARRANTIES OF MER-CHANTABILITY AND FITNESS FOR A PARTICULAR PURPOSE OR NONINFRINGEMENT. THIS SOFTWARE IS PROVIDED GRATU-ITOUSLY AND, ACCORDINGLY, BORLAND SHALL NOT BE LIABLE UNDER ANY THEORY FOR ANY DAMAGES SUFFERED BY YOU OR ANY USER OF THE SOFTWARE. BORLAND WILL NOT SUPPORT THIS SOFTWARE AND IS UNDER NO OBLIGATION TO ISSUE UPDATES TO THIS SOFTWARE.

3. While Borland intends to distribute (or may have already distributed) a commercial release of the Software, Borland reserves the right at any time to not release a commercial release of the Software or, if released, to alter prices, features, specifications, capabilities, functions, licensing terms, release dates, general availability or other characteristics of the commercial release.

4. Title, ownership rights, and intellectual property rights in and to the Software shall remain in Borland and/or its suppliers. You agree to abide by the copyright law and all other applicable laws of the United States including, but not limited to, export control laws. You acknowledge that the Software in source code form remains a confidential trade secret of Borland and/or its suppliers and therefore you agree not to modify the Software or attempt to decipher, decompile, disassemble or reverse engi-neer the Software, except to the extent applicable laws specifically pro-hibit such restriction.

5. Upon expiration of the Evaluation Period, you agree to destroy or erase the Software, and to not re-install a new copy of the Software. This statement shall be governed by and construed in accordance with the laws of the State of California and, as to matters affecting copyrights, trademarks and patents, by U.S. federal law. This statement sets forth the entire agreement between you and Borland.

6. Use, duplication or disclosure by the Government is subject to restric-tions set forth in subparagraphs (a) through (d) of the Commercial Computer-Restricted Rights clause at FAR 52.227-19 when applicable, or in subparagraph (c) (1) (ii) of the Rights in Technical Data and Computer Software clause at DFARS 252.227-7013, and in similar clauses in the NASA AR Supplement. Contractor/manufacturer is Borland International, Inc., 100 Borland Way, Scotts Valley, CA 95066.

7. You may not download or otherwise export or reexport the Software or any underlying information or technology except in full compliance with all United States and other applicable laws and regulations. In par-ticular, but without limitation, none of the Software or underlying infor-mation or technology may be downloaded or otherwise exported or reex-ported (i) into (or to a national or resident of) Cuba, Haiti, Iraq, Libya, Yugoslavia, North Korea, Iran, or Syria or (ii) to anyone on the US Treasury Department's list of Specially Designated Nationals or the US Commerce Department's Table of Deny Orders. By downloading the Software, you are agreeing to the foregoing and you are representing and warranting that you are not located in, under control of, or a national or resident of any such country or on any such list.

8. BORLAND OR ITS SUPPLIERS SHALL NOT BE LIABLE FOR (a) INCIDENTAL, CONSEQUENTIAL, SPECIAL OR INDIRECT DAMAGES OF ANY SORT, WHETHER ARISING IN TORT, CONTRACT OR OTH-ERWISE, EVEN IF BORLAND HAS BEEN INFORMED OF THE POSSI-BILITY OF SUCH DAMAGES, OR (b) FOR ANY CLAIM BY ANY OTHER PARTY. THIS LIMITATION OF LIABILITY SHALL NOT APPLY TO LIA-BILITY FOR DEATH OR PERSONAL INJURY TO THE EXTENT APPLIC-ABLE LAW PROHIBITS SUCH LIMITATION. FURTHERMORE, SOME STATES DO NOT ALLOW THE EXCLUSION OR LIMITATION OF INCIDENTAL OR CONSEQUENTIAL DAMAGES, SO THIS LIMITA-TION AND EXCLUSION MAY NOT APPLY TO YOU.

9. HIGH RISK ACTIVITIES. The Software is not fault-tolerant and is not designed, manufactured or intended for use or resale as on-line control equipment in hazardous environments requiring fail-safe performance, such as in the operation of nuclear facilities, aircraft navigation or com-munication systems, air traffic control, direct life support machines, or weapons systems, in which the failure of the Software could lead directly to death, personal injury, or severe physical or environmental damage ("High Risk Activities"). Borland and its suppliers specifically disclaim any express or implied warranty of fitness for High Risk Activities.